EXCELLENCE IN MANAGEMENT SCIENCE PRACTICE

EXCELLENCE IN MANAGEMENT SCIENCE PRACTICE

A Readings Book

Edited by

Arjang A. Assad
University of Maryland

Edward A. Wasil
American University

Gary L. Lilien
Pennsylvania State University

PRENTICE HALL, Englewood Cliffs, New Jersey 07632

Library of Congress Cataloging-in-Publication Data

Excellence in management science practice : a readings book / edited by
   I. Arjang Assad, Edward A. Wasil, Gary L. Lilien.
     p. cm.
  Includes bibliographical references.
  ISBN 0-13-297102-X
  1. Management science. 2. Operations research. I. Assad, Arjang
II. Wasil, Edward A. III. Lilien, Gary L.
  T56.25.E93 1991
  658.5—dc20   90-24075
                              CIP

Acquisitions Editor: *Valerie Ashton*
Editorial/production supervision: *Cyndy Lyle Rymer*
Cover Designer: *Franklin Graphics*
Prepress Buyer: *Trudy Pisciotti*
Manufacturing Buyer: *Robert Anderson*
Copy Editor: *Mary Haight*

© 1992 by Prentice-Hall, Inc.
A Simon & Schuster Company
Englewood Cliffs, NJ 07632

Please see page xv for list of publishers' acknowledgments.

Printed in the United States of America
10 9 8 7 6 5 4 3 2 1

ISBN 0-13-297102-X

Prentice-Hall International (UK) Limited, *London*
Prentice-Hall of Australia Pty. Limited, *Sydney*
Prentice-Hall Canada Inc., *Toronto*
Prentice-Hall Hispanoamericana, S.A., *Mexico*
Prentice-Hall of India Private Limited, *New Delhi*
Prentice-Hall of Japan, Inc., *Tokyo*
Simon & Schuster Asia Pte. Ltd., *Singapore*
Editora Prentice-Hall do Brasil, Ltda., *Rio de Janeiro*

CONTENTS

PREFACE *xi*

1 THE PRACTICE OF MANAGEMENT SCIENCE AND OPERATIONS RESEARCH *1*

1.1 PICTURES AT AN MS/OR EXHIBITION, 1
1.2 TEACHING MS/OR AND ITS PRACTICE, 6
1.3 CAPTURING MS/OR PRACTICE, 8
1.4 IMPLEMENTATION OF MS/OR STUDIES, 19
1.5 PLAN OF THE BOOK, 22
1.6 FURTHER READINGS, 24

2 PRODUCTION AND INVENTORY MANAGEMENT *30*

2.1 HIERARCHICAL PRODUCTION PLANNING FOR
A TILE MANUFACTURER, 31
2.2 INVENTORY AND PRODUCTION PLANNING
FOR AN APPAREL MANUFACTURER, 35
2.3 INVENTORY REDUCTION IN A
PHARMACEUTICAL FIRM, 41
2.4 AN OVERVIEW OF PRODUCTION PLANNING, 46
2.5 MANAGING INVENTORY SYSTEMS, 53
2.6 FURTHER READINGS, 59

v

A Hierarchical Production Planning System   67
Matthew J. Liberatore and Tan Miller

Blue Bell Trims Its Inventory   77
Jerry R. Edwards, Harvey M. Wagner, and William P. Wood

Development and Implementation of an Integrated
Inventory Management Program at
Pfizer Pharmaceuticals   98
P. P. Kleutghen and J.C. McGee

3 DISTRIBUTION   *116*

3.1 *DISTRIBUTING MEALS TO SENIOR CITIZENS, 119*
3.2 *SCHEDULING DELIVERIES OF*
    INDUSTRIAL GASES, 120
3.3 *IMPROVING THE OPERATIONS OF A*
    TRUCKLOAD CARRIER, 124
3.4 *IMPLEMENTATION OF VEHICLE*
    ROUTING SYSTEMS, 129
3.5 *MODELING MOTOR CARRIER OPERATIONS, 134*
3.6 *FURTHER READINGS, 138*

A Minimal Technology Routing System for Meals
on Wheels   148
John J. Bartholdi III, Loren K. Platzman, R. Lee Collins,
and William H. Warden III

Improving the Distribution of Industrial Gases
with an On-line Computerized Routing and
Scheduling Optimizer   156
Walter J. Bell, Louis M. Dalberto, Marshall L. Fisher,
Arnold J. Greenfield, R. Jaikumar, Pradeep Kedia, Robert G. Mack,
and Paul J. Prutzman

Maximizing Profits for North American Van Lines'
Truckload Division: A New Framework for Pricing
and Operations   174
Warren B. Powell, Yosef Sheffi, Kenneth S. Nickerson, Kevin Butterbaugh,
and Susan Atherton

4 MARKETING *194*

*4.1 SALES FORCE SIZING FOR A
PHARMACEUTICAL MANUFACTURER, 194*
*4.2 DEVELOPING A NEW ADVERTISING PROGRAM
FOR THE PHONE COMPANY, 195*
4.3 MARKETING DECISION PROBLEMS, 195
4.4 SALES FORCE MODELS, 199
4.5 ADVERTISING MODELS, 203
4.6 FURTHER READINGS, 208

Sales Force Sizing and Deployment Using a Decision
Calculus Model at Syntex Laboratories   211
   Leonard M. Lodish, Ellen Curtis, Michael Ness, and M. Kerry Simpson

The Development, Testing, and Execution of a New
Marketing Strategy at AT&T Long Lines   227
   Alan P. Kuritsky, John D. C. Little, Alvin J. Silk, and Emily S. Bassman

5 MATHEMATICAL PROGRAMMING *243*

*5.1 MODELING A FOREST PEST CONTROL AERIAL
SPRAY PROGRAM, 244*
5.2 IMPROVING GASOLINE BLENDING AT TEXACO, 245
*5.3 IMPROVING THE EFFICIENCY OF
CHECK PROCESSING, 247*
*5.4 THE FIELD OF
MATHEMATICAL PROGRAMMING, 248*
5.5 FURTHER READINGS, 254

Improving Efficiency in a Forest Pest Control
Spray Program   261
   David L. Rumpf, Emanuel Melachrinoudis, and Thomas Rumpf

OMEGA: An Improved Gasoline Blending
System for Texaco   271
   *Calvin W. DeWitt, Leon S. Lasdon, Allan D. Waren, Donald A. Brenner,
   and Simon A. Melhem*

Improving Transit Check Clearing Operations
at Maryland National Bank   286
   Robert E. Markland and Robert M. Nauss

6   QUEUEING AND SIMULATION   *294*

6.1 LOT SIZES AND LEAD TIMES IN A MANUFACTURING CELL, 295

6.2 CAPACITY PLANNING WITH A SIMULATION MODEL, 301

6.3 A GLANCE AT QUEUEING THEORY, 304

6.4 WAITING LINES IN BANKS AND TELEPHONE SERVICES, 309

6.5 OTHER APPLICATIONS OF QUEUEING MODELS, 317

6.6 SIMULATION AS A MODELING TOOL, 320

6.7 A SAMPLER OF SIMULATION APPLICATIONS, 323

6.8 FURTHER READINGS, 332

Lot-Sizing and Lead-time Performance in a Manufacturing Cell   341
Uday S. Karmarkar, Sham Kekre, Sunder Kekre, and Susan Freeman

An Application of Simulation and Network Analysis to Capacity Planning and Material Handling Systems at Tinker Air Force Base   349
A. Ravindran, B. L. Foote, A. B. Badiru, L. M. Leemis, and Larry Williams

7   DECISION-MAKING TECHNIQUES   *363*

7.1 RANKING SPORTS RECORDS, 364

7.2 ANALYSIS OF POSTAL AUTOMATION ALTERNATIVES, 370

7.3 A DECISION SIMULATOR FOR TIMBER PROCESSING, 376

7.4 FURTHER READINGS, 379

Ranking Outstanding Sports Records, 387
Bruce L. Golden and Edward A. Wasil

Postal Automation (ZIP+4) Technology: A Decision Analysis   397
Jacob W. Ulvila

Weyerhaeuser Decision Simulator Improves
Timber Profits 409
Mark R. Lembersky and Uli H. Chi

8 DECISION SUPPORT FOR GOVERNMENT SERVICES *418*

8.1 MAINTAINING ARIZONA'S HIGHWAY SYSTEM, *419*
8.2 REFUSE COLLECTION AND STREET CLEANING
IN THE UNITED STATES' LARGEST CITY, *423*
8.3 FURTHER READINGS, *425*

A Statewide Pavement Management System 431
Kamal Golabi, Ram B. Kulkarni, and George B. Way

Management Science in New York's Department
of Sanitation 447
Lucius J. Riccio

9 COMPANY-WIDE INTEGRATION OF MANAGEMENT SCIENCE MODELS *460*

9.1 MS/OR MODELS IN CITGO
PETROLEUM CORPORATION, *461*
9.2 A BRIEF LOOK AT IMPLEMENTATION ISSUES, *473*
9.3 FURTHER READINGS, *475*

The Successful Deployment of Management Science
Throughout Citgo Petroleum Corporation 482
Darwin Klingman, Nancy Phillips, David Steiger, and Warren Young

CONCLUSIONS *503*

PREFACE

As management science academics, we often deal with methodological issues, abstractions, models, mathematical techniques, and other esoteric matters. But our students demand explicit illustrations and examples or they tune out! Over the years, to illustrate the successes of our field for a varied audience of business school students in undergraduate, graduate, or executive programs, we have used a select set of applications papers that balance technical and managerial aspects of model building and implementation. This book grew out of our desire to make a collection of such articles accessible to a wide audience of students and instructors in management science.

SELECTION OF ARTICLES

In deciding what papers to include in this volume, our main goal was to exemplify the practice of management science and operations research (MS/OR). We sought clear, readable papers with a decided modeling and implementation (rather than technical) focus. Not surprisingly, many of the applications papers meeting these criteria had appeared in *Interfaces* and were often finalists in the annual competition for the Edelman Award for Management Science Achievement. We decided to select all our readings from *Interfaces*. To keep our examples current, we limited the selections to the period 1982–1989. During this time, *Interfaces* had a single editor (Gary Lilien), and the same managing editor and style maven (Mary Haight). Because the format of *Interfaces* was quite consistent over this period, the presentation of the readings is more uniform than is usual in a book of reprints. In total, we selected nineteen articles for this collection; five were winners of the Edelman Award, and another eight were finalists in that competition.

ORGANIZATION OF THE BOOK

The book has three parts: Part 1 clusters papers by area of application; Part 2 groups the reprints by management science methodology or tools; and Part 3 has a strong implementation focus. While we chose papers to populate the individual chapters evenly, we had to limit the number of papers in each chapter. We apologize if we have omitted anyone's favorite. After we selected the papers, we contacted the authors to solicit updates, additional references, and any corrections.

Given our intended audience, we strongly felt that this readings book should not be simply a collection of reprints. We therefore added a substantial body of new material to accompany the readings in each chapter. Each chapter starts with a synopsis of the papers that points out the salient features of the modeling and implementation effort and goes on to give a brief survey of the applications areas. We also present related and background readings.

In addition to material that relates directly to the papers, most chapters cite a variety of other applications papers. We generally describe these papers in brief. Occasionally, we give a more detailed account of one or two applications that illustrate modeling issues particularly well. Taken as a whole, these references provide a fairly comprehensive sample of the applications that appeared in *Interfaces* during the 1980s. In fact, most of the applications papers published in *Interfaces* are cited. For additional applications papers, we consulted the "Applications Reviews" column of *Interfaces* for 1982–1988, the "OR Practice" section of *Operations Research,* and the citations under "Applications" in the *OR/MS Cumulative Index* for 1982–1987.

We did not try to review the extensive literature on the MS/OR methodologies that the papers in this book used. We therefore limited our technical citations to well-known texts and overview or survey papers. We cited mainly papers that appeared in the last decade, but occasionally give earlier references for historical reasons. Throughout, our citations are meant to be representative, rather than comprehensive.

USING THE BOOK

We have three audiences in mind for this collection. The first is graduate students in business or engineering enrolled in a first, overview course in management science or operations research. The second group comprises undergraduates from these two disciplines. Finally, we hope that the book will also appeal to management science practitioners or managers with an interest in management science.

This collection can be used as a supplement to a first-level text in management science. A number of well-known texts now include short abstracts or summaries of selected applications. Our collection can complement such texts by adding detailed and realistic studies of modeling and implementation efforts. Alternatively, the book may form the basis of an introductory or second-level course focusing on modeling and implementation issues. Since the papers gathered here require no advanced technical knowledge, an introductory course can highlight the modeling issues rather than tools and techniques. For students in second-level courses who are already familiar with basic MS/OR techniques, instructors can elaborate on the technical aspects of model building and solution methods described in the technical appendices. The further readings in each chapter cover similar applications within each area.

ACKNOWLEDGMENTS

We thank the following authors of the papers in this collection for responding to our questionnaire: John J. Bartholdi, Marshall L. Fisher, Kamal Golabi, Uday S. Karmarkar, Paul P. Kleutghen, the late Darwin Klingman, Alan P. Kuritsky, Leon S. Lasdon, Mark R. Lembersky, Matthew J. Liberatore, John D. C. Little, Robert E. Markland, Tan Miller, Warren B. Powell, A. Ravindran, Lucius J. Riccio, David L. Rumpf, and Jacob W. Ulvila. Uday Karmarkar, Matt Liberatore, and Warren Powell were kind enough to read the material relating to their work and give us their comments. We also thank Carl Harris and Saul Gass for pointing out some valuable sources to us. We are grateful to Paul Prutzman of Air Products for obtaining permission to reprint the article he co-authored.

We followed our natural interests in writing the various chapters of the book. Arjang Assad assumed the primary responsibility for writing chapters 2, 3, 6, and 9; Ed Wasil did the same for chapters 5, 7, and 8; and Gary Lilien wrote chapter 4. The overall design of the book and the contents of chapter 1 reflect the joint thinking of the three of us. Mary Haight copy edited all of the material in the book, both the commentaries and the reprinted papers. She gave us extensive and detailed comments on our manuscript with the same thoroughness that has marked her tenure as managing editor of *Interfaces*. We sincerely thank her for her sustained commitment to this project. We greatly appreciate her numerous contributions to the style and presentation of this book and take full responsibility for all instances of what she termed "intentional violations of *Interfaces* style." Finally, we thank Dennis Hogan of Prentice Hall for his interest in this project at its inception, and we are grateful to Valerie Ashton, Cyndy Rymer, and Patty Phillips for seeing it through to completion.

PUBLISHER'S CREDITS

EXCELLENCE IN MANAGEMENT SCIENCE PRACTICE

1

THE PRACTICE OF MANAGEMENT SCIENCE AND OPERATIONS RESEARCH

1.1 PICTURES AT AN MS/OR EXHIBITION

Management science (MS) and operations research (OR) are disciplines dealing with scientific approaches to decision making or professions concerned with deciding how best to design and operate systems, usually under conditions requiring the allocation of scarce resources. This description does not fully convey the nature of MS/OR. After all, people "know" what a physician, a chemist, a computer programmer, or an accountant does for a living. Operations researchers and management scientists have to take some time to explain what they do. To communicate the nature of our profession to others, we prefer to use illustrations from the practice of MS/OR. In this spirit, we offer the following snapshots of MS/OR in action.

The Streets of New York City

In the 1970s, New York City's Department of Sanitation was fighting a losing battle to keep the city clean. Even with its work force of 11,000 and a budget exceeding $400 million, the department was hard pressed to keep more than half the streets in the city acceptably clean. The department's task was not simple. Each day four to five million pieces of litter weighing more than 100 tons were deposited along 6,000 miles of city streets and the department collected and disposed of over 22,000 tons of refuse daily. In 1978, a new commissioner of sanitation recognized the gravity of the cleanliness problem and took steps to "polish the Big Apple." Over the next three years, the department developed scientific techniques to improve sanitation operations, including four MS models for manpower forecasting, truck sizing, the assignment of loads to dump sites, and the effect of increased manpower on street cleanliness.

In a letter, Mayor Ed Koch praised the achievements of the department and noted that the modeling efforts resulted in a productivity improvement of over 17 percent for refuse collection over two years and resulted in much cleaner streets. He added, "Having a strong analytic background himself, Commissioner Steisel knew of the need to have a top technical support staff to help him move his department forward. He created the Office of Operations Planning, Evaluation, and Control to provide him with the operations analysis and planning capability he needed. . . . [The office's] contributions are used to support major decisions affecting millions of dollars of expenditures and the deployment of thousands of workers. . . . [This office] has given me and the Department of Sanitation the analytic support necessary to develop strategies and resolve overall service delivery issues."

Arizona Highways

Arizona has over 7,400 miles of highways to preserve and maintain. Each year, the state's department of transportation must allocate a multimillion dollar highway preservation budget by deciding which stretches of highway to repair and what repair actions to take. In the late 1970s, Arizona used MS/OR methods to develop a statewide pavement management system to support its decision making. The core of the system is a maintenance model that quantifies the effects of maintenance actions on the condition of a stretch of highway. The model captures the impact of weather conditions and traffic on the road surfaces, as well as the role of uncertainty. In its first year of use, this system saved the state $14 million for the fiscal year 1980-1981. Additional savings of $101 million were projected for the next five years. As a result of its success in Arizona, the system is used in Alaska, Colorado, and Kansas, and in other countries, such as Finland and Saudi Arabia.

Cutting for Profit at Weyerhaeuser

The Weyerhaeuser Company is one of the largest forest products companies in the world. In 1984, it enjoyed revenues of over $5.0 billion and felled an average of 100 trees a minute (15 million yearly) in the US. Suppose that a 75 foot Douglas fir tree has just been felled, delimbed, and topped. All that remains is a 65 foot stem. The worker in the forest must now cut the stem into logs, taking the shape and dimensions of the stem into account. Although there may be hundreds of different ways to cut the stem, the operator has to decide quickly because as many as six stems are cut per minute. As this decision affects the company's profit, the company has a keen interest in improving its cutting operators' decision-making abilities.

Weyerhaeuser developed a video-game-like software package called VISION for training its workers. Designed as a highly visual and interactive system, VISION simulated the stem-cutting decisions the operators faced in the forest. Moreover, VISION had optimizing power to produce profit-maximizing decisions: a dynamic programming model imbedded within the software found the optimal cutting decision for each stem and compared its profit to the profit resulting from the operator's decision. In this way, the system served as both a training device and a decision support system.

Weyerhaeuser has used VISION since 1977 and through 1985 cited benefits of over $100 million due to improved operations. Top level managers, including the company's Chief Executive Officer George Weyerhaeuser, have used the system. Donald Rush, Weyerhaeuser's Group Vice-President for Timberlands, remarked: "VISION changed our corporate behavior in ways that have made us more money, and these changes have persisted. The contributions to our bottom line have not only held up over the years, but have actually increased in importance over time and under adverse economic conditions. This is an advantage unique and exclusive to Weyerhaeuser, an advantage enjoyed currently by none of our competitors."

Trimming Inventory at Blue Bell

Blue Bell, Inc., the company that produces Wrangler jeans and Jantzen sportswear, ranks among the world's largest apparel manufacturers. In 1983, it enjoyed $1.2 billion of sales, operated 80 plants and 32 distribution centers in the US, and employed over 27,000 people worldwide. Faced with inventory carrying costs of over 25 percent, pressures for faster production and delivery response times, and demands for increased levels of service to its customers, Blue Bell started a major inventory reduction program in 1982. By using established MS/OR inventory management techniques, Blue Bell was able to cut its inventory by over 31 percent. Relying on an integer programming model to select markers that specify the patterns for cutting fabric into garment pieces, Blue Bell achieved significantly greater flexibility in varying its production quantities and still showed savings of $1.0 million in fabric costs.

Kenneth Tutterow, Blue Bell's Chief Financial Officer and Vice President for Finance, summarizes the program as follows: "Within a period of 21 months, management reduced inventory by $115 million. While inventory levels stood at $371 million in the second quarter of 1982, they had dropped to $256 million by the first quarter of 1984. In addition, net interest expense in 1983 was down $16 million from 1982, and fabric waste had been reduced by $1 million."

Planning and Distributing Petroleum Products at Citgo

Citgo Petroleum Corporation is the largest independent downstream marketer of petroleum products in the US; it supplies gasoline to numerous gas stations including most 7-Eleven convenience stores. In 1983, Citgo decided to reduce its working capital requirements by coordinating its production and distribution operations. To meet this goal, Citgo developed a supply, distribution, and marketing (SDM) modeling system to help top managers make logistical, marketing, and financial decisions. An on-line corporate data base and extensive report generation capabilities enable the system to make useful information available to managers at different levels of the company. At the heart of the system is a network flow optimizer that tracks products as they move between various locations and across time periods. This network has 3,000 nodes and 15,000 arcs per product.

R. E. Hall, Citgo's President and Chief Executive Officer, summarizes the benefits of the system as follows: "The combination of a much improved on-line corporate data base, an optimization-based SDM Modeling System, and a reoriented, better coordinated Citgo management team . . . has resulted in significant benefit to Citgo. Specifically, product inventories have been reduced by $116 million . . . This equates to a reduction of $14 million annually [in inventory carrying costs]. In addition, management improvements in coordination, pricing, and raw material and product purchasing decisions utilizing these new management tools have resulted in benefits estimated at $2.5 million annually."

These five examples, drawn from papers presented in this volume, have certain common features that help to make the description of MS/OR as a field more concrete. First, in all these cases, managers had to decide among various alternatives for planning or operating a complex system. There are different ways of cutting a log, various possible allocations of effort to street cleaning or highway maintenance, and many ways of allocating production and inventory among distinct products. Second, the studies tend to focus more on improving the way available technology is used, rather than on developing new technology: the goal is not to develop a better saw for cutting logs or an improved technique for repairing road services. Third, the ultimate contribution of each study is to identify and recommend superior decisions. Fourth, a model is constructed to capture the key factors affecting system performance and to quantify their impact in each study. Fifth, the model plays a key role in identifying superior decisions through quantitative analysis of some kind.

Of the preceding points, the last two help to set MS/OR applications off from a host of other productivity improvement exercises. As Gass [1983] puts it:

> The *scientific contribution* of OR is in the development of decision-aiding models. The OR resolution of a decision problem is based on the analyst's ability to translate the decision problem into a form—usually a mathematical model—that can be used to compare the extent to which each alternative solution satisfies the solution objective (p. 603).

The examples also reveal that MS/OR applications can differ substantially in scope and output. For instance, while the VISION software for Weyerhaeuser focused on the specific operation of cutting logs, Citgo's integrated SDM model was designed to capture the full range of its downstream operations. This diversity has been noted by other reviewers of OR applications. Larson [1988], for example, observes:

> An OR/MS product can assume many forms, from a computer program implemented in color graphics to a consultant's report, to card files, to a 'smart' machine tool, to an educational 'video game.' The numerous embodiments [of OR/MS] contribute to the field's fuzzy image . . . Due in part to the amorphous nature of its products and the highly technical nature of its process, as a profession OR/MS runs the risk of being absorbed by related and more easily identifiable fields such as computer science (p. 135).

Despite the danger that Larson alludes to, we feel that the versatility of MS/OR is its most important strength. Opportunities for applying MS/OR can be found in all parts of an organization. More importantly, MS/OR has provided managers with a common language and a new vocabulary for describing their complex environments. Wagner [1988] makes the following observation:

> Even a nonexpert can recognize and appreciate what has happened by listening to how the managers of such enterprises describe their tasks. For example, they speak of optimizing their "objective function," removing their "binding constraints," heeding the shadow costs, "updating the production coefficients," relieving the "bounds,"—technical phrases originally coined by operations researchers when the field was developing 40 years ago. Today's managers have gotten the vocabulary right even though they may never have studied the underlying mathematics . . . What is especially noteworthy about this shift in vocabulary is that the new concepts are far more sophisticated than the old: in effect, operations research models have helped managers

keep pace intellectually with the growing size and complexity of the enterprises they run (pp. 800-801).

The applications collected in this volume also point to the central role of the MS/OR specialist as modeler and analyst. This role is not limited to selecting or developing MS/OR techniques to solve a problem. Rather, the specialist also identifies areas that can benefit from the MS/OR methodology and sees the implementation process through. Indeed, some argue that MS/OR professionals are especially suited to lead interdisciplinary teams or studies [Batson 1987; Wagner et al. 1989]. Only extended descriptions of MS/OR applications can impart the true flavor of the interplay among these various tasks of the MS/OR practitioner.

1.2 TEACHING MS/OR AND ITS PRACTICE

Every thriving profession has its success stories and needs to revisit them periodically. Recently, a committee of 24 researchers and practitioners studied research directions for OR during the next decade [CONDOR 1988]. Their report begins with some of OR's important accomplishments during the last two decades. These accomplishments include several documented cases of successful MS/OR modeling and practice with measurable economic impact. These cases demonstrate the importance of well-documented success stories. As the CONDOR report puts it, "one of the great attractions of OR is its blend of deep intellectual content with a firm mandate for practice." The report also lists several factors that enhance the application of OR within the public and private sectors. The first factor has to do with the availability of data:

> Organizations now, more than ever, make major financial commitments to collect and maintain timely and accurate data . . . Availability of these data . . . has dramatically reduced the cost of developing and operating OR model-based systems because these systems no longer sustain the cost of data collection and maintenance. In fact, the quantities of data compel organizations to employ OR techniques to gain insight from the data (p. 620).

A related factor is the availability of more powerful and less costly computers and software. Many, including the authors of the CONDOR report, expect that the increasingly widespread use of personal computers and spreadsheet, data base, and project management software will lead to greater acceptance of quantitative models. Recognizing the importance of this technology, Wagner states:

The widespread availability of reliable software is as important as proper data treatment for successful operations research applications. Easy-to-obtain, easy-to-use computer programs are the most effective communications link between high-powered research teams and the average professional hoping to apply the research to other real-life situations [Wagner et al. 1989, p. 666].

The distinction between the high-powered research team and the average professional deserves comment. Two decades ago, addressing organizational problems through the use of some model-based approach involved the solution of the model by optimization, simulation, or other mathematical techniques. In many cases, these models were the domain of specialists who acted as the "high priests" of MS/OR. In the last decade or so, this has changed. Almost all recent graduates of business and engineering schools have been exposed to models and computers as decision-making aids. Many "average professionals" are now potential users of MS/OR expertise and may initiate most future applications of MS/OR.

Designing MS/OR Courses to Reflect Practice

As the impact of MS/OR is ultimately felt in its practice, MS/OR courses should familiarize students with applications in a serious fashion. This is particularly important in a first course. Borsting et al. [1988] believe that the aim of a first MS/OR course within an MBA program is "to prepare all students to be consumers of MS/OR information and to motivate those students who may be future producers of MS/OR to take other courses and learn the field in depth." Given this objective, they go on to list their view of the premises underlying such a course:

First, MS/OR is more than just a collection of techniques and classes of models. It is a way of perceiving, analyzing, and interacting with the world . . . The first course in MS/OR for MBA students should be more than just a survey of techniques and models. These techniques and models should be presented as tools to support decision making.

Second, the first course in MS/OR for MBA students should be relevant to the real world and to other courses in the MBA curriculum . . . The instructor should make the usefulness clear to the students, demonstrating the successful application of MS/OR in the real world and its use in other courses with a decision making orientation, such as finance, marketing, accounting, and business policy (p. 74).

Traditionally, however, most first courses in MS/OR have focused

on models and techniques. Borsting et al. recommend a shift of emphasis to problem formulation and the development of models that support
complex decision making. In particular, they recommend the use of
real-world applications and MS/OR success stories such as those published in *Interfaces* and the video tapes of the Edelman prize competition
presentations (see Section 1.3). Changing the focus of most MS/OR
courses from a concentration on tools and techniques to a consideration
of actual practice requires a new generation of texts and other teaching
materials.

Other approaches to achieving a focus on practice have also been
suggested: Giauque [1980] involved the students of his MBA classes in
field consulting, and Gelders [1981] designed an industrial management
curriculum that requires a master's thesis based on a formal project with
joint industry and university involvement. Zahedi [1984] cites a number
of other efforts or approaches in MS/OR education. Despite these efforts, giving students hands-on exposure to real MS/OR applications
requires resources and a level of coordination that are beyond the reach
of most introductory courses. However, such students can still experience the flavor of real-life applications vicariously, through published
accounts of the applications carried out by practicing MS/OR professionals. To serve this purpose, these accounts should go beyond a mere
description of tools to capture the full spectrum of MS/OR modeling
and implementation. We hope that the papers we have selected from
Interfaces for this volume will provide this documentation for the reader.

1.3 CAPTURING MS/OR PRACTICE

While it is important to make MS/OR tools more widely accessible, it is
equally important that the scope of MS/OR not be limited to building
and applying such tools. Reflecting on the early history of OR and how
its pioneers practiced their craft, Miser [1989] states:

> To sum up, any OR worker today must admire the rapid develop-
> ment and sophistication of our stock of models and our ability to
> analyze them, but this sort of work was not uppermost in the minds
> of our pioneers, nor should it today be the primary focus of OR
> work . . . [Building and analyzing models] were often the easy part of
> their work and a part that was often quickly accomplished; the hard,
> laborious, sometimes disappointing, and always time-consuming por-
> tions of their work were comparing the models with reality, using
> them to help in solving problems, persuading those in command to
> make effective use of the information generated by the analyses, and
> following up to see whether the actual effects compared favorably

with what was predicted. The success of these craft skills in combination yielded the birthright that we enjoy today (p. 73).

In this statement, Miser reminds us that the practice of MS/OR goes beyond model building and analysis. While technical developments and methodological contributions are generally straightforward to document and publish, chronicling the remaining components of MS/OR practice faces many barriers. It is difficult to document the processes of problem formulation, data collection, and implementation; and even harder to impart their true flavor.

One of the key goals of *Interfaces,* the journal from which all the articles in this book are drawn, is the exchange of information between managers and MS/OR professionals on issues related to practice. In addition to successful implementations of MS/OR methods, *Interfaces* also includes regular columns entitled "Misapplication reviews" and "20/ 30 hindsight" that extract lessons or insights from these less successful efforts. As MS/OR tools become more widely accessible and organizations increasingly rely on these tools instead of MS/OR professionals, misapplication errors are likely to increase.

In addition to *Interfaces,* the "OR Practice" section of the journal *Operations Research* also contains interesting applications of MS/OR. The editorial board of this section includes individuals with substantial experience as practitioners. For this section, the journal seeks reports on significant, nonroutine, or highly publicized examples of OR practice. It also solicits cases that failed in an instructive manner or cases that document major changes in the orientation or approach of a major application effort [Rothkopf 1989].

Despite the efforts of several journals, detailed reports of MS/OR applications are rarely published. The reason commonly advanced to explain this is that practitioners, unlike academics, are not rewarded for publishing articles. The internal recognition of the success of an MS/OR study is usually enough to reward the practitioner. Unless the firm decides to advertise its success, the practitioner is apt to just move on to the next assignment. The pressures of the next assignment often leave the individual little time to document past successes; and promotions or job turnover make this even less likely.

A more serious problem occurs at the level of the organization in which the study is performed. Many firms believe that releasing information on the methods they use can only benefit their competitors. Indeed, they often have structures in place to review, impede, or simply block the release of such information. But even from a purely economic point of view, this zero-sum mentality may be unjustified. In competitive bidding, for example, sharing information among firms may benefit all companies by eliminating the "winner's curse" where the winning bid may be unreasonably low because the firm had poor information on costs. To avoid such outcomes in joint bidding situations, oil companies routinely share seismological information and some have even published their bidding models.

The Franz Edelman Award

Aside from the persistence of the editors of *Interfaces* and the OR Practice section of *Operations Research*, the most effective mechanism for encouraging reports of successful MS/OR practice has been the Edelman Award. Through this award, The Institute of Management Sciences (TIMS) recognizes outstanding examples of MS/OR practice. In 1990, the invitation for submissions to the competition outlined the eligibility requirements:

> The prize is awarded for implemented work, not for a submitted paper or presentation describing a work . . . To be eligible, an entry must report upon a completed, practical application and must describe results that had a significant, verifiable, and preferably quantifiable impact on the performance of the organization under study.

With a 1989 membership of over 7,600 researchers, teachers, students, and practitioners, TIMS is one of the world's leading MS/OR professional organizations. One of its 19 special interest groups is the College on the Practice of Management Science (CPMS)—a group that seeks to focus the attention of the management community and the public at large on the value of MS/OR practice. In 1972, CPMS began sponsoring the Annual International Management Science Award Competition in the hopes of encouraging practitioners to document outstanding applications of MS/OR with proven benefits. In 1985, the award was renamed the Franz Edelman Award for Management Science Achievement in honor of the late Franz Edelman of RCA, a pioneer in the use of management science and management information systems.

Over the last two decades, the competition has steadily grown in prestige and visibility. In addition to cash prizes that totaled $10,000 in 1990, the winners receive wide recognition throughout the management science community: The finalists present their work during a day-long session at the national meeting of the MS/OR community, *Interfaces* annually publishes the papers of the competition's finalists in a special issue, and TIMS makes video tapes of the finalists' presentations.

Of the 19 papers in this book, five were winners and another eight were finalists in the Edelman Award competition in the years 1982 through 1988. From 1980 through 1989, *Interfaces* has published 53 papers by finalists of the 9th through the 17th annual prize competitions (some papers from the earlier years of the competition did not appear in *Interfaces*). A count of the published papers (Exhibit 1–1)

EXHIBIT 1–1. Papers by finalists in the competition for the Franz Edelman Award for Management Science Achievement are categorized by area of application. Some papers appear in more than one category. Papers are cited by the first author and the year in which the paper appears in *Interfaces*. From 1985 to 1989, papers appear in the first issue (Number 1, January–February). From 1980 to 1983, papers appear in the last issue (Number 6, December).

Facilities and Equipment Planning	Transportation	Government Services
Wind [1989]	Powell [1988]	Taylor [1989]
Ravindran [1989]	Holloran [1986]	Ulvila [1988]
Breitman [1987]	Welch [1986]	Riccio [1986]
Eaton [1985]	Sauder [1983]	Eaton [1985]
McMahan [1982]	Barker [1981]	Golabi [1982]
Graves [1982]	Dawson [1981]	
Swart [1981]	Brosch [1980]	

Production Planning and Scheduling	Marketing	Military
Vasko [1989]	Wind [1989]	Eiger [1988]
DeWitt [1989]	Lodish [1988]	Cochard [1985]
Box [1988]	Urban [1983]	Cooper [1980]
Dougherty [1987]	Kuritsky [1982]	Holz [1980]
Lembersky [1986]	Dyer [1982]	
Edwards [1985]	Oren [1980]	
Boykin [1985]		
King [1980]		
Cooper [1980]		

Inventory Management	Investment and Risk Analysis	Public Utilities
Chao [1989]	Bean [1987]	Chao [1989]
Edwards [1985]	Farrell [1983]	Terry [1986]
Kleutghen [1985]	Smith [1982]	Ikura [1986]
Hilal [1981]	Davidson [1980]	Graves [1982]
Brout [1981]		Showers [1981]
King [1980]		

Distribution and Logistics	Public Policy	Health Care
Powell [1988]	Kavrakoglu [1989]	Hilal [1981]
Klingman [1987]	Goeller [1985]	Pliskin [1981]
Blumenfeld [1987]	Graves [1982]	
Brown [1987]		
Bell [1983]		

reveals that the areas that received the greatest attention were production planning and scheduling (nine papers), transportation (seven papers), and facilities and equipment planning (seven papers). These counts can be compared with the results of surveys by Forgionne [1983] and Thomas and DaCosta [1979] who found that project planning, capital budgeting, production planning and inventory control, and forecasting were the most common areas of application for MS/OR in corporations.

Exhibit 1–2 categorizes the papers according to the techniques they use. The most widely used techniques are linear programming (11 finalists), integer programming (11 finalists), and simulation (10 finalists).

EXHIBIT 1–2. The papers by finalists in the competition for the Franz Edelman Award for Management Science Achievement are categorized by the primary MS tool used in the analysis and the application area. Papers that use more than one tool in a significant way appear in more than one category.

Tool	Paper	Area of Application	Problem Description	Firm or Agency
Linear Programming				
	Eiger [1988]	Military Manpower Management	Design system to support manpower planning	US Army
	Klingman [1987]	Logistics	Company-wide development of MS models	Citgo Petroleum
	Breitman [1987]	Facilities and Equipment Planning	Integrate facilities planning and strategic marketing	General Motors
	Holloran [1986]	Transportation	Schedule shiftwork at airline reservation offices and airports	United Airlines
	Goeller [1985]	Public Policy	Development national water management policy	Netherlands Rijkwaterstaat
	Graves [1982]	Public Policy Electric Utility	Develop long-term capital expansion policy	Potomac Electric Power Company
	Barker [1981]	Transportation	Achieve better service for a motor carrier	ANR Freight System
	Hilal [1981]	Health Care	Determine optimal quantity of heart valves to order from vendors	American Edwards Laboratory
	Holz [1980]	Military Manpower Management	Use goal programming to meet forecasts of Army strength	US Army

EXHIBIT 1–2. (*Continued*)

Tool	Paper	Area of Application	Problem Description	Firm or Agency
	Brosch [1980]	Transportation	Plan railroad freight car fleet size and mix to maximize long-term cash flow	Chessie System
	King [1980]	Production and Inventory	Develop an integrated system for production planning	Kelly-Springfield Tire
Integer Programming				
	Taylor [1989]	Government Services	Deploy patrol officers to maximize city coverage	San Francisco Police
	Vasko [1989]	Production	Design ingot molds and select ingot sizes	Bethlehem Steel
	Bean [1987]	Investment	Schedule divestiture of shopping malls and office buildings	Homart
	Brown [1987]	Distribution	Model real-time dispatching and scheduling of customer deliveries	Mobil
	Holloran [1986]	Transportation	Schedule shiftwork at airline reservation offices and airports	United Airlines
	Edwards [1985]	Production and Inventory	Reduce apparel inventory	Blue Bell
	Cochard [1985]	Military Operations	Improve aircraft utilization and responsiveness to airlift operations	US Air Force
	Boykin [1985]	Production	Optimize production cost per pound of chemical to meet target values	Monsanto
	Eaton [1985]	Government Services	Determine the locations of emergency medical service facilities	Austin, Texas
	Bell [1983]	Distribution	Design routes for vehicles that distribute industrial gases	Air Products and Chemicals
	McMahan [1982]	Facilities and Equipment Planning	Select energy improvement projects to maximize NPV	Exxon

(*Continued*)

EXHIBIT 1–2. (*Continued*)

Tool	Paper	Area of Application	Problem Description	Firm or Agency
Networks				
	Powell [1988]	Transportation Distribution	Optimize movements of trucks to points of need	North American Van Lines
	Klingman [1987]	Logistics	Company-wide deployment of MS models	Citgo Petroleum
	Blumenfeld [1987]	Logistics	Reduce costs of shipping parts and components from suppliers to plants	General Motors
	Ikura [1986]	Electric Utility	Optimize the flow of water released for hydroelectric plants	Pacific Gas and Electric
Nonlinear Programming				
	DeWitt [1989]	Production	Planning and scheduling gasoline blending operations	Texaco
	Dougherty [1987]	Production	Long-term planning of production facilities and decisions	Santos Ltd.
	Goeller [1985]	Public Policy	Develop a national water management policy	Netherlands Rijkwaterstaat
Dynamic Programming				
	Chao [1989]	Inventory Electric Utility	Manage coal inventories that fuel power plants	Electric Power Research Institute
	Lembersky [1986]	Manpower Training	Simulate decisions on how to cut logs	Weyerhaeuser
	Terry [1986]	Electric Utility	Determine the optimal allocation of hydro and thermal resources in Brazilian electric system	Centro de Pesquisas de Energia Electrica
	Golabi [1982]	Government Services	Develop optimal maintenance policies for highways	State of Arizona Department of Transportation
Optimization				
	Box [1988]	Production Scheduling	Scheduling caster to convert molten steel to solid steel slabs	LTV Steel
	Sauder [1983]	Transportation	Optimize train dispatching	Southern Railway
	Smith [1982]	Investment	Develop a computer-based lease portfolio planning model to improve profits	New England Merchants Leasing

EXHIBIT 1–2. (*Continued*)

Tool	Paper	Area of Application	Problem Description	Firm or Agency
	Showers [1981]	Communications	Finding good classification rules in credit screening	Bell System
Inventory Models				
	Chao [1989]	Inventory Electric Utility	Manage coal inventories that fuel power plants	Electric Power Research Institute
	Edwards [1985]	Production and Inventory	Reduce apparel inventory	Blue Bell
	Kleutghen [1985]	Inventory	Manage inventories in the production of pharmaceuticals	Pfizer
	Brout [1981]	Inventory	Controlling finished goods inventory of Planters Peanuts items	Standard Brands
	King [1980]	Production and Inventory	Develop an integrated system for production planning	Kelly-Springfield Tire
Simulation				
	Chao [1989]	Inventory Electric Utility	Manage coal inventories that fuel power plants	Electric Power Research Institute
	Ravindran [1989]	Facility Layout	Design jet engine repair facility at Tinker Air Force Base	US Air Force
	Eiger [1988]	Military Manpower Management	Design system to support manpower planning	US Army
	Lembersky [1986]	Manpower Training	Simulate decisions on how to cut logs	Weyerhaeuser
	Welch [1986]	Transportation	Analyze the capacity of a rail main line	Canadian National Railway
	Riccio [1986]	Government Services	Simulate the operations of sweeping street curbs	Department of Sanitation NYC
	Goeller [1985]	Public Policy	Develop a national water management policy	Netherlands Rijkwaterstaat
	Swart [1981]	Facility Planning	Improve efficiency, productivity, and sales of fast food restaurants	Burger King
	Dawson [1981]	Transportation	Planning canal capacity	St. Lawrence Seaway Authority

(*Continued*)

EXHIBIT 1–2. (*Continued*)

Tool	Paper	Area of Application	Problem Description	Firm or Agency
	Cooper [1980]	Production	Simulate phases of shipbuilding to diagnose causes of overruns	Ingalls Shipbuilding
Forecasting				
	Kavrakoglu [1989]	Public Policy	Diagnose causes of Turkish housing problem and suggest cures	Istanbul Chamber of Commerce
	Pliskin [1981]	Health Care	Develop a dialysis need-projection model	Massachusetts Department of Public Health
	Holz [1980]	Military Manpower Management	Use goal programming to meet forecasts of Army strength	US Army
Decision Analysis				
	Ulvila [1988]	Government Services	Assess impact of new postal equipment	US Postal Service
Investment and Risk Analysis				
	Bean [1987]	Investment	Schedule divestiture of shopping malls and office buildings	Homart
	Farrell [1983]	Portfolio Analysis	Develop an equity investment strategy	MPT Associates
	Smith [1982]	Investment	Develop a computer-based lease portfolio planning model to improve profits	New England Merchants Leasing
	Davidson [1980]	Risk Analysis	Analyze risk for corporate investment opportunities	Getty Oil
Marketing Science Models				
	Wind [1989]	Product Design	Design new hotel chain using conjoint analysis	Marriott
	Lodish [1988]	Sales Force Sizing and Deployment	Decide on sales force size and how it should be deployed using response functions	Syntex Laboratories
	Urban [1983]	New Product Sales	Forecast sales of new packaged goods using the ASSESSOR system	Armour-Dial Proctor & Gamble and others
	Kuritsky [1982]	Marketing Strategy	Develop strategy for residence long distance marketplace	AT&T

EXHIBIT 1–2. (*Continued*)

Tool	Paper	Area of Application	Problem Description	Firm or Agency
	Dyer [1982]	Merchandising Strategies	Develop new merchandising strategies using judgmental modeling and multiattribute utility theory	Standard Oil Company (Amoco)
	Oren [1980]	Brand Choice	Model consumer choice of computer printers	Xerox

For comparison, Harpell, Lane, and Mansour [1989] found that operations researchers used linear programming, statistics, and simulation most frequently in practice. Finally, Exhibit 1–3 lists the first-prize winners of the Edelman Award from 1980 to 1989.

1.4 IMPLEMENTATION OF MS/OR STUDIES

In 1960, the journal *Operations Research* published a cluster of papers from a 1958 symposium that revisited OR studies five years after their completion. In his introductory remarks, Churchman [1960] noted that "it is often difficult to learn what happened to a given case, because the published report stops before the implementation begins," and stated that many OR studies become more interesting the older they get. In one of the papers, Edie [1960] reviewed his 1953 study of the toll booths of the George Washington Bridge, performed for the Port of New York [Edie 1954], which won him the first Lanchester Prize ever awarded. Edie discussed the impact of the original study, compared the predictions of the queueing model with actual observations, and covered a host of other modeling and implementation issues that had emerged over the five-year period since 1953. He expressed the hope that a "Case Histories Ten Years After" symposium would take place to continue tracking the implementation process.

On a different note, within the same symposium, Ackoff [1960] dealt with unsuccessful case studies in OR and considered the reasons behind the lack of success. They included company reorganizations, lack of high-level management involvement, and economic pressures to reduce spending on outside services (consultants). This symposium was an interesting early attempt to review the challenges of implementing MS/OR models and was unique in following up studies after a number of years had transpired. Unfortunately, case studies covering implementation issues in detail have been rare in the quarter century following the symposium. As Stainton [1979] observes, "it is not normally possible to

EXHIBIT 1–3. First prize winners of the Franz Edelman Award for Management Science Achievement, 1980 to 1988.

Year	Authors	Title	Methodology	Comments
1988	Taylor and Huxley	A Break from Tradition for the San Francisco Police: Patrol Officer Scheduling Using an Optimization-Based Decision Support System	IP	A PC-based system that produces near-optimal schedules using an integer search procedure yields savings of $11 million per year.
1987	Lodish, Curtis, Ness, and Simpson†	Sales Force Sizing and Deployment Using a Decision Calculus Model at Syntex Laboratories	RF	A set of parameterized models helps Syntex increase its sales force size and change its deployment. Sales increase by 8 percent annually.
1986	Klingman, Phillips, Steiger, and Young†	The Successful Deployment of Management Science throughout Citgo Petroleum Corporation	LP, NT	The application of a wide variety of MS/OR tools turns around a money-losing company in two years. Profits improve $70 million per year.
1985	Lembersky and Chi†	Weyerhaeuser Decision Simulator Improves Timber Profits	DP	A video-game-like simulator that uses dynamic programming helps Weyerhaeuser make better decisions about cutting logs. Total operational benefits exceed $100 million.
1984	Goeller et al.	Planning the Netherlands' Water Resources	LP, NLP, SM	An integrated system of 50 models was used to develop a national water management policy that saved hundreds of millions of dollars in investment expenditures and saved $15 million per year by reducing agricultural damage.
1983	Bell et al.†	Improving the Distribution of Industrial Gases with an On-line Computerized Routing and Scheduling Optimizer	IP	Daily delivery schedules are generated for Air Products and Chemicals, Inc. by solving mixed integer programs with as many as 800,000 variables and 200,000 constraints to near optimality. Savings have been between 6 percent to 10 percent of operating costs.

Year	Authors	Title	Method	Description
1982	Golabi, Kulkarni, and Way†	A Statewide Pavement Management System	DP	Optimal maintenance policies are developed for the 7,400 miles of highways in Arizona. First-year savings amounted to $14 million.
1981	Barker, Sharon, and Sen	From Freight Flow and Cost Patterns to Greater Profitability and Better Service for a Motor Carrier	LP	Two decision models were constructed to help improve the strategic linehaul planning process for ANF Freight System, Inc. Savings are estimated at $9 million per year.
1980	King and Love	Coordinating Decisions for Increased Profits	LP, IN	An integrated "total system" is developed to coordinate sales forecasting, inventory control, production planning, and distribution management for Kelly-Springfield Tire Company. Benefits amounted to $5 million over a 10-year period.

DP	Dynamic Programming	NLP	Nonlinear Programming
IN	Inventory Models	NT	Networks
IP	Integer Programming	RF	Response Functions
LP	Linear Programming	SM	Simulation

† reprinted in this book

explore more deeply the published case studies, to examine how they evolved, and what conflicting objectives there might have been, and what impact personalities might have had." Drawing upon his experiences in developing a cutting stock model for a steel company, Stainton describes the different alternatives in formulating the problem and implementing the system. Another well-doumented implementation effort is the fire department deployment study performed by the New York City RAND Institute [Walker, Chaiken, and Ignall 1979]. Walker [1989] reflects on the lessons of this study and its development since 1974.

The familiar framework for conducting MS/OR studies comprises problem formulation, model construction, solution, testing, and evaluation [Agin 1978]. A general criticism of MS/OR publications and education is that they place a disproportionate emphasis on the technical issues related to formulating and solving models. In fact, scholarly publications in MS/OR devote the greatest amount of space to solution techniques and computational procedures. The processes of arriving at a suitable definition of the problem, or determining the scope and limits of the model are scarcely discussed. While these processes are difficult to capture and communicate, they contain valuable lessons. For example, the steps of the modeling process are iterative, rather than sequential. As Wagner et al. [1989] put it,

> Most operations research students, for example, get the idea that one starts with a model (that is, a conceptualization of variables, relationships, constraints, performance measures, etc.) and afterwards finds the data to support the conceptualization. In reality, however, the process between model conceptualization and data analysis is interactive (p. 665).

Similarly, model validation involves a complex web of issues and interacts with the other modeling steps [Gass 1983]. Authors usually discuss model verification—the process of demonstrating that a computer program associated with the model runs as intended. Validation, however, tests the agreement between the behaviors of the model and the real world; it is closely related to model construction and formulation. In evaluating the extent of this agreement, the very notion of a single model is perhaps misleading. As Miser remarks [Wagner et al. 1989],

> Most OR workers . . . tend to emphasize a central model as the core of interest in their work. But this is to ignore the fact that this model is almost always surrounded by many conceptions about the state of the surrounding world, about input data, about what variables can be treated as exogenous, and so on, that also can be thought of as models—and should be explored and judged just as the central

model. From this point of view almost every study involves a linked consortium of models—to all of which the careful analyst gives appropriate critical attention (p. 671).

Miser [1985] has emphasized the role of the interaction between the analyst and the client organization in the practice of systems analysis. Much of his discussion applies equally well to MS/OR. The importance of organizational and managerial factors grows as one approaches the implementation phase. The term implementation has different connotations for different groups. Schultz and Slevin [1979] point out that, to the OR analyst, implementation means "getting the results of OR work into the hands (minds) of managers;" while to managers, the term means "useful assistance in problem solving." The difference in viewpoints explains why an analyst once affirmed that a model has "already been implemented. They just are not using it!"

More generally, there is a distinction between *technical validity* (the model works as seen by MS/OR analyst) and *organizational validity* (the model fits within the organization). Schultz and Slevin explain the latter concept as follows:

[The model] must be compatible with organizational practices and user needs. It must not require tremendous energy devoted towards organizational change—or if it does, there must be a very clear and present benefit from the OR/MS innovation. This view of implementation suggests that the OR/MS researcher must be more than just a technical specialist . . . If he is not sensitive to what is happening in the organization, the likelihood of successful implementation is reduced (p. 4).

Schultz and Slevin mention a third dimension of implementation: the modified behavior (or decision making) of the users of the model should contribute to the organization's effectiveness as viewed by the top manager. In particular, a successful implementation must win the support of top management and enlist them as advocates. From this organizational perspective, implementation and the management of innovation has many common elements.

Some studies of implementation were based on surveys of MS/OR professionals or their clients. Watson and Marrett [1979] surveyed management scientists in a variety of nonacademic organizations to identify implementation problems. The barriers to implementation the respondents cited most frequently were problems in selling MS/OR to management, little appreciation for MS/OR among top or middle management due to educational background, and the lack of good clean data. Forgionne [1983] reported that inadequate data, poor communication, lengthy completion times of MS/OR studies, and lack of resources were the main impediments.

In the absence of a universal framework for implementation, case studies continue to provide a useful experiential base to guide the practice of MS/OR. Tomlinson, Quade, and Miser [1985] extract important lessons from a number of case studies in systems analysis. Wynne and Robak [1989] attempt to point out some common themes shared by the Edelman prize-winning studies. The papers in this volume do not completely expose the various implementation challenges and barriers the analysts encountered, but they do point out the crucial role that attention to organizational issues plays in successful MS/OR practice. In Chapter 9 and the conclusions, we revisit implementation issues and attempt to extract a few successful strategies for implementation indicated by the papers collected in this book.

1.5 PLAN OF THE BOOK

The 19 readings in this book cover a broad range of applications in both the private and public sectors. The nine chapters of the book fall into three parts. Part 1 groups articles by type of application and the functional areas within a firm to which they relate. Chapters 2, 3, and 4 focus on production planning, inventory management, distribution analysis, and marketing—all standard topics in the operations of a firm.

In Part 2, we take a methodological perspective and sample applications of well-known tools and techniques of MS/OR: mathematical programming, queueing and simulation, and decision-making aids. In grouping the readings around MS/OR tools in Part 2, we are following the current organization of most introductory texts and courses in MS/OR. We are aware that this scheme for presenting applications is debatable as it focuses on the tools. Nevertheless, we feel that as long as these techniques occupy such prominent places in MS/OR courses, students should be exposed to detailed studies that exemplify the application of these tools. Chapter 5 covers mathematical programming and presents applications of linear programming, nonlinear programming, and integer programming heuristics. The first paper in Chapter 6 combines simulation studies with queueing analysis to evaluate the performance of a manufacturing system, while the second uses simulation to plan capacity for a job-shop environment. Chapter 7 focuses on tools that help human beings make complex and challenging decisions. The chapter opens with a paper that uses a decision-making tool called the analytic hierarchy process to answer a question that should appeal to sports enthusiasts: Is there a methodical way of deciding upon the most outstanding sports records? The next paper considers an application of decision trees to the selection of equipment for the postal service. The final paper of Chapter 7 concerns an elaborate decision support system developed for a forest products company to guide the complex set of decisions associated with cutting up trees to produce logs.

The third part of the book focuses on implementation issues. While all the readings included in this book discuss implementation, the papers selected for Part 3 are particularly sensitive to implementation issues. Chapter 8 focuses on decision support for government services. Chapter 9 deals with the important issue of integrating MS/OR models into the complex web of information flow in a firm.

The readings in this book overlap in their application areas and techniques. For example, the application of MS/OR to production management is primarily captured in Chapter 2, but it is also illustrated in the two readings in Chapter 6, the gasoline blending problem of Chapter 5, and the CITGO study in Chapter 9. The reading for Chapter 9 could easily be integrated into Chapter 3 under the rubric of distribution management.

The Structure of Each Chapter

Each chapter introduces two or three readings that share the same applications or methodological area. We have also added a considerable amount of background and supplementary material to introduce the readings and to position them within the area of MS/OR to which they belong. This material is generally divided into three parts: an overview of the readings, a wide-angle view of the field, and an annotated list of further readings.

The overview has the dual purpose of summarizing and amplifying the readings. In its first role, it highlights the key points of each reading and summarizes its major contributions. In some cases, the overview explains certain parts of a reading in detail. While papers from *Interfaces* generally relegate discussions of mathematical models to appendices that follow the text, we integrate the presentation of the model into the overview.

The second part of each chapter typically reviews the area of application or methodology from which the readings are drawn. These sections focus on applications and serve as brief guides to additional sources in the area. In preparing these sections, we were guided by the following considerations:

1. Because the book focuses on applications, we limited the citations on methodologies and techniques to well-known texts and review articles.
2. We tried to cite most of the papers describing applications that appeared in *Interfaces* between 1980 and 1989 in the areas covered in our chapters. We looked especially for applications papers that detailed their application environments and were rich in institutional knowledge. At times, we cited

papers whose technical contents had little novelty if their application settings intrigued us.

3. In some chapters, we gave long summaries of a few applications that illustrated their areas particularly well (for example, in Chapters 2, 3, and 6). The papers summarized in this fashion were all good candidates to include as readings if we had had more space.

4. We tried to avoid presenting long lists of references with no further details. Instead, we include a brief description of each source we cite that brings out the nature of the application and its setting.

5. We tried to draw on accessible sources that students can find in most university libraries. We avoided references to proceedings, unpublished technical reports or dissertations, and scholarly journals that are not widely available. We occasionally deviate from this rule when the paper cited is intimately related to a paper included in this book.

In the last part of each chapter, we provide an annotated list of related and background readings. Related readings are limited to material directly relevant to the application or technique discussed in a given paper. Background readings draw upon a larger group of sources that discuss other applications of MS/OR to the same general area, or papers that apply the technique described in the reading in other settings.

We prepared this book because we firmly believe in the value of detailed accounts of applications of MS/OR in imparting the true flavor of our field and its challenges. Every field has its folklore and a collection of stories to go along with it. Ours is no exception. We hope that our selection of articles and our commentaries will help readers flesh out the bare bones of MS/OR techniques with concrete cases and stories that exemplify successful MS/OR practice.

1.6 FURTHER READINGS

- Several reports and articles review the past accomplishments and future directions of MS/OR. The report of the Committee on the Next Decade in Operations Research (CONDOR) is the result of a workshop conducted from May 31 to June 2, 1987 at the National Science Foundation [CONDOR 1988]. After reviewing some accomplishments of MS/OR in practice, the report outlines OR's research agenda in optimization, stochastic processes, the interface with artificial intelligence, operational and modeling sciences, manufacturing, and logistics. Commenting on this report, Wagner et al. [1989] make some keen observations about modeling, implementation, and MS/OR practice. Little [1988] discusses the future areas of research in the decision and management sciences that emerged from the 1984 workshop sponsored by the National Science Foundation. The promising cross-disciplinary research areas include choice theory, decision support, and the treatment of complexity.

- Certain reviews of MS/OR are richly illustrated with specific applications and examples from practice. In reviewing the role of OR in the service industries, Larson [1988] mentions many successful cases and applications; a number of these are extracted from articles that appear in this book. Wagner [1988] reviews the past accomplishments of OR, discusses how it produces value added for an industrial enterprise, and outlines the areas in which progress is likely to occur in the next decade. Throughout his discussion, Wagner draws upon his own experience in applying MS/OR to illustrate his points. Shubik [1987] gives an entertaining, personal account of the interplay between theory and applications in MS.

- In 1987, to commemorate ORSA's 35th anniversary, several past presidents of the society presented their views on OR in the journal *Operations Research*. All of these papers contain interesting stories, observations, and thoughts for the future. To mention a few examples, Miser [1987] argues that OR should develop a greater understanding of its domain and its professional practice. Gass [1987] comments on the meanings of professionalism in OR and argues that OR must develop a professional identity. In his highly critical account of OR's development, Ackoff [1987] argues that OR has failed to live up to its early promise, that it has become introverted, and that it no longer responds to the real needs of organizations. Blumstein [1987] believes that OR should continue its missionary role in providing a scientific base to other areas of management and goes on to respond to some of Ackoff's charges.

- To obtain better information about the composition and views of members of the MS/OR community, several large-scale surveys have been conducted. Balut and Armacost [1986] surveyed the members of ORSA to establish who the members are, why they joined or continue to renew, and what they think of the society's activities and publications. They found that 40 percent of ORSA's 7,000 members were employed at universities, 39 percent in corporations, 14 percent in government, and the rest in not-for-profit organizations. Approximately 1,000 of the members were students. King, Grover, and Nelson [1989] conducted a similar survey of TIMS members. They sent out questionnaires to all 5,967 members of TIMS in April 1988, and received over 2,400 responses. Over 60 percent of the respondents were academics, 31 percent were in business, and 8 percent were in government jobs. Close to eight percent identified themselves as students. These surveys of ORSA and TIMS memberships contain some information on salaries of MS/OR professionals. In a 1982 survey of TIMS members, Hall [1984] takes a close look at career paths and compensation levels. Bradbard et al. [1987] surveyed directors of MS/OR research of the 500 largest US industrial operations. Based on the results of their survey, Bradbard et al. discuss the profile of these directors and their hiring practices, and their evaluation of professional societies and their journals. Morgan [1989] reviews 15 surveys of the use of MS/OR in the private sector from 1958 to 1987. Her comparative review shows that companies have tended to decentralize MS/OR efforts.

- Education has been a key concern of the MS/OR community [Zahedi 1984]. Some recent reports have concentrated on the course offerings of business schools in MS/OR. Borsting et al. [1988] propose a design for a first MBA course in MS/OR that aims at preparing students to be consumers of MS/OR. They offer two sample course designs and describe the topics to be covered in each week of the 12-week course. A key goal of these integrative designs is to help students understand the role of modeling in managerial decision making. Consequently, the designers place less emphasis on tools or techniques and try to communicate the full process of decision support, instead of just one phase of the process. Carraway and Freeland [1989] surveyed 20 leading graduate business schools' course offerings in operations management and quantitative methods. They reviewed the contents of required and elective courses and concluded that the courses have become less mathematical and more managerial as compared to a decade ago.

- Certain researchers have investigated the use of MS/OR tools in practice. Harpell, Lane, and Mansour [1989] performed a longitudinal study of this issue by sending three pairs of questionnaires to ORSA members at five-year intervals (1973, 1978, and 1983). OR educators were asked about the quantitative techniques they spent most of their time teaching, while OR practitioners were requested to identify the techniques they found most useful in practice. Both groups consistently identified linear programming, simulation, and statistics as being most important, but practitioners recommended a more diverse set of techniques than did educators. In their surveys, Forgionne [1983] and Thomas and DaCosta [1979] identified the same tools with the addition of PERT/CPM. In a survey of industrial engineers, linear programming, simulation, network analysis, queueing analysis, and decision trees ranked as the five most widely used tools [Shannon, Long, and Buckles 1980].

- A number of studies have focused on the strategy and process of implementation efforts in MS/OR. Wysocki [1979] classifies 276 papers on this topic that appeared from 1953 to 1976; over 75 percent of these were published between 1970 and 1976. Interestingly, only 39 of these papers were case studies of actual implementations. Wysocki also lists 10 key papers that he used to build his research bibliography. Zahedi [1984] also briefly reviewed implementation issues. The book edited by Doktor, Schultz, and Slevin [1979] and the special issue of *Interfaces* in May/June 1987 are devoted entirely to MS/OR implementation. In their introduction to this special issue, Ginzberg and Schultz [1987] assess the status of implementation research and mention three themes in implementation studies: (1) things management can do to improve implementation success, (2) the effects of changing technology, and (3) changing views of the implementation process.

- Geisler and Rubenstein [1987] interviewed 24 managers in 18 manufacturing companies to investigate issues associated with implementing application software in production systems and reports how these managers ranked the importance of various factors that affect implementation. Similar studies with a specific focus that draw upon a sample of case studies appear in Doktor, Schultz, and Slevin [1979].

- Several studies focus on the role of the MS/OR analyst in the process of implementation. Eilon [1984] and Batson [1987] have pointed out the various roles that the MS/OR practitioner can play within the organization and argue in favor of a broader role and a more interdisciplinary approach in conducting MS/OR studies. Tingley [1987] also favors a broader view of MS/OR and recommends closer links between MS/OR and decision support systems. Jones and Smithin [1984] point out the importance of social and political skills in MS/OR studies and suggest that these factors should be analyzed explicitly. Hammond [1974] compared the roles of managers and management scientists in implementation and suggested that the sharp difference between them acts as an obstacle to implementation. Hammond [1979] describes a practitioner-oriented framework for implementation and illustrates it with a management science project from the food industry (a cheese manufacturer).

REFERENCES

Ackoff, Russell L. 1960, "Unsuccessful case studies and why," *Operations Research*, Vol. 8, No. 2, pp. 259–263.

Ackoff, Russell L. 1987, "OR, a post mortem," *Operations Research*, Vol. 35, No. 3, pp. 471–474.

Agin, Norman I. 1978, "The conduct of operations research studies," in *Handbook of Operations Research*, Vol. 1, eds. J. J. Moder and S. E. Elmaghraby, Van Nostrand Reinhold, New York, pp. 40–68.

Balut, Stephen J. and Armacost, Robert L. 1986, "ORSA as viewed by its members," *Operations Research*, Vol. 34, No. 6, pp. 945–953.

Batson, Robert G. 1987, "The modern role of MS/OR professionals in interdisciplinary teams," *Interfaces*, Vol. 17, No. 3, pp. 85–93.

Blumstein, Alfred 1987, "The current missionary role of OR/MS," *Operations Research*, Vol. 35, No. 6, pp. 926–929.

Borsting, Jack R.; Cook, Thomas M.; King, William R.; Rardin, Ronald L.; and Tuggle, Francis D. 1988, "A model for a first MBA course in management science/operations research," *Interfaces*, Vol. 18, No. 5, pp. 72–80.

Bradbard, David A.; Ford, F. Nelson; Cox, James F.; and Ledbetter, William N. 1987, "The management science/operations research industrial-academic interface," *Interfaces*, Vol. 17, No. 2, pp. 39–48.

Carraway, Robert L. and Freeland, James R. 1989, "MBA training in operations management and quantitative methods," *Interfaces*, Vol. 19, No. 4, pp. 75–88.

Churchman, C. West 1960, "Case histories five years after—A symposium," *Operations Research*, Vol. 8, No. 2, pp. 254–277.

CONDOR (Committee on the Next Decade in Operations Research) 1988, "Operations research: The next decade," *Operations Research*, Vol. 36, No. 4, pp. 619–637.

Doktor, Robert; Schultz, Randall L.; and Slevin, Dennis P., eds. 1979, *The Implementation of Management Science*, North-Holland, New York.

Edie, Leslie C. 1954, "Traffic delays at toll booths," *Operations Research*, Vol. 2, No. 2, pp. 107–138.

Edie, Leslie C. 1960, "Review of Port of New York Authority study," *Operations Research*, Vol. 8, No. 2, pp. 263–277.

Eilon, Samuel 1984, "Types of OR workers," *Omega*, Vol. 12, No. 2, pp. 99–107.

Forgionne, Guisseppi A. 1983, "Corporate management science activities: An update," *Interfaces*, Vol. 13, No. 3, pp. 20–23.

Gass, Saul I. 1983, "Decision-aiding models: Validation, assessment, and related issues for policy analysis," *Operations Research*, Vol. 31, No. 4, pp. 603–631.

Gass, Saul I. 1987, "A perspective on the future of operations research," *Operations Research*, Vol. 35, No. 2, pp. 320–321.

Geisler, Eliezer and Rubenstein, Albert H. 1987, "The successful implementation of application software in new production systems," *Interfaces*, Vol. 17, No. 3, pp. 18–24.

Gelders, Ludo F. 1981, "Introducing field consulting in the industrial management curriculum," *Interfaces*, Vol. 11, No. 2, pp. 1–7.

Giauque, William C. 1980, "Taking the classroom into reality: A field consulting experience for MBA's," *Interfaces*, Vol. 10, No. 4, pp. 1–10.

Ginzberg, Michael J. and Schultz, Randall L. 1987, "The practical side of implementation research," *Interfaces,* Vol. 17, No. 3, pp. 1–5.

Hall, John R., Jr. 1984, "Career paths and compensation in management science: Results of a TIMS membership survey," *Interfaces,* Vol. 14, No. 3, pp. 15–23.

Hammond, John S. 1974, "The role of the managers and the management scientist in successful implementation," *Sloan Management Review,* Vol. 15, No. 2, pp. 1–24.

Hammond, John S. 1979, "A practitioner-oriented framework for implementation," in *The Implementation of Management Science,* eds. R. Doktor, R. L. Schultz, and D. P. Slevin, North-Holland, New York, pp. 35–61.

Harpell, John L.; Lane, Michael S.; and Mansour, Ali H. 1989, "Operations research in practice: A longitudinal study," *Interfaces,* Vol. 19, No. 3, pp. 65–74.

Jones, Sue and Smithin, Tim 1984, "Using MS for the practice of MS," *Interfaces,* Vol. 14, No. 3, pp. 68–75.

King, William R.; Grover, Varun; and Nelson, Anthony 1989, "The evolution of the management sciences: A report of the 1988 survey of TIMS membership," *Interfaces,* Vol. 19, No. 6, pp. 10–24.

Larson, Richard C. 1988, "Operations research and the service industry," in *Managing Innovation,* ed. B. R. Guile and J. B. Quinn, National Academy Press, Washington, D.C., pp. 115–143.

Little, John D. C. 1986, "Research opportunities in the decision and management sciences," *Management Science,* Vol. 32, No. 1, pp. 1–13.

Miser, Hugh J. 1985, "The practice of systems analysis," in *Handbook of Systems Analysis: Overview of Uses, Procedures, Applications, and Practice,* ed. H. J. Miser and E. S. Quade, North-Holland, New York, pp. 281–326.

Miser, Hugh J. 1987, "Science and professionalism in operations research," *Operations Research,* Vol. 35, No. 2, pp. 314–319.

Miser, Hugh J. 1989, "The easy chair: What did those early pioneers have uppermost in mind, model building or problem solving?," *Interfaces,* Vol. 19, No. 4, pp. 69–74.

Morgan, Catherine L. 1989, "A survey of MS/OR surveys," *Interfaces,* Vol. 19, No. 6, pp. 95–103.

Rothkopf, Michael H. 1989, "OR Practice—Editorial statement," *Operations Research,* Vol. 37, No. 1, pp. 6–7.

Schultz, Randall L. and Slevin, Dennis P. 1979, "Introduction: The implementation problem," in *The Implementation of Management Science,* eds. R. Doktor, R. L. Schultz, and D.P. Slevin, North-Holland, New York, pp. 1–15.

Shannon, Robert E.; Long, S. Scott; and Buckles, Billy P. 1980, "Operations research methodologies in industrial engineering: A survey," *AIIE Transactions,* Vol. 12, No. 4, pp. 364–367.

Shubik, Martin 1987, "What is an application and when is theory a waste of time," *Management Science,* Vol. 33, No. 12, pp. 1511–1522.

Stainton, R. S. 1979, "Modelling and reality," *Journal of the Operational Research Society,* Vol. 30, No. 12, pp. 1031–1036.

Thomas, George and DaCosta, Jo-Anne 1979, "A sample survey of corporate operations research," *Interfaces,* Vol. 9, No. 4, pp. 102–111.

Tingley, George A. 1987, "Can MS/OR sell itself well enough?," *Interfaces,* Vol. 17, No. 4, pp. 41–52.

Tomlinson, Rolfe; Quade, Edward S.; and Miser, Hugh J. 1985, "Implementation," in *Handbook of Systems Analysis: Overview of Uses, Procedures, Applications, and Practice,* ed. H. J. Miser and E. S. Quade, North-Holland, New York, pp. 249–279.

Wagner, Harvey M. 1988, "Operations research: A global language for business strategy," *Operations Research,* Vol. 36, No. 5, pp. 797–803.

Wagner, Harvey M.; Rothkopf, Michael H.; Thomas, Clayton J.; and Miser, Hugh J. 1989, "The next decade in operations research: Comments on the CONDOR report," *Operations Research,* Vol. 37, No. 4, pp. 664–672.

Walker, Warren E. 1989, "Fire company relocation and the future of applied operations research," *Operations Research*, Vol. 37, No. 3, pp. 507–508.

Walker, Warren E.; Chaiken, Jan M.; and Ignall, Edward J., eds. 1979, *Fire Department Deployment Analysis: A Public Policy Analysis Case Study*, North-Holland, New York.

Watson, Hugh J. and Marrett, Patricia G. 1979, "A survey of management science implementation problems," *Interfaces*, Vol. 9, No. 4, pp. 124–128.

Wysocki, Robert K. 1979, "OR/MS implementation research: A bibliography," *Interfaces*, Vol. 9, No. 2, pp. 37–41.

Wynne, Bayard E. and Robak, Nicholas J. 1989, "Entrepreneurs enabled: A comparison of Edelman prize-winning papers," *Interfaces*, Vol. 19, No. 2, pp. 70–78.

Zahedi, Fatemeh 1984, "A survey of issues in the MS/OR field," *Interfaces*, Vol. 14, No. 2, pp. 57–68.

2

PRODUCTION AND
INVENTORY MANAGEMENT

To introduce some order into the plethora of decisions firms have to confront, it is common to group managerial decisions into three different classes—strategic, tactical, and operational. These three classes differ in scope and term, in the level of management involved, and in the degree of risk or uncertainty they present. In making strategic decisions, managers focus on formulating competitive strategy and the associated long-term capital acquisitions and investments. Tactical decisions focus on allocating resources efficiently in the medium term. For a manufacturing firm, tactical planning deals primarily with aggregate production planning—the process of determining capacity, the size of the work force, and target inventory levels over the next year or two. Finally, operational decisions concern detailed scheduling and inventory control on a weekly or daily basis. Such inventory replenishment decisions as how much and when to order properly belong to the operational group.

In this chapter, we present production and inventory planning systems of three different firms, spanning tactical and operational decisions. The first paper covers both aggregate and detailed production planning, while the other two deal with combined inventory and production planning.

The three implementation efforts have some important characteristics in common. First, the savings realized dwarfed the implementation cost in all three projects. At American Olean, development costs of $10,000 reduced the annual distribution costs by $400,000. Pfizer Pharmaceuticals invested only 1.5 man years to reduce inventory by nearly $24 million. Blue Bell's program took 21 months and involved 40 managers at its peak. However, even this cost is small compared to the benefits of reducing inventory by $115 million.

Second, all three implementations made good use of established production and inventory planning techniques. Among other tools, the studies used standard techniques of inventory management readily available in the literature. This does not detract from the firms' accomplishments; it is still a major challenge for any firm to implement such models fully and effectively. However, it does point out that in production and inventory planning, even standard and well-known "textbook" models can reduce costs with impressive results. Finally, all three adopted an integrative approach to system design in which forecasting, production planning, and inventory management are closely linked.

2.1 HIERARCHICAL PRODUCTION PLANNING FOR A TILE MANUFACTURER

Starting with projections of customer demand over time, manufacturing firms develop production plans to meet the demand in an economical way. The production plan must ultimately specify how much of each item a plant should produce in each time period of the planning horizon. The *master production schedule* consists of precisely this information. A firm may manufacture thousands of different items if all product variations (in sizes, colors, options, and so forth) are viewed as distinct items. A production plan that sets the weekly production quantities for 5,000 distinct items over the course of a year must specify over a quarter of a million numbers. To control the size of the planning problem, production planners often aggregate certain classes of items. For example, they may group the items by product line, by processing requirements, or by market demand characteristics. The way the firm defines these groupings and the criteria it selects for aggregating information are important decisions. The general approach, however, remains the same. Starting with the distinct items, several levels of aggregation ultimately lead to the highest level of aggregation where a single unit of measure is used for production—tons of output, or number of vehicles, for example. The use and presence of aggregate data characterizes *aggregate production planning*.

Liberatore and Miller [1985] developed a hierarchical production planning system for the quarry division of the American Olean Tile Company (AO). This division operates four plants that supply quarry tiles to some 120 sales distribution points (SDPs) across the United States. The various options for shape, size, color, and finish define several thousand distinct items. Each distinct item (a specific choice of shape, size, and so forth) is called a *stock keeping unit (SKU)*. While AO has thousands of SKUs, its product line can be aggregated into 10 families that represent several hundred items each.

The planners at AO begin by projecting the demand for the entire quarry division at the highest level of aggregation, expressing the annual sales of the division in square feet of tile. AO then disaggregates this overall projection to obtain forecasts of sales for each family at each SDP. The sales forecasts are expressed in terms of family-SDP pairs. The *plant/family/SDP assignment model* assigns these annual requirements to four plants across the country. A linear programming model minimizes the total cost of production and distribution. This model allows AO to consider the trade-offs between production and distribution costs. For instance, to take advantage of lower production costs at a given plant, AO may ship the finished goods over longer distances.

The capacities available at the four plants act as key constraints of the optimization model. To model the capacity limitations more realistically, Liberatore and Miller imposed bounds on the capacities of individual production lines within each plant. This refinement is necessary since an individual line can produce only a subset of the families. The output of the model specifies the annual production plan and the pattern of distribution of goods from plants to SDPs. The *master production schedule* specifies the weekly production requirements of each family at each plant during the upcoming quarter. It integrates the results of the assignment model with information on firm orders and short-term forecasts to specify production quantities by family.

The *family scheduling model* schedules production at the level of individual items within a plant to meet the master production schedule. The production requirements must be disaggregated from the family level to the item level. The family scheduling model is a large mixed integer program that seeks to minimize the sum of variable production costs, inventory holding costs, and line setup costs. Line setups reflect the fixed cost of switching from the production of one item to a different one. Once this changeover cost is incurred, the item is produced at a constant production rate in consecutive time periods until the line is set up again for another item (Exhibit 2–1). The family scheduling model focuses on scheduling carloads of tile as they move through the kiln, as this is the bottleneck operation at the plant.

The short-term production schedule must explicitly address the trade-off between changeover and holding costs: Once the line is set up for an item, it is reasonable to continue producing the item through several periods to avoid another costly setup. While an extended production run of one item reduces setup costs, it also builds up inventory that incurs holding costs. The optimal balance between these two cost components depends on the relative magnitude of setup and holding costs, but it is also influenced by the demand pattern for the item and the line's production rate for that item. The complexity of the problem

EXHIBIT 2–1. The decision variables of the family scheduling model for a single line specify the product manufactured in each time period and the periods when changeovers take place. A simple example with three products in the family and 12 time periods shows the values the decision variables assume for the particular production schedule displayed in the figure. The example assumes that the first line was not set up to produce the first product at the beginning of the first period. The objective function, which does not appear here, is the sum of changeover costs, variable production costs, and the cost of holding inventory.

Input Parameters

P = number of products
N = number of time periods
P_i = production rate of the line for product i

Decision Variables

$$x_{it} = \begin{cases} 1 & \text{if the line produces product i during period t,} \\ 0 & \text{otherwise.} \end{cases}$$

$$v_{it} = \begin{cases} 1 & \text{if production switches over to product i in period t.} \\ 0 & \text{otherwise.} \end{cases}$$

Relations among variables:

$$\sum_i x_{it} \le 1 \qquad t = 1,\dots, N \qquad (1)$$

$$v_{it} = \text{Max } \{x_{it} - x_{i,t-1}, 0\} \qquad (2)$$
$$t = 1,\dots, N$$
$$i = 1,\dots, P$$

Example

P = 3
N = 12
(P_1, P_2, P_3) = (40, 20, 50)

$$t = \quad 1\ 2\ 3\ 4\ 5\ \dots \qquad 12$$

$$i = \begin{matrix} 1 \\ 2 \\ 3 \end{matrix} \begin{bmatrix} 1\ 1\ 1\ 0\ 0\ 0\ 0\ 0\ 0\ 0\ 1\ 1 \\ 0\ 0\ 0\ 0\ 0\ 1\ 1\ 1\ 0\ 0\ 0\ 0 \\ 0\ 0\ 0\ 1\ 1\ 0\ 0\ 0\ 1\ 1\ 0\ 0 \end{bmatrix} = (x_{it})$$

$$\begin{bmatrix} 1\ 0\ 0\ 0\ 0\ 0\ 0\ 0\ 0\ 0\ 1\ 0 \\ 0\ 0\ 0\ 0\ 0\ 1\ 0\ 0\ 0\ 0\ 0\ 0 \\ 0\ 0\ 0\ 1\ 0\ 0\ 0\ 0\ 1\ 0\ 0\ 0 \end{bmatrix} = (v_{it})$$

Time period	1	2	3	4	5	6	7	8	9	10	11	12
Product produced	1	1	1	3	3	2	2	2	3	3	1	1
Production quantity	40	40	40	50	50	20	20	20	50	50	40	40

increases if each item can be produced on several different lines. For example, consider a single item that can be produced on two lines. Line 2 has the greater production rate. One can then compare two plans.

One schedules longer runs with infrequent setups on line 1, and the other uses shorter but more frequent runs on line 2. To address the full range of interactions among setup costs, variable production costs, holding costs, and production rates, one must formulate and solve a mixed integer programming model to optimize the short-term schedules.

The planning process at AO provides a clear example of the hierarchical process. Starting with highly aggregate information on demand and production, a sequence of models and decisions successively disaggregates, refines, and modifies the production plan to finally arrive at a short-term production schedule for each item. The link between aggregate planning and short-term planning deserves careful attention in any hierarchical model. The assignment model determines which plants will supply the product family demands at the SDPs. The monthly production quantities resulting from this schedule are combined with firm orders and short-term forecasts to construct the master production schedule.

The system at AO is specifically designed to integrate production planning at the family and item levels by linking the aggregate and detailed forecasts and inventories. The hierarchical planning process, by its very structure and design, is meant to overcome misalignments between medium-term and short-term production plans. In the past, these misalignments had in fact caused problems for AO.

The integration goes further to ensure that annual production plans set forth by the manufacturing department are aligned with the sales plan the marketing department produces for each SDP. Liberatore and Miller point out the importance of the level of aggregation in this coordination of marketing and manufacturing. In the past, AO based its manufacturing plan on the aggregate annual sales forecasts of the marketing department. Without more detailed planning, this means that certain sales territories may run out of products even though the total production matches the nationwide demand. When such regional imbalances occur, products must be shipped from SDPs with excess stock to other SDPs that need them. To avoid such costly redistributions, the plant/family/SDP assignment model gears production to the needs of individual sales territories by planning at the more disaggregate level of family-SDP pairs. Moreover, managerial involvement in planning improves communication, information flow, and coordination among managers. Given these benefits, integration should be an explicit design objective in hierarchical production planning.

American Olean has continued to develop the production planning model. Miller [1989] reports that the company is (1) enhancing the annual assignment model, (2) improving the quality of data inputs for planning, and (3) increasing the involvement of managers in supporting and using the model.

First, as AO increased its use of the annual assignment model, it decided to substitute a quarterly model for the annual one. Using four periods per year (instead of only one) facilitates more precise control of capacity and more detailed projection of inventory needs throughout the year. AO also enriched the model so that it would handle minimum run quantities to capture the manufacturing environment with more realism. This means that the model must be formulated as a mixed integer program instead of a linear program.

Second, to improve the quality of inputs to the overall planning system, AO refined the forecasting techniques and obtained more accurate production rates. The refined technique uses exponential smoothing to translate the annual forecast for the product line into forecasts for the distinct families that make up the product line. As the system depends on accurate production rates, AO has had to ensure corporate-wide agreement on the rates it uses. In fact, AO has found that production rates vary as a result of both technical and organizational factors. The company has been developing a clearer understanding of the impact of these factors (changing recovery rates, for example) on the production rates.

Accurate information flow is key to the success of implementing any system. AO has asked its managers and plant accountants to carefully evaluate, verify, and update inputs to the overall system. In addition to data on production rates, AO's management has examined production costs, inventory objectives, and sales histories. This is part of an effort to encourage managers and other users of the planning system to become closely involved in its development. To increase confidence in the model, the director of operations planning at AO regularly sends plant managers computer-generated reports based on the results of the model. Managers not only comment on the reports but use the data to support their own spreadsheet-based planning systems. This process has helped transform the planning system into an effective and reliable tool for decision making.

2.2 INVENTORY AND PRODUCTION PLANNING FOR AN APPAREL MANUFACTURER

The Wrangler Group of Blue Bell, Inc. is an international business that manufactures denim and corduroy jeans and other sports and casual apparel for men, women, and children. In basic styles of men's jeans alone, Wrangler makes 35 million pairs a year in 37 plants, accounting for over 10,000 individual SKUs. In the second paper of this chapter, Edwards, Wagner, and Wood [1985] describe Blue Bell's program for reducing its inventories.

Blue Bell wanted to drastically reduce its large investment in inventory at a time of very high interest rates (20 percent or more in 1982). In addition to the growth in inventory, Blue Bell was facing the following challenges associated with today's manufacturing environment:

1. Product proliferation. The number of distinct products had grown as Blue Bell tried to follow customer tastes (69 percent increase in the number of SKUs over six years). As jeans became fashion items, Blue Bell was forced to adopt a more market-oriented strategy that increased product variations.
2. Shrinking lead times. Retailers were placing orders closer to their desired delivery time, forcing Blue Bell to operate with shorter lead times. This pushed the company to move towards a just-in-time (JIT) approach to manufacturing.
3. Increased service demands. To remain competitive and to respond to the pressure of major chains of retailers, Blue Bell had to carry sufficient inventory to ensure prompt delivery.

Since finished goods inventories accounted for two-thirds of the total inventory at Blue Bell, inventory reduction required tight control of these inventories. To achieve this objective, Blue Bell had to re-examine its manufacturing practices. The integrated production planning process the company adopted starts with sales forecasting and eventually produces a detailed production schedule for individual items.

The Planning Process at Blue Bell

Wrangler products can be organized into a natural hierarchy (see Exhibit 2–2). A product group, such as jeans, is divided into several product lines or types of jeans (what fabric, for instance). A product line,

EXHIBIT 2–2. Blue Bell's hierarchical product structure has four levels. As one moves down the levels, the product specifications become known in greater detail, and further disaggregation of the product group takes place. There may be 75 lots in a product line, and a single lot may be produced in 50 different sizes.

Designation	Example	Comments
PRODUCT GROUP	Jeans	Highest level of aggregation.
PRODUCT LINE	Men's Corduroy	Specifies the customer group and the fabric.
LOT	Straight-leg Blue	Specifies the style and the color within the product line.
SIZE	Waist 34 Inseam 31	Fixes the waist and inseam measurements.

such as men's corduroy jeans, is further divided into lot numbers. Each lot number specifies a specific color and style (cut). Finally, each lot number, such as blue straight-leg men's corduroy jeans, is produced in a variety of sizes defined by waist and inseam measurements. Each size in a lot number constitutes a distinct SKU. The fact that a single product group can contain thousands of SKUs clearly shows the need for aggregation in the production planning process.

The planning process at Blue Bell reflects its product hierarchy. The first three steps of the production planning process (see Exhibit 2–3) address the more aggregate level of product lines. This process starts with sales forecasts and results in a production plan for each product line that incorporates seasonal inventories and safety-stock requirements. As is usual in aggregate planning, seasonal inventories are built up to smooth production. The product line requirements are disaggregated into lot requirements first, and the requirements of individual SKUs next. The last three steps of the planning process therefore deal with requirements for SKUs.

The Role of Markers

The first six steps of the planning process follow standard techniques in production and inventory control. The last step, however, is peculiar to Blue Bell's production process and brings out the curious interplay between production planning and inventory reduction. Blue Bell uses *markers* to cut pieces for garments out of several layers of fabric placed on a table two yards wide and up to 40 yards long. Markers are like cookie cutters that cut cookies of various shapes out of a layer of dough. Each marker contains the patterns for the parts of about 35 complete garments and produces only a subset of the SKUs in a lot.

The fact that a marker spans many different SKUs means that each marker links the production quantities of several SKUs in certain fixed proportions. Producing a certain SKU inevitably entails making other SKUs on the same marker. This presents no difficulties if requirements for different SKUs always follow certain fixed and stable proportions. However, the weekly net requirements of SKUs (generated by the sixth step of the planning process) exhibit great variability from one week to the next, and their sales volumes span a wide range. Some SKUs move 50 to 100 times faster than others. By fixing the relative proportions of production quantities of different SKUs, a marker used to produce a much-needed SKU may produce unwanted SKUs as well, thereby creating excess inventories of those finished goods.

The way markers produce combinations of items is related to the broader issue of *production mix flexibility*. The production process should be flexible enough to change the product mix rapidly as demand patterns shift or the inventory positions of stocked items fluctuate. For

EXHIBIT 2–3. The production and inventory planning process at Blue Bell comprises seven steps, each of which relies upon a different model. The models are processed sequentially; the output of one model serves as the input to the next.

PLANNING STEP	MODEL OR PROCEDURE
1 *SALES FORECASTING* Generate seasonal forecasts of monthly sales for the next 12 months.	MODEL 1 uses the Winters exponential smoothing technique with seasonal factors for each of the 12 months.
2 *SAFETY-STOCK PLANNING* Allocate safety-stock to each product line to protect against demand uncertainty over the lead time.	MODEL 2 relates the safety-stock required to the variability of forecast errors over the lead time.
3 *PRODUCT LINE PLANNING* Develop a production plan for the next 12 months for each product line. The plan must ensure adequate levels of safety-stock and seasonal inventories.	MODEL 3 is based on a graphical technique for production smoothing that compares cumulative production with cumulative demand.
4 *LOT PLANNING* Disaggregate the seasonal inventory and safety-stock of each product line into individual lot numbers.	MODEL 4 performs the disaggregation using managerial inputs and risk assessments for different lots.
5 *SIZE PLANNING* Disaggregate the requirements for each lot into requirements for the SKUs within the lot number.	MODEL 5 apportions the inventory of each lot into amounts for its constituent SKUs.
6 *NET REQUIREMENTS PLANNING* Convert the gross requirements of each SKU to net requirements for the item.	MODEL 6 simply adjusts the gross requirements by subtracting amounts of the SKU currently on hand or anticipated in the future. The resulting difference is the net requirement.
7 *MARKER SELECTION FOR PRODUCTION* Select the mix of markers to produce SKUs to meet the net requirements.	MODEL 7 uses linear programming to decide how many times each marker is used in each week.

Blue Bell, production flexibility is tied to its collection of markers. An extensive collection of markers would allow the planners to alter the product mix frequently to correct inventory imbalances. Exhibit 2–4

EXHIBIT 2–4. A simple example with two products shows how using a mix of markers instead of a single marker can reduce inventories. The first plan produces both items in every period with a single marker. The second plan alternates between two markers based on the demand for the two products. The average inventories of the items decrease from 850 to 512 for A and from 812 to 25 for B. The example is simplified to illustrate the main concept. In practice, each marker produces several (not just one or two) SKUs.

Weekly Production Rate	SKU A	SKU B
Marker 1	1500	300
Marker 2	1800	0

PLAN USING A SINGLE MARKER

SKU A

Week	1	2	3	4	5	6	7	8	Average Weekly Inventory
Net Requirements	1000	1000	1300	1300	1800	1700	1900	1800	
Production	1500	1500	1500	1500	1500	1500	1500	1500	
Ending Inventory	500	1000	1200	1400	1100	900	500	200	850

SKU B

Net Requirements	100	500							
Production	300	300	300	300	300	300	300	300	
Ending Inventory	200	0	300	600	900	1200	1500	1800	812

PLAN USING TWO MARKERS

SKU A

Week	1	2	3	4	5	6	7	8	
Net Requirements	1000	1000	1300	1300	1800	1700	1900	1800	
Production	1500	1500	1800	0	1800	1800	1800	1800	
Inventory	500	1000	1500	200	200	300	200	200	512

SKU B

Net Requirements	100	500							
Production	300	300							
Inventory	200	0	0	0	0	0	0	0	25

Marker Used	1	1	2	None	2	2	2	2

shows a simplified example with two SKUs in which using two markers instead of one reduces inventory.

In addition to increasing flexibility, the design of a marker should consider fabric waste. Since a marker cannot utilize 100 percent of the fabric for garment parts, the unused part of the fabric is wasted. To reduce such waste, Blue Bell designers in the past carefully grouped different SKUs onto the same marker, selecting them to minimize unused space. This approach, which builds dependencies into the production of different SKUs with the objective of reducing waste, is oblivious to demand patterns of the SKUs. The trade-off between reducing waste and controlling inventory drives the marker selection problem.

To address this trade-off, Edwards, Wagner, and Wood formulated a combinatorial optimization model for selecting the best mix of markers to use. The key output of the marker selection model is the set of marker and lay-up combinations used in each of the 16 weeks in the planning horizon. Each marker has patterns for several SKUs and the lay-up refers to the number of layers of fabric cut with the marker. Therefore, the marker and lay-up combinations planned for a given week completely specify the production quantities of all SKUs and the production schedule for that week. The model seeks to minimize the total fabric waste while meeting the projected weekly net requirements for all SKUs in a given lot number.

While the marker selection model is easy to formulate, its implementation raises a number of difficulties. First, the model cannot include all possible marker designs as potential candidates. For a lot with 75 SKUs (garment sizes), the number of possible marker designs can exceed 10^{66}, a hopelessly intractable number. Moreover, as markers are expensive to design, only markers that are used are produced. The limits on the size of the marker library lead to two problems. First, markers in the library must balance the needs for flexibility and for stability (new markers cannot be designed frequently). Second, the data on fabric waste associated with each marker, which the model requires as input, lacks precision: the exact waste can only be measured after the marker is designed. Edwards, Wagner, and Wood do not specify the extent of error in estimating waste prior to actual design, but it is clear that the waste figures that serve as cost coefficients to the marker selection model objective function are subject to uncertainty. To overcome these obstacles, Edwards, Wagner, and Wood restricted the model to a fixed library of markers. As the resulting integer programming problem was still too large to solve exactly, they solved it approximately as a linear programming problem.

With inventory reductions in excess of $115 million over 21 months, Blue Bell's inventory reduction program was an unqualified success. One may draw two lessons from the Blue Bell experience. First, it shows that well-established techniques of inventory planning are effective means of reducing inventory. Except for the marker selection model, all the models Blue Bell used are covered in standard texts and are regularly taught to students. Second, the goal of reducing inventory led Blue Bell to alter its production planning in order to increase production flexibility. A somewhat unexpected (but pleasant) result was that this increased flexibility did not entail a greater fabric waste. Instead, fabric waste was reduced by $1 million.

2.3 INVENTORY REDUCTION IN A PHARMACEUTICAL FIRM

Pfizer Pharmaceuticals is a division of an international company that develops, manufactures, and distributes a broad line of pharmaceuticals. Pfizer has developed trademarked antibiotics such as Terramycin and continues to develop new products. In the third paper of this chapter, Kleutghen and McGee [1985] discuss a major inventory management program at Pfizer that reduced inventories by $23.9 million while increasing the level of customer service. They attribute total annual savings of $7.93 million to this program.

As in many other successful inventory management programs, the key to inventory reduction at Pfizer is a clear understanding of the purpose served by inventories at different stages of the flow of materials through the manufacturing process. Within Pfizer, this flow starts with the purchase of raw materials and ends with distribution of finished products (called dosage forms) to the customers. Manufacturing occurs in two stages: two plants synthesize active organic ingredients, and four dosage plants blend these ingredients with other raw materials to produce dosage forms. To reduce inventories, Pfizer examined cycle stock, work-in-process, and safety stock inventories separately in each stage of its production process. It then developed simple models to determine the appropriate sizes of inventories of each kind at each stage (Exhibit 2–5).

Pfizer uses a material requirements planning (MRP) system to coordinate the timing of purchases with the projected production plan for finished goods. To improve this process, Pfizer fine-tuned the parameters of the MRP system, used a simple model to evaluate the purchasing economies associated with quantity discounts, and calculated safety-stock levels for purchased items. This reduced the inventory by $5.8 million.

The Inventory of Active Ingredients

In organic synthesis, the first stage of Pfizer's two-stage manufacturing process, batches go through a sequence of chemical reactions in reaction vessels to produce active organic ingredients. The capacity of these vessels limits the batch sizes. The synthesis process consists of up to 15

EXHIBIT 2–5. Inventories of different types are found at eight locations of the two-stage manufacturing process of Pfizer. The nature of each type of inventory and the savings realized through the inventory reduction program are shown. All figures are in millions of dollars.

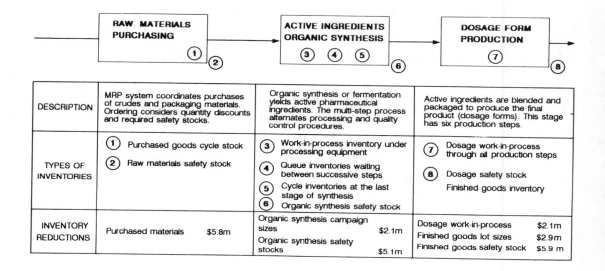

	RAW MATERIALS PURCHASING ①②	ACTIVE INGREDIENTS ORGANIC SYNTHESIS ③④⑤⑥	DOSAGE FORM PRODUCTION ⑦⑧
DESCRIPTION	MRP system coordinates purchases of crudes and packaging materials. Ordering considers quantity discounts and required safety stocks.	Organic synthesis or fermentation yields active pharmaceutical ingredients. The multi-step process alternates processing and quality control procedures.	Active ingredients are blended and packaged to produce the final product (dosage forms). This stage has six production steps.
TYPES OF INVENTORIES	① Purchased goods cycle stock ② Raw materials safety stock	③ Work-in-process inventory under processing equipment ④ Queue inventories waiting between successive steps ⑤ Cycle inventories at the last stage of synthesis ⑥ Organic synthesis safety stock	⑦ Dosage work-in-process through all production steps ⑧ Dosage safety stock Finished goods inventory
INVENTORY REDUCTIONS	Purchased materials $5.8m	Organic synthesis campaign sizes $2.1m Organic synthesis safety stocks $5.1m	Dosage work-in-process $2.1m Finished goods lot sizes $2.9m Finished goods safety stock $5.9 m

steps separated by careful quality checks. The lead time for the entire process can be as long as 49 weeks. A production run consists of a group of batches (called a *campaign*) that go through the production sequence together. Each batch maintains its identity throughout the process and its size is set by the vessels and the chemical process.

The problem in sizing each campaign is to determine the optimal number of batches that minimizes the sum of inventory carrying costs and changeover costs. However, the optimal campaign sizes cannot be calculated independently for each product since the products compete for equipment time. Kleutghen and McGee use an inventory model that includes the capacity constraint explicitly and optimizes the batch sizes for all products simultaneously.

To set up the campaign-sizing model, Kleutghen and McGee consider the effect of the campaign size on the three different types of inventory within the organic synthesis step (Exhibit 2–6). First, there is work-in-process (WIP) inventory involved in the individual production steps. As each step adds value, the work-in-process inventory must be assessed by taking an average of its value before and immediately after the step. Second, queue inventories form between successive production steps as the batches in a campaign emerge from one step, queue up for

EXHIBIT 2–6. The campaign-sizing model for organic synthesis seeks the optimal number of batches to use for each item's production run. The objective function is the sum of inventory carrying and changeover costs. The model has a single capacity constraint to capture the limited equipment time shared by all products. To avoid too much detail, some of the input data represent quantities lumped over the individual steps of the organic synthesis process.

The Campaign-Sizing Model

Input Data

J = number of products $(j = 1,...,J)$

K = annual availability of equipment time

I = annual inventory carrying costs as a percentage of product value

Decision Variables

N_j = number of batches of size B_j in the campaign of product j $(j = 1,...,J)$.

Data for Product j $(j = 1,...,J)$
D_j = annual demand
C_j = value of finished product

$CEPT_j$ = equipment processing time per unit of product j
CP_j = value of inventory undergoing value-adding operations
CQ_j = value of queue inventories awaiting the next processing step

Data associated with a single batch of product j
B_j = size of single batch
F_j = cumulative setup cost for a batch through all production steps
COB_j = cumulative changeover time over all production steps

Data associated with a campaign of a series of batches of product j
V_j = setup cost for a campaign through all production steps
COC_j = cumulative changeover time for a campaign over all steps

Capacity-constrained Optimization Model

$$\text{Minimize } \sum_j \left\{ \left(\frac{V_j}{N_j} + F_j \right) \frac{D_j}{B_j} + I \left[\frac{C_j}{2} + (CP_j + CQ_j) \right] N_j B_j \right\}$$

$$\text{subject to } \sum_j \left[\left(\frac{COC_j}{N_j} + COB_j \right) \frac{D_j}{B_j} + CEPT_j D_j \right] \leq K$$

$$N_j \geq 0 \quad \text{for all j.}$$

quality control tests, and then proceed to the next step. While waiting between two successive production steps, the WIP inventory remains at a constant value but incurs inventory carrying charges proportional to the length of time it waits in the queue. After the last production step, the inventory of the active ingredient produced in the campaign is held as cycle stock.

Apart from inventory carrying costs, the changeover costs in organic synthesis range from $15,000 to $95,000 for a single campaign. Initiating a campaign involves major changeover costs, while changing between different batches in a campaign incurs minor changeover costs. This cost structure is sometimes called the major-minor setup; Kleutghen and McGee call it the double changeover structure. The model must also account for losses in yield during the manufacturing process. The cost components of the model are expressed in terms of the decision variables that specify the size of a production run. There is a single capacity constraint that reflects the limited equipment time for all products. Kleutghen and McGee use the classical Lagrange multiplier technique to solve this model. The campaign sizes based on this model reduced inventory by $2.1 million.

Pfizer draws upon the inventory of finished active ingredients to produce dosage forms. Safety stocks of these ingredients are needed to protect against uncertainty in demand and supply. Uncertainty in demand is caused by variability in the amount of active ingredients drawn for dosage production. Since this variability is ultimately due to the variability of demand for dosage forms, safety stocks should provide protection over the combined lead times for producing active ingredients and for producing dosage forms. As the combined lead time can exceed 60 weeks and a very high service level is required, the safety stock can be expected to be high. The supply is uncertain because some batches within a campaign may be withheld for quality reasons. (This is similar to the uncertainty in supply other firms face when some of their incoming goods are rejected during inspection.) The organic synthesis safety stock model uses a simple probabilistic model to set safety stocks. By using a scientific procedure for determining safety stocks and taking the risk of stockouts into account explicitly, Pfizer was able to reduce its organic synthesis safety stocks by $5.1 million.

The Inventory of Dosage Forms

In the second stage of the production process, Pfizer produces dosage forms by blending active ingredients with other raw materials. In this stage, the potency of the product and its form (capsules, tablets, and so forth) are determined. The dosage production process, which takes six to 15 weeks, has six manufacturing steps and six quality control steps. The model for dosage WIP establishes target levels for WIP inventory by tracking how the value of this inventory increases as it moves through the manufacturing steps. Reductions in the dosage WIP inventory based on this model totalled $2.1 million.

Kleutghen and McGee use the well-known (s,S) inventory model to determine cycle and safety stock levels for the dosage forms. An (s,S) or min-max inventory system works as follows: If the inventory level is less than s when checked, an order is placed to bring it up to the maximum level S. Otherwise, no order is placed (Exhibit 2–7). The (s,S) model determines the levels of the cycle stock and the safety stock simultaneously. Generally, s incorporates the safety stock while the cycle stock is one half of the order quantity S-s.

The min-max inventory system is easy to implement and has been

EXHIBIT 2–7. In the (s,S) inventory replenishment policy under periodic review, the inventory level is reviewed every six weeks. If the inventory level is below s=40, then an order is placed to bring the inventory position up to S = 80 (A and C below). Otherwise, no order is placed (B). The delivery lead time is two weeks. The solid line shows the physical inventory over time and the dashed line is the inventory position including the amount on order.

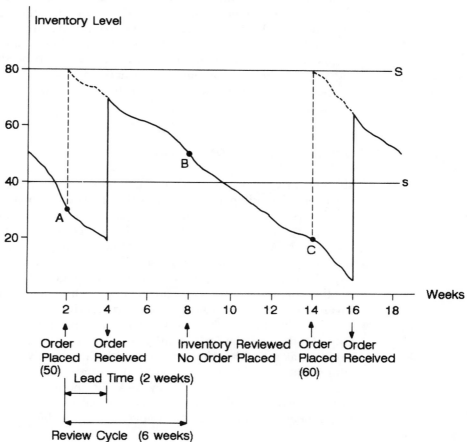

shown to be the optimal policy under a wide range of circumstances. The problem, however, lies in computing the optimal values of s and S. The exact determination of these values is too cumbersome for most applications. Instead, researchers have developed approximations to obtain near-optimal values of s and S. Kleutghen and McGee use an approximation that is easy to compute if the demand during lead time follows the normal distribution (see the related readings). Their model also considers backordering costs as this is an important service consideration for a pharmaceutical firm.

Pfizer was able to reduce its inventory of finished goods by $8.8 million as a result of implementing the (s,S) system. Of this, safety stock reduction accounted for $5.9 million, and the remainder was associated with lowering cycle inventories (lot sizes).

Paul Kleutghen [1989], the director of production planning and inventory control at Pfizer, Inc., states that the continuing inventory reductions resulting from the full implementation of the program have added up to $54 million. To decrease the cost of implementing the models and to widen their use within the organization, the models now operate on a PC-based local area network. The high changeover costs revealed by the analysis of the organic synthesis campaign sizes led engineering-operations to review the changeover procedures. Engineering improvements subsequently reduced synthesis changeover costs by 67 percent and acted as a catalyst for the move towards just-in-time production.

2.4 AN OVERVIEW OF PRODUCTION PLANNING

In the early 1950s, a large company invited four highly capable researchers (including two future Nobel laureates) to investigate its production practices. The company was interested in smoothing production in the presence of seasonal demand and reducing its inventory investment. Holt, Modigliani, Muth, and Simon [1960] collected the results of this study in their classic text on production planning. This masterful exposition provided the first complete statement of the aggregate production planning problem and related techniques of forecasting and inventory analysis. It still makes for delightful reading.

In what has come to be known as the HMMS model, Holt, Modigliani, Muth, and Simon formulated the aggregate production planning problem as a multi-period problem with the objective of minimizing the sum of the costs of regular payroll, overtime, hiring and firing, carrying inventory, and backorders. They took the monthly levels of production and the work force as the decision variables. By modeling each cost component as a quadratic (or linear) function, they were able to derive simple *linear decision rules* for setting the optimal levels of production and work force [Holt, Modigliani, and Simon 1955; Holt, Modigliani, and Muth 1956]. These rules specify the best choice of production (or work force) level for the current period in the form of a linear expression composed of the inventory and work force levels of the last period and estimates of future monthly sales. A full discussion of the HMMS model appears in Holt et al. [1960].

Over the years, many researchers have extended the HMMS model and have tested it in various applications. One attractive feature of linear decision rules was that they made it easy to compute the optimal policy. As faster and cheaper computers became available, it was natural for aggregate planning models to rely on powerful mathematical programming techniques such as linear programming to compute optimal policies. Hax [1978] reviews these developments in his comprehensive survey and highlights the hierarchical approach to production planning.

Hierarchical Production Planning

The guiding idea behind hierarchical production planning (HPP) is to distinguish between strategic, tactical, and operational decisions. In practice, production planning problems rarely allow all these decisions to be optimized simultaneously within a single monolithic model. Even if such a giant model could be solved, HPP proponents believe that the nature of managerial decision making argues against lumping the decisions together. Instead, it is more effective to define different levels of aggregation to make the planning process more intelligible at each level. Hax [1978] and Meal [1984] discuss these conceptual underpinnings of the HPP framework.

Hax and Meal [1975] apply the HPP framework to plan capacity for a major manufacturer that produces over 10,000 different final products (items) at four plants. The firm had to plan production to respond to a seasonal demand pattern. Inadequate planning had led to deteriorating customer service despite the company's large investment in inventory. In approaching this problem, Hax and Meal first had to define suitable aggregations of the firm's products. Three distinct levels of aggregation emerged. On the lowest level, *items* refer to individual finished products (SKUs). The next level of aggregation collects items into families. A *family* is a collection of items that are produced together as they share similar processing requirements (items share a common major setup). Usually, this means that the machines producing these items are set up in the same way. A *type* is a group of items with the same seasonal demand pattern and inventory carrying costs. The 10,000 items in the firm formed 200 families and 5 types.

The HPP process has four major steps (Exhibit 2–8):

EXHIBIT 2–8. The four modules of the hierarchical production planning system determine the production quantities for product types, families, and items. Each module constrains the production quantities of the next module. The seasonal planning module fixes the amount of time allocated to each type. The families within a single type must be produced within this time (T_k), and the run quantities (RQ_{ij}) of the items in the same family must sum to the run quantity for that family ($RQ_{j.}$). Forecasting models provide forecasts with different levels of detail to these modules. Initially, the economic item and family run lengths are determined without capacity constraints and fed into the modules for family and item scheduling. The overstock limits place upper bounds on the amount of inventory of each item.

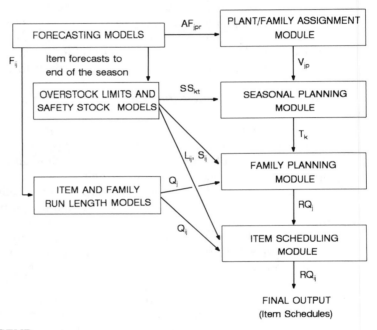

FINAL OUTPUT
(Item Schedules)

LEGEND

V_{jp}	=	production of family j allocated to plant p
T_k	=	production time allocated to family k
RQ_j	=	run quantity of family j
RQ_{ij}	=	run quantity of item i in family j
AF_{jpr}	=	annual forecast demand of family j for plant p in region r
F_{ij}	=	forecast usage of item i in family j
SS_{kt}	=	safety stock for family k in period t
S_{ij}	=	safety stock required for item i of family j
L_{ij}	=	overstock limit for item i of family i
Q_j	=	economic run length of family j
Q_{ij}	=	economic run length of item i in family j

1. The process starts with the annual assignment of families to plants. A mixed integer program decides which plant (or plants) should produce each family to minimize the sum of fixed production costs and variable

production and transportation costs. This *plant/family assignment module* is similar to the one Liberatore and Miller [1985] use, but it omits plant capacity constraints. Once the families assigned to each plant are fixed by this model, the system proceeds to plan production at individual plants.

2. The *seasonal planning module* operates at the level of types. Using a 15-month planning horizon to fully capture the seasonal cycle, a linear programming model ensures that the production plan meets the seasonal demand and fulfills the requirements for safety stock in each period. The objective of this problem is to minimize the total cost of overtime and carrying inventory. Constraints limit the amounts of regular and overtime production across all types. With five types and seven time periods, the linear program has about $3 \times 5 \times 7 = 105$ decision variables and about 90 constraints. A linear program of this size must be solved for each plant (some plants that do not produce all types have smaller linear programs). The model allocates production hours to each product type in each time period.

3. Taking the production hours for each type as input, the *family scheduling module* determines the size of the production run (or run quantity) for each family in the next month. The run quantities are governed by several considerations. First, the total production time for all families within a product type must equal the aggregate production time allocated to that type by the previous module. Second, the family run quantities must be based on the economic order quantity for that family to strike a balance between changeover costs and the costs of carrying inventory. Third, adequate safety stock levels must be maintained for each item to ensure high levels of customer service. Finally, overstock limits rule out an unreasonable accumulation of inventory for any item. In their procedure, Hax and Meal first determine the families that require production in the next time period, modify their economic order quantities (if necessary) to observe overstock limits, and then inflate or deflate the run quantities to ensure that the aggregate production hours match the amount allocated to the type.

4. Finally, the *item scheduling module* disaggregates the run quantity of each family into production quantities for its constituent items, attempting to equalize the run-out times of the items in the family. As before, overstock limits continue to apply to each item.

HPP is a four-step sequential planning problem: the output of a module at one level of aggregation specifies the input to the module at the next lower level of aggregation. Silver and Peterson [1985] work through a detailed numerical example to illustrate the procedures of the last three steps. Hax and Meal [1975] report that the implementation of their HPP system took about two years and cost under $200,000. They estimated that the annual savings exceeded $200,000 at each of the firm's four plants.

Hax and his coworkers have refined the basic methodology in a number of studies. Hax and Golovin [1978] compare four different disaggregation schemes for the family-scheduling problem (step 3 of the preceding four-step process). One scheme finds the run quantities of families by explicitly minimizing the total setup cost incurred by families within a single type. Bitran and Hax [1977] formulate this as a continuous nonlinear knapsack problem. They also show that the results of HPP compare favorably with the "true optimum" obtained from a large mixed integer programming formulation of the production planning problem that avoids aggregation altogether. These tests revealed that the largest deviations occurred in the presence of high setup costs. Bitran, Haas, and Hax [1981] introduced certain refinements in HPP to handle this case. Another interesting development is the extension of HPP to manufacturing processes with two or more stages. In a fabrication-assembly process, for example, parts are manufactured in the first stage of production and subsequently assembled into the finished products in the second stage. Such processes are often controlled with MRP systems. To extend HPP to the two-stage process, Bitran, Haas, and Hax [1982] perform two aggregations, one for parts and another for the finished products. Hax and Candea [1984] provide a comprehensive overview of the research on the HPP methodology.

Several detailed implementations of HPP have appeared in the literature. In their text on applied mathematical programming, Bradley, Hax, and Magnanti [1977] present two detailed accounts of the hierarchical approach. In the first, they discuss strategic and tactical planning for a large fully integrated aluminum company with six plant locations. At each plant, a smelter produces molten aluminum metal, which is cast into ingot form. The strategic model plans capacity expansion for the entire firm. There are 10 possible sources for shipping products to customers: six existing smelters, a new smelter location, and three swapping sources. A linear programming model finds the optimal allocation of capacity to these sources by minimizing the sum of the costs of production (reduction plus casting), in-transit inventory, and transportation. The tactical model assigns customer orders for ingots to the four domestic plants on a weekly basis. This tactical model operates on a more detailed level. It considers 13 product groups (instead of eight in the strategic model) and plans the assignments to individual casting machines at each of the four plants (40 in total). This results in a large linear programming problem that minimizes the sum of casting, inventory, and reassignment costs (for transferring orders from one plant to another).

In their second account of HPP, Bradley, Hax, and Magnanti [1977] describe a two-level hybrid model for planning machine configuration and manpower needs at a naval tender job shop. Naval tenders are special-purpose ships that perform various maintenance functions for the US Navy fleet. The aggregate model uses mixed integer programming to plan the number of machines of each type required in each time period and the associated manpower needs to meet demand. The detailed model is a job-shop simulation model that captures the detailed scheduling environment of the tender. Meal [1984] discusses some other manufacturing settings for HPP.

Oliff and Burch [1985] describe a three-level hierarchical production scheduling system for the Owens-Corning Fiberglas (OCF) plant in

Anderson, South Carolina. OCF is a leading manufacturer of glass fiber products that produces over 200 distinct items. The Anderson facility has two production lines and seven possible combinations of work shifts. The aggregate planning module, which has a planning horizon of three to 12 months, determines how to switch among different production levels to minimize the sum of the costs of payroll, overtime, hiring or firing, and inventory. The resulting aggregate plan sets target inventory levels for the disaggregate model. This mixed integer programming model generates lot sizes and line assignments for each product in each time period. The variables of this model are similar to those in Exhibit 2–1. Oliff and Burch solve this model as a large linear program with 10,000 variables and 10,000 constraints. On the third level of the hierarchical approach, a sequencing heuristic schedules individual jobs and special orders on each line while seeking to minimize the sequence-dependent changeover costs. By using this model, OCF was able to decrease its changeovers from a monthly average of 70 in 1981 to less than 40 in 1982 and 1983. This resulted in an estimated annual savings of $100,000 or more.

Oliff and Leong [1987] give a detailed account of the production switching rule for aggregate planning and compare the results of this procedure with the aggregate production plan at OCF. The plan generated by the switching rule cost about $1.1 million as compared to OCF's total costs of approximately $1.3 million. Oliff [1987] describes the disaggregate model he used to assign products to production lines and to determine lot sizes.

Van Wassenhove and Vanderhenst [1983] describe a hierarchical approach to production planning in the bottleneck department of a large chemical firm, where three huge machines produce about 20 different types of chemicals. Since the total capacity of these machines exceeds annual demand, there are planned idle periods when the machines are shut down. Because the setup costs (for stopping and starting machines) are very high, these idle periods must be planned carefully. The hierarchical method developed by the authors has three steps:

1. Determine the idle periods of the machines—A zero-one integer programming model plans the idle periods of all machines to minimize the sum of the costs of carrying inventory and setup costs. The idle times of the three machines must be determined simultaneously since there is a constraint on the maximum number of machines that can operate in any time period.

2. Plan the production lots—For each machine, a lot-sizing model determines the run quantities for the product groups by trading off setup costs against inventory carrying costs.

3. Determine the production sequences—The sequence in which the products are produced on a single machine affects the total costs because the setup times are sequence-dependent (the changeover cost depends on the two products produced before and after each changeover). Once the pro-

duction lots in each time period are determined, the optimal production sequence can be determined by solving a traveling salesman problem for each machine.

Van Wassenhove and Vanderhenst implemented this hierarchical model in the company, where it is run once every two weeks. Its major benefit is to plan idle times while taking preventive maintenance requirements into consideration.

Finally, Axsäter and Jonsson [1984] use the data from a Swedish manufacturer of drilling equipment to perform a simulation study of a hierarchical production planning system. The three main types of light-weight rock drilling equipment are assembled from 78 items produced by the company and 92 parts or components purchased from outside vendors. The authors use an aggregate planning model to plan produc-tion and then adjust the output of the MRP system to match the output of the aggregate plan. Their simulation tests show that aggregate plan-ning can reduce costs significantly as compared to the case when the MRP system is run without such planning.

Other Applications of Production Planning

There are many applications of production planning around the world. Gelders and Van Steelandt [1980] developed a two-level production planning system for an aluminum mill in Belgium that performs found-ing, rolling, and finishing operations. The firm employs 1,500 people and produces 8,500 tons of product per month to cover an average of 100 incoming orders a day. The aggregate model is run weekly to simulate future machine loads and optimize machine utilizations. It pro-vides the marketing department with valuable information on delivery lead times and the types of orders it should seek. The detailed model develops the daily operational schedule for manufacturing individual orders.

Garg and Tsai [1986] consider production planning at a large wire and cable plant in Taipei that produces communication cables for a single customer. Since the sole customer controls the production re-quirements, the plant must plan its production based on how the con-tract quantity compares with its available capacity. When the detailed orders fall below the plant capacity, the plant's goal is to decide upon the product mix and then to produce this mix with the minimal number of setups. If the detailed orders exceed capacity, however, the objective shifts to one of minimizing tardiness since some orders must be delayed beyond their due dates. Garg and Tsai demonstrated that revised pro-duction plans could reduce setups by more than 50 percent in the former case and save approximately $10,000 per month in penalty costs in the latter case.

Van Wassenhove and De Bodt [1983] consider the medium-term production planning problem for the injection molding department of a Belgian manufacturer that produces about 100 end items and 3,500 components. The firm wanted to smooth its production to avoid subcontracting. Using a capacitated lot-sizing procedure, the authors accomplished this objective and also reduced total setup and inventory costs by about 20 percent. Tang, Adulbhan, and Zubair [1981] developed an aggregate planning model for a manufacturer of heavy mechanical equipment in Pakistan.

Lingaraj [1980] describes a simple but interesting application of production and inventory planning in the beedi industry. The beedi is a small roll of finely cut tobacco, wrapped in a leaf and held together by a thread, smoked by workers in south Asia. Beedi production is essentially a cottage industry; subcontractors use workers to roll beedis at home. Lingaraj discusses how the contractor should set safety stocks for his leaf inventory. He also analyzes the contractor's production plan to meet the company's requirements. This plan involves carrying seasonal inventories since production capacity is higher in the monsoon season while the demand is level. Jensson [1988] uses linear programming to plan daily production for Icelandic fish-processing firms. In this problem, the production planner has to respond to the randomness in the supply of raw materials (fish) by changing the product mix and the utilization of machinery and labor. The linear programming model determines production quantities and allocates man-hours to maximize net revenue.

Going back to applications in the US, Baker et al. [1987] describe a microcomputer-based model for planning production and cost analysis used by Bethlehem Steel Corporation. The system analyzes product flows through the production facilities to evaluate different production plans and uses a spreadsheet package to perform the calculations.

2.5 MANAGING INVENTORY SYSTEMS

In many manufacturing firms, inventory management is a major element of logistics planning. Manufacturers often carry inventories of raw materials, purchased parts, semifinished goods, assemblies, and finished goods. Even such nonmanufacturing firms as distributors and retailers need to track and control their inventories. The same is true of firms in the service industry: the inventory of a blood bank is subject to spoilage with age and must be closely managed; car rental companies (and major railroads) have to balance and position their inventories of cars across the nation.

It is convenient to classify inventory according to the function it serves within the firm. Hax and Candea [1984] identify four basic categories:

1. *Pipeline inventories* result from the flow of goods in the production and transportation stages and include work-in-process and in-transit inventories.

2. *Cycle stocks* or lot-size inventories result from procuring, transporting, or producing items in batches to take advantage of certain lot size economies or to meet technological constraints.

3. *Seasonal inventories* result when the demand for a product is seasonal; the firm builds inventory during low-demand periods in anticipation of the peak periods.

4. *Safety stocks* protect against uncertainties in demand for the goods or unreliable supply of inputs. Safety stocks reduce the risk of shortages during surges of demand or when the supply of goods is interrupted.

To be successful, an inventory reduction program must assess the firm's inventory requirements in each of the four categories. Different decision rules govern the allocation of each type stock. These rules provide scientific answers to the question "how much inventory is enough?"

The use of mathematical modeling in deriving decision rules for inventory has been an active area of research for nearly 80 years. As Erlenkotter [1989] has recently established, Harris's celebrated economic order quantity formula dates back to 1913. According to Hadley and Whitin [1963], the first full-length book devoted to inventory problems was F. E. Raymond's *Quantity and Economy in Manufacture*, published in 1931. Arrow, Karlin, and Scarf [1958] review the roots of inventory theory in the economic literature prior to 1950. Following the publication of the seminal paper by Arrow, Harris, and Marschak [1951], researchers produced a large body of mathematical work on inventory theory. The volume by Arrow, Karlin, and Scarf [1958] is representative of this research. Since the early 1960s, a number of texts have focused on practical techniques for managing inventory. These techniques translate the theory into decision rules that firms can implement to manage inventory systems with a large number of items. Standard references on inventory management include the texts by Brown [1967], Hadley and Whitin [1963], Love [1979], and Silver and Peterson [1985]. Brown [1978b] gives a very concise review of the area.

Inventory Reduction Programs

Despite their accessibility, inventory management techniques are still not used universally. Blue Bell and Pfizer Pharmaceuticals both reduced their inventories dramatically by using "textbook" techniques. Brout [1981] describes how the Planters Division of Standard Brands, the market leader in such nut products as peanuts, controlled its finished goods inventories. In 1980 Planters produced over 100 distinct items at three plants within the US and shipped them through 12 warehouses. Planters' finished goods inventory equalled five to eight weeks of forecast demand (reflecting the sizeable seasonality in demand) and ranged from $20 million to $50 million in value. Planters wanted to improve its inventory control techniques to reduce its inventory without lowering customer service. The company needed a practical approach that could be implemented rapidly at all of its 12 locations.

Planters decided to use a programmable hand-held calculator for inventory control. In the new system, each item had its own card which recorded data magnetically. The calculator was programmed to update forecast errors and to determine order quantities, reorder points, and levels of safety stock for all items using standard inventory control models. To use this tool, the operator only needed to follow a few simple instructions. The implementation started in January 1980 and all warehouses were using the system 29 weeks later. Brout reports that Planters reduced its total finished goods inventory by 23 percent after one year. This $9.9 million reduction in the value of inventory translated into an annual savings of $2.5 million in the cost of carrying inventory. Planters also improved its customer service; the rate of unfilled demand decreased by 36 percent. Other benefits included reduced order processing costs (due to placing fewer orders), fresher product and smaller losses due to aging, and better management information and control.

Cohen and Dunford [1986] report another case involving Manitoba Telephone Systems, a Canadian company that leases and repairs telephone equipment through its phone centers. By carefully analyzing the distribution of its uncertain demand and its impact on the customer service level, this company reduced its on-hand inventory 45 percent. Barron [1985] used a simple newsboy model to help inventory managers at Hallmark set order quantities. By using payoff matrices, managers can explicitly evaluate the trade-off between salvage value and shortage costs in the presence of uncertain demand, thereby avoiding large orders that may result in obsolete inventory. Lingaraj and Balasubramanian [1983] describe an inventory management and materials information system for an aircraft plant that supplies the Indian Air Force. They classify inventory items by combining ABC classification (based on item value) with a measure of how essential the item is (based on its procurement lead time and its production requirements). They use this classification to determine order quantity and safety stock levels. The system saved about $400,000 annually and increased the availability of materials. Mason et al. [1984] describe an inventory reduction plan at General Motors' carburetor assembly plant at Tuscaloosa, Alabama. This plant had to determine what portion of its inventory of 8,000 end items and 20,000 components could be tagged as excess stock. By eliminating this excess stock, the company gained the one-time benefit of its salvage value as well as the recurrent savings of future carrying costs. A combi-

nation of forecasting and economic analysis resulted in a one-time savings of $420,000 and recurrent annual savings of $135,000.

In his study of the retail segment of the inventories of US naval
supply centers, Gardner [1987] demonstrates the effectiveness of shifting the investment in inventory between cycle and safety stocks. Typically, a supply center stocks an average of 80,000 items worth about $25
million. Both cycle stock and safety stock are carried for all items, but a
budget constraint mandated by law requires that the average inventory
investment equal approximately 2.5 months of demand. Prior to
Gardner's study, safety stock accounted for 1.5 months and the remaining month went into cycle stock; the analysis revealed the reverse allocation to be superior. Larger cycle stock implies that orders are placed less
frequently so that the workload associated with reordering items decreases. In this application, the annual number of orders decreased
from 240,000 to 184,000 with no loss in the service level. The associated
20 percent reduction in work load saved the Navy about $2 million in
manpower costs. Gardner used exchange curves [Brown 1967; Silver
and Peterson 1985] to model the trade-off between customer service and
reordering work load, keeping the total inventory investment fixed. As
this study shows, aggregate exchange curves are powerful tools for high-
lighting trade-offs between different components of inventory costs.

In ABC analysis, a well-known technique for managing inventories,
stock items are divided into different classes based on an appropriate
measure of their importance to the company. The most important items
are placed in class A, followed by class B, and so on [Silver and Peterson
1985]. Quick [1982] uses ABC analysis to examine the public drug
procurement programs of developing countries. In these programs, government agencies purchase pharmaceuticals in large quantities (equivalent to one year's consumption, for example) from their suppliers. The
purchasing pattern must balance carrying, ordering, and stockout costs.
In practice, the manager of a drug procurement program must provide
the highest service level possible given a limited budget. To evaluate and
compare different patterns of purchasing, Quick calculates the cost of
carrying cycle and safety stocks for items in different classes. Finally,
Gelders and Van Looy [1978] describe an application of ABC analysis in
a large petrochemical company that had 22,500 different items. Among
other benefits, their decision rules reduced the inventory of slow-
moving items by over 25 percent.

More Complex Inventory Systems

In certain applications, evaluating inventory policies requires more elaborate or customized model building, including the use of simulation
models. The reduction of wood chip inventories at Weyerhaeuser pulp
mill plants provides one example. To hedge against uncertainties in

demand, supply, and price, pulp mills store as much as 100,000 tons of wood in chip form, an inventory valued at $5.0 million. It costs the corporation $750,000 annually to carry this inventory. Moreover, since wood chips deteriorate with age, even a five percent annual loss due to deterioration costs another $250,000. To justify inventory holding costs of this magnitude, the risk associated with stockouts must be carefully analyzed. The SPRINT model described by Finke [1984] uses simulation to find the probability of stockouts and assesses stockout costs, which are then balanced against inventory carrying costs. SPRINT uses probabilistic beta distributions to project chip inflows and usage over the planning horizon. By using SPRINT, Weyerhaeuser was able to reduce its wood chip inventory by 190,000 dry tons at six pulp mills over three years, lowering annual inventory costs by over $2.0 million.

The fuel inventory problem an electric utility faces is somewhat similar to the one just described for pulp mills. Electric power plants carry inventories of coal or gasoline, which they burn to generate power. Many power plants carry inventories large enough to cover four to five months of usage. According to Chao et al. [1989], the industry spends $1.6 billion to carry this inventory each year. These large inventories are meant to protect against the risks of running out of fuel under conditions of uncertain supply and fluctuations in the demand for electricity (due to extreme temperatures, for example). In 1982, the research arm of the electric utility industry—the Electric Power Research Institute (EPRI)—started to develop the Utility Fuel Inventory Model (UFIM) to address the trade-off between the risks of fuel shortages and the costs of holding fuel inventories. UFIM is composed of three submodels [Chao et al. 1989, Morris et al. 1987]. The first submodel uses a Markov decision model (see Chapter 10) to find the optimal inventory policy under normal conditions. The second submodel specifically handles disruptions of a finite duration within a probabilistic framework. Finally, the simulation submodel simulates the behavior of the entire system to collect statistics on expected costs and variances.

UFIM provides fuel managers of utilities with a valuable decision-making tool. The managers can use it to evaluate the impact of specific inventory policies and to customize these policies by season or by plant. Because the model quantifies the risks of shortages, it allows managers to reduce inventory and face the risks in a calculated and justifiable manner. These benefits translate into economic gains. The implementation of UFIM at three plants of Consumers Power of Jackson, Michigan generated savings that ranged from $800,000 to $15.0 million. Chao et al. [1989] report that the model has been successfully transferred to nearly 80 utilities. They estimate savings of $0.75 million per year for each user and cite documented savings of $125 million to date for UFIM users.

Controlling inventories becomes much more complex in systems where the inventory is located at different levels or at multiple locations that interact (a central warehouse that supplies its satellites, for example). Fincke and Vaessen [1988] describe the inventory system at Ciba-Geigy, a multinational producer of chemicals, pharmaceuticals, and agricultural products. They studied the two-level inventory system where the parent company supplies the inventories at its wholly-owned subsidiaries (called group companies). An important decision was whether to keep safety stock centralized in the parent company or distributed among the group companies. Fincke and Vaessen used simulation to evaluate the impact of two alternatives on the total distribution costs and the service level. The study revealed that while a fully decentralized policy minimizes the total amount of safety stock in the system, the policy with the least total cost is to maintain inventories at the parent company. This cost advantage of the centralized policy was due to the higher costs of carrying inventory at the group companies and the low variable costs of the new highly automated distribution center.

Cohen et al. [1990] describe a system called Optimizer that IBM implemented to control the spare parts inventory of its US service support operations. The IBM parts distribution network forms a complex multi-echelon system with two central automated warehouses, 21 field distribution centers, 64 parts stations, and 15,000 outside locations. The system controls over 200,000 parts numbers to support the operations of about 1,000 IBM products. Optimizer derives its stocking policies from sophisticated algorithms for stochastic inventory control. Its implementation helped IBM reduce parts inventories by 20 to 25 percent without lowering its service levels and led to operational efficiencies that save IBM about $20 million a year.

Classical inventory systems generally assume that items used to fill demand leave the system forever. In certain inventory systems, such as supply systems for spare parts in the military, items are repairable and can return to the system for repeated use. Tedone [1989] describes an interesting example of such a system at American Airlines for managing the spare aircraft parts the company needs to support its fleet of over 400 aircraft. Each time an aircraft departs, it is thoroughly inspected. If a part is judged to be defective, it is replaced with a spare unit. While the stock rooms at the airports keep spare parts on hand, they do not repair defective parts; a base facility both stocks and repairs parts. When the airport issues a spare part, the base facility ships an identical unit to the stock room that supplied the spare part. At the same time, the defective part is shipped to the repair facility. As the average value of a part is about $5,000, the inventory of repairable parts must be kept small and managed carefully to avoid stockouts. Tedone describes the microcomputer-based decision support system that American Airlines uses to forecast the demand for repairable parts and to allocate parts to different airport locations. The system uses regression to relate the monthly demand for parts to the number of flying hours in each month. In allocating parts to different locations, the system minimizes the sum of inventory ownership cost and the expected shortage cost, subject to a constraint on the minimum expected system availability.

According to Tedone, the system is currently accepted as the standard tool for allocating repairable parts at American Airlines; it recommends allocations for over 5,000 different parts. The system has provided a one-time savings of $7 million, and a recurring annual savings of $1 million. In addition to these economic benefits, it has increased the productivity of materials management analysts and enabled them to analyze parts more frequently, with greater insight into the performance of the overall parts inventory.

The last two studies provide a glimpse of the complex issues that arise in multi-level and multi-location inventory systems. Schwarz [1981a] has collected a number of studies on multi-level production and inventory systems, including a useful review of repairable systems by Nahmias [1981]. Schwarz [1981b] gives a short and accessible review of multi-location distribution systems. Finally, major inventory reductions often occur when firms redesign their logistics systems to reduce total distribution costs. Chapter 9 contains several examples of firms that have dramatically reduced their logistics costs.

2.6 FURTHER READINGS

Related Readings

Liberatore and Miller Paper

- The design of the hierarchical system at American Olean follows the framework developed by Hax and Meal [1975] as described in Section 2.4. Because American Olean (AO) has few product families, Liberatore and Miller use only two levels of aggregation—families and items—while Hax and Meal use types as well to aggregate families.
- The AO family scheduling model is a generalization of a mixed integer programming model Liberatore [1984] developed for the production of two products on a single line. For the case of two products, a single variable suffices for specifying the product the line produces in each time period. Liberatore [1984] generalizes this single-line model to the multiproduct case and adds constraints on the minimum and maximum size of a production run. For P products and N time periods, the resulting model has 4PN decision variables and approximately 10PN constraints. For instance, a problem with two products and a 26-week horizon has about 208 variables and 546 constraints. Liberatore presents some computational experience with problems of this size. The model Oliff [1987] developed for Owens-Corning Fiberglas addresses similar production scheduling decisions. Cattrysse, Maes, and Van Wassenhove [1990] and Fleischmann [1990] present different solution techniques for this problem and report

their computational experience with problems that have up to 50 products and eight to 122 time periods.

- In discussing implementation issues for AO's hierarchical models, Miller and Liberatore [1988] emphasize the importance of communication across corporate departments and point out the need for an accessible corporate data base to support modeling activities. Miller and Liberatore [1989] describe a simpler hierarchical planning model that AO implemented in its ceramic mosaic division.

Edwards, Wagner, and Wood Paper

- The Blue Bell study relies on some standard techniques of production planning and inventory control. Edwards, Wagner, and Wood [1985] cite the pages of the well-known text of Peterson and Silver [1979] where these techniques are discussed. We mention the first three models of the Blue Bell planning system here and refer to the new edition of the same text [Silver and Peterson 1985].

    The sales forecasting model uses the Winters exponential smoothing model with seasonal indices [Silver and Peterson 1985, pp. 115-126]. In forecasting sales, this model takes both trend and seasonality into account. Twelve seasonal indices estimate the relative magnitude of sales in each month as compared to the whole year. Inventory control systems often use exponential smoothing to forecast demand. Gardner [1985] reviews the status of this general class of forecasting techniques.

    The safety stock planning model establishes the amount of safety stock carried for each item. Safety stock protects against the variability of demand over the lead time for producing the product and hence should move with the standard deviation of this demand. A widely used method for determining safety stocks is to use the standard deviation of forecast errors over a lead time as a measure of the variability of demand. This standard deviation is then multiplied by a safety factor that depends on the desired service level [Silver and Peterson 1985, pp. 269-276]. The standard deviation of forecast errors of lead time demand must be estimated from historical data. In planning its safety stocks, Blue Bell assumed that this standard deviation is proportional to the lead time raised to a certain power and estimated this exponent from past demand data [Silver and Peterson 1985, pp. 131-133].

    The third model is a variation on the graphical method for aggregate production planning [Silver and Peterson 1985, pp. 543-547]. Using this technique, a company can smooth its production rate over the course of the year by carrying seasonal inventories. Since the method is easy to understand, most production management texts describe this technique and provide numerical examples.

Kleutghen and McGee Paper

- Pfizer Pharmaceuticals uses the (s,S) inventory policy to set lot sizes for producing finished goods and to determine levels of safety stock (see Exhibit 2–7). This policy fixes values of s and S to minimize the expected costs of ordering (setup), carrying inventory, and backordering. Researchers have investigated the mathematical properties of (s,S) policies since the

1950s, and Scarf [1963] presents a masterful survey of the early theoretical work. While (s,S) policies were shown to be optimal under fairly general conditions, the computational burden of finding the optimal settings of s and S stood in the way of using optimal policies in practice. To overcome this difficulty, Wagner [1975, Section 19.7] presents an empirical approximation to the optimal policy that makes calculation of s and S easy. The approximation is based on a detailed study where Wagner, O'Hagan, and Lundh [1965] compared approximate and optimal policies. Kleutghen and McGee use the Wagner procedure to calculate their (s,S) policies.

The idea behind the Wagner approximation is to set the difference $S-s$ equal to the economic order quantity (the optimal batch size), which is easily calculated from the well-known square root formula. The value for s is then determined to balance the costs of carrying inventory and backordering. Assuming a normal distribution for demand simplifies these calculations considerably. However, if the cost parameters indicate that orders should be placed more frequently than once every other period, this approach is modified to focus primarily on the trade-off between carrying and backordering costs.

In more recent years, a technique Ehrhardt [1979] developed for computing (s,S) policies has received much attention. This approach, called the *power approximation*, uses theoretical results to set up expressions that approximate the optimal values of $S-s$ and s. These expressions have specific functional forms but involve parameters that must be determined through regression analysis. Ehrhardt and Wagner [1982] present a detailed account of their experience with this approach and also cover recent advances of practical importance in inventory modeling. Ehrhardt, Schultz, and Wagner [1981] investigate (s,S) policies for a two-level system where a wholesaler's demand originates from other facilities that follow (s,S) policies to replenish their inventories. Finally, Jacobs and Wagner [1989] demonstrate that effective statistical estimation of the parameters of the demand distribution can reduce the total system cost in inventory systems that follow (s,S) replenishment policies. They incorporated the new estimators into Ehrhardt's power approximation method and applied it to US Air Force data to measure the savings in total cost.

Background Readings

Many implementation studies that serve as background readings for the three papers were discussed in Sections 2.4 and 2.6. In this section, we mention some additional sources and overview papers.

- Forecasting is an integral component of successful inventory management. In one of the original and influential texts in this area, Brown [1959] presents many of the principles behind forecasting for statistical inventory control. In his text, Brown [1977] adopts a modular approach in presenting the building blocks of forecasting and inventory management. The text is organized around a library of programs and contains samples of the output these programs produce. Brown [1978a] gives a short synopsis of the established techniques. Gardner [1985] takes stock of exponential smoothing models—models that have been widely used for forecasting demand within inventory systems.

- Aggregate production planning is now covered in many standard production and operations management texts [Hax and Candea 1984; Silver and Peterson 1985]. Vollmann, Berry, and Whybark [1988] give a comprehensive overview of manufacturing planning and control with emphasis on medium-term and short-term production planning. In their reviews of production planning, Gelders and Van Wassenhove [1981] and Hax [1978] emphasize aggregate planning, while Graves [1981] concentrates on production scheduling. Maxwell et al. [1983] present a useful summary of production planning for multi-stage assembly systems. Bahl, Ritzman, and Gupta [1987] review lot-sizing and capacity issues within production and inventory planning. They divide production planning problems into single-level and multi-level problems and subdivide each class into problems with unconstrained resources and problems with limited resources. They survey the literature on each of these four groups of problems. Goyal and Gunasekaran [1990] review models of multi-stage systems that manufacture products in several stages and must control work-in-process inventories occuring between successive stages. They cite 121 articles that represent research in this area. In his chapter in a forthcoming book, Shapiro reviews mathematical programming models of production planning. In addition to hierarchical planning, he discusses models for process manufacturing, lot sizing, and job-shop scheduling. Kusiak and Chen [1988] review the role of artificial intelligence and expert systems in production planning. The March 1990 issue of the *European Journal of Operational Research* (Volume 45, No. 1) focuses on production planning and contains two articles on hierarchical production planning.

- Most texts on production management present a broad view of its role within the firm [Fogarty and Hoffman 1983; McLeavey and Narasimhan 1985; Vollman, Berry, and Whybark 1988]. Silver [1981] critically reviews the role of operations research in inventory management. Schwarz [1981b] surveys the analytical work on physical distribution. Schwarz [1981a] has edited a volume that includes mathematical analyses of multilevel inventory along with good review papers. We did not mention the recent work on just-in-time production systems and their role in reducing inventories. Schonberger [1987] discusses this topic and reviews the experiences of various manufacturers with JIT techniques.

- Blue Bell used an optimization procedure to select markers in such a way as to minimize fabric waste. The underlying optimization is similar to the well-known cutting stock or trim-loss problem. In this problem, a manufacturer must decide on patterns for cutting large units into pieces of the sizes ordered by the customers. In the paper industry, for example, the basic unit may be a wide roll of paper that must be cut into rolls of smaller widths required by the customers. This defines a one-dimensional trim-loss problem since the length of the roll is fixed. Blue Bell's problem, on the other hand, is a two-dimensional problem with intricate patterns. Hinxman [1980] surveys trim-loss problems in one and two dimensions and reviews solution techniques proposed for these problems. Haessler [1988] discusses heuristic techniques for solving one-dimensional trim-loss problems from a practical viewpoint. He presents five different roll-trim problems arising in the paper and film industries and the heuristics used to solve them. The January 1990 special issue of the *European Journal of Operational Research* (Vol. 44, No. 2) is devoted to cutting and packing problems in one, two, and three dimensions. In an article in this collection, Dyckhoff [1990] develops a typology of different cutting and packing problems and cites much of the relevant literature.

REFERENCES

Arrow, Kenneth J.; Harris, Theodore E.; and Marschak, Jacob 1951, "Optimal inventory policy," *Econometrica*, Vol. 19, No. 3, pp. 250–272.

Arrow, Kenneth J.; Karlin, Samuel; and Scarf, Herbert 1958, *Studies in the Mathematical Theory of Inventory and Production*, Stanford University Press, Stanford, California.

Axsäter, Sven and Jonsson, Henrik 1984, "Aggregation and disaggregation in hierarchical production planning," *European Journal of Operational Research*, Vol. 17, No. 3, pp. 338–350.

Bahl, Harish C.; Ritzman, Larry P.; and Gupta, Jatinder N. D. 1987, "Determining lot sizes and resource requirements: A review," *Operations Research*, Vol. 35, No. 3, pp. 329–345.

Baker, Gordon L.; Clark, William A., Jr.; Frund, Jonathan J.; and Wendell, Richard E. 1987, "Production planning and cost analysis on a microcomputer," *Interfaces*, Vol. 17, No. 4, pp. 53–60.

Barron, F. Hutton 1985, "Payoff matrices pay off at Hallmark," *Interfaces*, Vol. 15, No. 4, pp. 20–25.

Bitran, Gabriel R.; Haas, Elizabeth A.; and Hax, Arnoldo C. 1981, "Hierarchical production planning: A single stage system," *Operations Research*, Vol. 29, No. 4, pp. 717–743.

Bitran, Gabriel R.; Haas, Elizabeth A.; and Hax, Arnoldo C. 1982, "Hierarchical production planning: A two-stage system," *Operations Research*, Vol. 30, No. 2, pp. 232–251.

Bitran, Gabriel R. and Hax, Arnoldo C. 1977, "On the design of hierarchical production planning systems," *Decision Sciences*, Vol. 8, No. 1, pp. 28–55.

Bradley, Stephen P.; Hax, Arnoldo C.; and Magnanti, Thomas L. 1977, *Applied Mathematical Programming*, Addison-Wesley, Reading, Massachusetts.

Brout, Donald B. 1981, "Scientific management of inventory on a hand-held calculator," *Interfaces*, Vol. 11, No. 6, pp. 57–69.

Brown, Robert G. 1959, *Statistical Forecasting for Inventory Control*, McGraw-Hill, New York.

Brown, Robert G. 1967, *Decision Rules for Inventory Control*, Holt, Rinehart, and Winston, New York.

Brown, Robert G. 1977, *Materials Management Systems*, John Wiley & Sons, New York.

Brown, Robert G. 1978a, "Forecasting," in *Handbook of Operations Research*, Vol. 2, ed. J. Moder and S. E. Elmaghraby, Van Nostrand Reinhold, New York, pp. 3–26.

Brown, Robert G. 1978b, "Inventory Control," in *Handbook of Operations Research*, Vol. 2, ed. J. Moder and S. E. Elmaghraby, Van Nostrand Reinhold, New York, pp. 173–212.

Cattrysse, Dirk; Maes, John; and Van Wassenhove, Luk N. 1990, "Set partitioning and column generation heuristics for capacitated dynamic lotsizing," *European Journal of Operational Research*, Vol. 46, No. 1, pp. 38–47.

Chao, Hung-Po; Chapel, Stephen W.; Clark, Charles E., Jr.; Morris, Peter A.; Sandling, M. James; and Grimes, Richard C. 1989, "EPRI reduces fuel inventory costs in the electric utility industry," *Interfaces*, Vol. 19, No. 1, pp. 48–67.

Cohen, Morris; Kamesam, Pasumarti V.; Kleindorfer, Paul; Lee, Hau; and Tekerian, Armen 1990, "Optimizer: IBM's multi-echelon inventory system for managing service logistics," *Interfaces*, Vol. 20, No. 1, pp. 65–82.

Cohen, Rochelle and Dunford, Fraser 1986, "Forecasting for inventory control: An example of when simple means better," *Interfaces*, Vol. 16, No. 6, pp. 95–99.

Dyckhoff, Harald 1990, "A typology of cutting and packing problems," *European Journal of Operational Research*, Vol. 44, No. 2, pp. 145–159.

Edwards, Jerry R.; Wagner, Harvey M.; and Wood, William P. 1985, "Blue Bell trims its inventory," *Interfaces*, Vol. 15, No. 1, pp. 34–52.

Ehrhardt, Richard A. 1979, "The power approximation for computing (s,S) inventory policies," *Management Science*, Vol. 25, No. 8, pp. 777–786.

Ehrhardt, Richard A.; Schultz, Carl R.; and Wagner, Harvey M. 1981, "(s,S) policies for a wholesale inventory system," in *Multi-level Production/Inventory Control Systems*, ed. L. B. Schwarz, North-Holland, New York, pp. 145–161.

Ehrhardt, Richard A. and Wagner, Harvey M. 1982, "Inventory models and practices," in *Advance Techniques in the Practice of Operations Research*, ed. H. J. Greenberg, F. H. Murphy, and S. H. Shaw, North-Holland, New York, pp. 250–332.

Erlenkotter, Donald 1989, "An early classic misplaced: Ford W. Harris's economic order quantity model of 1915," *Management Science*, Vol. 35, No. 7, pp. 898–900.

Fincke, Ulrich and Vaessen, Willem 1988, "Reducing distribution costs in a two-level inventory system at Ciba-Geigy," *Interfaces*, Vol. 18, No. 6, pp. 92–104.

Finke, Gary F. 1984, "Determining target inventories of wood chips using risk analysis," *Interfaces*, Vol. 14, No. 5, pp. 53–58.

Fleischmann, Bernhard 1990, "The discrete lot-sizing and scheduling problem," *European Journal of Operational Research*, Vol. 44, No. 3, pp. 337–356.

Fogarty, Donald W. and Hoffmann, Thomas R. 1983, *Production and Inventory Management*, South-Western Publishing, Cincinnati, Ohio.

Gardner, Everette S., Jr. 1985, "Exponential smoothing: The state of the art," *Journal of Forecasting*, Vol. 4, No. 1, pp. 1–38.

Gardner, Everette S., Jr. 1987, "A top-down approach to modeling US Navy inventories," *Interfaces*, Vol. 17, No. 4, pp. 1–7.

Garg, Udai and Tsai, Chin-Yang 1986, "Modeling and analysis of a large wire and cable plant operation," *Interfaces*, Vol. 16, No. 6, pp. 77–85.

Gelders, Ludo F. and Van Looy, Paul M. 1978, "An inventory policy for slow and fast movers in a petrochemical plant: A case study," *Journal of the Operational Research Society*, Vol. 29, No. 9, pp. 867–874.

Gelders, Ludo F. and Van Steelandt, Frank V. 1980, "Design and implementation of a production planning system in a rolling mill: A case study," *AIIE Transactions*, Vol. 12, No. 1, pp. 54–58.

Gelders, Ludo F. and Van Wassenhove, Luk N. 1981, "Production planning: A review," *European Journal of Operational Research*, Vol. 7, No. 4, pp. 101–110.

Goyal, Suresh K. and Gunasekaran, A. 1990, "Multi-stage production-inventory systems," *European Journal of Operational Research*, Vol. 46, No. 1, pp. 1–20.

Graves, Stephen C. 1981, "A review of production scheduling," *Operations Research*, Vol. 29, No. 4, pp. 646–675.

Hadley, G. and Whitin, T. M. 1963, *Analysis of Inventory Systems*, Prentice-Hall, Englewood Cliffs, New Jersey.

Haessler, Robert W. 1988, "Selection and design of heuristic procedures for solving roll trim problems," *Management Science*, Vol. 34, No. 12, pp. 1460–1471.

Hax, Arnoldo C. 1978, "Aggregate production planning," in *Handbook of Operations Research*, Vol. 2, ed. J. Moder and S. E. Elmaghraby, Van Nostrand Reinhold, New York, pp. 127–172.

Hax, Arnoldo C. and Candea, Dan 1984, *Production and Inventory Management*, Prentice-Hall, Englewood Cliffs, New Jersey.

Hax, Arnoldo C. and Golovin, Jonathan J. 1978, "Hierarchical production planning," in *Studies in Operations Management*, ed. A. C. Hax, John Wiley & Sons, New York, pp. 400–428.

Hax, Arnoldo C. and Meal, Harlan C. 1975, "Hierarchical integration of production planning and scheduling," in *Studies in Management Sciences, Logistics*, Vol. 1, ed. M. A. Geisler, North-Holland, New York, pp. 53–69.

Hinxman, A. I. 1980, "The trim-loss and assortment problems: A survey," *European Journal of Operational Research*, Vol. 5, No.1, pp. 8–18.

Holt, Charles C.; Modigliani, Franco; and Muth, John F. 1956, "Derivation of a linear decision rule for production and employment scheduling," *Management Science*, Vol. 2, No. 2, pp. 159–177.

Holt, Charles C.; Modigliani, Franco; Muth, John F.; and Simon, Herbert A. 1960, *Planning Production, Inventories, and Work Force*, Prentice-Hall, Englewood Cliffs, New Jersey.

Holt, Charles C.; Modigliani, Franco; and Simon, Herbert A. 1955, "A linear decision rule for production and employment scheduling," *Management Science*, Vol. 2, No. 1, pp. 1–30.

Jacobs, Raymond A. and Wagner, Harvey M. 1989, "Reducing inventory system cost by using robust demand estimators," *Management Science*, Vol. 35, No. 7, pp. 771–787.

Jensson, Pall 1988, "Daily production planning in fish processing firms," *European Journal of Operational Research*, Vol. 36, No. 3, pp. 410–415.

Kleutghen, Paul P. 1989, private communication.

Kleutghen, Paul P. and McGee, J. C. 1985, "Development and implementation of an integrated inventory management program at Pfizer Pharmaceuticals," *Interfaces*, Vol. 15, No. 1, pp. 69–87.

Kusiak, Andrew and Chen, Mingyuan 1988, "Expert systems for planning and scheduling manufacturing systems," *European Journal of Operational Research*, Vol. 34, No. 2, pp. 113–130.

Liberatore, Matthew J. 1984, "A dynamic production planning and scheduling algorithm for two products processed on one line," *European Journal of Operational Research*, Vol. 17, No. 3, pp. 351–360.

Liberatore, Matthew J. and Miller, Tan 1985, "A hierarchical production planning system," *Interfaces*, Vol. 14, No. 4, pp. 1–11.

Lingaraj, B. P. 1980, "Production and inventory planning in the beedi industry," *Interfaces*, Vol. 10, No. 6, pp. 97–102.

Lingaraj, B. P. and Balasubramanian, R. 1983, "An inventory management and materials information system for aircraft production," *Interfaces*, Vol. 13, No. 5, pp. 65–70.

Love, Stephen F. 1979, *Inventory Control*, McGraw-Hill, New York.

Mason, J. Barry; Mellichamp, Joseph M.; Miller, David M.; Gilligan, Thomas P.; and Cook, Garady 1984, "A joint industry-labor-university cost saving venture," *Interfaces*, Vol. 14, No. 6, pp. 70–79.

Maxwell, William; Muckstadt, John A.; Thomas, L. Joseph; and VanderEecken, Jacques 1983, "A modeling framework for planning and control of production in discrete parts manufacturing and assembly systems," *Interfaces*, Vol. 13, No. 6, pp. 92–104.

McLeavey, Dennis W. and Narasimhan, Seetharama L. 1985, *Production Planning and Inventory Control*, Allyn and Bacon, Boston, Massachusetts.

Meal, Harlan C. 1984, "Putting production decisions where they belong," *Harvard Business Review*, Vol. 62, No. 2, pp. 102–111.

Miller, Tan 1989, private communication.

Miller, Tan C. and Liberatore, Matthew J. 1988, "Implementing integrated production and distribution planning systems," *International Journal of Operations and Production Management*, Vol. 8, No. 7, pp. 31–41.

Miller, Tan C. and Liberatore, Matthew J. 1989, "Production and distribution planning in a process firm," *Production and Inventory Management Journal*, Vol. 30, No. 1, pp. 44–48.

Morris, Peter A.; Sandling, M. James; Fancher, Richard B.; Kohn, Michael A.; Chao, Hung-Po; and Chapel, Steven W. 1987, "A utility fuel inventory model," *Operations Research*, Vol. 35, No. 2, pp. 169–184.

Nahmias, Steven 1981, "Managing reparable item inventory systems: A review," in *Multi-level Production/Inventory Control Systems*, ed. L. B. Schwarz, North-Holland, New York, pp. 253–277.

Oliff, Michael D. 1987, "Disaggregate planning for parallel processors," *IIE Transactions*, Vol. 19, No. 2, pp. 215–219.

Oliff, Michael D. and Burch, E. Earl 1985, "Multiproduct production scheduling at Owens-Corning Fiberglas," *Interfaces*, Vol. 15, No. 5, pp. 25–34.

Oliff, Michael D. and Leong, G. Keong 1987, "A discrete production switching rule for aggregate planning," *Decision Sciences*, Vol. 18, No. 4, pp. 582–597.

Peterson, Rein and Silver, Edward A. 1979, *Decision System for Inventory Management and Production Planning*, John Wiley & Sons, New York.

Quick, Jonathan D. 1982, "Applying management science in developing countries: ABC analysis to plan public drug procurement," *Socio-Economic Planning Sciences*, Vol. 16, No. 1, pp. 39–50.

Scarf, Herbert E. 1963, "A survey of analytic techniques in inventory theory." in *Multistage Inventory Models and Techniques*, ed. H. E. Scarf, D. M. Gilford, and M. W. Shelly, Stanford University Press, Stanford, California, pp. 185–225.

Schonberger, Richard J. 1987, *World Class Manufacturing Casebook: Implementing JIT and TOC*, The Free Press, New York.

Schwarz, Leroy B., ed. 1981a, *Multi-level Production/Inventory Control Systems: Theory and Practice*, North-Holland, New York.

Schwarz, Leroy B. 1981b, "Physical distribution: The analysis of inventory and location," *AIIE Transactions*, Vol. 13, No. 2, pp. 138–150.

Shapiro, Jeremy F., forthcoming, "Mathematical programming models and methods for production planning and scheduling," in *Handbooks in Operations Research and Management Science*, Volume 4: Logistics of Production and Inventory, ed. S. Graves, A. Rinnooy Kan, and P. Zipkin, North-Holland, New York.

Silver, Edward A. 1981, "Operations research in inventory management: A review and a critique," *Operations Research*, Vol. 29, No. 4, pp. 628–645.

Silver, Edward A. and Peterson, Rein 1985, *Decision Systems for Inventory Management and Production Planning*, second edition, John Wiley & Sons, New York.

Tang, John C. S.; Adulbhan, Pakorn; and Zubair, Tahir 1981, "An aggregate production planning for a heavy manufacturing industry," *European Journal of Operational Research*, Vol. 7, No. 1, pp. 22–29.

Tedone, Mark J. 1989, "Repairable part management," *Interfaces*, Vol. 19, No. 4, pp. 61–68.

Van Wassenhove, Luk N. and De Bodt M. A. 1983, "Capacitated lot sizing for injection molding: A case study," *Journal of the Operational Research Society*, Vol. 34, No. 6, pp. 489–501.

Van Wassenhove, Luk N. and Vanderhenst, P. 1983, "Planning production in a bottleneck department: A case study," *European Journal of Operational Research*, Vol. 12, No. 2, pp. 127–137.

Vollmann, Thomas E.; Berry, William L.; and Whybark, D. Clay 1988, *Manufacturing Planning and Control Systems*, second edition, Richard D. Irwin, Homewood, Illinois.

Wagner, Harvey M. 1975, *Principles of Operations Research*, second edition, Prentice-Hall, Englewood Cliffs, New Jersey.

Wagner, Harvey M.; O'Hagan, Michael; and Lundh, Bertil 1965, "An empirical study of exactly and approximately optimal inventory policies," *Management Science*, Vol. 11, No. 7, pp. 690–723.

A Hierarchical Production Planning System

Matthew J. Liberatore
Tan Miller

Production planning can be seen as a hierarchy of managerial decision-making activities. The hierarchy ranges from strategic planning through tactical planning to operations control [Anthony 1965]. In formulating strategy, the firm decides on its objectives, such as profitability, growth, and market and technological position. In analyzing its environment, the firm determines whether existing or new products will better enable it to achieve its objectives during the planning period. Manufacturing policies are established to help close some of the gaps between projected and desired performance. These may call for changes in the capacity, location, and configuration of the firm's physical facilities. What financial, human, and material resources are available to operating management over the planning horizon are also defined.

These upper management decisions form a framework for tactical (medium-term) production planning, which allocates capacity to product lines and establishes the sources of product supply for the various levels in the distribution chain (warehouses, sales centers, and so forth). This tactical plan must be put into operation by determining a short-term production schedule for each manufacturing facility. The firm's hierarchical production planning and scheduling activities must be integrated to insure coordination between the various organization levels responsible for developing and executing plans [Gelders and Van Wassenhove 1982]. Also the hierarchy of managerial decisions must be consistent to avoid excessive suboptimization, recognizing that it is usually impossible to construct one all-encompassing model for analyzing decisions at all levels.

Such a hierarchical production planning system has been developed at American Olean Tile Company (AO) because of AO management's interest in using computer-based decision aids to integrate

(1) The development of the annual production plan and source of supply,

(2) Short-term production scheduling activities at each of the plants, and

(3) Inventory control procedures at the sales distribution points (SDPs).

An annual production-planning and sourcing model has been successfully implemented, and a short-term computerized scheduling model is being field tested. The master production schedule is based on forecasts from a computerized inventory control system at the SDPs, as well as on firm, scheduled orders.

Our modeling approach generally follows the framework developed by Hax and Meal [1975]. However, our product aggregation-disaggregation scheme is quite simplistic, while our approach to short-term scheduling is based on a mixed-integer-programming model. The literature contains few reports on the practice of hierarchical planning and integration. Notable exceptions include the implementation of Hax and Meal [1975], case studies in a rolling mill [Gelders and Van Steelandt 1980] and a medium-sized chemical firm [Gelders and Van Wassenhove 1982], and an integrated production, distribution, and inventory planning system for a large chemical fertilizer company [Glover et al. 1979]. The need for additional descriptions of industrial applications in designing coordination schemes and integrated systems has been suggested [Gelders and Van Wassenhove 1982].

COMPANY BACKGROUND

The American Olean Tile Company, founded in 1923 as the Franklin Tile Company, manufactures a wide variety of ceramic tile products. These products range from tile produced for walls (indoor and outdoor applications) and for floors (both light residential and heavy commercial), to tiles produced for elaborate mural designs. AO currently operates eight factories located across the US from New York to California that supply approximately 120 sales distribution points, a combination of marketing sales territories and company-owned warehouses. These factories utilize several different production processes, all of which begin with a crushing and milling procedure, and which eventually lead to the firing of the tile in large kilns. AO produces three basic lines of tile products: (1) glazed tile, (2) ceramic mosaics, and (3) quarry tile. The quarry division operates four factories at three locations (Quakertown, Pennsylvania; Lewisport, Kentucky—two plants; and Roseville, California), while the glazed and ceramic mosaic divisions have two and one manufacturing sites, respectively.

In recent years, AO's distribution network has expanded quite rapidly, and this trend continues today. The growth of this network prompted AO's management to initiate a modeling program designed to assist manual planning of production and distribution. The modeling began with the quarry division, which has the largest distribution network of the three divisions (Figure 1). In implementing the annual production planning model, the need for coordinating it with short-term production scheduling at the plants and inventory control at the SDPs became apparent. It became clear that full benefits from proper plant, product, and SDP assignments cannot be obtained when short-term scheduling and inventory control decisions are not aligned with the annual plan or the assumptions underlying it. A hierarchical production planning system was developed to improve the integration of the annual plan, short-term scheduling, and inventory control.

PRODUCTION PLANNING FRAMEWORK

The design of any product aggregation scheme depends on product structure,

FIGURE 1. Quarry tile distribution network for American Olean Tile Company.

■ Plant Sales Offices
▲ Sales Service Centers
● Distributors

and consistency and feasibility are the principal objectives and constraints [Gelders and Van Wassenhove 1982]. The quarry tile product line was aggregated into 10 families, each of which comprises several hundred items or stock-keeping units (SKUs). Because the number of product families is small, demand seasonality is incorporated at the family level in our system. The Hax-Meal approach [1975] groups families into types having similar seasonality patterns. The level of aggregation employed at AO is appropriate to both the nature of the tile product and its manufacturing process.

In most general terms, tile can be classified into two product types: flat tile and trim tile. Flat tile constitutes approximately 90 percent of total quarry sales and is produced in approximately seven to 10 basic shapes (for example, 4″ x 8″ or 6″ x 6″). Trim tiles are pieces of tile specially shaped to form a border between the sur-

face covered by the flat tile and the surface next to the flat tile (for example, the border where a floor and a wall intersect). The demand for trim tile is dependent (in a materials requirements planning sense [Orlicky 1975]) on flat tile demand. Once we have set the production schedule for flat tile, the amount of associated trim production required is determined through a known flat-to-trim selling ratio. Decisions about trim production are derived directly from decisions on flat production, and often the trim associated with a particular flat product is fired concurrently on the same production line.

The flat tile production process itself made it logical to further condense SKUs into major product families. In addition to a basic shape and color, flat tile is made in several different surfaces (for example, regular and abrasive), and in several variations of the basic color (for example, Grey and Grey Flash). However, tiles made from one basic flat shape in one color all require very similar raw materials and have virtually identical manufacturing cost and capacity constraints. Therefore, several major flat tile SKUs can be aggregated into one major product family with minimal impact on the accuracy of our model results. The aggregation process resulted in the formation of 10 major product families encompassing over 98 percent of total quarry sales.

Figure 2 summarizes the framework for the hierarchical integration of the production planning and scheduling activities for the AO quarry tile division. The planning process begins with an annual, subjective sales forecast for total quarry division sales expressed in square feet of tile. The director of market planning, in consultation with other top management, generates this sales projection based upon a combination of economic trends and specific quarry market developments. This forecast is allocated to each product family and apportioned to the SDPs based on the ratio of their annual total sales to the total of all quarry tile sales during the previous year. Some adjustments are then made by the planning and marketing staffs. Analysis of recent historical demand patterns has revealed that AO's sales mix remains essentially constant in the short run (12–18 months). These forecasts and the current configuration of AO's plants and SDPs, as well as production line and freight costs, are incorporated into a model which assigns annual family demand by SDP to plants within available capacity.

FIGURE 2. Hierarchical production planning and scheduling framework for American Olean Quarry Tile Division.

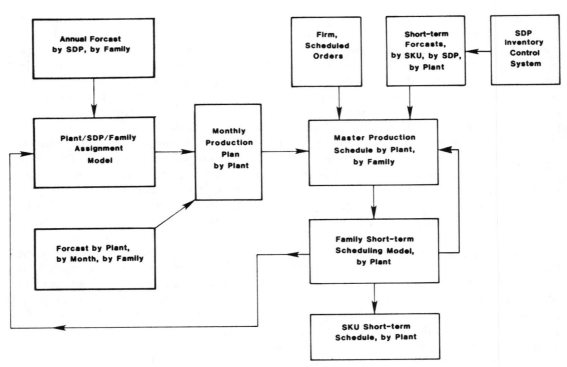

A monthly production plan is then developed by plant-level production personnel based on these assignments and seasonal inventory targets and demand patterns. The monthly production plan, scheduled orders received from larger customers, and short-term demand forecasts generated at each SDP are combined into a master production schedule (MPS) (by family) at each plant. The planning horizon for the MPS is the upcoming quarter, and the length of the planning period is typically one to two weeks.

AO currently uses IBM's Inventory Management Program and Control Techniques (IMPACT) for both SDP short-term forecasting and inventory management (see Chase and Aquilano [1981, pp. 500–506] for a good summary of IMPACT's functions and objectives). The SKU demand forecasts are generated by exponential smoothing with trend and seasonality adjustments [Brown 1962; Tersine 1982, pp. 45–59]. A standard order point-economic order quantity (EOQ) system is used for inventory control, where customer service is measured as percentage of demand filled from stock on hand [Tersine 1982, pp. 158–161]. Forecast errors are measured and tracked using mean absolute deviation (MAD).

Process industries tend to schedule capacity first and then materials [Taylor, Seward, and Bolander 1981]. This differs from materials-oriented systems, such as Materials Requirements Planning (MRP), which are used extensively by the fabrication and assembly industries. Our system uses a short-term scheduling model which first determines the assignment of production lines by planning period to meet the MPS, while minimizing the sum of variable manufacturing, setup, and inventory costs. (This model is currently being field tested. It is the critical link between the divisional annual planning, plant-level pro-

duction scheduling, and SDP inventory control activities.) Then, based on SKU demand forecasts for each family and derived demand for trim products, a short-term SKU production schedule and the associated materials requirements for each plant are established. The mathematical formulations of the plant, family, and SDP assignment model and the family short-term scheduling model are described in the appendices.

IMPLEMENTATION

The process of implementing the revised plant, family, and SDP assignment patterns suggested by our modeling results has required at least as much effort as the model development process itself. It became evident during initial field testing that a successful implementation would hinge on the interest and support of two distinct sets of individuals: (1) key production and distribution personnel at corporate headquarters; and (2) field personnel, such as plant managers. Each group expressed a variety of concerns regarding the changes implied by the model's results. However, two factors provided the most compelling arguments for gaining their support.

First and most importantly, we emphasized the potential savings resulting from model implementation. Management interest was heightened by the fact that the benefits would be ongoing. Second, the use of a staged process for implementation allowed changes to be made at an acceptable rate. Massive reassignments were not requested at the outset, nor would they have been approved by upper management. For example, the model suggested many changes in source of supply for the SDPs. However, only a few assignments were altered during each stage.

This facilitated a smooth transition and avoided the turmoil and resistance which might otherwise have arisen.

In a staged implementation, it is necessary to evaluate each step separately. The affected personnel consider each step on its own merits, not as part of a larger, overall plan. Therefore, the success of each step, and ultimately of the entire plan, depends upon developing self-supporting stages. Each stage must be evaluated for any potential "suboptimization" effects. Specifically, the impact of staged revisions on the entire system must be considered before implementation.

This process has been completed for the quarry tile division, and a similar process is under way for the glazed division. Its LP is substantially larger, with 440 decision variables and 2440 constraints. Because the family scheduling model is currently being field tested, a detailed discussion of implementation issues is not yet possible. However, current efforts focus on implementation at one of the three locations, while the remaining sites will be converted in a second stage.

COSTS AND BENEFITS

The development costs fall into two basic categories: (1) man-months committed to data and model development, and (2) expenditures for computer software. Because several system components were already in place, the development costs to date are much less than they would be for the complete system. Specifically, IMPACT and the annual aggregate forecasting process were already in use and were incorporated into the overall framework.

The family short-term scheduling model is still under development, making it difficult to estimate a total cost now.

Concerning the plant, SDP, and family assignment model, more accurate estimates can be given. Development required approximately five man-months of an analyst's time distributed over a nine-month period. The computer model was developed and stored on a commercial time-sharing system at a cost of under $10,000. Software development costs of the short-term family scheduling model will exceed the $10,000 level, since an efficient mixed integer programming capability is required.

An integrated hierarchical system for planning and scheduling production offers many benefits at both the individual component and the system-wide level of an organization. These benefits range from improved coordination and communication between departments to substantially reduced production and distribution costs. As a whole, the system significantly enhances American Olean's ability to position itself more competitively in the marketplace. AO has used the annual assignment model results in developing the production and distribution allocation plan for the quarry division. This plan saves between $400,000 and $750,000 per year. The suggested plan did not substantially alter the capacity loadings at the individual plants. However, it did suggest significant changes in their family mixes. Thus, the model uncovered comparative cost advantages in terms of delivered cost (variable production costs and freight) from each plant.

The development of the assignment model required a sales forecast by family for each SDP. Previously, in the absence of these forecasts, the annual production plans of the manufacturing department did not always coincide with the SDP sales plans of the marketing department. The manufacturing department had always based annual production goals upon the marketing department's annual sales forecast. However, without a detailed forecast, production could not be based on the demands of individual sales territories.

As an indirect benefit, the process of developing the model stimulated closer coordination between the marketing and manufacturing departments in meeting the needs of the sales territories. AO also derived several other indirect benefits, which are also difficult to quantify. Specifically, this methodology produces a general pattern of lower delivered costs at AO's sales distribution points. This offers top management the marketing option of lowering product prices (or at least minimizing any price increases) while maintaining AO's required profit margins on an item-by-item basis.

The annual planning model can help AO management measure the financial impact of adjusting some medium-term manufacturing and distribution strategies. For example, a plant may have stopped making a particular product because the cost of a major raw material has become too high. The model can determine the system-wide change in annual manufacturing and distribution costs if a less costly alternative material can be found. Other examples include determining what cost savings would result from such capital investment decisions as adding new production capacity to a plant, and what financial penalty would accompany controlling the usage rate of a scarce material at a producing location.

The annual assignment model also helps to reduce unplanned redistribution costs which occur every year. These "hidden" costs arise when one SDP transships a product to a second SDP which is out of stock. These costs are reduced because assignments are now tied more closely to demand patterns within each SDP's market area.

Although the short-run family scheduling model has been developed and solved using actual production, cost, and MPS data for one plant location, we have not yet fully implemented it. We anticipate that its principal impact will be cost savings from improved short-run production plans. For example, even at a plant with a relatively straightforward production process (say, five production lines and five families), the number of potential production combinations over even a short-term planning horizon (for example, four two-week time buckets, or eight weeks) is very large. It is virtually impossible to evaluate manually the total costs associated with even a small subset of potential production schedules. The family scheduling system will be able to make such evaluation easily and should lead to significant cost savings. In addition, this model and the other components of the system will increase labor productivity by freeing many man-weeks previously devoted to manual planning efforts.

In summary, the hierarchical production-planning system offers a modeling approach which integrates decision making and communication across corporate and plant level organizations, enabling more consistent medium- and short-term production-planning and scheduling decisions.

APPENDIX 1: Plant/Family/SDP Assignment Model

The following definitions are used:

Y_{ijpk} = square feet of family i produced on line j at plant p and shipped to SDP k.

C_{ijpk} = the unit square footage cost of

producing family i on line j at plant p and shipping (at truck-load rates) to SDP k.

D_{ik} = square footage demand of family i at SDP k.

S_{ijp} = square footage annual production capacity of product i produced on line j at plant p.

Integer assignment variables are not required since annual SDP demand is sometimes in practice split over several locations. Also since AO planned to operate all current plants during the strategic planning horizon (five years), fixed manufacturing costs were excluded from the analysis.

The problem can then be stated in a transportation-type linear programming format.

Minimize

$$\sum_i \sum_j \sum_k \sum_p Y_{ijkp} C_{ijkp} \qquad (1)$$

subject to

$$\sum_p \sum_j Y_{ijkp} = D_{ik}, \qquad (2)$$

for all possible i, k (family-SDP) combinations

$$\sum_i (1 / S_{ijp}) \sum_k Y_{ijkp} \leq 1, \qquad (3)$$

for all possible j, p (line-plant) combinations

$Y_{ijkp} \geq 0$, for all i, j, k, p.

The multiplier $(1/S_{ijp})$ is needed in equation (3) to adjust for the different capacity level (or equivalently, production rates) for each family which can be produced on a given line. The three locations in the quarry tile division have four, six, and two production lines, respectively. There are 10 families, which are produced on different subsets of these 12 lines, and the 120 SDPs stock some or all of these families.

The problem can be solved on any large-scale linear programming system. In this case, a matrix generator was used to simplify the input and editing process, and the resulting model was run on MPS III. The model has approximately 1660 decision variables and 570 constraints.

APPENDIX 2: *Family Scheduling Model*

The AO family scheduling model minimizes the total of variable production, line setup, and inventory holding costs over the short-term planning horizon while meeting the MPS. Production rates by family by production line are constant during each scheduling period. Backlogging of demand is not permitted. The mathematical fomulation is a generalization of a single production line model developed for a chemical processing plant [Liberatore 1984]. The model itself is a mixed integer linear program, and the formulation is given below.

Where

X_{ijt} = *1*, if product i is produced on production line j during period t
= *0*, otherwise.

V_{ijt} = *1*, if a production changeover to product i on line j occurs during time t
= *0*, otherwise.

C_{ij} = the unit cost of producing product i on line j.

P_{ij} = the production rate per period of product i on line j.

S_{ij} = the fixed cost to set up product i on line j.

D_{it} = the demand for product i during period t.

H_i = the end-of-period holding cost for product i.

I_{it} = the inventory of product i at the end of period t.

L_i = the set of all production lines which can be scheduled to produce product i.

M_j = the set of all products which can be scheduled on production line j.

P = the number of products to be scheduled.

L = the number of production lines available.

N = the number of periods in the planning horizon.

t = the time period, expressed in units of one week.

The problem can be stated as minimize

$$\sum_{t=1}^{N} \sum_{j \in L_i} \sum_{i=1}^{P} C_{ij} P_{ij} X_{ijt} + S_{ij} V_{ijt} + \sum_{t=1}^{N} \sum_{i=1}^{P} H_i I_{it} \quad (4)$$

subject to

$$I_{it} \geq 0, i = 1, 2, \ldots, P, \quad t = 1, 2, \ldots, N, \quad (5)$$

$$\sum_{j \in M_j} X_{ijt} \leq 1, \quad j = 1, 2, \ldots, L, \quad (6)$$

$$t = 1, 2, \ldots, N,$$

$$V_{ijt} \geq X_{ijt} - X_{ij,t-1}, \quad i = 1, 2, \ldots, P, j \in L_i, \quad (7)$$

$$t = 1, 2, \ldots, N,$$

X_{ijt}, V_{ijt}, binary, where I_{io}, X_{ijo} given as initial conditions.

Finally, ending inventory is defined as

$$I_{it} = I_{i0} + \sum_{k=1}^{t} \sum_{j \in L_i} P_{ij} X_{ijk} - \sum_{k=1}^{t} D_{ik} \quad (8)$$

$$i = 1, 2, \ldots, P, \quad t = 1, 2, \ldots, N.$$

Equation (5) prevents backlogging of demand, while equation (6) insures that at most one product is scheduled on a given line during each period (an assignment-type constraint). Equation (7) relates the changeover variable (V_{ijt}) to the production scheduling variables in the current and

previous periods (X_{ijt} and $X_{ij,t-1}$, respectively). A changeover to product i on line j occurs during period t and only if $X_{ijt} = 1$ and $X_{ij,t-1}$ is 0. Thus even if the line was idle during period $t-1$, we assume that a changeover occurs to i if it is then scheduled during period t. It is easily shown that equation (7) forces V_{ijt} to be 1 only if $X_{ijt} = 1$ and $X_{ij,t-1}$ is 0; in all other cases V_{ijt} must be 0. Thus, V_{ijt} need not be specified as a binary variable.

The inventory variables can be eliminated from the formulation, and after grouping terms and simplifying, we obtain minimize

$$\sum_{t=1}^{P} \sum_{j \in L_i} \sum_{t=1}^{N} [C_{ij} + (N - t + 1)H_i] \quad (9)$$

$$P_{ij} X_{ijt} + S_{ij} V_{ijt}$$

subject to

$$\sum_{k=1}^{t} \sum_{j \in L_i} P_{ij} X_{ijk} \geq \sum_{k=1}^{t} D_{ik} - I_{i0}, \quad (10)$$

$$i = 1, 2, \ldots P, \quad t = 1, 2, \ldots, N,$$

$$\sum_{i \in M_j} X_{ijt} \leq 1, \quad (11)$$

$$j = 1, 2, \ldots L, \quad t = 1, 2, \ldots, N,$$

$$V_{ijt} \geq X_{ijt} - X_{ij,t-1}, \quad i = 1, 2, \ldots, P, \quad j \in L_i, \quad (12)$$

$$i = 1, 2, \ldots, N.$$

X_{ijt} specified as binary; I_{io}, X_{ijo} given. We define $C(Z)$ to be the cardinality of the set Z. It follows that

$$\sum_{i=1}^{P} C(L_i) = \sum_{j=1}^{L} C(M_j) = V,$$

where V is the number of distinct product production line scheduling combinations. Therefore, the problem defined by equations (9)—(12) is a mixed integer program, with $2NV$ decision variables, NV of which must be specified as binary, and $(P + L + V)N$ constraints.

A variety of techniques and approaches has been suggested in the literature (for example, Crowder, Johnson, and Padberg [1983]; Guignard and Spielberg [1981]) which improve the performance of searching algorithms for binary integer programming. To reduce the time required to find an acceptable integer solution for the family scheduling model, a series of *redundant constraints* was added to the problem formulation. These serve to increase the optimal cost of the linear programming (LP) relaxation of the problem and tend to force more variables to assume binary values. The amount of searching time required to find both an initial feasible binary solution and a good solution is drastically reduced. Initial results were dramatic: for one sample problem, the number of branches checked to find an initial feasible solution dropped from 2000 to 15. Depending upon the actual data, some of these redundant constraints may be more effective than others so that additional testing is required before final implementation.

REFERENCES

Anthony, Robert N. 1965, *Planning and Control Systems: A Framework for Analysis*, Harvard University, Graduate School of Business Administration, Division of Research, Boston, Massachusetts.

Brown, Robert G. 1962, *Smoothing, Forecasting and Prediction of Time Series*, Prentice-Hall, Englewood Cliffs, New Jersey.

Chase, Richard B. and Aquilano, Nicholas J. 1981, *Production and Operations Management* (third edition), Richard D. Irwin, Homewood, Illinois.

Crowder, Harlan; Johnson, Ellis L.; and Padberg, Manfred 1983, "Solving large-scale zero-one linear programming problems," *Operations Research*, Vol. 31, No. 5 (September–October), pp. 803–834.

Gelders, L. F. and Van Steelandt, F. V. 1980, "Design and implementation of a production planning system in a rolling mill: A case study," *AIIE Transactions*, Vol. 12, No. 1, pp. 54–58.

Gelders, L. F. and Van Wassenhove, Luk N. 1982, "Hierarchical integration in production planning: Theory and practice," *Journal of Operations Management*, Vol. 3, No. 1 (November), pp. 27–35.

Glover, Fred; Jones, Gene; Karney, David; Klingman, Darwin; and Mote, John 1979, "An integrated production, distribution, and inventory planning system," *Interfaces*, Vol. 9, No. 5 (November), pp. 21–35.

Guignard, Monique and Spielberg, Kurt 1981, "Logical reduction methods in zero-one programming," *Operations Research*, Vol. 29, No. 1 (January–February), pp. 49–74.

Hax, A. C., and Meal, H. C. 1975, "Hierarchical integration of production planning and scheduling," in *Studies in the Management Sciences*, M. A. Geisler, editor, Vol. 1, *Logistics*, North Holland, Amsterdam.

Liberatore, Matthew J. 1984, "A dynamic production planning and scheduling algorithm for two products processed on one line," *European Journal of Operational Research*, Vol. 17, No. 3 (September), pp. 351–360.

Orlicky, Joseph 1975, *Material Requirements Planning*, McGraw-Hill, New York.

Taylor, Sam G.; Seward, Samuel M; and Bolander, Steven F. 1981, "Why the process industries are different," *Production and Inventory Management*, Vol. 22, No. 4, pp. 9–24.

Tersine, Richard J. 1982, *Principals of Inventory and Materials Management*, second edition, Elsevier North Holland, New York.

A letter from Linwood A. Kulp, Jr., Director, Distribution Services at American Olean Tile states that: "This model now represents the major annual production planning tool utilized by American Olean's quarry and glazed white body tile divisions. It also forms the basis for distribution decisions. As this modeling system at AO matures, it should yield an estimated savings of over \$400,000 annually. . . . The short-run mixed integer scheduling model discussed in the paper would represent the next component to AO's distribution and production planning system. AO's plant managers have expressed interest in this model. However, as noted, plans for this model remain in the developmental stages at present."

Blue Bell Trims Its Inventory

Jerry R. Edwards
Harvey M. Wagner
William P. Wood

An unusual management science success took place at Blue Bell, Inc. that had a significant impact on the economic well-being of the entire enterprise. The substantial improvements, which are apparent in the corporation's annual report, include an impressive reduction in inventory, growth in net income, and a reduction in short-term debt. This management science project influenced all levels of executives, including the chairman of the board, the president, the management committee, the division presidents and their staffs, and the plant managers and their employees. It was an exciting experience for Blue Bell, particularly since the improvements occurred in only 21 months—astonishing for a turnaround of this magnitude.

When this effort began, the economic and competitive pressures that Blue Bell faced were severe. The high cost of carrying inventory had become particularly acute. Short-term interest rates were hovering at 20 percent, and as a result, net interest expenses for Blue Bell had ballooned from $1.1 million in 1979 to $21.9 million in 1982. Financing inventory had dramatically pushed up Blue Bell's cost of doing business.

No "quick fix" approach was going to work, because the contributing factors were both internal and external to the firm. Management science provided the means for senior executives and other managers to swiftly take effective action to turn the situation around. A new production planning process was designed, tested, and implemented that reduced inventories more than 31 percent (from $371 million to $256 million) without a decrease in sales or customer service. The new process also reduced manufacturing costs by approximately $1 million. The strong support of top management was a major factor in this achievement, and that support was communicated down the line so that employees at every level became enthusiastically involved.

LOOKING AT BLUE BELL

Blue Bell is one of the world's largest apparel manufacturers. In fiscal year 1983, sales totaled $1.2 billion and yielded $48 million in net income. Headquartered in Greensboro, North Carolina, Blue Bell employs over 27,000 people worldwide. Domestic operations are supported by 80 plants and 32 distribution centers located primarily in the Southeast, but with sizeable facilities in the Southwest, Northwest, and Puerto Rico. International operations are conducted by 15 plants and 17 distribution centers.

Blue Bell has three major businesses. The largest is the Wrangler Group, which is the business in which the production planning process was developed. Wrangler manufactures denim and corduroy jeans and several other product lines in sports and casual apparel. Wrangler markets to men, women, and children in the USA and also has a substantial international business. Red Kap, the second largest business, makes a variety of durable garments used for on-the-job wear by production, service, and white-collar personnel. Jantzen, the third major business, manufactures a variety of sports and casual apparel product lines, including popular lines of swimwear and sweaters.

To understand the context of the inventory-reduction work, it is important to know that within these businesses Blue Bell has from one to four profit centers, each focused on specific product lines, which break down into styles, lots, and sizes or stock keeping units (SKUs) (Figure 1). Each of the four profit centers in

FIGURE 1. The product hierarchy for jeans.

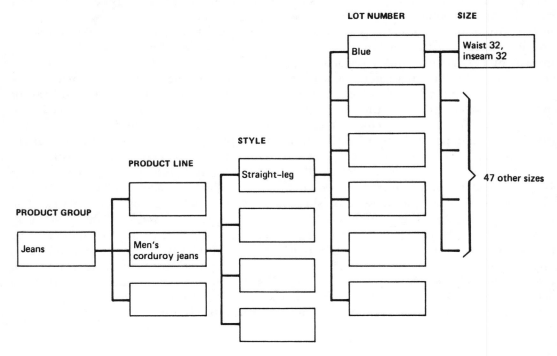

Wrangler (menswear, womenswear, boyswear, and "kids") is organized functionally with sales, merchandising, manufacturing, operations, and finance departments. Operations, responsible for production planning and inventory control, strives to interface the market-oriented needs of merchandising with the constraints and resources of manufacturing. It must balance service to the customer against the costs of manufacturing and maintaining inventory.

UNDERSTANDING THE URGENCY AND COMPLEXITY

In the spring of 1982, Blue Bell management became concerned about its high investment in working capital. In this working-capital-intensive business, inventory and accounts receivable comprise three-fourths of the asset base. Management's preliminary analysis indicated that inventory represented the greatest opportunity for reduction in working capital.

Management's incentives were compelling. For the 12 months ending March 1982, inventory averaged over $371 million, or more than 50 percent of Blue Bell's asset base. Annual charges for maintaining inventory (including short-term borrowing or opportunity cost of capital tied up, warehousing, and obsolescence) totaled at least 25 percent of the inventory investment.

Management realized that to reduce inventory significantly would require extensive improvement in production planning and inventory control. Any solution would have to accommodate the increased complexities in product line and increased service demands of the environment. The number of product lines, styles, and SKUs had grown tremendously, over 69 percent from 1976 to 1982. The production proc-

ess had incorporated several new automated manufacturing operations—embroidery, screenprinting, and various finishing treatments such as prewashing—in response to changes in customer tastes. This increasing complexity meant that the number of decision variables had grown dramatically. Consequently, an unprecedented degree of coordination and execution was required to effectively control Blue Bell's business.

At the same time, service demands were increasing. Blue Bell's customers include national and regional chain stores, department and specialty stores, mass merchandisers, variety stores, and catalog houses. Two major transformations were taking place with these customers:

(1) *Lead time on orders was decreasing.* By 1982 retailers had become sensitive to the high cost of financing their own inventory and had begun to order products closer to when they needed them for sale. This shortened Blue Bell's order lead time and reduced the information from which the company could plan production. More and more, Blue Bell had to produce to stock and also faced more demand uncertainty in its production planning.

(2) *Service demands were increasing.* The retail apparel industry, once highly fragmented, was becoming increasingly concentrated as major chains and discounters took a larger share of the business. As these accounts gained leverage over suppliers, they came to expect higher product availability, more on-time shipments, and shipment of complete orders. Blue Bell, recognizing the competitive importance of superior customer service, could not reduce inventory at the expense of customer service.

With these joint pressures of a complex

product line and increased service expectations, improvements in production planning and inventory control would require a new planning process. It would have to coordinate the functions of sales, marketing, manufacturing, operations, and finance within each profit center.

FORMING A TASK FORCE

The financial magnitude of these issues convinced Blue Bell management to organize a working capital task force. The vice president of finance oversaw the task force and ensured that the desired results were achieved. The task force included three managers. One, from the data processing (DP) systems group, had strong experience in operations research and management science. The second, a chief engineer from the manufacturing func-

tion, had extensive experience in manufacturing and production planning. And the third, a profit center controller, had a strong commitment to minimizing inventory investment.

The task force was asked to (1) diagnose the inventory-reduction opportunity, (2) develop a comprehensive program for reducing inventory, and (3) implement the program.

Work began with the Wrangler Group, comprised of womenswear, menswear, boyswear, and kids profit centers. In basic styles of men's jeans, Wrangler makes 35 million pairs of jeans a year in 37 plants. There are over 10,000 individual SKUs manufactured and stocked. Thus, the magnitude of the task force's job was large.

What happened at each phase of the Wrangler project is shown in Figure 2.

FIGURE 2. The chronology of the Blue Bell inventory reduction project from June 1982 to December 1983.

Diagnosis	Development	Stage 1 Implementation	Stage 2 Implementation
June to July 1982	August to December 1982	January to March 1983	March to December 1983
Performing competitive analysis Running computer simulation Assessing reduction potential	Building the inventory planning models Planning and selecting markers Economizing on fabric waste Utilizing cutting-room capacity Developing the marker planning and selection model Developing the recommendations	Setting up the DP project team Designing and developing prototypes Testing the system in a profit center Testing in parallel with current planning process on a single lot Testing "live"	Rolling out to all divisions Implementing other supporting recommendations

DIAGNOSING THE PROBLEM

The task force's first assignment was to assess what opportunity existed for inventory reduction and investigate how inventory could be reduced without curtailing service or increasing manufacturing costs. The team compared Blue Bell's inventory levels to those of similar companies and found that more than $150 million in inventory reduction was possible. Management had reservations about relying solely on a comparison with similar companies for it is difficult to identify truly comparable companies. Within the apparel industry, there are great differences in product-line mix, seasonality of demand, outside contracting policies, level-production practices, desired service levels, and accounting rules. All of these differences can significantly affect the balance sheet levels of inventory. Therefore, the task force needed to confirm the opportunity for reduction through an internal Blue Bell analysis. It developed a scientific inventory-planning computer simulation model for this purpose.

The model explicitly recognized the characteristics of Wrangler's business, namely, the product-line mix, demand seasonality, level production, contracting policies for raw materials, and desired service levels. The model focused on finished goods inventories, since they made up two-thirds of the total and were the component most out of line with comparable companies. (Later, raw material inventories were modeled as well.)

Blue Bell management wanted a production policy that maintained an even workforce throughout the year. Consequently, the simulation model calculated a smooth production plan based on an annual sales forecast for each lot in a product line (Figure 1). The model assessed the forecast error distribution and, with a given production lead time, computed the end-of-the-month target safety stock to provide the desired level of customer service. Using actual sales history, the simulation then calculated the resulting monthly inventory levels, comprising preseason build-up stock and safety stock. The model was applied to every lot in Wrangler's largest product line.

The simulation results convinced senior management that a quantum opportunity existed: simulated finished goods inventories on the tested product lines were half the historical levels throughout the entire year. The results were credible to the executives because the management science model reflected the specific characteristics of Blue Bell's business.

The size of the opportunity confirmed, the task force next investigated how to achieve the reduction. First it examined in depth the current production planning and inventory control operation. Through quantitative analyses, interviews with all the key personnel in the planning process, and several plant visits, the task force identified two key analytic tasks that would lead to inventory reduction.

The first task was to determine a better approach for managing and allocating capacity, measured by labor hours per month per plant. A more effective methodology was needed to establish the right overall capacity level and efficiently allocate this capacity to the production of specific lots. The proper solution would control aggregate inventory throughout the business.

The second task was to find a better balance of the cost of carrying inventory against the risk of shortages. Data analysis by the task force showed that inventory had not been well balanced at the SKU level. Some SKUs showed months of supply whereas others were out-of-stock. Thus, unless a systematic approach could be developed to consistently achieve a "balanced" inventory at the SKU level, it would be difficult for Blue Bell to attain the dramatic reductions in inventory envisioned.

The team constructed seven scientific models that addressed the two tasks: (1) sales forecasting, (2) safety-stock planning, (3) product-line planning, (4) lot planning, (5) size planning, (6) net requirements planning, and (7) marker design and selection. Because the initial six models are adaptations of well-known management science approaches, we will not explain them in detail but refer the reader to the appropriate pages in Peterson and Silver's recent text [1979].

PLANNING INVENTORY AND PRODUCTION REQUIREMENTS

A product line, such as men's corduroy jeans, can be disaggregated into lot numbers that designate the style, such as straight leg or flare leg, and the color, such as blue or brown (Figure 1). There can be as many as 75 lot numbers in a line. The first three models yield a product-line plan.

The sales forecasting model produces a cumulative estimate of what Wrangler's own customers will want. Sales volume is not uniform throughout the year. For example, orders for boys' jeans peak prior to the start of school. The forecasting model weights historical demand with bookings to date. It produces 12 monthly forecasts, updated every month [Peterson and Silver 1979, pp. 118-127].

Given management's policy of providing a high level of customer service, a safety stock must be added to the forecast to

hedge against demand forecast uncertainty. The safety-stock model is based on a statistical fit, using log-log regression, of monthly forecasts versus actual demands [Peterson and Silver 1979, pp. 136-139]. The model produces a formula for safety-stock quantities depending on forecast sales, production lead time, target service level, and a normal distribution of forecast errors [Peterson and Silver 1979, pp. 221-225].

The product-line planning model indicates the cumulative production needed at each of the next 12 months. It reflects Blue Bell's policy of keeping the workforce level throughout the year. At each month, the difference between planned cumulative production and forecast cumulative sales consists of the targeted safety-stock and the preseason build-up inventory (Figure 3) [Peterson and Silver 1979, pp. 609-612].

Given the planned safety-stock and build-up inventory at the product-line level, the fourth model disaggregates this inventory down to lot numbers (Figure 1). The model is not a simple arithmetic allocation. It accommodates forecasting risk and managerial assessment of market strength. As a result, staple, less risky lots,

FIGURE 3. A graphic representation of inventory planning models.

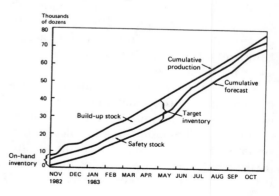

such as men's straight leg blue denims, may have a proportionately greater inventory build-up than a fashion jean.

The fifth model takes the planned inventory of a lot at a specific week and apportions the stock to sizes, or SKUs [Peterson and Silver 1979, pp. 118-127]. A jean size is designated by waist and inseam measurements. The sales volume of a popular size can be up to 50 times greater than that of a slow-moving size. This model yields the planned gross requirements for each SKU at the specified week.

The sixth model calculates the net requirements from the preceeding gross requirements for each SKU. The calculations involve a straightforward netting out of inventory-on-hand and work-in-process [Peterson and Silver 1979, pp. 208-209]. Typically, for any week the net requirements differ considerably from the gross requirements. The factors that affect the transformation involve economical production batch sizes, shifting customer order patterns, production variances, and systematic forecast errors. There also is considerable variation in the net requirements for a SKU from one week to another. It is essentially this variability that makes the task of keeping inventory in balance so difficult. The seventh model, described below, addresses this problem.

DESIGNING AND SELECTING MARKERS

A plant must cut fabric to meet each week's net requirements at the SKU level. The cutting department spreads the appropriate fabric on a table one layer at a time to achieve a specified "lay-up" (number of layers). Then, a "marker" (a pattern containing parts of garments) is spread on the fabric and used as a cutting guide

FIGURE 4. Example of marker.

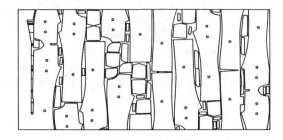

(Figure 4). The cutting department needs to know how many layers to lay on the cutting table and which marker to use. To meet a week's requirements for all SKUs within a lot number, the cutting department may use several markers, each with a different mix of SKUs and a different lay-up.

It is important to recognize that prior to planning the week's cutting, the necessary markers must have been designed and produced. Usually, the cutting department limits its marker selection by choosing from a pre-existing library that may contain several dozen markers for a given lot and fabric width. Blue Bell's existing marker library was not well designed to produce only the SKUs that are needed to meet the week's net requirements. What happened repeatedly was that the markers utilized to make the required SKUs also made SKUs that were not needed that week. One important reason is that marker design and utilization had focused on minimizing fabric waste.

The plant always recognized the problem of having to make unneeded SKUs and had the option of specially ordering markers when the balance problem was serious. But since the lead time for a new marker can be as long as two weeks and the process is expensive, requests for new markers had to be infrequent.

Therefore, the task force addressed the

problem of redesigning the entire marker library. This task was a critical challenge, because there are severe manufacturing cost penalties associated with an ill-thought-out approach to marker planning and selection. A poorly designed library adversely affects both fabric waste and capacity utilization.

ECONOMIZING ON FABRIC WASTE

Fabric represents over 50 percent of the cost of producing a garment, so an increase in fabric waste severely increases manufacturing costs. The area of a marker between pattern parts represents the wasted fabric. The efficiency of a marker is measured by the ratio of waste area to the total area, and waste is typically 15 percent of the fabric used. Unlike waste in paper, metal, and chemical processes, fabric scrap cannot be recycled and may incur added disposal costs. So a marker library must be designed and selected not only to meet changing weekly manufacturing requirements but also to economize on fabric waste. There are two key marker design elements that affect fabric waste:

(1) *Number of garments in a marker.* As the number of garments in a marker increases, fabric waste declines. Having more garments in a marker offers a larger number of options for fitting patterns into a more efficient design.

(2) *Distribution of sizes in a marker.* As the variety of sizes in a marker increases, fabric waste declines. Having different sizes in a marker provides an assortment of shapes and dimensions that facilitates efficient design.

The actual fabric waste of a marker cannot be measured until after the marker is designed. Thus, the efficiency of a marker cannot be known until after the

investment in the marker design has been made.

The marker library may have to change over time in order to reflect constantly changing size-percent forecasts. When a specific size's percent of sales changes (and consequently, its size-percent forecast), the set of existing markers may become inappropriate.

A marker library for each lot number must be flexible enough to meet the week-to-week fluctuation in the SKU mix and, in particular, to accommodate enormous volume differences among the higher and lower volume sizes. (Higher-volume sizes of jeans move 50 to 100 times faster than lower-volume sizes.) Blue Bell's existing library contained efficient markers; the waste percentages were low. But prior operating experience had made it clear that the library was not sufficiently flexible and caused extreme inventory imbalances.

UTILIZING CUTTING ROOM CAPACITY

Another crucial issue is efficient use of the cutting room capacity, as this manufacturing stage is highly automated and capital-intensive. A cutting table is approximately two yards wide and up to 40 yards long. To maintain efficiency, it is desirable to use markers that are as long as the table allows. Cutting fabric in many layers at a time also increases efficiency.

These considerations, however, must be balanced against inventory needs. While longer markers utilize cutting table capacity better, they may not produce the required size mix. And a particular week's manufacturing requirements may be better met through fewer, rather than more, layers.

Marker design and selection must effectively handle fabric waste, SKU balance, and capacity utilization as they relate to the week's needs. The process must provide a library of designs which encompass the weekly variations in size requirements and be flexible enough to indicate when additional markers must be added to the library.

DEVELOPING THE MARKER PLANNING AND SELECTION MODEL

The decision problem of selecting markers each week is one of simultaneously choosing a subset of the markers, most of which have been planned already and are in the library, and computing the lay-up for each in order to produce the quantities needed to meet weekly requirements, maintain high cutting-capacity utilization, and economize on fabric waste.

To accomplish this, the task force formulated a linear programming (LP) model (see appendix). Before embarking on redesigning the entire library, the task force had to be confident that the balance problem could be solved by improving marker selection. Therefore the LP model was tested on a microcomputer. The existing marker library was used first, and the results showed that it was inadequate. The LP was then used to test a more effective library. The new markers that were designed using the LP process proved to be

economical over a wide range of size percent distributions and performed consistently above historical standards for fabric waste. The task force had accomplished the second of its key analytical tasks.

DEVELOPING THE RECOMMENDATIONS

Implementing the solution was the next step. Blue Bell had to develop DP systems to execute the various models and to adopt several management and organizational changes.

The analytical approaches described above required comprehensive and integrated DP system support to install an array of production planning and inventory control systems. The planning process had to be responsive to short lead times for plant scheduling. Early in the study, the task force had agreed that the currently available planning systems were inadequate; they did not have the capability to incorporate the new planning models and decision rules.

Also, new management systems were needed that included procedures, guidelines, and policies necessary for running a production planning process. The new process needed more discipline, structure, and cross-functional coordination (Figures

FIGURE 5. Annual planning cycle at the product group level.

	January–March	April–May	June Week 1	Week 2	Week 3	Week 4
Wrangler Group						
Director of Marketing	Releases market planning guidelines					
Director of Manufacturing				Reviews over/under report		Approves capacity planning

(Continued)

FIGURE 5. (*Continued*)

	January–March	April–May	June Week 1	Week 2	Week 3	Week 4
Profit Center						
President		Communicates top-down strategy	Approves business plans, capacity summary		Approves capacity planning	
Merchandising		Develops business plan		Reviews over/under report		
Operations		Develops product plans	Initiates capacity planning		Completes capacity planning	
Manufacturing		Prepares capacity summary		Reviews over/under report	Reviews capacity planning	Assigns product lines to divisions and plans

FIGURE 6. Monthly planning cycle at the product line level.

	Week 1		Week 2		
	Wednesday	Thursday/Friday Monday	Tuesday	Wednesday	Thursday
Merchandising Manager/VP Merchandising	Attends planning meeting		Attends planning meeting		
	Reviews forecast		Discusses/resolves plan		
Director of Operations	Reviews production position	Develops new capacity plan	Reconvenes planning meeting		Commits to fabric
	Convenes planning meeting	Evaluates capacity options	Discusses/resolves/finalizes/plan		
VP Manufacturing/Chief Engineer	Develops capacity summary		Attends planning meeting		Directs implementation of plan
	Attends planning meeting		Discusses/resolves plan		

FIGURE 6. (*Continued*)

	Week 1			Week 2	
	Wednesday	Thursday/Friday Monday	Tuesday	Wednesday	Thursday
Profit Center President	Attends planning meeting		Attends planning meeting	Reviews/approves capacity plan	
Controller	Attends planning meeting		Attends planning meeting		

5, 6, and 7). More explicit roles and responsibilities had to be developed for all key players in the planning process to achieve execution and coordination.

Finally, the new process necessitated organizational changes. The task force had to ensure that qualified people were carrying out the planning function and that they were trained in the concepts as well as the operation of the new planning systems; the organization needed to be streamlined to establish a smooth decision-making process; and, most important, senior managers had to become more involved in the planning process to truly strengthen production planning and inventory control at Blue Bell.

In December 1982, at the end of the development phase, the task force presented its overall recommendations to Blue Bell's management committee:

(1) Adopt the new planning approaches and techniques of the inventory-planning model and the marker planning and selection model,

(2) Develop a comprehensive set of DP systems to execute planning concepts,

(3) Implement a new production planning management system to provide the necessary coordination, and

(4) Strengthen the management organization to support the new planning approach.

FIGURE 7. Weekly planning cycle at the lot and SKU level.

	Week 1: Master scheduling				
	Monday	Tuesday	Wednesday	Thursday	Friday
Product Manager	Reviews product line position	Attends operations planning meeting Agrees to revised master schedule inputs		Reviews master schedule	

(*Continued*)

FIGURE 7. (*Continued*)

	Week 1: Master scheduling				
	Monday	Tuesday	Wednesday	Thursday	Friday
Operations Planner	Reviews production position	Convenes operations planning meetings Agrees to revised master schedule inputs	Develops master schedule		Finalizes master schedule Inputs master schedule to SKU system
Division Planner				Reviews master schedule	
Fabric Coordinator		Attends operations planning meeting	Schedules fabric deliveries		
Division Manager				Reviews master schedule	

	Week 2: SKU scheduling				Week 3: Cuts		
	Monday Tuesday	Wednesday	Thursday	Friday	Monday Tuesday	Wednesday Thursday	Friday
Operations Planner	Reviews marker decisions						
Division Planner	Reviews SKU report and selects markers Develops week's cuts	Orders new markers Delivers week's cuts to detail planner	Reviews daily cuts				
Manufacturing Division Manager	Reviews week's cuts						
Detail Planner		Receives week's cuts	Develops daily cut schedule				

FIGURE 7. (*Continued*)

| | Week 2: SKU scheduling | | | | Week 3: Cuts | | |
	Monday Tuesday	Wednesday	Thursday	Friday	Monday Tuesday	Wednesday Thursday	Friday
			Inputs cuts to master schedule system				
			Releases first day's cuts	Releases balance cuts			
Cutting-Room Supervisor					Executes Day 1 and Day 2 cuts	Executes Day 3 and Day 4 cuts	Executes Day 5 cuts
Pattern Department Supervisor		Receives marker orders					

These recommendations represented a comprehensive and integrated plan for improving production planning and inventory control at Blue Bell.

SETTING UP THE DP TEAM

Top management, already actively involved, now demonstrated its resolve through several unprecedented moves (Figure 8). The task force leaders, who had been pursuing this project in addition to their normal line-management duties, were relieved of all other responsibilities to spend full time on the effort. The chief financial officer, the management committee member directly responsible for the project, became more closely involved on a day-to-day basis. The project began reporting directly to him.

The most visible sign of Blue Bell's commitment to the project, however, was management's decision to accelerate the design and development of the new DP systems. The existing systems could not accomplish the task of significantly reducing inventory without harming customer service or increasing manufacturing costs.

Blue Bell senior management questioned whether the traditional approach to systems development would be successful. The sheer magnitude of the systems work needed was assessed by the task force members. Getting all the new systems to work on an accelerated timetable would require an extraordinary effort.

Blue Bell management took attention-getting action. A team of eight DP professionals was selected and organized to work solely on this project. For the first time, Blue Bell set up a dedicated project team to do systems work. The DP systems manager, who had been on the task force from

FIGURE 8. Top management involvement during the project.

	1982	1983
	J J A S O N D	J F M A M J J A S O N D
Formed the working capital task force (Management Committee)	——	
Reviewed preliminary findings (CFO and Wrangler Group VP)	——	
Reviewed production planning system (CEO)	——	
Reviewed findings and recommendations (Management Committee)	—	
Charged profit centers with responsibility to make program work (Management Committee)	——	
Set up unprecedented, accelerated DP team on site (Management Committee)	——	
Provided CFO involvement on day-to-day basis; project began reporting directly to CFO	————————	
Reviewed progress on DP systems prototypes (Management Committee)	——	
Reviewed results of implementation and new systems (Management Committee)	——	
Participated in seminar for training management in planning concepts and systems (Management Committee and division presidents)	——	

the start, was named project leader, and the dedicated DP team members were moved from the administrative building, where DP services were located, to Wrangler headquarters, where the users were located. Microcomputers, mainframe terminals, and printers were physically relocated.

These moves quickly and unambiguously communicated to Blue Bell personnel that management was serious about developing the necessary systems support as rapidly as possible. The ambitious charge from the management committee was to complete all major DP systems within three months and begin implementation immediately thereafter. Specifically, six new DP systems were required: (1) sales forecasting, (2) capacity planning, (3) lot master planning, (4) size forecasting, (5) size planning, and (6) marker planning and selection. These systems encompassed the seven management science models.

DESIGNING AND DEVELOPING PROTOTYPES

Several unusual characteristics of the development phase allowed the task force to succeed in that time frame. First of all, the critical parts of the systems, especially the on-line features, were prototyped on either a microcomputer or the mainframe. The prototype approach concentrates on designing output screens and formats, and testing computational logic and design. The prototypes are not written to be efficient in running time or storage requirements. Attention to machine efficiency is postponed until the prototype design is reviewed by users and tested for its logical adequacy.

Prototyping substantially shortened the development time and, most important, dramatically increased the level of user involvement. The prototypes were easily changed to try out user suggestions, which encouraged users to make their ideas known. An unexpected benefit was the help the prototypes provided in educating users about the new concepts. This enabled the task force to bring the users on board quickly as part of the systems development team. Because they understood the logic in the models, users developed a healthy trust in the output and enthusiasm for using the systems in their planning.

Also important in the systems design and development phase was the requirement for on-line applications. Management was concerned with the length of the planning cycle—specifically, with the time it took for changes in demand to trigger changes in production scheduling. In order to shorten the cycle, the new systems required on-line applications with overnight batch updates. The on-line feature reduced the planning cycle substantially.

Given the extensive on-line requirements and the time pressure to develop the systems quickly, the SAS® on-line product (under TSO®) was used to develop the prototypes on the mainframe. In addition to being a statistical processor, SAS® also permits the design of reports

and tabular arithmetical operations. Using SAS® made it possible to change systems easily—even after they were on the mainframe—and substantially reduced the systems development time.

Also significant and unusual during design and development was top management's constant review of the progress of the task force and their understanding of the nature of the systems (Figure 8). The management committee, including both the president and the chairman of the board, spent an entire day reviewing the inputs, the processing logic, and the outputs of each system. They studied all user console screens and management reports. In fact, the chairman of the board spent two days examining the DP systems and another day reviewing the management planning process.

This intense top-management involvement was critical to successful implementation of the new planning systems. The reviews enabled the task force to demystify the systems and planning models. Instead of viewing them as a "blackbox" effort, senior management understood the systems in detail and thus fully supported their implementation in the profit centers. This top-down pressure for implementation was extremely effective in accelerating the rollout of the new planning process.

The unconventional approach taken in the systems design and development phase succeeded. In 90 days, the DP systems team had actually developed and tested all six major systems.

TESTING THE SYSTEMS

The systems design and development phase proceeded on schedule. Nevertheless, the planning models incorporated in the systems had to be exhaustively tested prior to full-scale implementation. The models made sense theoretically. But, given the potential negative impact on service and manufacturing costs, the systems would first have to be tested in a real-life, low-risk environment.

Another key issue that needed testing was the ability to balance stocks. It was uncertain whether or not the planning models and systems were sufficiently responsive to achieve a consistently balanced inventory position at the SKU level.

A final issue concerned incremental costs that would be associated with the new approach to marker design and selection. The new planning process required entirely new markers. Markers were expensive, and the capacity to make markers was limited. Whether the cost and capacity issues associated with the new markers were justified had to be confirmed.

TESTING IN PARALLEL

To test these issues, the task force concentrated on a single-profit center of Wrangler. Working with that center's management, the team selected one lot for the initial, limited test environment. The initial testing stage involved parallel planning. In other words, the new approach was used to plan a lot in parallel with the current planning process. However, the new process was not used for production.

TESTING "LIVE"

Once the task force and users were satisfied with the progress in the parallel test, the test then moved to "live" planning. The new planning approach and systems were used to actually schedule production. Again, the test was limited to one lot.

The task force worked closely with manufacturing personnel at the plant. Weekly trips were made from Greensboro to the test manufacturing plant in Alabama. After several weeks, the team and the users jointly decided to expand the test to a larger group of lots. A few weeks later, the new planning systems and approach were ready for broad-scale implementation within the profit center.

Two factors were important to success during the testing phase. First, the users were not just onlookers but equal partners on the task force. At the beginning of the test, the users learned about the systems and the logic of the planning models. In response to the users' comments and suggestions, the task force set the pace for the testing program. There were agreed-upon milestones and agreed-upon go/no-go points. The users determined when to proceed to the next stage of the testing program.

Second, top management participated in the initial testing process. At the beginning, a kick-off meeting was held with the management of the test profit center. The new planning approach and the testing program were explained in detail to the profit center officers, including the president. They were then asked by a member of the management committee to take responsibility for "making it work." The visible role of top management in the testing phase ensured that the project quickly achieved its goals.

ROLLING OUT TO ALL DIVISIONS

With successful completion of the test at the product-line level, rollout then began by manufacturing division. In each Wrangler division, a standard format was followed. A kick-off meeting with all the profit center managers was followed by an educational period for both the managers and the personnel in the plants. Initially, the team conducted a testing program with one lot to understand and identify any issues particular to that manufacturing division. Finally, after the initial testing, the systems were expanded to the entire division.

IMPLEMENTING OTHER SUPPORTING RECOMMENDATIONS

An organizational task force was formed to consider four remaining organizational issues:

(1) *Training and development.* What training and skills were needed to effectively execute the new planning process? How would training in fundamental planning techniques and DP systems be accomplished?

(2) *Organizational structure.* What shifts in the organizational structure of the planning function were needed to successfully implement the new program? What changes in roles, responsibilities, and reporting relationships were needed to streamline the decision flow and ensure execution and coordination?

(3) *Staffing.* What backgrounds, experience, seniority, and other traits should the staff have? What should be the key policies for managing human resources?

(4) *Top-management's role.* What role should top management play in production planning and inventory control? What issues should top management be involved in? How would top management ensure excellence in this important control function?

The organizational task force worked for 10 weeks to analyze, resolve, and rec-ommend a program to address each of these issues. They presented their report to the management committee at the end of the 10-week charter. The report was approved, and implementation responsibilities were assigned. These organizational recommendations were an integral part of the solution for achieving a long-term improvement in production planning and inventory control.

ASSESSING THE DIRECT BENEFITS

Several significant and tangible benefits resulted from the comprehensive effort of the working capital task force; the most important and substantial was a $115 million reduction in inventory levels from $371 million in the second quarter of 1982 to $256 million in the first quarter of 1984. This reduction occurred without any reduction in sales volume or narrowing of the product line. Because of the decreased need for working capital, short-term debt averaged only $47.4 million in fiscal year 1983 as compared to $111.6 million in 1982 (with no increase in long-term debt). In addition, cash and marketable securities totaled over $90 million at the end of 1983, versus $8 million in 1982.

Along with the inventory reduction came a decline in carrying cost, which significantly bolstered fiscal year 1983 operating results. As the management committee stated in the 1983 annual report, "A key factor to these stronger final quarters was a commitment to reduce inventories, which resulted in a sharp decrease in interest expense during 1983." Net interest expense in 1983 was down $16 million from net interest expense in 1982.

The second tangible benefit of this project was reduced raw-material costs. A paramount concern at the start of this study was whether the new process would increase fabric waste while trying to balance inventories. In fact, at the onset, the task force warned that a trade-off in fabric waste might have to be made if Wrangler were to substantially reduce its inventories and keep them in balance. Surprisingly, results today indicate that there is no increase in fabric waste. To the contrary, fabric waste has slightly decreased under the new approach. While annual fabric-cost savings are estimated at $1 million, the real "good news" story is that the planning system saved Wrangler from having to make the classic manufacturing trade-off between cost and flexibility.

ASSESSING THE INDIRECT BENEFITS

The primary indirect benefit has been the improvement of service levels. In the original test division, on-time shipments increased and order cancellations declined even with significantly less inventory. In other divisions, service has remained at traditional high levels, again with significant inventory reductions. The key to this service performance is the ability to balance inventory stocks and, therefore, to have in stock only those items that would be shipped. The task force believes that the servce potential of the new planning systems has only begun to be tapped. The new approach may well allow Blue Bell to aggressively respond to the growing service demands of its changing retailer environment.

A second indirect benefit of this project is the model it established for systems design and development. The methods used to achieve such high user understanding and acceptance have been identified by Blue Bell for use in future systems projects. These include the formation of a dedicated project team, the close involvement of users as partners in the development process, and the intense involvement of top management.

SUMMARIZING THE SUCCESS STORY

Blue Bell's massive inventory reduction resulted from a broad-scale, corporate-wide mobilization, led by a special task force. At its peak, over 40 Blue Bell managers were directly involved, 11 of them full-time. The effort was widespread and comprehensive and so was the solution. It required new planning models and systems as well as organizational changes. Further, it focused top management's attention on production-planning and inventory-control issues.

Management science was essential in achieving these benefits. The simulation model developed during the diagnostic phase enabled the task force to convince top management that, with realistic assumptions about Blue Bell's business, a dramatic reduction in inventory could be achieved. The model provided a tangible, highly motivating target to shoot for, and it persuaded management to commit the huge amount of resources required to succeed.

More important, however, management science provided an analytical approach for maintaining customer service and economizing manufacturing cost while simultaneously lowering inventories substantially.

The uniqueness of this project lies in the way management science was supported by top management to improve an entire company's operating performance. The control problem faced by Blue Bell was neither esoteric nor isolated but fundamental and broad-scale. It could not be solved by focusing only on management science models, nor could it be solved by ignoring them. Once the comprehensive analytic "answer" had been constructed, an equally aggressive effort was needed for implementation and execution. And that effort had to have the support and involvement of top management.

In summary, the combination of these two factors—management science and top-management support—allowed Blue Bell to achieve dramatic results through a fundamental and comprehensive turnaround.

APPENDIX

This appendix provides the mathematical description of the marker selection optimization model.

Let N be the total number of different SKUs (waist and inseam combinations) for a specific lot. For a men's jeans lot, N usually is about 75, but for some popular lots, N can be as large as 125. Each SKU comprises a dozen or more pattern parts that, when assembled, form the finished garment (Figure 4).

Let T be the number of weeks in the planning horizon. In the Blue Bell application, T equals 16, in order to reflect production lead times.

Let the cumulative net requirements through the first t weeks of the horizon be R_{tq} for SKU q. This represents the sum of the weekly demand forecasts up to week t plus the build-up and safety stock targeted for week t less inventory on hand and in the production pipeline at the beginning of the horizon.

The design of a specific marker m is described by a vector of N non-negative integers $(A_{1m}, \ldots, A_{qm}, \ldots, A_{Nm})$, where A_{qm}

is the number of times the group of pattern parts making SKU q appears in marker m (Figure 4). Given the width and length of the lay-up tables in Blue Bell plants, the sum $\Sigma_{i=1}^{N} A_{im}$ is approximately 35 finished garments, and so an individual marker makes only a subset of SKUs in a lot.

The precise value of the sum depends on the lot, the particular combination of SKUs included, and the width of the fabric to be cut. Denim used for blue jeans frequently is made in widths 54″, 60″, and 62″. Consequently, the number of possible efficient markers that could be designed for a specific lot number using denim is of the order of magnitude $3N^{35}$. (The feasible number of markers is much larger, because it is possible to have a marker with k sizes, where k can be any number less than 35. But markers with small k represent an inefficient use of cutting capacity.) Designate as L the number of markers that actually are in the library and available to produce the lot.

Let w_m be the value of the fabric waste associated with marker m. Only after a marker with the quantities $(A_{1m}, \ldots, A_{qm}, \ldots, A_{Nm})$ has actually been designed can the value of w_m be known precisely. Prior to the design, however, w_m can be approximated using a percentage of the non-waste fabric.

For manufacturing efficiency, a lay-up for the cutting of a marker is between 60 and 70 layers. Let p denote the lay-up quantity, where $60 \leqslant p \leqslant 70$. Then designate the selection variable x_{tmp} as the number of uses of marker m, with lay-up p, to complete production in week t.

The optimization model is

$$\text{minimize} \quad \sum_{t=1}^{T} \sum_{p=60}^{70} \sum_{m=1}^{L} pw_m x_{tmp}$$

subject to $\displaystyle\sum_{t=1}^{\tau} \sum_{p=60}^{70} \sum_{m=1}^{L} pA_{qm}x_{tmp} \geq R_{\tau q}$

for
$$\tau = 1,...,T$$
$$q = 1,...,N$$

x_{tmp} non-negative integer.

This discrete linear optimization model, as stated, is impractical to solve because of its size. A library of all efficient markers would be enormously large and too expensive to actually design in order to determine the actual values of w_m. The computational burden of solving each week such a large-scale optimization with integer-valued variables is too great to be feasible in a scheduling environment that necessitates real-time planning of hundreds of lot numbers at a plant. Thus, to make the application possible, it is necessary to formulate a relaxation of the above model that yields a practical-sized linear programming optimization.

The key ideas used in the relaxation are to restrict L to a fixed set of markers that gives a specially structured matrix, to employ a rolling horizon, to use a single non-negative continuous variable y_{tm} the number of lay-ups of marker m used in week t, instead of a set of px_{tmp}, and to design an on-line computational support system that permits the scheduler to adjust optimal y_{tm} to give efficient lay-ups.

The linear programming model has many similarities to the classic cutting-stock-problem [Faaland 1981; Gilmore and Gomory 1961a, 1961b; Salkin and de Kluyver 1975; Wagner 1975], but there are several essential differences. In the cutting-stock problem, it is possible to mathematically calculate the trim waste. In the marker problem, knowing only $(A_{1m}, \ldots, A_{qm}, \ldots, A_{Nm})$ for a marker is not sufficient to exactly compute its waste fabric. The marker actually has to be designed, which is costly and time-consuming of a scarce resource. In typical cutting-stock situations, the blades must be set manually for each individual roll cut, no matter what the chosen cut widths. Consequently, the cut combinations need not always be the same from day to day. This flexibility in the cutting blade settings makes the Gilmore-Gomory [1961, 1963] algorithm attractive. In the marker application, however, the marker library ought to remain stable, so that new combinations do not have to be designed very often. Only occasionally should it be necessary to add new markers in order to adjust for evolving shifts in the relative volume of demand for the individual N sizes.

REFERENCES

Brown, R. G. 1977, *Material Management Systems: A Modular Library,* John Wiley and Sons, New York.

Faaland, B. H. 1981, "The multiperiod knapsack problem," *Operations Research,* Vol. 29, No. 3 (May–June), pp. 612–616.

Gilmore, P. C. and Gomory, R. E. 1961, "A linear programming approach to the cutting stock problem I," *Operations Research,* Vol. 9, No. 6 (November–December), pp. 849–858.

Gilmore, P. C. and Gomory, R. E. 1963, "A linear programming approach to the cutting stock problem II," *Operations Research,* Vol. 11, No. 6 (November–December), pp. 863–888.

Peterson, R. and Silver, E. A. 1979, *Decision Systems for Inventory Management and Production Planning,* John Wiley and Sons, New York.

Salkin, H. M. and de Kluyver, C. A. 1975, "The knapsack problem: A survey," *Naval Research Logistics Quarterly,* Vol. 22, No. 1, pp. 127–144.

Wagner, H. M. 1974, "The design of production and inventory systems for multifacility and multiwarehouse companies," *Operations Resarch,* Vol. 22, No. 2 (March–April), pp. 278–291.

Wagner, H. M. 1975, *Principles of Operations Research,* Prentice-Hall, Englewood Cliffs, New Jersey.

A letter from Kenneth E. Tutterow, Chief Financial Officer and Vice President —Finance, Blue Bell, Inc. states that "the award recognizes an unusual success story that unfolded at Blue Bell, Inc., in the years 1982 and 1983. Within a period of 21 months, management reduced inventory by $115 million. While inventory levels had stood at $371 million in the second quarter of 1982, they had dropped to $256 million by the first quarter of 1984. In addition, net interest expense in 1983 was down $16 million from 1982, and fabric waste had been reduced by $1 million. Blue Bell was assisted on this project by McKinsey & Company, Inc. (Atlanta Office)."

Development and Implementation of an Integrated Inventory Management Program at Pfizer Pharmaceuticals

P. P. Kleutghen

J. C. McGee

Pfizer was founded in Brooklyn, New York in 1849 by two young emigrants from Germany and, during its first 100 years, produced and sold fine chemicals in bulk to the chemical and food processing industries. During World War II, the company's application of its large tank fermentation expertise resulted in a significant breakthrough in the manufacture of penicillin. When penicillin was released for commercial use after the war, Pfizer was producing 85 percent of the US supply.

Following a worldwide soil-screening program in the late 1940s, Pfizer scientists discovered a new antibiotic, trade-marked Terramycin, which proved extremely effective. The company subsequently made four decisions that dramatically changed its pattern of growth. In 1950, it established an antibiotics division (the forerunner of Pfizer Laboratories) to introduce its new discovery, marking Pfizer's entry into the pharmaceutical industry. The second strategic decision was to establish its foreign trade subsidiaries (now Pfizer International) in 1951. Third, in 1952 the company moved into animal health, establishing its agricultural division. This move toward market diversification led to the fourth component of the strategy, growth through acquisition, which dramatically broadened Pfizer's base of business. Today Pfizer operates in 65 countries with businesses in five major categories: agriculture, specialty chemicals, materials science, consumer, and the dominant healthcare group, which includes the pharmaceutical segment, contributing more than 50 percent of the company's sales.

US pharmaceutical sales are supported by three marketing divisions selling a broad line of ethical pharmaceuticals in five major therapeutic classes: cardiovascular, antibiotic, central nervous system, anti-diabetes, and anti-inflammatory.

The cornerstone of Pfizer's growth strategy is its continuing investment in research and development. The company's rate of investment in R & D more than quadrupled during the 1970s. Currently, increases in research investment are programmed at approximately 20 percent per year. Pfizer's strategy has paid off in a highly successful series of pharmaceutical product launches over the past few years and in a strong pipeline of compounds at various stages of clinical development in all of the therapeutic classes listed above.

We focus here on the US pharmaceutical manufacturing organization. Pfizer is a vertically integrated company that manufactures key intermediates or chemicals used in its finished products (called dosage forms). The supply chain can be summarized in three steps. First, the active pharmaceutical ingredients are produced through fermentation or organic synthesis; second, these actives are combined with other raw materials in the dosage; third, the finished product is distributed to the company's customers. The US pharmaceutical group manages two organic synthesis plants and four dosage plants.

BACKGROUND AND OBJECTIVES

A few years ago, the combination of high interest rates, rapid growth of the pharmaceutical business, and historically high inventories dictated a more focused approach to managing inventory. Divisional management therefore embarked upon a program to (1) control and improve inventory turnover, (2) understand and manage the forces behind the swings in inventory levels, and (3) improve the accuracy of dollar inventory forecasts and thus improve cash-flow projections.

THE PROGRAM

The inventory management program proceeded in four phases over a period of

3.5 years but with only 1.5 man years of effort involved:

(1) Analysis of historical performance data and definition of problems and opportunities (early 1980 to mid-1981),

(2) Definition of a plan of action (mid-1981) including what management science (MS) models were needed to effectively manage inventories,

(3) Definition, design, and development of MS-based models to manage inventories (late 1981 to late 1982), and

(4) Implementation of the program (early 1982 through mid-1983).

PHASE 1: ANALYSIS

The initial step in the inventory management program was a comprehensive analysis of the inventory management function as it existed. It revealed the following problems and opportunities:

(1) The lack of an accurate and adequately detailed data base to support the analysis and monitoring of inventory performance confused the management process.

(2) Responsibility for inventory management was assigned to several organizations. Raw materials and work-in-process (WIP) inventories were managed at the local plant level, while finished goods inventories were managed and planned by the headquarters production planning and inventory control (PPIC) function.

(3) Inventories were not part of the performance evaluation objectives at the plant level.

(4) Inventory data was highly aggregated and did not allow meaningful trend analysis nor an understanding of how management intervention affected inventories.

(5) Methods for inventory management were not consistent among the different plants.

(6) The methods used in inventory management were not "state-of-the-art."

(7) Inventory forecasting was manual, time consuming, inaccurate, and not routine.

(8) The impact on inventory management of the operating differences between the dosage and organic synthesis phases of production was not clearly understood.

(9) Inconsistent definition of different classes of inventories among plants (what belongs in finished goods, WIP, raw materials, and so forth) prevented meaningful interplant comparisons.

(10) The quantitative impact of capacity constraints, degree of vertical integration, and product mix on inventory was not fully understood and resulted in inaccurate and counterproductive comparisons between plants and divisions within the company.

PHASE 2: DEFINITION OF A PLAN OF ACTION

The plan of action proposed to senior management can be summarized as follows:

— A centralized function for divisional inventory management was needed to assure that appropriate, up-to-date management techniques were developed and applied consistently across the divisional locations.

— Major inventory categories (such as finished goods, WIP, purchased materials, and so forth) needed to be defined accurately, and inventory data reported consistently throughout the division. This required changes in the divisional inventory accounting and reporting systems.

— Management science models specifically tailored to the operational needs of dosage and synthesis plants had to be created.

— Inventories would become part of the objectives in overall performance evaluation at plant level. This would require a functional reporting system and the definition of quantitative targets against which performance could be measured. These objectives would be set using the output of the MS models.

— A computer based inventory forecasting system would be designed and implemented to improve the speed and accuracy of all inventory forecasts.

PHASE 3: MODEL DEFINITION AND DESIGN

Inventory models had to meet several criteria:

(1) Output from the models would become the quantitative objective of a performance measurement system.

(2) Since local management would have to agree to the objectives, the models needed to be intuitively understandable.

(3) Since the new methods were to be phased in over a short period of time, they had to be easy to implement, especially in data processing and programming.

(4) All models had to be cost-effective, that is, the expected cost savings in inventory investment had to be greater than the cost of model design and implementation.

Detailed models and techniques were designed and introduced for the following applications:
— Finished goods lot sizes and safety stocks,
— Target work-in-process inventories in the dosage plants,
— Organic synthesis "campaign sizes" (run quantities) in the chemical plants,
— Organic synthesis safety stocks,
— Inventory forecasting, and
— Purchased materials inventory strategies, using MRP.
Elements of an existing, fragmented data base were brought together into a new data base that not only supported the centralized sales forecasting and master-planning systems, but also the newly developed inventory management program, including the MS models described in detail below.

FINISHED GOODS LOT SIZE AND SAFETY STOCKS

Finished goods inventory targets are computed using the well-known Wagner approximation to the optimizing (s,S) model. The Wagner heuristic provides near-optimal results, is computationally efficient, easy to program, has the advantage of being a model that includes backorder cost, and simultaneously answers lot-sizing and safety-stock questions. Implementation of the Wagner model necessitated some preliminary analysis and some special definitions.

The heuristic requires that the probability distribution function of demand be known. Statistical tests were completed on five years of sales history of a sample of products that covered over 20 percent of the items in the product line. These tests

confirmed that the normal distribution provided a good statistical model for over 90 percent of the product items.

Statistical tests also revealed that the variance of sales around the mean remained nearly constant through time. This implied that the variance around the historical mean could be used as an efficient estimator of the variance of sales around the future (or forecasted) mean. The computer program introduced to compute the (s,S) quantitites reflects this assumption.

The back-order cost parameter in the model was set equal to the gross margin to assure that historical high rates of customer service would be maintained.

The setup cost used in the model is the total of the setup costs at each manufacturing step through which the product is processed. This practice is acceptable because batches keep their integrity throughout the production process and are not combined at any point. This separation of batches is mandatory within the pharmaceutical industry.

The output of the (s,S) system is used as follows. The s quantity is considered to be safety stock and the difference $(S\text{-}s)$ is considered to be batch size. These quantities are locked in for a one-year period, although policies for all items produced are reviewed every quarter to see whether any changes in sales forecasts or profitability warrant different inventory policies. Experience has shown that for products with an annual growth or decline rate of less than 20 percent a one-year fixed policy is acceptable.

In applying the model, we discovered a number of high-volume items where the $(S\text{-}s)$ portion of inventories (that is, the order quantity) was larger than the largest batch that could be manufactured. To circumvent the problem, scheduling policies were changed so that series of batches would be processed that in total approximated the proposed (*S-s*) quantity. This "campaigning" of lots through the manufacturing chain resulted in higher inplant efficiencies as the number of major cleanups and changeovers was reduced. This lowered manufacturing costs because of the reduced downtime and higher productivity. It might seem contradictory that inventory reductions could be brought about by increasing run quantities, but in these high-volume cases, the increased cycle stock inventories were more than offset by decreased safety stocks yielding a net inventory decrease.

The quantitative impact of the introduction of the (*s,S*) based management system can be summarized as follows:

(1) Reduction in finished goods inventories of $8.8 million over a two-year period. These savings were estimated by costing out average inventories on a product-by-product basis, using "old" and "new" inventory polices.

(2) Annual savings in changeover costs totaled $250,000 estimated by comparing changeover costs under "old" and "new" scheduling policies for those products where multiple-batch quantities were introduced.

In addition, a series of management control benefits result from the application of the model. The (*s,S*) quantities are interpreted as a min-max control range, within which the inventory position should vary. Exception reporting systems flag inventory levels below the *s* level and above the *S* point. Items with inventories outside the control range are subject to immediate management action and follow-up. This system targets management action and uses managerial time more efficiently.

The (*s,S*) quantities for each product can be translated into dollar inventory goals that can be aggregated to product

line or plant-dollar targets by adding up the midpoint levels between the *s* and *S* quantities. These goals can then be compared against actual dollar inventories, available from the accounting system, to track performance. In addition, the fact that goals are built from the bottom up (that is, on a product-by-product basis) and are consistent with current sales forecasts and manufacturing policies greatly enhances the credibility of the system and makes it an ideal base for accurate inventory forecasting.

DOSAGE WORK IN PROCESS

Dosage WIP covers the production chain that ultimately delivers product for sale. This chain is a series of steps from the blending and compounding of active and other raw materials through processes that determine the ultimate potency and form (such as tablets or capsules) of the product and the bottle sizes. A typical product is processed through six dosage manufacturing steps and a similar number of quality control steps during six to 15 weeks.

WIP inventory value increases as labor and equipment dollars are added at each manufacturing step but remains constant during each phase of quality control since further processing is postponed pending satisfactory completion of testing. This production and quality control system yields a distinctive WIP curve (appendix).

Average WIP inventory can be approximated (see Appendix 1) by establishing a functional relationship between the following readily available parameters: manufacturing lead time in weeks, unit sales forecasts per year, the full standard cost of the product, and the fraction of raw material cost to full standard cost per unit. This simplified model was validated for accuracy in the Puerto Rico dosage plant before it was programmed for general use by the other facilities. Validation results showed a 90 percent error for a product that is made once per year, less than 10 percent for high-turnover items, and less than five percent for a series of products aggregated into a single product line. Because the model averages WIP inventories of a single batch over a full year, accuracy increases as the number of batches increases.

The product data base, mentioned above, is used as input to the model, which implies that all WIP inventory forecasts are automatically consistent with current sales forecasts and manufacturing policies.

The model is used to quantify dosage WIP inventory targets on a monthly basis. These targets are well understood in that they are built up from dosage detail. Comparing actual and target levels reveals those product lines that require management action. Detailed analysis of the initial application of the model identified a series of erroneous lead-time parameters, used in the MRP master-planning system, that unnecessarily lengthened the time between start-up and due dates. Correction of these parameters resulted in shorter WIP queues and an overall reduction of WIP inventory levels of $2.1 million. These savings were estimated by comparing historical and current WIP levels for those product lines where planning parameters were changed. Another major use of the approach is to forecast WIP inventory levels by using projected sales volumes.

ORGANIC SYNTHESIS CAMPAIGN SIZING

The chemical synthesis of pharmaceutical actives presented a new challenge in inventory management. The synthesis operation produces the active ingredients that are the key inputs to dosage production through a production process spread over a sequence of chemical reactions controlled in batches, which are constrained by the physical size of the reaction vessels. Quality control tests are performed after each synthesis step to insure that the product meets physical and chemical requirements.

The management problem is to determine the optimal production run or "campaign" (series of batches) to minimize the combined inventory investment and changeover costs over all products and production steps. The task, however, is aggravated by considerations typical of the pharmaceutical industry that complicate the model formulation, specifically:

(1) A double changeover structure had to be introduced in the formulation. At every production step a major changeover occurs at the beginning of a series of batches (a campaign). In addition, there are minor changeovers between batches within a campaign. Very high costs for cleanup (to avoid cross-contamination between different products) are typical of synthesis operations within the pharmaceutical industry. At Pfizer, changeover costs across all production steps for a full campaign of a product vary between $15,000 and $95,000.

(2) Batch sizes at each production step are constrained by technological or equipment limits.

(3) A quality-control check takes place after each production step. Each batch is tested separately which keeps substantial inventories in a "QC queue" that is integrated into the inventory cost portion of the model and affects the campaign size decision.

(4) The model is formulated as a multi-

product, capacity constrained optimization. This not only changes the solution compared to single product and unconstrained formulations but introduces an optimal solution for a total facility, rather than for a portion of a facility.

(5) The model has been adapted to the multistep production process typical of synthesis operations. Yield losses occur at each step. Few solution procedures are available for a multistep, capacity constrained environment, and those that use iterative or dynamic programming methods become difficult to apply for processes of more than three steps (for example, the Johnson [1972] and the Jensen and Kahn [1972] methods). This model is a one-step analytical procedure readily programmed on a microprocessor-based commercial spreadsheet package.

The mathematical model developed quantifies the optimal campaign size for each product within a facility, taking into account the staggered setup cost structure, the multistep production process, the constraints for the facility, the queue lead times between production steps, and reactor vessel size constraints. The model minimizes total setup and changeover costs and inventory costs during the lead time for production and quality control, subject to capacity and reactor vessel size constraints. It is formulated as a multiproduct, nonlinear, constrained optimization (see Appendix 2).

The model can be solved analytically, in contrast to iterative or dynamic programming formulations that are difficult to program and implement. The solution method has been set up as a LOTUS 1-2-3 application, which is ample proof of its ease of implementation. In addition, the model formulation is quite broad, making it applicable to other chemical industry problems.

An interesting problem arose during implementation. Plant management objected to the campaign sizes initially generated. They pointed out that the first batch in a campaign invariably has a lower yield than the ensuing batches. Therefore, a substantial shortening of campaign sizes (as proposed by the model) would severely reduce campaign yields. Favorable inventory performance would then be offset by unfavorable production performance. We decided to add the yield differential (in cost) to the setup cost of the campaign which increased the campaign sizes, although they remained well below historical run quantities. This made the reduced run quantities palatable to plant management, and the new quantities were implemented in less than three months.

Application resulted in a reduction of $2.1 million in WIP inventories, estimated by costing out the decrease in inventories resulting from the "old" and "new" policies. The model was originally introduced in the Puerto Rico facility and is to be introduced in the Brooklyn chemical plant in 1984 with projected savings of $.6 million.

ORGANIC SYNTHESIS SAFETY STOCKS

Synthesis safety stocks assure supply of the active ingredient to the dosage plant. These safety stocks tend to be high for several reasons:

(1) The lead time for synthesizing an active ingredient of up to 15 steps over a 49-week period, and

(2) The high penalty for stockouts in the pharmaceutical industry.

Historically, synthesis safety stocks were set by management judgment without quantification of the risks of stockout. We realized that these safety stocks could be reduced early in the program.

To calculate what safety stock levels were necessary to support high customer service, a mathematical model was developed that included the following parameters: the optimal campaign size of the previous model, the estimated annual consumption of active ingredients by the dosage plant, the standard deviation of demand during the manufacturing lead time in both the dosage and synthesis plants, and the probability that a number of batches within a campaign are delayed for quality reasons (see Appendix 3).

The model can be readily understood by non-MS professionals and computed with a desktop calculator or with a commercial spreadsheet package on a microcomputer. Thus, it is very transportable from plant to plant and inexpensive and quick to implement.

The first application of the model recommended a decrease in inventories so substantial that management decided on a two-year phased-in implementation to make sure that a plant would not be forced to severely decrease production in one year with unfavorable impact for employment levels and product cost.

The program test in the Puerto Rican plant resulted in inventory reductions of $5.1 million over a two-year period calculated by comparing the previous safety-stock policies to the proposed and implemented levels.

INVENTORY FORECASTING

Early in the program, Pfizer recognized the need to accurately forecast inventories over both short- and long-term planning horizons. Detailed, long-range projections

(five years) had been made once per year by a time consuming manual process (six man weeks), which had less than the desired accuracy. Short- and medium-term forecasts (less than one year) were generated quarterly and consisted merely of updating the previous long-range plan as major assumptions (such as sales forecasts or new product launch dates) changed.

A real-time, on-line model was designed to assist in forecasting inventories. The model uses a two-step approach:

(1) In step one, the base inventory level for a given product line is expressed as the total of the inventory targets of the major inventory components: finished goods safety stocks and cycle stocks, dosage WIP, organic synthesis campaign sizes and safety stocks, and purchased materials. The data is taken from the models described earlier. For finished goods, dosage and synthesis WIP, data are first aggregated from the item to the product line level.

(2) In step two, the base inventory forecast is extrapolated by projecting real growth and rates of increase in production costs for each product line. The results are then summarized into five-year forecasts, quarterly in the first year, and annually in the later years.

Analysis of the different MS models shows that finished goods and organic synthesis safety stocks and dosage WIP vary according to demand. Finished goods cycle stocks and synthesis campaign sizes vary with the square root of demand, tending to reduce the impact of changes in real growth on inventory levels. With this in mind, we made two simplifying assumptions to escalate the base case inventories into forecasts. First, we assumed that for each product line finished goods and organics safety stocks, dosage WIP, and inventories of purchased materials vary linearly with the real growth rate of the product. Second, finished goods cycle stocks and organic synthesis campaign sizes are kept constant over the planning horizon except for an inflation adjustment.

Projections for individual product lines are sound because they are based on the latest forecast updates that are driving the finished goods master plan and the materials requirements plan. Inventory forecasting, by design, is therefore integrated with all other parts of the management program. This integration results in highly accurate forecasts since the major inventory components are individually managed to vary within relatively narrow and well-understood target bands (min-max ranges). Forecast data can be readily aggregated from the product line to the plant and divisional level.

Projections for new product launches can be added to the model within the planning horizon, inventories can be evaluated either in current or in constant dollars through time, and the impact of changes to sales forecasts or inventory policies can be simulated. A full five-year forecast on a product line and plant basis can be generated in 15 minutes. Computerization of this effort saves nearly six man weeks per year and permits more frequent forecast updates of the long-range plan.

Experience with the model over three years shows that, on a one-year horizon, forecast accuracy is within one percent of actual results and, on a two-year horizon, is within three percent.

In addition to accuracy and speed, several other benefits result from application of the model. It provides a concise summary of all information needed to manage inventories at various levels of detail:

product line, inventory category, and plant. The forecast data can then be used as source data in the reporting and control programs used to track performance. With the model, planning is less subjective and based more on objective, quantitative, and well-understood inputs.

PURCHASED MATERIALS

Purchased materials are largely crudes and packaging components, whose inventory levels are managed through an integrated MRP system. The central sales forecasting system drives a centralized master-planning module for each plant. Time phased finished goods production is exploded through the bills-of-materials into component requirements, which are then translated into actual purchase orders. Analysis of the system revealed that it was working well but that it could be enhanced to further reduce inventories.

We found that suppliers were willing to hold inventories at their expense in exchange for longer-range firm commitments which would allow them to plan more efficient runs. This resulted in lower inventory levels for Pfizer and more stable product cost.

Our main effort in materials purchasing focused on integrating the systems to forecast sales, plan production, manage inventories, and control the procurement of raw materials. The models developed emphasized improvement of the decision parameters that the MRP package used to generate purchase orders. A simple quantity-discount purchase model was introduced to guide buyers in issuing purchase orders for designated quantity-discount items. A methodology was introduced to calculate safety-stock levels for purchased items using finished goods demand, variability of demand, and supply lead time as parameters.

The introduction of MRP by itself resulted in a drop in raw material inventories. This decline was compounded through the introduction of new purchasing strategies, facilitated by the availability of MRP. The impact of the new purchasing strategies and the changes in MRP planning parameters decreased net inventory by $5.8 million. These savings were estimated by comparing inventory performance in purchased materials before and after implementation of the program.

PHASE 4: PROGRAM MANAGEMENT

The full implementation of the new inventory management program depended on organizational changes and top management support:

(1) The production planning and inventory control (PPIC) organization was restructured to emphasize the increased focus on inventories. The job of inventory manager was created to provide centralized expertise and to develop state-of-the-art management techniques.

(2) A control system was designed that used the output of the MS models as control parameters. In addition, a reporting system was instituted to track inventory performance, to maintain program visibility, and to identify opportunities for reducing inventory.

(3) Routine communication of performance and standards of performance was crucial to the successful implementation of the program. Individual targets for each of the major inventory categories at each plant were agreed upon in advance with local manage-

ment, insuring that all principals in the organization understood and accepted the objectives. Acceptance of the inventory program was not immediate, particularly given its innovative nature and the initial concern about headquarters becoming more involved in plant matters. As with all such programs, strong commitment from senior management was a must. During development, the PPIC group used this commitment and numerous formal presentations to keep the program visible and to encourage local organizations as progress was made. With this approach, the inventory management program became a cooperative venture between headquarters and plant management. This insured a broad base of support, sustained commitment, and an ultimately successful program.

COSTS AND BENEFITS OF THE PROGRAM

The full design and implementation took only 1.5 man years over a period of three calendar years. Several student interns programmed the models, and the full expense for the program totaled less than $100,000.

The main impact was in inventory reductions in the following areas: finished goods lot sizes, $2.9 million; finished goods safety stocks, $5.9 million; purchased materials, $5.8 million; organic synthesis safety stocks, $5.1 million; organic synthesis campaign sizes, $2.1 million; and dosage WIP, $2.1 million; for a total of $23.9 million in inventory reductions.

The positive cash-flow benefit of $23.9 million results in a permanent savings in interest and insurance expenses of $3.6 million per year, estimated at an average, conservative carrying cost of 15 percent. The drop in inventory levels alone resulted in a significant increase in the return on investment for the US pharmaceutical group. Further opportunities for reduction of $7.9 million have been formally included in the 1984 pharmaceutical operating plan, and opportunity for an incremental $8.9 million are targeted for 1985 through 1988.

The increased emphasis on inventory management has been extended to other PPIC areas which led to some unexpected positive results in customer service, particularly a dramatic decrease in weekly national back orders, from an average of $778,000 in 1980 to $31,000 in 1983. In 1983 customer service jumped to an unprecedented 99.98 percent, a record high for the division and at the leading edge of performance within the US pharmaceutical industry as reported in surveys issued by the industry's trade association. Although the positive impact of decreased back orders is difficult to quantify, it is estimated internally that 10 percent of back orders result in lost sales. By comparing the difference in weekly back orders between 1980 and 1983 and assuming a 10 percent lost sales rate, we estimate increases in sales at $3.8 million per year.

The introduction of the (s,S) finished goods model triggered a series of schedule policy changes for high-volume products. They are now campaigned under an optimal policy which reduces total setup costs and increases equipment efficiency and productivity. The impact of these policy changes is a reduction in annual setup costs of $250,000.

Finally, as a result of the improved product supplies, total freight costs were reduced by $280,000 per year: air shipments, formerly needed to avoid stockouts

in branch warehouses were needed to a lesser extent. These savings were estimated by comparing direct freight billings and were not adjusted to reflect the fact that shipping volumes doubled over a period of three years.

The total annual savings directly attributable to the inventory management program are as follows:

Inventory carrying costs	$3,600,000
Increased sales	3,800,000
Savings in setup costs	250,000
Reduced freight costs	280,000
	$7,930,000

EXTENSIONS

The program, including the reporting and control system, was designed to be readily transferable. Sister divisions have begun implementing both organic synthesis models at several synthesis plants. The two synthesis models can be generally applied throughout the chemical industry, although they may have to be tailored to local constraints.

The (s,S) Wagner model can be applied to virtually any industry, particularly since the model gives near-optimal results and is easy to implement. While the dosage WIP model is particularly suited to the pharmaceutical industry, it could be used in any company that is characterized by intermediate queue inventories yielding the distinctive WIP curve. The reporting and control system provides a sound framework for managing inventories in an industrial environment and can be readily instituted in a variety of businesses.

CONCLUSIONS

The introduction of MS techniques to inventory management at Pfizer Pharmaceuticals resulted in significant and permanent benefits. The importance of the effort, however, extends beyond the classic quantitative factors.

The inventory management system is not only state-of-the-art, flexible, and easily understood, but has been developed into an integrated management system that covers sales forecasting, production planning, materials requirements planning, and purchasing as well as inventory management for six distinctly different plants.

The theoretical advances made in Pfizer's program, such as the organic-synthesis campaign-size model, and the synthesis safety stock and dosage WIP models, have enhanced the inventory management theory that is applicable in the process industry. The inventory forecasting and simulation tools introduced are novel additions to applications literature and to the inventory field in general.

APPENDIX 1: Development of a Model to Project Dosage Work-in-Process Inventories

Assume a manufacturing process where material is routed through a series of steps. Value is added at each step, and time is consumed in between steps (for example, schedule lead time, queue time, quality control release time). Also, assume that the product is manufactured in discrete, equal-sized batches. Work-in-process, for a single batch, can be graphically depicted as shown in Figure 1.

The WIP inventory value of a batch increases in a stepwise fashion as the batch goes through different production steps. At the beginning of the process, the value is that of the materials; each step adds labor and equipment pool dollars, plus possible additional materials dollars. After

FIGURE 1. Work-in-progress for a single batch increases in value with each step.

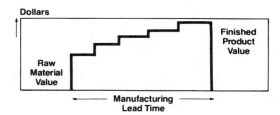

completion of the final step, the product is at full manufacturing cost.

Total WIP inventory equals the area under the stepwise curve. This area, however, can be approximated by the area constrained by the trapezoid that is obtained by connecting the initial and final point of the stepwise curve by a straight line.

We introduce the following variables:

D = demand in units per year.

Q = batch size in units.

LT = manufacturing lead time in weeks.

C = finished goods production cost of the product.

p = the fraction of raw materials cost at the first step, to full cost at the final step ($0 \leqslant p \leqslant 1$)

The "cost" of goods in inventory is approximated as being halfway between raw material cost and their finshed product value. Then the total WIP inventory value for a single batch during the lead time can be approximated as

$$(1 + p)CQ/2. \qquad (1)$$

And from (1) one can calculate the average WIP of a product of which multiple batches are made throughout the year as

$$\left(\frac{(1 + p)}{2} \right) \left(CQ \frac{LT}{52} \right) \frac{D}{Q}. \qquad (2)$$

And (2) can be reduced to

$$\left(\frac{(1 + p)}{2}\, C\right) \frac{LT}{52}\, D. \qquad (3)$$

Note that the formula (3) becomes independent of batch size and could thus be taken as a formula that is fairly generally applicable.

APPENDIX 2: Development of Optimal Production Run Quantities in Batch-Constrained, Capacity-Constrained Chemical Processes

Assume a manufacturing process with the following characteristics:

— Product is routed through a series of manufacturing steps.
— Product is manufactured in runs ("campaigns") of a series of batches.
— Individual batches maintain their identity throughout all steps of the production process.
— Major changeovers take place at each production step prior to the startup of a campaign of batches.
— Minor changeovers occur at each step prior to the startup of an individual batch within a campaign.
— Batch sizes are constrained by technological limitations (for example, size of reactor vessels).
— After each production step all batches will remain in a queue before progressing to the next step (for example, to complete quality testing).
— Total inventories are composed of work-in-process (WIP) inventories (covering the gradual buildup in value between the first and the last step) and finished product inventories (covering the inventories of released final step material).

FIGURE 2. Synthesis WIP increases as campaign progresses.

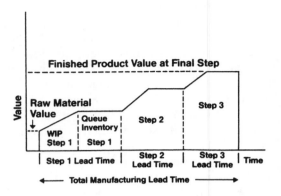

Finished product inventories follow the traditional sawtooth pattern, but WIP inventories can be depicted as shown in Figure 2.

The following abbreviations will be used:

D_j = annual demand for the jth product ($j = 1, \ldots, J$).

C_{oj} = raw material value of one unit of product j at the beginning of step 1.

C_{ij} = standard cost of one unit of product j at the completion of the ith manufacturing step ($i = 1, \ldots, M_j$).

C_j = value of the product after the last production step.

M_j = the number of production steps for product j.

a_{ij} = the yield between the ith to last step for the jth product ($0 < a_{ij} \leqslant 1$).

F_{ij} = the setup cost (per batch) at step i, product j, to change a reactor over from one batch to another.

F_j = the cumulative setup cost for

one batch of product j to go through all production steps

$$= \sum_i F_{ij} , \quad i = 1, \ldots, M_j.$$

V_{ij} = the setup cost for a campaign of a series of batches of product j at step i.

V_j = the cumulative setup cost of a campaign of product j to go through all manufacturing steps

$$= \sum_i V_{ij} , \quad i = 1, \ldots, M_j$$

B_j = maximal size of a single batch of a product j at the last manufacturing step. This quantity is constrained by the smallest batch, adjusted for yield losses that can be made at any of the manufacturing steps.

N_j = the number of batches that make up a campaign of product j.

I = annual inventory carrying charge (percent per year).

COB_{ij} = cleanup, setup, and changeover time for a batch of product j at step i (hours per batch).

COB_j = cumulative changeover time for a product over all production steps

$$= \sum COB_{ij}, \quad i = 1, \ldots, M_j.$$

COC_{ij} = changeover time for a campaign of a series of batches of product j at step i (hours per campaign).

COC_j = cumulative changeover time for a campaign of a series of batches product j over all manufacturing steps

$$= \sum_i COC_{ij} , \quad i = 1, \ldots, M_j.$$

K_{ij} = equipment time needed to process one unit (kg) of product j at the ith step.

K = maximal available equipment time in a processing facility (process, idle, changeover, setup, and cleanup times) (hours per year).

Q_j = campaign size of a series of batches of product j ($Q_j = N_j B_j$).

T = number of hours per year. Note that $K \leq T$, that is, total operating time has to be less than or equal to total available time per year.

k = cost per hour changeover in a facility. This cost is a constant and is the same for each product and step combination.

LT_{ij} = the lead time (in years) that product j waits after completion of step i before it can move on to step $i+1$. This lead time is necessary for QC release, schedule queue, and so forth.

Total costs to be minimized are made up of
(1) Changeover costs at the beginning of a campaign of N batches, at every step of the production process,
(2) Changeover costs before every batch within a production run (at every step),
(3) Average inventory during production of the product at each step,
(4) Inventories during the queue lead time after each production step, including the last step to release material before final use of the product, and

(5) Average finished product inventories after release from the final production step.

These individual components can be quantified as follows:

$$V_j(D_j/N_jB_j) \tag{1}$$

= the cumulative changeover costs for a run of N_j batches of product j through all (M_j) manufacturing steps. The number of production runs (campaigns) is given by dividing annual demand by the size of the production run (N_j times the batch size B_j).

$$F_j(D_j/B_j) \tag{2}$$

= changeover costs associated with producing D_j/B_j batches to cover annual demand D_j.

$$N_jB_jIC_j/2 \tag{3}$$

= average cost of inventory at the last step M_j of product j, resulting from a campaign of N_j batches of size B_j.

$$\left[\sum_i \frac{C_{ij}LT_{ij}}{a_{ij}} \right] N_jB_jI \tag{4}$$

= cumulative average inventory carrying cost of a run of N_j batches of size B_j over the "queue" lead time (LT_{ij}). This inventory is costed out at the product value appropriate for each step for the duration of the lead time. The batch size is adjusted for the yield loss (a_{ij}) between the ith and last step.

$$\left[\sum_{i=0}^{M_j-1} \left(\frac{K_{ij}}{T} \frac{(c_{i+1,j} + c_{ij})}{2} \frac{1}{a_{i+1}} \right) \right] N_jB_jI \tag{5}$$

= cumulative average inventory investment during the production time. This component is made up of the total run quantity (N_jB_j) adjusted by the yield loss between the ith and last step (a_{ij}). Total production time at each step is given by

the time required to process one unit of product j at step i (K_{ij}/T) times the campaign size. The average value of the product during production is half the difference between the product value at the end of step $i+1$ ($C_{i+1,j}$) and the beginning of step $i+1$ (C_{ij}).

Capacity within a facility is consumed by

(1) Changeover time for each batch of product j at each step i,

(2) Changeover time for each production run of N_j batches of product j at each step, and

(3) Time to produce N_j batches of product j through all production steps.

These components can be quantified as follows:

$$\left[\sum_i (COB_{ij}) \right] \frac{D_j}{B_j} \tag{6}$$

= total changeover time for all batches of product j, over all production steps equals the number of batches (D_j/B_j) times the cumulative setup time for one batch over all production steps

$$\left[\sum_i (COC_{ij}) \right] \frac{D_j}{N_jB_j} \tag{7}$$

= total changeover time for a full production run of N_j batches of product j equals the number of production runs (D_j/N_jB_j) multiplied by the cumulative setup time for each campaign at every production step $\sum_i COC_{ij}$

$$\left[\sum_i \frac{K_{ij}}{a_{ij}} \right] D_j \tag{8}$$

= cumulative production time to produce D_j units of product j over all production steps equals total volume D_j, adjusted by the yield (a_{ij}) at step i, multiplied by the time needed to process one unit of product j at step i.

We introduce the following definitions:

$$C1_j = \sum_i \frac{C_{ij}LT_{ij}}{a_{ij}} \text{ , and substitute in (4);}$$

$$C2_j = \sum_{i=0}^{M_j-1} \left(\frac{K_{ij}}{T} \frac{(C_{i+1,j} + C_{ij})}{2} \frac{1}{a_{i+1}} \right),$$

and substitute in (5);

$$C3_j = \sum_i COB_{ij} \text{ , and substitute in (6);}$$

$$C4_j = \sum_i COC_{ij} \text{ , and substitute in (7);}$$

$$C5_j = \sum_i \frac{K_{ij}}{a_{ij}} \text{ , and substitute in (8).}$$

The problem can now be rewritten as

$$\min \ f(N_j) = \sum_j \left[\frac{V_j D_j}{N_j B_j} + \frac{F_j D_j}{B_j} + \frac{N_j B_j I C_j}{2} \right.$$
$$\left. + (C1_j + C2_j)N_j B_j I \right] \quad (9)$$

subject to

$$\sum_j \left[\frac{C3_j D_j}{B_j} + \frac{C4_j D_j}{N_j B_j} + C5_j D_j \right] \leq K. \quad (10)$$

The objective function defines total setup costs (for each campaign and each batch within a campaign) and total inventory costs (average inventory after the last step during production and during queue lead time).

The constraint defines total capacity consumed in changeovers (for each campaign and all batches within a campaign) plus capacity consumed in production. We introduce the Lagrange Function $L(N_j)$

$$L = \left[\sum_j \frac{V_j D_j}{N_j B_j} + \frac{F_j D_j}{B_j} + \frac{N_j B_j I C_j}{2} \right.$$

$$\left. + (C1_j + C2_j)N_j B_j I \right]$$
$$+ \lambda \sum_j \left[\frac{C3_j D_j}{B_j} + \frac{C4_j D_j}{N_j B_j} + C5_j D_j - K \right]. \quad (11)$$

The solution to the problem (11) is found by differentiating L with respect to N_j and λ, which results in the following set of simultaneous equations:

$$\frac{\delta L}{\delta N_j} = \frac{-V_j D_j}{N_j^2 B_j} + \frac{B_j I C_j}{2}$$

$$+ (C1_j + C2_j)B_j I - \frac{\lambda C4_j D_j}{N_j^2 B_j} = 0 \quad (12)$$
$$(j = 1, \ldots, J).$$

$$\frac{\delta L}{\delta \lambda} =$$
$$\sum_j \left[\frac{C3_j D_j}{B_j} + \frac{C4_j D_j}{N_j B_j} + C5_j D_j - K \right] = 0. \quad (13)$$

Solving (12) for N_j yields

$$N_j^* = \frac{1}{B_j} \sqrt{\frac{2 D_j (V_j + \lambda^* C4_j)}{I [C_j + 2 (C1_j + C2_j)]}}$$

λ^* can be found by substituting N_j^* in equation (13), and by substituting V_j by $kC4_j$.

After some algebra, this yields

$$\lambda^* = \frac{1}{2} \left[\frac{\sum_j \sqrt{C4_j D_j I (C_j + 2 C1_j + C2_j)}}{K - \sum_j \frac{(C3_j D_j + C5_j D_j)}{B_j}} \right]^2 - k .$$

APPENDIX 3: Development of Safety-Stock Policies for Organic Synthesis Operations

The following model has been developed to compute safety-stock policies for chemical operations that are integrated with finishing operations. The finishing steps use material produced by the preceding chemical process, which by itself occurs over a series of production steps.

The following abbreviations will be used:

$m1$ = the number of weeks to complete a campaign of a given active ingredient from start to finish.

$m2$ = the number of weeks required to complete a lot of finished goods from blend to packaged material, using material produced in the previous (chemical synthesis) step.

N = the number of batches of the last step of a synthesis campaign.

P = the probability that a single batch within a campaign is held up for quality reasons (p is higher than the final rejection rate in order to add a degree of conservatism).

q = the number of batches within a campaign that are on QC hold for any period of time (yet may be released at some point in the future).

D = the annual active ingredient draw by the finishing operation that follows the synthesis step (kgs per year).

WD = the average weekly active ingredient draw ($D/52$) (kgs per week).

$SD(WD)$ = the standard deviation of the weekly active ingredient draw based on variability of finished goods demand.

B = the batch size of the last step of a synthesis campaign (kg).

$K = B/WD$, = the number of weeks for which one batch of finished active ingredient can fill finished goods demand.

Max (WD) = the maximal amount of bulk that would be required to cover demand over the total dosage and synthesis work-in-process lead time ($m1 + m2$).

We define

$$\text{Max } (WD) = (m1 + m2) \, WD + 3.0 \, (SQRT \, (m1 + m2)) \, (SD(WD)).$$

= the demand plus three times the standard deviation of this demand over the total dosage and synthesis lead time and as such covers full demand with nearly 100 percent certainty.

$(N-q)$ = the number of batches within a campaign without any QC holds, in other words, immediately releasable material.

$(N-q)^*K^*WD$ = finished goods demand translated into kilos of active ingredient that can be covered by $(N-q)$ problem-free batches of active ingredient.

The safety stock required to cover the possibility of a stockout resulting from the release delay of q of a campaign of N batches is equal to the maximal demand over the total WIP lead time minus the demand that can be covered by the $(N-q)$ released batches, or

$$\text{Max } (WD) - (N-q) \, (K) \, (WD) = \text{safety stock.} \tag{1}$$

Equation (1) has to be weighted by the probability of rejection of q batches in an N batch campaign, $Pr \, [q]$ and summed over the total number of rejection scenarios within a campaign ($q = 1, 2, 3, \ldots, N$), or

$$\sum_q [\max(WD) - (N - q)(K)(WD)] \Pr[q]$$

= bulk safety stocks.

The probability of rejecting q batches of an N batch bulk campaign can be found in statistical tables of the summarization of terms of Poisson's exponential binomial limit.

REFERENCES

Jensen, P. A. and Kahn, H. A. 1975, "Scheduling in a multistage production system with static deterministic demand," *AIIE Transactions*, Vol. 4, No. 2, pp. 126–133.

Johnson, Lynwood A. 1972, "Multistage economic lot size problems with static, deterministic demand," *Technical papers of the 23rd Annual Conference of the American Institute of Industrial Engineers*, pp. 387-392.

Vander Eecken, J. and Lambrecht, M. 1975, "Voorraadmodellen met meerdere produkten en beperkingen" (translation: Multi-product, constrained inventory models), *Tijdschrift voor Ekonomie en Management*, Vol. 20, No. 2, pp. 1-27.

Wagner, Harvey M. 1972, *Principals of Operations Research with Applications to Management Decisions*, Prentice-Hall, Englewood Cliffs, New Jersey.

A letter from John W. Mitchell, Vice President, Production at Pfizer Pharmaceuticals states that "The work described in the paper 'Development and Implementation of an Integrated Inventory Management Program at Pfizer Pharmaceuticals' has resulted in several benefits to the company including inventory reductions of nearly $24 million and a significant reduction in average backorder levels.

In addition, several of the MS models introduced in Pharmaceuticals have been implemented in sister divisions at Pfizer. Indications are that the total benefit to Pfizer of the work done by Messrs. McGee and Kleutghen will exceed those listed in the above referred paper."

3

DISTRIBUTION

Firms routinely have to transport goods to customers who are widely scattered over the geographic area served by the firms' facilities. This chapter presents three studies of firms that distribute goods with a fleet of vehicles. Typically, each vehicle visits a number of customer locations. *Vehicle routing* involves planning the operation of a fleet of vehicles to deliver goods or to provide services. Vehicle routing problems vary considerably in size and complexity. Consider two simple examples: A mid-size bakery may use a small fleet of vehicles to carry its products to various customers within a single city. A local newspaper may use small vans to carry its papers from the printing facility to certain drop points. In these examples, each vehicle starts out loaded from the central facility, makes a sequence of stops at the delivery points, and returns to the facility after its last stop. The routing problem becomes progressively more difficult for larger operations as the number of facilities, the number of customers, the area of service, and the size of the fleet increase. In the last two decades, operations researchers and transportation scientists have developed powerful techniques to carry out this distribution function efficiently.

The key decision in vehicle routing is to design routes for the vehicles. A *route* is a sequence of stops that a vehicle visits between two successive visits to the depot. The simplest routing problem occurs when we seek a single route that visits all customers and minimizes the total travel time. This is the celebrated *traveling salesman problem* (Exhibit 3–1). Suppose, however, that a single vehicle cannot handle all the customers in a single trip because its capacity or time are limited. The customers must then be divided among a fleet of vehicles with the

EXHIBIT 3–1. The traveling salesman problem involves finding the minimum-cost itinerary for visiting a fixed set of customers. The vehicle covering the itinerary must visit each customer exactly once and return to its point of origin. In the formulation shown for this problem, the objective function is the total cost of the tour. Constraints (1) and (2) ensure that each customer is visited exactly once. Constraint (3) ensures that the tour forms a connected cycle. The depot is included for convenience alone and is not an essential feature of the problem.

The Traveling Salesman Problem

Inputs

n = number of customers
a depot location (customer 0)
c_{ij} = cost of traveling from customer i to customer j

Decision Variables

$$x_{ij} = \begin{cases} 1 & \text{if the vehicle travels from customer } i \text{ to customer } j, \\ 0 & \text{otherwise.} \end{cases}$$

Integer Programming Model

Minimize $\displaystyle\sum_{i=0}^{n} \sum_{j=0}^{n} c_{ij}\, x_{ij}$

subject to $\displaystyle\sum_{i=0}^{n} x_{ij} = 1$ for all i (1)

$\displaystyle\sum_{j=0}^{n} x_{ij} = 1$ for all j (2)

$\displaystyle\sum_{i \in S} \sum_{j \in \bar{S}} x_{ij} \geq 1$ for every proper non-empty subset S of $\{0, 1, \ldots, n\}$ (3)

$x_{ij} = 0$ or 1 for all i and j

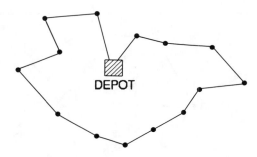

Illustration of a traveling salesman tour

EXHIBIT 3–2. The vehicle routing problem involves finding a set of trips, one for each vehicle, to deliver known quantities of goods to a set of customers. The objective is to minimize the travel costs of all trips combined. There may be upper bounds on the total load of each vehicle and the total duration of its trip. The problem can be formulated using two linked sets of variables. One set assigns customers to vehicles and determines the subsets S_k. The other set determines the sequence in which each vehicle visits the customers assigned to it. These routing variables are similar to the variables in Exhibit 3–1. To keep the description simple, the variables are not defined explicitly here. Also, only the vehicle capacity is constrained in each trip. A similar constraint can be defined for the trip's duration.

The Vehicle Routing Problem

Inputs	*Decision Variables*
$n =$ number of customers	Assignment variables that fix the set of
$K =$ number of vehicles available	customers S_k assigned to vehicle k
a depot location designated customer 0	
$c_{ij}^k =$ cost of traveling from customer i to	Routing variables that describe the tour
customer j for vehicle k (for all i, j, k)	traversed by vehicle k, (k = 1, . . . , K)
$d_i =$ demand of customer i (i = 1, . . . , n)	
$b_k =$ capacity of vehicle k (k = 1, . . . , K)	

Statement of the Problem

Minimize the total travel costs of the fleet
subject to

— each customer must be visited by a vehicle
$$\bigcup_k S_k = \{1, \ldots, n\}$$

— the demand assigned to vehicle k must not exceed its capacity
$$\sum_{i \in S_k} d_i \leq b_k, \text{ for all } k$$

— the tour for vehicle k begins at the depot, visits all customers in S_k, and returns to the depot

---

In this illustration, the vehicle capacity is 100. The numbers give the customer demand at each site (n = 14, K = 5).

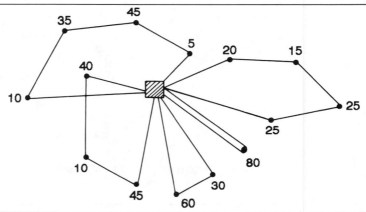

objective of minimizing the total cost of all the routes. This is called the *vehicle routing problem* (Exhibit 3–2). When the times of visits to customers become important, for example if customers can be visited during certain hours only, it is necessary to provide more information about a route. In addition to specifying all activities of a vehicle, a *vehicle schedule* attaches times to these tasks. For example, the schedule associates arrival and departure times with the visit to each customer site. This information must be included if the customer accepts deliveries only within certain time windows. In practice, vehicle routes and schedules must be designed to comply with a host of constraints besides time windows. For example, certain stops may have to precede others, the fleet may have different types of vehicles, or certain work rules may constrain the activities of the vehicle crew.

The vehicle routing problem forms the subject of the first two papers of this chapter. In the first paper, Bartholdi et al. [1983] describe a simple application of routing in a low-technology setting. In the second paper, Bell et al. [1983] describe a large, complex distribution problem involving the delivery of industrial gases. The focus of the last paper shifts to a commercial truckload carrier that provides trucks and drivers to transport the goods of its customers. In this application, Powell et al. [1988] describe a network-based system they developed to improve the assignment of drivers to loads at North American Van Lines.

3.1 DISTRIBUTING MEALS TO SENIOR CITIZENS

Bartholdi et al. [1983] discuss routing for a Meals on Wheels program in Georgia. This program uses three or four vehicles to deliver meals to approximately 200 elderly customers. As all lunches must be delivered within the four hours between 10 a.m. and 2 p.m., it is not possible to serve all the clients with a single vehicle. Instead, the customers are divided into three or four roughly equal groups and each group is assigned to a different vehicle.

Bartholdi et al. describe a heuristic technique for solving this vehicle routing problem approximately. They first find a "giant tour" that visits all the customers and then divide this tour to form individual routes for the vehicles. To construct the giant tour, they use a new *spacefilling-curve* heuristic that solves the traveling salesman problem approximately with very little computational effort.

Currently, sophisticated algorithms can optimally solve large traveling salesman problems with 600 to 2,000 customers. Good heuristics can handle much larger problems and provide near-optimal solutions whose costs are within a few percent of the optimum. But these techniques require computer runs and accurate data on travel times. The spacefilling-curve heuristic solves the traveling salesman problem by using the (x,y) coordinates of customers to establish the order in which customers are to be visited. This order is then used for the particular subset of customers requiring service on any particular day.

The routing system designed by Bartholdi et al. requires minimal technology: it works without a computer, is easy to operate, and requires little in the way of resources beyond two Rolodex™ card files. Despite its frugal requirements, the minimal technology system reduced travel time by about 13 percent. However, its main contribution is not so much to reduce travel time (which, after all, constitutes only 30-40 percent of the total delivery time), but to provide a convenient low-cost tool for carrying out the daily routing activity. Over 10 Meals on Wheels operations in the United States, Canada, and England use this system.

As a heuristic, the spacefilling-curve algorithm has certain attractive features that Bartholdi and Platzman [1988] point out. The algorithm is

— *abstemious*: it is frugal in its data requirements, using only 2n coordinates for n customers. In contrast, the amount of data required to record distances between all pairs of customers is proportional to n^2.
— *extremely fast*: it has the same running time as sorting. The running time grows as n on the average and as nlogn in the worst case.
— *agile*: it can update solutions quickly. A customer can be added to or deleted from the database of n customers in about logn steps.
— *trivial to code*: the code is only 30 lines long and can be implemented on a personal computer using integer arithmetic only.

These features have made the spacefilling-curve heuristic useful in different applications where it is impractical to expend a large amount of computational time or effort. Taking advantage of the speed of the spacefilling-curve heuristic, one commercial software package for vehicle routing uses it as a first cut to produce initial route configurations called "instantaneous routes." The user can then modify these routes by invoking other procedures. The algorithm is also used to control the movements of pen plotters in real time and to assign bin numbers in warehouses.

3.2 SCHEDULING DELIVERIES OF INDUSTRIAL GASES

Air Products and Chemicals uses a sophisticated computerized system to distribute industrial gases. In contrast to the Meals-on-Wheels application, this system can be characterized as high-technology in its use of advanced algorithms. Air Products has a fleet of 340 trucks that travel over 22 million miles a year to serve 3,500 customers out of 23 plants and depots. At each depot, the scheduler dispatches 10 to 30 trucks to visit 150 to 400 customers. The firm is committed to a high level of automation, and the scheduling module is integrated with existing order-entry and demand-forecasting modules. The ROVER scheduling module, which requires extensive and accurate data, relies on advanced techniques in mathematical programming to handle the large size and the various complicating constraints of the vehicle scheduling problem. Bell et al. [1983] describe how Air Products developed and implemented the ROVER system.

Air Products transports liquefied gases (oxygen and nitrogen) from its plants to the storage tanks of its customers. Its goal is to replenish customers' tanks periodically to ensure that the supply of gas in each tank stays above a specified minimum level. To do this, Air Products must forecast the inventory levels of all its customers and time its deliveries accordingly. The distribution problem is therefore driven by two considerations:

1. *Inventory replenishment*—deliveries must be made before the level of gas in the customer tank runs too low, and
2. *Routing*—vehicle trips must be designed to avoid high travel costs and low utilization of the vehicles.

The interaction between these two considerations accounts for the richness of this delivery problem. As Bell et al. point out, their scheduling problem is different from the traditional vehicle routing problem (Exhibit 3–2) in several ways. First, the problem is multi-period in nature since routes must be designed over five days instead of a single day. This adds another degree of freedom to the problem as deliveries to customers can "slide" from one day of the week to another. Second, the same customer location may be visited by more than one truck. While local delivery operations generally do not split orders (fill a single customer's demand with two trucks), the interaction between the customers' requirements and the timing of deliveries may make this an attractive option for Air Products. Even when a single truck visits a customer, the amount delivered to the customer is a decision variable: a tanker does not have to fill up the customer's tank. Finally, while geographical proximity is often a good guide for clustering customers or assigning them to the same route, in this problem inventory considerations may cause other groupings of customers to be superior. In other words, temporal considerations compete with spatial ones in the design of vehicle schedules. Bell et al. give a small but telling example to show how these subtler clusterings might elude the dispatcher.

Bell et al. use a model based on the *set-covering* approach to vehicle routing problems (Exhibits 3–3 and 3–4). In this approach, a *route generator* produces a collection of possible routes and tests them for feasibility. Each route covers the needs of certain customers and has an associated cost that captures the cost of running the entire route. A *route optimizer* then selects the optimal subset of the routes to serve the customers at mini-

EXHIBIT 3–3. In the set-covering approach to vehicle routing, the input data includes a set of candidate routes. Each route is represented by a column of zeros and ones. The entries of this column correspond to customers: a one in the column indicates that the route visits or "covers" the customer corresponding to that entry. The cost of the column is the total cost of running the route. The set covering problem seeks to select a minimum-cost subset of columns that covers all customers. In the integer programming formulation of this problem, the covering constraints (2) ensure that each customer is visited at least once. Reversing this inequality results in the set packing problem; changing (2) to equality constraints produces the set partitioning problem.

Set Covering Problem

Inputs

m = number of customers
n = number of routes
A collection of routes $j = 1, \ldots, n$

$$a_{ij} = \begin{cases} 1 & \text{if customer i is on route j} \\ 0 & \text{otherwise} \end{cases}$$

c_j = cost of route j

Decision Variables

$$y_j = \begin{cases} 1 & \text{if route j is selected} \\ 0 & \text{otherwise.} \end{cases}$$

Integer Programming Model

$$\text{Minimize} \quad \sum_j c_j y_j \tag{1}$$

$$\text{subject to} \quad \sum_i a_{ij}\, y_j \geq 1 \qquad (i = 1, \ldots, m) \tag{2}$$

$$y_j = 0 \text{ or } 1 \ (j = 1, \ldots, n)$$

---

mum cost. To select the collection of routes that meet demand at minimum cost, one must solve the set covering problem as an integer program.

Two complications generally plague this approach. First, it may be impractical to enumerate all possible routes because their number is extremely large. Second, once the candidate routes are specified, a good algorithm is needed to solve the resulting set covering problem. In the Air Products application, route selection is more complicated as it goes beyond deciding upon the sequence of customers to visit. The vehicle serving the route, its start time, and the amount delivered to each cus-

EXHIBIT 3–4. The matrix A displays the candidate routes in this small example of the set-covering approach. Two different solutions of the set covering problem and the corresponding routes are shown: solution A uses routes 1, 5, and 7; and solution B selects routes 4, 8, and 9. Customer 6 is visited twice in solution B.

The matrix $A = (a_{ij})$ composed of 10 routes for 8 customers.

Customer 1	1	1	0	0	0	0	0	1	0	1
2	1	1	0	0	0	0	0	1	0	0
3	1	1	0	1	0	0	0	0	0	0
4	0	1	1	1	1	0	0	0	0	0
5	0	1	1	0	1	1	0	0	1	0
6	0	0	1	0	0	1	1	1	1	1
7	0	0	1	0	0	1	1	1	0	1
8	0	0	1	0	0	0	1	1	0	1

Routes: 1 2 3 4 5 6 7 8 9 10

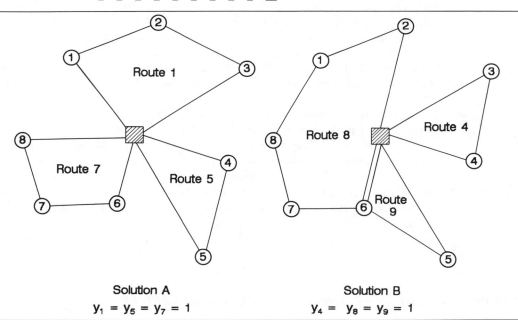

Solution A
$y_1 = y_5 = y_7 = 1$

Solution B
$y_4 = y_8 = y_9 = 1$

tomer on the route must all be specified to obtain a complete vehicle schedule.

In devising the set-covering approach, Bell et al. needed to avoid an explosion in the size of the route optimization problem. The structure of Air Products' routes proves to be critical in this connection—the average number of customers per route is very small (two on average and rarely more than four). The route generator enumerates a collection of routes that satisfy certain feasibility requirements. At this stage, the routes correspond to simple itineraries that list the sequence of customers to be visited; they do not specify the vehicle to be used or the start time.

The route optimizer solves a mixed integer programming problem to select the best routes from the candidate routes. The zero-one (binary) decision variables of this problem simultaneously select the route itinerary, assign a vehicle to this route, and fix a start time for the vehicle schedule. The continuous variables specify the amount delivered to each customer. To appreciate the size of the problem, consider a typical scheduling session where 15 vehicles must be scheduled to serve 54 customers. The route generator produces 377 routes. Given the 15 choices for vehicles and the 120 choices for start time, this creates 15 x 120 x 377 or 678,600 binary decision variables. However, many of these combinations do not produce feasible routes so that only 164,196 survive (still a large number of zero-one variables by integer programming standards). With this number of binary variables, 380,481 continuous variables, and 166,166 constraints, the mixed integer programming problem is intractable unless its special structure is fully exploited. By relying on a powerful mathematical programming technique called Lagrangian relaxation (see the background readings), Bell et al. can solve such a problem in 0.3 to 3.0 minutes of CPU time and obtain solutions with total costs within 0.5 to 2.0 percent of the optimum.

The implementation of this model presented many interesting issues. Bell et al. had to build an interactive interface for the model. They had to distinguish between hard and soft constraints of the problem (hard constraints cannot be violated, while soft constraints can be violated at a cost). They also had to estimate the benefits of the routing system—a question of great practical significance. Air Products and similar industries generally use such aggregate measures as miles driven per gallon. Bell et al. describe the challenges of obtaining a suitable performance measure for a complex scheduling system, especially when customer usage patterns vary over time.

3.3 IMPROVING THE OPERATIONS OF A TRUCKLOAD CARRIER

Both Meals on Wheels and Air Products rely on their own fleets of vehicles to distribute goods. A firm that owns or leases a fleet of vehicles for delivery operations must schedule the activities of both vehicles and drivers. However, many firms relegate this task to commercial common carriers. The common carrier must then pick up the loads at their origins and deliver them to the specified destinations. Depending on the nature of the loads, the firm may use *truckload* (TL) or *less-than-truckload* (LTL) trucking to distribute its goods. TL and LTL trucking are two very different operations within the motor carrier industry. In 1986, the nation's freight bill for ICC-authorized intercity transportation amounted to $58.1 billion, of which TL trucking accounted for $43.7 billion.

A truckload carrier has to advertise its prices for carrying loads between various locations. This pricing decision is a complex problem for the TL carrier. Even after a price is established, the carrier must decide whether to accept a shipper's load or not. Finally, to serve the loads it has accepted or the loads that it may accept in the future, the carrier needs to dispatch its vehicles and drivers over its entire region of operation. In the last paper of this chapter, Powell et al. [1988] describe a system for supporting these decisions on an operational basis used by North American Commercial Transport (NACT)—a division of North American Van Lines. This carrier, whose annual revenues exceed $260 million, manages a fleet of over 5,800 trailers. The system focuses on dispatching the fleet in such a way as to reduce empty miles and maximize the contribution from both known movements (by reducing empty moves) and future uncertain moves.

Customers request the carrier to pick up a load at its origin and deliver it to its destination. The carrier's dispatcher assigns a driver to this load, trying to select a driver who is close to the origin of the load. Having vehicles close to the origins of loads is important since it reduces the distance vehicles have to travel empty. If a driver completes the delivery and there is no load nearby, the dispatcher may ask the driver to wait for a future assignment or move to an area where additional assignments are more likely to be found. This decision must be made quickly as the driver is often waiting on the telephone. If a carrier does not have trucks close by when a load is called in, a competitor may get the load. The issue of deciding which loads to accept (or reject) is called *load acceptance*.

The TL *vehicle allocation problem* is different from the traditional vehicle routing problem in some important ways:

1. Uncertain demand—At the beginning of a typical day, the carrier knows only 30 to 40 percent of the demand for that day and only 10 percent of the demand for the next day.
2. Real-time environment—Apart from tracking truck positions in real time, dispatchers must react to new information that flows in over the course of the day.
3. Load evaluation and acceptance—The carrier can reject unattractive loads but must decide quickly when orders are called in.
4. No fixed base—The trucks are not based at a fixed depot and can therefore "wander" over the entire network, going through a sequence of loaded and empty moves.

If all loads are known in advance and the vehicles are based at depots, then the vehicle allocation problem becomes a vehicle scheduling problem in which tours must be designed for the trucks. Each tour will be a sequence of pickup and delivery pairs, with possible deadhead legs between the destination of one load and the origin of the next load. If the problem requires that all demand be served, then the objective is to minimize the cost of deadheading. Bodin et al. [1983] call this the tractor-trailer scheduling problem with full loads. Fisher, Huang, and Tang [1986] describe a large instance of this problem with 3,400 trucks in Shanghai.

The LOADMAP System

The uncertainty of the customers' future loads requires a model that can handle stochastic effects explicitly and consistently. In developing the LOADMAP model, Powell et al. wanted to capture the uncertain dispatching environment of NACT, and yet provide usable and realistic answers. The main tool of the model is a network algorithm that can optimize current and future movements of trucks through NACT's 60-80 geographical regions of operation. Because the nodes of this network represent geographical regions at particular time periods, the underlying structure is called a *space-time network*.

Researchers had previously used space-time networks to capture movements of vehicles with deterministic demands, for instance in optimizing the movements of empty railcars over a rail network. The novelty of the work of Powell et al. is to use the network to capture the stochastic movements of trucks, movements that are not known with certainty at the time of dispatch. As only a small fraction of future demand is known for certain on any given day, estimating the revenues of future (uncertain) movements of a vehicle has an important effect on how the vehicles are dispatched.

The overall structure of the vehicle allocation system and its inputs and outputs appear in Exhibit 3–5. A key module of LOADMAP is the *regional impact model* that quantifies the attractiveness of dispatching an additional truck to different regions. This model divides the current and future movements of a single truck into three stages (Exhibit 3–6). Stage 1 consists of known movements of the truck, which take it from its current location to the destination of the last known movement. Stages 2 and 3 cover all uncertain future moves of the truck out of this region, but differ in one important way: stage 2 captures the first uncertain truck movement for which only the origin is known. In stage 3, the origins and destinations of future truck movements are both unknown. To give an example, suppose that the last known movement of the truck terminates in region 5 on day 3. To assess the economic benefits of having trucks in region 5, Powell et al. perform a marginal truck analysis that estimates the contributions of successive trucks sent into region 5 on day 3. These marginal values are computed by propagating the future (uncertain) trajectory of the truck probabilistically. The dispatch probabilities specify the

EXHIBIT 3–5. The vehicle allocation system uses a large network model to optimize vehicle movements. Uncertain movements of vehicles in the future appear as stochastic arcs in this network. The regional impact model determines the costs of these arcs. The output of the network model specifies which of five possible dispatching options should be selected for each truck in order to maximize the expected net revenues of the entire system.

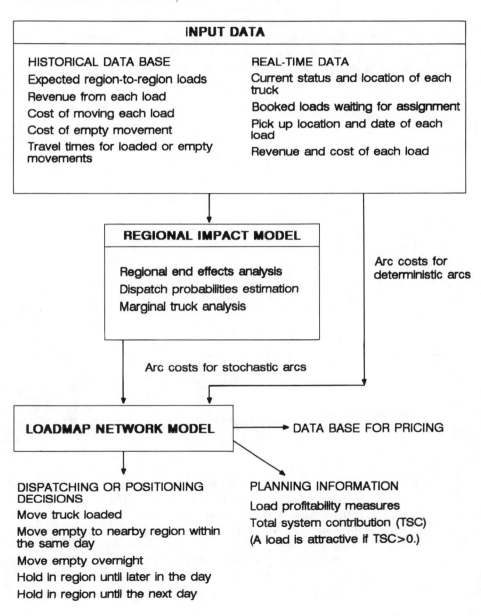

INPUT DATA

HISTORICAL DATA BASE
Expected region-to-region loads
Revenue from each load
Cost of moving each load
Cost of empty movement
Travel times for loaded or empty movements

REAL-TIME DATA
Current status and location of each truck
Booked loads waiting for assignment
Pick up location and date of each load
Revenue and cost of each load

REGIONAL IMPACT MODEL

Regional end effects analysis
Dispatch probabilities estimation
Marginal truck analysis

Arc costs for deterministic arcs

Arc costs for stochastic arcs

LOADMAP NETWORK MODEL → DATA BASE FOR PRICING

DISPATCHING OR POSITIONING DECISIONS
Move truck loaded
Move empty to nearby region within the same day
Move empty overnight
Hold in region until later in the day
Hold in region until the next day

PLANNING INFORMATION
Load profitability measures
Total system contribution (TSC)
(A load is attractive if TSC>0.)

EXHIBIT 3–6. The current and future movements of a vehicle are divided into three stages. Stage 1 consists of known movements; the truck is scheduled to move loaded from region 2 to region 4, move empty from 4 to 1, and loaded again from 1 to 5. At the end of stage 1, the truck is available for use in region 5, on day 3. Stage 2 captures the first uncertain dispatch out of region 5. Stage 3 consists of all uncertain movements beyond stage 2. The dynamic programming model of stage 3 computes the end effects that measure the value of a truck in region j on day s. The marginal analysis model determines the probabilities of different dispatch options out of region 5 to assess the value of sending additional trucks into region 5. This calculation uses the end values to capture the contributions of stage 3.

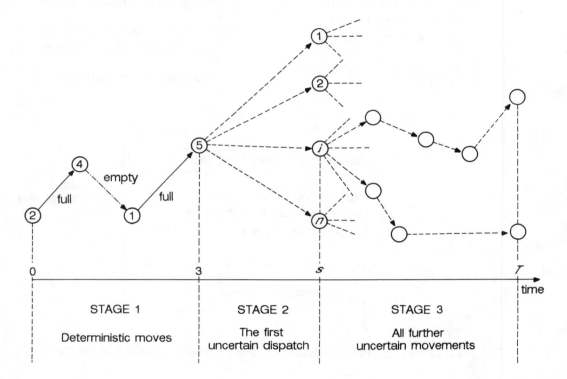

relative frequencies with which different options are selected for sending an additional truck out of region 5. These probabilities are computed from a Poisson model that uses historical data on average vehicle flows. Once in stage 3, a truck is assumed to follow the observed historical frequencies with which different dispatching options were chosen until the end of the planning horizon. The *end effects* capture the contribution of these movements in stage 3.

The main output of the regional impact model is a set of arc costs for the stochastic arcs in the network. In the network, the contribution of each additional truck sent into a given region on a certain day is represented as the cost on a stochastic arc that can carry at most one unit of flow. Once the arcs for deterministic movements are also added in, the entire problem can be solved with an efficient network flow code. The network model for NACT has 10,000 links but takes only 2.0-4.0 CPU seconds to solve on an AMDAHL 580 computer. The full LOADMAP system takes less than 15 seconds and is run four times daily to incorporate new information that becomes available as the day unfolds. In the operational mode, the network solution positions the trucks optimally by selecting one of five dispatching decisions for each truck (Exhibit 3-5). The model can also be used in planning mode to provide valuable information on profitable loads and pricing carrier services.

How does one measure the benefits of a complex model like LOAD-MAP? Clearly, the model's results should be compared to what human decision makers can accomplish in the real-time environment. Powell et al. use a simulation model to make this comparison, as described in the last section of the paper. Essentially, they compare the results of the model with those obtained by teams of dispatchers in controlled simulation games. Based on these comparisons, they estimate that the model can save $2.49 million annually.

Powell [1989] informs us that he is working on a new group of models that are more mature than the LOADMAP model. A major carrier with approximately 1,000 tractors is currently using this technology for its real-time truck dispatching operations. Powell sums up the current status of modeling for the carrier industry as follows: "The evolution of sophisticated planning models in the motor carrier industry is slow but steady. Unlike some applications of operations research in other industries, these models address the most central, important planning problems faced by a motor carrier. As a result, the sincere adoption of these techniques within the industry requires complete support at all levels of management, from the president down to the planning staff in charge of implementing the recommendations. In time this support will come, but at this stage, it is only fair to say that we are still in a confidence building mode."

3.4 IMPLEMENTATION OF VEHICLE ROUTING SYSTEMS

For a firm that distributes goods, vehicle routing or dispatching is the final step in a chain of activities that starts with order entry and extends through order picking in the warehouse and vehicle loading. Over the years, order entry and warehouse control have been increasingly automated, but this automation has not been fully extended to dispatching yet. Many firms with sophisticated order entry and inventory control systems still rely on slips of paper (route slips) to assign orders to vehicles. After this assignment, sequencing the stops on the route is frequently left to the driver.

In the last 15 years, interest in vehicle routing has intensified considerably. The pace of algorithmic advances and implementation efforts has quickened, and the economic benefits of computerized vehicle routing have been recognized. Noting the obvious gap in the use of computerized systems for vehicle routing, firms have started to develop and market commercial vehicle routing packages in the 1980s. Over 30 microcomputer-based systems are now available with prices ranging from hundreds of dollars to over $50,000. The aggressive marketing of these packages has certainly increased distribution managers' awareness of the benefits of computer-assisted routing. With the active participation of academic researchers, several companies, such as Air Products, have implemented customized routing systems. This has strengthened the interplay between research and practice. Companies now realize that large routing problems can be solved efficiently despite a host of real-life complications and constraints.

Although many firms have installed routing systems over the last 10 years or so, there are few detailed reports of these implementation efforts. Companies generally protect the results of such efforts as proprietary information. In fact, most of the published accounts describe projects that involved university-based groups. It would be useful to complement these studies with reviews of actual industry practices similar to Golden and Wasil's [1987] account of computerized routing in the soft drink industry.

Algorithms for Vehicle Routing Systems

When Dantzig and Ramser introduced the classical vehicle routing problem in 1959, they used an example with 12 customers and could only conjecture the value of the true optimum for this small problem. While researchers continued to work on vehicle routing algorithms in the '60s and the '70s, research activity in this area has greatly increased during the last 20 years.

From an algorithmic point of view, the vehicle routing problem is more challenging than the traveling salesman problem. In fact, one can view the problem as consisting of two stages. First the customers are divided among the various vehicles. Next, an optimal tour is produced for each vehicle by solving a variant of the traveling salesman problem. Exact algorithms are currently unable to solve the vehicle routing problem optimally if more than 300 customers are involved. But this limit may soon increase substantially; the success of mathematical programming-based techniques for solving traveling salesman problems has kindled more research in this area. However, even when the vehicle routing problem is not solved to optimality, ideas from mathematical programming can guide the construction of algorithms or define subproblems that are solved exactly. Magnanti [1981] reviews routing problems and their formulations from this point of view and Christofides [1985] lists some algorithmic approaches to vehicle routing that capitalize upon mathematical programming techniques. Laporte and Nobert [1987] review the research on solving integer programming formulations of the vehicle routing problem and its variants.

Heuristic methods have been used for solving vehicle routing problems since 1964, when Clarke and Wright [1964] developed their well-known procedure. Heuristic procedures can currently handle problems with a thousand customers or more and are generally flexible enough to work in the presence of various constraints. Bodin et al. [1983] review most routing heuristics developed prior to 1982. Most of these techniques continue to be used in solving practical problems. To give one example, Nambiar, Gelders, and Van Wassenhove [1989] used heuristics to construct routes for tankers in the Malaysian rubber industry. These tankers transport latex from smallholder's collection stations to factories that process the rubber. The problem has time windows since latex is a perishable good. The authors selected six well-known heuristics from the literature and compared the routes they generated for this application.

A number of sources cover the developments in vehicle routing during the last 10 years. The collection of papers edited by Golden and Assad [1988] is representative of the algorithmic and practical advances in this field and gives a flavor of the diversity of routing applications. Desrochers, Lenstra, and Savelsbergh [1990] introduce a scheme for classifying different types of vehicle routing and scheduling problems. The scheme is based on four fields that describe the network addresses, the vehicles, the network and service characteristics, and the objective function of each problem. Ronen [1988] concentrates on routing problems for road vehicles (trucks) and lists the different characteristics they exhibit in practice. Golden and Assad [1986] describe some of the more recent algorithmic developments and implementations. Assad [1988] focuses on modeling and implementation issues that arise in practice. Solomon and Desrosiers [1988] survey routing problems that are constrained by time windows. Ronen [1983] describes routing and scheduling of cargo ships and vessels.

Three Applications of Vehicle Routing

Fisher et al. [1982] described their experience with the Clinical Systems Division of Du Pont, a nationwide distributor of clinical supplies and equipment. This division delivered consumable chemical products for use in clinical analyzers. Analyzers are machines that automate most routine tests performed in medical laboratories. The firm had to plan 50 routes to serve 1,500 customers in 1,000 cities. The typical vehicle tour spanned a week (Monday through Friday) to visit 20-50 customers, covering from several hundred miles to 2,000 miles before returning to the base. In addition, the routing problem was further complicated by other constraints, such as two different types of vehicles and limits on continuous driving times.

The routing system used a two-stage approach and relied on a powerful mathematical programming problem called the *generalized assignment problem* to assign customers to trucks [Fisher and Jaikumar 1981; Fisher, Jaikumar, and Van Wassenhove 1986]. A color graphics interface displayed routes and allowed dispatchers to track the progress of the algorithm. Fisher et al. report a 15 percent reduction in delivery costs as a result of using the system. They also used the model in planning mode to make recommendations for the location of facilities. The use of the model for strategic planning identified new configurations for the distribution system that had even greater savings potential.

Yano et al. [1987] implemented a microcomputer-based vehicle routing system for Quality Stores, a Michigan-based chain of some 40 stores. Most stores are located within 250 miles of the distribution center near Toledo, Ohio. A fleet of 11 trucks delivers goods to the stores, visiting an average of 15 stores each day. *Backhauls* constitute an interesting feature of this application. Once a truck has delivered the goods loaded onto the truck at the warehouse, it would be empty and would normally deadhead back to the warehouse. To avoid this unproductive move, dispatchers regularly seek opportunities for the truck to pick up a load from vendors on its way back (that is, on the backhaul). Normally, backhaul moves consist of only pickups, and these pickups occur only after all deliveries are completed. Yano et al. actually consider more complicated backhaul movements: the truck can leave the warehouse with goods to deliver to A, B, and C, complete these deliveries, pick up loads at vendors P and Q, deliver a portion of the goods just picked up (at Q) to D, and finally return to the warehouse.

This mixture of pickups and deliveries on the same route complicates the vehicle routing problem. At Quality Stores, the number of stops on a route was limited to four deliveries plus four pickups; backhauls could not start until the truck was empty. The small number of stops per route is crucial to the model Yano et al. used. Their system uses a set-covering approach (see Section 3.2) that remains viable if the number of feasible routes does not explode. In this application, the number of feasible routes is typically under 250, and it takes only a few seconds on a personal computer to generate them in advance. The system can solve problems with 20 to 50 stops in 10 to 30 minutes. Through efficient routing and by using backhauls, Yano et al. reduced the transportation budget of Quality Stores by $450,000 in 1986 as compared to 1985.

Brown et al. [1987] describe the centralized computer-assisted dispatching (CAD) system that helped Mobil reduce its operating expenses for delivering light petroleum products by $3 million per year. In each of Mobil's 23 dispatch areas across the nation, dispatchers must assign trucks to carry petroleum products from Mobil's terminals to gas stations and other customers. Customers place orders for specific products (mostly, three grades of gasoline) and request a particular delivery date and shift. Although dispatchers focus on a single dispatch area at a time, they still face a complicated task. In the Los Angeles basin area, for example, 30 trucks deliver 329 product orders products from seven terminals to 116 customer locations in a single shift.

From a modeling point of view, the dispatching decision is a vehicle routing problem with multiple depots and complicated capacity, compatibility, loading, and sequencing restrictions. The design of a multi-stop route for a tanker truck involves solving a traveling salesman problem. However, even when the list of orders assigned to a single truck is fixed, the loading of these products into the truck compartments is far from trivial as various weight, volume, and safety restrictions apply. CAD uses mathematical programming to solve the loading problem. From the start, the developers of CAD were aware that the system should respond very rapidly. Out of the five to ten minutes the dispatcher typically allots to each dispatch, only five to ten seconds are spent on reviewing the results of the optimization run. CAD performs the optimization for routing and loading in less then one second.

By using CAD, each dispatcher at Mobil was able to handle twice as many orders. This gain in efficiency allowed Mobil to combine three separate dispatch centers into a small central office in Valley Forge, Pennsylvania that handles 600,000 customer orders a year nationwide.

Interactive Routing Systems

Mobil's CAD system is a good example of how algorithmic and interactive features can be combined within a single system. CAD was specifically designed to assist human dispatchers, not to replace them. It uses optimization to evaluate different assignments of orders to trucks or different loading alternatives, performing repeated feasibility checks and costing computations that the dispatcher would find very frustrating to duplicate. The optimization modules produce a good candidate solution for presentation to the dispatcher. The dispatcher can then interact with the system and override it prior to final acceptance.

In a large number of routing problems encountered in practice, a host of such constraints as time windows, loading restrictions, and crew constraints will challenge any routing algorithm. As no single model can capture all of these constraints, system support for user interaction is a necessary condition for success in the field. Belardo, Duchessi, and Seagle [1985] emphasize the role of computer graphics and interactive screens in solving the routing problem of the Southland Corporation (the owner of

7-11 stores). In this application, which involved 1,500 customers daily, an interactive system with modest algorithmic capabilities saved $1,000 per day by eliminating one route out of the 35 formed daily. Fisher and Rosenwein [1989] describe another interactive scheduling system for ships that pick up and deliver bulk cargo.

Interactive systems depend upon users to modify the routes proposed by the system in order to improve their quality. This notion of quality, which Assad [1988] discusses in greater detail, is based on a variety of constraints and desirable features the dispatcher has in mind in evaluating routes. Duchessi, Belardo, and Seagle [1988] have recently enhanced their interactive system by adding knowledge-based expert system modules to guide the generation of quality routes. If these efforts are successful, future routing systems may expand into general decision support systems linked to major geographical data bases.

3.5 MODELING MOTOR CARRIER OPERATIONS

The research on vehicle allocation may be traced back to the late '60s when a number of researchers considered the problem of distributing empty cars over a rail network. Since estimates indicate that the typical railcar in the US rail system is empty 40 percent of the time, managing empty cars is important economically. The purpose of an operational model is to coordinate loaded and empty moves so that the empty railcars are positioned where they are needed. In one of the pioneering papers in this area, White and Bomberault [1969] optimized the positioning of empty freight cars using a network model that took the time element into account explicitly. Later, White [1972] modeled the distribution of empty containers in a similar way. The flows in these applications occur on space-time networks. In a space-time network, a node represents a given time period as well as a specific location and arcs represent movements over time as well as space. This network structure has been used ever since and is one component of the model developed by Powell et al. [1988]. Dejax and Crainic [1987] provide a detailed review of empty vehicle allocation models with special emphasis on rail and trucking modes.

Much of the work on railcar distribution has focused on deterministic models in which forecasts of future demands are assumed to be known. In this case, the empty car distribution problem can be solved by efficient transshipment algorithms applied to the space-time network. According to Powell [1988], Schnieder National Inc., a large national truckload carrier in Green Bay, Wisconsin, uses a model that assumes all future demands are integers, known with certainty. According to Powell, virtually all other truckload carriers have to deal with uncertainty. Historical data reveals that the flow of trucks between two regions fluctuates significantly from one day to the next and often averages under 0.5 trucks. Thus, handling uncertainty becomes all-important in modeling TL operations.

Jordan and Turnquist [1983] developed one of the first major models to incorporate uncertainty explicitly. Powell, Sheffi, and Thiriez [1984] adopted a similar stochastic framework by treating the number of loaded vehicles moving between regions i and j as random variables with known means and variances. However, this model did not account for a key issue encountered in practice: trucks that cannot move full are often not moved at all. The model should therefore avoid forcing empty movements in favor of holding trucks over when the actual demand falls below the number of trucks allocated. Powell [1986] developed an extended model to allow for this option. This model uses a network with stochastic flows because the number of vehicles moving loaded over a link is random. Although the model uses sophisticated logic to account for uncertainty, it is still not completely realistic since if a vehicle in region A cannot move loaded to region B, it may still be dispatched loaded to another region C. Moreover, solutions to this model produce fractional vehicle flows that are not directly usable in an operational setting. These considerations led to the regional impact model described in this chapter.

Powell's subsequent work on the vehicle allocation problem has clarified the relationship between the regional impact model, which he now calls nodal recourse, and his earlier work [Powell 1988]. It is now clear that nodal recourse is a significant generalization of the earlier models and is therefore expected to work better. Moreover, it has the added advantages of being both simple and computationally effective.

Less-than-Truckload Carriers

Less-than-truckload (LTL) motor carriers form another important segment of the trucking industry. In LTL trucking, shipments ranging from 300 to 10,000 pounds are transported by trucks that can carry up to 45,000 pounds. Each LTL shipment has a point of origin and a destination. Unlike TL trucking, the LTL industry provides service according to a regular schedule between pairs of locations. The main issue in this industry is to consolidate freight to reduce transportation costs without incurring large handling costs or impairing customer service.

An LTL transportation network operates with two types of terminals. *End-of-line terminals* (or end-of-lines, for short) act as origins or destinations of linehaul moves, while *breakbulk terminals* (or breakbulks) serve as consolidation and transshipment points for the freight (Exhibit 3–7). Typically, several end-of-lines (a1, a2, and a3) are associated with a primary breakbulk center (A). A given LTL shipment that originates near a1 and is destined for a location served by c2 may go through the following moves:

EXHIBIT 3–7. The breakbulk terminal A is the primary breakbulk center for terminals a1, a2, and a3 in this small example of an LTL network. Direct services are provided between a1 and B, and also between A and c3.

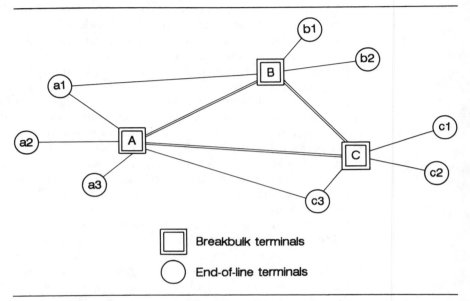

— local pickup at the point of origin and delivery to end-of-line terminal a1,
— linehaul movement from a1 to the primary breakbulk A,
— sorting and consolidation at A,
— movement from A to B,
— handling and consolidation at B for movement to C,
— movement from B to C,
— shipment from C to its satellite c2, and
— local delivery from c2 to its destination.

Heavy traffic from a1 to B may justify a direct service to B that avoids intermediate handling at A. Direct services almost always originate from or terminate at breakbulks. For a carrier to provide direct service between two terminals, it must be sure of a certain minimum weekly trailer flow (say, three to five trailers per week). To ensure good customer service, the carrier must also serve some links at established minimum frequencies. Essentially, the carrier's trade-off is between operating costs and the level of service.

The *load planning* problem for an LTL carrier can be broken down into four key decisions:.

1. Where to establish direct services,
2. How to route freight over a given network of direct services,

3. How to integrate and route TL freight (LTL carriers also handle some TL freight), and
4. How to route empty trailers to balance the flow of freight cars.

The objective of the problem is to minimize the sum of the costs of direct transportation, of handling at the terminals, and of empty or loaded truck movements. In the terminology of network optimization, the first two decisions are called *network design* and *routing*. These decisions interact because a change in the service network requires a rerouting of the flows. The combined result of these decisions is a set of rules that govern traffic flow. For example, shipments at terminal i headed for destination j must be put on the trailer headed for breakbulk B. LTL carriers usually view the third decision as being subservient to the first two. TL traffic generally acts as the backhaul for the LTL moves. Once the LTL moves are determined, the carrier tries to create demand for such profitable backhauls. Finally, the fourth problem can be solved with an efficient network flow code that balances the empties created by both LTL and TL traffic.

Powell and Sheffi [1986, 1989] describe the load-planning system APOLLO that they developed for PIE Nationwide. This national LTL carrier (originally known as Ryder Truck Lines and later as Ryder/PIE) has over 300 terminals throughout the United States, of which about 30 are breakbulks. The number of terminals is an important measure of the difficulty of the network design problem since one can associate a zero-one decision variable with each pair of terminals to decide whether the resulting link is in the network of direct services. Even though direct service links must have a breakbulk at one endpoint, this still results in 17,000 links in the case of PIE. However, only 2,000 of these are actually used in practice. The system must therefore have a good mechanism for pruning the links to identify potentially useful ones. The large problem size is further complicated by the nonlinear (fixed charge) linehaul cost structure that results from the requirements for providing service with certain minimum frequencies. This implies that the cost of providing service over a link is initially constant until the weekly flow of trailers exceeds the minimum frequency for that link (Exhibit 3–8).

APOLLO is an interactive optimization system. The user interacts with the system to fix the first decision, while the system provides automatic support for decisions 2 and 4. In addressing the network design problem, the system ranks the links by evaluating the impact of the addition or deletion of each link on the total cost. For a network with 15,000 potential links, this process takes 10-20 seconds on an IBM 3081 to complete and is by far the most time-consuming part of the system. The user can then select and confirm some of these suggestions. The routing decision relies on shortest path logic with override capabilities that the user can invoke.

EXHIBIT 3–8. The plot of the cost function for less-than-truckload service reveals the fixed charge. The cost is constant until the flow exceeds the minimum frequency, and it increases linearly thereafter. In this plot, the vertical axis measures the costs in multiples of the cost of hauling one trailer.

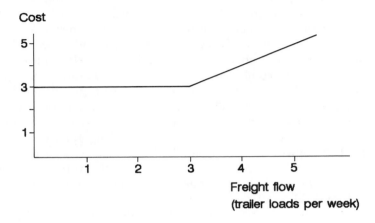

Implementing the system was a major undertaking that took three years. It was completed in 1985 and is still used at PIE. The resulting system cost $500,000 to develop, has a 300-page user's manual, and contains over 40,000 lines of code. APOLLO reduced the length of time for load planning from four months to several days. This meant that load planning could be performed more frequently and more responsively. Powell and Sheffi [1986] estimate the annual savings resulting from the system at $30-40 million. One study identified an annual savings of $7-10 million out of total operating costs of $400 million. In addition to this study, Powell and Sheffi [1989] present many other interesting observations on system implementation at PIE. In an update, Powell [1989] reports that the APOLLO load planning system is now called SUPERSPIN. This system, which comprises 80,000 lines of code, is being used by both PIE and Yellow Freight System. With approximately 600 terminals, the Yellow network is effectively four times larger than the PIE network.

3.6 FURTHER READINGS

Related Readings

Bartholdi et al. Paper

- Bartholdi and Platzman [1988] generalize their heuristic for the traveling salesman problem to a generic spacefilling curve heuristic that is applicable to a number of interesting combinatorial problems, such as the K-median problem. A curious application proposed by a strategic defense initiative (star wars) contractor involves using spacefilling curves to "route" a laser weapon through 1,000-30,000 moving targets. As these targets are incoming missiles whose positions change rapidly, the algorithm must react quickly in real time to obtain and update solutions. Bartholdi and Platzman also use the heuristic to assign bin numbers to locations of different items in a warehouse.

- Bartholdi and Platzman first introduced the spacefilling-curve heuristic in 1982 for the planar traveling salesman problem and followed this with an application to the minimum-weight matching problem in the plane [Bartholdi and Platzman 1983]. The authors derive some basic mathematical properties of the algorithms. For example, they show that if n customers are randomly and independently distributed over some region, and Euclidean distances are used to compute tour lengths, then as n gets large, the spacefilling-curve heuristic generates tours that are no more than 25 percent larger than optimum.

- Chauny et al. [1987] used a three-dimensional version of the spacefilling-curve heuristic to direct a numerically-controlled machine for cutting a flat workstock. The machine loads tool bits from a rotating drum for each operation. In sequencing operations, one must consider both planar movements along the workstock and the rotation of the drum to access the next tool bit. These two considerations can be combined into a generalized travel cost in three-dimensional space. A desirable sequence would then minimize the generalized travel cost between operations.

Bell et al. Paper

- Golden, Assad, and Dahl [1984] describe liquid propane distribution—another problem that combines inventory and routing considerations. The firm in their application delivers about 100 million gallons of propane annually, operating out of 60 districts. A district has three or four trucks that deliver propane to approximately 3,000 customers within a 25-mile radius of the depot. These customers consume propane for heating or industrial uses and require deliveries with frequencies ranging from once a day to three times per year. The firm has to forecast the propane level in customer tanks and replenish this supply periodically while minimizing some aggregate measure of distribution costs. This problem has many of the features of the Air Products application with one important difference: A single truck can deliver propane to 60 to 100 customers daily. Because the number of stops per route is much larger than in the Air Products problem, the set-covering approach is inappropriate. Instead, a two-stage heuristic first selects the customers to receive delivery on a given day and then solves a vehicle routing problem to route the trucks that visit the customers selected in the first step.

- Ball [1988] discusses a class of routing problems he calls *allocation routing* that involve two components—an allocation component that assigns customers to days, and a routing component that constructs routes to visit all the customers assigned to the same day. In addition to the distribution of industrial gases and liquid propane products, this class includes *driver-sell* applications. In this mode of operation, which is popular in the beverage industry, the driver visits customers with some suitable frequencies without knowing their demands for certain. Once again, the goal is to keep the inventory at retail stores replenished. However, in this case the routes generally have a periodic nature and the definition of driver territories is an important practical consideration (also see Golden and Wasil [1987]). Anily and Federgruen [1990] analyze integrated replenishment strategies for distributing goods to a set of retailers using a fleet of vehicles based at a single depot.

Powell et al. Paper

- In a companion paper to the one in this chapter, Powell [1987] describes the dynamic vehicle allocation problem in greater detail. In particular, he shows that the model can be interpreted as associating a reward structure with vehicle movements that are governed by a Markov chain. He also discusses the end effects of the model more carefully. Powell [1990] gives a short review of the dynamic optimization for TL carriers and describes an interactive graphic simulation system called MIDAS on which competing algorithms for the problem can be compared.
- The major challenge of the dynamic vehicle allocation problem is to choose a modeling methodology that would capture the uncertainty of the operational environment in a realistic way. It is important to realize that this choice is not uniquely determined. Powell [1988] looks at four methodological approaches that approach the vehicle allocation problem from different perspectives: stochastic networks, Markov decision processes, stochastic programming, and deterministic networks. Using the language of stochastic programming, he shows that vehicle allocation models differ in the choice of a recourse strategy. The regional impact model, which represents nodal recourse, results from a linearization of the downstream recourse function. More recently, Franzeskakis and Powell [1990] have proposed a stochastic programming formulation of the vehicle allocation problem that enables them to solve it as a pure network problem, thereby capitalizing on the speed and efficiency of exisiting network optimization procedures.

Background Readings

Bartholdi et al. Paper

- While Bartholdi et al. use a very simple and fast heuristic for the traveling salesman problem, this celebrated problem has a long history in the literature of operations research. Dantzig, Fulkerson, and Johnson [1954] used a linear programming formulation of the traveling salesman problem to find the optimal solution of a 49-city problem—a problem that was considered to be large at the time. After providing a detailed exposition of their solution technique, they concluded their paper by stating: "It is clear that we have left unanswered practically any question one might pose of a theoretical nature concerning the traveling salesman problem."

Since that time, the traveling salesman problem has motivated some of the most powerful combinatorial optimization techniques developed to date. In July 1986, Padberg and Rinaldi [1987] reported the exact solution of three large symmetric traveling salesman problems with 532, 1,002, and 2,392 cities, the largest problems solved optimally up to that time. They used an integer programming formulation of the problem that has n(n-1)/2 zero-one variables for a problem with n cities. Their solution technique is based on a branch-and-cut approach that uses sophisticated concepts from polyhedral theory and mathematical programming to generate good cuts in the solution space [Grotschel and Padberg 1985]. The solution time for the 532-city problem, which has 141,246 binary decision variables, was five hours and 58 minutes on the CYBER 205 supercomputer. The two Euclidean traveling salesman problems with 1,002 cities and 2,392 cities took seven hours and 18 minutes and 27 hours and 20 minutes, respectively.

- While research on solving large scale traveling salesman problems continues, problems with 100 to 300 nodes are within the reach of algorithms implemented on personal computers. Boyd, Pulleyblank, and Cornuejols [1987] describe a PC-based software package called TRAVEL for solving Euclidean traveling salesman problems. The package includes the spacefilling curve heuristic of Bartholdi and Platzman [1982] along with several standard heuristics for tour construction. Once an initial tour is available, the package uses tour improvement procedures to reduce the length of the tour. Finally, the package includes an effective mathematical programming-based bounding technique developed by the authors to obtain lower bounds on the tour length. The quality of these bounds is good: they are within two percent of the optimum solutions for 100-city random Euclidean problems. The animated graphics of the package display the results as the algorithms are running, thereby making it a pedagogically appealing tool.

- The text edited by Lawler et al. [1985] offers encyclopedic coverage of the traveling salesman problem. In their lead article, Alan Hoffman and Peter Wolfe trace the historical roots of the problem. The other papers in this book examine the structure of the traveling salesman problem and present exact and heuristic techniques for solving it. Finally, Nemhauser and Wolsey [1988, pp. 469-495] describe some of the newer integer programming-based techniques for solving traveling salesman problems and illustrate them on a 67-city problem.

- The spacefilling-curve approach identifies a tour through all customers a priori. On a given day, however, only a subset of the customers are visited. Jaillet [1988] presents an interesting probabilistic analysis of how an a priori ordering of the customers performs when the customers visited each day are chosen randomly.

Bell et al. Paper

- The set-packing approach Bell et al. used for Air Products can be modified and applied to other routing problems such as scheduling ships for the pickup and delivery of bulk cargo. Fisher and Rosenwein [1989] used the approach to schedule a fleet of 20 ships lifting 28 cargos for the Military Sealift Command of the US Navy. An interesting feature of this problem is that some cargo can be assigned to an outside carrier, so the fleet does not have to serve all of the demand. The set packing problem can be used as a model since each ship lifts only a small number of cargos. This integer programming model is embedded within an interactive scheduling system. Fisher, Huang, and Tang [1986] outline a similar approach for the trucking problem in Shanghai where 3,400 trucks transport 6,000-7,000 orders daily. Both papers cite other applications of the set-covering approach.

- Brown, Graves, and Ronen [1987] use a set-partitioning approach to solve the tanker routing and scheduling problem of a major oil company that is similar to the problem Fisher and Rosenwein [1989] solved. The company uses a fleet of several dozen tankers to ship crude oil from the Middle East to Europe and North America. As a tanker costs $10,000 per day and consumes fuel at the rate of $5,000 to $40,000 daily, there is a large economic incentive to optimize the tankers' schedules. Given a planning horizon of about three months, the company has a slate of cargos to transport during this period. Each cargo corresponds to a full shipload and must be moved from its loading port (origin) to its discharging port (destination). However, the company's fleet does not have to move all cargos; some can be spot chartered to outside carriers. A typical problem has a planning horizon of 10 to 80 days, 50 cargos, 24 tankers, three loading ports, and nine discharging ports. Tankers carry an average of 1.0 to 3.2 cargos per schedule. The set-partitioning approach is viable for this problem because the number of cargos per schedule remains small.

Starting with the standard set partitioning model, Brown, Graves, and Ronen add surplus and slack variables to allow the constraints of the model to be violated at a cost. In this way, penalty terms are used to drive the algorithm towards feasibility. The authors use a code they had developed for mixed integer programming problems with elastic penalties. From a cold start, the algorithm takes approximately 80 seconds on an IBM 3033 to select the optimal shipping plan from the 7,349 candidate schedules of the 80-day problem. Armed with even a simplistic initial plan, the algorithm can solve the same problem in less than eight seconds. The algorithm performs even better if a human scheduler provides manual assistance.

- Bell et al. use the Lagrangian relaxation technique to solve the large mixed integer program they formulate for the industrial gases distribution problem. This technique has proved to be a powerful and practical approach to combinatorial problems since its application to the traveling salesman problem in 1970. Essentially, the Lagrangian relaxation technique involves relaxing certain complicating constraints and including in the objective function terms that penalize the violations of these constraints. Once the complicating constraints are relaxed, the remaining problem is usually easy to solve. For example, the relaxed problem may decompose into many smaller but significantly easier problems. The key to the success of Lagrangian relaxation lies in finding the set of constraints that produces this effect.

Fisher's [1985] highly readable tutorial on Lagrangian relaxation, briefly describes over 10 different successful applications of the technique. Shapiro [1979] and Fisher [1981] cover Lagrangian techniques in greater technical detail, while Geoffrion's [1974] account remains a classical exposition of the basic theory. Fisher, Jaikumar, and Van Wassenhove [1986] use Lagrangian relaxation to obtain good bounds in a branch-and-bound algorithm for the generalized assignment problem. They show that the improved bounds can reduce the number of nodes of the branch-and-bound tree by nearly two orders of magnitude. Their computational results includes test problems arising from vehicle routing problems [Fisher and Jaikumar 1981] that had up to 17 vehicles and 200 customers. Beasley [1990] presents a heuristic algorithm based on Lagrangian relaxation for set covering problems in which columns have unequal costs. He compares this heuristic with two other algorithms on a set of test problems with 100 to 1,000 rows and 400 to 10,000 columns.

- Desrosiers, Sauvé, and Soumis [1988] use Lagrangian relaxation to solve a time-constrained routing problem that arises in school bus scheduling. In the morning, school buses make a number of trips to carry students from pickup points to school. The itinerary of each trip consists of a sequence of pickup points with the school as the last stop. While the trips' itineraries are fixed in advance, there is some freedom in scheduling a trip: the key scheduling constraint is that students must arrive at their schools within certain time windows. Once the students picked up during a single trip are delivered to school, the bus can start another trip. Therefore, the morning schedule for each bus consists of a number of consecutive trips. In the afternoon, buses perform trips that pick up the students at schools and carry them back home. The problem is to minimize the number of buses required to cover all trips. In their computational experience with the Lagrangian relaxation-based approach, the authors solve problems in which the number of trips ranges from 48 to 223.

- Miller [1987] discusses the scheduling problem for Ethyl Corporation's fleet of bulk tankers that deliver gasoline antiknock compounds to distribution and customer terminals around the world. The routing and scheduling of these tankers has an inventory component that is similar to Air Product's problem: tankers must visit terminals before their inventories of product run out. Ethyl uses a fleet of four tankers to deliver a mix of 20 different products to approximately 30 terminals. The tankers have 8 to 10 compartments and typically carry six or seven products. The planning horizon for this scheduling problem is 18 months. During this period, each ship makes four or five voyages, and each terminal is visited from 1 to 10 times. Each voyage corresponds to a sequence of stops the ship visits between two successive loadings at the company's loading ports.

  The firm must design ship schedules that specify all voyages made by each ship during the planning horizon (together with arrival and departure times) and determine the amounts of each product delivered to each terminal. The schedules must observe a host of restrictions. For example, some ships cannot call on certain terminals, visits must be made within certain time windows, and the cargo on the ship must obey certain loading conditions to avoid instability problems at sea. Although the problem can be modeled as a very large space-time network, the network for a typical problem has over a million nodes and 20 million arcs. Instead of attempting to solve this intractable problem, the scheduling system solves portions of the problem and relies upon computer-aided interaction with the user to modify or improve solutions. The system implemented at Ethyl has four subsystems: a feasible schedule generator, a simulator, a report and graphics generator, and an improvement module. Miller reports that the system has been successful in producing acceptable solutions that meet Ethyl's complicated operating constraints.

- In such transportation areas as the airline industry and public transit, it is difficult to schedule vehicle crews even after the itinerary of the vehicles is specified. Set partitioning and set covering models are commonly used to solve this problem. Gershkoff [1989] describes the set partitioning model that American Airlines uses to solve its airline crew scheduling problems. In this application, the rows of the set partitioning problem represent flights to be covered and the columns correspond to candidate crew trips. These crew trips consist of sequences of flight segments that start and end at the same location. Each crew trip must obey a set of work rules and has a cost associated with it. The model finds the set of crew trips that minimizes the cost of covering all flight segments. Blais, Lamont, and Rousseau [1990] describe the successful HASTUS system that they developed for generating bus and driver schedules in Montreal. HASTUS uses network flow techniques, optimal matching, and heuristics to optimize vehicle and crew schedules. Its success in Montreal, where the system has generated annual savings of $4,000,000 in manpower and vehicle operating costs combined, has led to installations in 40 major cities worldwide.

Powell et al. Paper

- A rich and multi-faceted literature covers the operations and economics of commercial motor carriers. Taff [1986] describes the operations of different carriers, their equipment, and the regulations governing this field.

- Crainic and Roy [1988] describe a tactical planning model for freight transportation that is applicable to both rail and LTL transportation. The model simultaneously determines the frequencies with which different services are provided and the routing of freight through the resulting service network. The objective of the model comprises transportation costs and penalty terms that penalize low service levels. The authors tested the model on data from CN Express, the LTL transportation division of Canadian National. The CN network had 34 terminals, 959 origin-destination pairs across Canada, and 289 different services.

- Barker, Sharon, and Sen [1981] describe a system used by the subsidiaries of ANR Freight System (ANFRS), a Detroit-based corporation whose primary business is LTL freight. In 1980, ANFRS provided service to 200 cities and earned $400 million in revenues. It developed systems to handle LTL freight as well as the associated TL traffic. The developers did not pursue a mathematical-programming approach for the LTL model due to nonlinearities in the model and the prediction that it would "be difficult to solve at a reasonable cost." As with Powell and Sheffi, they also felt that a black box approach was not suitable to the planning environment in LTL freight planning. This paper contains a good overview of the LTL industry and also addresses implementation issues and experiences at some length. Powell and Sheffi [1989] cite a number of other efforts in the use of MS/OR techniques in LTL planning.

- Less-than-truckload trucking and express parcel delivery are two examples of the class of many-to-many logistics problems. In these problems, goods are shipped from many origins to many destinations dispersed over a wide geographical region. Certain questions arise naturally in many-to-many systems. Should breakbulk terminals be used? If so, how many? How should the frequency of service be determined? Daganzo [1987] attempts to answer these questions by analyzing the characteristics of many-to-many operations with as little data as possible. His analysis uses approximate expressions to capture the main cost components of the delivery operations in order to reveal the basic economies of different system configurations. Daganzo's paper cites other applications of this approach to transportation problems.

REFERENCES

Anily, Shoshana and Federgruen, Avi 1990, "One warehouse multiple retailer systems with vehicle routing costs," *Management Science*, Vol. 36, No. 1, pp. 92–114.

Assad, Arjang A. 1988, "Modeling and implementation issues in vehicle routing," in *Vehicle*

Routing: Methods and Studies, ed. B. Golden and A. Assad, North Holland, New York, pp. 7–45.

Ball, Michael O. 1988, "Allocation/routing: Models and algorithms," in *Vehicle Routing: Methods and Studies*, ed. B. Golden and A. Assad, North Holland, New York, pp. 199–221.

Barker, Henry H.; Sharon, Ed M.; and Sen, Dilip K. 1981, "From freight flow and cost patterns to greater profitability and better service for a motor carrier," *Interfaces*, Vol. 11, No. 6, pp. 4–20.

Bartholdi, John J. and Platzman, Loren K. 1982, "An O(NlogN) planar traveling salesman heuristic based on spacefilling curves," *Operations Research Letters*, Vol. 1, No. 4, pp. 121–125.

Bartholdi, John J. and Platzman, Loren K. 1983, "A fast heuristic based on spacefilling curves for minimum weight matching in the plane," *Information Processing Letters*, Vol. 17, pp. 177–180.

Bartholdi, John J. and Platzman, Loren K. 1988, "Heuristics based on spacefilling curves for combinatorial problems in Euclidean space," *Management Science*, Vol. 34, No. 3, pp. 291–305.

Bartholdi, John J.; Platzman, Loren K.; Collins, R. Lee; and Warden, William H. 1983, "A minimal technology routing system for Meals on Wheels," *Interfaces*, Vol. 13, No. 3, pp. 1–8.

Beasley, J. E. 1990, "A Lagrangian heuristic for set-covering problems," *Naval Research Logistics*, Vol. 37, No. 1, pp. 151–164.

Belardo, Salvatore; Duchessi, Peter; and Seagle, J. Peter 1985, "Microcomputer graphics in support of vehicle fleet routing," *Interfaces*, Vol. 15, No. 6, pp. 84–92.

Bell, Walter J.; Dalberto, Louis M.; Fisher, Marshall L.,; Greenfield, Arnold J.; Jaikumar, R.; Kedia, Pradeep; Mack, Robert G.; and Prutzman, Paul J. 1983, "Improving the distribution of industrial gases with an on-line computerized routing and scheduling optimizer," *Interfaces*, Vol. 13, No. 6, pp. 4–23.

Blais, Yves; Lamont, Jacques; and Rousseau, Jean-Marc 1990, "The HASTUS vehicle and manpower scheduling system at the Societe de transport de la Communaute urbaine de Montreal," *Interfaces*, Vol. 20, No. 1, pp. 26–42.

Bodin, Lawrence D.; Golden, Bruce L.; Assad, Arjang A.; and Ball, Michael O. 1983, "Routing and scheduling of vehicles and crews: The state of the art," *Computers & Operations Research*, Vol. 10, No. 2, pp. 63–211.

Boyd, Sylvia C.; Pulleyblank, William R.; and Cornuejols, Gerard 1987, "TRAVEL—an interactive traveling salesman problem package for the IBM personal computer," *Operations Research Letters*, Vol. 6, No. 3, pp. 141–143.

Brown, Gerald G.; Ellis, Carol J.; Graves, Glenn W.; and Ronen, David 1987, "Real-time, wide area dispatch of Mobil tank trucks," *Interfaces*, Vol. 17, No. 1, pp. 107–120.

Brown, Gerald G.; Graves, Glenn W.; and Ronen, David 1987, "Scheduling ocean transportation of crude oil," *Management Science*, Vol. 33, No. 3, pp. 335–346.

Chauny, Fabien; Haurie, Alain; Wagneur, Edouard; and Loulou, Richard 1987, "Sequencing punch operations in a flexible manufacturing cell: A three-dimensional spacefilling curve approach," *INFOR*, Vol. 25, No. 1, pp. 26–45.

Christofides, Nicos 1985, "Vehicle routing," in *The Traveling Salesman Problem*, ed. E. L. Lawler et al., John Wiley & Sons, New York, pp. 431–448.

Clarke, G. and Wright, J. W. 1964, "Scheduling of vehicles from a central depot to a number of delivery points," *Operations Research*, Vol. 12, No. 4, pp. 568–581.

Crainic, Teodor G. and Roy, Jacques 1988, "OR tools for tactical freight transportation planning," *European Journal of Operational Research*, Vol. 33, No. 3, pp. 290–297.

Daganzo, Carlos F. 1987, "The breakbulk role of terminals in many-to-many logistics networks," *Operations Research*, Vol. 35, No. 4, pp. 543–555.

Dantzig, George B.; Fulkerson, R.; and Johnson, S. 1954, "Solution of a large traveling salesman problem," *Operations Research*, Vol. 2, No. 4, pp. 393–410.

Dantzig, George B. and Ramser, J. H. 1959, "The truck dispatching problem," *Management Science*, Vol. 6, No. 1, pp. 80–91.

Dejax, Pierre and Crainic, Teodor G. 1987, "A review of empty flow and fleet management models in freight transportation," *Transportation Science*, Vol. 21, No. 4, pp. 227–247.

Desrochers, Martin; Lenstra, Jan Karel; and Savelsbergh, Martin W. P. 1990, "A classification scheme for vehicle routing and scheduling problems," *European Journal of Operational Research*, Vol. 46, No. 3, pp. 322–332.

Desrosiers, Jacques; Sauvé, Michel; and Soumis, François 1988, "Lagrangian relaxation methods for solving the multiple traveling salesman problem with time windows," *Management Science*, Vol. 34, No. 8, pp. 1005–1022.

Duchessi, Peter; Belardo, Salvatore; and Seagle, John P. 1988, "Artificial intelligence and the management science practitioner: Knowledge enhancements to a decision support system for vehicle routing," *Interfaces*, Vol. 18, No. 2, pp. 85–93.

Fisher, Marshall L. 1981, "The Lagrangian relaxation method for solving integer programming problems," *Management Science*, Vol. 27, No. 1, pp. 1–18.

Fisher, Marshall L. 1985, "An applications-oriented guide to Lagrangian relaxation," *Interfaces*, Vol. 15, No. 2, pp. 10–21.

Fisher, Marshall L.; Greenfield, Arnold J.; Jaikumar, R.; and Lester, Joseph T. 1982, "A computerized vehicle routing application," *Interfaces*, Vol. 12, No. 4, pp. 42–52.

Fisher, Marshall L.; Huang, Jiegang; and Tang, Bao-Xing 1986, "Scheduling bulk-pickup-delivery vehicles in Shanghai," *Interfaces*, Vol. 16, No. 2, pp. 18–23.

Fisher, Marshall L. and Jaikumar, R. 1981, "A generalized assignment heuristic for vehicle routing," *Networks*, Vol. 11, No. 2, pp. 109–124.

Fisher, Marshall L.; Jaikumar, R.; and Van Wassenhove, Luk N. 1986, "A multiplier adjustment method for the generalized allocation problem," *Management Science*, Vol. 32, No. 9, pp. 1095–1103.

Fisher, Marshall L. and Rosenwein, Moshe B. 1989, "An interactive optimization system for bulk-cargo ship scheduling," *Naval Research Logistics*, Vol. 36, No. 1, pp. 27–42.

Franzeskakis, Linos F. and Powell, Warren B. 1990, "A successive linear approximation procedure for stochastic dynamic vehicle allocation problems," *Transportation Science*, Vol. 24, No. 1, pp. 40–57.

Geoffrion, Arthur M. 1974, "Lagrangian relaxation and its uses in integer programming," *Mathematical Programming Study*, Vol. 2, pp. 82–114.

Gershkoff, Ira 1989, "Optimizing flight crew schedules," *Interfaces*, Vol. 19, No. 4, pp. 29–43.

Golden, Bruce L. and Assad, Arjang A. 1986, "Perspectives on vehicle routing: Exciting new developments," *Operations Research*, Vol. 34, No. 5, pp. 803–810.

Golden, Bruce L. and Assad, Arjang A., eds. 1988, *Vehicle Routing: Methods and Studies*, North-Holland, New York.

Golden, Bruce L.; Assad, Arjang A.; and Dahl, Roy W. 1984, "Analysis of a large scale vehicle routing problem with an inventory component," *Large Scale Systems*, Vol. 7, Nos. 2 and 3, pp. 181–190.

Golden, Bruce L. and Wasil, Edward A. 1987, "Computerized vehicle routing in the soft drink industry," *Operations Research*, Vol. 35, No. 1, pp. 6–17.

Grotschel, Martin and Padberg, Manfred W. 1985, "Polyhedral theory," in *The Traveling Salesman Problem*, ed. E. L. Lawler et al., John Wiley & Sons, Chichester, England, pp. 251–360.

Jaillet, Patrick 1988, "A priori solution of a traveling salesman problem in which a random subset of the customers are visited," *Operations Research*, Vol. 36, No. 6, pp. 929–936.

Jordan, William C. and Turnquist, Mark A. 1983, "A stochastic, dynamic model for railroad car distribution," *Transportation Science*, Vol. 17, No. 2, pp. 123–145.

Laporte, Gilbert and Nobert, Yves 1987, "Exact algorithms for the vehicle routing problem," *Annals of Discrete Mathematics*, Vol. 31, pp. 147–184.

Lawler, Eugene L.; Lenstra, Jan Karel; Rinnooy Kan, Alexander H. G.; and Shmoys, David B. 1985, *The Traveling Salesman Problem: A Guided Tour of Combinatorial Optimization*, John Wiley & Sons, Chichester, England.

Magnanti, Thomas L. 1981, "Combinatorial optimization and vehicle fleet planning: Perspectives and prospects," *Networks*, Vol. 11, No. 2, pp. 179–214.

Miller, David M. 1987, "An interactive computer-aided ship scheduling system," *European Journal of Operational Research*, Vol. 32, No. 3, pp. 363–379.

Nambiar, Jay M.; Gelders, Ludo F.; and Van Wassenhove, Luk N. 1989, "Plant location and vehicle routing in the Malaysian rubber smallholder sector: A case study," *European Journal of Operational Research*, Vol. 38, No. 1, pp. 14–26.

Nemhauser, George L. and Wolsey, Laurence A. 1988, *Integer and Combinatorial Optimization*, John Wiley & Sons, New York.

Padberg, Manfred W. and Rinaldi, G. 1987, "Optimization of a 532-city symmetric traveling salesman problem by branch and cut," *Operations Research Letters*, Vol. 6, No. 1, pp. 1–7.

Powell, Warren B. 1986, "A stochastic formulation of the dynamic vehicle allocation problem," *Transportation Science*, Vol. 20, No. 2, pp. 117–129.

Powell, Warren B. 1987, "An operational planning model for the dynamic vehicle allocation problem with uncertain demands," *Transportation Research*, Vol. 21B, No. 3, pp. 217–232.

Powell, Warren B. 1988, "A comparative review of alternative algorithms for the dynamic vehicle allocation problem," in *Vehicle Routing: Methods and Studies*, ed. B. Golden and A. Assad, North-Holland, New York, pp. 249–291.

Powell, Warren B. 1989, private communication.

Powell, Warren B. 1990, "Real-time optimization for truckload motor carriers," *OR/MS Today*, Vol. 17, No. 2, pp. 28–33.

Powell, Warren B. and Sheffi, Yosef 1986, "Interactive optimization for motor carrier load planning," *Journal of Business Logistics*, Vol. 7, No. 2, pp. 64–90.

Powell, Warren B. and Sheffi, Yosef 1989, "Design and implementation of an interactive optimization system for network design in the motor carrier industry," *Operations Research*, Vol. 37, No. 1, pp. 12–29.

Powell, Warren B.; Sheffi, Yosef; Nickerson, Kenneth S.; Butterbaugh, Kevin; and Atherton, Susan 1988, "Maximizing profits for North American Van Lines' truckload division," *Interfaces*, Vol. 18, No. 1, pp. 21–41.

Powell, Warren B.; Sheffi, Yosef; and Thiriez, Sebastien 1984, "The dynamic vehicle allocation problem with uncertain demands," in *Proceedings of the Ninth International Symposium on Transportation and Traffic Theory*, ed. J. Dormuller and R. Hamersalg, VNU Science Press, The Netherlands, pp. 357–374.

Ronen, David R. 1983, "Cargo ships routing and scheduling: Survey of models and problems," *European Journal of Operational Research*, Vol. 12, No. 2, pp. 119–126.

Ronen, David 1988, "Perspectives on practical aspects of truck routing and scheduling," *European Journal of Operational Research*, Vol. 35, No. 2, pp. 137–145.

Shapiro, Jeremy F. 1979, "A survey of Lagrangian techniques for discrete optimization," *Annals of Discrete Mathematics*, Vol. 5, pp. 113–138.

Solomon, Marius M. and Desrosiers, Jacques 1988, "Time window-constrained routing and scheduling problems," *Transportation Science*, Vol. 22, No. 1, pp. 1–13.

Taff, Charles A. 1986, *Commercial Motor Transportation*, seventh edition, Canell Maritime Press, Centreville, Maryland.

White, W. W. 1972, "Dynamic transshipment networks: An algorithm and its application to the distribution of empty containers," *Networks*, Vol. 2, No. 3, pp. 211–236.

White, W. W. and Bomberault, A. M. 1969, "A network algorithm for empty freight car allocation," *IBM Systems Journal*, Vol. 8, No. 2, pp. 147–169.

Yano, Candace A.; Chan, Thomas J.; Richter, Lori K.; Cutler, Theodore; Murty, Katta G.; and McGettigan, David 1987, "Vehicle routing at Quality Stores," *Interfaces*, Vol. 17, No. 2, pp. 52–63.

A Minimal Technology Routing System for Meals on Wheels

John J. Bartholdi, III

Loren K. Platzman

R. Lee Collins

William H. Warden, III

Routing problems—where vehicles visit many delivery points distributed over a geographical region and return to the depot within minimal time—are notoriously difficult to solve. Even the most powerful computers available today would require years to exactly solve routing problems of moderate size. Consequently recent research has focused on heuristic methods, simple procedures that enable computers to generate good (but not optimal) solutions.

Unlike computers, humans have a knack for generating good routes, but they get bogged down in details when the problem is large. With our colleagues at the Production and Distribution Research Center of the Georgia Institute of Technology, we have been investigating interactive computer methods, in which a computer with color graphics is used as an "intelligent scratchpad" by a human operator who designs the routes. In the course of these activities we unexpectedly discovered a heuristic so simple that a computer is not even required [Bartholdi and Platzman 1982].

We recognized that our idea applies wherever routing must be performed quickly without computers or technically trained personnel. From previous experience we knew of a charitable organization that faced routing problems of this type. To validate our method and to help a worthy cause, we worked with the charity to implement a routing system based on our idea.

MEALS ON WHEELS

Senior Citizen Services, Inc. is a private, nonprofit corporation in Atlanta, Georgia whose purpose is to provide social services for the elderly, especially the elderly poor, in Fulton County. One of their major services is the "Meals on Wheels" program (MOW), which delivers prepared lunches to people who are unable to shop or cook for themselves. As for many charitable organizations, the funding for MOW is unstable, chronically insufficient, and occasionally desperate. Any additional resources are used to purchase more food for needy people, so the administrative facilities of MOW remain the bare minimum necessary to function.

MOW operates Monday through Friday each week. At 8:30 a.m. the prepared meals are delivered by an institutional caterer to Senior Citizen Services in mid-Atlanta. There they are heated in a holding oven until about 9:15 a.m. when four paid, part-time employees arrive. They load the meals into insulated bulk containers and then into their four vehicles. Each driver is given a "route manifest" which lists all of his delivery locations' in a suggested order of visitation. Each then drives his route, delivering 40-50 meals to 30-40 locations between 10 a.m. and 2 p.m.

Because the delivery vehicles are usually station wagons, they can easily carry sufficient meals, so vehicle capacity is not an effective limitation. The only constraint is that all meals must be delivered within four hours, the length of time the insulated containers will keep the meals properly warm. However, drivers complete their routes within the limit so time constraints are usually not active. In fact, neither vehicle capacity nor delivery time is likely to become an active constraint unless the system grows considerably, an unlikely event for a charitable organization during lean times.

MOW maintains two lists of clients: an *active* list of those to whom meals are currently delivered, and a *waiting* list of those hoping to join the system when space or additional resources become available. A special feature of this delivery problem is

TABLE 1. Changes in the Meals on Wheels active client list from August 1981 through November 1982. About 80% of these clients received their meals through the routing system; the rest were served by volunteers.

Month	People Served	People Added	People Lost
July 1981	159	—	—
August	167	15	7
September	169	8	6
October	195	29	3
November	225	40	10
December	256	37	6
January 1982	?	?	?
February	273	31	?
March	299	41	15
April	327	36	8
May	341	26	12
June	353	22	10
July	358	5	20
August	278	2	62
September	240	2	40
October	227	8	21
November	246	40	21

that the lists are quite volatile (Table 1). In fact, the lists change at a rate of about 14% each month because of the nature of the clients: most are elderly or ill. They may die, or recover from illness, or receive care elsewhere (in a hospital, nursing home, or family) and so leave whichever list they are on. Clients may be added to the active list either from the waiting list, or as emergency special cases (perhaps referred to MOW by a social worker).

The volatility of the active list is further increased by the special way in which MOW is funded. Senior Citizen Services receives operating revenues from three primary sources, the federal government, the state of Georgia, and United Way. Unfortunately, all three administer their grants under different fiscal calendars.

The federal government begins its fiscal year on October 1, the State of Georgia on July 1, and United Way on January 1. The multiple fiscal years cause continuous turmoil at MOW because each grant must be spent during its respective fiscal year. Consequently it is not unusual for a large number of people to be added to the active list during the close of a fiscal year and then to be removed to the waiting list during the beginning of a new fiscal year.

MOW is managed by a devoted, energetic woman who is a full-time employee of Senior Citizen Services. As in many charitable organizations, the manager tends to be overworked. Her responsibilities are many, and include management of the MOW budget, and responsibility for all technical aspects of meals: planning menus, ordering meals from the caterer, monitoring the quality of meals, maintaining the insulated containers for the meals, and supervising part-time employees. In administering the delivery of meals she maintains the list of delivery locations, maintains routes to be followed by the delivery trucks, and supervises the four part-time drivers. She also recruits and trains volunteers, and coordinates her services with social workers. The manager has little time (and essentially no resources) to devote to routing.

We set out to design a method to help the busy manager quickly generate efficient routes from a volatile list. This method could not rely on a computer, nor even on appreciable clerical effort, for such resources are not within the means of MOW.

THE NEW HEURISTIC

The routing system we implemented is based on a new traveling salesman heuristic [Bartholdi and Platzman 1982] which is

FIGURE 1. The spacefilling curve is an infinitely crinkly version of the pattern below. The heuristic tour visits the points as they appear along the spacefilling curve.

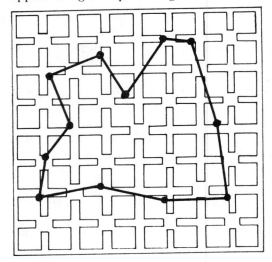

extremely simple and yet provides good tours on the average. The idea behind this algorithm is a "spacefilling curve" (Figure 1), which may be imagined to visit all the points of the unit square. The algorithm has the following structure:

Step 1. For each location (x,y) calculate its relative position, θ, along the spacefilling curve.

Step 2. Sort the locations from the smallest to largest θ.

Thus the points to be visited are sequenced according to the order in which they appear along the spacefilling curve. Details of the calculations as well as a complete study of the heuristic can be found in Bartholdi and Platzman [1982].

We have shown that this heuristic generates tours that are about 25% longer than optimum (on the average, for random point sets). The quality of this solution is competitive with other commonly

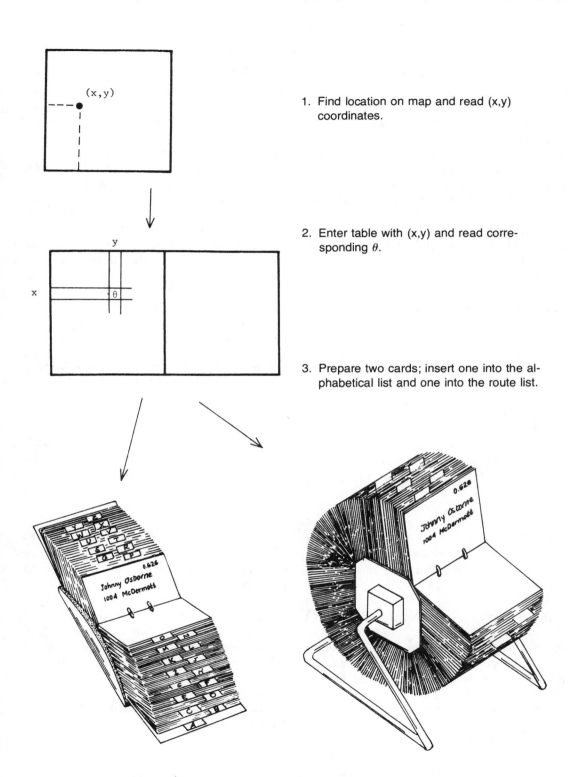

1. Find location on map and read (x,y) coordinates.

2. Enter table with (x,y) and read corresponding θ.

3. Prepare two cards; insert one into the alphabetical list and one into the route list.

FIGURE 2. How to add a client to the system.

considered heuristics and it is an order of magnitude faster. Moreover, several novel features of this new heuristic make it especially attractive. First, it requires minimal data: to route to n locations requires only the $2n$ values of the coordinates (x,y). In fact, the $O(n^2)$ distances between points are never required! Second, points may be easily inserted into or removed from the heuristic tour. There is no need to re-solve the entire problem. In contrast, tours generated by other methods are not so easy to modify. It is the minimal requirements of this algorithm together with the ease of insertion and removal that suit it so well to the MOW routing problem.

THE ROUTING SYSTEM

The routing system we built for MOW consists of a map, a table of θ values, and two Rolodex™ card files.

The map is a standard Department of Transportation street map of Atlanta. It is mounted under a plastic grid so that one can read the (x,y) coordinates for any location.

We pre-computed a table for MOW so that they do not need to calculate θ. It allows one to enter with values for (x,y) and read a corresponding θ value. It fits easily on six sheets of paper.

Each of the two card files contains a complete list of active clients. A card lists a client's name, address, and telephone number, together with miscellaneous notes, such as special handling required for meals, etc. In addition, each card has the client's θ number. Each client is represented by two identical cards, one for each file. The first file is sorted alphabetically by name, and the second is sorted numerically by θ.

The card files permit simple insertion and removal of clients so that the system can easily handle the volatility of the lists. To remove a client, one just looks up his name in the alphabetical list, notes his θ value, and removes the card, then looks up his θ value in the route list and removes that card also. To insert a client, one simply goes to the map and measures the (x,y) coordinates of the client's location, then enters the table with (x,y) and reads the corresponding θ value. Two identical file cards are prepared for the client. One card is inserted into the alphabetical list and the other is inserted into the numerically sequenced list (Figure 2).

The second card file is the implementation of the heuristic. It maintains all client locations in the sequence that a *single* delivery vehicle would follow when obeying our heuristic. We convert this to subroutes for four vehicles by simply partitioning the cards of the card file into four roughly equal sets of contiguous cards (Figure 3). Then each vehicle drives approximately one-fourth of the single vehicle route. The idea of partitioning a single route into subroutes is similar to that of Fredrickson, Hecht, and Kim [1978], who prove nice worst-case bounds for a stricter implementation of the method.

This route-partitioning scheme gives great flexibility to the manager. If a driver or vehicle is unavailable, it is simple to partition the route list into three sets of cards to immediately determine three routes. We expect that this flexibility will be even more important for other MOW programs where the drivers are unpaid volunteers whose number varies daily.

IMPLEMENTATION, OPERATION, AND PERFORMANCE

We had some initial difficulty in implementing the system because the drivers did not want to change their routes. Each

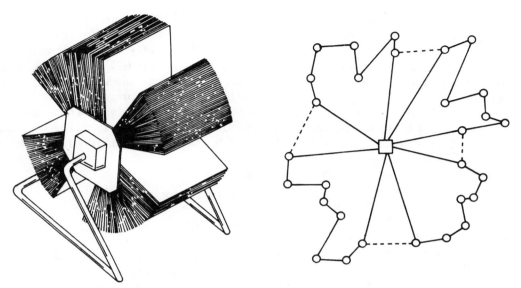

FIGURE 3. The sorted cards give an efficient single-vehicle tour. Partitioning the cards gives efficient subtours for many delivery vehicles.

was familiar with his area of the city and general sequence of locations. Moreover, there was concern that too much change would upset the clients. Most of the clients are old, sick, and isolated, and for them the regular visit of a familiar driver is an important part of their day. However, because of budget reductions in July 1982, MOW had to severely reduce its active list and restructure the routes accordingly. Since major changes had to be made anyway, we implemented our system at that time.

Because the routing algorithm is a heuristic, we expected it to occasionally choose sequences that could easily be improved. Accordingly we advised drivers to consider their sequence a suggestion to which they should make local improvements if possible. In fact no clear improvements were found and we had trouble with drivers erroneously thinking they knew an improvement to the sequence. After that we recommended that the sequence be maintained exactly as determined by the heuristic.

We discovered that partitioning the single route into subroutes caused some concern. The manager naturally wanted "ideal" routes, that is, those that look efficient on a map *and* balance total delivery time among the drivers. She was worried because the routes derived by partitioning tend to have somewhat large travel times to each first or from each last delivery. It seemed more reasonable, she felt, to go to someplace close first. But when we measured the routes, the relatively long initial and final legs of each were generally found to be an insignificant part of total delivery time. This was partly because the heuristic reduced total driving time to only 30-40% of total delivery time for each route. Thus occasional travel time aberrations from imperfectly partitioned routes are unimportant. However, the MOW manager preferred to hunt and make adjustments until she determined an acceptable partition. Since repartitioning is done only occasionally, this seemed satisfactory.

The routing system is generally used as expected, with one exception. In practice, the manager tends to make additions to the active list by "eyeballing" the map, and not by looking up θ immediately. She does this because daily changes are small and she is rushed. Later, when time permits, she looks up the θ values and files them appropriately. But there is a danger of our system degenerating if the θ values are not maintained.

The manager tries to balance the work of the four drivers. Because they are paid by the hour, none wants an unusually short route, and trading routes among the drivers is not acceptable because that would disrupt the driver-client relationship. Fortunately, the partitioning scheme works quite well in this regard. Because travel time is only 30-40% of total delivery time, the total delivery time depends mostly on how many meals are to be delivered. Consequently, partitioning the route file into equal sets of cards tends to produce routes for which the total delivery times (although not travel times) are nearly equal. Table 2 summarizes the routes as of November 1982.

Because the client list changes so quickly, it was not possible to directly compare the driving times and distances of our routes with previous routes. We did, however, submit a previous client list to our heuristic and determined that our routes were about 13% shorter as measured by Euclidean distance.

The most important improvement, however, is the facility with which the system may now incorporate changes in the client list or the number of drivers.

FUTURE WORK

There are other programs similar to MOW in several counties immediately surrounding Atlanta. While their active lists are smaller (typically half that of MOW) they cannot afford paid deliverers. Consequently they are dependent on volunteer drivers, whose number may vary from day to day. We expect a system like ours to help these organizations too. Accordingly, we are preparing a booklet describing how to implement such a system, giving θ tables, and so forth. We hope to make the booklet available to Meals on Wheels organizations throughout the country.

Our method may also be useful to various profitable delivery ventures as well, especially if it is not possible to justify a major investment in computer equipment and appropriately trained personnel. Potential application areas might include package, parts, or newspaper deliveries.

TABLE 2. Summary of the routes as of November 1982.

	Routes			
	1	2	3	4
Meals	48	47	55	45
Locations	25	35	38	36
Approximate miles	23	28	41	37
Approximate total delivery time (hours)	3½	3½	4	4

REFERENCES

Bartholdi, J. J., III and Platzman, L. K. 1982, "An $O(n \log n)$ planar travelling salesman heuristic based on spacefilling curves," *Operations Research Letters*, Vol. 1, No. 4 (September), pp. 121-125.

Frederickson, G. N., Hecht, M. S., and Kim, C. E. 1978, "Approximation algorithms for some routing problems," *SIAM J. Computers*, Vol. 7, No. 2 (May).

Barbara M. Dimorier at Senior Citizen Services of Atlanta writes that, "With this new method, we were able to reduce the number of miles driven and to consolidate five routes into four. Because of the method we now have an easy, inexpensive, and quick way to adjust our drivers' routes as we remove and add new clients."

Improving the Distribution of Industrial Gases with an On-line Computerized Routing and Scheduling Optimizer

Walter J. Bell

Louis M. Dalberto

Marshall L. Fisher

Arnold J. Greenfield

R. Jaikumar

Pradeep Kedia

Robert G. Mack

Paul J. Prutzman

The principal products of the industrial gas industry are oxygen, nitrogen, hydrogen, argon, and carbon monoxide. In the industry's formative years, these were sold as highly compressed gases stored in heavy metal cylinders. Air Products and Chemicals, Inc. (Air Products), a leading supplier of industrial gases, was founded by the late Leonard P. Pool in 1940, on the strength of a simple, but then revolutionary idea: the "on-site" production of industrial gases, primarily oxygen. Air Products built oxygen generating facilities adjacent to large volume users so that oxygen could be piped directly from the generator to the point of use. This reduced distribution costs and was a technical and economical success. It launched a history of rapid growth at Air Products based upon high technology innovations in distribution.

During the 1950s, Air Products acquired several independent regional gas distributors, and a marketing concept known as "piggybacking" was introduced in which extra gas liquefaction capacity was added to the "on-site" plants. This enabled Air Products to serve its "on-site" tonnage base-load gas customers, such as steelmakers, while serving additional smaller customers in the surrounding area by distributing the liquefied gas in insulated tank trucks.

During the past 20 years, Air Products has been instrumental in developing new applications for industrial gases. These include oxygen in cupolas; oxygen for copper smelting; inert atmospheres for heat treating; liquid nitrogen for the quick freezing of meats and other food products; and liquid nitrogen for grinding various materials and recovering scrap metals from them.

Today, Air Products is one of the world's largest industrial gas producers supplying world-wide a broad range of industrial gases and related production and distribution equipment. Air Products also produces industrial and specialty chemicals and provides engineering, construction, and maintenance services.

Air Products has grown from a company with sales of $8,300 in 1940 to an international corporation with sales exceeding $1.5 billion in 1982, 18,900 employees, and facilities in 13 countries.

A spirit of innovative progress has flourished in the distribution function of the Industrial Gas Division. Headed by Vice President of Operations Stan Roman and Manager of Distribution Byron Trammell, the department has been a leader in developing computer applications that improve productivity and enhance management reporting for private fleet transportation. Examples include regular identification of chronically underutilized cylinder delivery trucks and routes, exception reports to identify trips not meeting established goals, a matrix of fuel mileage by driver and tractor, and an integrated product line vehicle activity and accounting system. Programs in driver safety and energy efficiency have been recognized by a presidential award for energy efficiency and the American Trucking Association's president's award for safety programs. The latter award is especially significant because it is the only one ever awarded to a private carrier.

By the 1970s, the plants, trucks and other equipment used by Air Products for the manufacture and distribution of liquid gases were highly engineered and automated. This was in sharp contrast to the completely manual system for scheduling the delivery of these liquid gases. It was clear that a further competitive edge in the industry would depend on automation of delivery scheduling. This goal was first officially recognized in the company's strategic plan written in 1975. Fuller appreciation of the importance of this goal requires a detailed understanding of the economics of industrial gas distribution.

ECONOMICS OF INDUSTRIAL GAS DISTRIBUTION

Liquid oxygen and nitrogen are manufactured in highly automated plants by repetitive compression and expansion of air to lower its temperature. At specific temperatures, the cooled gases liquefy and are removed via a distillation column. The plants also serve as supply depots where liquefied gases are stored in large tanks at temperatures less than $-320°F$. The liquefied gases are distributed in cryogenic bulk tankers to industrial users and hospitals. Storage tanks at customer sites are provided under long-term contracts by the supplier, who monitors the inventory in the tank and delivers product as needed. Air Products currently operates 23 plant/depots throughout the United States supplying about 3,500 customers. The depots operate independently and serve their own designated set of customers. Customers are assigned to depots by a linear programming model which minimizes total system production and distribution costs. Liquid oxygen and nitrogen customer deliveries are made by a fleet of about 340 trucks that travels over 22 million miles a year. The trucks assigned to each depot are controlled by a single scheduler, aided by coordinators.

Because the cost of manufacture is fairly uniform across different suppliers, competition in the industry is based on service, technical marketing, pricing and lower costs obtained through more efficient distribution. The degree of freedom available to distribution management at

Air Products is greater than in any other industry. They decide when to supply a customer based on the inventory level in the customer tank, how much to deliver, how to combine the different loads on a truck and how to route the truck. Thus inventory management at customer locations is integrated with vehicle scheduling and dispatching.

The ability to control inventory makes this fleet scheduling problem different from the traditional and much studied vehicle routing problem. In the traditional problem, customer demands are fixed and must be served by a fleet of trucks within a fixed period of time, frequently a day. Usually, customer orders cannot be split between two or more trucks. The goal in the traditional problem, to minimize the distance traveled in making the required deliveries, is usually accomplished by serving customers that are near to each other with the same truck.

To see how the inventory dimension changes the nature of the problem, consider the simple example illustrated in Figure 1. There are four customers, each with a specified tank capacity and daily usage. The numbers on lines joining customers specify mileages. Suppose we have a single truck that can transport 5,000 gallons per trip and can make up to two trips per day. Currently, all customer tanks are full. How should we schedule our truck to accomplish required deliveries while traveling minimum miles? The most obvious schedule in this example would have two trips a day. One trip would deliver 1,000 gallons to customer 1 and 3,000 gallons to customer 2. The other trip would deliver 2,000 gallons to customer 3 and 1,500 gallons to customer 4. The total distance traveled each day under this schedule is 420 miles. Although this schedule looks reasonable, it is possible to do better. On

FIGURE 1. A simple example of the bulk delivery problem.

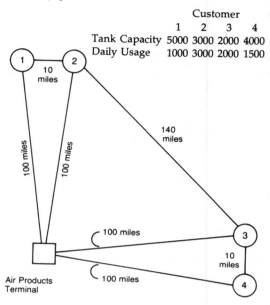

	Customer			
	1	2	3	4
Tank Capacity	5000	3000	2000	4000
Daily Usage	1000	3000	2000	1500

day one, we drive a single trip to customers 2 and 3 delivering 3,000 and 2,000 gallons respectively. On day two, we drive two trips. The first trip delivers 2,000 gallons to customer 1 and 3,000 gallons to customer 2. The second trip delivers 2,000 gallons to customer 3 and 3,000 gallons to customer 4. On successive days, the schedule repeats, using the day one schedule on odd days and the day two schedule on even days. The total mileage for two days is 760 miles, or a daily average of 380 miles. This is nearly 10% less than the daily average of 420 miles in the more obvious schedule.

In this simple example, a scheduler would have little difficulty in finding the superior solution by simply enumerating the various possibilities. In reality, things are not so simple. Typical problems involve several hundred customers and about 20 trucks, so that the scheduler must make simplifying assumptions. The most natural assumption is to focus on the spatial dimension of the problem and place customers who are near each other on the same trip. The possibility of driving 140 miles from customer 2 to customer 3 when there is a customer 10 miles away is unlikely to be considered by a scheduler who has limited time to make a large number of decisions.

In addition to the large number of customers and trucks, several other factors complicate the real situation. To start with, just getting the data that is presented in Figure 1 is a challenging task. Before the development of a computer system, mileages between customers were known only approximately from a plot of the customer locations on a map. Usage rates are difficult to estimate and vary considerably over time as a function of the customer's operation. Because of the uncertainty in customer demand, it is not possible to let customer inventory drop to 0 as we've assumed in the example. Rather, inventory must be maintained above a specified safety-stock level. Customers are not open for delivery on every day of the week or during every hour of the day and trucks must make their deliveries within certain prescribed time windows which can vary among customers. The trucks in the fleet differ in characteristics such as capacity and operating costs. Moreover, the capacity of a truck is imposed by state laws specifying the maximum loaded truck weight. These legal weight limits differ from state to state, so the capacity of the truck actually changes when it crosses a state boundary. Finally, some trucks are incapable of serving certain customers because they are too big, require an external power source for an electric pump, and so forth. The availability of trucks, drivers and product is limited. At any particular time, any of these factors can constrain the set of feasible scheduling options.

The costs that must be considered in scheduling include driver pay, tolls, and vehicle-related costs such as depreciation, fuel, and maintenance. In addition to costs that are directly related to mileage, there are costs that do not vary directly with mileage but depend upon the time spent by drivers loading the truck at the terminal, unloading at customer sites and performing various set-up functions. The rules governing driver pay are complicated and vary considerably. For example, depending on the nature of the trip, a driver may be paid by the hour or by the mile.

Prior to the development of the system described here, the complicated scheduling function was performed completely manually by a staff of dedicated and capable individuals at the depots. The concept of using a computer to assist these schedulers was appealing. At the same time, it was clear that any computerized vehicle scheduling system had to be carefully designed to consider all of the important complexities of the problem, to insure the availability of relevant data, and to complement, rather than replace, the efforts of the existing schedulers.

THE VEHICLE SCHEDULING SYSTEM

The increasing attention that was given by Air Products to the possibility of a computerized vehicle scheduling system culminated in January 1980 with the formation of a team (the authors) charged with developing a computerized vehicle scheduling system. This team has since been involved in the design, development and implementation of the vehicle scheduling system described in this section. The system first went live at the Wharton, New

Jersey, depot in October 1981. Subsequently, depots have been added to the system at a steady rate until currently 11 depots are using the system.

The vehicle scheduling system is depicted in Figure 2. The program modules and data of the system reside on an AMDAHL 470/V8 at Air Products corporate headquarters in Allentown, Pennsylvania. The system is accessed by schedulers at the plants via CRTs linked to the AMDAHL by dedicated telephone lines. The scheduling module is used daily at each depot to produce a detailed schedule for a two- to five-day horizon, with the first day's schedule being the most important one. Delivery data and customer requirements are updated interactively as they are received. The schedule is also changed interactively as required.

Six data files are used by the system. The customer file contains a description of each customer served by Air Products, including the capacity of all tanks, safety

FIGURE 2.   The vehicle scheduling system.

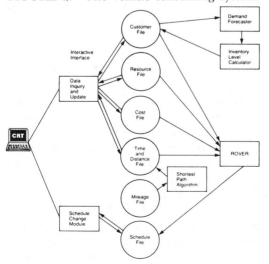

stock levels, and historical product usage. The demand forecaster uses the historical demand data with a time series model to obtain a forecast of demand for each customer. This forecast is used by the inventory level calculator to project the inventory level in each customer tank at any point in time.

The resource file contains a description of each truck in the system, giving its capacity by state and a list of customers that can be feasibly served by the truck. Also included in the resource file is the availability of liquid nitrogen, liquid oxygen, and delivery drivers by day for at least five days into the future.

The cost file includes all relevant costs, including a per-mile rate for vehicle fuel and maintenance, and extensive data describing driver pay regulations.

The mileage file is a network representation of the road system of the United States. A shortest route algorithm [Glover and Klingman 1977] is used with this file to obtain the distance, travel time and toll cost between any pair of customers. This data is stored in the time and distance file.

All of this data can be accessed and updated in real-time by the scheduler using the various programs in the data inquiry and update module.

All data is used by the scheduling module which is called ROVER, for Realtime Optimizer for Vehicle Routing. ROVER produces a list of trips to be performed over the next two to five days. The data given for each trip includes the start time, the scheduled vehicle, the amount of product to be delivered to each customer, the time at which delivery to each customer will be completed, the length of the trip and the cost of the trip. The schedule change module allows the scheduler to examine the ROVER output and make changes as necessary due to contingencies.

ROVER obtains a schedule by solving a very large (up to 800,000 variables and 200,000 constraints) mixed integer program to proven near optimality using a Lagrangian relaxation algorithm developed for this project and reported in Fisher et al. [1982]. The mixed integer programs solved by ROVER, with hundreds of thousands of variables and constraints, are apparently the largest integer programs ever solved to near optimality on a routine basis. The Lagrangian relaxation algorithm developed as part of this project extends the theory of optimization.

The distances between customers are obtained from a detailed network model of the US highway system. This network contains information on 65,000 road segments (links) and 40,000 road intersections (nodes). The length, travel time and any toll charges are stored for each link. A state-of-the-art shortest route algorithm [Glover and Klingman 1977] is used to obtain the shortest path between each pair of customers.

An on-line network is used to link the scheduler at each depot to the vehicle scheduling system at corporate headquarters. This network allows the functions of the system to be performed on-line in real time. This is particularly important since some decisions, such as the appropriate response to an emergency order, are required quickly. A user-friendly interface allows the scheduler to query and update data, execute the ROVER scheduling module, and change the schedule as desired. The decision support system assists, rather than replaces, the scheduler.

DEMAND FORECASTING AND INVENTORY LEVEL CALCULATOR

Deciding when to deliver to customers and how much to deliver requires a forecast of the rate at which each customer is consuming product and a calculation of the latest possible time the customer needs a delivery. The forecasting method used is exponential smoothing. Ten values of the smoothing constant are evaluated each time a new forecast is computed and the value that minimizes the absolute error for the most recent five usage rate forecasts is chosen. The most recent 15 customer inventory levels with corresponding dates and times are stored in the on-line customer file and used to make this point estimate of customer usage.

This process is complicated because usually the only known customer inventory levels are those recorded before and after each delivery. Since the time between deliveries is chosen by the scheduling module on a dynamic basis, the interval between deliveries is generally not uniform (as it is in all other time series forecasting problems of which we are aware). Because of this nonuniformity we must determine the hours of day that a customer is operating and using product and consider this operating pattern in determining usage rates. For example, if a customer does not operate on weekends and a five-day interval between deliveries includes a weekend, the usage per operating day would be one-third of the total usage for the five-day period. In the system, we identify for each eight-hour shift of each day the level of operations at each customer.

Because the forecasted usage rates are subject to forecast error, safety stocks are established at each customer to protect against stockouts. Customers with a high level of variability are often telephoned, as well, to establish their exact inventory level prior to the time at which they have been projected to need the product.

Using forecasted usage rates, the estimated inventory level at 8:00 am is calculated for all customers daily. We also project when safety and empty levels will be reached. Forecasts and level calculations are then available on-line for inquiry. A daily forecast results report shows on the horizontal time-axis the most recent seven days' history of deliveries and projections of the latest time in the future at which a customer must receive a delivery. The format is similar to that used by the manual system, which helped the schedulers to make the transition from manual to computer operations. On the report, the forecast error for each customer is shown and provides the basis for manual changes.

In addition to receiving the daily batch calculation of the inventory levels, the scheduler can interactively inquire when a customer will reach a specified level or what level is forecasted for a specified time.

TIME AND DISTANCE DATA

The travel time and distance between combinations of customers and between each customer and the depot is an important input to the scheduling module. The common approach of computing straight line distances from coordinates of latitude and longitude and then adjusting by some factor to approximate road miles was judged to be too inaccurate for our application, especially in metropolitan areas, and it provides no information about travel times. At a large depot with 300 customers there are about 45,000 different intercustomer travel times and distances. To achieve the necessary level of detail for distances and travel speeds in a practical manner, a vendor was contracted to develop to our specifications a comprehensive computerized data base of the net-

work of highways in the United States. This data base contains about 65,000 road segments (links) and about 40,000 intersections of road segments (nodes). The roads specified for inclusion in the data base were all the interstate and federal highways, most state highways, and selected county, local, and city roads. For each road segment, the length of the segment and the toll cost is specified. Instead of a travel speed for each segment, five major characteristics are specified which are then used to compute travel speed: road type (limited access, divided, undivided, city street), number of lanes, urbanization (as a proxy for traffic density), terrain, and road ownership (interstate, federal primary, state, and so forth).

Each possible intercustomer distance and travel time is then determined by finding the "shortest" path between pairs of customers through the highway network. The criterion used to determine the "shortest" path is not solely distance, but is a travel-cost value found from a combination of travel time, distance, and tolls. The time-related component of travel cost reflects the case when drivers are paid an hourly rate while the distance component primarily reflects vehicle costs such as fuel, maintenance, and tractor depreciation. The shortest route algorithm itself is an efficient dynamic programming algorithm developed by Glover and Klingman [1977].

REAL-TIME OPTIMIZER FOR VEHICLE ROUTING (ROVER)

ROVER uses all the data described above on customer usage rates, costs, distances, travel times and availability of drivers, product, and trucks to produce a schedule for the next two to five days.

ROVER is based on a large mixed-integer-programming formulation of the problem of making deliveries efficiently subject to resource constraints. To formulate the bulk-delivery problem as a mixed-integer problem, we first generate a set of possible vehicle routes, where a route is a set of customers to be delivered on one trip that begins and ends at the depot. The order of customer stops on the route is specified, but not the delivery amounts or the start time of the route. The model is formulated to optimally select from this menu of possible routes a subset to actually be driven, specifying the time each route should start, the vehicle to be used, and the amount to be delivered to each customer on the route.

The major advantage of the route generation approach is that essentially any route constraints and cost function can be accommodated. An obvious limitation is the potentially large number of possible routes. This is not a difficulty here because the number of customers on a route is small, on average about two and rarely more than four. This means that the number of technically feasible routes is not unreasonably large. Further, many routes can be discarded as uninteresting because they have a high cost or because their combined demand requirements differ greatly from truck capacity.

A program was written to generate the set of possible routes to be included in the mixed-integer-programming model. Not all technically-feasible routes are generated, and the program uses some complicated heuristics to decide whether or not to include a particular route. For example, a route would be excluded if the amount of product that could be delivered to the customers on the route was significantly less or significantly more than a truckload. We would exclude a route to two cus-

tomers each of whom could take a full truckload of product on the assumption that a single stop trip to each of these customers would be more efficient. Once a route has been generated, the least-cost sequence in which to visit the customers on the route is determined by complete enumeration.

The mixed-integer-programming formulation contains two kinds of variables. A set of 0-1 variables is used to select routes. A particular 0-1 variable equals one if a designated route is selected to be driven by a particular vehicle at a fixed starting time. The two- to five-day horizon of the model is divided into one hour intervals and a separate 0-1 variable is defined for each route and vehicle for each possible starting hour. The other variables in the model are continuous variables that specify the amounts of product delivered to each customer on a route.

For each customer a value per unit of product delivered by the end of the planning horizon has been defined. The object of the model is to maximize the value of the product delivered less the costs incurred in making these deliveries. The costs considered by the model include driver pay, vehicle depreciation, fuel, and specify the amount of product to be delivered to each customer on a particular route-vehicle-starting time combination.

The constraints of the model consist of customer-demand constraints and resource constraints imposed by the availability of trucks, drivers, and product. The customer demand constraints impose lower and upper limits on the amount of product that must be delivered by any point in time to each customer, limit the time at which a customer is open for delivery, and define the set of vehicles that can feasibly serve a customer. The resource constraints in the model impose vehicle capacity, the times at which each vehicle is available, the availability of driver time, and the availability of the two products scheduled by the model, liquid oxygen and liquid nitrogen.

The size of the problems that are run daily varies from depot to depot. The number of trucks ranges from about 10 to 30, and the number of customers from 150 to 400.

The dimensions of the mixed-integer-programming formulation are enormous. The number of 0-1 variables has ranged from about 100,000 to 200,000; the number of continuous variables from about 300,000 to 600,000; and the number of constraints from about 100,000 to 200,000. Clearly, problems of this magnitude are far beyond the current state-of-the-art in mixed-integer programming. Fortunately, large problems such as this are usually endowed with a sparse coefficient matrix and special structure that can be exploited in their solution. We were able to apply Lagrangian relaxation to decompose the problem into a set of knapsack problems—one for each vehicle. An algorithm based on this Lagrangian relaxation has obtained feasible solutions that are proven to be within one-half to two percent of optimality in a modest amount of computing time. By working with a relaxed version of the problem one avoids setting up the 800,000 variable mixed-integer program alluded to previously. That monster problem is solved implicitly, not explicity. A statement of the integer-programming model algorithm is provided in the Appendix. Further technical details are available in Fisher et al. [1982]. A technical spin-off of this work is reported in Fisher et al. [1983].

Our Lagrangian algorithm appears to have expanded the size problems that are solveable to near optimality on a routine

basis. Our computational experience is illustrated by a recent typical run. The problem had 15 vehicles, 54 customers, and 120 time periods (five days). The route generator produced a menu of 377 possible routes. If all combinations of routes, trucks and starting times were feasible, the number of 0-1 variables would be 377 x 120 x 15 = 678,600. However, because constraints on when a customer can receive a delivery and from which trucks exclude many combinations of routes, trucks, and starting times, the number of 0-1 variables was 164,196. The number of continuous variables was 380,481. The model contained 166,166 constraints.

The AMDAHL 470/V8 required 2 minutes 51.83 seconds of CPU time to execute the input of data, the generation of routes, and the Lagrangian relaxation algorithm described [Fisher et al. 1982, Section 2.4]. This produced a feasible solution with a total cost of $9,064.67. Solution of the Lagrangian relaxation also produced a bound on the optimal solution that exceeded the feasible value by $46.80 or .5 percent of total cost. The daily runs of the system usually require 20 seconds to 3 minutes of computer time and produce feasible solutions that differ from the upper bound by .5—2 percent of total costs.

INTERACTIVE INTERFACE

The schedule developed by ROVER is used in an operating environment where reaction to contingencies is a daily way of life. These contingencies include changes in a customer's requirement (either drastic change in usage or a request for a specific delivery) and changes in the delivery resources available (such as trucks, drivers, and product available for delivery). The schedule change module provides the capability to change schedules interactively in response to contingencies. In addition, most schedulers have developed a great deal of expertise at creating opportunities for productivity improvement. For example, depot personnel often anticipate orders and will call customers who otherwise would not permit delivery to arrange early delivery.

The features included in the schedule change module enable the scheduler to add or delete a trip, add or delete a customer on a trip, change the trip start-time, change the vehicle assigned to the trip, and find a customer to add to a trip in progress. With the exception of finding a customer to add to a trip in progress, the scheduler specifies the basic elements of the change and the schedule change module then performs feasibility checks on customer/vehicle compatibility, customer delivery time restrictions, vehicle availability, product availability, and driver availability; determines the sequence of stops; and computes the quantity to be delivered to each customer. Both components of the scheduling module (ROVER) objective function, the cost of the trip and the value of the trip, are calculated and shown to the scheduler together with any feasibility violations. Based on this information, the scheduler can either accept the change or continue with additional changes. The scheduler also has the option of specifying the sequence of stops and the quantities to be delivered. Finding a customer to add to a trip in progress is used when there is product remaining in the truck after the final scheduled stop has been made.

Because the schedule change process requires extensive interaction between the scheduler and the computer system, we have emphasized ease of use and "friend-liness" in the schedule change module to maximize the scheduler's effectiveness. Similarly, in all other on-line functions, especially the frequent entry of delivery data, very special attention has been given to ease of use.

IMPLEMENTATION

Development work on the vehicle scheduling system began in January 1980 and culminated in October 1981 when the first implementation site, Wharton, New Jersey, began to use the system to produce operational schedules. During the 1980-81 development period the project team created and tested the modules and data bases described in the previous section. Components of the system were tested on historical data from the Wharton, New Jersey and Delaware City, Delaware depots.

The Wharton depot was chosen as the first installation site because it was close to corporate headquarters and had a large, diverse customer population that would thoroughly exercise all features of the system. Since the Wharton installation, eleven additional depots have gone live on the vehicle scheduling system. One of these depots (Delaware City) was closed in May 1983 and all oxygen and nitrogen operations discontinued. The location and dates of the implemented depots are listed in Table 1.

It is highly likely that five depots will be added during the fiscal year ending in September 1984. The remaining seven depots are very small and it is not clear at this point if the economic benefits of vehicle scheduling will justify the cost of dedicated phone lines and hardware at the depots. This picture could change as hardware costs decrease and additional applica-

TABLE 1. The depots at which the computerized vehicle scheduling system has been implemented, their dates of implementation, and the number of months they have been in operation.

Site	Implementation Date	Number of Months Operational as of October 31, 1983
Wharton, NJ	October 1981	25
Glenmont, NY	January 1982	22
Delaware City, DE	May 1982	12
LaSalle, IL	August 1982	15
Granite City, IL	September 1982	14
North Baltimore, OH	October 1982	13
Conyers, GA	November 1982	12
Pryor, OK	February 1983	9
LaPorte, TX	April 1983	6
Dallas, TX	April 1983	6
El Segundo, CA	May 1983	5
Lancaster, PA	July 1983	3
		142

tions are added to the on-line network.

The combined use of the vehicle scheduling system by the 12 depots represents a significantly long history of 142 months. Since the system is run at least once every weekday at each implemented depot, the ROVER optimization module and other programs of vehicle scheduling system have now been executed on operational data more than 3,000 times.

On the day when vehicle scheduling went live at Wharton, New Jersey in October 1981, the authors of this paper breathed a collective sigh of relief. Together with supporting personnel, we had invested 24 man years over a two-year period in developing the vehicle scheduling system. However, our relief was temporary when we realized that the hardest part of the project lay ahead of us— making it work!

The process of "making it work" actu-

ally began before the Wharton implementation and continues even today. We can now understand this process; it consists of the following activities:

— Introducing inexperienced computer users to state-of-the-art technology,
— Identifying and solving unforeseen problems, and
— Integrating the system into existing depot activities.

The schedulers who would be using the system were unfamiliar with computers and the discipline and precision required by the management science approach. To facilitate the implementation under such conditions, depot-personnel training was conducted in a phased approach which allowed schedulers the opportunity to become comfortable with the system as each functional area was added. The psychological impact of computerization on individuals was a major consideration in our training approach. We considered the trainees' feelings and took them into account in our decisions, managing them carefully so that the implementation program would continue at a steady rate. Major emphasis was placed on developing users' confidence in the computer system, a key to their acceptance of the changes that accompany computerization. It was important to stress that the computer would not "threaten" jobs but rather "enhance" them.

One unforeseen problem resulted from the fact that the integer-programming model of the delivery problem required "hard" constraint limits. By contrast, a human scheduler knows that many of the constraints in the problem are somewhat "soft" and makes judicious adjustments where necessary to improve the quality of the schedule. To illustrate, in one early run of the ROVER model, there were three adjacent customers that each required about one-third of a truckload of product by 12 noon of the first day of the schedule horizon. The obvious decision was to send a single truck to satisfy the three customers' requirements. However, if such a trip were started at the beginning of the scheduling horizon, delivery would be completed at the first customer by 12 noon, at the second by 12:30 pm and at the third by 1:00 pm. Because this violates the constraints of the model, the trip was not scheduled. Instead, a separate truck was sent to each of the customers, much to the amusement of the scheduler, who pointed out in rather direct language that delaying delivery by one hour to customers receiving deliveries about once a week is no big deal.

What's at issue here is possibly the most fundamental problem in applying integer-programming models. Because of integrality restrictions, small changes in constraint limits can cause large changes in the optimal value. Because the data in most models can be changed slightly at little cost, these models can give misleading results. To overcome this difficulty, we determined from the nature of our problem those constraints to which the model was highly sensitive and set their limits to relatively loose values. For example, the problem above was found to occur only for customers that were a considerable distance from the depot and required delivery relatively early in the scheduling horizon. For these few customers, the delivery time-limit was relaxed slightly.

The project team carefully designed the man-machine interfaces so that the vehicle scheduling system would fit into the daily work flow of existing depot activities. Changes were made to screen-formats and on-line dialogues as we observed bottlenecks, problems, and opportunities for enhancements. One key improvement that became the cornerstone of the implementation process was revamping the daily forecast results report. As initially designed, the report was oriented towards a strict inventory control perspective and was not compatible with the way the scheduler evaluated customer demand patterns. This initial report did not lend itself to replacing manual customer records, and as a result both a manual and automated forecasting system were maintained. A new report was designed which replicated the manual customer records and added other enhancements.

During the implementation phase, the model's solution was critically evaluated in parallel with the manual scheduling process. Schedulers had to accept or revise the model's daily solutions. Each scheduler had certain routes that he was accustomed to using out of habit, even though other more efficient routes existed. It was often troubling to schedulers when ROVER produced routes that differed greatly from those they were used to. At this point we had the choice of "winning the battle" by forcing the scheduler to use the routes produced by the system or "winning the war" by allowing the scheduler to exercise control over the system and thereby gain confidence in it.

We opted for the latter course and were able to employ a technical feature of the system that had not been intended for this purpose. Each customer had a specified "neighborhood" of other customers that could be combined with that customer on the same route. Neighborhoods were originally introduced to reduce the amount of data that needed to be stored and were set up to contain about 50 customers. We now found that by carefully reducing the neighborhoods, we could limit the system to producing routes similar to those the scheduler was used to seeing. This proved invaluable in making schedulers feel comfortable with the system. Once they felt "in control" of the system, most schedulers began to ask that the neighborhoods be expanded in size to allow more options.

IMPACT

In 1979 when this project was undertaken, the economic environment was severe. The nation was entering a recession and double digit inflation was having a serious effect on Air Products' distribution expenses. The industrial gas industry was in an overcapacity position that was further squeezing already tight profit margins. Although there was a good manual scheduling system in place, Air Products' management saw room for improvement,

and people throughout the organization were capable and willing to accept change. Within this background, the management committee of Air Products approved this high technology, high risk project. Senior management decided to undertake this project as a demonstration and a use of high technology computer methods "to enter the 21st century on the run." The impact of the project has completely confirmed the wisdom of their decision.

The most direct tangible benefit has been a reduction in delivery expenses resulting from the increased productivity of the drivers and vehicles. The methodology we employed to measure this reduction is reasonably straightforward. Since delivery costs correlate strongly with miles driven, the miles driven per gallon of product delivered were monitored continuously before and after implementation of the vehicle scheduling system. In interpreting changes in the miles driven per gallon of product delivered, care was taken to control for the fact that customer usage rates change over time. For example, if the usage rate decreased significantly for several customers that were relatively far from a depot, this would cause a reduction in the miles traveled per gallon delivered, even if there were no improvement in scheduling efficiency. To control for this effect, we also computed on a continual basis a "weighted delivery radius." The weighted delivery radius for a period equalled the amount delivered to each tank times the distance of that tank from the depot summed over all tanks and divided by the amount delivered.

The effect of the vehicle scheduling system can be evaluated by measuring over time the miles per gallon delivered relative to the weighted delivery radius. The weighted delivery radius for a terminal is computed by multiplying each customer's usage rate times his distance from the terminal, summing over all customers and dividing by total customer usage. Generally, the savings increased over time as the schedulers became familiar with using the system. In the case of liquid nitrogen deliveries at Wharton, the average miles per gallon delivered has decreased by 9.1 percent since introduction of the vehicle scheduling system. To this must be added the impact of the weighted delivery radius which has increased by 1.3 percent, yielding a total mileage savings of 10.4 percent. The average savings for a system of 16 depots is estimated at 6 percent to 7½ percent or $1.54 million to $1.72 million annually. Obviously, the dollar value of annual savings will increase as Air Products business continues to grow or if the inflation in the cost of transportation persists.

Another benefit derived from increased tanker productivity is a reduction in future requirements to purchase additional tankers to meet growing business needs. In the future, savings from avoiding capital expenditure should reach $445,000 annually, representing a reduction in capital spending of $3.1 million.

A third area for savings lies in greater utilization of the existing telephone line and computer network. Once the network exists, new applications can be added at a small incremental cost. One such application under development would replace the present practice of mailing completed shipment receipts to regional teleprocessing centers who subsequently transmit them electronically to the billing system at corporate headquarters. Instead, completed shipment receipts would be directly transmitted and result in a net present value cash flow exceeding $100,000 over several years.

The major intangible benefit is that the complex and powerful decision support system is used continuously each day by depot personnel. The interactive schedule change module and the extensive data base at the customer-tank-level of detail offer schedulers the opportunity to be more comprehensive in evaluating and selecting trips. The ready availability of the cost of alternative pairings is particularly valuable and is a crucial element of the system.

Using the vehicle scheduling system has reduced the clerical effort in scheduling, and thereby increased the time available for planning. The scheduling module (ROVER) also serves as a catalyst in training others to do scheduling, thereby reducing the reliance upon a single individual.

The availability of the time/distance data base and associated road network offers the potential to more effectively determine what roads vehicles will take. The continually shifting schedule means there are few "standard" routes. Initial efforts in this area showed that there are tradeoffs; the shortest route is not necessarily the best route. Work is underway at two depots to better define the criteria for selecting routes, with the ultimate objective of creating a comprehensive cross-reference of distances and routes between delivery locations.

A number of further benefits are expected in the future. We are continuing to refine and enhance the system, and the schedulers are becoming more familiar with its use. Both tend to further reduce costs. In the future, consideration will be given to extending the system to other industrial gas product lines. We also believe this methodology is applicable outside the industrial gas industry for scheduling delivery of such products as petroleum, liquid propane, and home heating oil, or for scheduling of raw materials and products internally within a company.

Currently the safety-stock inventory level in each customer tank is determined manually by the scheduler. This process could be improved by considering in a more rigorous fashion variability in usage and distance from the depot. Using the vehicle scheduling system to determine the optimal tank size for new and existing customers is also being considered. The vehicle scheduling system would provide very accurate distribution-cost information which could then be combined with other financial considerations, including tank investment and installation cost, to determine the optimal tank size.

A final benefit of this project is the experience we gained in developing this large-scale operational decision support system in an inter-disciplinary environment. The internal project development team included individuals from the management science, business systems, and user communities, acting in consort with outside consultants. The development process was a powerful catalyst cementing the relationship between the various management information and end-user functional areas. This relationship makes it markedly easier to develop other similar projects. The lessons we all learned from this experience offer valuable insights into ways to better manage a developmental project of this magnitude and scope.

The project has received widespread support and interest among top management of the company. At a recent financial conference with securities analysts sponsored by Air Products, A. P. Dyer, Air Products Group Vice President—Gases Groups, briefly described the vehicle scheduling system: "I've simplified an extremely complex process which is designed to significantly reduce distribution costs. Thus far we have implemented the program in eight of our terminals. The savings in the first year of implementation including the usual start-up problems have been about 7 percent per terminal. We are highly optimistic for the future of this program. I might mention that other companies involved in similar bulk distribution have exhibited keen interest in the program" [1982].

ACKNOWLEDGEMENTS

We would like to give special acknowledgement to Stan Roman, Vice President of Air Products Industrial Gas Division Operations, and Byron Trammell, Manager of Air Products Industrial Gas Division Distribution, for their continuing support of this project. Significant contributions to the design, development, and implementation of the system were made by the other members of the Air Products project team: Ken Bailey, Paul Fehr, Dennis Houser, Charlie Lewis, Pete Peluso, Al Russell, and Tracey Smith. We would also like to acknowledge Roger Bast, Manager of Management Sciences at Air Products, for his contributions to this project. Special thanks are due the personnel at the initial system implementation sites in the Eastern Region for their help in making the system work. We would also like to thank Peter Kolesar and Janet Showers for their review and comments on this manuscript.

Marshall Fisher's work was supported in part by ONR contract N00014-78-C-0307 P0007.

REFERENCES

Fisher, M. L.; Greenfield, A. J.; Jaikumar, R.; and Kedia, P. 1982, "Real-time scheduling of a bulk delivery fleet: Practical application of Lagrangian relaxation," University of Pennsylvania, Decision Sciences Working Paper, October 1982.

Fisher, M. L.; Jaikumar, R.; Kedia, P.; and Solomon, M. 1983, "A Lagrangian relaxation approach to solving large set partitioning-packing problems with side constraints," talk at the Chicago ORSA/TIMS Meeting, April 1983.

Fisher, M. L. forthcoming, "A practitioner's guide to Lagrangian relaxation," *Interfaces.*

Glover, F., and Klingman, D. 1977, "Network applications in industry and government," *AIIE Transactions,* Vol. 9, No. 4 (December), pp. 363-376.

"Managing Growth—Planning Profitable Change" 1982, A compilation of the presentations to representatives of the financial community at Air Products Corporate Headquarters during the week of December 6, 1982, Air Products & Chemicals, Allentown, Pennsylvania.

APPENDIX: MIXED-INTEGER-PROGRAMMING FORMULATION AND ALGORITHM SUMMARY

This appendix is extracted from Fisher et al. [1982], which contains a more extensive discussion of the technical aspects of our algorithm. The following definitions are used in our formulation.

Indices

k = possible route index

v = vehicle index

i = customer index

t = time index

T = length of the planning horizon.

The index t ranges from 0 to T.

Customer Data

D_{it} = upper limit on the amount that can be delivered to customer i during the interval from 0 to t

d_{it} = lower limit on the amount that must be delivered to customer i during the interval from 0 to t

vd_i = per unit value of deliveries to customer i

VEH_i = set of vehicles that can feasibly service customer i. A vehicle could be infeasible for a customer because, for example, it was too large to fit at the unloading dock or because it required an external power source for unloading that was unavailable at the customer site.

A_1 = set of customers that can receive any number of deliveries

A_2 = set of customers that must receive exactly one delivery

A_3 = set of customers that can receive at most one delivery

($A_1 \cup A_2 \cup A_3$ is the set of all customers)

$TIME_i$ = set of times at which a delivery at customer i can be completed. This set is defined because many customers are not open 24 hours a day and are constrained as to when they can receive deliveries. Also, by definition of d_{it} and A_2, delivery to a customer $i \in A_2$ is infeasible at any time greater than t if $d_{it} > 0$.

Vehicle Data

CAP_v = capacity of vehicle v

c_v = per unit unloading cost for vehicle v

Possible Routes Data

S_k = set of customers on route k in delivery order

R_i = set of routes on which customer i appears

= $\{k \mid i \in S_k\}$

TL_k = time that a vehicle is occupied in driving route k (assumed integral)

tc_{ik} = time after the start of route k until delivery to customer i is completed (assumed integral)

T_k = times at which route k can start

= $\{t \mid t \in \{0, 1, \ldots, T\}, t + tc_{ik} \in$

$TIME_i$ for all $i \in S_k\}$

V_k = vehicles that can drive route k

= $\bigcup_{i \in S_k} VEH_i$

K_v = routes that vehicle v can drive

= $\{k \mid v \in V_k\}$

FC_{kv} = fixed cost for vehicle v driving route k. FC_{kv} includes all costs that are independent of the amount delivered to each customer on route k. In the application considered here, FC_{kv} is determined from the mileage of route k, driver pay regulations, fuel costs and vehicle depreciation per mile.

Variables

y_{ktv} = 1, if route k starts at time t on vehicle v, 0, otherwise

x_{iktv} = amount delivered to customer i on route k by vehicle v starting at time t.

Route Selection Model

$$\max \sum_k \sum_{v \in V_k} \sum_{t \in T_k} [\sum_{i \in S_k} (vd_i - c_v) \, x_{iktv}$$

$$- FC_{kv} \, y_{ktv}] \tag{1}$$

subject to

$$d_{it} \le \sum_{k \in R_i} \sum_{v \in V_k} \sum_{\substack{\tau \in T_k \\ \tau \le t - tc_{ik}}} x_{ik\tau v} \le D_{it},$$

for all t and $i \in A_1$ \hfill (2.1)

$$\sum_{k \in R_i} \sum_{v \in V_k} \sum_{t \in T_k} y_{ktv} = 1, \, i \in A_2 \tag{2.2}$$

$$\sum_{k \in R_i} \sum_{v \in V_k} \sum_{t \in T_k} y_{ktv} \le 1, \, i \in A_3 \tag{2.3}$$

$$\sum_{i \in S_k} x_{iktv} \le CAP_v \, y_{ktv}, \text{ for all } ktv \tag{3}$$

$$\sum_{k \in K_v} \sum_{\substack{\tau = t - TL_k \\ \tau \in T_k}}^{t-1} y_{k\tau v} \le 1, \text{ for all } tv \tag{4}$$

$$y_{ktv} = \quad 0 \text{ or } 1, \text{ for all } ktv \tag{5.1}$$

$$D_{i,t+tc_{ik}} \ge x_{iktv} \ge 0, \text{ for all } iktv \tag{5.2}$$

$$x_{iktv} \ge d_{iT} \, y_{ktv} \quad , \text{ for all } ktv \tag{5.3}$$

and $i \in S_k \cap A_2$.

The objective of the route selection model is to maximize the value of all deliveries less the fixed and variable costs of making those deliveries. Constraints (2.1) through (2.3) represent customer demand for the three types of customers. In constraint (2.1) note that $x_{ik\tau v}$ is not the amount delivered to customer i at time τ, but at time $\tau + tc_{ik}$. This explains the requirement for $\tau \le t - tc_{ik}$ in the summation over t. The summation over $x_{ik\tau v}$ is the amount delivered to customer i during the time interval from 0 to t. Constraints (2.2) and (2.3) express the requirement that 1, or at most 1, delivery should be made to customers in A_2 or A_3. Constraints on the volume of these deliveries are imposed by (5.2) and (5.3). Constraint (5.3) expresses the requirement that the single delivery received by a type 2 customer must be sufficient to supply his needs for the entire planning horizon. The sets A_1 A_2 and A_3 would normally be defined by management policy. Generally, A_2 and A_3 will contain smaller customers for whom multiple visits in a single planning horizon would be uneconomical. The customers in A_3 have the further property that $d_{iT} = 0$.

Constraint (3) is similar to constraints that arise in warehouse location models if we think of y_{ktv} as the variable that determines whether a warehouse is open and the x_{iktv} as variables representing flows from that warehouse. If a particular route-time-vehicle combination ktv is not selected, then $y_{ktv} = 0$ and constraint (3) requires that $x_{iktv} = 0$ for all i contained in S_k. On the other hand, if a ktv combination is selected, then $y_{ktv} = 1$ and this constraint requires that deliveries on this route not exceed vehicle capacity. It is understood in constraints (3) and (5) that the indices ktv will run only over values that are allowed by the sets T_k and V_k.

Constraint (4) imposes the requirement that vehicle v cannot be driving more than one route during the time interval from $t-1$ to t.

Constraints (5.1) to (5.3) impose integrality requirements and natural lower and upper bounds on the continuous variables. The parameters d_{it} and D_{it} are determined from the forecast of the demand for customer i. As described in the section on demand forecasting and inventory level calculation, the forecast of future demand can be used to predict what the customer inventory level would be at any point in time if no further deliveries were made. Then, D_{it} is set to the capacity of the storage tank minus the predicted inventory level at time t. If forecast inventory is above the safety stock level at time t, then d_{it} is set to 0. Otherwise, d_{it} is set to the safety stock level minus predicted inventory at time t.

The parameters vd_i are used to represent the effect of model decisions on events that occur beyond the horizon of the model. In the short run horizon considered by the model, there is considerable discretion in the amount of product that can be delivered to a particular customer. However, the amount delivered in the long run is determined by customer demand. Hence, each gallon scheduled for delivery to customer i within the model

horizon reduces the amount that must be delivered in the future. This effect is accounted for by setting vd_i to an estimate of the cost per unit of delivering to customer i at a point in time outside the planning horizon of the model.

Lagrangian relaxation was the central concept used in analyzing the route selection model. As described in Fisher [1984], the goal in formulating a Lagrangian relaxation is to dualize a set of constraints whose removal greatly simplifies the problem, but still admits a tight bound on the optimal objective value. This purpose is accomplished here by dualizing constraints (2.1)—(2.3).

The key observation in solving the Lagrangian problem is that removing constraints (2.1)—(2.3) greatly simplifies the dependence of x_{iktv} on y_{ktv}. As a result, we are able to solve for values of x_{iktv}, $i \in S_k$ that are optimal in the Lagrangian problem if $y_{ktv} = 1$. Once the x_{iktv} have been determined, the Lagrangian problem reduces to a problem for each vehicle that resembles the knapsack problem and can be solved by dynamic programming.

In our computational algorithm we first use a multiplier adjustment method to determine values for the Lagrange multipliers that provide a tight upper bound on the optimal value. We then execute a primal heuristic that uses the Lagrange multipliers to obtain a feasible solution to the route selection model.

Finally we have built a branch and bound algorithm around this Lagrangian procedure. However, branch and bound has not played a major role in our computational work because the upper bound and feasible solution that come from the procedures just described have always been sufficiently close for practical purposes.

Maximizing Profits for North American Van Lines' Truckload Division: A New Framework for Pricing and Operations

Warren B. Powell

Yosef Sheffi

Kenneth S. Nickerson

Kevin Butterbaugh

Susan Atherton

The basic operating characteristics of a truckload motor carrier are deceptively simple: shippers provide information on trailer loads of freight to be hauled from an origin city, on a given day, to a destination city. The carrier must provide a truck at the origin at the right time or potentially lose the load. While en route, the truck is dedicated to its assignment; once the load is delivered at the destination, the truck is available for another dispatch. Thus the freight is not handled at intermediate locations, as would be the case with less-than-truckload carriers, and in general, the trucks do not visit multiple origins and multiple destinations on a single trip, as would be the case with household movers. In a truckload operation, the vehicle fleet typically moves in response to demand without any base terminals or fixed schedules.

This seemingly simple technology actually poses some difficult challenges to large truckload carriers who operate thousands of trucks and can dispatch hundreds of drivers per hour. Dispatchers must assign individual drivers to loads while minimizing *deadhead* miles (empty miles from a driver's location to a pickup point). Thus, in order to satisfy the customers' needs and minimize its own costs, a carrier must have its trucks placed as close as possible to the pickup locations. Truck positions, however, are the result of previous dispatching decisions, and so current decisions affect future service and profitability. Thus, when assigning individual trucks to loads, dispatchers try also to ensure that these trucks will be well positioned once their mission is complete.

Randomness in shipper demands makes this task very difficult. At the beginning of a typical day a carrier may know only 30 to 40 percent of the loads it will carry that day and as little as 10 percent of the next day's loads, and thus dispatchers are never certain of what will be available at the end of each run. In addition, decision lead times are very short. When a driver calls in, the dispatcher must either assign the truck to a known load, dispatch it empty to a *deficit* region (one in which there are typically more loads than trucks), or hold the truck in anticipation of a future load at its current location. These decisions are made continuously by dozens of dispatchers simultaneously over the entire fleet positioned across the country. In this environment the Operations Department tends to respond to immediate problems with little time for gathering information and little opportunity for planning ahead.

CARRIER ISSUES

An important management concern in truckload operations is minimizing empty miles. Empty movements result both from structural imbalances in freight flows between producing and consuming regions and from the random nature of shipper demands. The structural imbalances create a recurring need to reposition trucks from surplus to deficit regions. Even if flows were perfectly balanced, however, randomness would cause demand requests to materialize in places and times which did not correspond exactly to current truck positions. As a result, the need to maintain a high level of equipment utilization would force additional deadheading. In fact, random effects are strong enough to cause a traditional surplus region to become a deficit region on any given day.

The high pressure environment, coupled with the demand uncertainty, provides only limited time for the carrier to plan each dispatch, creating the potential for excessive empty miles. The more serious effect of this fire-fighting mode of dispatching, however, is that the carrier passes up business opportunities without knowing they were there. The carrier's

loss of this "invisible freight" results from the fact that shipper representatives often call for service following a list of approved carriers. A carrier ranked high on this list will get as many loads as it has trucks on the day and at the place where the loads are available. It will lose any load which it cannot commit to carrying, even though such loads may be very profitable.

In addition to getting enough hauling capacity to the right locations, truckload carriers evaluate each load request before accepting it. (Different loads may carry different revenues even between the same origin-destination pair.) Freight from certain large shippers with which the carrier has long-term relationships is always accepted if trucks are available. Other loads, however, can be accepted or rejected depending on whether they add positive marginal contributions to the system.

How much a given load contributes to the carrier's profit should be determined by taking into account not only the revenue minus direct cost (direct contribution) of that load, but also the expected earnings of the trailer upon its arrival at the destination. These earnings in turn should reflect the outbound loaded opportunities at the destination and the supply of trucks there. Furthermore, the entire contribution of each load has to be balanced against the availability of other loads and the opportunity cost of using a trailer to carry the load under study. In short, load acceptance is an important issue for truckload carriers, and it should be based on systemwide considerations that account for all regions at all future time periods. The carrier cannot carry out such an analysis manually in the short time it has to respond to the shipper, and thus loads are typically accepted if the direct contribution is positive and the capacity is there.

Beyond load acceptance and truck dispatching, truckload carriers also have to determine movement prices. Since all carriers use the same equipment and provide the same service in comparable transit times, pricing is very important. Without the infrastructure and fixed schedules of other transportation modes, the underlying structure supporting a truckload carrier is the market itself—the multidirectional patterns of loads and empties that move continuously throughout the country. In addition to dispatching trucks and screening load requests, truckload carriers are engaged in an extremely delicate balancing act of setting prices in thousands of interrelated traffic markets simultaneously. These prices must reflect complex backhaul opportunities, which are a function of the flows in the system, which in turn are a function of prices.

Interestingly, these issues are less problematic for small truckload carriers that operate a few trucks in a limited number of traffic lanes. While such carriers are more susceptible than large ones to demand fluctuations, they can easily solve issues of dispatching, load screening, and pricing due to the virtual lack of interactions across truck assignments and traffic lanes.

NORTH AMERICAN COMMERCIAL TRANSPORT (NACT)

The truckload market in the US is currently characterized by excess capacity and therefore by strong competition. It is a market where many customers (shippers) perceive the product offered as generic in terms of the equipment and level of service offered.

The Commercial Transport Division of North American Van Lines is one of the nation's largest truckload motor carriers,

with annual revenues in excess of $260 million and a fleet of more than 5,800 trailers. In its competitive market, NACT strives to be customer-oriented rather than operations-oriented. In other words, NACT does not operate in a fixed pattern and expect shippers to use its services whenever they fit their needs. Instead, it tries to understand its customers' needs and to tailor trucking services to fit those needs. This emphasis on a high level of service, in conjunction with the competition from hundreds of small but highly efficient regional operators, challenges NACT to utilize its size to its advantage. Properly managed, a large carrier can provide shippers with the right truck at the right place at the right time more often than any small operator or a combination of small operators.

To achieve these advantages, NACT proposed the development of a computer model that would help it manage the complexities of a large operation and reap the benefits of its scale. While research on the theoretical aspects of this problem had been going on at universities for several years, no satisfactory solution was available.

The project resulted in a sophisticated new package named LOADMAP (Load Matching and Pricing) that challenges fundamental operating procedures used by truckload carriers. Standard practices of minimizing empty miles within artificial boundaries have been replaced with logic which single-mindedly maximizes profits and, interestingly, also increases service levels systemwide. Outputs from the model also assist sales and marketing personnel to identify those loads and traffic lanes with the highest marginal contribution to profits.

The development of LOADMAP required more than an application of existing management science techniques. It involved the development of a new stochastic network optimization model that handles forecasting uncertainties in a novel way, overcoming important practical difficulties in deterministic models [White 1972; Ouimet 1972] and in simpler stochastic models that have been tried previously [Jordan and Turnquist 1983; Powell, Sheffi, and Thiriez 1984]. Following Powell [1987], this new modeling framework is, in fact, directly applicable to solving a wide range of problems which have spatial, temporal, and stochastic elements (such as rail car distribution and rental vehicle management).

THE MODELING APPROACH

The problem LOADMAP solves can be grasped by focusing on the decision to dispatch a truck to haul a load from, say, region 1 on Monday, arriving at region 5 on Wednesday (Figure 1). Once the truck arrives at region 5, it may be dispatched in any one of five different directions, arriving at a new destination anywhere from Thursday to Monday. From these points the truck may find yet another five possible outbound dispatches, creating 25 different possible trajectories by the end of its second move (beyond the one evaluated). Using a more realistic average of 30

FIGURE 1. The dispatch of a truck from region 1 to region 5 must be evaluated in the context of the different dispatches that may be made out of region 5, which in turn must account for any subsequent downstream dispatches.

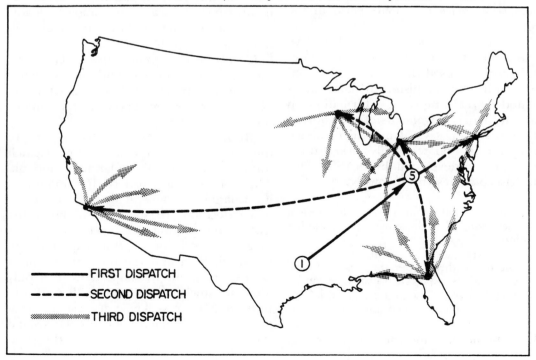

FIRST DISPATCH

SECOND DISPATCH

THIRD DISPATCH

possible outbound dispatches from a region, after three moves there would be $30^3 = 27{,}000$ possible trajectories. In addition, since we do not know what loads will actually be available as the truck arrives in each destination, we can only probabilistically guess which trajectory should be used. This is further complicated by the presence of other trucks in those destination regions — these trucks may take these "probabilistic loads" before the truck under study. The problem then is to decide how to evaluate the contribution of a movement, given all its possible ramifications.

Note that the movement from region 1 to region 5 has to be compared with a possible move from region 1 to other regions — with all possible trajectories out of those regions. It also has to be compared with the possibility of holding the truck in region 1, out of which many potential trajectories may materialize in the future.

To solve this problem LOADMAP builds on a set of 60-80 geographically defined regions used by NACT. It then works with a set of historical data that is updated in real time with information on loads and truck movements. The historical data is based on several months of actual loads and is updated daily using time-series models developed by NACT. This data base includes the following:

- The expected number of loads between each pair of regions over the planning horizon,
- The expected direct contribution (revenue minus direct operating costs) of each load and its expected transit time, and
- The expected cost and transit time for moving empty between any two regions.

The real-time data includes the following:

- The current location and status of each truck in the system (including the expected arrival time of trucks in transit and the estimated time for them to be ready for a new assignment),
- A list of all known (booked) loads which have been called in by shippers but not yet assigned to a driver, and
- The direct contribution of each known load, its pickup date and the time required for the move.

This information is used to develop an estimate of what will happen to a truck once it is sent into a region. The complex and uncertain set of possible trajectories is handled by tracing the future path of a truck in three stages:

(1) *The deterministic movements* are the sequence of one or more movements whose characteristics (revenue, cost, departure time and arrival time) are known at the time of the first dispatch. These movements include carrying known loads, empty moves, and holding a truck in position.

(2) *The first uncertain dispatch* represents the first movement beyond the sequence of deterministic moves. The characteristics of that move are not known at the time of the first dispatch.

(3) *All further uncertain movements* are those beyond the first uncertain dispatch until the end of the planning horizon. These three stages reflect the amount of information available at the time of a dispatch decision. In stage 1, we know the exact contribution of each movement (negative if it is an empty move) and both the destination and the time of arrival at each destination. In stage 2, we can only estimate stochastically the outbound opportunities, but we know at least the location of a truck when it begins the second stage (since we are able to track the vehi-

cle deterministically through the first stage). By the time we get to stage 3, not only are we forced to forecast the available opportunities, but we do not even know the location of the truck.

Our solution approach models each stage with a level of detail that matches the quality of the information available.

STAGE 3: END EFFECTS

Stage 3 deals with those truck movements that are the furthest into the future. It is modeled by developing a single number, $p(j,s)$, termed an *end effect*, which gives the value of a truck in region j on day s. This number is calculated by using

FIGURE 2. The average contribution of a truck in different regions, relative to region 1, becomes constant as the planning horizon is increased, suggesting that planning past 10 or 15 days will have no impact on decisions today.

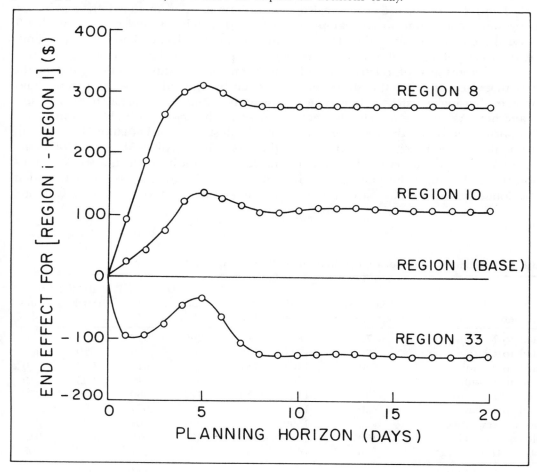

dynamic-programming-style recursions to track the forward trajectory of a truck based on historical loaded and empty flows (see appendix). An end effect is thus an estimate of the expected contribution of a truck, until the end of the planning horizon, independent of the forecasted number of trucks in a region. It indirectly reflects, however, the past supply of trucks and the opportunities available to them in that region on that day of the week.

Figure 2 shows the relative end effect values of three regions calculated for each day until the end of a 20-day planning period. The relative end effects are calculated by subtracting some base region (in this case the end effect of region 1) from the end effects of each of the other regions. The importance of relative end effects is that they describe the short term advantage of using a truck in one region over another. As the curves clearly show, after approximately 10 days the end effects for all regions become constant.

Figure 2 is based on actual data and it demonstrates that once the planning horizon is longer than 10 days, the relative

end effects would not change by increasing the planning period. (LOADMAP sets this period to 20 days as a safety factor.) Figure 2 also highlights the fact that the value of a truck in different regions can be very different, reflecting the dispatch opportunities out of that region.

STAGE 2: THE MARGINAL TRUCK

The goal in modeling stage 2 of a truck trajectory is to capture the marginal value of an additional truck in a region at some future time. It is modeled by looking at what a dispatcher would do, say, on day 3 in Boston. We do not know with certainty what options will be available to the dispatcher, but we can consider what might happen by evaluating historical trends and assuming that the dispatcher will use trucks in the most profitable manner. Table 1 illustrates the situation by showing the first nine possible ways (out of many more possibilities) in which a truck in Boston on day 3 might be used: first, loaded to Pittsburgh, second, loaded to Chicago,

TABLE 1. Possibilities open to a truck located in Boston on day 3.

Assignment	Expected Contribution	End Effect	Total	Dispatch Probabilities			
				Truck 1	Truck 2	Truck 3	Truck 4
Loaded to Pittsburgh	75	1880	1955	.295	.049	.006	0
Loaded to Chicago	190	1741	1931	.167	.080	.020	.004
Loaded to Miami	250	1567	1817	.021	.013	.004	0
Loaded to Baltimore	40	1500	1540	.015	.010	.003	0
Loaded to New York	55	1452	1507	.427	.580	.449	.259
Loaded to Dallas	330	1175	1505	.027	.077	.109	.102
Empty to New York	-35	1509	1474	.001	.004	.007	.007
Loaded to Denver	450	1014	1464	.007	.023	.036	.038
Empty to Harrisburg	-40	1478	1438	.030	.117	.227	.298
Expected Contribution				1713	1550	1477	1433

and so on. If, when we actually reach day 3, there is a load to Pittsburgh, the historical average contribution of that load (revenue minus direct operating costs) is $75 (see the "expected contribution" column). We then need to factor in how valuable a truck will be in Pittsburgh, where it might be leaving on day 5. This is given by the end effect, which in this (realistic) example is $1,880. The $1,880 is the expected total contribution a truck will earn starting in Pittsburgh on day 5 until the end of the planning horizon (which was set at 20 days for this example). The $1,880 by itself is not meaningful; what is important is its value relative to the end effects of other regions.

Adding the direct contribution to the end effect, we can rank the different options that may be available to the dispatcher in terms of expected profitability as shown in Table 1 (see the "total" column). We can now assume that if the dispatcher were to have one truck in Boston on day 3, he would use it on the highest ranked available option. The second truck would then be used on the next highest option and so on. As a result, we can develop the probability of dispatching the first, second, ... *k*-th truck from Boston on day 3 to any one of the possible assignments it might have. (The idea here is that the first truck in a region has all the options open to it out of the loads available then and there, the second truck has all the options except the best one taken by the first truck, and so on.) The dispatch probabilities for the first four trucks for each of the nine assignment options are shown in the last four columns of Table 1.

Since they are based on historical data, the dispatch probabilities incorporate the forecasted number of loads from Boston on day 3 to each of the potential destina-

tions. Thus, the first truck has a 29.5 percent probability of being dispatched on the first option (loaded to Pittsburgh) but its most likely dispatch is loaded to New York City, an assignment that ranks only fifth on the list. The second truck has a lower probability of being dispatched to Pittsburgh but an even higher probability of moving loaded to New York.

Consider now the column labeled "Truck 1" in Table 1, depicting the dispatch probabilities of the first truck. Multiplying these probabilities by the total expected contribution of each assignment (the "total" column in Table 1), the column sum total will be the expected contribution of the first truck in Boston on day 3. These calculations can be performed for all possible trucks to give the value of each additional truck in the region and day under study. As should be expected, the marginal truck values decline monotonically from one truck to the next.

The calculation of the marginal truck values for each potential truck in each region at each point in time is the heart of the model. These calculations mean that LOADMAP handles forecasting uncertainties in a natural and rigorous way, capturing relationships between total profits and the number of trucks sent into a region. The smoothness of the trade-off between the number of trucks in a region and the value of each additional truck gives the model considerable stability in both dispatching and the calculation of the value of an additional load into a region.

STAGE 1: KNOWN CONTRIBUTIONS

Having developed a probabilistic model of truck movements through the second and third stages of its trajectories (in decreasing detail), modeling the first stage is .

more straightforward. It simply requires adding up the direct contributions of the deterministic loaded and empty moves that make up this stage. Thus if LOAD-MAP evaluates a movement from the current location of a truck to, say, Washington, DC, arriving on day 2, and from there to Boston, arriving on day 3, the contribution of that part of the movement is simply the sum of these two known direct contributions (to Washington, DC, and then to Boston). The challenge here is to choose among the many thousands of possible sequences of loaded and empty moves.

THE NETWORK STRUCTURE

Now that we know how to evaluate a given move, the problem is to determine how to optimally dispatch the trucks to maximize both customer service and total expected profits over the planning horizon. This problem can be represented by a time/space network model in which each node represents a particular region on a given day.

To handle correctly intra-regional deadhead movements, each region/day is actually represented by a set of three nodes: an inbound node, an outbound node, and a node for the stochastic cluster emanating from the region/day under consideration. The link from an inbound node to an outbound node of the same region is associated with intra-regional deadheading cost. Loaded move links lead from the outbound node of one region to the inbound node of another, while empty move links lead from the inbound node of one region to the outbound node of another. Such a representation models the fact that the empty movements go directly to a pickup point within a region, while loaded move-

ments have to drop off the load and then deadhead to a pickup point. Notwithstanding this three node representation of each point, we assume in the remainder of this paper that each region/day is represented by a single node, for clarity of exposition.

The LOADMAP network incorporates two types of links: (1) "*deterministic*" *links*, which are used to represent the movement of specific known loads, possible empty moves, or holding a truck in a region (capturing the stage 1 movements); and (2) "*stochastic*" *links*, which are used to capture the value of an additional truck in a region (representing the movements in stages 2 and 3).

FIGURE 3. A cluster of stochastic links gives the value of each additional truck in a region on a given day until the end of the planning horizon. Each additional truck is worth less due to the reduced opportunities available.

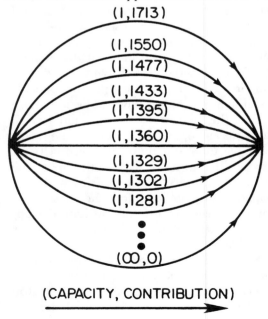

(1,1713)
(1,1550)
(1,1477)
(1,1433)
(1,1395)
(1,1360)
(1,1329)
(1,1302)
(1,1281)
⋮
(∞,0)

(CAPACITY, CONTRIBUTION)

The stochastic links are arranged in clusters where a cluster emanates from each node (region/day combination) in the network, in addition to all other links that may emanate from it. Figure 3 depicts one such cluster, in which each of the stochastic links, except the last one, has an upper bound of one (truck) and a link contribution which equals the value of that marginal truck. While Figure 3 depicts only 10 links (the first four of which correspond to the example in Table 1), an actual cluster might contain up to 50 stochastic links. The last link, with zero contribution and no upper bound, is added to the cluster in case the model sends a larger-than-expected number of trucks to that region/time.

A simplified view of the resulting time/space network is shown in Figure 4. In this network the links represent possible truck movements. Solid links represent known loads each with a known contribution, dashed links represent empty moves or holding actions (also with known contributions) and the stochastic links are drawn in boxes. Every truck enters the network on the region/day where it first becomes available. The trucks then "flow" over the network, "picking up" positive and negative contributions as they move across each link.

The network structure used by LOAD-MAP means that at the beginning of any given day the following options are available for each truck: (1) holding in place for

FIGURE 4. Loaded and empty moves out of the first time period can be represented using a time/space network, with each path ending in a cluster of stochastic links.

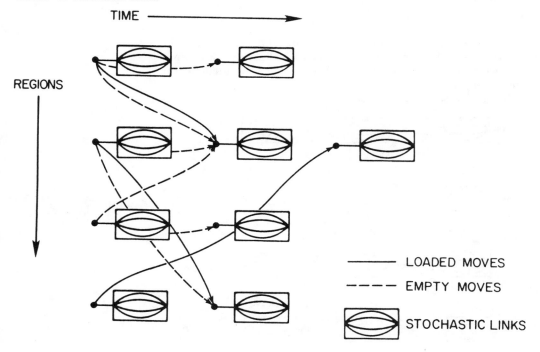

TIME ⟶

REGIONS

——— LOADED MOVES

- - - - EMPTY MOVES

STOCHASTIC LINKS

loads that may be called in later in the day (the value of this option is quantified by stochastic links emanating from the current region on the first day); (2) moving loaded if a load is available; (3) moving empty to a nearby region arriving later the same day ("same day empties"); (4) moving empty over a longer distance, arriving the next day ("overnight empties"); or (5) holding in the region until the next day ("moving into" either the deterministic or stochastic links emanating from the next day's node).

Regardless of the type of movement chosen, all truck trajectories ultimately end in a movement over one of the stochastic links. This link then summarizes all future expected costs and revenues from the time it is entered through the end of the planning horizon. Note that the deterministic portion of the network extends as far into the future as there are known loads. When the model runs out of known loads, it simply generates one last set of stochastic links and stops. This is shown in Figure 5, which depicts known loads emanating from future time points and the corresponding extension of the network into the future. Note that the actual network structure connects the end of each stochastic link cluster to a single "super-sink" node; this is not drawn in Figures 4 and 5 for clarity of presentation.

This structure gives LOADMAP the ability to build automatically on the amount of information available to the carrier. When more loads are called in earlier, the number of deterministic links grows, and a larger portion of each truck trajectory within the planning period is known with certainty. Dispatching decisions will then automatically become more accurate. This property also means that the model can be used to quantify the value of advanced booking.

FIGURE 5. Multiple dispatches over known loads and empty repositioning can be represented in an expanded network. The network extends until all known loads are represented, with each truck eventually ending in a cluster of stochastic links.

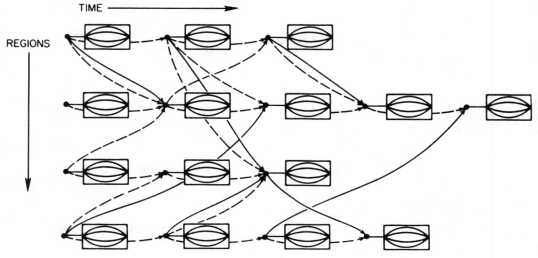

OPTIMIZATION OF TRUCK DISPATCHING

At North American, the model is run four times a day to provide updated instructions based on current conditions. Using a tailored start procedure and an efficient adaptation of the network simplex code, LOADMAP optimizes a 10,000 link network in 2-4 CPU seconds. The total run time of the model is less than 15 CPU seconds on an AMDAHL 580 computer.

One of the crucial decisions that the model has to make when no known loads are available in a given region is whether to send the truck empty elsewhere or to hold it for loads that may come in later that day. To do this correctly, the model has to forecast what will happen in the remainder of each day, as the day is unfolding and loads are called in. The modeling logic here is based on a detailed statistical analysis of historical data, where we assumed that loads are booked in accordance with a Poisson process at a rate that varies over the course of the day. The expected number of loads that have yet to be called in is then updated each time the model is run, thus providing an accurate estimate of the value of holding a truck versus repositioning it at another region.

This logic implies that the value of holding a truck in place at the beginning of a day is generally much higher than, say, at 3:00 PM, when 95 percent of the expected loads may have already been called in. As a result, the model is more likely to recommend an empty move at the end of the day than in the morning. When such a move is made, it is intended to position the truck for loads that are expected to be called in the next day.

The structure of the network underlying LOADMAP derives from state-of-the-art analytical and numerical considerations. Aside from mathematical elegance, these considerations offer critical practical features in two areas: the optimization that LOADMAP performs and the way it handles the uncertainty inherent in the problem.

In the first area, LOADMAP explicitly maximizes expected profits over the entire system. Every dispatch decision (loaded or empty) is automatically balanced against all other opportunities for the truck under consideration, including the possibility of holding it for a load that may be called in later. On a practical level this means that LOADMAP's recommendations may include the following:

— Refusal to take certain loads due to their overall negative impact on the system (even though the *direct* contribution of a refused load may be positive).
— Recommending long or unusual empty moves by correctly estimating the marginal contribution of such a movement.

In the second area, LOADMAP handles the future uncertainty explicitly, creating a unique stochastic network structure that distinguishes between known and forecasted information. By contrast, other models treat demand forecasts deterministically, a process that creates practical problems ranging from heuristic truncation of the planning horizon to unreasonable sensitivity of immediate decisions to forecasted data. These problems create difficulties in implementing model recommendations. (For example, a deterministic model may recommend moving loaded trucks out of a region that has no loads to be shipped.)

Such issues are never a problem with LOADMAP, which handles those and other problems in a way that is both rigorous and intuitive. Particularly useful features of the model include the following:

— The farther a forecast is in the future, the less effect it has on decisions made today.

— Loads that have already been called in have a greater impact than forecasts for future loads.

— Increasing the planning horizon (beyond the usual 15 to 20 days) has no effect on the size of the network and has only a small effect on execution times. Furthermore, for theoretical reasons, increasing the planning horizon beyond approximately 20 days has no effect on dispatch decisions made today.

The blending of actual optimization with explicit treatment of uncertainty allows LOADMAP to make unique tradeoffs in optimizing the dispatching decisions. For example, it is willing to take high risks in repositioning trucks into a region for high margin freight, whereas it will insist on a high probability of finding a load out of regions with low margins. This ability to balance probabilities with profit margins allows North American to leverage its size and mitigate the effects of randomness in demand. LOADMAP's recommendations to position trucks where customers are likely to have loads to be shipped allow the carrier to provide a higher level of service while maximizing its profits.

ESTIMATION OF SHIPMENT PROFITABILITY

As the previous sections show, LOADMAP is a unique tool that allows NACT dispatchers to maximize profits on a realtime basis. It also is being used by Sales and Marketing to help develop sales priorities, identifying traffic lanes where additional freight will have the highest marginal contribution to total system profits. Thus, what would normally be considered a purely operational model is in fact an important tool for tactical planning and marketing. Indeed, LOADMAP's most profound impact is the framework it provides for understanding the economics of trucking.

We can illustrate the power of this framework by considering one of the most important and difficult problems in truckload planning — quantifying the profitability of a load to the system. Load profitability analysis is needed both for screening loads in real-time and for evaluating traffic lanes and shippers.

A widely used approach to calculating load profitability is to subtract from the revenue generated by the load the direct operating cost along with some portion of the empty costs incurred before or after the loaded move. This allocation of empty miles is not only arbitrary but also ignores the opportunity cost of using a truck on a given load, as well as the larger impact of accepting that load on the rest of the system.

Our alternative approach works as follows. Let

$r(i,j)$ = the revenue earned on a load going from i to j (where i and j represent nodes in the LOADMAP network, that is, each represents a given region on a given day).

$c(i,j)$ = direct operating cost of hauling a load from i to j.

$VP(j)$ = the marginal contribution of an additional truck at j.

$VM(i)$ = the marginal contribution of one less truck at i.

Network optimization experts will quickly recognize the relationship between the dual variables at nodes i and j *(node duals)* and the quantities *VP(j)* and *VM(i)*. Unfortunately, the node duals generated by the network simplex algorithm only approximate *VP(j)* and *VM(i)*. The reason is that due to the network flow constraints the value of the dual variable associated with adding a truck at a (region/day) node is not the same as the value of the variable associated with subtracting a truck there. The simplex node duals, however, can give either one of these values or even some intermediate number. Thus these variables can be highly unstable, creating problems in their practical application.

To solve these problems we developed a special post optimality logic to calculate *VP(j)* and *VM(i)* directly in a rigorous way. For example, to consider the value of adding a truck in a region/time node, we consider opportunities to either increase flow into that node or decrease flow out of it. This requires finding a path from that node to the "supersink" node at the end of the planning horizon, along which we can increase flow (or decrease flow when going against a link's direction). Using this logic we can calculate the total system contribution (TSC) of a load going from region/time *i* to region/time *j* as follows:

$$TSC = r(i,j) - c(i,j) + VP(j) - VM(i).$$

The term *VP(j)* incorporates the downstream effect of sending another truck into region *j* while *VM(i)* balances the opportunity cost of not using the truck on some other activity out of *i*. If the TSC is positive, the load is considered attractive, whereas loads with a negative TSC should be avoided. Note that apparently profitable loads may have a negative TSC if there are even more profitable opportunities being passed up. At the same time a seemingly poor load can appear attractive

if the best alternative is to hold the truck in a poor region or move it empty.

The TSC statistic is not only an intuitively reasonable measure of the value of a load to the system, it also rests on a solid mathematical foundation. The expression is drawn from optimization theory where it is known as a shadow price or reduced cost. The practical application of this approach is in its ability to give the planner the value (to the system) of each load over the entire planning horizon. This statistic, in conjunction with longer-term considerations of customer relations, is used by NACT to make clear accept-or-reject recommendations.

MARKETING AND PRICING

Aside from their use for evaluating each incoming shipment, TSC statistics can be used in marketing and market performance analysis, where they can identify markets with high profit potential, as well as markets which are not performing up to standard. After each run of LOAD-MAP, the TSC statistic of each load is calculated and stored in a special data set. Then, from time to time, the average TSC of all the loads moving in each lane is computed and reported to the marketing department. Similarly, the average TSC statistic for each customer and customer location is calculated and reported to marketing.

If a lane has a low average TSC relative to other lanes outbound from a region, it indicates that the prices in that lane do not adequately reflect systemwide balance conditions and other opportunities out of that region. Since the TSC reflects global balance conditions, a lane may have a high TSC even though prices are relatively low, if it is generally a backhaul lane. Conversely, a heavy head haul lane may exhibit a low TSC if the prices, while relatively high, are not high enough to offset backhaul costs and other opportunities.

In addition to its use in evaluating lane performance and in tactical marketing, the average TSC statistic is also used to provide an input to pricing decisions. While pricing must take into account many factors, including current market conditions and competitive pressures, the TSC statistic gives the lowest price that should be charged in a given lane on a short-term basis. Since we require that the TSC should be greater than zero, the average price in a lane, $r(i,j)$, should satisfy

$$\underline{r}(i,j) > \underline{c}(i,j) + \underline{VP}(j) - \underline{VM}(i)$$

where the underlined quantities represent moving averages of the corresponding values. This expression helps avoid underpricing in highly competitive lanes and adds a quantitative perspective that mitigates the tendency that may exist in marketing organizations to drop prices as low as required to attract business.

In using the average lane TSC values, North American has been able to develop better sales priorities, which simultaneously reflect market and operating conditions. The implications are significant. Truckload motor carriers typically exhibit the traditional tension between Operations, which is encouraged to reduce empty miles, and Marketing, which strives to maximize revenues. With a network model that maximizes profits and a method for identifying markets with the highest profit contribution, North American has a system that gives both Operations and Marketing the same objective — to maximize profits.

IMPLEMENTATION

We developed LOADMAP in 1985 and installed it at North American in February 1986. After several months of testing, a number of refinements to the forecasting logic, and the addition of several reports, the model went on-line early in the summer of 1986.

IMPACT ON MANAGEMENT PHILOSOPHY

Some of the most significant impacts of LOADMAP are the changes in management philosophy it produces. NACT management has compiled the following list of observations regarding the model's long-term impact on the way the truckline has been managed:

Planning ahead in Operations: Prior to LOADMAP, Operations reacted to loads as they became available. LOADMAP, however, requires load forecasts and anticipation of truck movements to meet current and future demand. Operations now forecasts loads for each day and the next and receives feedback on its forecasting performance.

Operating on a national scope: Planners, who each manage a group of regions, used to give priorities to loads in their own regions. With LOADMAP, planners often reposition trucks across regional boundaries since each load and move is evaluated on the basis of its contribution to system-wide profit.

Unifying Sales and Operations objectives: Sales and Operations often have conflicting goals on which their performance is evaluated; thus Sales gauges load volume and revenue while Operations measures empty miles. LOADMAP provides the total system contribution for every move as a means to measure the performance of both departments.

Short-term pricing: The use of LOAD-MAP's minimum prices (based on the requirement of a positive TSC) demonstrated how rates on incremental loads priced on a daily basis can improve margins and help balance vehicle flows.

Customer priority by operating lane: Based on historical TSC statistics, North American can now develop customer priority lists by traffic lane based on the contribution level of each shipment. Sales then reviews the list to modify priorities based on long-term customer commitments and national contracts. This provides both Sales and Operations a common goal in servicing customers and understanding the worth of the customer's entire volume to the system.

Real-time load evaluation: Prior to LOAD-MAP, Operations and Sales would almost always accept loads from customers, then determine how to provide a truck to service the load. Now management believes that through the use of LOADMAP's results, loads can be screened at order entry for impact on the current system. Loads can then be accepted or rejected on the basis of the customer's priority and the load's contribution at the time of order registration. This alleviates the problem of accepting a load and then not being able to perform the service.

Recognition of each region's "booking profile": The forecasting model requires the development of profiles of how loads are called in over the course of the day. This has increased the dispatchers' sensitivity to the timing of shipment bookings in each region and to the time when vehicles could be released or held to meet anticipated demand.

BOTTOM-LINE IMPACTS

Two approaches were taken to develop hard numbers on the impact LOADMAP has had on North American's bottom line. The first included analysis undertaken internally by North American, comparing LOADMAP's dispatching decisions over a period of three weeks to what actually happened in the field. This analysis was limited by the fact that it ignored LOAD-MAP's ability to better position the fleet, thereby increasing total revenue. (During the test period trucks were not actually dispatched by LOADMAP, so there was no reliable way of estimating the effect.) Instead, attention was focused purely on LOADMAP's ability to minimize total empty miles by optimizing across the entire fleet. The results showed that if 100 percent of LOADMAP's recommendations had been followed, the loaded movement ratio (that ratio of loaded to total miles) would have improved by 3.8 percent as a result of the reduction in empty miles. This translates to potential annual savings of $4,980,000. In practice, however, not all of the recommendations can be followed (due to restrictions in the management of the owner-operator fleet) and the consensus was that only half of these savings were truly achievable, giving a conservative estimate of $2,490,000 in annual savings.

SIMULATING THE OPTIMIZATION

In reality, there will be an impact on the revenue side as LOADMAP produces better positioning for the right loads. Unfortunately, it is impossible to measure directly the amount or quality of this invisible freight in the system. Instead, we designed an experiment that tests the dispatching capabilities of the model with a degree of precision and detail that we have not seen documented elsewhere.

First, we wrote a large-scale Monte-Carlo model that encompasses LOADMAP to simulate the entire operation of a truckload carrier. The simulation imitates the process of loads being called in and the movement of drivers with a very high level of detail. This includes simulation of such activities as drivers exceeding their duty time limits and going to sleep, matching different truck types with load types, dispatching single and double teams, and accounting for actual driver compensation schedules (based on a driver's experience and the length of haul of a load). Five times during each simulated day the simulation calls LOADMAP to determine how drivers should be dispatched and, following the execution of LOADMAP's instructions, the clock is advanced to the next dispatch period.

This simulation approximates the operation of a truckline that uses LOADMAP, and thus some of the effects of the model can be learned by running it with actual data and comparing the results to actual performance. Such an experiment, however, cannot entirely capture the invisible freight since the carrier usually does not know about freight not carried due to insufficient capacity. To measure this effect we developed a truck dispatching game built around the simulation model. In this game, teams of six dispatchers compete against each other by making dispatch decisions with the objective of maximizing total contribution while servicing the customer demands. Each team member operates a dispatch computer terminal and can execute any dispatch from his or her region. As in actual operations, team members cooperate with each other by sending empties across regional boundaries and alerting teammates to developing problems. Each dispatch is recorded by the computer, and at the end of each day all loads that were not carried are recorded as "refused."

In a game in July 1986, starting with the same truck locations and using an identical set of loads, a team of Princeton students competed against a team of MIT students. In August 1986, three teams of logistics and carrier executives competed against each other during an MIT summer course; at the end of 1986, the game was run with teams of Princeton students; and in February 1987, with teams of NACT managers. All experiments used data from NACT, factored down by 60 percent (to speed the game up) and randomized enough to mask actual loads. We followed each of the above experiments (games) by a simulation/LOADMAP run using the same data. The results all showed that LOADMAP consistently produces an 8-10 percent profit increase over the teams, all of whom performed similarly. (The NACT teams performed somewhat better than the others but still within the same range.) This profit percentage amounts to about two million dollars annually for NACT.

While these results support the (independently obtained) NACT estimate, it is interesting that in all cases both costs and revenues in the simulation/LOADMAP runs were higher than those of the teams. LOADMAP tended to run more empty miles but also to take more loads. In fact, LOADMAP typically left behind significantly fewer loads than did the teams. More importantly, out of the "must take" loads (loads tendered by important clients) LOADMAP refused only one or two versus 18 to 23 such loads refused by the teams (these numbers are for a standard

12-day game or simulation run). These results demonstrate that, consistent with NACT philosophy, LOADMAP increases customer level of service while maximizing profit.

The merit of better service cannot be measured strictly in the light of short-term profit. The main value of these results is that they demonstrate how LOADMAP can increase the carrier's ability to provide the right truck at the right place at the right time all the time. In that sense, LOADMAP is not only just a management science model that saves money; it is a management science model that makes money.

APPENDIX

Two elements of the algorithm need to be explained in greater detail: the end effects, $p(j,s)$, and the dispatch probabilities shown in Table 1.

The end effects are calculated using a simple backwards recursion. For notational simplicity, assume that out of a given region i on day s we have $n = 1, 2, \ldots, N$ options available to a truck, where an option might be to move loaded or empty to another region, or to hold in the same region until tomorrow. Now define

P = number of periods in the planning horizon;

$u_n(i,s)$ = the average number of trucks historically used for the n-th dispatch option;

$q_n(i,s)$ = the fraction of trucks out of region i, day s used for the n-th option,

= $u_n(i,s) \, / \sum_k u_k(i,s)$;

$t(i,j)$ = the number of time periods (= 1, 2,. . .) required to move loaded or empty from region i to region j (the model uses two different travel times for these movements, but for simplicity we will assume here that they are the same);

$r_n(i,s)$ = direct contribution of the n-th option, where it is usually positive if the movement is loaded and is minus the empty movement costs if the option is an empty movement; and

$w_n(i,s)$ = the expected value of the n-th option.

The last quantity, $w_n(i,s)$, is calculated as follows:

If $s + t(i,j) < P$, then

$$w_n(i,s) = r_n(i,s) + p(j, s + t(i,j));$$

If $s + t(i,j) \geq P$, then

$$w_n (i,s) = r_n(i,s) \, [(P-s)/t(i,j)],$$

where the last equation accounts for contributions within the planning horizon if the movement ends beyond the planning horizon. The first equation puts the expected value of the n-th option as the direct contribution from that option plus the expected value of terminating at the destination, given by the end effect.

The end effects can now be calculated by starting at $s = P$ and then working backwards through time. Initially set

$$p(j,P) = 0 \text{ for all } j.$$

Now start with $s = P - 1$, then $P - 2$, and so on, calculating at each step

$$p(j,s) = \sum_n q_n(j,s) \, w_n(j,s) \text{ for all } j.$$

An important property that can be

shown easily is that as P becomes very large (in practical terms, large means 15 or 20 days), the end effects can be expressed in the following form:

$$p(j,s) = g_j + b (P - s)$$

where g_j is a region specific adjustment factor (which captures the differences between regions) and b is a growth factor that does not depend on the region a truck starts in. This means that if the planning horizon is sufficiently large, the end effects simply grow linearly at the same rate for all regions. As a result, for large P we can write the relative value of a truck in region i on day t versus region j on day s using

$$p(i,t) - p(j,s) = g_i - g_j + b (s - t),$$

which of course is independent of the length of the planning horizon. It is this important property that makes our model independent of the length of the planning horizon.

Having calculated the end effects, the next step is to find the truck dispatch probabilities, shown as the last four columns in Table 1. We will assume below that the options have been ordered so that $w_1(i,s) \geq w_2(i,s) \geq \ldots \geq w_N(i,s)$. Assume we are working out of region i on day s, and let

$d(k,n)$ = the probability the k-th truck is dispatched on the n-th option,

f_n = the forecasted number of trucks that will be used on the n-th option (if the n-th option represents an empty move, this is typically taken to be the historical number of empties used for this purpose),

X_n = a random variable, with mean f_n, denoting the actual number of

trucks used for the n-th option,

Y_n = a random variable denoting the cumulative number of trucks used on the top n options,

$$= \sum_{i=1}^{n} X_i .$$

The probability that the k-th truck is dispatched on the n-th option is equivalent to the joint probability that Y_{n-1} is less than k (if it were greater than or equal to k, then we would have dispatched the k-th truck on one of the first $n-1$ options) and that Y_n is greater than or equal to k (if this were not true, we would be dispatching the k-th truck on option $n + 1$ or greater). Thus

$$d(k,n) = \text{Prob} [Y_{n-1} < k \text{ and } Y_n \geq k].$$

which after some manipulations becomes

$$d(k,n) = \text{Prob} [Y_{n-1} < k] - \text{Prob} [Y_n < k].$$

We assume that the random variables X_n are distributed according to a Poisson distribution with mean f_n, and hence the variables Y_n also have Poisson distributions. Thus the dispatch probabilities are simply differences between two Poisson distributions.

REFERENCES

Jordan, W. C. and Turnquist, M. A. 1983, "A stochastic dynamic model for railroad car distribution," *Transportation Science*, Vol. 17, No. 2, pp. 123-145.

Ouimet, G. P. 1972, "Empty freight car distribution," *MS thesis*. Queens University, Kingston, Ontario.

Powell, W. B. 1987, "An operational planning model for the dynamic vehicle allocation problem with uncertain demands," *Transportation Research*, Vol. 213, No. 3, pp. 217-232.

Powell, W. B.; Sheffi, Y.; and Thiriez, S. 1984, "The dynamic vehicle allocation problem with uncertain demands," *Proceedings of the Ninth International Symposium on Transportation and Traffic Theory*, Dormuller and Hamersalg, eds., VNU Science Press, The Netherlands, pp. 357-374.

White, W. W. 1972, "Dynamic transshipment network: An algorithm and its application to the distribution of empty containers," *Networks*, Vol. 2, No. 3, pp. 211-236.

Keith J. Margelowsky, Vice-President, Administration, North American Commercial Transport Division, A Division of North American Van Lines, Inc., PO Box 988, Fort Wayne, Indiana 46801-0988, writes "The impact of this system on our operation is divided into these areas:

Changes in Management Philosophy

More proactive management in daily truckload operations.

Operation on a national scope rather than regional.

Common goals between Sales and Operations Departments.

Pricing decisions which consider daily incremental impacts.

Major Uses of LOADMAP

Recommended repositioning of vehicles.

Load prioritization.

Evaluation of potential loads.

The impact of LOADMAP can be measured by the improvement to divisional contribution margin. We have performed a number of evaluations, and our conservative estimate is a $2.9 million improvement."

4

MARKETING

From the viewpoint of a manager or decision maker, marketing deals with deciding what products to offer under what terms and conditions to what potential customers. To make those decisions soundly, marketers must understand how their customers and their competitors are likely to respond to the products and terms they offer.

Among the many tools at the marketer's disposal are the means to transmit information about product benefits to potential customers (through the sales force and other media), and the content of the selling message itself.

This chapter presents examples of management science approaches to two common marketing problems: determining the size of a sales force, and evaluating the effectiveness of a new advertising program.

4.1 SALES FORCE SIZING FOR A PHARMACEUTICAL MANUFACTURER

At Syntex Laboratories, a pharmaceutical manufacturer, Lodish et al. [1986] helped determine the firm's sales force management strategy— the size of the sales force and the allocation of sales effort across the company's products and customers. They needed to develop sales response functions to feed a relatively simple decision model. The model had to be simple both because it had to be understood by the firm's top management and because data were just not available to justify a more sophisticated approach to parameterize the sales [Little 1970]. While judgmental calibration has both critics and advocates [Chakrabarti,

Mitchell, and Staelin 1981 and Little and Lodish 1981], the successful results of the project testify to the quality of the data obtained by this method.

This project convinced Syntex top management to greatly increase the size of its sales force and to deploy the sales force in a different manner than had been the case historically. The result was a recurring $25 million increase in sales that top management concedes is due to the use of the model.

4.2 DEVELOPING A NEW ADVERTISING PROGRAM FOR THE PHONE COMPANY

In the late 1970s, Kuritsky et al. [1982] at AT&T Long Lines created a marketing program to bring the level of use of the long-distance phone network more closely into balance across the day. Their program of research was classical: it followed all of the steps of a top quality market research program leading to effective marketing action. The most impressive aspect of the study is the large scale market experiment designed to evaluate the effectiveness of the new program. During a 26-month period, AT&T monitored the calling habits of 16,000 customers in a balanced, "split-cable" television advertising experiment. As AT&T maintains complete data on the timing of phone calls as well as on the timing of the ads, this experiment provided an excellent demonstration of the impact of advertising copy on sales. The model projected over a $100 million profit increase following use of this advertising copy strategy for five years.

4.3 MARKETING DECISION PROBLEMS

The major decisions that marketers address fall into two categories, strategic and tactical. Strategic marketing decisions address such questions as what new products should a firm develop and how should it manage the interactions among its line of products. Tactical marketing decisions deal with the management of what marketers call the "marketing mix" (the price, advertising, selling, service, and other related decisions) for a specific product.

To describe the role and use of MS/OR and mathematical models in marketing, we will first outline some of these decision areas in a bit more detail and then indicate what makes the marketing environment difficult to predict and control.

Strategic marketing decisions include decisions about new products and product lines. In deciding whether to market new products, one must answer the following questions: What is the sales level and market share for a new product likely to be? When is the best time for a new product to be introduced? How do the marketing mix elements affect the likely sales rate and market share for the product?

One must also consider questions about the company's product line: How do the related products of a firm interact with one another in the market? Are they synergistic (Polaroid film and Polaroid cameras)? Do they compete with one another for business (New Coke and Coke Classic)? How should the marketing mix for this line of products be managed over different markets and over time?

The company must also consider higher level questions concerning the firm's overall strategy: What is the appropriate marketing route to healthy growth for the firm? Through existing (or new) products? In existing (or new) markets? As a leader, follower, or niche player in these markets?

Tactical marketing or deciding on the marketing mix concerns the physical design of products, the pricing strategy, distribution, advertising, and the sales force: What features (performance level, options, warranty period, and so forth) should products incorporate? What line of products should be produced? In what package sizes? How should the products be presented, psychologically, in the market place—as high performance products? As luxury products? As high-value products?

In considering pricing strategy, the firm must decide what the price should be for the product or products. How should that price vary over time, by order size, by geographic region, by type of customer (original equipment manufacturer versus end user, for example)? How should a line of products by priced? How should complementary products be priced? (The price of razors versus the price of blades, for example.) How should the firm react to pricing variations of competitive products?

In considering distribution strategy for the product, one must ask, What is the most profitable way to reach the market? Should the firm use distributors, go direct to customers with its own sales force, or use some combination? How should that distribution strategy vary by type of customer (large or small), region, or country? How many levels of middlemen should be included in the channel of distribution? Where should distribution facilities be located? In what markets? At what specific locations in each market area?

Advertising and promotion decisions concern the following questions: How much should be spent to advertise and promote the product or products? How should that spending vary over time? (Should it be steady? Vary by season? Or be pulsed?) How much advertising and promotion should be directed to the consumer and how much to intermediaries (distributors and retailers)? What media should be used to communicate the advertising messages (print, direct mail, television, or radio)? What specific set of programs or magazines should carry the ad? What advertising copy or message is best for selling the product?

The company must consider how to use its sales force in marketing the product: What role should the sales force take? (Is direct selling, distributors' effort, or advertising to play the primary role in selling the product?) How much should be spent to sell the product? How large should the sales force be? How should sales force effort be allocated to customers, to products, and to sales territories over time? How should the sales force be motivated and compensated to ensure optimal productivity?

Several characteristics of the marketing environment make it difficult to predict and control: Advertising spending may have almost no effect until a certain amount has been spent, because so many messages bombard us all each day. But the effect of advertising on sales must reach a point of diminishing returns; a market's ability to absorb a product has some limit. (How much Coke can you drink?)

Marketing mix decisions have strong interactions. Advertising spending may affect price elasticity: advertising aimed at clear product differentiation is designed to make consumers less sensitive to price. But advertising that stresses a product's value for the money ("Cutrate brand works as well as Premium at a fraction of the price!") may increase price elasticity in the market. Advertising and selling efforts may complement or substitute for one another. The same may be true for advertising and promotional activities. And these effects and interactions may vary over the product life cycle.

Marketing decisions are made in highly sensitive and competitive environments, where it is critical for the firm to respond to competitive activities and to anticipate competitors' responses to those actions. An increase in a firm's spending on advertising may spur one competitor to lower its prices and another to introduce a glassware-giveaway promotion: that increase in advertising, by stimulating competitive response, may even lead to lower product sales!

Marketing decisions must be made in the face of these and many other uncertainties, not the least of which is the often meager and outdated information available about product performance and other activities in that market (sales, price, advertising levels, and the like, for both the marketer and its competitors). Even when good data are available, one must always question whether the market will behave in the future as it has in the past.

Because marketing systems are too complex to manage in all of their detail, people deal with models of them, employing the MS/OR approach. Even simple models can prove quite powerful in practice.

Example

H. J. Heinz, in promoting one of its products, began an analysis of promotional effectiveness in 1972. A preliminary study indicated that promotional effectiveness, in terms of effect on market share, was different for different package sizes within a district and varied across districts. A model, based on the results of the initial study, showed wide variation in promotional effectiveness across markets. That simple regression model linked share of features and promotions by package size to market share. An overall analysis indicated that a budget reallocation might be in order. Specifically, for the fiscal year 1973-1974, Heinz reduced the total number of promotions by 40 percent from what it had been the previous year and concentrated mostly on those promotions that the model showed was effective. Heinz's market share was increased by more than three share points [Shapiro 1976, p. 86].

This example of marketing modeling and analysis has several important points:

— Standard business practice (the prior promotional policy) may be less than cost-effective.
— Marketing models do not have to be complex to be valuable.
— Models may help isolate situations where profitability can be increased by reallocating resources or by cutting spending.
— Models help firms to focus on the key variable of interest (the market-varying, promotional-response parameter) and serve as vehicles for analyzing its impact.

The nature and the diversity of marketing decisions makes the area a bit different from some of the other functional areas, in that there are few, generic "marketing models" per se. Rather, marketing models have been built and applied that differ widely according to their

— Mathematical form: Some marketing models are linear, some are nonlinear, but linearizeable, and some are inherently non-linear.
— Static or dynamic nature: Some marketing models take a static view of the world while others look at the flow of actions over time. Dynamic models vary depending on whether they look at the world at discrete intervals or continuously.
— Probabilistic or deterministic nature: While nothing in a market is known with certainty, marketing modelers sometimes ignore the uncertainty (deterministic models), deal with uncertainty by appending it to a deterministic model (deterministic with stochastic error), or build an inherently stochastic model (probability model).
— Level of aggregation: Individual behavior can be modeled directly and then aggregated up to a market level, or total market response can be modeled directly.
— Level of demand: Product or brand sales can be modeled directly, or sales can be viewed as the product of the sales of the product class and market share.

Exhibit 4–1 elaborates on this framework and gives some mathematical examples.

We are faced with a diverse set of marketing problems and a

EXHIBIT 4–1. Mathematical models in marketing can be classified along five dimensions.

Dimension	Examples
1. Mathematical Form	
Linear in parameters and variables	$Q = a_o + a_1X$
Nonlinear in variables, linear in parameters	$Q = a_o + a_1X + a_2 X^2$
Nonlinear in parameters, linearizable	$Q = a_o X_1{}^{a_1} X_2{}^{a_2}$
Inherently nonlinear	$Q = a_o (1 - e^{-a_1 x})$
2. Dynamic Effects	
Discrete time	$Q_1 = a_0 + a_1 X_t + \lambda Q_{t-1}$
Continuous time	$\dfrac{dQ}{dt} = \dfrac{rX\,(V - Q)}{V} - \lambda Q$
3. Uncertainty	
Deterministic	$Q = a_0 + a_1 X$
Deterministic with stochastic error	$Q = a_0 + a_1 X + \epsilon$
Inherently stochastic	$p = f$ (past purchase behavior)
4. Level of Aggregation	
Individual	$p = f$ (past behavior, marketing variables)
Segment or market	$Q = a_0 + a_1 Q$
5. Level of Demand	
Product class	$Y = f$ (demographic trends, total marketing spending)
Brand sales	$Q = SV$
Market share	$S = \dfrac{us}{us + them}$

diverse set of models that can be used to address them. We will focus on only two areas: sales force models, and advertising models.

For a broader perspective, the most comprehensive book available on the MS/OR approach to marketing is Lilien and Kotler [1983] (a revised version is projected for 1991). The book has more than 1,100 references, and each chapter includes an extensive review of the literature in the area, citing important applications. Clark [1987] is the most comprehensive case book currently available, providing detailed illustrations of the business situations in which many of these models have been used. Lilien [1986, 1988] provides Lotus 1-2-3 templates that permit easy construction of many models.

4.4 SALES FORCE MODELS

Exhibit 4–2 shows the four main phases in managing personal selling. First, the firm must define the role of personal selling in its marketing

EXHIBIT 4–2. Sales force decision problems can be tackled at four levels that interact with one another, as seen here. (Source: Montgomery and Urban, 1969, p. 244. Used with permission.)

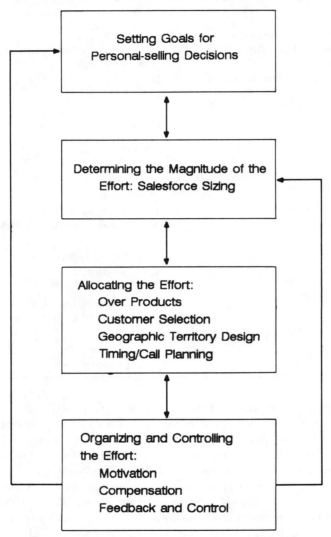

mix by establishing goals or criteria for use in making decisions about the sales force. Second, it must commit resources to the effort; it must develop a sales force budget and determine the size of the sales force. Third, the firm must allocate resources and decide how effort is to be spread among customers, products, sales territories, and time (that is, how calls are to be scheduled). Finally, it must consider the organization, motivation, and control of the selling effort: the firm must set the structure of the sales force and the levels of reporting responsibility; it must establish motivation and compensation schemes; it must monitor the training and assignment of salespersons; and it must monitor the results of the selling effort—sales performance—and feed these results back into the other decision areas to help the firm to adapt to changing market conditions.

As the two-directional flows in Exhibit 4–2 suggest, this process is cyclical rather than sequential. Sales force goals affect the magnitude of the effort, but the size of the effort limits what goals are possible as well. The size of the sales force affects its allocation, but at the allocation stage the firm may discover that sales response is greater (or smaller) than expected, and therefore profitability may be enhanced by allocating more (or fewer) resources to personal selling. The initial sales-force-sizing decision may also be updated in light of customer and territory allocations. Simultaneous determination of these management problems would be ideal, but, in practice, firms usually allocate resources sequentially across the dimensions.

We will focus on the issues of determining sales force size and allocating sales effort. Across a wide variety of industries, firms spend somewhere between five and 15 percent of sales on the sales force, and so deciding on the sales-force size and allocating sales effort are very important.

Sales Force Sizing

To decide on the size of their sales forces, many firms use either an arbitrary percentage of sales or they follow industry guidelines. In the percentage-of-sales method, a percentage of the past or anticipated future sales level is allocated to the sales-force budget. In the industry guidelines method, the firm determines its level of spending by observing what other "similar" firms seem to spend.

Neither of these methods has much to recommend it except simplicity, since each ignores the interaction between the number of salespeople and the level of sales.

Ideally, the firm would like to be able to relate the level of sales to a sales response function and maximize profit:

$$\max Z = PQ(X) - C(Q) - D(X) \text{ or}$$

$$\max \text{Profit} = \text{price} \times \text{quantity} - \text{production and marketing costs,}$$

where

Z = profit,

P = selling price,

$Q(X)$ = quantity sold as a function of selling effort level X,

C(Q) = cost of producing and merchandising Q units,

D(X) = total cost of a selling effort of level X.

The equation above assumes that all other elements in the marketing mix are fixed (price, advertising, and so forth), no carryover or competitive effects exist, a single product is sold by the salesperson, and so on. The equation is naive, but it points out the key unknown relationship: while the elements P, C(Q), and D(X) are likely to be known or readily estimable, the quantity Q(X)—the sales response function—is generally more difficult to obtain. Lodish et al. [1986] provide an approach for developing an estimate of this quantity.

Allocation of Effort

To allocate selling effort, the firm must answer two basic questions: (1) How can salespersons best utilize their time, allocating it between existing customers and prospects? and (2) How should selling effort be allocated to products?

Many procedures exist to help the salesperson and the sales manager address these questions. We will outline one well-known and successful procedure:

CALLPLAN [Lodish 1971] is an interactive salesperson's call-planning system. Its objective is to determine call-frequency norms for each client (current customer) and each prospect (account not currently buying from the salesperson). Call frequencies are the numbers of calls per effort period, which is the time period on which the allocations are based (usually one to three months).

The model is based on the assumption that the expected sales to each client and prospect over a response period (usually a year) are functions of the average number of calls per effort period during that response period. The response period is assumed to be long enough so that such phenomena as carryover in call effort from one period to the next are considered.

The CALLPLAN procedure has two phases:

1. The calibration stage, in which the expected profit associated with different call policies for each customer and prospects is determined; and,
2. The optimization phase, in which optimal allocation of time to customers and prospects is established.

Interestingly, a controlled experiment was run at United Airlines on the use of CALLPLAN [Fudge and Lodish 1977]. United Airlines has a sales force to promote passenger travel and another to promote air freight operations. Account call frequency determines, to a large degree, the efficiency of the sales force's time allocation.

Twenty salespersons (16 passenger representatives and four cargo representatives) participated in the experiment; 10 pairs of salespersons (five in New York and five in San Francisco) were matched by local management. Ten CALLPLAN participants were chosen randomly, one from each pair. Then the remaining 10 salespersons comprised the control group. This group was told they were participating in an experiment and they manually estimated their own call-frequency policies and anticipated sales for each account to compare with CALLPLAN. Therefore major sources of potential contamination were largely controlled for.

After six months, the CALLPLAN group had an 11.9 percent increase in sales from the previous year, while the control group had only a 3.8 percent increase; thus the CALLPLAN users realized an 8.1 percent higher level of sales. This difference was significantly different from 0 at the 0.025 level. The actual sales improvement over that of the control group for just these 10 people was "well into seven figures."

4.5 ADVERTISING MODELS

One of the most important and bewildering promotional tools of modern marketing management is advertising. No one doubts that it is effective in presenting information to potential buyers. There is also widespread agreement that it can be persuasive to some extent and can reinforce buyer preference for a company's product.

Advertising is bewildering because, among other reasons, its effects typically play out over time, may be nonlinear, and can interact with other elements in the marketing mix in creating sales. Currently, no one knows what advertising really does in the marketplace. However, what advertising is supposed to do is fairly clear: advertising is undertaken to increase company sales or to increase profits over what they otherwise would be. However, it is rarely able to create sales by itself. Whether the customer buys also depends on the product, the price, packaging, personal selling, services, financing, and other aspects of the marketing process.

Aaker and Myers [1975] define three decision areas for advertising: (1) setting objectives and a budget (what advertising should do and how much to spend), (2) deciding on copy (what message), and (3) deciding what media to use. Although we address these three points separately here, they are closely interrelated: advertising objectives drive copy decisions, and copy effects, varying by response group, affect media decisions. In addition, time is an issue for all three decision areas. For budgeting, dollars must be spent over time, and pulsing versus more continuous spending patterns must be evaluated. Furthermore, advertising copy varies in its effectiveness over time, eventually wearing out. New copy must be phased in. Finally, media decisions are closely connected with the timing and scheduling of messages, as well as with the selection of media.

Advertising Response Phenomena

Little [1979] identifies three sets of controversies for advertising sales response models: shape, dynamics, and interaction. He also reviews many empirical examples in a rare attempt to unify and generalize what we have observed (Exhibit 4–3). First, advertising increases sales here: sales increase considerably when substantial new advertising dollars are introduced. Also, the sales rate increases within a month or so, substantially faster than many managers purport to be the case.

Exhibit 4–3 also shows sales leveling off under the new spending

EXHIBIT 4–3. Sales rate of a packaged good rises quickly under increased advertising but declines slowly after it is removed. (Source: John D.C. Little, 1979. Used with permission.)

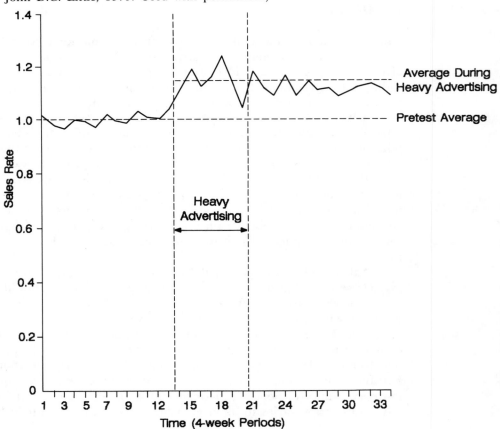

regime: apparently, the total effect of the advertising was seen before spending stopped.

Finally, the exhibit shows the beginning of decay following the lowering of advertising. Furthermore, sales decayed more slowly than they grew. Two separate phenomena are involved: the rise is related to advertising communications, while the decline is related to product experience, a different phenomenon. The decline therefore should be expected to occur at a different rate.

Exhibit 4–4 shows the sales of a line of products that have never been advertised. Supermarkets and department stores are full of house brands, price brands, and other products that sell quite well with no advertising. Therefore an advertising response model should admit the possibility of sales with zero advertising.

Perhaps the most interesting set of controversies in advertising deals with nonlinearities in the response curve. Logic suggests that a linear response curve is unreasonable: a product with a linear response would have an "optimal" advertising rate of either zero or infinity, and its sales could be made increasingly large by continuing to increase

EXHIBIT 4–4. The healthy sales of a line of unadvertised food products showing that advertising is not always required to sell something. (Source: John D.C. Little, 1979. Used with permission.)

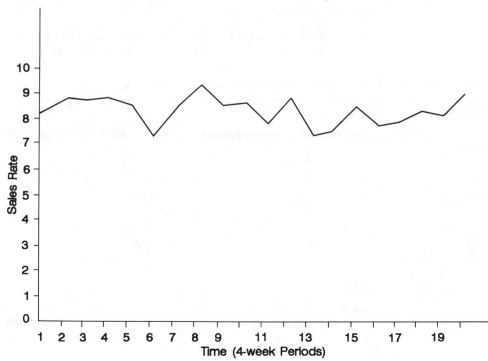

spending on advertising. On the other hand, nonlinearity covers many alternatives, the two most important of which are diminishing returns and an S shape.

Exhibit 4–5 shows two products that display concavity, or diminishing returns to advertising. Although there is some argument to the contrary, both the practice of pulsing (justified on the theory that small amounts of advertising do little good but that medium amounts are effective) and empirical evidence support the S-shaped response hypothesis.

Finally, Little [1979, p. 644] summarizes his observations with a list of five phenomena that a good advertising response model should admit:

1. Sales respond dynamically upward and downward, respectively, to increases and decreases of advertising and frequently do so at different rates.
2. Steady-state response can be concave or S-shaped and will often have positive sales at zero advertising.
3. Competitive advertising affects sales.
4. The dollar effectiveness of advertising can change over time as the results of changes in media, copy, and other factors.
5. Products sometimes respond to increased advertising with a sales increase that falls off even as advertising is held constant.

Frequency Phenomena

For media planning and scheduling, knowledge of the effect of advertising exposures over time is critical. Naples [1979, pp. 63-81] summarizes

EXHIBIT 4–5. Two examples of nonlinear response show the phenomenon of diminishing returns at high advertising rates. (Source: John D.C. Little, 1979. Used with permission.)

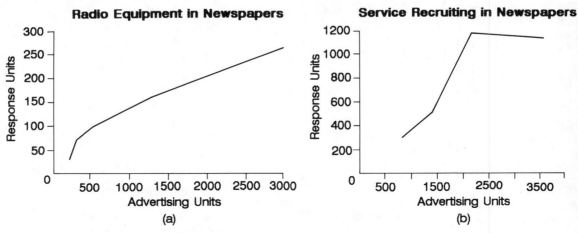

the results of an extensive review of the published literature and offers the following conclusions:

1. Optimal exposure frequency appears to be at least three exposures within a purchase cycle.
2. Beyond three ad exposures, effectiveness increases but at a decreasing rate.
3. Frequency by itself does not cause wear-out, although it can advance the decline of an effective campaign.
4. Response to advertising appears smaller for the brand with dominant market share.

Over the years many systematic procedures have been developed to support media decisions. These procedures can be categorized via three components: (1) their objective function, which assigns a value (profit/effective exposure, for example) to a schedule; (2) the solution strategy (optimizing; expert system; rules of thumb, for example) and (3) the constraints (budget and other).

In the 1960s the development of media decision models surged. Many were very sophisticated and required enormous amounts of data and computational power to generate schedules. After a decade of trial, advertising agencies found a number of heuristic procedures they could use to generate very good (if not "optimal") schedules with much less time and effort. In addition, media planners understood these heuristic procedures easily. Today, heuristic procedures are the dominant tools used in media selection.

Copy Phenomena

Copy research involves investigation of a myriad of phenomena, from how the physical and mechanical aspects of ads relate to recognition, recall, and other measures to the humor and seriousness of TV ads. In his review of a large number of copy-testing studies, Ramond [1976, pp. 49-51] provides the following principles, where the term *principle* implies a basic finding with implications for future practice. These principles, like the observations above, hold in many circumstances:

1. The bigger the print ad, the more people will recognize it later, possibly as a function of the square root of the size increase.
2. Color ads are recognized by more people than black-and-white ads.
3. Product class has a significant effect on recognition or recall of both TV and print ads.
4. Sex, humor, and fear have no consistent effect in what advertising communicates.
5. Awareness and attitude changes are sensitive to differences in TV-commercial execution and can predict changes in brand choice.
6. Ads need not be believed to be remembered.

While these observations have not been sufficiently understood or generalized to justify the term *theory*, they do represent what appears to be general agreement about the effects of advertising copy. Research in this area continues. For example, Hanssens and Weitz [1980] reported that industrial-ad recall and readership scores were strongly related to a variety of characteristics, such as size and position in magazines.

Because of the noisy nature of the marketplace, as well as the often long delays between advertising and its impact on sales, most advertising copy is tested in laboratory-like settings or theaters, and immediate response as well as delayed response (day-after recall) are used to indicate the effectiveness of the advertising.

Occasionally, field experiments in a test market city are used to evaluate a new advertising strategy; such experiments increasingly are using so-called split-cable technology in which adjacent neighborhoods in the same city view the same television programs but see different commercial messages. In many cases, it is still difficult to measure the differences in advertising effect because the sales from these adjacent neighborhoods are not easily decoupled. The paper by Kuritsky et al. [1982] describes a situation in which this decoupling problem was overcome.

4.6 FURTHER READINGS

Related Readings

Lodish et al. Paper

- Lodish [1971] develops an interactive salesperson's call-planning system (CALLPLAN) in a slightly different context (that is, individual salespeople allocate effort to customers). Fudge and Lodish [1977], in a previous Edelman finalist paper, report the results of a controlled field experiment at United Airlines using CALLPLAN. Clark [1987] gives a more complete description of the Syntex story, and also provides a Lotus 1-2-3 spreadsheet in which the student can study the response modeling directly.

Kuritsky et al. Paper

- Little [1979] provides an excellent overview of the advertising response models and the phenomena that they attempt to model. Gross [1972] wrote a classical paper on the controversies surrounding how much to spend on creating versus testing ads. His conclusion was that ad agencies were in a conflict of interest situation, by both creating ads and acting as agents for media (taking a commission on media sales) and that the industry might operate more efficiently if it were organized differently. McGuire [1977] provides a good description of the concepts behind split cable advertising experiments and their basic design. Lilien and Kotler

[1983, Chapter 14] and Rust [1986] provide extensive reviews and guides to the model-based work in the advertising area.

Background Readings

Lodish et al. Paper

- Lilien and Kotler [1983, Chapter 16] provide an overview of sales-force models, focusing on those models that have been useful for sales-force sizing, as here, as well as effort allocation (across products as well as across customers), sales territory design, sales motivation and compensation models, and integrative models for sales-force decisions.
- Zoltners and Sinha [1980] and Cravens [1979] provide useful review articles. Zoltners and Sinha provide 48 references for integer programming models of sales-force allocation models alone, while the Cravens provides a useful comparative assessment of 22 sales-force decision models.
- Hutt and Speh [1989, Chapter 17], Johnson [1976], and Shapiro [1977] are all fine texts discussing sales-force decision problems.

Kuritsky et al. Paper

- Aaker and Myers [1975] is a good text, providing a background and overview of both management and behavioral science perspectives on advertising problems. Dunn and Barban [1986], Rossiter and Percy [1987], and Shimp and DeLozier [1986] are all good, contemporary advertising texts.

REFERENCES

Aaker, David A. and Myers, John G. 1975, *Advertising Management*, Prentice-Hall, Englewood Cliffs, New Jersey.

Chakrabarti, Dipankar; Mitchell, Andrew; and Staelin, Richard 1981, "Judgmentally based marketing decision models: Problems and possible solutions," *Journal of Marketing*, Vol. 45, No. 4, pp. 12–23.

Clark, Darral G. 1987, *Marketing Analysis and Decision Making: Text and Cases with Lotus 1-2-3*, The Scientific Press, Redwood City, California.

Cravens, David W. 1979, "Salesforce decision models: A comparative assessment," in *Sales Management: New Developments from Behavioral and Decision Model Research*, ed. R. Bagozzi, The Marketing Science Institute, Cambridge, Massachusetts, pp. 310–324.

Dunn, S. Watson and Barban, Arnold M. 1986, *Advertising*, The Dryden Press, New York.

Fudge, William K. and Lodish, Leonard M. 1977, "Evaluation of the effectiveness of a model-based salesman's planning system by field experimentation," *Interfaces*, Vol. 8, No. 1, Part 2, pp. 97–101.

Gross, Irwin 1972, "The creative aspects of advertising," *Sloan Management Review*, Vol. 15, No. 1 (Fall), pp. 83–110.

Hanssens, Dominique M. and Weitz, Barton A. 1980, "The effectiveness of industrial print advertisements across product categories," *Journal of Marketing Research*, Vol. 17, No. 3, pp. 294–306.

Hutt, Michael D. and Speh, Thomas W. 1989, *Business Marketing Management: A Strategic View of Industrial and Organizational Markets*, The Dryden Press, New York.

Johnson, H. Webster 1976, *Sales Management: Operations Administration Marketing*, Merrill Publishing, Columbus, Ohio.

Kuritsky, Alan P.; Little, John D. C.; Silk, Alvin J.; and Bassman, Emily S. 1982, "The development, testing, and execution of a new marketing strategy at AT&T long lines," *Interfaces*, Vol. 12, No. 6, pp. 22–37.

Lilien, Gary L. 1986, *Marketing Mix Analysis with Lotus 1-2-3*, The Scientific Press, Redwood City, California.

Lilien, Gary L. 1988, *Marketing Management: Analytic Exercises with Lotus 1-2-3*, The Scientific Press, Redwood City, California.

Lilien, Gary L. and Kotler, Philip 1983, *Marketing Decision Making: A Model Building Approach*, Harper and Row, New York.

Little, John D. C. 1970, "Models and managers: The concept of a decision calculus," *Management Science*, Vol. 16, No. 8, pp. B466–485.

Little, John D. C. 1979, "Aggregate advertising models: The state of the art," *Operations Research*, Vol. 27, No. 4, pp. 629–667.

Little, John D. C. and Lodish, Leonard M. 1981, "Commentary on 'Judgement Based Marketing Decision Models,' " *Journal of Marketing*, Vol. 45, No. 4, pp. 24–29.

Lodish, Leonard M. 1971, "CALLPLAN: An interactive salesman's call-planning system," *Management Science*, Vol. 18, No. 4, Part 2 (December), pp. 25–40.

Lodish, Leonard M.; Curtis, Ellen; Ness, Michael; and Simpson, M. Kerry 1986, "Salesforce sizing and deployment using a decision calculus model at Syntex Laboratories," *Interfaces*, Vol. 18, No. 1, pp. 5–20.

McGuire, Timothy W. 1977, "Measuring and testing relative advertising effectiveness with split cable TV panel data," *Journal of the American Statistical Association*, Vol. 72, No. 360, pp. 736–745.

Montgomery, David B. and Urban, Glen L. 1969, *Management Science in Marketing*, Prentice-Hall, Englewood Cliffs, New Jersey.

Naples, Michael J. 1979, *Effective Frequency*, Association of National Advertisers, New York.

Ramond, Charles 1976, *Advertising Research: The State of the Art*, Association of National Advertisers, New York.

Rossiter, John R. and Percy, Larry 1987, *Advertising and Promotion Management*, McGraw-Hill, New York.

Rust, Roland T. 1986, *Advertising Media Models: A Practical Guide*, Lexington Books, Lexington, Massachusetts.

Shapiro, Arthur 1976, "Promotional effectiveness at H. J. Heinz," *Interfaces*, Vol. 6, No. 2, pp. 84–86.

Shapiro, Benson S. 1977, *Sales Program Management: Formulation and Implementation*, McGraw-Hill, New York.

Shimp, Terry A. and DeLozier, M. Wayne 1986, *Promotion Management and Marketing Communication*, The Dryden Press, New York.

Zoltners, Andris A. and Sinha, Prabhakant 1980, "Integer programming models for sales resource allocation," *Management Science*, Vol. 26, No. 3, pp. 242–260.

Sales Force Sizing and Deployment Using a Decision Calculus Model at Syntex Laboratories

Leonard M. Lodish

Ellen Curtis

Michael Ness

M. Kerry Simpson

Deciding on the appropriate amount to spend on the sales force is a very difficult practical problem. Theoretically, money should be invested in the sales force as long as marginal returns on that investment are greater than other alternative places for corporate investment. However, determining the rate of return on different sales force investments is very difficult for most marketing managers. The biggest determinant of investment in the sales force is the number of people in the force. Relating incremental sales to incremental changes in the sales force size and then relating those incremental sales to profitability over different planning horizons is very difficult. It is hard to isolate the effect of the sales force from all the other effects in the marketplace that might cause sales to go up or down. These effects include pricing, advertising, changes in distribution, changes in market needs, and changes in competitive behavior.

For ethical pharmaceutical firms, the sales force investment decision is even more crucial, because the sales force is the prominent way of marketing their products. Early in 1982, Syntex Laboratories' management realized that the decision on sales force size for the next three years would be very important for the company. One of the idiosyncratic characteristics of decisions on sales force size is that they involve what may be the worst kind of costs for a company. They are variable costs when they are added, that is, each salesperson adds an amount of compensation plus expenses plus sales management time to the cost of the firm. However, it is difficult to cut back sales force size significantly. The morale of the salespeople who remain may be hurt, and the training costs that have been incurred to get a salesperson up to speed are foregone. Management's primary concern was to determine the size the sales force needed to be to optimally support the existing products.

Since 1982, a model-based methodology has been used by Syntex Laboratories to help determine direction for their sales force size and associated decisions on strategic deployment and the product portfolio. Trade-offs were needed in model building and model implementation to make the model practical and implementable for Syntex.

THE COMPANY

Syntex Corporation began in 1940 with topical steroid preparations prescribed by dermatologists and then introduced products for birth control, which were prescribed by gynecologists. By 1982, Syntex Corporation was an international company that developed, manufactured, and marketed a wide range of health and personal care products. In fiscal 1981 (ending July 31), consolidated sales were $710 million with $98 million in net income. Syntex had recorded a 23 percent compound annual growth rate since 1971. Syntex Laboratories, the US human pharmaceutical sales subsidiary, was the largest Syntex subsidiary. Syntex Laboratories' sales for fiscal 1981 increased 35 percent to $215 million and had grown as a percentage of total pharmaceutical sales to 46 percent. Syntex Laboratories' profit percentage of the international operation was greater, however, than their sales percentage, because sales in the US were much more profitable than sales around the world. More detail on the company and the initial model building can be obtained from Clarke, D. [1983].

In 1982, the Syntex product line was made up of seven major products grouped into four categories: nonsteroidal antiarthritic (NSAI) drugs, analgesics, oral contraceptives, and topical steroids. The NSAI product, Naprosyn, was by far the largest and most successful, while birth control and topical steroid products represented the company's early development

as a drug manufacturer. Naprosyn, introduced in 1977, was the third largest selling drug in the NSAI therapeutic class in the US. Naprosyn had become quite successful, because the dosage was flexible, it was prescribed twice a day, less frequently than competing products, and it seldom had side effects. Naprosyn had been introduced first to rheumatologists, who specialize in treating arthritis, and then to general physicians. Anaprox, an analgesic, was launched early in 1981. Anaprox was targeted for analgesic use and for the treatment of menstrual pain. The total number of prescriptions written for analgesics was twice as large as for antiarthritic drugs in the US. Naprosyn and Anaprox are chemically similar products.

Syntex produces two topical steroid creams for treating skin inflammations, Synalar and Lydex. Growth in these products in fiscal 1981 was only slightly ahead of sales in 1980. During 1980's fiscal year, Syntex was the only established company to increase total prescription volume in topical steroids, and two new entries had grown from small shares. Syntex had a very strong following among dermatologists. In 1981, 21 percent of all new topical steroid prescriptions written by dermatologists were for Syntex products.

Syntex's oral contraceptive products, Norinyl 1 + 35 and Norinyl 1 + 50, were available in three dosage forms that together garnered 10 percent of the oral contraceptive market. Sales volume for oral contraceptives in 1980 had grown by 23 percent. However, the growth in dollar volume was primarily the result of price increases. The low dose segment was the growth segment of the oral contraceptive market.

Nasalide is a steroid nasal spray for the treatment of hay fever and allergies, and it had just been approved for United

States marketing by the government authorities early in fiscal 1982.

MARKETING AND SALES AT SYNTEX LABORATORIES

The role of the sales force is to visit physicians and encourage them to prescribe Syntex drugs for their patients. Other marketing elements in the pharmaceutical industry in the US include advertising in medical journals, direct mail, giving physicians samples of products, and other specialized forms of product promotion, such as medical symposia and convention booths. Physicians, the target market for Syntex, could be segmented in many ways. One would be by their specialty (family practice, general practice, internal medicine, orthopedics, rheumatology, Ob/gynecology, dermatology, allergies, and otolaryngology). Data were available on the sizes of each of these specialty groups. Other means of segmenting physicians by number of prescriptions written or innovativeness in trying new products have also been used in the pharmaceutical industry. However, precise data to segment physicians are very expensive to obtain and were not available in 1982 to Syntex.

When a physician prescribes a Syntex drug for a patient, the prescription can be filled at any pharmacy, not necessarily in the same area as the physician. The pharmacies, in many cases, do not buy directly from Syntex but through large wholesalers. Thus, it is very difficult to isolate specifically sales that are influenced by the salesperson's calls on a particular physician. The salesperson does not know whether a sale is made or its amount.

During a sales call, a sales rep normally provides a physician with samples and information about the dosage levels and possible uses for various drugs. Typically, a Syntex salesman is able to describe or "detail" between two and three products during one sales call. It is difficult in many cases to get appointments with busy physicians, and a number of competing sales reps vie for physicians' time.

In late 1981, Ellen Curtis and Michael Ness of the marketing research department consulted with Len Lodish and Kerry Simpson after surveying the literature on sales force management. They then recommended to marketing management that a new approach be used to better answer the question of sales force size at Syntex Laboratories. These four became the model building and development team. The situation at the time was summed up by the then senior vice-president for sales and marketing as follows:

> Our history had been one of increasing the sales force size in relatively small steps. I've never been really satisfied that there was any good reason why we were expanding by 30 or 40 representatives in any one year other than that was what we were able to get approved in the budget process. Over the years, I'd become impatient with the process of going to the well for more people every year with no long-term view of it. I felt that if I went to upper management with a more strategic, or longer-term viewpoint, it would be a lot easier to then sell the annual increases necessary to get up to a previously established objective in sales force size and utilization [Clarke 1983, p. 9].

Syntex Laboratory's management felt it needed a more substantive long-term approach to the issue of optimal sales force size. Corporate management was in turn requiring more thorough analysis to support major expenditures.

MODEL BUILDING TRADE-OFFS

The model-building trade-offs that were needed to handle this problem were challenging. First, because of the way products are distributed in the pharmaceutical industry, there was no available data for trying to estimate empirically what the response had been to sales force size in the past. Syntex did not have data that some pharmaceutical firms do have, which describe wholesaler shipments to small geographical areas. Second, as this decision on sales force size was risky, because of the difficulties of reversing it, convergent procedures to develop sales force size estimates would have been useful. Third, if subjective estimates were to be used, management would devote only a limited amount of time to estimating parameters for a procedure that had not been proven or used in the past by the company. If management were to estimate parameters, it was important that they be able to estimate response realistically. That is, could managers and other people making estimates realistically imagine response scenarios? The problem also had to be structured so that the solution was realistic and made sense. Therefore the model needed to be complete on the important issues of sales force size. It was also very important to involve the managers who were to implement the solution in the model-building process. Summarizing the model-building objectives, the team felt that we should do the best we could with the people and data available.

THE INITIAL MODELS

We first had to decide what kind of sales response estimates to use. We felt that having managers estimate directly what sales response would be with different size sales forces was too broad. To make such direct estimates a manager would need to know (at least implicitly)

(1) Where the increase or decrease in sales force personnel would be employed,

(2) What products would have more or less effort applied to them, and

(3) Which market segments would have more or less effort applied to them.

Alternatively, the response estimates could be made at a very micro level, such as for physicians of a certain specialty in one region. In this case, it would be very difficult for anyone to make response estimates to details for a particular product. Hundreds of estimates would be needed for each product, region, and specialty. Thus, the way the problem was structured or the market divided in order to estimate sales response was a critical trade-off the team had to make.

We decided to develop two similar but separate versions of the model, each one to help estimate sales response to increased or decreased sales force size. The first model sought to determine the optimal number of sales presentations (details) to be allotted to each Syntex product; the second sought to decide the number of sales representative visits to physician specialties. The first model involved sales response estimates of the effect on sales if the emphasis on particular products were changed, while the second model looked at estimates of sales changes if the effort applied to various market segments were changed. By estimating or approximating the effects of sales force size independently of each other, the two models could provide convergent estimates and thus reduce risk.

The structure of the two models was mathematically identical. Each was based upon the existing strategic plan for the next three years. This plan had been constructed following the same method Syntex Laboratories had used for many years. The plan assumed the sales force would remain the same for the next three years but did include all other changing elements of the environment and competition of which the planners were aware when they made the forecast. Also included in the models were hard data on the cost per sales representative, which included compensation, expenses and prorated management time for regional and district managers in the sales force. The variable cost for producing and distributing each product was also a necessary input to convert sales to incremental contribution to fixed costs. These costs were estimated both by product and on average for sales by specialty, depending on the average product mix that was anticipated by specialty. The final bit of hard information utilized by the models was the current allocation of sales force effort by products and market segments. These data were available from company records and syndicated sources. In each sales call (visit), the sales rep makes several presentations (or details). The required transformation of salespersons to number of presentations (details) and the number of calls was available also from syndicated data.

The important element of the models

for which data were not available was the sales response of products or market segments to changes in sales force effort over a future three-year period. We chose the three-year period as long enough for new products to achieve maturity and get through the introductory diffusion process. A time period shorter than three years would not allow this to happen. Some managers felt uncomfortable with a longer time horizon because they felt they could not estimate sales response over such a long period.

THE MODELS

Both the models for product and segment allocation were based upon the strategic plan for fiscal year 1985. Each model modified the plan's sales levels by a response function which related sales changes to changes in sales effort. These sales levels were multiplied by an adjustment factor that reflects incremental contribution margin or other corporate product/segment priorities. The mathematical program maximizes adjusted sales subject to sales resource constraints. See the appendix for a detailed description of the model and solution procedure.

SUBJECTIVE PARAMETER ESTIMATION

Estimating response functions was the most important activity of the model-building and implementation effort. The estimation required knowledge from many different vantage points within the corporation. Different people's responsibilities within the corporation caused them to have different points of view on what sales response might be. For example, a product manager would be very attuned to his particular product's sales response but might not be very familiar with or sympathetic to other products that compete for sales force attention. The estimation procedure also attempted to minimize the group domination that might happen if one strong individual were able to dominate a discussion. The procedure also tried to isolate the relevant assumptions that went into sales response so that they could be looked at and evaluated over time.

A series of special estimation meetings were held in conjunction with the annual marketing planning meetings which took place in a conference center location off-site. The corporate personnel involved in the estimation meetings were the senior vice-president of sales and marketing, the vice-president of sales, two people from the market research department, two product managers, two regional sales managers, and two salespeople. Given constraints on available people, this was our best attempt at developing a group that would be collectively expert on sales response to sales force effort.

We began the meeting with a short lecture on sales response modeling and an exercise in which a small problem was solved manually by people in the group. We did this so that the group would understand what the model was trying to accomplish and to motivate the participants to go through Delphi estimation sessions.

The main purpose of the meetings was to come to a group consensus on the likely response of each Syntex product and physician specialty to sales rep effort. On Monday, the first day of the annual meetings, we distributed work sheets to the participants which asked them to estimate what change in sales for each of seven

Syntex Labs' products and nine physician specialties would result from different levels of sales rep activity. Each manager responded to the following question for each product and specialty: "According to the strategic plan, if the current level of sales force effort is maintained from 1982 to 1985, sales of Product A would be the planned level. What would happen to Product A's 1985 sales (compared with present levels) if during this same time period it received

(1)   No sales effort?
(2)   One half the current effort?
(3)   50 percent greater sales effort?
(4)   A saturation level of sales effort?"

These four points would then be used to fit a smooth curve to represent the response function (see appendix).

Each manager filled out his initial response estimates without discussing them with other members of the group. The responses of the group were then summarized on a computer. The summaries included quartiles, medians, and minimum and maximum answers for each of the questions. These summaries were discussed by the group, and those members of the group who were at the far ends of the group norms were encouraged to discuss the reasons for their estimates.

This discussion was extremely fruitful because it isolated a lot of the critical assumptions that were necessary for doing a realistic job of response modeling. Elements, such as the competitive situation, the role and ability of the sales force to influence physicians, and environmental effects, were thoroughly discussed for each product and market segment. After this discussion, we passed out new work sheets, and again each person independently developed his or her response judgments, but in this round participants could take into account the discussion and the summary of the previous estimations. After the second round, the summary showed that the group had reached a fine consensus.

During the three-day national sales meeting, we ran the model and produced output. The group then reconvened after the planning meeting, the model output was presented, and the results were discussed. The initial model output looked reasonable to the group, and it required only a small amount of fine tuning. The senior vice-president of sales and marketing said after the conclusion of the modified Delphi sessions, "Of course, we knew that the responses we estimated were unlikely to be the 'true responses' in some absolute knowledge sense, but we got the most knowledgeable people in the company together in what seemed to me to be a very thorough discussion and the estimates represented the best we could do at the time. We respect the model results, but we'll utilize them with cautious skepticism" [Clarke 1983, p. 10].

The national sales manager summarized his feelings: "We did the best we could to estimate the model. At first we were uncomfortable at having to be so specific about things we weren't too sure about, but by the end of the discussions, we were satisfied that this was the best we could do" [Clarke 1983, p. 10].

THE MODEL RESULTS

Table 1 shows the input to the product allocation model. Table 2 shows the first report made available by the model, the step report. This report shows incrementally which products or segments enter the solution, at what levels, as resources are added to the sales force. At any level or step, an output report is available that summarizes the allocation by product or

TABLE 1. Model input.

Maximum number of sales people: 1,000
Cost per rep by region: $55,498.70
Effort (details or calls) per salesperson per year: 3,677.4

	Naprosyn	Anaprox	Norinyl 1+35	Norinyl 1+50	Synalar	Lydex	Nasalide
Strategic adjustment factor (contribution) for each product:							
	.811	.633	.837	.837	.616	.616	.616
Minimum effort (calls or details) for each product:							
	0	0	0	0	0	0	0
Response functions based on 100 for each product:							
Number of calls	47	15	31	45	56	59	15
One half	68	48	63	70	80	76	61
Present number	100	100	100	100	100	100	100
50 percent more	126	120	115	105	111	107	146
Saturation	152	135	125	110	120	111	176
Normal planned effort (details) for each product:							
	357,853	527,581	195,443	88,817.7	101,123	110,351	210,225

TOTAL DETAILS: 1.59139M

TABLE 2. Step report on the sales force strategy model for fiscal year 1985.

Step	Number of reps	Change in reps	Sales (000)	Change in sales (000)	Change in marginal contribution per rep (000)	Allocated to:
1	0	0	161,129	0	0	NA
2	115.0	115.0	297,965	136,836	909.5	Naprosyn
3	123.9	8.8	307,720	9,754.9	838.8	Naprosyn
4	132.7	8.8	316,326	8,605.8	733.4	Naprosyn
5	152.5	19.8	333,930	17,604.3	690.2	Norinyl 1 + 50
6	161.3	8.8	341,488	7,558.0	637.4	Naprosyn
7	163.5	2.2	343,136	1,648.1	572.8	Norinyl 1 + 50
8	172.3	8.8	349,757	6,621.4	551.5	Naprosyn
9	181.2	8.8	355,553	5,795.5	475.8	Naprosyn
10	190.0	8.8	360,626	5,073.6	409.6	Naprosyn
11	192.2	2.2	361,834	1,207.6	404.8	Norinyl 1 + 50
12	201.1	8.8	366,280	4,446.1	352.1	Naprosyn
13	221.1	20.0	379,083	12,802.9	338.9	Synalar
14	223.6	2.5	380,596	1,512.6	317.2	Synalar
15	232.4	8.8	384,498	3,902.7	302.3	Naprosyn
16	234.9	2.5	385,797	1,298.5	264.5	Synalar
17	243.8	8.8	389,230	3,432.6	259.2	Naprosyn
18	252.6	8.8	392,256	3,026.3	221.9	Naprosyn
19	255.1	2.5	393,362	1,106.0	217.0	Synalar
20	257.6	2.5	394,386	1,024.2	196.9	Synalar
21	266.5	8.8	397,061	2,674.8	189.7	Naprosyn
22	310.0	43.5	409,278	12,216.9	179.7	Norinyl 1 + 35
23	314.8	4.8	410,602	1,324.7	174.0	Norinyl 1 + 35
24	323.6	8.8	412,973	2,370.5	161.8	Naprosyn
25	326.1	2.5	413,835	861.6	156.8	Synalar
26	335.0	8.8	415,941	2,106.4	137.6	Naprosyn
27	339.8	4.8	417,027	1,086.4	132.7	Norinyl 1 + 35
28	342.3	2.5	417,752	725.1	123.2	Synalar
29	344.5	2.2	418,217	464.8	121.7	Norinyl 1 + 50
30	353.3	8.8	420,094	1,877.0	116.6	Naprosyn
31	362.2	8.8	421,771	1,677.0	98.2	Naprosyn
32	364.7	2.5	422,383	611.6	95.2	Synalar
33	366.9	2.2	422,766	383.4	90.6	Norinyl 1 + 50

34	371.7	4.8	423,586	819.5	86.5	Norinyl 1+35
35	380.6	8.8	425,088	1,502.5	82.2	Naprosyn
36	511.0	130.4	453,321	28,233.1	81.5	Anaprox
37	524.0	13.0	456,113	2,791.9	80.0	Anaprox
38	526.5	2.5	456,631	517.6	72.1	Synalar
39	553.8	27.3	462,174	5,543.1	69.7	Lydex
40	562.7	8.8	463,523	1,349.6	68.2	Naprosyn
41	564.9	2.2	463,843	319.5	66.3	Norinyl 1+50
42	569.7	4.8	464,514	670.7	60.7	Norinyl 1+35
43	572.2	2.5	464,953	439.9	52.9	Synalar
44	644.9	72.8	477,648	12,694.8	49.2	Nasalide
45	647.1	2.2	477,917	268.9	47.0	Norinyl 1+50
46	649.9	2.7	473,360	442.9	44.5	Synalar
47	654.7	4.8	478,910	550.1	39.3	Norinyl 1+35
48	657.2	2.5	478,286	375.6	37.1	Synalar
49	662.4	5.2	480,060	774.1	33.9	Nasalide
50	675.4	13.0	481,887	1,827.3	33.2	Anaprox
51	677.6	2.2	482,115	228.2	31.5	Norinyl 1+50
52	680.1	2.5	482,437	322.2	23.9	Synalar
53	685.0	4.8	482,890	452.9	23.0	Norinyl 1+35
54	690.2	5.2	483,544	653.5	19.9	Nasalide
55	692.4	2.2	483,739	195.3	19.0	Norinyl 1+50
56	705.4	13.0	485,259	1,519.6	18.3	Anaprox
57	707.9	2.5	485,536	277.7	12.9	Synalar
58	712.7	4.8	485,911	374.8	9.4	Norinyl 1+35
59	714.9	2.2	486,090	168.4	8.7	Norinyl 1+50
60	720.1	5.2	486,629	549.6	8.0	Nasalide
61	722.9	2.7	486,905	276.1	6.8	Lydex
62	735.9	13.0	488,170	1,265.0	5.9	Anaprox
63	738.4	2.5	488,411	240.5	3.8	Synalar
64	740.6	2.2	488,557	146.2	0.2	Norinyl 1+50
65	745.4	4.8	488,869	312.1	−1.4	Norinyl 1+35
66	750.6	5.2	489,331	461.8	−2.2	Nasalide

segment that is optimal for that level of resources. For example, the allocation by product of the sales force for 381 representatives (Step 35) and 511 representatives (Step 36) is shown in Tables 3 and 4. The reason that there is such a large difference in resources between these two solutions is that Anaprox was the marginal product to be allocated. It was optimal to allocate either no effort or at least 130 sales reps to it. This phenomenon was due to increasing returns in the parts of the response curve for Anaprox. Table 5 shows the current policy evaluation of 433 representatives for comparison.

The recommended optimal sales force sizes computed from either the product or specialty model were reasonably close together (over 700 representatives). The models differed considerably, however, in their estimation of the incremental contribution per added sales rep at levels between the current sales force size of 433 and 600. Both models indicated that the current sales force was too small, and they both showed that the allocation of effort of the current force was suboptimal. For example, even with the solution for 381 sales reps (52 people fewer than the current size) for the model by product, sales would be approximately $50 million higher and profits $45 million higher if the sales force were to reallocate its effort.

The management implications of the model output were somewhat surprising, but they were also ideas that some members of the management team had been thinking about for quite a while but had not really conceptualized or made explicit. After the model had been digested, Mike Ness said,

When Len (Lodish) asked how far out he should run the thing, we were standing at 430 reps, and I said, "Why don't

you run it out to 550 or the maximum, whichever comes first." We knew we weren't paying enough attention to Naprosyn because our major competitors outnumbered us so far, and that's our biggest and most important market. We also knew that Naprosyn was our most important product, but we didn't really know to what *degree* it was our most important product. We had the perception that a lot of the attention given to launching three new products had been at the expense of our smaller products, but the model showed it had come out of Naprosyn and that was exactly what we hadn't wanted to happen [Clarke 1983, p. 14].

A subsequent meeting of the model design and building team developed the four following conclusions:

(1) Until the size of the sales force approached 700 general representatives, profitability would not be a constraint to adding representatives.

(2) From the FY 1981 base of roughly 430 representatives, Syntex Labs should grow to an optimal allocation of sales effort rather than redeploy the current sales force. This could be done by devoting additional sales resources largely to the primary-care audience (general practitioners, internists, and family practice physicians).

(3) Naprosyn was the largest product in Syntex's product line, the most sales-responsive, and highly profitable. Thus Syntex Labs should make it the driving force behind nearly all deployment and allocation decisions.

(4) Syntex should consider itself a major generalist company, since optimal deployment would require the greatest portion of a large sales force to be devoted to the generalist physican audience.

We presented these conclusions and the model-based derivation behind them to

TABLE 3. The model output report of the sales force strategy model covering a new policy based on having 381 sales representatives on board in fiscal year 1985.

Product	Number of reps allocated	Presentations	Sales in dollars
Naprosyn	257	943,432	308,029,056
Anaprox	0	0	5,475,000
Norinyl 1+35	58	213,211	22,019,448
Norinyl 1+50	29	104,966	38,048,152
Synalar	37	137,894	41,222,456
Lydex	0	0	8,614,000
Nasalide	0	0	1,680,000
Total	381	1,399,503	425,088,112

TABLE 4. The model output report covering a new policy based on having 511 sales representatives on board in fiscal year 1985: run number 3.

Product	Number of reps allocated	Presentations	Sales in dollars
Naprosyn	257	943,432	308,029,056
Anaprox	130	479,619	33,708,128
Norinyl 1+35	58	213,211	22,019,448
Norinyl 1+50	29	104,966	38,048,152
Synalar	37	137,894	41,222,456
Lydex	0	0	8,614,000
Nasalide	0	0	1,680,000
Total	511	1,879,122	453,321,240

TABLE 5. A model output report of the sales force strategy model covering a continuation of the present policy until fiscal year 1985.

Product	Number of reps allocated	Presentations	Sales in dollars
Naprosyn	97	357,853	202,001,792
Anaprox	143	527,581	36,500,000
Norinyl 1+35	53	195,443	20,113,592
Norinyl 1+50	24	88,818	35,992,408
Synalar	27	101,123	36,894,000
Lydex	30	110,351	14,600,000
Nasalide	57	210,225	10,471,728
Total	433	1,591,394	356,573,520

senior management at Syntex Laboratories and to the board of directors of Syntex Incorporated. During the next three years, the company added approximately 200 salespeople to the sales force. This was the largest number that could be added because of limitations on the ability to train and deploy salespeople. About one year after the original model had been developed, we developed a more complicated model that simultaneously allocated sales effort to segments and products; it was based on subjective estimates by the same group. Because the conclusions of this model corroborated those of the previous runs, the company continued to increase the sales force. It was difficult to completely reorient the existing sales force to pay a lot more attention to the general practitioner and take effort away from the other products and markets that the company had been serving since its inception. However, the model seemed to cause people to change direction somewhat in terms of allocating incremental resources to products and segments.

One unanticipated outcome of the model occurred when a corporate person whose responsibility was liaison between R & D and Marketing heard a presentation about the model exercise. He realized that a decision to have a new product marketed by the Syntex Laboratories sales force involved trade-offs between sales force time on the new product and time on existing products. He developed a model similar to the one described here to evaluate whether new products could be profitably assigned to the sales force or whether they could be more profitably licensed to other pharmaceutical firms because the opportunity costs of time taken from the established products were too great to put those new products into the line. Thus the resource allocation model

not only affected strategic sales force size and deployment decisions, but also affected strategic decisions on the product portfolio for Syntex Laboratories as a whole.

THE IMPACT OF THE MODEL IMPLEMENTATION

Early in 1985 we analyzed the actual deployment since the development of the model. We compared model forecasts with the strategic plan forecasts. We developed the model forecasts by taking the actual deployment over the previous two years for each product and applying the response function estimated by the Delphi group for that level. That response function was then multiplied by the base forecast from the strategic plan for fiscal year 1984 (see appendix). Both the model forecast and the base strategic plan forecast were adjusted for three unforecastable events. One of them was the withdrawal from the market of Zomax, a product competitive to Anaprox. External estimates said that that was worth $9.3 million in sales for Anaprox. We therefore adjusted both forecasts by $9.3 million. A new way of dispensing the birth control pills caused a $6 million increase, which we added to both forecasts. Finally a solution form developed for Synalar added $0.6 million to its sales for filling up the pipelines at the wholesale level.

Table 5 shows the forecasts for the strategic plan and for the model for fiscal year 1984, two years after the estimates were developed. In only one instance did the model do significantly worse than the strategic plan in predicting sales. That was for Nasalide, the new product introduced in 1982. The strategic plan and the adjustment made by the model significantly underestimated what actually happened

(Table 6). However, even at the actual level of sales of $12 million in fiscal year 1984, the opportunity cost in lost sales of other products because of effort given to Nasalide was still not enough to justify the effort that was deployed to it. In all the other cases the model predictions were excellent. Over all seven products the model had a mean absolute deviation of $1.51 million compared to a median absolute deviation of $6.44 million for the strategic plan. The model's forecasts were much better than those of the strategic plan.

Sales were $25 million higher than the strategic plan forecast. These sales changes were in the direction forecasted by the model and are directly related to changes in deployment and sales force size in the directions recommended by the model. Considering the extra cost of the additional salespeople and the incremental profitability of the sales increase, the return on the sales force investment is at least 100 percent. All indications are that the increased sales due to increasing the sales force size will continue for at least the next few years. Another outcome of the modeling effort was that management realized how important response function estimates are. During the last year, the market research department has begun developing data so that empirical estimates of response functions can be developed. So far these empirical regressions have supported the basic directions that the subjective estimates encouraged.

TRANSPORTABILITY OF THE TECHNIQUE

The general technique used by Syntex Laboratories has been used by at least 10 other pharmaceutical firms and by other firms whose businesses are largely dependent on their sales forces, including banks and chemical, steel, and rubber companies. The same technique is also being used

TABLE 6. How accurate were the original response estimates? How to read this table: Using the Anaprox example, the "base" fiscal year 1984 forecast for Anaprox, according to the strategic plan, was $26 million. This number was adjusted to reflect the positive impact of the Zomax withdrawal (+$9.3 million) to equal $35.3. The model forecast for fiscal year 1984, at the actual detailing level, was $18.3. The Zomax adjustment was then added, showing that the deployment model was a better predictor of actual sales achievement than the strategic plan.

Product	Strategic Plan "Base" FY84 Forecast	Strategic Plan Base + Adjustment	Actual FY84	Model + Adjustment	Model FY84 Forecast
Naprosyn	$175	$175	$204	$203.2	$203.2
Anaprox	26	35.3	28	27.6	18.3
Norinyl 1+35	15.2	20.7	20.4	20.7	15.2
Norinyl 1+50	36.8	37.3	39	38.8	38.3
Synalar	33.8	36.2	34.9	33.8	31.4
Lydex	14	14	13.1	12	12
Nasalide	7.3	7.3	11.9	5.2	5.2

to determine where charity solicitors should deploy their limited resources.

OBSERVATIONS FROM 20/20 HINDSIGHT

The group that developed and implemented the model would have done some things differently had we perfect 20/20 hindsight. One important task we could not convince management to spend the time to do was to develop estimates for one year out as well as three years out. One year after the model had been developed and sales force size had started to increase significantly, management asked the natural question, "How are we doing compared to what we should be doing?" It was difficult, if not impossible, to answer that question, because no group consensus was available on how long it would take for salespeople to get up to speed and what would happen one year after sales force size had been changed. A difficult period ensued when no one was sure whether the increase in sales force size was working because in fact it took over a year for sales growth to change incrementally as a result.

This kind of problem occurs many times in model-building activities. The criteria for judging the application and its success are not operationally defined at the beginning of the project. Had we 20/20 hindsight, we would have done this much more explicitly than we did.

We also would have tried to influence more greatly the evaluation, motivation, and control of the sales force to ensure that a greater part of the possible increases in sales and profits would be obtained, as they could have been by a more severe reallocation of sales force resources.

There was much opportunity to improve the deployment of the sales force during the first two years of the increase in its size which was not seized. We compared the actual fiscal year 1984 sales with the fiscal 1984 sales predicted if the optimal details recommended by the model had in fact been applied. The difference of $36 million in sales was foregone because deployment was not changed as radically as would have been desirable. It proved very difficult to change the patterns of salespeople who had been habitually visiting specialty physicians selling products which were now supposed to receive much less emphasis according to the model.

CONCLUSION

Even though the building, estimation, and implementation of the model could have been improved, it had a significant positive impact on the performance of Syntex Laboratories in the three-year period, 1982-1985. Sales were eight percent higher than they would have been if the status quo had continued, and management and research personnel realized how important the size and deployment of the sales force is to the strategic success of the company.

The one-time, out-of-pocket cost for developing and running the model was $30,000. This small investment resulted in an ongoing yearly revenue stream $25,000,000 higher than it would have been without the use of the model. The return is extremely high and recurs each year. There are now on-going efforts to continually improve and evaluate sales force deployment and sales force size using both subjective and empirically-based methodologies.

Both the models for product and segment allocation were based upon the strategic plan. Let S_p be the strategic plan forecast for fiscal year 1985 for product p, ($p = 1, \ldots, P$) with the status quo sales force allocation. Let $r_p(x_p)$ be the sales response of product p to a level of sales effort x_p where x_p is scaled as an index with $x_p = 100$ being the current sales effort for product p. r_p is also scaled as an index where 100 is equated to the strategic plan forecast, S_p. Let a_p denote the contribution margin per incremental dollar of sales for product p. Given the model objectives, this factor may also reflect corporate priorities on products. If one dollar of sales is worth more on product A than product B because of long term considerations, then the a_A factor for product A would be higher then a_B. Thus, in general we can term a_p a strategic adjustment factor. The strategic plan sales resource allocation by product is denoted e_p for effort per product. For a particular sales force size S, the mathematical programming problem becomes

(1) Maximize $z = .01 \sum_{p=1}^{P} r_p(x_p) \; S_p a_p$,

(2) $\qquad\qquad s.t. \; \sum_{p=1}^{P} x_p e_p \leq S.$

The segment model is identical in structure to the model above with segments replacing products.

This knapsack problem can be solved by incremental marginal analysis of a concave envelope of the r_p functions. These concave envelopes cause the solution procedure to take advantage of all economies of scale in allocations of sales effort to products or segments. These concave envelopes overlook parts of the response functions which show increasing returns to scale. The incremental analysis procedure for this "loose knapsack" problem will only solve for certain sales force sizes which take advantage of economies of scale. However, these solutions are optimal for those sales force sizes. Furthermore, any sales force sizes that are not picked by the incremental analysis routine would not be optimal in the sense that the marginal return on sales resources would be higher at the levels picked by the "loose" knapsack incremental analysis routine.

SOLUTION PROCEDURE

Each $r_p(x_p)$ function is discretized so it is evaluated for increments of x_p. This discretized function is then approximated by a piecewise linear, concave function r'_p which is always above or touching the original function at each discretized increment of x_p. For more detail, see Lodish [1971] from which this section is adopted.

These approximations are constructed for each product p as follows:

Let $x_{p,o} =$ either 0 or a required minimum amount of effort. Let $x_{p,1}$ be a value of x_p such that $\{(r_p(x_p) - r_p(x_{p,o}))/(x_p - x_{p,o})\}$ is a maximum over all possible values of x_p.

In general, $x_{p,l}$ is the value of x_p such that $\{(r_p(x_p) - r_p(x_{p,l-1})) / (x_p - x_{p,l-1})\}$ is a maximum for all possible values of x_p greater than $x_{p,l-1}$. Let $b_{p,l}$ denote this maximum value. These b's are the slopes of the piecewise linear, concave approximations to the original r_p function, denoted r'_p. r'_p is defined recursively

(3) $r'_p(x_p) = r_p(x_{p,o}) + b_{p,1}(x_p - x_{p,o})$
   for $x_{p,o} \leq x_p \leq x_{p,1}$, and

(4) $r'_p(x_p) = r_p(x_{p,l-1}) + b_{p,l}(x_p - x_{p,l-1})$
   for $x_{p,l-1} \leq x_p \leq x_{p,l}$.

Note that r'_p has constant or diminishing returns and that at every point where r'_p changes slope the approximation is exact, that is $r'_p = r_p$.

The mathematical program (1) and (2) is solved "loosely" as follows:

Step 1: Calculate the incremental ratio IR_p for each product, where $IR_p = b_{p,l} S_p a_p / e_p$. IR_p is the incremental adjusted sales (gross margin) per sales effort unit for product p.

Step 2: Choose the product p that has the highest IR_p and allocate effort to it up to the highest effort level that has the slope used in the IR_p calculation.

Step 3: For this product, change its slope to the next one in the IR_p calculation. Update the sales effort units used so far.

Step 4: If the sales effort allocated violates any constraints, then stop. Otherwise, go to Step 2.

FITTING THE RESPONSE CURVES

The model used pieces of two four-parameter curves for different areas of the response curve. The four-parameter curve is of the form

$$(5) \quad r_p(x_p) = ZER + \frac{(SAT - ZER) x_p^{DEL}}{GAMMA + x_p^{DEL}}$$

The parameters ZER, SAT, $GAMMA$, and DEL are uniquely determined by four input data points. This curve is used twice to obtain the complete response function. For fitting the points from zero through the present effort level, the curve in (5) is fit through the zero, one half percent level, present level, and saturation points. For fitting points greater than the present level, the curve is fit through zero, present, present + 50 percent, and saturation. This procedure for generating smooth curves has some possible theoretical problems, but works very well in practice. See Lodish [1971] for details. Little [1970] introduced the function to marketing.

REFERENCES

Lodish, L. M. 1971, "CALLPLAN, an interactive salesman's call planning system," *Management Science*, Part II, Vol. 18, No. 4 (December), pp. 25–40.

Clarke, D. 1983, "SYNTEX Laboratories (A)," Harvard Business School case number 9-584-033.

Little, John D. C. 1970, "Models and managers, the concept of a decision calculus," *Management Science*, Vol. 16, No. 8 (April), pp. B466–485.

The Development, Testing, and Execution of a New Marketing Strategy at AT&T Long Lines

Alan P. Kuritsky

John D. C. Little

Alvin J. Silk

Emily S. Bassman

How can the benefits of an advertising campaign be established? That question has been debated for years. Does advertising have much impact at all? If it does, how can that impact be measured? A recent article in the *Wall Street Journal* compared advertising to religion. It stated that most companies were not quite certain exactly what happened when they advertised. However, many of these companies had almost a blind faith that by repeatedly pursuing the practice of advertising, eventually something good would happen to their firm. There is little consensus in the advertising industry about how, and under what conditions, advertising works or even about how to test the effectiveness of a campaign [Ramond 1976]. The best measure would be actual purchase or use of the product. Because purchase and use can be difficult to measure, advertisers rely on other processes or surrogate measures such as top-of-mind awareness, recall, preference, and purchase intent.

AT&T Long Lines has introduced a national advertising campaign for its residential long distance customers to enhance its highly successful "Reach Out" campaign. A substantial part of the multimillion dollar annual advertising budget is devoted to this new "Cost of Visit" campaign. The campaign, which stresses how inexpensive a twenty-minute telephone "visit" can be, is more than just a switch from an emotional to a pragmatic appeal. Careful research segmented the long distance market and found a group of people who have reasons to call long distance but limit their calls because of a price barrier. "Cost of Visit" uses a new way to present the price of long distance calling to this consumer. It also encourages calling during off peak hours.

The concept behind the new campaign resulted from a concerted, long term effort using various research tools in an almost "textbook" approach. However, the final decision to go ahead with the new campaign was based on the results of an experiment used to test the "Cost of Visit" strategy. This procedure was unusual in a number of respects, including its precision. The experiment was conducted on a dual cable television system which enabled the performance of the new campaign to be compared to that of the established "Reach Out" strategy. AT&T's own long distance usage tracking system was used to measure the effects each had upon long distance telephone usage.

The most gratifying result of the experiment was that the "Cost of Visit" campaign produced a statistically and economically significant increase in calling over "Reach Out." For the company that means millions of calls made during off peak hours. Because services are not as much in demand during those hours and the additional traffic can be handled at little additional expense, these incremental calls are highly profitable. Estimates for 1982 show that by switching $30 million in advertising from "Reach Out" to "Cost of Visit," the company will gain $22 million more for its investment. In five years, that figure should top $100 million—all with very little extra expense for the company.

BACKGROUND

American Telephone and Telegraph, the world's largest company, is the foremost supplier of telecommunications services in the United States. Prior to 1969, long distance phone service in the US was a regulated monopoly. During the 1970s, however, the Federal Communication Commission began encouraging competition in the long distance telecommunications marketplace. As a result, AT&T began competing with other companies to provide long distance service to residential customers. Since 1980 the number of those competitors has grown dramatically and they are no longer fledgling firms.

RESEARCH PROGRAM

The research leading to "Cost of Visit" began in 1975 and culminated in 1980 with the field experiment. This research program consisted of four projects: (1) a segmentation study of the residential long distance market, the first conducted by the Bell System; (2) tracking studies to test customer awareness of interstate phone rates; (3) qualitative research on customer attitudes to develop an advertising concept; and (4) a large scale field experiment that measured the effect of alternative advertising strategies in the marketplace. The total cost of the research was approximately $1 million.

THE RESIDENTIAL LONG DISTANCE USAGE STUDY

In 1975, a residential Long Distance Usage Study was conducted which divided the market into "Heavy, Medium, Light and Non-users" segments. The most important discovery was that a large group of light telephone users looked a lot like heavy users in terms of demographics and psychographics, except for a psychological "price barrier." Since the "lights" had, on average, four or more friends or relatives living more than 50 miles away, and their demographic characteristics did not prevent them from being potentially heavier users, they were designated "Potential Telephone Users" (PTU's). Researchers hypothesized that this group's usage might be stimulated through advertising, and the groundwork was laid for the development of "Cost of Visit." The PTU's represented a substantial portion of the residential market —even a slight increase in this group's phone use could represent a large increase in overall long distance calling.

CUSTOMER INTERSTATE RATE AWARENESS STUDY

For several years AT&T Long Lines has conducted an annual study which focuses specifically on long distance rate awareness. Some 3,000 residential telephone users are surveyed by mail. Each year the same general conclusion is drawn: most customers do not know the cost of a long distance call or when it's cheaper to call. Most overestimate the cost of those calls by 50%.

The long distance rate structure consists of three rate periods:

— Full rate period: 8 a.m. to 5 p.m., Monday through Friday
— Discount calling period: 5 p.m. to 11 p.m., every night except Saturday
— Deep discount calling: Friday 11 p.m. until Sunday 5 p.m. and every week night from 11 p.m. till 8 a.m.

Calls were discounted 35% during the discount calling period and 60% during the deep discount calling period. (In 1982 the 35% discount increased to 40%.)

CONCEPT DEVELOPMENT STUDY

The next step was a three-phase concept development project carried out in 1977.

Phase I: The attitudinal data collected in the 1975 segmentation study were used to identify possible alternative advertising positions. Each of the 68 individual attitudinal items employed in that study was screened as a possible positioning concept using two types of criteria. The first was essentially statistical and concerned the extent to which the attitude varied across the usage segments. The second type was judgmental relating to whether or not the particular item represented an attitude that might be influenced by means of advertising. Seventeen attitudinal items emerged from this screening process as potential advertising concepts or themes. These items were then sorted judgmentally on the basis of similarity of content into five position alternatives.

Phase II: The five position alternatives were then translated into written concept statements and further developed and tested in focus group interviews conducted with PTU's. These sessions provided insights into the psychological aspects of long-distance calling which were used to refine the initial concepts.

The revised position conceptualizations were then exposed to a second round of focus groups. The final copy positions used were:

(1) *Lifeline:* It's easy to drift apart when you're far away from family and friends. Long distance can help keep you together.
(2) *Cost of Visit:* Many people are still depriving themselves of long distance because they think it costs too much. If they only knew how cheap it really is!
(3) *Feel Good:* When you're feeling happy, it can make you even happier. When you're feeling down, it can cheer you up. However you feel, long distance can make you feel better.
(4) *Letters:* When you stop to think of the advantages of long distance calling, you've got to wonder why some people still only write letters.
(5) *Comfortable:* A lot of people don't realize how easy it is to have a relaxed long distance conversation.

Phase III: The five positions were subsequently turned into slide-tape presentations and used in individual in-depth interviews. These interviews were conducted with small samples of both PTU's (light users) and heavy or medium users to ensure that the strategy developed for lighter users would not "turn off" those who already called frequently.

"Cost of Visit" emerged as the dominant alternative as judged by various structured and unstructured measures of respondent reaction following exposure to the five positions. It was the only strategy that successfully attacked people's rigid perceptions of price/value. After viewing the commercial, customers indicated that a 20-minute call was reasonable in length and a relaxing way to visit someone, a marked contrast to their perceptions of previous strategies where customers felt the "rate meter" was running after three minutes. In addition, "Cost of Visit" dealt directly with another common problem— although customers sometimes know how much off-peak calling is discounted, they usually miscalculate the discount's effects on rates. For instance, some mistakenly believed that under full rates, a 20-minute long distance call could cost as much as $20.00. When they heard that calls were being discounted 60 percent, they calculated that the call would still cost them $8.00. In fact, during 1979 a 20-minute long distance call during the weekend before 5 p.m. on Sunday was *never* more than $3.33. Finally, "Cost of Visit" also promoted visiting by telephone as pleasurable. (Figure 1 presents the story boards for one of the "Cost of Visit" commercials.)

The "Cost of Visit" theme contained several important elements:

— Surprise (most people are unaware of the low calling cost),
— The appropriateness of 20-minute visits (a reasonable amount of time to talk),
— The cost of less than $3.33,

— No hidden extra costs (all taxes included).

These elements were incorporated in the finished TV commercials which were then tested in a field experiment.

LARGE SCALE FIELD EXPERIMENT

To test "Cost of Visit's" effectiveness in stimulating calling, a study was designed using the AdTel Company's dual cable television system in a particular geographical area. (Under the terms of a contract with the cable company, the test location cannot be disclosed publicly.) In the AdTel system, two cables are used to distribute signals to subscribing households who can receive both regular (that is, network) and restricted-access channels and programming. The geographical area is subdivided into a checkerboard pattern where each square consists of a cluster of 40 to 50 subscribers. Households within a given square receive their signal from one cable but those in an adjacent square are served by the second cable. Signals transmitted over the two cables can be controlled through a cut-in facility making it possible to vary the frequency, timing or content of the commercials aired over the two cables. Using this capability, one group of cable subscribers received the "Reach Out" campaign, being broadcast on national network television, while the second group was exposed to the "Cost of Visit" commercials cut into the same programming and time slots as those in which "Reach Out" was aired.

Split cable facilities have been widely used for advertising experiments. Rhodes [1977] provides detail on the AdTel system. His paper and that of Adler and Kuehn [1969] report some of AdTel's ex-

AT&T Long Lines Residence

Title: "Sister"
Commercial No.: AXLL2074
Length: 30 Seconds

(MUSIC UNDER)

WOMAN VO: On Saturday nights, my sister

Laurie was official perfume tester

and

make-up adviser.

An all around little miss fix-it.

And she's still my biggest fan,

even though we're miles apart.

WOMAN (OC): We call each other most every weekend, when it's cheaper so we can visit longer.

ANNCR VO: Stay close to someone you love this weekend,

when a 20-minute state to state call is only $4.06 or less, tax included.

SINGERS: Reach out, reach out and touch someone.

Figure 1. The storyboard for a typical "Cost of Visit" advertisement—1982 execution.

perience in advertising experimentation, including case examples. Technical accounts of split cable advertising experiments concerned with spending levels may be found in McGuire [1979] and Winer [1980].

To measure the relative effectiveness of two advertising strategies is an ambitious undertaking and so steps were taken to obtain high precision. Whereas split cable experiments usually measure sales effects by using panels of say 2,000 households, the present experiment involved a much larger number of approximately 16,000 from the two cables. About 8,000 households were on each cable.

Furthermore, unlike consumer products that are distributed through middlemen and so are subject to uncontrolled variations in price, availability, and display, the opportunity to use the telephone is relatively constant and stable. Finally, records of actual telephone usage obtained from the telephone company's household billing system were used in the analysis. (To protect customer anonymity individual names and addresses of customers were not identified.)

The experiment, which lasted for slightly more than two years, was structured into three phases: the Pre-Assessment (5 months), Treatment Period (15 months), and Post-Assessment (6 months).

1. *Pre-Assessment:* During the Pre-Assessment phase, records of all households in the sample of cable subscribers were tracked for long distance calls of over 50 miles in order to establish their normal calling behavior. In addition, sample households were sent questionnaires to obtain demographic and attitudinal information. One of the major uses of these data was to check the equivalence of the two groups of cable subscribers. Question-

naires were returned by 22,068 respondents representing 15,311 telephone numbers. A representative subsample of 3,600 was analyzed, and as expected, it was found that the two groups were well-balanced and essentially equivalent with respect to usage, demographic, and community of interest variables (number of close friends and relatives living more than 50 miles away or outside the US).

The pre-assessment questionnaire also included 32 attitude items, which were grouped into seven factors comparable to those found in the 1975 national segmentation study. The attitudes of the cable groups and those of the previous national segmentation study were found to be similar, which increased our confidence in the projections of results from the AdTel study to other groups throughout the nation.

2. *Treatment Period:* During the treatment period the two advertising campaigns were aired over the two cables in the same program and time slots. The advertising rate on the cables was approximately 300 gross rating points per week or, on average, each household received three exposures per week. The average number of active telephone numbers tracked during the period was 7,192 for the "Cost of Visit" cable, 7,334 for "Reach Out." Measures of the effects of the two alternative strategies were in terms of calls/telephone number, minutes/call, and revenue/telephone number. These variables were examined during the daytime full rate period, the evening discount period, and the weekend/night deep discount period.

The objective of the "Cost of Visit" campaign was to encourage all user groups to call during discount off-peak periods—particularly the 60% "deep discount" period. In addition, specific attention was given to the light users who traditionally made only 2 or 3 calls a month. The basic hypothesis was that this substantial "Potential Telephone User" group would respond to the "Cost of Visit" campaign.

The results of the study supported the strategy that grew out of the earlier segmentation and developmental research. The "Cost of Visit" strategy resulted in more long distance calling during the treatment period than "Reach Out," especially among the light users (see Figure 2). "Cost of Visit" had its greatest advantage in stimulating calls over "Reach Out" during the 60% discount period among all usage segments, especially during the weekend. Overall, calling during the deep discount period increased by an average of over a half a call per household over the 15 month post-test period. These results were highly significant in statistical terms (at the 99% confidence level) and in

Figure 2. For all usage segments combined, the cumulative difference in calls per telephone number during the 15 month treatment period shows the greatest increase in calls during the night/weekend deep discount period.

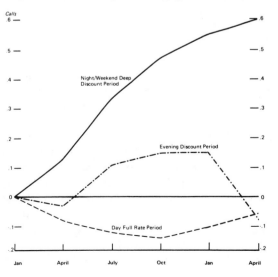

economic terms. They also indicate the high precision of the experiment. Furthermore, the targeted lighter users increased calls by an average of over one and a half calls per household during the 15 months. Households were changing their normal behavior and calling more during off-peak hours—all because of a change in the advertising copy. In addition, the group which was the target of the research, the light user, responded the most (see Figure 3).

Comparing "Cost of Visit" to "Reach Out," there was significant improvement in revenue. For the targeted light user groups, revenue increased by over 15% during the night/weekend period. For all user groups and rate periods combined, the revenue increase was approximately 1%. This increase was particularly notable because the standard for comparison was the "Reach Out" strategy, already a proven winner.

3. *Post-Assessment:* In the post-assessment phase the test commercials were withdrawn from the cable systems and replaced with the current Long Lines national campaign being run elsewhere at that time. Tracking of household long distance calling was continued for six months to evaluate the durability of the treatment effects. During the post-assessment phase usage differences remained positive but were much smaller and no longer statistically significant. This raises interesting questions for future research regarding the interactions between sequential copy treatments and the role of continued advertising in reinforcing customer behavior.

Because attitude research played a key role in the development of "Cost of Visit" strategy, we were interested in determining whether pre-post shifts in customer attitudes toward long-distance calling could be detected. As well, the relationship be-

Figure 3. For the targeted light usage segment, the cumulative difference in calls per telephone number during the 15 month treatment period shows a migration from light to heavier use.

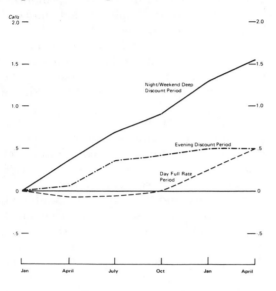

tween attitude change and behavior change is a perplexing and highly controversial matter in advertising research [Ramond 1976]. Analysis of the post-assessment data showed that there were numerous shifts in attitude, generally in a positive direction. These shifts were typically small—one-to-two-tenths of a point on a six point scale, or 4-5% of the respondents. More important, different effects on attitudes toward rates were observed between the two cable samples (Table A-2). The two attitude items were: "I think the cost of a long distance call is a good value for the money" and "when I make a long distance call to keep in touch, I don't worry how long I talk."

The fact that caller attitudes toward rates and lengths of calls changed favorably is consistent with the increase in calling experienced with the "Cost of Visit" campaign. However, since the attitude change was so slight when compared with the actual behavior change, national projections of the results were done by weighting groups with similar calling habits, rather than attitudes. In general, usage has traditionally been superior to attitude as a method of predicting future behavior.

One issue arose during the actual implementation of the ad campaign. During late 1981 AT&T raised its long distance rates. Now the question was whether it still made sense to make customers aware of exactly how much it cost to make a long distance call. A separate series of customer focus group sessions indicated that the answer was still yes—continue with the "Cost of Visit" campaign with the revised rates. Since customers had previously overestimated the cost of calling by over 50%, awareness of the revised rates still produced an overall perception of lower prices. Also, customers said they expected to see gradual price increases during an inflationary period and that long distance rates were not rising as much as other things they bought.

BENEFITS

The "Cost of Visit" campaign successfully persuaded customers to call during times that are both cheaper for them and more profitable for the company. This marketing campaign helped solve a classical "peak-load" problem. It also lowered peoples' perceptions of AT&T long distance calling prices, which should have a high payoff for the company in today's newly-emerging competitive telecommunications market. When projected nationally, the increase in calls for 1979 would have been about fifteen million using

"Cost of Visit." Since the annual revenue base for all of AT&T residential Long Distance calling was over $7 billion, a one percent increase in revenue would be approximately $70 million in incremental dollars per year on a national basis. A separate study on the "Reach Out" campaign concluded that if $30 million were spent on "Reach Out," approximately $150 million in incremental revenue would be generated over 12 months. By using that $30 million instead for "Cost of Visit" advertising on a limited geographic basis during 1982, some $172 million in revenue will be realized. The difference between the two campaigns in 1982 alone will be $22 million, given the planned advertising schedule. The $22 million represents only a portion of the $70 million of incremental revenue that would be realized if the entire media budget was spent on "Cost of Visit" in all areas of the country. Conservatively projecting the use of this ad campaign over the next five years it will produce about $100 million more than the "Reach Out" campaign (see Appendix for a description of the projection model).

This project is one of a handful of published studies that has reported finding a significant effect on purchasing or usage behavior due to changes or variations in advertising copy strategy [Bloom, Jay, and Twyman 1977; Rao 1978; Rhodes 1977]. Failures to find copy effect in sales experiments have been known to occur (for instance, Dhalla 1975) and negative results are probably underrepresented in the literature. Such evidence has high managerial relevance now when long-standing criticisms of traditional advertising pretesting procedures appear to have escalated to new levels of severity [Honomichl 1981]. As Little [1979] has shown, the accumulation of empirical studies can contribute to the advancement of management science in advertising by revealing important phenomena that decision models should encompass. Much remains to be learned about the dynamics of response to changes in copy strategy and the durability of such effects. The present work also lends support to the types of creative advertising policy advocated by Gross [1972] in the sense that it represents a case where the difference in the potential profitability between the alternative strategies was clearly sufficiently large to justify the heavy expenditures required to develop alternative campaigns and test their relative effectiveness in a full scale sales experiment.

CONCLUSIONS

AT&T Long Lines has embarked on the new national "Cost of Visit" campaign with confidence because of the extremely precise experiment that proved that strategy was more effective than the highly successful "Reach Out" campaign with a target segment of the market. Most encouraging is the fact that the market segment most responsive to the new campaign was the target group of customers who make few long distance calls. Further, measures of attitudinal responses showed positive change in some items related to long distance rates.

The national television campaign starts with $30 million during 1982. Over the next five years the company can expect to earn at least $100 million more from primarily light users than it hoped to gain using "Reach Out" alone.

Further, this $100 million requires little expense to the company since existing telephone facilities will be used to handle the incremental calling and advertising costs will not increase above their originally projected levels.

ACKNOWLEDGEMENTS

Any management science project this large has benefited from the contributions of many people along the way. We would especially like to acknowledge the efforts of R. Emond, R. Brookmeyer, and B. Carlson who had primary responsibility for the project during the segmentation study and initial design of the field experiment; W. West, M. Leone, D. Dolan, and J. Redfern who were product managers of residence interstate service; R. Golden of N. W. Ayer, who contributed to the concept development process; M. E. Caro, S. Marg, and G. Smit of AT&T Long Lines and S. Chow and J. Lattin of MIT, who contributed to the data analysis of the field experiment; and B. Wood of AT&T Long Lines, who assisted in writing this article.

REFERENCES

Adler, J. and Kuehn, A. A. 1969, "How advertising works in market experiments," *Proceedings,* 15th Annual Conference, Advertising Research Foundation, New York, pp. 63–70.

Bloom, D., Jay, A., and Twyman, T. 1977, "The validity of advertising pretests," *Journal of Advertising Research,* Vol. 17, No. 2 (April), pp. 7–16.

Dhalla, N. K. 1975, "Setting of advertising budgets with econometric techniques," *Proceedings,* Business and Economics Section, American Statistical Association, Washington, pp. 304–307.

Gross, I. 1972, "The creative aspects of advertising," *Sloan Management Review,* Vol. 15, No. 1 (Fall), pp. 83–110.

Honomichl, J. 1981, "TV copy testing flap: What to do about it," *Advertising Age,* Vol. 52, No. 3 (January 19), pp. 59–61.

Little, J. D. C. 1979, "Aggregate advertising models: The state of the art," *Operations Research,* Vol. 27, No. 4 (July–August), pp. 629–667.

McGuire, T. W. 1977, "Measuring and testing relative advertising effectiveness with split-cable TV panel data," *Journal of the American Statistical Association,* Vol. 72, No. 360 (December), pp. 736–745.

Ramond, C. 1976, *Advertising Research: The State of the Art,* Association of National Advertisers, New York.

Rao, A. 1978, "Productivity of the marketing mix: Measuring the impact of advertising and consumer and trade promotion on sales," paper presented at the Association of National Advertisers Advertising Research Workshop, New York.

Rhodes, R. 1977, "What AdTel has learned: Six recommendations for increased payout from television advertising research," paper presented at the Advertising Research Conference, American Marketing Association, New York, March.

Winer, R. S. 1980, "Estimation of a longitudinal model to decompose the effects of an advertising stimulus on family consumption," *Management Science,* Vol. 26, No. 5 (May), pp. 471–482.

TECHNICAL APPENDIX

Several different analytical tools were used in this series of studies, including cluster analysis, factor analysis, linear regression, analysis of variance, and contingency table analysis.

The national segmentation study consisted of a survey sample based on an area probability sample projected to four regions served by the Bell System. A total of 806 households were interviewed. In married households, both the male and female head were separately interviewed, and this resulted in 1351 total interviews.

The validity of the sample was checked by comparing the demographics of the participants to those of the total population as reported by census data. In addition, a comparison was made of the long distance usage rates of respondents vs. nonrespondents. Both of these checks demonstrated that the sample was a valid and projectable one (see Table A-1 for sample-census comparison).

The first step was a factor analysis of

TABLE A-1. The 1975 national segmentation study showing the demographics of the sample contrasted to 1970 census data.

	Sample for this Study %	1970 Census %
Marital Status		
Married	84	75
Divorced, Widowed, Separated	12	19
Never Married	4	6
Age		
Under 34	34	37
35–44	18	17
45 to 54	17	17
55 or over	28	29
Sex		
Male	45	48
Female	55	52

the 68 survey attitude items included in the survey. The specific factor analysis technique used was a principal component analysis with a varimax rotation. The second multivariate analysis involved the grouping of individual respondents according to the similarity of their factor scores. The end result of this analysis was a set of segments of individuals with relatively similar patterns of responses to the attitude items. In other words, respondents grouped through this procedure into a segment had a unique pattern of responses to the attitude items that are different from the patterns of all other segments. The specific cluster analysis technique used in this study was the Howard-Harris Profile Similarity Program.

The final step in the analysis involved the tabulation of the responses to the questionnaire items for the various consumer clusters or segments. This analysis allowed for a comparison of each seg-

ment's long distance usage, media habits, life style, etc., and guided the formulation of marketing strategies to stimulate long distance usage among those segments judged to have the highest potential.

The concept development study process looked at these attitude items and judgmentally selected out 24 items which appeared changeable. These items were again judgmentally sorted into five factors to be used as a basis for advertising copy positions. A comparison of these five concept development factors to the factors generated in the segmentation study indicated that they were the same top five factors. With this confirmation, the ad copy was generated and tested using individual questionnaire measures on an eleven point scale of "intent to call" as the criterion to rank order the copy positions.

In the AdTel strategy experiment, the measure of interest for the behavioral data was the relative advantage of "Cost of Visit" (Cable B) over "Reach Out" (Cable A). For each variable (calls, minutes, revenue), the overall average difference between cables was calculated for each weekly interval. Using linear regression, these weekly values were analyzed in order to determine the percentage increase. Briefly, the technique compared the pretest average with the test period average (i.e., the difference between Cable B and Cable A in the test period average minus the difference between Cable B and Cable A during the pre-period).

In projecting the results to the nation, base behavioral measures were first obtained for the whole Bell System. Then the incremental gains in percentages observed in the test market were applied to those base figures separately for each usage segment and each rate period. For instance, light users in the 60% discount period showed a particular gain in the test market. For any other geographical area, this gain can be applied to the base behavior shown by light users in the 60% discount period in that area. This was done for each usage segment and each rate period for the Bell System as a whole. The separate results were summed to obtain an overall result, which represents the incremental gain that could have been expected if "Cost of Visit" had been implemented nationwide.

The AdTel analyses were done at MIT, where research on several issues is continuing using data from the AdTel strategy segment.

AdTel USAGE ANALYSIS

In marketing one normally expects different behavior from light and heavy users. In the present instance, the "Cost of Visit" strategy was designed specifically to appeal to light users. Accordingly, five usage segments were defined based on calling behavior in the pre-period.

Specifically, all households (i.e., telephone numbers) were classified into one of the five segments based on the calls over 50 miles made in the 4-week period, October 15—November 11, 1978. This time period was chosen because it was after the summer vacation period and before the high calling periods of Thanksgiving and Christmas.

Even if a household makes no calls in the 4-week definitional period, it does not mean that the household never makes long distance calls. In fact the zero-call group averaged 1.3 calls/4-weeks over the 15 months of the treatment period. It was clear, however, that the segmentation identified large differences in average calling behavior and hence the operational defini-

tions of the usage segments were indeed meaningful.

All analyses were done by segment and expressed in terms of usage/household/unit of time. The measures of usage were calls, minutes of calling, and revenue in cents. Only calls over 50 miles were considered.

When we wished to show overall population effects in the experimental groups, we used the comparisons within individual segments on a usage/household basis and then synthesized the total population effect by weighing each individual segment effect by its fraction of the total population. The fractions were calculated across the two cables combined.

This is different and substantially more accurate than comparing two groups in aggregate (see Importance of Segmentation).

CALCULATION OF STRATEGY EFFECT

The calculation of the differential effectiveness of the strategies administered to, say, Group 1 and Group 2 is:

[average usage/household/week in Group 1 during treatment period − average usage/household/week in Group 1 during pre-period].

[average usage/household/week in Group 2 during treatment period − average usage household/week in Group 2 during preperiod].

The possible groups are the 2 cables.

Usage may variously be calls, minutes or cents.

An easy way to do this calculation and at the same time develop standard errors and confidence limits based on econometric techniques is to use linear regression. For example, let

USDF = difference in usage/household per week between treatments ("Cost of Visit" minus "Reach Out")

UNOFF = dummy variable for existence of advertising difference by week

$$= \begin{cases} 0 \text{ for pretest weeks} \\ 1 \text{ for treatment weeks} \end{cases}$$

$\epsilon =$ Disturbance factor

The regression:

$$USDF = \alpha + \beta * UNOFF + \epsilon$$

will model the difference in usage/household/week between cables as a pre-period constant, α, and a treatment period constant $\alpha + \beta$, where the regression will calculate α to be the mean difference between cables in the pre-period and $\alpha + \beta$ the mean difference in the treatment period. Then $\beta(= \alpha + \beta - \alpha)$ is the mean treatment period difference adjusted for the pre-test difference. β is the desired strategy in units of usage/household/week. The week-to-week variations in USDF provide a measure of error in a standard econometric way. Various graphical analyses and other checks indicated that a single parameter regression model was the appropriate choice for analysis. In calculating USDF or any other usage variable that cuts across segments, the usage differences were calculated by individual segment and aggregated by weighting with the segment fractions of the two cables combined.

Cumulative plots were the principal device for displaying the data and standard regression methods were used to carry out the appropriate statistical analyses. Several properties of the cumulative plots should be noted.

(1) A constant difference in effect between cables appears as a constant slope on the cumulative.
(2) A period of no difference between cables creates a flat segment on the cumulative plot.
(3) The units on the vertical axis are incremental calls per household to date. In other words, the number of calls at the end of the experiment is the total cumulative incremental calls made by the average household over the course of the 15 months. We obtain the same number by multiplying the advertising coefficient from the regression by 65 weeks.

The four pre-period weeks used to define segments were omitted from the regression. This is considered to be a conservative procedure to protect against any possible threat from "regression to the mean" phenomena. The threat seems minor because of the controlled nature of the experiment but we take the step as an extra precaution. In addition, for individual segment analyses, the definitional weeks were clearly atypical and would distort standard error estimates.

AGGREGATE RESULTS FOR THE CABLE POPULATION

The overall results show the cumulative difference in usage/household measured from the start of the experimental treatments on January 1, 1979. The cumulative effect over the entire 15-month treatment period was looked upon as the natural measure of effectiveness for evaluating the strategies. Since the difference calculated is "Cost of Visit" less "Reach Out," positive values indicate incremental usage for "Cost of Visit." The difference has been adjusted by the pre-period average (see Figures 2 and 3).

The experiment is remarkable for its high level of precision. The standard errors for the aggregate results are about 0.5 calls, 5.7 minutes and $1.24 per household over a 15-month period. These standard errors are calculated by multiplying 65 (the number of weeks in 15 months) times the per week value of the standard error. In Figure 3, for example, the t statistic is 3.85 with a 99% confidence level for the light user segment. The standard errors at other points on the cumulative curves can be closely estimated by multiplying the appropriate value of the standard error by the number of weeks since the start of the treatment.

ATTITUDE CHANGE ANALYSIS

Table A-2 summarizes the pre-post shifts in attitudes relating to long distance rates observed for the two treatments. We analyzed the pre-post attitudinal changes in two different ways and compared the results. Each approach has its own advantages and limitations but in certain respects the methods complement one another.

First, we made use of an analysis of variance for repeated measures. The ANOVA

TABLE A-2. Difference in the mean of attitude items concerning reasonable rates measured before and after the test period for each of the advertising strategies. Ratings are on a 6-point scale, in which a higher score indicates more agreement. *Wording of item is such that a decrease in the mean score indicates an increase in the favorability of the respondents' expressed attitude toward long distance calling.

Question	Attitudinal Item	RO	COV	
B4*	I try very hard to limit my long distance calling in order to keep the phone bill down.	4.757	4.701	Pre
		4.701	4.650	Post
		+.056	+.051	Difference
B17	I make a special point of waiting for the low rate time for most of my long distance calls.	5.055	5.011	Pre
		5.049	5.047	Post
		−.006	+.038	Difference
B25*	I think the cost of a long distance call is a good value for the money.	4.320	4.403	Pre
		4.429	4.615	Post
		+.109	+.212	Difference
B29*	I would probably make many more long distance calls than I do now if the rates were cheaper.	4.882	4.926	Pre
		4.802	4.806	Post
		+.078	+.120	Difference
B31*	When I make a long distance call to keep in touch, I don't worry how long I talk.	3.108	3.185	Pre
		3.087	3.284	Post
		−.021	+.099	Difference

TABLE A-3. Raw data from the week of October 15, 1978.

	Cable 3	
	household	calls
low segments	5,074	1,292
high segments	2,795	6,911
total	7,869	8,203

	Cable 4	
	household	calls
low segments	5,277	1,277
high segments	3,054	7,482
total	8,331	8,748

Analysis: Calls/household

	Cable 3		Cable 4
low segments	0.2546	>	0.2399
high segments	2.4726	>	2.4499
combined	1.0426	<	1.0501

method is well suited to detecting differential strategy effects but, of course, requires that the necessary distributional assumptions be met. A weakness of the repeated measures ANOVA method here was that it assumed that the pretest level does not influence the magnitude of change and it does not provide a test for the presence of an interaction of the treatment effect with the pretest.

The second method involved comparisons of contingency tables formed by cross-tabulating the pretest and post-test ratings for each treatment sample and carrying out χ^2 tests to detect differential patterns of change between samples. Here the attitude ratings were treated as discrete measures and the hypothesis tests required no special distributional assumptions. An advantage of this mode of analysis here was that it allowed comparisons to be made between samples with respect to post-test attitudes controlling for between-samples differences in the pretest attitudes.

IMPORTANCE OF SEGMENTATION

Early in the process of analyzing the data we found that, when the cables were compared in simple aggregation, often little or no effect was found, but when the cables were compared segment by segment, effects emerged. The reason is that modest imbalances in numbers of household in different segments can distort the aggregates. This is most easily seen in an example. Close inspection of the numbers below, which are drawn from actual data, will show the surprising result that

(1) Cable 3 has greater calls/household than Cable 4 in *both* "low" and "high" segments.

(2) Cable 4 has greater calls/household than Cable 3 in aggregate.

Clearly the segment by segment analysis is the appropriate one. If we wish to determine the calls/household for an aggregate population we can weight the segment calls/household by the average (across cables) number of households in each segment.

PROJECTION MODEL

The purpose of the revenue potential model was to project the results obtained in the AdTel experiment cities to other geographic areas. Of special interest is the Bell System as a whole.

One may think of the revenue potential calculation as consisting of a data base, inputs, the model itself, and outputs. The model combines data base and inputs to produce the outputs. The data base contains strategy response measurements from the AdTel cities experiment and geographic usage data from AT&T's Market Analysis of Revenue Calls (MARC) system.

From the AdTel experiment comes the incremental percentage gains of the "Cost of Visit" (COV) strategy relative to the "Reach Out" (RO) strategy on calls, minutes and dollars per household. The gains (which in certain cases can be negative) are broken out by rate period (full rate, 35% discount, and 60% discount) and by usage segments defined in terms of prior telephone usage by the households. MARC provided 1979 annual data on calls, minutes and revenue per household for a set of selected geographic areas and for the total Bell System. This is broken out in the same catagories as the AdTel response data. Throughout the experiment and in the projection, only calls over 50 miles are considered. "Household" is used to refer to a residence telephone number or account.

The model consists of a cell by cell projection and aggregation. Thus incremental usage is calculated by applying the experimentally determined percentage gains to each combination of usage segment and rate period for a geographic area and summing to obtain the total effect. The basic projection assumption is that the households of a usage segment in an arbitrary area will, on average, respond to the COV strategy in the same percentage terms as the households in the corresponding usage segment in the test cities. However, the actual incremental gains will differ considerably from area to area because of different numbers of people and variations in their calling habits.

The inputs to a run of the model are the Advertising Areas of Dominant Influence (ADI's) to be considered and the type of output desired. It is also possible to make "what if" assumptions about strategy response by segment and rate period. Outputs are incremental usage for the ADI's or Bell System, broken out by whatever aggregations of the basic data may be requested.

The model involves individual population cells whose projected calling behavior is calculated from past usage and experimental results. Summation over cells yields the projected effect for the total population of interest. Let

$i = 1, \ldots, I$ = index of cells (usage segments),

$j = 1, \ldots, J$ = index of calling categories (rate periods),

z_{ij} = usage measure/household in cell i for calling category j for an ADI Area of Dominant Influence,

n_i = number of households in cell i for the ADI,

p_{ij} = percent increase (expressed as a fraction) in usage/household for COV relative to RO in cell i and category j,

y = incremental usage in the ADI.

Then

$$y = \sum_{i=1}^{I} n_i \sum_{j=1}^{J} z_{ij} P_{ij} .$$

5

MATHEMATICAL PROGRAMMING

Over the last 30 years, mathematical programming has evolved into a key decision-making support tool within operations research. Two factors underlie the efficacy of mathematical programming models. First, the optimization of a system performance measure subject to a set of constraints constitutes a powerful conceptual framework that is widely applicable in practice. Second, the sophisticated algorithms and computers now available to solve these optimization models allow practitioners to attack large problems and complicated systems. The readings in this chapter illustrate both the power and usefulness of linear, nonlinear, and integer programming in solving practical planning and operational problems.

The first paper describes a medium-size linear program used to determine the most cost-effective way of aerial spraying insect-infested forests in the state of Maine. In the second paper, the classic OR problem of blending petroleum stocks to produce gasoline is modeled as an NLP. Analysts at Texaco use a decision support system built around an accurate and efficient algorithm for solving NLPs to plan the monthly schedule for gasoline blending. The third paper in this chapter focuses on the problem of how local banks can efficiently return checks to out-of-state banks so that funds can be collected quickly. The authors modeled the transit check-clearing problem as a facility location problem, formulated it as a large integer program, and developed an efficient technique to solve it. The use of this model at Maryland National Bank in Baltimore has improved the efficiency of check clearing and has saved the bank more than $100,000 per year.

5.1 MODELING A FOREST PEST CONTROL AERIAL SPRAY PROGRAM

The spruce budworm is a destructive pest that infests spruce and fir trees in the northern United States and Canada. In the mid 1980s, it was responsible for damaging over five million acres of forest in the state of Maine alone. Since 1972, the Maine Forest Service has conducted large-scale aerial spraying of pesticides in northern and eastern parts of the state in an attempt to control the spruce budworm. In 1983, for example, 850,000 acres of trees were sprayed during the months of May and June by 24 aircraft that operated out of six different airfields.

Planning the spraying operation begins many months in advance: the Forest Service identifies infested areas (known as spray blocks) and determines which types of aircraft and airfields to use in the project. It may consider as many as four types of aircraft and eight airfields. Prior to 1984, the Maine Forest Service relied on experience and judgment in assigning spray blocks to nearby airfields and then assigning aircraft to spray specific blocks. This decision process required data on the sizes of the spray blocks (in acres) and their distances from airfields.

Rumpf, Melachrinoudis, and Rumpf [1985] improved the efficiency of Maine's aerial spray operation by developing a linear program that assigns spray blocks to specific airfields and aircraft to minimize the total cost of spraying. The constraints ensure that each block is entirely sprayed and also take into account the limited amount of time that each airfield and aircraft combination is available for effective spraying. This LP formulation will not determine which of, say, K airfields to open and use in the spraying operation, but rather requires that the user fix the number and location of airfields in advance of running the model. Thus, the user must make separate runs to examine several different airfield combinations. These runs allow the user to add fixed airfield costs to each objective function value in order to determine the solution with the least cost overall. In this way, the user can investigate the trade-off between the cost of flying longer distances to the spray blocks from fewer airfields and the cost of flying shorter distances from more airfields. Thus, increasing the number of airfields results in higher fixed costs in return for shorter flight distances.

This LP model was used to develop an operations plan for the 1984 spraying season; it used four types of aircraft (including a new long-range single engine plane) to cover 283 blocks from four to six airfields. The four-airfield LP model contained 748 variables and 292 constraints and was solved on a VAX-11/780 minicomputer. The resulting flying cost was $594,000 while the fixed cost for the four airfields was $40,000. In contrast, the flying and fixed costs for a six-airfield model were $575,000 and $60,000, respectively. As expected, flying costs decrease but fixed costs increase with more airfields.

5.2 *IMPROVING GASOLINE BLENDING AT TEXACO*

Blending petroleum stocks to produce final gasoline products is a very complex operation. At a typical Texaco refinery, crude oil is first distilled and processed to produce intermediate gasoline stocks. As many as 15 different stocks are then sent to storage tanks to await blending into high-quality gasolines.

Each stock exhibits different properties, like the amount of lead and the percent sulfur, and the availability of each stock for blending is limited. Each grade of final gasoline product, such as premium unleaded or leaded regular, must satisfy a set of quality specifications. To determine a blend, one must consider 14 different characteristics (like octane rating). The challenge for Texaco's analysts is to specify how much of each stock should be allocated each month to each blend of gasoline so that they meet all quality and supply restrictions and optimize a specified objective (such as profit).

EXHIBIT 5–1. This LP model will determine the optimal way of blending m gasoline stocks into n blends of gasoline to maximize profit. The objective function (1) calculates profit as the difference between gasoline sales and the cost of input stocks. The octane rating and percent lead content of each blend must meet prespecified requirements. Constraints (2) and (3) use a weighted average to meet the required qualities for a barrel of each gasoline blend. Constraint (4) ensures that the refinery does not exceed the available number of barrels of each stock.

Input Parameters	*Decision Variables*
c_i = cost per barrel of stock i	x_{ij} = barrels of stock i used in gasoline blend j
p_j = sales price per barrel of blend j	
a_i = available barrels of stock i	
o_i = octane rating of stock i	
l_i = percent lead content of stock i	
r_j = minimum octane rating of blend j	
m_j = maximum lead content of blend j	

Linear Programming Model

$$\text{maximize} \quad p_1\sum_i x_{i1} + p_2\sum_i x_{i2} + \ldots + p_n\sum_i x_{in} \qquad (1)$$
$$- c_1\sum_j x_{1j} - c_2\sum_j x_{2j} - \ldots - c_m\sum_j x_{mj}$$

subject to

$$\sum_i o_i x_{ij} \geq r_j\sum_i x_{ij} \ (j = 1, 2, \ldots, n) \qquad (2)$$
$$\sum_i l_i x_{ij} \leq m_j\sum_i x_{ij} \ (j = 1, 2, \ldots, n) \qquad (3)$$
$$\sum_j x_{ij} \leq a_i \qquad (i = 1, 2, \ldots, m) \qquad (4)$$
$$x_{ij} \geq 0 \qquad (i = 1, 2, \ldots, m; \\ j = 1, 2, \ldots, n)$$

Analysts might rely on past experience, previous blending recipes, or output from a mathematical model to help produce a final set of products. In the early 1950s, one of the first industrial applications of linear programming was to the gasoline blending problem. Exhibit 5–1 shows a simple LP model of this problem.

DeWitt et al. [1989] describe their development, testing, and calibration of an optimization-based decision support system called OMEGA (Optimization Method for the Estimation of Gasoline Attributes) that is designed to help analysts at Texaco plan a monthly schedule for gasoline blending. OMEGA is an easy-to-use, on-line, interactive system that runs on mainframe computers, superminis, and microcomputers. It has been installed in seven refineries in the United States, as well as refineries in Canada and Wales. Texaco estimates benefits of more than $30 million per year from using this state-of-the-art system.

OMEGA relies on a nonlinear program (NLP) to model the gasoline blending problem. In this model, some restrictions take the form of weighted averages of stock qualities much like the linear constraints shown in the LP model. However, constraints involving distillation (the process of separating crude oil components by boiling point ranges) and octane blending are complex, nonlinear expressions. Sample constraints are shown in Exhibit 5–2.

At the algorithmic heart of OMEGA is a powerful reduced gradi-

---

EXHIBIT 5–2. In the gasoline blending problem, certain constraints for distillation and octane blending assume nonlinear forms. The natural logarithm of the weighted average is taken in constraint (1) and quadratic and interaction terms are used in constraint (2).

Input Parameters	*Decision Variables*
$d_i =$ distillation point for stock i	$x_{ij} =$ barrels of stock i used in gasoline blend j
$s,t =$ distillation constants	
$v_j, w_j =$ lower and upper bounds for distillation blending	
$a,d,g =$ octane blending constants	
$b_i, c_i, e_i, f_i, h_i, k_i, l_i =$ quality indices for stock i	
$r_j =$ minimum octane rating of blend j	

Distillation Blending Constraints

$$v_j \leq s + t \left[\ln \left(\sum_i d_i x_{ij} / \sum_i x_{ij}\right)\right] \leq w_j \qquad (j = 1, 2, \ldots, n) \qquad (1)$$

Octane Blending Constraints

$$a \left[\sum_i b_i^2 x_{ij} / \sum_i x_{ij} - \sum_i [c_i x_{ij} / \sum_i x_{ij}]^2\right] + d \left[\sum_i e_i x_{ij} / \sum_i x_{ij} - (\sum_i f_i x_{ij} / \sum_i x_{ij})^2\right]^2$$
$$+ g \left[\sum_i (h_i / \sum_i x_{ij} - [k_i x_{ij} / \sum_i x_{ij}][l_i x_{ij} / \sum_i x_{ij}])\right] \geq r_j \qquad (j = 1, 2, \ldots, n) \qquad (2)$$

ent procedure for solving NLPs. The implemented algorithm is very accurate and quite efficient. For example, OMEGA solves a blending problem with 40 variables and 71 constraints in about five seconds on a large IBM mainframe computer.

5.3 IMPROVING THE EFFICIENCY OF CHECK PROCESSING

Markland and Nauss [1983] focus on the problem of how local banks can efficiently return checks to out-of-state banks so that funds can be collected quickly. Modeling this problem is complicated by several factors. First, checks can be returned directly to the drawee bank or they can be cleared either through a private bank or a Federal Reserve Bank. Check-clearing charges as well as clearing speeds are usually different for the three banks. Second, the alternative modes of transporting the checks to the clearing agency (such as direct courier service) differ in cost and availability during the day.

Markland and Nauss modeled the check-clearing problem as a 0-1 integer program that is similar in structure to the *simple* or *uncapacitated plant location problem* (SPLP). Given customers with known demands, the SPLP decides which facilities to open to minimize the sum of the fixed costs for the facilities and the transportation costs for shipments to the customers. Exhibit 5–3 provides the model formulation as a mathematical programming problem. This model imposes no capacity constraints on the facilities. Thus, once the open facilities are specified, the assignment of customers to plants or warehouses is obvious. Each customer is supplied by the facility that yields the cheapest transportation cost (customer j is supplied out of the facility i* that minimizes c_{ij} over all i with $y_i = 1$). This simple assignment rule fails if the facilities have finite capacities. Such complications as multiple products, more complex cost structures (including production-related costs), multi-level distribution features (from plant to warehouse to retailer), and multi-period planning (time-phasing) can be incorporated into this facility location model to enhance its realism.

Markland and Nauss treated the out-of-state checks as the customers and the clearing methods as the facilities in their SPLP model. They sought a solution technique that could solve large-scale problems, containing 200 to 300 facilities, 2,000 customers, and 15,000 to 20,000 facility-customer connections, without requiring excessive core computer storage (capacity for storage was limited at Maryland National Bank). These considerations led them to use a branch-and-bound heuristic rather than an exact optimal algorithm. However, the computational results for five problems showed that the heuristic was both accurate (all problems were solved to optimality) and efficient (the solution time is under 60 seconds for each problem). Their model continues to be used

EXHIBIT 5–3. In the simple plant location problem, facility locations must be selected out of m possible sites to minimize the total cost of serving n customers. The objective function (1) represents the total costs. Constraint (2) requires that the demand of each customer be satisfied. Constraint (3) links the location and customer assignment decisions: if facility i is not open ($y_i = 0$), it cannot ship to any location. Accordingly, constraint (3) forces $x_{ij} = 0$ for all j when $y_i = 0$. This constraint is automatically satisfied when $y_i = 1$ since total shipments out of a facility never exceed the total demand.

Input Parameters	*Decision Variables*
m = number of possible sites	x_{ij} = amount shipped from facility i to customer j
n = number of customers	
c_{ij} = per-unit transportation cost for shipping from facility i to customer j	$y_i = \begin{cases} 1, & \text{if facility i is opened} \\ 0, & \text{if facility i is not opened} \end{cases}$
f_i = fixed operating cost for facility i	
d_j = demand of customer j	

Integer Programming Model

minimize

$$\sum_i \sum_j c_{ij}x_{ij} + \sum_i f_i y_i \tag{1}$$

subject to

$$\sum_i x_{ij} = d_j \qquad (j = 1, 2, \ldots, n) \tag{2}$$

$$\sum_j x_{ij} - y_i \left(\sum_j d_j\right) \leq 0 \qquad (i = 1, 2, \ldots, m) \tag{3}$$

$$x_{ij} \geq 0 \qquad (i = 1, 2, \ldots, m; \; j = 1, 2, \ldots, n)$$

$$y_i = 0 \text{ or } 1 \qquad (i = 1, 2, \ldots, m)$$

by Maryland National Bank and has also been implemented at First Bank in Minneapolis.

5.4 THE FIELD OF MATHEMATICAL PROGRAMMING

Over the last 40 years or so, decision makers in industry and government have been able to mathematically model and solve important large-scale real-world problems. Mathematical programming models and especially linear programming models have been used to represent a wide range of problems including airline crew scheduling, chemical blending and distribution, production scheduling, electric power flow, land use planning, tanker scheduling, and municipal waste collection. The airline, chemical, steel, and petroleum industries, as well as the military, have been frequent users of mathematical programming models.

Bradley, Hax, and Magnanti [1977] provide a well-written, accessible overview of the entire field of mathematical programming that covers application and theory. They include introductory material on linear, integer, nonlinear, and dynamic programming, network models, and more advanced material on formulating and solving large-scale linear programs. They devote four chapters to actual real-world applications of mathematical programming techniques, including an LP model to determine the best composition and mission of the US Merchant Marine Fleet and a mixed integer programming model for designing a naval tender job shop. Shapiro [1979] gives a highly theoretical treatment of mathematical programming that covers many of the important results and solution algorithms in such areas as LP, NLP, IP, and network optimization.

Several books are designed to familiarize readers with the broad range of mathematical programming models. Salkin and Saha [1975] present 14 papers that describe the application of linear programming to important problems in industry and agriculture and in other areas such as investment planning and transportation. Williams [1978] describes the basic principles of building linear, nonlinear, and integer programming models and then presents the formulation and solution of 20 problems that range from refinery optimization to manpower planning. Levary [1988] contains a collection of papers that focus on applying mathematical programming techniques to a wide variety of interesting problems in structural, chemical, and mining engineering, and aeronautics and astronautics. For example, one application describes the use of a nonlinear programming model to help design fins that stabilize the roll of a ship, while another paper constructs a nonlinear 0-1 program to locate drillholes for mine planning.

The entire July–August 1990 issue of *Interfaces* is devoted to the practice of linear programming with some discussion of integer and nonlinear programming. The issue contains a total of 13 papers: three applications papers, two historical pieces, two reminiscences, five tutorials (including papers on network-related formulations, tabu search, and interior point methods), and a paper that offers some thoughts on mathematical programming practice in the 1990s.

There are many fine textbooks that focus primarily on a single branch of mathematical programming. Space limitations prevent us from discussing even a small subset of the best textbooks in each field. However, in Exhibit 5–4, we provide a brief annotated bibliography of current and classical references in the three areas, that is, LP, NLP, and IP, represented by the readings in this chapter. A sampler of references for network optimization—a very important and practical branch of mathematical programming—appears in Chapter 9.

There are several excellent articles that either provide a survey of

EXHIBIT 5–4. A partial list of classical and current textbooks that cover the theory and application of linear programming, nonlinear programming, and integer programming.

Title Author(s)	Comments
Linear Programming Textbooks	
Linear Programming and Extensions Dantzig [1963]	This book is written by the developer of the simplex algorithm. The 28 chapters cover the theory of linear programming and classical applications such as the transportation problem, the transshipment problem, and the maximal flow problem.
Optimization Theory for Large Systems Lasdon [1970]	Many of the most important algorithms for solving large-scale LPs and NLPs are developed and then illustrated by numerical examples. Powerful procedures including Dantzig-Wolfe decomposition and Benders' partitioning algorithm are presented.
Linear Programming Chvátal [1983]	The four parts of this textbook focus on the theory of linear programming, selected applications (including the cutting stock problem and game theory), network flow problems, and such advanced techniques as generalized upper bounding. The ellipsoid method is outlined in an appendix. The book is written in a style that is suitable for readers with high-school level mathematics.
Linear Programming: Methods and Applications Gass [1985]	The first edition of this book was published in 1958, making it one of the earliest monographs on linear programming. The current version contains chapters on the theoretical and computational aspects of the simplex algorithm, as well as chapters on degeneracy, parametric linear programming, and the decomposition of large-scale systems. Two chapters are devoted to applications including transportation problems, diet problems, and network flow problems.
Theory of Linear and Integer Programming Schrijver [1986]	This is a highly theoretical treatment of linear and integer programming. It covers some of the latest results including Karmarkar's algorithm for linear programming and Lenstra's procedure for

EXHIBIT 5–4. *(Continued)*

Title Author(s)	Comments
	integer programming. Schrijver was awarded the 1986 Lanchester Prize for this book. (This prize is given annually to the author of the best English language paper or book in operations research.)

Nonlinear Programming Textbooks

Title Author(s)	Comments
Nonlinear Programming: A Unified Approach Zangwill [1969]	The three main sections of this book cover the formulation of nonlinear programming problems, indentification of an optimal solution, and explanation of solution algorithms including conjugate directions, conjugate gradient, and penalty and barrier methods. Much of the book focuses on the covergence of an NLP algorithm to the solution of a specified problem.
Nonlinear Programming: Theory and Algorithms Bazaraa and Shetty [1979]	This is a highly theoretical treatment of three major topics: convex analysis, optimality conditions and duality, and algorithms and convergence. An extensive 37-page bibliography focuses on articles and books that cover NLP theory.
Nonlinear Programming: Theory, Algorithms, and Applications McCormick [1983]	Although much of this book is devoted to traditional NLP algorithms for constrained and unconstrained problems, several chapters present applications. Formulations of chemical equilibrium, inventory, engineering design, and water pollution control problems are included.
Linear and Nonlinear Programming Luenberger [1984]	This book is divided into three parts. The first part focuses on a theoretical development of the simplex method, duality, and the transportation and network flow problems. The second and third parts derive optimality conditions and present a variety of algorithms that solve NLPs.

Integer Programming Textbooks

Title Author(s)	Comments
Integer and Combinatorial Optimization Nemhauser and Wolsey [1988]	Describes the theoretical underpinnings of algorithms that can solve discrete optimization models. The first seven chapters present the mathematical

(Continued)

EXHIBIT 5–4. (*Continued*)

Title Author(s)	Comments
	foundations and the next six are devoted to a discussion of general integer programming issues including branch-and-bound and cutting-plane algorithms. The final three chapters focus on integral polyhedra, matching, and matroids.
Foundations of Integer Programming Salkin and Mathur [1989]	This book concentrates on algorithms for general integer programming problems. It covers cutting planes, enumerative methods, decomposition methods, and the group theoretic method. One chapter of the text discusses fixed charge problems and the plant location problem in particular.

LP, NLP, and IP applications or present background on important breakthroughs in each area. In their early annotated bibliography of linear, nonlinear, and dynamic programming, Riley and Gass [1958] cataloged over 1,000 articles, books, monographs, proceedings, and corporate and government reports that cover a wide range of theoretical issues and application areas. Gass [1985] provides a selective bibliography of over 400 linear programming applications that were published mostly in the 1970s and early and mid 1980s in 20 diverse areas, including agriculture, banking, energy, environment, health care, public policy, and university management. For readers interested in the history of LP, Dantzig [1963, 1982] traces the origins of linear programming and the influences which led to its development. Dorfman [1984] presents a controversial look at the discovery of linear programming.

Although the simplex method is the most widely used procedure for solving LPs, researchers have tried to develop a better algorithm. L. G. Khachiyan [1979] introduced the ellipsoid method for linear programming that was proven to be theoretically efficient. However, in practice, Khachiyan's method is quite slow in solving LPs, especially when compared to the simplex method. Bland, Goldfarb, and Todd [1981] present a comprehensive survey of the ellipsoid method together with its theoretical and practical properties. In an article designed for readers unfamiliar with LP concepts, Bland [1981] illustrates the ellipsoid method and also discusses the issues of computational complexity that arise when the performance of algorithms is compared.

As mentioned earlier, the simplex method performs quite well in practice. For many years, researchers did not understand why the procedure was so efficient. In 1982, K. Borgwardt was awarded the Lanchester Prize for his work on analyzing the performance of the simplex method. This important area of research is summarized and extended in Borgwardt [1987].

N. Karmarkar [1984] of AT&T Bell Laboratories introduced a projective scaling method for linear programming that was also proven to be an efficient procedure. However, when applied to very large LPs, Karmarkar's procedure seemed to be faster than the simplex method. Hughes [1989] describes some computational experience in solving LPs for the Military Airlift Command. A simplex-based optimizer on a mainframe computer required four hours to solve a problem with 36,000 variables and 10,000 constraints. Karmarkar's method running on an AT&T mini-supercomputer solved a similar problem with more than 150,000 variables and 12,000 constraints in one hour. Hooker [1986] provides an intuitive explanation of the approach and covers some of the theory behind the method. Schrijver [1986] gives a highly theoretical description of Karmarkar's method.

Lasdon and Waren [1980] present a comprehensive survey of nonlinear programming models in three areas where NLPs have had a significant impact: (1) the oil and chemical industries, (2) nonlinear networks, and (3) economic planning. They discuss the application of NLP models and solution procedures to such problems as petroleum product blending, managing hydroelectric systems, and traffic flow in an urban transportation network. They include a bibliography of over 190 citations.

In their well-known textbook on integer programming, Garfinkel and Nemhauser [1972] gave a comprehensive picture of this area as it had developed since the late 1950s. An indication of the great expansion of this area is the recent comprehensive textbook by Nemhauser and Wolsey [1988]. It is two and a half times as long as the earlier text and contains over twice as many citations. In addition to its quantitative growth, the field of integer programming has gone through a qualitative change. The emphasis has shifted to combinatorial properties of classes of integer programming problems and the exploitation of their special structures. In Chapter 1 of their textbook, Nemhauser and Wolsey review the key themes of the research in integer programming and list a variety of sources and references on this subject. A synopsis of these key themes is available in their chapter-length review of integer programming [Nemhauser and Wolsey 1989].

Schrijver [1986] devotes the latter half of his book to a systematic exposition of the role of polyhedral theory and the geometry of lattices in integer programming.

Texts on combinatorial optimization often contain good chapters on integer programming techniques or models with special combinatorial structure. Papadimitriou and Steiglitz [1982] and Parker and Rardin [1988] cover matching problems, covering and packing problems, and cutting planes.

During the past four decades, the computer hardware and software used to solve mathematical programs has changed dramatically. A desktop microcomputer now boasts the computing power of a mid-1970s mainframe. Analysts can now use microcomputers to accurately and efficiently solve LPs with several thousand variables and constraints and NLPs with several hundred variables and constraints. Networks with thousands of nodes and arcs can also be modeled on microcomputers. Wasil, Golden, and Sharda [1989] review the state of the art in micro-based LP and NLP software. They provide a brief account of the evolution of mathematical programming software and review six different systems with respect to such factors as user-interface and user-control capabilities. Wasil, Golden, and Liu [1989] survey the features exhibited by six commercially-available NLP systems for the microcomputer and test them for accuracy and efficiency on a set of NLPs. Waren, Hung, and Lasdon [1987] present a status report on NLP software that focuses primarily on mainframe-based packages and new algorithmic developments. Sharda [1988] highlights key advances and improvements in 20 different LP packages for the microcomputer. The most significant achievement has been the development of spreadsheet-compatible LP packages that allow users to model and solve LPs easily.

5.5 FURTHER READINGS

Related Readings

Rumpf, Melachrinoudis, and Rumpf Paper

- Rumpf, Rumpf, and Melachrinoudis [1988] present additional details concerning model development and implementation for the aerial spray program. The overall cost of the modeling effort was $18,000 and took about one year. They devoted five months to evaluating candidate models and formulating an appropriate LP. Collecting data on the different types of aircraft, airfields, and spray blocks took four months and testing a code to successfully solve the LP took three months. The authors also modified the flight plans selection model reported in the *Interfaces* paper by relaxing the time window constraints. This allowed a 220-block, five-airfield, four-aircraft problem to be solved in under 10 minutes on a microcomputer. The 1985 spray program was evaluated using this modified LP and was run on a microcomputer in the Maine Forest Service's office. Recently, David Rumpf [1989] informed us that the microcomputer-based model that was used extensively in the 1985 project is still in working order, but it has not been used since then. It seems that enough mature trees have been harvested to force the budworm into remission and the forests have not required spraying.

- In the flight plans selection LP, different airfield and aircraft combinations are not treated as decision variables but must be fixed by the decision maker prior to solving the model. Melachrinoudis, Rumpf, and Venegas [1987] remedy this and other shortcomings of the earlier modeling effort by developing a mixed integer programming (MIP) formulation. The enhanced model selects the aircraft teams and airfields to use in the spraying operation and also determines where to station the aircraft teams. The MIP formulation shown in Exhibit 5–5 resembles the original

EXHIBIT 5–5. The MIP model of the aerial spray operation to suppress spruce budworms takes into account the fixed costs of using an airfield, stationing specific aircraft types at an airfield, and costs associated with airfield landing rights. The constraint (4) forces $t_{ijk} = 0$ for all i in A_k and all j when airfield k is not used. If $y_k = 0$, then no aircraft are stationed at the airfield and no blocks of forest can be sprayed from that airfield. The fixed costs associated with using airfield k are incurred if $y_k = 1$. The constraint (5) ensures that the total amount of time for aircraft team of type i does not exceed the number of available hours.

Input Parameters		*Decision Variables*	
e_k	= fixed cost of using airfield k	t_{ijk} =	total time for aircraft team type i flying to block j from airfield k
h_i	= fixed cost for aircraft team type i per spray season	x_i =	number of aircraft teams of type i used in the project
L	= airfield landing rights cost	$y_k = \begin{cases} 1, \text{ if airfield k is used} \\ 0, \text{ otherwise} \end{cases}$	
c_i	= cost per hour of flying aircraft team type i		
u_{ijk}	= fraction of flying time in t_{ijk}	$z_{ik} = \begin{cases} 1, \text{ if one or more aircraft teams of type i is stationed at airfield k} \\ 0, \text{ otherwise} \end{cases}$	
A_k	= set of aircraft types that can be stationed at airfield k		
S	= set of feasible flight plans		
s_i	= spray speed for aircraft team type i		
r_{ijk}	= fraction of spraying time in t_{ijk}		
a_j	= area of block j		
T_{ik}	= total number of aircraft hours available, including all teams of type i that can be supported at airfield k		
M	= very large number		
W_i	= number of hours aircraft team type i available during spray season		

(continued)

EXHIBIT 5–5. (*Continued*)

Mixed Integer Programming Model

$$\text{minimize} \sum_k e_k y_k + \sum_i h_i x_i + \sum_k \sum_{i \in A_k} Lz_{ik} + \sum \sum_{(i,j,k) \in S} \sum c_i u_{ijk} \ t_{ijk} \tag{1}$$

subject to

$$\sum_k \sum_{i \in A_k} s_i r_{ijk} \ t_{ijk} \geq a_j \qquad (j = 1, 2, \ldots, m) \tag{2}$$

$$\sum_j t_{ijk} \leq T_{ik} \ z_{ik} \qquad (k = 1, 2, \ldots, p; \ i \in A_k) \tag{3}$$

$$\sum_j \sum_{i \in A_k} t_{ijk} \leq My_k \qquad (k = 1, 2, \ldots, p) \tag{4}$$

$$\sum_j \sum_k t_{ijk} \leq W_i x_i \qquad (i = 1, 2, \ldots, n) \tag{5}$$

$$t_{ijk} \geq 0 \qquad (i, j, k) \in S$$

$$y_k = 0 \text{ or } 1 \qquad (k = 1, 2, \ldots, p)$$

$$z_{ik} = 0 \text{ or } 1 \qquad (k = 1, 2, \ldots, p; \ i \in A_k)$$

$$x_i \geq 0 \text{ and integer} \qquad (i = 1, 2, \ldots, n)$$

LP model but includes three new decision variables (x_j, y_k, and z_{jk}), two new constraints, and three new terms in the objective function that account for such fixed costs as airfield office space costs, the cost of transporting aircraft to Maine, and equipment storage costs. Using data from the 1985 spray project, they formulated and solved LP and MIP models. The MIP model was solved on a minicomputer using the LINDO software package, while the LP was solved on a microcomputer. A comparison of the solutions of the LP and MIP models revealed that the MIP solution was nearly $47,000 cheaper than the best LP solution. This represents a gain of seven percent in going to the more sophisticated MIP model.

Markland and Nauss Paper

- The companion paper to this article is Nauss and Markland [1985]. It contains additional modeling issues, computational work, and implementation experience with the transit check-clearing problem.

- The location of lock boxes is a related facility location problem in banking. Lock boxes are post office boxes operated in various locations to which customers of a corporation direct their payments. Well-planned locations of such boxes allow the corporation to collect its funds more quickly. In fact, Nauss and Markland used the procedure they designed for the lock box problem as a basis for their branch-and-bound procedure for the transit check-clearing problem. Nauss and Markland [1981] give a complete description of the lock box problem along with computational results.

- In order to maximize its available funds, a corporation may decide to pay a client's bill from a bank that has a long check-clearing time (a slow bank). In this case, the corporation wishes to optimally locate banks so that check-clearing times are maximized. Cornuejols, Fisher, and Nemhauser

[1977] give an excellent presentation of the bank account location problem and provide computational results for approximate solution algorithms. For its mathematical analysis of the location problem, this paper received the 1977 Lanchester Prize for the best published contribution in operations research in the English language.

Background Readings

DeWitt et al. Paper

- In the early 1950s, the petroleum industry was one of the first adopters of the new linear programming methodology. LPs were used to model the problems of gasoline blending and refinery scheduling. The pioneering work in the field was carried out by Charnes, Cooper, and Mellon [1952]. Manne [1956] describes much of the early effort in applying mathematical models to oil refinery scheduling problems. Garvin et al. [1957] survey the first-generation applications of linear programming to drilling and production, manufacturing, and marketing and distribution problems found in the oil industry. Bodington and Baker [1990] give a very nice decade-by-decade description of mathematical programming in the petroleum industry from the 1940s to the present.

- Many of the mathematical programming models used by the petroleum and refining industries rely on nonlinear functions. For example, as we illustrated earlier, gasoline blending constraints can assume nonlinear forms. Over the past 20 years, analysts in the oil industry have used successive linear programming (SLP) to successfully solve large-scale non-linear programs. Basically, the algorithm uses a sequence of LPs to solve an NLP. Baker and Lasdon [1985] describe the various types of nonlinearities found in the oil industry and discuss some of the nonlinear modeling techniques used at Exxon. They present an efficient SLP algorithm and its application to six industrial problems within Exxon, including refinery planning and gasoline blending. The largest problem contained 720 rows and 1,276 columns and solving it required 12.60 minutes of CPU time on an IBM 370/168 computer. Palmer [1984] describes the development of a software system that supports LP applications at Exxon. The system has been used to model and solve problems in 100 diverse areas including petroleum product blending and investment planning.

Markland and Nauss Paper

- Hess [1975] wrote one of the earliest papers on the transit check-clearing problem; however, it primarily concerned the expansion of a check-processing facility. In a related paper, Davis et al. [1986] discuss the location of check-processing centers where there is also a routing component.

- The banking industry is a major user of optimization, simulation, and forecasting models. Cohen, Maier, and Vander Weide [1981] review the use of management science tools in such banking areas as bond portfolio management, bank operations, and loan portfolio management. Zanakis, Mavrides, and Roussakis [1986] present a comprehensive classification of 164 articles that focus on applications of management science in banking. The *European Journal of Operational Research* has devoted a special issue to

OR in banking (Volume 30, Number 1, June 1987). While this issue focuses on banking in Europe, it conveys the breadth of planning issues in banking where OR is useful.

- When locating branch facilities for banks, demographic and competitive issues must be considered in detail. Sevosi and Troiani [1987] discuss these considerations for the Sicilian bank system. Their work illustrates how locational decisions go beyond what simpler cost minimization models can adequately capture.

- There is a vast literature on plant and facility location. Nemhauser and Wolsey [1988] devote special attention to integer programming models of plant location and covering problems. In their text, Love, Morris, and Wesolowsky [1988] cover the field of facility location in an accessible manner. The survey by Brandeau and Chiu [1989], which contains 238 references, indicates the diversity of the field. Krarup and Pruzan [1983] review the literature on the simple plant location problem—a model that has been studied exhaustively from a theoretical perspective.

REFERENCES

Baker, Thomas E. and Lasdon, Leon S. 1985, "Successive linear programming at Exxon," *Management Science*, Vol. 31, No. 3, pp. 264–274.

Bazaraa, Mokhtar S. and Shetty, C. M. 1979, *Nonlinear Programming: Theory and Algorithms*, John Wiley & Sons, New York.

Bland, Robert G. 1981, "The allocation of resources by linear programming," *Scientific American*, Vol. 244, No. 6, pp. 126–144.

Bland, Robert G.; Goldfarb, Donald; and Todd, Michael J. 1981, "The ellipsoid method: A survey," *Operations Research*, Vol. 29, No. 6, pp. 1039–1091.

Bodington, C. E. and Baker, T. E. 1990, "A history of mathematical programming in the petroleum industry," *Interfaces*, Vol. 20, No. 4, pp. 117–127.

Borgwardt, Karl H. 1987, *The Simplex Method: A Probabilistic Analysis*, Springer-Verlag, Heidelberg, West Germany.

Bradley, Stephen P.; Hax, Arnoldo C.; and Magnanti, Thomas L. 1977, *Applied Mathematical Programming*, Addison-Wesley, Reading, Massachusetts.

Brandeau, Margaret L. and Chiu, Samuel S. 1989, "An overview of representative problems in location research," *Management Science*, Vol. 35, No. 6, pp. 645–674.

Charnes, Abraham; Cooper, William W.; and Mellon, Bob 1952, "Blending aviation gasolines—A study in programming interdependent activities in an integrated oil company," *Econometrica*, Vol. 20, No. 2, pp. 135–159.

Chvátal, Vasek 1983, *Linear Programming*, W. H. Freeman, New York.

Cohen, Kalman J.; Maier, Steven F.; and Vander Weide, James H. 1981, "Recent developments in management science in banking," *Management Science*, Vol. 27, No. 10, pp. 1097–1119.

Cornuejols, Gerard; Fisher, Marshall L.; and Nemhauser, George L. 1977, "Location of bank accounts to optimize float: An analytic study of exact and approximate algorithms," *Management Science*, Vol. 23, No. 8, pp. 789–810.

Dantzig, George B. 1963, *Linear Programming and Extensions*, Princeton University Press, Princeton, New Jersey.

Dantzig, George B. 1982, "Reminiscences about the origins of linear programming," *Operations Research Letters*, Vol. 1, No. 2, pp. 43–48.

Davis, Samuel G.; Kleindorfer, George B.; Kochenberger, Gary A.; Reutzel, Edward T.; and Brown, Emmitt W. 1986, "Strategic planning for bank operations with multiple check-processing locations," *Interfaces*, Vol. 16, No. 6, pp. 1–12.

DeWitt, Calvin W.; Lasdon, Leon S.; Waren, Allan D.; Brenner, Donald A.; and Melhem, Simon A. 1989, "OMEGA: An improved gasoline blending system for Texaco," *Interfaces,* Vol. 19, No. 1, pp. 85–101.

Dorfman, Robert 1984, "The discovery of linear programming," *Annals of the History of Computing,* Vol. 6, No. 3, pp. 283–295.

Garfinkel, Robert S. and Nemhauser, George L. 1972, *Integer Programming,* John Wiley & Sons, New York.

Garvin, W. W.; Crandall, H. W.; John, J. B.; and Spellman, R. A. 1957, "Applications of linear programming in the oil industry," *Management Science,* Vol. 3, No. 4, pp. 407–430.

Gass, Saul I. 1985, *Linear Programming: Methods and Applications,* McGraw-Hill, New York.

Hess, Sidney W. 1975, "Design and implementation of a new check clearing system for the Philadelphia federal reserve district," *Interfaces,* Vol. 5, No. 2, pp. 22–36.

Hooker, John N. 1986, "Karmarkar's linear programming algorithm," *Interfaces,* Vol. 16, No. 4, pp. 75–90.

Hughes, George, C. 1989, "Karmarkar algorithm finds a home at MAC," *OR/MS Today,* Vol. 16, No. 3, pp. 22–23.

Karmarkar, Narendra 1984, "A new polynomial-time algorithm for linear programming," *Combinatorica,* Vol. 4, No. 4, pp. 373–395.

Khachiyan, L. G. 1979, "A polynomial algorithm in linear programming," *Soviet Mathematics Doklady,* Vol. 20, No. 1, pp. 191–194.

Krarup, Jakob and Pruzan, Peter M. 1983, "The simple plant location problem: Survey and synthesis," *European Journal of Operational Research,* Vol. 12, No. 1, pp. 36–81.

Lasdon, Leon S. 1970, *Optimization Theory for Large Systems,* Macmillan, New York.

Lasdon, Leon S. and Waren, Allan D. 1980, "Survey of nonlinear programming applications," *Operations Research,* Vol. 28, No. 5, pp. 1029–1073.

Levary, Reuven R., ed. 1988, *Engineering Design: Better Results Through Operations Research Methods,* North-Holland, New York.

Love, Robert F.; Morris, James G.; and Wesolowsky, George O. 1988, *Facilities Location: Models & Methods,* North-Holland, New York.

Luenberger, David G. 1984, *Linear and Nonlinear Programming,* Addison-Wesley, Reading, Massachusetts.

Manne, Allan S. 1956, *Scheduling of Petroleum Refinery Operations,* Harvard University Press, Cambridge, Massachusetts.

Markland, Robert E. and Nauss, Robert M. 1983, "Improving transit check clearing operations at Maryland National Bank," *Interfaces,* Vol. 13, No. 1, pp. 1–9.

McCormick, Garth P. 1983, *Nonlinear Programming: Theory, Algorithms, and Applications,* John Wiley & Sons, New York.

Melachrinoudis, Emanuel; Rumpf, David L.; and Venegas, Ramon 1987, "Mixed integer programming improves spray operation planning," *Canadian Journal of Forest Research,* Vol. 17, pp. 1602–1608.

Nauss, Robert M. and Markland, Robert E. 1981, "Theory and application of an optimizing procedure for lock box location analysis," *Management Science,* Vol. 27, No. 8, pp. 855–865.

Nauss, Robert M. and Markland, Robert E. 1985, "Optimization of bank transit check clearing operations," *Management Science,* Vol. 31, No. 9, pp. 1072–1083.

Nemhauser, George L. and Wolsey, Laurence A. 1988, *Integer and Combinatorial Optimization,* John Wiley & Sons, New York.

Nemhauser, George L. and Wolsey, Laurence A. 1989, "Integer programming," in *Optimization* (Handbooks in Operations Research and Management Science, Volume 1), ed. George L. Nemhauser, Alexander H.G. Rinnooy Kan, and Michael J. Todd, North-Holland, New York, pp. 447–527.

Palmer, Kenneth 1984, *A Model-Management Framework for Mathematical Programming,* John Wiley & Sons, New York.

Papadimitriou, Christos H. and Steiglitz, Kenneth 1982, *Combinatorial Optimization: Algorithms and Complexity,* Prentice-Hall, Englewood Cliffs, New Jersey.

Parker, R. Gary and Rardin, Ronald L. 1988, *Discrete Optimization,* Academic Press, San Diego, California.

Riley, Vera and Gass, Saul I. 1958, *Linear Programming and Associated Techniques: A Comprehensive Bibliography on Linear, Nonlinear, and Dynamic Programming,* The Johns Hopkins Press, Baltimore, Maryland.

Rumpf, David L. 1989, private communication.

Rumpf, David L.; Melachrinoudis, Emanuel; and Rumpf, Thomas A. 1985, "Improving efficiency in a forest pest control spray program," *Interfaces,* Vol. 15, No. 5, pp. 1–11.

Rumpf, David L.; Rumpf, Thomas A.; and Melachrinoudis, Emanuel 1988, "Systems analysis for large-scale forest protection programs: Operational modeling in a spruce budworm spray project," *Journal of Forestry,* Vol. 86, No. 2, pp. 18–24.

Salkin, Harvey M. and Mathur, Kamlesh 1989, *Foundations of Integer Programming,* North-Holland, New York.

Salkin, Harvey M. and Saha, Jahar, eds. 1975, *Studies in Linear Programming,* North-Holland, New York.

Schrijver, Alexander 1986, *Theory of Linear and Integer Programming,* John Wiley & Sons, Chichester, England.

Sevosi, Angela and Troiani, Marilena 1987, "The banking system in Sicily: A territorial analysis for planning and marketing purposes," *European Journal of Operational Research,* Vol. 30, No. 1, pp. 55–67.

Shapiro, Jeremy F. 1979, *Mathematical Programming: Structures and Algorithms,* John Wiley & Sons, New York.

Sharda, Ramesh 1988, "The state of the art of linear programming on personal computers," *Interfaces,* Vol. 18, No. 4, pp. 49–58.

Waren, Allan D.; Hung, Ming S.; and Lasdon, Leon S. 1987, "The status of nonlinear programming software: An update," *Operations Research,* Vol. 35, No. 4, pp. 489–503.

Wasil, Edward A.; Golden, Bruce L.; and Liu, Li 1989, "State-of-the-art in nonlinear optimization software for the microcomputer," *Computers & Operations Research,* Vol. 16, No. 6, pp. 497–512.

Wasil, Edward A.; Golden, Bruce L.; and Sharda, Ramesh 1989, "Mathematical programming software for the microcomputer: Recent advances, comparisons, and trends," in *Impacts of Recent Computer Advances on Operations Research,* ed. Ramesh Sharda, Bruce Golden, Edward Wasil, Osman Balci, and William Stewart, North-Holland, New York, pp. 263–272.

Williams, H. P. 1978, *Model Building in Mathematical Programming,* John Wiley & Sons, Chichester, England.

Zanakis, Stelios H.; Mavrides, Lazaros P.; and Roussakis, Emmanuel N. 1986, "Applications of management science in banking," *Decision Sciences,* Vol. 17, No. 1, pp. 114–128.

Zangwill, Willard I. 1969, *Nonlinear Programming: A Unified Approach,* Prentice-Hall, Englewood Cliffs, New Jersey.

Improving Efficiency in a Forest Pest Control Spray Program

David L. Rumpf

Emanuel Melachrinoudis

Thomas Rumpf

The spruce budworm is the most destructive defoliator of spruce-fir forests in all of North America. Over five million acres of Maine's forests have been severely infested in recent years. The Maine Forest Service has conducted annual aerial spray programs since 1972 to control budworm damage to the forest and to mitigate an anticipated shortage of wood as documented by the Sewall Company's Maine spruce-fir demand analysis [1983].

Yearly spraying of treatment acreage takes place during May and June; the infested areas are located in remote northern and eastern Maine. Aircraft, crews, and support personnel are stationed at each of the airfields. Only eight fields were suitable for use during the 1983 project (see Figure 1). Aircraft teams consisted of one or more spray aircraft, a guide plane with pilot and navigator, and a monitor plane with pilot and observer. The navigator used LORAN, a radio wave location system, to determine exactly when to start and stop spraying. Several teams of aircraft may be stationed at an airfield;

for example, in 1983 four C-54 teams, one M-18 team, and two Thrush teams were based at Presque Isle, the most active site. C-54's are large four-engine aircraft with relatively long range and high spray speed which fly individually as an aircraft team. The Thrush or Air Tractor is a workhorse of the agricultural spray industry. A single engine aircraft, it flies slowly, has a short range but provides very accurate spraying; it flies as a team of three aircraft. The M-18 is a large single engine aircraft with longer range and larger payload than the Thrush which can also apply spray very accurately; it flies as a team of two aircraft.

Project planning begins in the fall with aerial and ground analysis of insect danger. The state, in cooperation with landowners, makes a preliminary determination of acreage requiring treatment. While the Maine Forest Service coordinates the operation, spraying activities are subcontracted. A spray operator employing agricultural pilots performs spraying, another contractor performs chemical mixing and

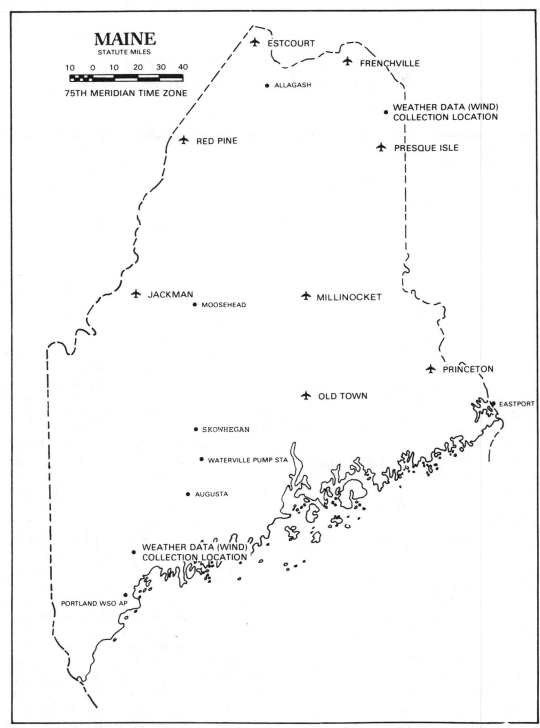

FIGURE 1: Map of Maine Showing the Airfields Considered for 1983 Spray Project

delivery. Bid specifications are prepared during January, bids are received by the end of February, and contracts awarded by March. The Forest Service develops operational plans, works out logistics with the sub-contractors, decides when blocks can be sprayed, and monitors every spray trip to insure effectiveness and environmental protection.

The weather is an important factor. The insecticide attains effective dispersion and deposit on tree foliage only under dry conditions and moderate wind speeds of three to 15 miles per hour. These requirements generally restrict spraying to early morning or evening hours. The spraying must also occur during a specific stage of insect development, a requirement which limits spray activity to a period of three to seven days for a given site (spray block). The total time window for a particular airfield lasts for two to four weeks depending on the number and location of blocks sprayed. Total project duration for all airfields is from three to six weeks.

In 1983, 24 spray aircraft, operating from six separate airstrips in northern and eastern Maine, sprayed nearly 850,000 acres. The contracting costs for the aircraft and crews represent one-third or more of total costs for the project each year. In an attempt to maximize the efficiency of aircraft assignments and reduce aircraft needs and contracting costs, the Forest Service investigated computer software which could analyze the costs of spray block treatment by aircraft type and airstrip assignment.

MODEL FORMULATION

The literature on managing agricultural and forest pests is dominated by biological models (see Wirewick [1977]; Feldman and Curry [1982]). Although Clark et al. [1979] discuss the relationship between ecological and policy sciences, they focus on improving the use of the results of biological modeling in management decisions. Banaugh and Ekblad [1981] develop equations for determining the treatment cost for a single spray area (spray block); however, the technique has not yet been applied. There are to our knowledge no published accounts of mathematical models improving the efficiency of agricultural or forest spray operations.

During the past two years, we have developed a cost-minimizing mathematical model which assigns spray blocks to aircraft and airfields. In previous years, spray blocks were assigned to airfields by partitioning the map into regions around each airfield. Aircraft types were then assigned to blocks on the basis of the block's size and distance from the airfield.

Initially we tried to formulate the problem either as a network-flow problem or as an integer-programming problem. A network-flow approach, although very attractive because of the efficiency of existing algorithms (see Glover and Klingman [1977]), was excluded because of lack of realism in the model. The integer programming formulation was prohibitively large. After these unsuccessful attempts, we developed a linear programming formulation and carried it through to solution. It is not only computationally efficient by nature, but models the situation quite realistically.

Given a set of airfields and the characteristics of the different types of spray aircraft, the model determines the lowest cost set of flight plans which will accomplish the required spraying. The ability to evaluate alternative scenarios, for example the effect of closing certain airfields or using a different type of spray aircraft, is one major advantage of the model.

The major assumption of the mathematical model, detailed in Appendix I, is that an aircraft team sprays one block, then sprays additional blocks until it has no insecticide left; that is, until its full load is delivered. Most of the time this is a realistic assumption.

The decision variables are the times allocated to each aircraft team flying out of each airfield to spray each block. Each includes spraying time, turning time, void time, orientation time, ferrying time, and ground time (see Appendices I and II for definitions). If less than a full load of insecticide is used for a block, only a corresponding part of ferrying and ground time is allocated to that block. Only the variables which can be identified with feasible flight plans, that is allowable combinations of blocks, aircraft, and airfields, are considered. An allowable combination is such that the block is within the operating range of the aircraft flying out of a particular airfield, the aircraft is allowed to spray the insecticide specified for that block, and there are one or more aircraft teams of the type specified stationed at the airfield.

Two types of constraints are imposed on the variables. First, the time used exclusively for spraying each block should be sufficient to guarantee complete spraying, and that time depends on the location and geometry of the block and the aircraft and airfield characteristics. The second type of constraint takes into consideration the limited time window for each aircraft and airfield combination during which weather conditions and pest development allow for effective spraying. The function to be minimized is the total spraying cost. The objective function sums spraying cost for all chosen flight paths. The decision varia-

ble, time allocated to spray the block, is multiplied first by a ratio representing actual flying time over total time (flying and ground) then by cost per flying hour. The cost per flying hour includes both direct and indirect costs for an aircraft team (see Appendix II).

DATA COLLECTION AND DETERMINATION OF MODEL PARAMETERS

Each year before the bidding process starts, the Maine Forest Service prepares a large-scale map displaying the airports and the blocks to be sprayed. We used this map to calculate distances. The map was given a rectangular system of coordinates with x,y axes running east-west and north-south; the origin of the coordinate system was selected in such a way that all blocks and airfields fall within the first quadrant. We measured the coordinates of the centroids of blocks for block locations and the centroids of airfields for airfield locations and calculated distances.

The time available for spraying is a complex probabilistic function of both weather conditions and the budworm development cycle. Rather than predicting available spray windows through a multifactor causative model, we estimated the spray window on the basis of previous experience. First, the average number of morning and afternoon spray periods was calculated on the basis of three years of data (1980-1982). Since data were available for only four airfields, the number of spray periods for additional airfields were set equal to the geographically closest known airfield. The Edson report [1982] details time from takeoff to final shutdown for a number of morning and afternoon spray periods. These data, supplemented by hand-collected data from the 1983 project, were used to calculate the mean time per period for the C-54 and Thrush. In 1983, a new type of aircraft, the M-18, was first used. This plane is similar to the Thrush but has a larger capacity and a range of 110 miles round trip versus 70 miles for the Thrush. The M-18's mean time per period was defined to be equal to that for a Thrush.

The total time window available is a function of location (weather patterns) and aircraft type (smaller aircraft can be quickly loaded and airborne to take advantage of short spells of good weather). We assumed that for each aircraft type and airfield the time window was approximately a normally distributed random variable. Sample means and variances were used as estimators, and one standard deviation was subtracted from the mean to insure with over 80 percent confidence that we would indeed observe the defined time window. The total hours available for each aircraft and airfield combination are equal to the time window times the number of aircraft teams which can be supported at the given airfield. The mathematical model determines the number of teams of each type required according to the overall minimum spray cost criterion.

The costs associated with each spray aircraft were determined by first calculating the fixed and variable costs assigned to it. Then, fixed costs were divided by the estimated total time window to obtain an hourly cost, which was added to the hourly variable costs to obtain the cost per hour for each spray aircraft and airfield combination (see Appendix II). Data for each type of aircraft were obtained from manufacturer's specifications. Personnel cost data for each aircraft team were supplied by the aircraft contractors and the Maine Forest Service.

The parameters for time spent actually spraying and for all flying time were derived by splitting the total aircraft time allocated to a block into several task times and taking appropriate fractions (Appendix II). We collected data on orientation time, turning time, ground time, and efficiency during the 1983 spray operation. We measured the east-west distances and the percent "out" on the map. The "outs" are marshes or other wetlands which are not sprayed. The Maine Forest Service provided all remaining data.

USE OF MODEL

Since the Maine Forest Service contracts out the aerial spray operation, the model served both to guide preparation of contract specifications and to support operational planning for aircraft location and reassignment during the project. Eight airfields were considered for use in 1983 (Figure 1). The over 300 spray blocks defined for the 1984 project were roughly within the convex hull defined by these eight airfields. We evaluated the effect on cost for a variety of possible project specifications and determined the best set of flight plans given the airfields and aircraft types available. The spray project staff were especially interested in the effect of closing one or more airfields. They were also interested in observing the effect of a change in aircraft characteristics such as ferry distance or speed.

An important planning decision is the number and location of the base airfields. The decision to use an airfield is political, logistic, and analytic. It is political because one airfield experienced demonstrations against the spray project in the past and logistic because both food and lodging are required for the pilots and project staff.

The analytic aspect (consideration of block location, aircraft characteristic, and airfield location) is incorporated in the model and thus is reflected in the results.

Several major changes had occurred since the 1983 project which made specifying contract requirements more difficult. First, the project lost a centrally located airfield, Red Pine, which was the base airfield for 20 percent of the spraying during 1983. Second, a new type of spray aircraft became available. The new type, defined as long-range single engine (LRSE), included Airtractors with long-range gas tanks, Agcat B with long-range gas tanks, and the Bull Thrush. The new aircraft were as maneuverable as the Thrushes but had twice the range. These changes provided a rapidly changing context for testing model usefulness.

Initially, a post hoc analysis of the 1983 project proved the realism of the model. A baseline run satisfying all spray requirements and aircraft constraints was compared to actual 1983 operations results. Project staff, including the director and the airport flight managers, confirmed the validity of the results. A "what if" scenario demonstrated that the loss of the Red Pine airfield would have increased the cost of the 1983 project by 20 percent.

Use of the model to analyze the 1984 project began only a few weeks before the deadline for bid specifications when spray acreages first became available. The most immediate need was to evaluate the effectiveness of the new long-range single engine aircraft (LRSE). Project staff roughly estimated cost per hour for the two-airplane LRSE team to be $1,600 with spray capacity equal to the M-18 team and a slightly higher spray speed of 118 mph. In the time available we decided to consider the following three scenarios: case A, no restrictions; case B, no LRSE for blocks

within 25 miles of an airfield; case C, a test of the sensitivity of LRSE cost and capacity estimates. The new aircraft proved very efficient (see case A, Table 1), flying more hours than Thrushes and C-54's combined. Given that the availability of this new aircraft type was restricted, in case B we limited LRSE's to blocks 25 miles or further from an airfield. This modification replaced 25 percent of LRSE hours with Thrushes; however, costs increased by less than one percent. Thus the Thrush team proves to be nearly as efficient as the LRSE for nearby spray blocks. Case C was evaluated because LRSE includes several new aircraft whose exact specifications were unclear. Thus we raised the cost to $1,800 and lowered the capacity to that of a Thrush team. Higher cost and reduced capacity lowered LRSE hours to 129, less than half of case A, while costs increased by five percent.

The project staff used the model exten-

Table 1. Scenarios for the preliminary 1984 project which covers 314 spray blocks. Case A has no restrictions; case B uses no long-range single engine aircraft within 25 miles of the airfield; and case C, in addition to the conditions of case B, raises the LRSE cost and lowers capacity to an amount equal to a Thrush team.

	Case A	Case B	Case C
Number of airfields	7	7	7
Cost	$918,000	$922,000	$961,000
Flying hours per team			
C-54	205	205	226
LRSE	275	210	129
Thrush	33	101	169
Number of teams required			
C-54	4	4	5
LRSE	5	4	2
Thrush	1	2	3

sively in preparing bid specifications. They produced a more efficient spray plan which led to a lower bid cost than would have been possible without the model. Previous projects had specified more aircraft than were necessary.

Reevaluation of harvesting plans, insect damage hazards, and environmental concerns resulted in a one-third reduction in 1984 spray acreage. Several scenarios (sets of assumptions concerning airfields and aircraft types) were evaluated to support decisions about which airfields to open as spray bases, how many spray teams to locate at each field, and which blocks of spray acreage to assign to each airfield and aircraft combination. Model results include a detailed report listing the optimal aircraft and airfield assignment for each spray block. Using this information speeds preparation of the operations plan and insures a lowest cost plan. Summary results for several scenarios are shown in Table 2.

The actual operations plan for 1984 followed case 1. The use of the LRSE reduced the number of airfields required. Since the setup cost for each airfield is about $10,000, such savings can be significant. Cases 2, 3, and 4 evaluate the effect of modifying airfield decisions (2 and 3) or aircraft choice (4). Case 2 shows an operating cost reduction of $4,000 that resulted from opening an additional airfield for Thrush aircraft at Millinocket which caused the ferry distance to be shorter for the spray blocks near that airfield. The net effect, however, is an overall cost increase of $6,000 when airfield setup costs are included. Case 3 shows a cost savings of $24,000 if Red Pine, the centrally located airfield, is substituted for Estcourt, a more peripheral airfield. Unfortunately, the forest service has been denied access to Red Pine. However, the size of the savings suggests that building a new airfield

Table 2. Scenarios for final 1984 project which covers 283 blocks. In case 1, long-range single engine aircraft (LRSE) cannot spray within 25 miles of an airfield. This allows efficient use of Thrushes and corresponds to the operating conditions chosen for the 1984 project. In case 2, case 1 is modified by opening Millinocket airfield. In case 3, case 1 is modified by replacing Estcourt with Red Pine airfield. In case 4, case 1 is modified by replacing LRSE with M-18 aircraft.

	Case 1	Case 2	Case 3	Case 4
Number of airfields				
	4	5	4	6
Aircraft flying hours				
C-54	122	122	103	105
LRSE	228	211	203	180
				(M-18)
Thrush	60	77	100	128
Flying Cost	$594,000	$590,000	$570,000	$575,000
Setup Cost	40,000	50,000	40,000	60,000
Total Cost	$634,000	$640,000	$610,000	$635,000

might be economically justified. Case 4 replaces the LRSE with the M-18, the shorter-range aircraft used in the 1983 project.

The replacement would mean opening two additional airfields to keep all spray blocks within range of at least one aircraft and airfield combination. The total increase in cost for the aerial spray operation (savings of $19,000 offset by $20,000 setup cost) is $1,000. In addition, two extra air bases further complicate the logistics for providing aircraft teams and increase the cost of providing insecticide.

Case 1 for the final 1984 project consists of 748 variables and 292 constraints. The model was solved using a revised simplex algorithm written in Fortran by the authors. All runs were executed on a Digital Equipment Corporation VAX-11/780 minicomputer.

SUMMARY

A mathematical model of the spruce budworm suppression project's aerial spray operation has saved time and reduced costs for the Maine Forest Service. The model successfully applies mathematical programming in support of natural resources management. Future plans include implementing the model on the Forest Service's microcomputers and training project staff to run the model as required.

ACKNOWLEDGMENT

We thank the referees for their valuable comments and suggestions.

APPENDIX I: Linear Programming Formulation

The following definitions are used in the formulation:

Indices

i = aircraft team type index
j = spray block index
k = airfield index
p = insecticide type index

Spray Block Data

(b_{1j}, b_{2j}) = location of block j in a rectangular system of coordinates (miles)

h_j = insecticide to be used for block j

ew_j = maximum east-west distance of block j (miles)

n_j = proportion of the interior of block j which should not be sprayed

a_j = area of block j to be sprayed (acres)

Airfield Data

(f_{1k}, f_{2k}) = location of airfield k (miles)

A_k = set of aircraft team types allowed to be stationed at the airfield k

Aircraft Team Data

c_i = cost of flying aircraft team type i (\$ / hour)

or_i = operating range of aircraft team type i (miles)

f_i = ferry speed of aircraft team type i (miles/hour)

1_{ip} = area sprayed by aircraft team i fully loaded with insecticide type p (acres)

s_i = spray speed for aircraft team type i (acres/hour)

g_i = ground time of aircraft team type i (hours)

ta_i = turning time of aircraft type i; time between completing one swath and beginning another (hours)

G_i = set of insecticides allowed to be sprayed by aircraft team type i

sw_i = swath width of aircraft team type i (miles)

Other Data

d_{jk} = distance between block j and airfield k (miles)

T_{ik} = total time window for aircraft team type i stationed at airfield k, a probabilistically determined upper limit which is dependent on weather conditions, insect development, and number of aircraft teams type i stationed at airfield k

r_{ijk} = fraction of t_{ijk} exclusively for spraying

u_{ijk} = fraction of t_{ijk} including all flying times, that is, all times except the ground time

Variables

t_{ijk} = total aircraft time for aircraft team type i flying from airfield k to spray block j where less than full load trips incur fractional ferry time allocations; includes spraying time, ferrying time, orientation time upon arrival at the block, turning time to align at the beginning of each swath, and ground time

Flight Plans Selection Model

$$\text{Min} \sum_{(i,j,k)\in S}\sum\sum c_i u_{ijk} t_{ijk} \qquad (1)$$

subject to

$$S = \{(i,j,k) : d_{jk} \le or_i \text{ and} \qquad (2.1)$$

$$h_j \in G_j \text{ and } i \in A_k\},$$

$$\sum_k \sum_{i\in A_k} s_i r_{ijk} t_{ijk} \ge a_j \qquad \forall_j , \qquad (2.2)$$

$$\sum_j t_{ijk} \le T_{ik} \qquad \forall_k , \quad i \in A_k , \qquad (2.3)$$

$$t_{ijk} \ge 0, \qquad (i, j, k) \in S.$$

APPENDIX II: Aircraft Cost Data and Derivation of r_{ij} and u_{ij}

THRUSH

Three-plane spray team, plus one guide plane with pilot and guide, one spotter

Fixed Costs

— fly up to 1,500 miles at $2,000/plane	$6,000
— 3 pilots for 1.5 months	18,000
— guide plane lease	3,000
— guide pilot	6,000
— guide	3,000
— spotter	3,000
— one/half contractor representative	3,000
— food/lodging 8.5 people, 45 days, $22/day	8,400
— transportation	500
Total fixed costs	$50,900

Assume 55 hours of flying time

Fixed costs per hour	$925
Variable Costs	
— depreciation at $100/hour, 3 planes	300
— fuel, 3 planes at 40 gal/hour, 1 at 10	260
— maintenance, 4 planes at $20/hour	80
Total cost/hour for Thrush team	$1,565

M-18

Two-plane spray team, one guide plane with guide, one spotter

Fixed Costs

— fly up to 1,500 miles at $2,500/plane	$ 5,000
— two pilots	12,000
— guide plane lease	3,000
— pilot for guide plane	6,000
— guide	3,000
— spotter	3,000
— one/half contractor representative	3,000
— transportation	500
— food/lodging, 7.5 people, 45 days, $22/day	7,400
Total fixed costs	$42,900

Assume 55 hours of flying time

Fixed costs per hour	$780
Variable Costs	
— depreciation, $120/hr for two planes	240
— fuel, 50 gal/hour for two planes	
10 gal/hour for 1 plane	220
— maintenance at $75/hour for 2 planes	
$20/hour for 1 plane	190
Total cost/hour for M-18	$1,430

C-54

One-plane team

Fixed Costs

— fly up from Arizona (base airfield for C-54)	$15,000
— pilot for 1.5 months	8,000
— copilot for 1.5 months	4,000
— spotter	3,000
— food/lodging, 5.5 people, 45 days, $22/day	5,400
— one/half contractor representative	3,000
— transportation costs	500
Total fixed costs	$38,900

Assume 40 hours of flying time

Fixed costs per hour of flying time	$972
Variable Cost	
— depreciation at $100/hour	$100
— fuel at 250 gal/hour	500
— maintenance	100
Total cost/hour for C-54	$1,672

The derivation of r_{ijk} and u_{ijk} requires definition of several task times:

— orientation time, that is, flying time required for the aircraft team to orient itself upon arrival at the spray block. The average orientation time is independent of the aircraft team type and equal to five minutes or .0833 hours.

— spraying time (a_j/s_i)

— void time, that is, total time spent flying within the boundaries of the block over no-spray areas (outs) such as ponds, meadows, streams, and so forth. It was approximated by the percentage of void area versus spray area multiplied by the spraying time $(n_j/(1-n_j))$ (a_j/s_i).

— turning time, that is, time between completing one swath and beginning another. Since the aircraft usually spray along north-south or south-north directions, the turning time is $(\lceil ew_j/sw_i - 1\rceil)$ (ta_j) where $\lceil\ \rceil$ denotes the least upper bound integer value.

— share of the ferry time taken proportional to the block's area $((2d_{jk}/f_i)(a_j/1_{ip}))$. Note, this allows for multiple trips to one block.

Assuming 90 percent efficiency, r_{ijk} was computed as

$$r_{ijk} = \frac{\text{spray time}}{\text{total aircraft time}}(.9).$$

Similarly, u_{ijk} was computed as

$$u_{ijk} = 1 - \frac{\text{ground time}}{\text{total aircraft time}}$$

REFERENCES

Banaugh, R. and Ekblad, R. 1981, *A Method for Comparing Cost and Productivity of Aerial Spray Delivery,* US Department of Agriculture — Forest Service, Equipment Development Center, Missoula, Montana.

Clark W. C.; Jones, D. D.; and Holling, C. S. 1979, "Lessons for policy design: A case study of ecosystem management," *Ecological Modeling,* Vol. 7, No. 1, pp. 1-53.

Edson, D. T. 1982, *Aircraft Efficiency/Block Design,* Final Report, The James Sewall Company, Old Town, Maine.

Feldman, R. M. and Curry, G. L. 1982, "Operations research for agricultural pest management," *Operations Research,* Vol. 30, No. 4 (July-August), pp. 601—618.

Glover, F. and Klingman, D. 1977, "Network applications in industry and government," *AIIE Transactions,* Vol. 9, No. 4 (December), pp. 363-375.

James W. Sewall Company 1983, *Spruce Fir Wood Supply Demand Analysis,* Final Report submitted to State of Maine Department of Conservation, The James Sewall Company, Old Town, Maine.

Wirewick, K. 1977, "Mathematical models for the control of pests and infectious diseases: A survey," *Theoretical Population Biology,* Vol. 11, No. 2 (April), pp. 182-238.

A letter from Kenneth G. Stratton, Director of the Maine Forest Service, states: "Work with the model has enabled our budworm division to improve the efficiency of spray operations through the reduction in numbers of airports and spray aircraft teams. In addition, the model has provided us with a previously unavailable tool for analyzing a variety of potential changes in the administration and nature of the spray operation."

OMEGA: An Improved Gasoline Blending System for Texaco

Calvin W. DeWitt
Leon S. Lasdon
Allan D. Waren
Donald A. Brenner
Simon A. Melhem

In the late 1970s, the oil companies began to experience downward pressures on profitability due to rapid and continuing changes in the external environment. Contributing factors included large variations in crude oil prices, lower quality crudes, and changing gasoline specifications mandated by new government regulations and by the changing requirements of automobile engines. Partially in response to these pressures, Texaco's computer and information systems department (now the information technology department or ITD) developed an improved on-line interactive gasoline blending system called OMEGA (optimization method for the estimation of gasoline attributes).

This new system consists of a data acquisition and query module, linear and nonlinear equations that predict output blend qualities given input stock qualities and volumes, the GRG2 nonlinear optimizer [Lasdon and Waren 1978], and an interactive user interface. The system enables a user to retrieve a variety of data from up-to-date refinery data bases and to interactively examine and modify the data after it is inserted into the OMEGA data base. These data include information on stock qualities and availability, as well as on blend specifications and demands. Furthermore, the user, by selecting appropriate menu options, can construct and solve a nonlinear optimization problem that determines how much of each stock to allocate to each blend so that all quality specifications are met, stock availability and blend demand constraints are satisfied, and the selected objective is optimized.

OMEGA was first installed in 1983 and is now used in all seven Texaco USA refineries and in two foreign plants. We chose the initial site, the Convent, Louisiana plant, because of its intermediate complexity and well-established data acquisition and in-line blending equipment. As OMEGA use was extended to other refineries, we encountered some resistance from users who had developed their own blending models or had noted differences between the blends recommended by the system and existing blending practice. Analysis showed that these differences were due to the increased accuracy of the OMEGA input data and model formulation, and to the improved robustness and accuracy of its optimizer. To promote its acceptance, we made trial runs of OMEGA using the existing blend compositions as a starting point. OMEGA's final solutions consistently showed a much higher profit. Subsequent blending and testing in the laboratory verified that the predicted blend qualities were more accurate than those generated by the older methods.

The economic benefits attained by using OMEGA are difficult to measure since market conditions and refinery configurations have changed since its installation. However, taking the compositions of blends used prior to OMEGA as initial values for OMEGA's optimizer, we have observed increases in gasoline profits of up to 30 percent for some batches. Using more conservative and refinery specific estimates of per batch benefits, Texaco estimates total ongoing economic gains stemming from OMEGA to be more than $30 million annually.

GASOLINE BLENDING

Figure 1 is a simplified diagram of a refinery. The incoming crude oil contains a wide range of materials, from light ones, such as gasoline, to the heaviest ones, such as industrial fuel oil and asphalt. The crude oil is split into various component streams by distillation, which separates the

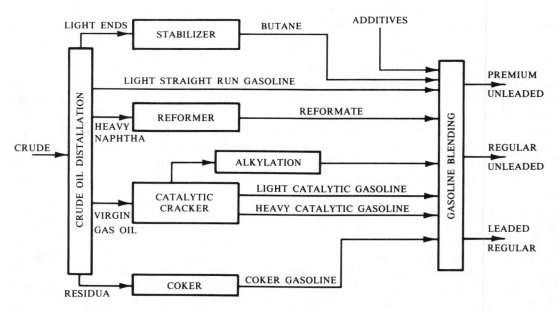

FIGURE 1: Illustrated above is the flow of gasoline stocks through a refinery. Crude oil enters the crude units and is refined by the various processes into high quality gasoline stocks. The stocks are then blended to yield one of four grades of gasoline: regular leaded, unleaded, unleaded plus, and premium unleaded.

components by boiling point ranges. Only a small portion of the distillate can go directly to gasoline blending. Most of the output streams from the distillation unit are sent to other processing units where the molecules are reformed to improve their quality or are cracked and recombined into lighter, more valuable ones. These resulting products, of widely different qualities, are then sent to intermediate storage tanks from which they are blended into gasoline.

Refining involves many complex processing steps. Some of these activities are batch operations, and others involve continuous processing to transform crude oil into components that have greater value in the marketplace. Gasoline blending is primarily a batch process. It must, however, be synchronized with other batch processes and with continuous processes to maintain a balanced and profitable ongoing plant operation. In addition, the entire refinery operation needs to be coordinated with parallel activities in crude supply, marketing, and product distribution. Linear programming was applied to refinery scheduling and gasoline blending problems as early as the 1950s. See, for example, the books by Manne [1956] and Charnes and Cooper [1961].

Generally, Texaco develops aggregated plans at a wide functional horizon and decreases the horizon and increases the rigor of the analysis as the operating time frame draws closer. For example, it creates a monthly operating plan for the entire downstream operation of a regional subdivision of the company. This plan is based on simplified representations of each operating function. A linear programming model for the refinery is used as part of this process. The blending portion of this LP model is usually linear. On the other hand, the company supports the day-to-

day scheduling of blending operations by a rigorous representation of the blending dynamics in the form of a nonlinear blending model.

Gasoline blending involves mixing a variety of available stocks, along with various additives, to produce a set of required blends in an optimal fashion. The required blends are leaded regular, unleaded regular, unleaded plus, and super unleaded gasolines. The stocks are the intermediate products from the refinery, such as straight run gasoline from a distillation column, reformate from a reformer, and catalytic gasoline from a catalytic cracker. Lead and other octane enhancers, such as MMT, are some of the additives. Stocks are produced by one of the refinery process units and are stored in intermediate storage tanks. The selected stocks are blended together, either by an in-line blender or in a blend tank, to create the blends. The in-line blender periodically samples the blend and automatically tests the properties of the samples on-line. This information is used to adjust stock flow rates so that the blend will meet its quality specifications in spite of unanticipated fluctuations in the properties of the stocks. On occasion, as many as 15 stocks are blended to yield up to eight blends.

The qualities of the blend are determined by the qualities of the stocks. The blend qualities are the various blend attributes or properties that must be controlled for each blend. The optimization problem is to calculate the volume of each stock to be used in each blend, subject to availability constraints on each stock and demand and quality specifications for each blend, so that an appropriate objective function is optimized. As many as 14 different characteristics may be involved for each blend.

Typical stock properties include Reid

vapor pressure, percent sulfur, percent aromatics, the temperatures at which various fractions of the blend boil off, octane indices including research, motor, and road octanes, and lead content (Figure 2). Equations relating blend qualities to stock qualities and volumes are presented in more detail in the appendix. Blend volatilities and octanes are nonlinear functions of the input stock qualities, whereas most of the other qualities are assumed to blend linearly with respect to volume fractions.

For a problem with I stocks and J blends, there are $J*(I + 3)$ decision variables and approximately $16*J + I$ constraints. For an analysis involving seven input stocks and four output blends, the optimization problem will consist of 40 variables (most with bounds) and 71 constraints.

Currently, blending models that incorporate nonlinearities are single period ones. Those models used for operations planning include the blending requirements for an entire month in the problem definition. In this case, neither the sequence of the blending operations nor

their impact on intermediate inventory is considered. This type of run is generally made once a month, or more often if there is a marked departure of the boundary values (stock production, blend offtake) from the values assumed in the previous analysis. Those models used for actual blending consider only a single blend at any one time, but the model may be used in this mode on a daily basis.

THE EVOLUTION OF BLENDING MODELS AT TEXACO

By the early 1960s Texaco had installed computers in some of its refineries. These computers were used primarily for accounting, data acquisition, process control, and refinery modeling. During this period, gasoline blend compositions were provided by a combination of trial and error, experience, and the use of average response tables. As computers became more readily available, mathematical models were developed to aid the gasoline blender. These mathematical models at-

```
                STOCK  QUALITIES                              02
        SELECT THE STOCK NUMBER WANTED: 1            PRESS H FOR HELP
_____
                        STOCK NAME: HOBG              TANK NUMBER: 1
    IBP: 100.00      90%: 220.00      RVP: 10.000     RONO:    94.0
    10%: 110.00       EP: 250.00    SULFUR:   .000    RON+C:  100.00
    20%: 120.00                        API: 68.0000    MONO:   80.00
    30%: 122.00                       AROM:  5.00     MON+C:   85.00
    50%: 136.00                       OLEF: 65.00      BROM:   99.00
    70%: 178.00                     PB HEEL:   .00    VALUE:   33.00
_____
FILENAME: TEST
```

FIGURE 2: The stock qualities screen is a typical OMEGA input screen. The user selects the stock desired by entering a stock number. If the refinery has data acquisition facilities, the properties will be filled in automatically and the user can review the properties modifying any erroneous readings. Without data acquisition capabilities the user enters the correct properties.

tempted to predict the characteristics of each blend based on the properties of the stocks available and on the blend proportions suggested by the blender. They were quite useful for case studies to augment the blender's intuition and experience.

During the 1960s, computer hardware and software advanced significantly. Refinery engineers began to use linear programming to solve large planning models that included linearized blending submodels. In 1965, IBM introduced POP II, their process optimization program for nonlinear optimization, which used a successive linear programming algorithm to solve nonlinear programming problems [Smith 1965]. Shortly thereafter, Texaco developed a gasoline blending optimization system, GOP, which used the POP II program.

Investigation of the blending process at Texaco in the early 1980s revealed that the GOP system was not being used routinely by all refineries. Further study uncovered several problems that inhibited its use. The blending model used in GOP was not sufficiently accurate, and therefore the actual blends frequently did not meet their specifications. The FORTRAN code was also difficult to maintain. In addition, during the optimization process, the POP II algorithm would often stop at an infeasible solution. Moreover, not only was POP II very slow but its results appeared inconsistent as it would often stop at different values if started from different starting points. This reduced confidence in the results.

The refining industry had also changed significantly during the 1970s. The average qualities of the crude oils available for refining were different than for previously available crudes (that is, they were heavier and had a higher weight percent of sulfur). This led to changes in refinery processing and to gasoline stocks with inferior qualities. At the same time, automobile manufacturers modified automobile engines so that they required higher octane fuels. The greatest impact, however, came from new government regulations. For example, the EPA mandated that lead use was to be reduced from 1.7 grams per gallon of total gasoline produced in 1975 to 0.8 grams in 1978. Since adding lead to the blend increases its octane, other means for meeting octane specifications were required and they typically increased the cost. These changes resulted in blend specifications being more difficult and more expensive to meet.

These more restrictive blend specifications, together with the changes in input stock qualities, resulted in POP II being even more unreliable. As a result, in 1980 Texaco began looking for other nonlinear optimization packages. Experience with POP II indicated that a method that first tried to satisfy all constraints and then maintained feasibility while improving the objective would be desirable. This suggested that reduced gradient algorithms might be effective.

One of the authors (Brenner) had attended a TIMS/ORSA meeting in 1981, at which Lasdon presented results on the performance of the generalized reduced gradient algorithm, GRG2, developed by Lasdon and Waren [1978]. This presentation led him to test GRG2. Test results verified that the algorithm was very robust and reliable. The ability to imbed it within a larger system by calling it as a subroutine was also important, since Texaco planned to build a new interactive blending system around the optimizer. Based on these factors, Texaco decided to use GRG2 as the foundation for a new and improved gasoline blending and optimization system.

THE DEVELOPMENT OF OMEGA

Texaco began developimg their new nonlinear gasoline blending optimization system, OMEGA, early in 1982. The first phase in this development was to replace POP II with GRG2 as the optimizer. The second phase was to improve the accuracy of the mathematical blending model being used. This model is used to calculate the output blend properties, other constraint values, and the value of the objective function. The equations in the new model were obtained from several sources: the GOP model, literature in the public domain, and internal Texaco studies. The software that generates the model was developed by Texaco's information technology department (ITD), using structured programming techniques. ITD is also responsible for maintaining the software. Interfacing the model to the optimizer was such a straightforward process that it was not regarded as a separate phase in the OMEGA development.

The next development phase was to design and implement the user interface. Texaco defined ease of use as a top priority. Hence, OMEGA was developed as a full screen, menu-driven, interactive system. All inputs and options are entered through the menus.

Because of the large amount of input data, we also developed automatic data acquisition capabilities. We designed the system to interface with Texaco's refinery data acquisition systems, which automatically record tank inventories and production flow rates and identify stock volumes available for blending. OMEGA can also access laboratory test results on stock properties, which are also recorded in the data acquisition system. This ability to access the data acquisition system has proven

to be a useful feature for the day-to-day blending of gasoline.

Once OMEGA was running, the next development phase was to tune the GRG2 optimizer and the model. Prior to tuning, OMEGA was occasionally starting-point dependent. We adjusted the GRG2 parameters, made minor modifications to GRG2, and scaled the OMEGA model. These actions effectively eliminated the problem of starting-point dependency. During this phase, we also extended the system to allow the user to start from the previous optimum solution. In practice, however, the stocks available for blending vary so much from day to day that the blender usually enters a new set of starting values for each run.

INSTALLATION

The next phase in the OMEGA implementation program was its installation at an actual refinery. It is very important that the first installation be successful in order to promote acceptance at other sites. Much thought went into selecting the first site. A refinery with in-line gasoline blending was desirable since this gives the user better control over the blend qualities during the blending process. Texaco felt that the initial refinery needed to have engineers and nontechnical personnel (the blenders) who were familiar with computers so that the we would not have to deal with problems associated with introducing computers in addition to the problems of installing a new blending system. Automatic data-acquisition facilities were also desirable to take advantage of OMEGA's automatic data-capture capabilities. In addition, we chose a refinery that was neither the most complex nor the simplest so that it would be truly representative.

The first installation of OMEGA was successful. Texaco then began installing OMEGA in all of its refineries in the United States. We encountered some resistance from various engineers and blenders. Many of the refineries had developed and maintained their own models, and the engineers argued that they already had a tool that worked for their purposes (the "not invented here" syndrome). Another perceived difficulty was that the OMEGA output blends differed in composition from the products that they were blending. The blenders had obtained the recipes for these output blends from the GOP system, from case studies using other models, from trial and error, or from experience.

Comparative analysis of OMEGA blend compositions and the compositions predicted by the plant personnel led to the identification of several factors that contributed to their differences. One factor was that the OMEGA model is more accurate than the GOP model. Another is that the OMEGA optimizer finds optimal solutions more often than the POP II algorithm did and also gives more accurate results, so it responds well to small changes in stock composition. Another factor adding to the difference in blend recipes is that, in the past, POP II would stop at an infeasible point due to the inaccuracies in the model or because the POP II algorithm would go infeasible during optimization and would not become feasible again. This made it more difficult for the blenders to determine a feasible recipe that satisfied the required specifications. As a result, blends would often have to be reblended. During the reblending process, stocks were manually added until the spec-

ifications were satisfied, leading to blends that were more costly than necessary.

Identifying these factors contributed to the gradual acceptance of OMEGA. However, it took three years before OMEGA was widely accepted. As the engineers used OMEGA more frequently, they gained more confidence in it. Personnel at the first refinery installation were extremely helpful in answering questions and providing aid to engineers at the other refineries. Furthermore, OMEGA was very easy to use and significantly more flexible than the other procedures, and this also contributed to its increasing popularity.

One of the features that promoted the use of OMEGA was the inclusion of a quality giveaway objective. Usually this quality is octane. Prior to using OMEGA, the finished blends would often overshoot or exceed some of their specifications. For example, a blend specification might require a minimum of 87 MON (Motor Octane Number) whereas the actual blend might have an 87.5 MON. This excess octane in the output blend increases costs over what could be achieved with no giveaway. Since most of the components do not have well-established market prices, it is very difficult to obtain an accurate cost or profit objective. Such objectives, therefore, tend to be used for planning studies, and other objectives are used for daily blending.

Previously the giveaway had not been considered to be very significant. However, as governmental regulations lowered the amount of lead allowed in regular gasoline, octane specifications became more difficult to meet. The government also required new automobiles to use unleaded gasoline. With these new regulations, the higher octane stocks with good volatility qualities were in more demand. The value of the higher octane blending stocks began to increase greatly, and the price of gasoline varied a great deal during this period of time. Giveaway had become a significant factor in determining blending profitability.

To convince the blenders that the previous method of blending was not economical, we made a trial run of OMEGA at these refineries to show what additional profit could be gained. The composition of the last batch of gasoline blended at the refinery without using OMEGA was fed into OMEGA as the starting point. OMEGA was then run in optimization mode, typically giving a much more profitable final blend recipe. The blender was encouraged to blend, in the laboratory, a sample of gasoline following the optimal blend composition reported by OMEGA and to test the sample to verify that the blend did indeed meet its specifications. The successful outcome of this process provided convincing evidence of OMEGA's value.

OMEGA is now installed in all seven of Texaco's domestic refineries and in its refineries in Pembroke, Wales and in Nanticoke, Canada. It currently runs on IBM mainframes, on Data General supermini computers, and on IBM personal computers. CPU times vary greatly from case to case. A typical planning problem with 40 variables and 71 constraints run on an IBM 3090 computer takes about five seconds, and as an operational problem run on a Data General MV8000 in a refinery takes about two minutes.

MAINTENANCE

As mentioned earlier, OMEGA is maintained centrally by Texaco's information technology department. It is constantly being updated and extended. When new governmental regulations are invoked, modifications are made to OMEGA to reflect these regulations. In recent years, for example, the EPA required a lead phasedown for regular leaded gasoline. This made it necessary to modify the OMEGA model so that it would be more accurate for these lower levels of lead. The new model also reflects the fact that the laboratories are now testing the octane response of blend stocks to lead at lower levels. This phasedown also led to the use of other octane improvers, such as MMT and oxygenates, which had to be incorporated into the model.

Other business changes also led to model modifications. For instance, refinery upgrades and the refining of different crudes (heavier crudes with higher sulphur contents) have resulted in blend stocks with significantly different properties than those previously encountered. The quality equations in the model had to be extrapolated to predict the resulting blend qualities.

OMEGA is continually modified to reflect changes in refinery operations. Even during the installation phase, as new refineries began to use OMEGA, differences in refineries required changes to the system. For example, some refineries needed to account for the effects of heels. A heel is the blend left in a blend tank after pumping out all of the blend that is normally pumped from the tank. Hence, the composition of the next blend to be added to the tank should take into account the qualities and quantity of the heel. In addition, some refineries required that special consideration be given to mix stocks. Mix stocks occur when several stocks are fed into the same storage tank prior to blending. Modifications were made to OMEGA to accommodate both heels and mix stocks.

When Texaco began installing OMEGA in their foreign refineries, we had to make additional changes to handle the different requirements for each country appropriately. Furthermore, enhancements to OMEGA are constantly needed to enable it to answer the new and unanticipated what-if questions refinery engineers ask.

THE USER INTERFACE

Simple interactive input makes OMEGA very easy to use. All input data can be entered manually. However, OMEGA can interface with the refinery data acquisition system to retrieve blend specifications, stock-flow rates, stock inventory, and stock qualities. The user specifies a file name for input data when he or she first enters the system, and this name is displayed in the lower left-hand corner of the main menu. The main menu allows the user to choose any of seven input screens or one of the two automatic data selection screens. The user can access stock qualities, stock availabilities, blend specifications, blend requirements, starting values and limits, optimization options, automatic stock selection, automatic blend specifications selection, and several other options from this menu. Figure 2 shows the stock qualities screen, which is typical of most of the OMEGA screens.

Several features aid the user in performing planning functions. By choosing option 7 from the main menu, the user obtains the optimization options screen. From this screen, the user can select one of the following objective functions: maximum profit per barrel, maximum profit, minimum octane (quality) giveaway, or a weighted linear combination of profit and quality giveaway. The objective function chosen depends on the problem that is being solved and the characteristics of the refinery. If the stocks available in the refinery have relatively low octane numbers, then the octane giveaway objective function would be desirable for daily blending. If superior quality stocks are prevalent, then profit would be used. The profit objective is usually used for planning studies.

One of the more difficult problems encountered while blending gasoline stocks is how to ensure that the holdover stocks will be easily blendable. Holdover stocks are those input stocks that are left over after blending all of the products actually required by Texaco's current blending plan. Since OMEGA looks at only one time period, if the objective function is solely to maximize profit then the holdover might contain only stocks with inferior characteristics. To counter this tendency to use all of the higher grade stocks in the required blends, the user can select quality giveaway as the objective function. The user can also place limits on the amount of a particular stock that can be used in a blend and on the amount that can be left in inventory.

Another option is available to ensure that the leftover stock will be blendable. The user specifies that all of the leftover stock must be blended into holdover blends with specified qualities. This allows the objective function to be optimized subject to both the quality constraints for today's required blends and the quality constraints for future blends (the holdover blends). Of course, this option can sharply increase problem size. The user can also specify the maximum amount of any specific holdover blend based on marketing information for the next time period.

Each refinery uses a different set of features depending on the stocks it has available for blending. These vary depending on the refinery configuration and on the particular crudes being refined. The availability and ease of use of the many features in OMEGA has provided the engineers and blenders with a powerful and very useful tool.

THE UNIQUENESS OF OMEGA

Many companies in the process industries have used nonlinear programming to perform on-line and off-line optimization. Applications vary in scope from individual sections of equipment within a process unit to plant-wide optimization including many interconnected units. Organizations reporting such experience include Shell [Gochenour and Preston 1987; Cutler and Perry 1983] and Chevron [Justice 1985]. In particular, Chevron has developed an interactive nonlinear blending system called GINO (Gasoline Inline Optimization) and is using it in several refineries. To the best of our knowledge, no one has developed a dedicated blending system with OMEGA's scope and features nor has anyone integrated such a system so thoroughly into their blending operations both for medium-range planning and short-term scheduling. Recently, Texaco has begun licensing OMEGA for use by other companies.

OMEGA USAGE

Each refinery uses OMEGA to varying degrees and for various purposes depending on the needs, complexity, and configuration of the refinery. We will describe how the system is typically used, starting from medium range (monthly) planning, and proceeding to real-time blending.

On a monthly basis, refineries use OMEGA to develop a gasoline blending plan for the month. The plan is generated five to 10 days before the first of the month. Planning is performed on a monthly basis because the overall refinery planning models, which select the refinery crude slate and determine the anticipated gasoline stock volumes and stock qualities that will be produced, are run monthly, and because tax considerations make it desirable to minimize refinery stock inventories on the first of the month.

The refinery planning model's projected blending stock volumes are input to OMEGA. The stock qualities used in OMEGA are either the stock properties projected by the refinery-planning model or the actual average stock properties from the previous month. This varies among the refineries depending on which approach the planner believes is the most accurate.

The blending planner typically calculates three to eight blends in a single OMEGA run. Each blend is one of the four grades of gasoline that Texaco manufactures. Often the blender will create two blends for each grade, a blend for the fixed volume of the grade that has been committed during the planning process, called a "required" blend, and a blend for any additional amount of that grade that the refinery can make, a "holdover" blend. The blender may also create a blend for each method by which a grade of gasoline is to be transported. For example, the blender may create one unleaded regular blend for the pipeline and another for truck pickup at a terminal. This separation gives the blender a better conceptual view of the blending operation, and it is often required: a pipeline may deliver the gasoline grade to a geographical region that has different quality specifications than the region being supplied by truck or barge.

The refinery planning model's blend compositions are input into OMEGA as starting values. OMEGA is then executed with a 'blend-all' feature for all stocks except butane. The blend-all feature requires that all of the available stock must be blended into some blend. Butane is excluded because it is such an economical blending stock that as much will be blended as is allowed by the quality constraints and more will be purchased if refinery volumes are not adequate. The blend-all feature minimizes end-of-month stock inventories and prevents OMEGA from using all the high quality stocks and leaving only the low quality stocks behind.

OMEGA then creates a monthly blending plan. This blending plan displays the grade splits, that is, the proportion that each blend constitutes of the total gasoline output. This plan is reviewed to determine if it is reasonable (not all of the possible real-world constraints are part of the blending model). If not, additional constraints are placed on the blend compositions or the blend volumes, and OMEGA is rerun.

Once a reasonable blending plan has been developed, the marketing department is contacted to discuss the resulting grade splits. Marketing takes into account the current state of the gasoline market and the production by alternate refining sources and may make suggestions for modifying the grade splits. A finalized blending plan will then be developed for the month. The refinery uses the blending plan grade splits to determine gasoline production targets for the month.

Individual blend compositions are determined by running OMEGA with the current actual stock flow rates and stock qualities. The grade splits for OMEGA may either be fixed according to the monthly blend plan or may be allowed to vary from the plan by a small percentage (usually five percent). Low stock percentages, however, are not permitted because of in-line blender limitations. The resulting compositions are then given to the scheduler or blender. As the month progresses, these blend recipes may have to be recalculated because the availability and qualities of stock may deviate from what was expected. Normally this recalculation occurs every seven to 15 days.

The scheduler determines when each of the grades will be blended. This scheduling must take into consideration when specific blends are to be delivered, current actual stock and blend tank inventories, and the in-line blender capacity. If a particular stock inventory is low, the scheduler may rerun OMEGA, restricting the use of this limited stock and allowing the others to vary from the blend recipe by plus or minus some small amount, typically five percent.

The scheduler gives the blender the daily blend recipe(s). The blender uses the recipe(s) to determine the flow rates for the input stocks. During blending, these rates must be adjusted to account for variations in stock properties as well as any minor inaccuracies in OMEGA's model. Many factors can account for variations in stock qualities. For example, if stock is being withdrawn from a stock tank and added to the tank at the same time, stratification can occur in the tank, causing different levels to have different characteristics.

For batch blending after the blend is completed, quality assurance personnel take a sample and test it in the laboratory. If the blend does not meet a particular specification, additional stock(s) must be added, perhaps two or three times. This process can take one or two days.

With in-line blending, product qualities are measured automatically by on-line testing equipment. The testing interval ranges from seven to 20 minutes, depending on the specific attribute under test. If some property specifications are not met, the stock rates are adjusted. In most refineries with in-line blenders, a single stock will be adjusted for each unsatisfied specification. The scheduler or planner will tell the blender which stock rate, the so-called trim stock, to adjust for each quality.

In Texaco's Nanticoke (Canada) refinery, the in-line blender has a process control computer associated with it. The partial derivatives of the objective function and of the active constraints are downloaded from OMEGA to the process control computer. This linearized model is used to adjust the stock flow rates on-line to meet the quality specifications while minimizing quality giveaway.

BENEFITS

OMEGA has now been installed in all seven of Texaco's US refineries, as well as in its refineries in Pembroke, Wales and in Nanticoke, Canada. Over the last three years, these refineries have steadily increased their usage of OMEGA. This commitment to installation and expanded use of OMEGA is clear evidence that OMEGA is perceived as contributing to overall profitability. However the extent of this contribution is very difficult to measure. Even ignoring indirect and nonquantifiable benefits, its direct contribution to profit is not clear since there are so many changing factors involved in profitability. Market demand, profit margins, and even the refineries themselves have changed. Some refineries, for example, have added in-line blenders and stock tank mixers that are used to help minimize stratification. These continuing changes make it difficult to determine the actual dollar benefit directly attributable to daily blending with OMEGA.

In an effort to get the best possible measure of actual benefits, we tried several different methods. The first method, a comparison of the blend compositions that the blenders used without OMEGA to those used with OMEGA, was carried out at three refineries prior to installing OMEGA. The blenders were asked to collect information about all of the blends that they blended during a one-week period. This information included stock availability, stock qualities, blend-quality specifications, blend demands, blend values, and the blend compositions that were used.

This information was input into OMEGA. The blenders' blend compositions were used as starting values and OMEGA was allowed to optimize. The resulting profit for the OMEGA blend was compared to that obtained by the blender. In some batches OMEGA achieved as much as a 30 percent increase in profits. The average increase in profit was approximately five percent of the gross gasoline revenue.

In late 1984, in an attempt to verify these results, we asked each refinery that was using OMEGA heavily to provide its own estimates of the benefits achieved with OMEGA. The refineries estimated the benefits as a direct increase in profit. The profit estimates ranged from two to five percent of gross gasoline revenues, with some of the refineries specifying a range within this interval. These estimates correspond to a range of 1.0 to 2.5 cents per gallon in benefits.

However, recognizing that all of the theoretical benefits from an optimization system cannot be realized in real life, we have taken half of the most conservative estimate, reducing the benefit to 0.5 cents per gallon. Applying this to all of Texaco's domestic gasoline production, six billion gallons of gasoline annually, we estimate the benefits at 30 million dollars per year.

More difficult to quantify are the intangible benefits. If OMEGA is used to calculate blending recipes, fewer blends fail to meet their quality specifications. OMEGA's more reliable gasoline grade split estimates provide significant aid to those developing marketing strategies and refinery production targets. They also provide good octane blending index estimates for the linear programming refinery planning model.

Another source of intangible benefits is the use of OMEGA for what-if case studies. These studies are performed for various reasons, such as economic analysis of refinery improvement projects and analysis of how proposed governmental regulations would affect Texaco. No attempt was made to quantify the benefits for such case studies, although some refinery and manufacturing headquarters personnel believe that these benefits are as significant as those for daily blending.

In addition, OMEGA's features have provided Texaco with capabilities to do things that were not possible with the previous blending system. One feature allows the user to deal with mix stocks. This is useful in refineries with complex piping or in plants that have a large number of stocks. The excess blend feature enables the refinery to consider new grades of gasoline, such as unleaded plus and 10 percent ethanol gasoline, to determine whether they are profitable to produce. The ability to specify a minimum and maximum volume of stock and blend inventory, along with the blend-all feature, gives the user substantially more control of inventory. With OMEGA the user can easily incorporate lead/MMT premixes and other future additives. OMEGA's features make it easy and quick to explore new avenues of profitability for a refinery; such exploration was difficult or essentially impossible without OMEGA.

ACKNOWLEDGMENT

The authors acknowledge the significant contribution of Mr. B. J. Purrington to OMEGA. Mr. Purrington was involved in the development of GOP (OMEGA's predecessor) and was responsible for developing OMEGA's model. In addition, he was the project leader in charge of OMEGA from its conception until he retired from Texaco in 1985.

APPENDIX

The qualities of a blend are determined by the qualities of the stocks used in the blend. The optimization problem is to determine the volume of each input stock in each blend so that the objective function is optimized subject to the output blends satisfying their quality specifications, stock availability constraints, and blend demand constraints. Most of the blend quality equations are of the following form:

$$Vf_{i,j} = X_{i,j} / \left(\sum_{i=1}^{I} X_{i,j} \right)$$

$$Q_{j,k}(x_j) = \sum_{i=1}^{I} (S_{i,k} * Vf_{i,j})$$

where

$X_{i,j}$ are the independent variables, the amount of stock i in blend j;

$S_{i,k}$ is the kth quality index for stock i;

$Q_{j,k}$ is the kth quality index for blend j;

$Vf_{i,j}$ is the volume fraction of stock i in blend j;

x_j is a vector with ith component X_{ij}.

Such weighted averages of stock qualities have been used in linear specification blending models for many years. However, the distillation and octane blending equations have more complex forms. There are many published forms for these qualities, usually containing exponentials, logarithms, and quadratic and other interaction terms. Two commonly used equations follow:

Distillation Blending

$$D_{j,k}(x_j) = b_k + c_k * ln\left(\sum_{i=1}^{I}(S_{i,k}*Vf_{i,j})\right)$$

where b_k and c_k are constants,
S_{ik} is the kth distillation point for stock i,
D_{jk} is the kth distillation point for blend j.

Octane Blending

$$Oct_{j,k}(x_j) = a_k*\left(\sum_{i=1}^{I}(Vf_{i,j}*b_i^2) - \sum_{i=1}^{I}(Vf_{i,j}*c_i)^2\right)$$

$$+ d_k*\left(\sum_{i=1}^{I}(Vf_{i,j}*e_i) - \left(\sum_{i=1}^{I}Vf_{i,j}*f_i\right)^2\right)^2$$

$$+ g_k\sum_{i=1}^{I}\{(Vf_{i,j}*h_i) - (Vf_{i,j}*j_i)*(Vf_{i,j}*k_i)\}$$

where

a_k, d_k, and g_k are constants,
b_i, c_i, e_i, f_i, h_i, j_i, and k_i are quality indexes for stock i,
$Oct_{j,k}$ are the various octane indexes for blend j.

The optimization problem then becomes

min or max $f(x)$
subject to

$\underline{Q_{j,k}} \leqslant Q_{j,k}(x) \leqslant \overline{Q_{j,k}}$, for all j; $k = 1, \ldots, 7$;

$\underline{D_{j,k}} \leqslant D_{j,k}(x) \leqslant \overline{D_{j,k}}$, for all j; $k = 1, \ldots, 4$;

$\underline{Oct} \leqslant Oct_{j,k}(x)$, for all j; $k = 1, 2, 3$;

$\underline{Sv_i} \leqslant \sum_j X_{i,j} \leqslant \overline{Sv_i}$, for all i;

$\underline{Bv_j} \leqslant \sum_i X_{i,j} \leqslant \overline{Bv_j}$, for all j;

$X_{i,j} \leqslant \overline{Pb_j}$, for all j; $i =$ the index for grams of lead in blend j.

Symbols with underbars (overbars) are specified lower (upper) limits and Sv and Bv are the limits on stock and blend volumes, respectively.

REFERENCES

Charnes A. and Cooper, W. W. 1961, *Management Models and Industrial Applications of Linear Programming*, John Wiley and Sons, Inc., New York.

Cutler, C. R. and Perry, R. T. 1983, "Real time optimization with multivariable control is required to maximize profits," *Computers and Chemical Engineering*, Vol. 7, No. 5, pp. 663–667.

Gochenour, G. B. and Preston, R. F. 1987, "Equations based process simulation," in *Foundations of Computer Based Process Simulation*, eds., G. V. Rehlactis and H. D. Spriggs, Elsevier, New York, pp. 333–348.

Justice Jr., L. E. 1985, "Refinery planning and optimization with microcomputers in Chevron," NPRA Computer Conference, Paper #CC-85-101.

Lasdon, L. S. and Waren, A. D. 1978, "Generalized reduced gradient software for linearly and nonlinearly constrained problems," in *The Design and Implementation of Optimization Software*, ed. H. Greenberg, Kluwer Academic Publications, Norwell, Massachusetts, pp. 363–397.

Manne, Alan S. 1956, *Scheduling of Petroleum Refinery Operations*, Harvard University Press, Cambridge, Massachusetts.

Smith, H. V. 1965, "A process optimization program for nonlinear systems: POP II," Share General Program Library 7090 H9 IBM 0021.

Mike Killien, the acting vice-president of Texaco USA, describes OMEGA as "A state-of-the-art blending system, which includes the unique GRG2 nonlinear optimizer, an online database, and an interactive user interface. OMEGA was first installed in 1983 and is now used in all seven of Texaco's refineries in the United States and in two international refineries. Texaco estimates the total ongoing economic benefits from OMEGA to be more than thirty million dollars annually.

"In an effort to measure the benefits, before OMEGA was installed, a comparison of the blend compositions used by the blenders without the help of OMEGA was made to those suggested by OMEGA. In some batches the resulting profit for the OMEGA blend was as much as 30 percent greater. The average increase in profit was approximately five percent of the gross gasoline revenue or about 2.5 cents per gallon. If this calculation were applied to all the gasoline manufactured by Texaco USA last year the profit increase would be approximately 150 million dollars.

"In late 1984 refineries that were using OMEGA heavily were asked to provide their own estimate of the benefits achieved with OMEGA. Two refineries gave an estimate of the increased value of the product blended. The Louisiana refinery estimated this increase in value to be between two and four percent. This gives a range of from 1.0 to 2.5 cents per gallon in benefits. However recognizing that all of the theoretical benefits from a computer optimizer cannot be realized in real life, we have taken half of the most conservative estimate, reducing the benefit to 0.5 cents per gallon. Applying this to all of Texaco's domestic gasoline production, six billion gallons of gasoline annually, the benefits are 30 million dollars per year.

"With OMEGA fewer blends fail to meet their quality specifications because the blend property predictions are better. OMEGA's more reliable gasoline grade split estimates result in better marketing strategies as well as better refinery production targets. The result of these better planning numbers are fewer late trading changes and better control of inventories. OMEGA also provides good octane blending index estimates which are used in the refinery LP planning models thus improving those models. Another source of intangible benefits is the use of OMEGA for "what-if" case studies. No attempt was made to quantify the benefits for such case studies although some refinery and manufacturing headquarters personnel believe that these benefits are as significant as those for daily blending."

Improving Transit Check Clearing Operations at Maryland National Bank

Robert E. Markland
Robert M. Nauss

Reducing the time required for processing checks is foremost among the problems commercial banks confront to improve productivity [Gambs 1976]. Improving the efficiency of check processing is critical for two reasons. First, check volume is extremely large and is increasing at an estimated rate of 7% per year [Powers 1976]. Second, the passage of the Depository Institution's Deregulation and Monetary Control Act of 1980 changed the banking system of the United States: the Federal Reserve System began charging for its check processing services on September 1, 1981 [*Business Week* 1981]. This has increased the costs of check processing for the banking industry, and in order to offset the increased cost banks must process checks more efficiently.

A major aspect of the time (and, hence cost) component of check processing involves the "clearing" of checks. Check clearing means making the funds actually available to the bank in which the check was originally deposited.

The problem a typical bank (for exam-

ple, Maryland National Bank, Baltimore) faces in clearing checks can be described as follows: Once the checks have been collected at a bank's operations center and have been tabulated, microfilmed, and sorted, they are divided into three categories: on-us, local, and out-of-town (transit). The on-us category denotes checks drawn on the bank itself. The local category includes all checks drawn on banks in the immediate metropolitan area as well as certain government checks. The transit category includes all other checks.

The on-us checks are cleared immediately using the bank's internal reconciliation accounting for customer accounts. The local checks are generally cleared daily in the mid-morning at a local clearinghouse where each local bank sends a representative to present checks drawn on other local banks. Accounts between banks are reconciled at that time. The clearing procedures for on-us and local checks are straightforward and require little analysis. However, the clearing of transit checks poses a much more difficult problem.

The design of transit check clearing operations is a complex combinatorial problem. Consider a check deposited by a customer at Maryland National Bank in Baltimore that is drawn on a bank in Chicago. Once Maryland National Bank has processed the check internally it must clear the check by sending it back to the Chicago bank on which it was originally drawn. This can be done in at least three ways. First, the check may be taken to the Federal Reserve Bank in Baltimore, and the Federal Reserve System used to transport the check to the Chicago bank. This may take as long as two days. Second, the check may be sent to a private clearing bank which transports the check to the Chicago bank. This service may be quicker than the Federal Reserve System, but will also probably be more expensive. Third, Maryland National Bank could arrange for direct courier service to the Chicago bank. This is probably the quickest of the three, but it is also the most expensive. A flat fixed charge of $25 to $75 would be incurred for a courier, while a nominal per check charge on the order of 1 to 10 cents would be assessed in the other two cases.

Deciding which clearing method to use is further complicated by two factors. First, the decision is a function of the time of day and the day of the week. For example, a check arriving on Friday morning might be sent by courier in order to reach Chicago by Friday afternoon, and thus clear on Friday. If the Federal Reserve System were used, a check arriving on Friday might not be cleared until Monday. Second, a clearing decision must be made for every check. Transit check clearings at Maryland National Bank averaged over 500,000 daily.

To develop a criterion for deciding which method to use it is important to understand the concept of a bank *avail-ability schedule*. Each bank in the United States has an availability schedule which outlines the number of days required to clear checks drawn on various banks in each region of the country. For example, checks with a Federal Reserve District (FRD) identification number of 210 are drawn on New York banks. Thus, Maryland National Bank may state in its availability schedule that such checks are guaranteed to clear in one business day if the checks are deposited at the bank by 4:00 p.m. This means that the customer who deposits such a check will have the funds from the deposited check credited to his account by the next business day. If the check does not actually clear by the next business day Maryland National Bank still must credit the customer's account and the bank "eats the float" on the funds. The Federal Reserve System also has its own availability schedule which in turn guarantees to clear a check in so many days if the check is presented at a Federal Reserve Bank by a certain time of day (cutoff time). In the situation posed above, if Maryland National Bank were to clear the check through the Federal Reserve System and the check clearing were delayed, the Federal Reserve System would "eat the float" rather than Maryland National Bank.

Savings in float can sometimes be achieved by increasing the amount spent for transportation. For example, sending checks directly to the bank on which they are drawn (a "direct send") will speed up the process of collecting funds and will reduce float costs. Different transportation modes may be available at different times of day. One commonly employed option consists of a truck courier to the airport, an airline to the destination (direct-send city), and a truck courier to the endpoint (direct-send bank). Furthermore, stops may be made at more than one bank within the destination city, or if an airplane is chartered, other destination cities and endpoint banks may be included as legs within an overall transportation plan. In order to select the least costly method of clearing checks, it is necessary to take into account not only float reduction, but also transportation costs, charges imposed by clearing banks, and the complexities of achieving the cutoff times quoted for the "direct send" banks.

MODELING THE PROBLEM

The transit check clearing problem may be modeled as a large scale 0-1 integer linear program. The structure is similar to the classical uncapacitated facility location problem. (A detailed mathematical formulation is included in the appendix.)

Two types of 0-1 decision variables are used in the model. First, there is a decision variable for each potential clearing method indexed by each time period (and day) in which the clearing method may be used. For example, suppose direct send flights to New York City leave each day of the week at 8:00 a.m., 1:00 p.m., and 4:00 p.m. With three flights on each of seven days, the number of 0-1 variables representing New York City direct sends alone would be 21.

The second decision variable is for each check type indexed by each of its potential clearing methods by each time period (and day). For example, consider checks drawn on a New York City bank that are ready for clearing at 7:00 a.m. on Monday. These checks could be cleared using any of the New York City direct sends as well as any potential direct sends to other cities. Thus, decision variables must be explicitly created for all such possibilities. However, it is possible to reduce the number of these alternatives, under certain conditions, through the use of straight forward dominance relations [Nauss and Markland 1982].

The objective of the integer programming formulation is to minimize the sum of the opportunity cost of float, the variable (per check) charges, and the fixed transportation charges for the direct sends. There are two sets of constraints. First, each check type must be cleared by exactly one method. Second, each check type may not be cleared by a particular method of clearing in a given time period on a given day unless that method is selected for use (that is, the fixed cost is assessed).

DATA REQUIREMENTS

In order to actually solve the bank transit check clearing problem the following information is necessary:

(1) The total dollar amount and the number of checks for each drawee check classification that are processed and sorted by the bank by the hour and day of week. There are over 100 different check classifications each represented by a four digit FRD number. In addition, individual bank eight digit Federal Reserve District American Banking Association (FRDABA) classifications may be processed, sorted, and cleared independently of the FRD classifications.

(2) Private clearing bank and Federal Reserve Bank availability schedules for both four digit FRD classifications and individual bank eight digit FRDABA numbers.

(3) A list of potential courier schedules with pickup times and delivery times to specified clearing banks and Federal Reserve banks for each day of the week.

(4) The fixed and variable (per check) charges for all possible modes of check clearing.

(5) The marginal rate of investment for the bank.

The decision making time period used for this study was one week, with one month of data collected in four weekly segments and then averaged to generate a representative week.

SOLVING THE PROBLEM—PROBLEM SIZE AND COMPLEXITY

In practice, the decision to use particular direct sends is not made on a day-to-day basis. Rather, each day's direct send decisions are linked to the following day's decisions. For example, a collection of checks (commonly called a cash letter) processed on a Monday afternoon could be cleared via the Federal Reserve and given two day availability. The same cash letter could be held overnight until Tuesday and then be sent on a Tuesday direct send to gain immediate availability (one day from Monday). Thus, it may be better to hold a cash letter until the next day to improve availability.

Because holding a cash letter overnight is a possibility, the formulation must consider the entire one week cycle of seven consecutive days. To visualize the size of the problem consider the following: Suppose each day is divided into 48 half-hour time periods. In seven days there would be 336 time periods. Further, suppose there are 100 four digit FRD's and 50 eight digit FRDABA's which are sorted and processed during each day. Finally, suppose there are 75 potential direct sends which could be made either daily or on particular days of the week. Before calculating the size of the problem we can make the following observations. First, each of the 150 FRD and FRDABA categories do not generally appear in every

possible time slot during the week. Second, certain potential direct sends can be made only on the weekend or only during the weekdays depending upon airline connections and the receiving bank's availability schedule. Under these conditions the number of decision variables for each potential clearing method indexed by each time period (and day) may range from 100 to 400, and the number of decision variables for each check type indexed by each potential clearing method and by each time period may range from 2,000 to 25,000. The magnitude of the problem could be reduced by considering two, three, or four days of check processing rather than the entire week.

The size of this complex combinatorial problem is a major obstacle to its efficient solution. We developed an efficient branch and bound algorithm that solves such problems, as an outgrowth of previous work in the area of lock box modeling [Nauss and Markland 1981]. Mathematically, the two problems are similar, but with two important differences. First, the arcs (or connections) from cash letters to direct sends do not form a dense set. Rather, each cash letter generally has between two and fifteen arcs. That is, each cash letter could be sent on anywhere from two to fifteen direct sends. In the lock box problem each customer zone may be assigned to any potential lock box. The second difference is that the check clearing problem is much larger than the lock box problem. A large lock box problem might have 80 potential lock boxes, 125 customer zones, and 10,000 arcs (or connections). A large check clearing problem could have about 200 direct sends, 1500 cash letters, and 20,000 arcs (or connections).

The relative sparsity of the check clearing problem allows economies in core requirements and allows programming techniques which take advantage of that sparsity. For example, using linked lists and vector storage can reduce both storage and computation times. (Complete algorithmic development and theoretical results are given in Nauss and Markland 1981 and 1982.)

COMPUTATIONAL EXPERIENCE AND OUTPUT RESULTS

Computationally the algorithm implementation appears to be quite efficient (Table 1).

The transit check clearing model produces five types of reports which are used by management for making decisions (Exhibits 1-5). In addition it produces a standard set of reports that detail the dollar volume and item endpoint volume by time of day and day of the week.

The first report (Exhibit 1) generates aggregation information combining for each time slot the dollar and item volumes for a particular endpoint (or FRD classification). Thus, for FRD 110-0000 (Boston

TABLE 1. The Computational Results for Maryland National Bank (AMDAHL 470/ V7—excluding input/output time). The third column indicates the number of check type to direct send connections. The fourth column indicates CPU time in seconds to generate and prove optimality of solutions.

Potential Direct Sends	Check Types	Check/Send Connections	CPU Time/Sec.
103	1230	11205	1.66
57	1290	12725	2.87
87	2216	21222	21.23
200	1400	10505	17.75
200	1400	10460	58.73

EXHIBIT 1. Aggregation of cash letters to combine for each time slot the dollar and item volumes for a particular endpoint.

Aggregations for FRD 110-0000 processed on Tuesday

AGGREGATE
  2130
  2200
  2230
  2300

Aggregations for FRD 111-0000 processed on Tuesday

AGGREGATE
  2100
  2130

AGGREGATE
  2200
  2230

City) processed on Tuesday, the checks for 2130, 2200, 2230, and 2300 hours may be combined in one cash letter that is ready for clearing at 2300 hours. This is because there was no difference in potential availability on all potential direct sends for 110-0000 items processed during these times.

The second report (Exhibit 2) lists the three best routing alternatives for each endpoint (or FRD classification) for each aggregated time slot independent of direct send fixed costs. Thus, checks drawn on banks with FRD's 110 or 2110 processed on Tuesday at 2300 hours comprising 886 items and $791,896 may be given one day availability if sent on the direct send named Boston 1 on Wednesday and delivered to bank 390 in Boston. The per item cost is 1.6 cents. One day availability would also be granted if the endpoint checks are sent on the direct send named New York 1 on Wednesday and delivered to bank 607. The per item cost in this case, however, would be 2.3 cents. Once again, FRD 110 items could be sent directly to bank 390 in Boston or they could

EXHIBIT 2. The three best routing alternatives for each endpoint.

Day when checks are processed is Tuesday.

End points	Time Slot	Items	Dollars	Best Direct Send Availability	Best Direct Send $-Float + per item cost	Best Direct Send Item Cost	Second Best Direct Send Availability	Second Best Direct Send $-Float + per item cost	Second Best Direct Send Item Cost	Third Best Direct Send Availability	Third Best Direct Send $-Float + per item cost	Third Best Direct Send Item Cost
				Boston 1	W390							
Boston City							New York 1	W607		Boston 2	W 391	
110 2110	2300	886	791896.	1.00	339.61	.016	1.00	345.81	.023	1.00	346.70	.024
				Windsor Locks 1	W396		New York 2	W 601		New York 1	W 601	
Windsor Locks RCPC	2130	969	433953	2.00	374.21	.018	2.00	386.65	.031	2.00	386.65	.031
111 118 119 211												
2111 2118 2119 2211												

EXHIBIT 3. The optimal solution and the second and third best routings.

Wednesday Link Index = 20 Direct Send is New York 1 Departure time = 0830

FRD	Day Processed	Time Slot	Items	Dollars	Opp. Cost of $-Float + per item cost	Availability	Second Best Routing: Bank Delivered to	Second Best Routing: Direct Send	Second Best Routing: Bank Delivered to	Second Best Routing: Opp. Cost of $-Float + per item cost	Third Best Routing: Direct send	Third Best Routing: Bank Delivered to	Third Best Routing: Opp. Cost $-Float + per item cost
110-0000	Tu	2300	886	791896	345.81	1.00	607	Boston 2	391	346.70	Philadelphia 1	322	350.20
111-0000	Tu	2130	969	433953	386.65	2.00	601	Buffalo 1	406	396.34	Philadelphia 2	306	406.21
210-0000	Wed	0600	901	1583789	20.72	0.00	607	New York 2	601	688.79	New York 3	604	691.82

Direct Send Cost of Airport= 74.20

Incremental (Delivery Costs) = 11.00

Total Cost for Direct send = 85.20

Total Per Item Charges = 71.14

be sent to bank 607 in New York with the New York bank in turn processing the items and sending them to Boston.

The third report (Exhibit 3) gives the optimal solution to the problem; it lists the direct sends that are to be used and the endpoints (FRD and FRDABA classifications) that are to be sent on each direct send. In addition, it gives the second and third best routing for all the direct sends used in the optimal solution. Thus, for example, FRD 110 items are sent on the New York 1 direct send leaving at 0830 hours on Wednesday. The items receive one day availability from Tuesday (when they were processed). For the same availability, but a slightly higher per item charge, these items may be sent on the Boston 2 or Philadelphia 1 direct sends.

The fourth report (Exhibit 4) presents the optimal solution by ordering the pertinent information by the day processed, then by endpoint, and finally by time slot. The fifth and final report (Exhibit 5) orders the information in the optimal solution first by the day processed, then by the time slot, and finally by the endpoint.

SUMMARY AND CONCLUSIONS

The computer-based system described has been developed, tested, and implemented for check processing at Maryland National Bank in Baltimore, Maryland. This bank typically processes over 500,000 checks worth over $250,000,000 each day. Application of the model has saved the Maryland National Bank more than $100,000 per year using a data base of availability schedules which is being expanded to include additional potential direct sends. Additional savings should be realized when this is completed. We are currently working with several other large banks to develop and enhance the model and its associated computer system.

REFERENCES

Business Week, "A new expense: clearing checks," August 3, 1981, p. 74.

Gambs, C. M. 1976, "The cost of the U.S. payments system," The Journal of Bank Research, Vol. 7, No. 4 (Winter), pp. 240-244.

Nauss, R. M. and Markland. R. E. 1981, "Theory and application of an optimization procedure for lock box location analysis," Management Science, Vol. 27, No. 8 (August), pp. 855-865.

Nauss, R. M. and Markland, R. E. 1982, "Optimization of bank transit check clearing operations" Working Paper, University of Missouri-St. Louis.

Powers, W. R. 1976, "A survey of bank check volumes," Journal of Bank Research, Vol. 7, No. 4 (Winter), pp. 245-255.

APPENDIX

The transit check clearing problem may be modeled as a large scale 0-1 integer linear program. The structure is similar to the classical uncapacitated facility location problem.

$$x_{ijk} = \begin{cases} 1 \text{ if check type } i \text{ is cleared by} \\ \text{method } j \text{ in time period } k \\ 0 \text{ if not} \end{cases}$$

$$y_{jk} = \begin{cases} 1 \text{ if clearing method } j \text{ is used in} \\ \text{time period } k \\ 0 \text{ if not} \end{cases}$$

c_{ijk} = opportunity cost of float for checks of type i cleared by method j in time period k

v_j = variable (per check charge) for clearing method j

f_{jk} = fixed cost of clearing method j in time period k

$J(i) = \{j \mid$ check type i cleared by method $j\}$

d_{ik} = number of checks of check type i ready for clearing in time period k

where $i = 1, \ldots, n$; $j \epsilon J(i)$; $k = 1, \ldots, m$;

EXHIBIT 4. Optimal solution presented by day processed, endpoint, time slot.
Day when checks are processed is Tuesday.

FRD	Time Slot	Direct Send	Day Sent	Bank	Items	Dollars	Opp. Cost of $-Float + per Item Cost	Availability
110-0000	2300	New York 1	Wednesday	607	886	791896	345.81	1.00
111-0000	2130	New York 1	Wednesday	601	969	433953	386.65	2.00

EXHIBIT 5. Optimal solution presented by day processed, time slot, endpoint.
Day when checks are processed is Tuesday.

Time Slot	FRD	Direct Send	Day Sent	Bank	Items	Dollars	Opp. cost of $-Float + per Item Cost	Availability
2300	111-0000	New York 1	Wednesday	601	969	433953	386.65	2.00
2130	113-0000	Buffalo 1	Wednesday	406	268	69022	72.09	2.00
2200	710-0000	Chicago 2	Wednesday	242	781	140989	138.84	2.00
2200	711-0000	Chicago 2	Wednesday	242	901	1040016	448.67	1.00
2300	110-0000	New York 1	Wednesday	607	886	791896	345.81	1.00

$L = \{j \mid j \epsilon J(i), i = 1, \ldots, n\}$. Then, the transit check clearing problem may be formulated as:

$$\text{Minimize} \quad \sum_{i=1}^{n} \sum_{j \epsilon J(i)}^{m} \sum_{k=1}^{m} c_{ijk} x_{ijk}$$

$$+ \ v_j d_{ik} x_{ijk} + \sum_{j \epsilon L} \sum_{k=1}^{m} f_{jk} \ y_{jk} \qquad (1)$$

$$x_{ijk} = 0,1$$

$$y_{jk} = 0,1$$

$$\sum_{j \epsilon J(i)} x_{ijk} = 1 \ \text{all} \ i = 1,\ldots, n; \ k=1, \ldots, m; \qquad (2)$$

$$x_{ijk} \leq y_{jk} \ \text{all} \ i=1, \ldots, n; \ j \epsilon J(i); \ k=1, \ldots, m. \qquad (3)$$

The objective function simply adds the opportunity cost of float, the variable (per check) charges, and the fixed transportation charges. Constraint (2) requires that each check type i during each time period k be cleared by exactly one clearing method $j \epsilon J(i)$. Constraint (3) assures that a check type i during time period k can only be cleared if the corresponding clearing method j in time period k is being used. An additional constraint:

$$\sum_{j \epsilon L} \sum_{k=1}^{m} y_{jk} \leq K \qquad (4)$$

may also be added to the formulation if a limit is to be placed on the number (K) of direct sends which may be made.

We have received a letter from David L. Kot, Senior Operations Officer of Maryland National Bank which says, "We estimate that Maryland National has saved approximately $100,000 through a combination of improved availability of funds, lower cost transportation routes and reduced fees paid to the Federal Reserve and correspondent banks."

6   QUEUEING AND SIMULATION

If mathematical programming techniques form one arm of the body of MS/OR methodology, then queueing and simulation jointly constitute the other. Mathematical programming models are best suited for optimizing deterministic systems; queueing and simulation are tools designed specifically for systems with stochastic components or random behavior.

Although queueing and simulation each have an independent and extensive body of literature, these methodologies are in fact complementary from a modeling perspective. The strength of queueing models lies in the exact or approximate analytical results they provide for the behavior of a waiting line. These results are useful and offer many insights but depend on a simplified representation of the real-world system to make the mathematics tractable. Simulation models, on the other hand, can capture a vast amount of detail to faithfully mirror the complexities of the real system. This gain in realism comes at a cost: simulation models cannot provide useful relations between the performance of the system and its input parameters. At best, these relations must be extracted from repeated runs of the model. In many complex stochastic systems, however, simulation can serve to empirically validate the analytical results obtained from queueing theory and its approximations.

The two studies discussed in this chapter use queueing and simulation to model parts manufacturing in a streamlined job shop. Karmarkar et al. [1985] investigate the important problem of reducing manufacturing lead times within a manufacturing cell at Eastman Kodak. They consider the effect of batch sizes on lead times and develop a combined queueing-optimization model for finding optimal batch sizes. They proceed to validate the recommendations of the mathematical model with a detailed simulation model of the production process.

In the second study, Ravindran et al. [1989] describe a detailed simulation model of the modular work centers within a large engine repair facility at Tinker Air Force Base. They use the simulation model to determine the number of machines to place within each work center and the size of the waiting area for work-in-process inventory. This model uses a detailed record of the parts repaired by the facility to simulate the performance and capacity needs of each work center. The authors bring out the challenges of designing and implementing a large simulation model for planning purposes.

6.1 LOT SIZES AND LEAD TIMES IN A MANUFACTURING CELL

Many manufacturing firms fabricate a wide variety of parts within job shops. A *job shop* typically consists of several work centers. Each work center houses one or more machines that focus on a certain type of operation, such as drilling, grinding, or welding. Based on the operations it requires, a part visits different machine centers according to its prescribed *routing* until all the necessary operations have been completed. In such a job shop, the grouping of machines into work centers is based on the similarity of the operations they perform. The organization of the job shop is therefore *functional*.

A different principle of organization called *group technology* organizes machines with different capabilities into manufacturing *cells* that fabricate parts with similar shapes and processing requirements. The design principle behind a manufacturing cell is to separate the production of a group of items from the more complex job shop environment so that the flow of parts through the specialized group of machines within the cell can be streamlined. Ideally, the cell becomes similar to a small assembly line and runs more efficiently.

A key problem in controlling a job shop is to manage manufacturing lead times. The overall lead time for an item is the total amount of time the item spends within all work centers it visits. Typically, less than 10 percent of that time is actual processing time. During the rest of its time in the job shop, the item simply waits in queues. Congestion increases the size of the queues and the associated delays. If the job shop does not have much excess capacity, items often have to wait in queues for machines to become available. If the machine requires a setup to produce an item, all the other items in queue are further delayed. Setups also eat into the productive machine time available.

Manufacturing lead times greatly affect the performance of a manufacturing facility. As Karmarkar [1987a] explains, long lead times cause a host of problems that increase production costs. First, long lead times increase work-in-process inventories and safety stocks, both of which incur carrying costs. Second, long lead times mean that the production schedule cannot be changed over long periods. In practice, however, schedule changes do occur and a job shop cannot realistically freeze its production schedule if the lead times are too long. Third, long lead times create undesirable delays between the fabrication of parts and their incorporation into the finished goods. These delays reduce the overall responsiveness of the manufacturing system and also work against maintaining good information on quality.

In the first paper in this chapter, Karmarkar et al. investigate the effect of batching decisions on manufacturing lead times. They study a manufacturing cell at Eastman Kodak that produces 13 parts with similar processing characteristics on 15 machines. In the past, the cell had exhibited both long lead times and high work-in-process inventories. Accordingly, Karmarkar et al. chose the length of manufacturing lead times and the level of work-in-process inventories as the key performance measures for the cell.

The Effect of Batch Sizes

To illustrate the effects of batching, Karmarkar et al. use the simple M/M/1 queueing model for a single machine that processes only one item. In the M/M/1 model, customers arrive randomly at a single service facility. The customer arrivals and the service times are both stochastic in nature. In particular, the arrivals follow a Poisson process, which means that the times between successive arrivals follow an exponential probability distribution. Similarly, the service time of each customer is an exponential random variable. With these assumptions, there is a simple formula that expresses the average time each customer spends in the system in terms of the arrival and service rates (see Exhibit 6–1). Since the manufacturing cell processes units in batches, a batch of Q items corresponds to a single customer. Karmarkar et al. are interested in how the average time T a batch spends in the system depends on the batch size Q.

To understand the impact of lot sizes on lead times, consider what happens when a batch enters the system. First, the batch may have to wait in queue until the batches that arrived earlier are processed. Then it waits while the machine is set up for the operations this batch requires. Finally, the batch must wait until all units in the batch are completed. This run time is proportional to the batch size on the average. The average service time per batch is simply this processing time plus the fixed setup time. However, batch size also affects the rate at which batches arrive at the machine. If we assume that the demand expressed as the total number of units per month is constant, then a larger batch size means that batches arrive less frequently. In other words, the arrival

EXHIBIT 6–1. In the M/M/1 queueing model, customers arrive according to a Poisson process so that the time between two successive arrivals is exponentially distributed. A single service facility serves the customers with exponential service times. The performance measures on the size of the queue and average waiting time remain of key interest in other queueing models. The relation between these two measures is given by Little's Formula, which generalizes to more complicated queueing systems.

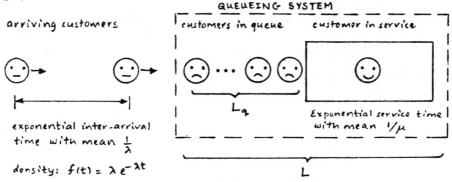

Model Parameters

λ = arrival rate (customers per unit time)

μ = service rate (customers per unit time)

$\rho = \dfrac{\lambda}{\mu}$ utilization factor

Model Performance Measures

L = average number of customers in the system

L_q = average number of customers waiting in queue

W = average amount of time that a customer spends in the system

W_q = average amount of time that a customer waits in queue

Queueing Results

$$W = \frac{1}{\mu - \lambda} = \frac{1/\mu}{1 - \rho} \qquad\qquad L = \frac{\rho}{1 - \rho}$$

$$W_q = \frac{\lambda}{\mu(\mu - \lambda)} = \frac{1}{\mu}\,\frac{\rho}{1 - \rho} \qquad\qquad L_q = \frac{\rho^2}{1 - \rho}$$

Little's Formula: $L = \lambda W$ and $L_q = \lambda W_q$

rate of batches is inversely proportional to Q. Therefore, the basic trade-off is between frequent arrival of small batches (which result in frequent setups) and infrequent arrival of large batches (each requiring a large amount of processing time which ties up the machine for an extended period).

The queueing formulas from the M/M/1 model allow us to investigate the behavior of the function T(Q), which expresses the average

EXHIBIT 6–2. The effect of lot-sizing in a simple M/M/1 queueing system can be evaluated by expressing the average waiting time for each batch as a function of the batch size Q.

Input Parameters	*Decision Variable*

$D=$ demand (units/month) $Q =$ batch size
$P=$ processing rate (units/month)
$u=$ productive utilization $= D/P$
$\tau=$ setup time per batch (months)

Parameters of the M/M/1 Queue

$\lambda =$ arrival rate (number of batches per month) $= D/Q$

$\bar{x} =$ average processing time per batch (months) $= \tau + \dfrac{Q}{P}$

$\mu =$ service rate (batches/month) $= 1/\bar{x}$

$\rho =$ utilization rate or traffic intensity $= \dfrac{\lambda}{\mu} = u + \dfrac{D\tau}{Q}$

Objective Function

    $T(Q) =$ average time a batch of size Q spends in the system

$$T(Q) = \frac{\tau + Q/P}{1 - u - D\tau/Q}$$

Properties of T(Q)

— The minimum value of $T(Q)$ is $\tau(1 - \sqrt{u})^{-2}$

    and is attained at
$$Q^* = \frac{D\tau}{\sqrt{u} - u}$$

— $T(Q)$ increases to infinity as Q approaches $Q_{min} = D\tau / (1 - u)$

— For large Q, $T(Q)$ behaves as the linear function $\dfrac{\tau}{1-u} + \dfrac{Q}{(1-u)P}$

time a batch spends in the system as a function of batch size. Following queueing terminology, this average time in the system includes both the processing time and the wait in the line. With this understanding, we will simply call $T(Q)$ the waiting time.

Exhibit 6–2 presents the basic relations for the queueing model with lot sizing. Exhibit 6–3 gives a numerical example of these relations. The plot in Exhibit 6–3 shows that the waiting time function has a V-shaped (convex) curve. For large values of Q, the processing time dominates the setup time for each batch and the waiting time per batch increases approximately linearly with batch size. Karmarkar et al. call this the *scale effect*. As the batch size is reduced, the waiting time goes through a minimum and then starts to increase very sharply as the

EXHIBIT 6–3. A plot of the average waiting time as a function of the batch size Q for a numerical example shows its basic properties in the M/M/1 model with lot sizing. The waiting time goes to infinity when Q approaches Q_{min}, the minimum possible batch size. As Q increases, the arrival rate decreases, the average processing time per batch goes up, and the utilization factor for the queue decreases. The calculations are performed in time units of months using the relations of Exhibit 8–2; the figures are multiplied by 30 to convert to days.

Values of the Parameters

D = 750 units per month

P = 1,000 units per month

u = D/P = 0.75

τ = setup time = 0.02 months

Q_{min} = 60 units

Q* = 129 units

T(Q*) = 1.114 months or
33.43 days

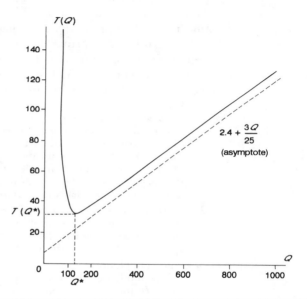

Batch size Q	Arrival rate $\lambda = D/Q$	Average processing time per batch $\tau + Q/P$		Utilization factor $\rho = \dfrac{\lambda}{\mu}$	Average waiting time per batch T(Q)	
		months	days		months	days
75	10	0.095	2.85	0.95	1.9	57.0
150	5	0.170	5.1	0.85	1.133	34.0
300	2.5	0.320	9.6	0.80	1.6	48.0
750	1	0.77	23.1	0.77	3.348	100.4
1,500	0.5	1.52	45.6	0.76	6.333	190.0
3,000	0.25	3.02	90.6	0.755	12.326	369.8

batch size approaches the minimum batch size Q_{min}. Below this batch size, the processing facility cannot keep up with the arrivals and the M/M/1 model ceases to apply. Choosing a small batch size close to this minimum size means that arrivals are frequent and the queue builds up rapidly, as increasingly more time is spent on setups rather than on productive processing. The large increase in waiting time reflects the effects of congestion. The usual indicator of these effects is the ratio of the arrival rate to the service rate: the *utilization factor*. As Q decreases and approaches Q_{min}, the utilization factor approaches one and the average waiting time goes to infinity.

The Q-LOTS Model

While simple, the M/M/1 model clearly shows the dependence of the waiting time on batch size. This relationship remains qualitatively the same if the M/M/1 model is replaced with more complicated queueing models. Indeed, Karmarkar et al. develop a more sophisticated queueing-optimization model called Q-LOTS that bridges the gap between the idealized M/M/1 scenario and the complexities of the manufacturing cell. Constructing Q-LOTS involves the following steps:

1. Each work center is represented by a more complicated queueing model that retains the assumption of Poisson arrivals but allows a general probability distribution for the service time and more than a single machine at the work center. This means that the M/M/1 queue is replaced with the M/G/c queue (c stands for the number of machines). Results from queueing theory provide an expression for the average waiting time at the work center that depends on the arrival time and service characteristics.

2. Since the cell produces 13 different items, the queueing model must be modified to handle the multi-item case. Naturally, this means that 13 batch sizes must be determined simultaneously, one for each item. The search space therefore consists of 13-tuples corresponding to batch size vectors.

3. The model must account for the flows between work centers. This involves modeling the cell as a *queueing network* where the output of one work center (itself modeled as a queueing system as described in the preceding step) feeds into the work centers the items visit next. Thus, the departures from various work centers constitute the arrival process for a work center "downstream." As the analysis of queueing networks is notoriously complicated, the model must account for flow between work centers in a heuristic manner.

4. An optimization component must determine the best lot sizes using the waiting time formulas derived from the queueing network approximation. In general, the optimization step solves a nonlinear program with the components of the lot-size vector as decision variables.

The lot-sizing problem for the manufacturing cell has a multi-objective nature. The ultimate goal is to reduce the average lead times of all parts manufactured in the cell. Karmarkar et al. use a single objective that represents a weighted sum of lead times for all items. Naturally, this objective does not prevent the reduction of the lead time for one item at the expense of the lead times of other items. However, by using the item demands as weights, the model attaches greater priority to the reduction of lead times for high-volume items. Q-LOTS produces an optimal set of lot sizes, one for each item, that attempts to minimize this objective.

How does one validate the results of a model such as Q-LOTS? In principle, one can implement the recommended lot sizes in the cell and measure the improvement in the weighted lead time and the work-in-process (WIP) inventory. This approach, however, will likely be costly and run into numerous practical measurement difficulties. Karmarkar and his coworkers chose another viable approach to model validation that increased the confidence in their results even though it stopped short of full implementation. They evaluated the results of Q-LOTS on Eastman Kodak's detailed simulation model of the manufacturing cell.

In the latter half of their paper, Karmarkar et al. compare Q-LOTS and the simulation model in some detail. The main advantage of Q-LOTS is that, by relying on analytical queueing relations, it can optimize the choice of the lot-size vector. With the simulation model, on the other hand, one must rely on multiple runs and heuristic search techniques to arrive at a lot-size vector with reasonable performance measures. A simulation run with the lot sizes obtained from this search procedure exhibits a weighted average lead time of 9.08 days. If the cell is simulated with the lot size recommendations of Q-LOTS, the lead time measure decreases to 7.26 days. This 20 percent improvement in the average manufacturing lead time demonstrates that the lot sizes produced by Q-LOTS outperform the best batching policy based on the simulation model alone. As compared to the previous practice based on the usual economic order quantity, lead times and WIP were reduced by as much as 70 percent.

According to Karmarkar [1989], Kodak is using scaled-down lot sizes in its plant. Kodak has used a commercial scheduling system called OPT [Chase and Aquilano 1989, Chapter 17] to determine lot sizes since Q-LOTS was not designed as a "production" code. Kodak has therefore been able to compare lot sizes determined by OPT with those recommended by the Q-LOTS model; the results were similar.

6.2 CAPACITY PLANNING WITH A SIMULATION MODEL

In the second paper in this chapter, Ravindran et al. [1989] describe the design of a modular repair facility at Tinker Air Force Base (TAFB) in Midwest City, Oklahoma. This facility, which occupies over 900,000 square feet of production floor space, overhauls and repairs 2,000 aircraft and jet engines annually. The layout design of this facility had two key components: (1) to assess capacity needs at each modular repair center and (2) to design a conveyor system to transport parts between these centers. This section focuses on the detailed simulation model that Ravindran et al. developed to plan capacity.

The TAFB repair facility operates as a large job shop organized into 13 modular repair centers. When an engine arrives for repair, it is disassembled, and the defective parts are routed to the appropriate centers for repair. A part may visit more than one work center, but eventually, when it has been repaired, it returns to the reassembly area for assembly back into an engine. In the past, TAFB had used a functional organization for its work centers, grouping them according to the basic processes involved. This meant that a part had to be transported from one center to another as many as 50 times. The new organization clustered work centers around families of parts with the same geometry, metal type, and processing operations. For instance, a single *modular repair center* (MRC) repairs the turbine blades of all engine types. This is similar to the manufacturing cell Karmarkar et al. [1985] analyzed, but there is more interaction between various MRCs at TAFB.

A standard method of analyzing job shops is to collect statistics on the flows of parts between pairs of work centers. At TAFB, parts move between different MRCs (inter-MRC flows) but movements also occur between individual machines within the same MRC (intra-MRC flows). Ravindran et al. analyze the inter-MRC movements to design an automated conveyor system for TAFB. Because parts move on pallets, the flow of parts must be converted into pallet flows. These flows occur on the arcs of a network model with 56 nodes that they use to model the system. Shortest paths analysis of this network allowed Ravindran et al. to design an efficient conveyor system that decreased materials handling by 50 to 80 percent.

While the network model for the conveyor system uses inter-MRC flows as its key data, the simulation model concentrates on flows within the repair centers, considering a single MRC at a time. In each MRC, parts move between machines so that different operations can be performed. When these operations are completed, the parts leave the MRC. Since in a group layout, the machines within each MRC are tailored to manufacture a specific family of parts, parts do not have to leave the MRC very frequently. Occasionally, however, a part is sent away from its primary MRC to some general purpose shop for operations such as painting or heat treatment. When this external service is completed, the part returns to its primary MRC. The simulation model records such movements into and out of each MRC and accounts for the delays associated with such movements; it does not attempt to follow the part while it is out for external service.

Each MRC acts like a small job shop and exhibits congestion effects that cannot be ignored. Queues build up in front of the machines, and since the queue area is limited, a part that is unable to join a machine queue must wait elsewhere. The MRC has a stacker that stores these parts in a waiting area. Ravindran et al. use the Tinker Integrated Planning Simulation model (TIPS) to determine the number of machines needed at each MRC and the size of the stacker area. The number of machines must be large enough to guarantee that a machine will be available 95 percent of the time when a component arrives. Repeated runs of the simulation model with different numbers of machines allow one to determine the number of machines needed to meet this availability goal. By tracking the stacker queue buildup, TIPS can size the stacker area. By collecting statistics on parts moving across the boundary of each MRC, TIPS also helps determine the materials-handling requirements to support such movements.

The simulation model requires a large amount of detailed data to capture the actual operations of each MRC. This data can be organized into seven groups:

1. *Work Control Documents (WCDs).* Each engine part has a WCD that specifies its primary MRC and the sequence of machines the part visits within the MRC. The WCD identifies the operations needed by the part and the routing of the part through the repair facility. There are 2,600 different WCDs, corresponding to different parts with different processing requirements. When a single MRC is simulated by TIPS, the WCDs determine the contribution of the part to the intra-MRC flows, as well as the movements across the boundary of the MRC.

2. *Annual engine repair requirements.* The load on the repair facility is determined by engines of different types that need repair each year. These repair requirements are similar to a master production schedule since each engine is an assembly containing different parts that need repairs. Given data on the relative frequencies with which different WCDs of an engine need repair, the engine requirements can be exploded into WCD requirements.

3. *Units Per Assembly (UPA) factors.* Since identical units of the same part follow the same sequence of operations, they require only one WCD. For example, 10 identical turbine blades have a single WCD attached as they move through the shop. The UPA factors specify how many identical units occur in each WCD.

4. *The arrival process.* The simulation model must know how the various jobs arrive at each MRC. While many stochastic simulation models build some randomness into the arrival process, TIPS uses a deterministic arrival process: the arrivals of each part are evenly spaced over the year.

5. *Service times.* The machine processing times TIPS uses vary within five percent of the average values of these processing times. Over this range, they are described by truncated normal distributions.

6. *Labor requirements and rules.* To estimate labor needs, TIPS requires data on the operator time for processing parts on each machine. It also explicitly keeps track of the availability of operators by modeling the absences of workers due to training, illness, or vacation.

7. *Machine breakdowns.* Breakdowns of machines within the job shop and their subsequent repair introduce another element of randomness that TIPS models explicitly. The input parameters for TIPS specify the rate at which each machine breaks down and the distribution of its repair time. The time to repair a machine is an exponentially-distributed random variable.

The preceding input data for the simulation amounted to over a quarter of a million individual elements. Because any data base of this size is likely to contain errors, Ravindran et al. developed data checking and verification programs to locate errors automatically.

TIPS uses the data to simulate the operations of an MRC over time. Basically, the simulation model traces the movement of each part through the MRC and collects statistics on such performance measures as average times for processing, waiting, and handling; queue lengths at the machines and the stacker; and machine utilization levels. The TIPS model uses a uniform structure to simulate all MRCs and is coded in the SLAM simulation language.

The size and complexity of the MRCs varies considerably within TAFB. A small MRC may repair approximately 820 items a year that represent five different parts (WCDs). A large center may handle 329 different parts and process over 100,000 items annually. The limiting factor on the size of the simulation model is the maximum number of concurrent items within a single MRC. SLAM sets this limit at 70,000 entities. MRCs exceeding this limit were broken down into smaller modules by segregating the inflow of parts into several streams. Thus, even a single MRC can result in too large a simulation model. This explains why Ravindran et al. treated each MRC in isolation: it is clearly impractical to capture the whole facility (all 13 MRCs) within a single model.

Verifying and validating a simulation model is a major task in itself. Ravindran et al. tested the TIPS model to ensure that it behaves reasonably and consistently as its input data changes. They also had to make sure that the results of the model match the actual (historical) performance of the job shop. Ravindran et al. performed this key test on a representative MRC.

The TAFB study resulted in substantial benefits in the design of both the materials-handling system and the work centers. The flow times for parts decreased by 35 to 50 percent while the percentage of defective items dropped two years in a row. The savings in equipment purchases amounted to $4.3 million, and annual labor savings averaged over $2.0 million. Remarkably, the authors developed and verified the model in only three months! For large simulation models, the data collection and verification steps alone often take several months to complete. In this study, the university team of Ravindran and his coworkers was able to meet the needs of TAFB promptly when some national consulting firms estimated that the task would require a year or more.

According to Ravindran [1989], since the TAFB project was completed, over 60 organizations asked to review the TIPS model for possible use. The Air Logistics Center at San Antonio is one of a number of centers that have decided to use this model to reconfigure their production systems.

6.3 A GLANCE AT QUEUEING THEORY

Queueing theory is about 80 years old. Its official "birth" is usually traced back to the paper of Erlang [1909] entitled "The theory of probabilities and telephone conversations." As this title suggests, queueing theory has its origins in telecommunications where, as busy signals remind us, waiting for service plays a key role. The literature of mathematical queueing theory burgeoned in the 1950s. Saaty [1961] cites 910 sources from the queueing literature through 1960 and his 1966 update adds about half this number for the work published between 1961 and 1966. Today, queueing theory is a standard tool in many applications areas, including data communications, computer networks, transportation systems, traffic flows, and urban emergency systems.

Basically, a queueing system consists of a service facility and customers who arrive and wait for service. The key characteristics of a queueing system are the arrival pattern, the number of servers and their processing rates, and rules that govern how customers are served (queue discipline). Exhibit 6–4 summarizes some of the variations that occur in these characteristics and also presents the convenient shorthand notation common in queueing theory. While Exhibit 6–4 focuses on a single queue, more complex queueing systems arise naturally. The job-shop environment Karmarkar et al. [1985] analyzed involved a network of queues, one at each machine center. This is one example of applications that involve several interconnected queues where the output of one queue serves as input for other queues. Indeed, the area of queueing networks is highly active in view of its numerous applications to manufacturing, computer systems, and data communications [Bertsekas and Gallagher 1987, Kleinrock 1976].

Queueing theory analyzes the behavior and performance characteristics of a queueing system mathematically. Such performance measures as the average queue length, the average waiting time for each customer, and the availability of servers are often of interest. However, queueing theory cannot provide answers to the full range of questions on the behavior of stochastic systems. In their assessment of the first three decades of research in queueing theory, Larson and Odoni [1981] summarize its strengths and weaknesses as follows. Almost all mathematical results of queueing theory describe systems in equilibrium conditions; very few results describe the transient behavior of queues. Even for equilibrium conditions, most of the exact results require exponentially distributed inter-arrival or service times. Finally, queueing theory is generally successful in obtaining information about the mean and variance of such key performance measures as queue length but relatively deficient in specifying the probability distributions of these measures. In spite of these limitations, queueing theory provides a great deal of useful information on the behavior of queueing systems.

Queueing theory and its applications are covered in many good texts. Exhibit 6–5 lists a few of the better-known texts that deal entirely or primarily with queueing theory. To this exhibit, we must add a number of other sources that cover queueing theory within the larger context of probability theory and stochastic processes. For the novice with

EXHIBIT 6–4. The basic characteristics of a single-server queueing system are captured by the arrival and service patterns and the queueing discipline. The standard queueing notation provides a convenient shorthand for some well-studied queues. Thus, an M/G/2/K queue denotes a system with Poisson arrivals, a general service time distribution, two parallel servers, and a limit of K on the number of customers in the system.

ARRIVAL PATTERN	• distribution of inter-arrival times • arrivals in single units or in groups • lost calls or balking—some arrivals do not enter the system • feedback or recycling—some of the queue output reenters the system
SERVICE CHARACTERISTICS	• distribution of individual service times • number of service channels or servers • number of service stages
SYSTEM CAPACITY	• maximum number of customers in the system • maximum allowable queue length
QUEUE DISCIPLINE	• FCFS (FIFO)—First come, first served • LCFS (LIFO)—Last come, first served • SIRO—Service in random order • PRI—Priorities, preemptive or non-preemptive (some customers have priority over others for receiving service)
CUSTOMER BEHAVIOR	• balking—customer refuses to join the queue (if line is too long or too slow) • jockeying—customer switches between queues • reneging—customer leaves the queue before receiving service
QUEUEING NOTATION	A / B / s / C / Q A–Arrival time distribution (M, D, E_k, GI) B–Service time distribution (M, D, E_k, G) s– Number of parallel channels (1 to infinity) C–Capacity of the system (1 to infinity) Q–Queue discipline (FCFS, LCFS, SIRO, PRI, or other)
DISTRIBUTION SYMBOLS	M –Exponential distribution D –Deterministic value E_k –Erlang of order k GI–General distribution, independent G –General distribution

very little mathematical background, Ross [1989] provides a particularly engaging and insightful treatment of simple queueing systems. In their well-known text, Hillier and Lieberman [1986, Chapters 17 and 18] also introduce queueing theory and present a detailed application. Larson

EXHIBIT 6–5. These well-known texts provide full-length treatments of queueing theory. They all cover the fundamentals, but the more recent texts devote considerable attention to queueing networks and approximations.

Title, Authors	Comments
Introduction to Queueing Theory Cooper [1981]	This clearly written text covers standard birth-and-death and Markovian models. It also includes chapters on the control of queues and the simulation of queueing models.
Queues Cox and Smith [1961]	This short monograph has long served as a quick and intuitive introduction to queueing.
Introduction to Queueing Networks Gelenbe and Pujolle [1987]	Intended as an accessible primer on queueing networks and their applications to communications systems, this text covers Jackson and BCMP networks, approximate methods, and flows.
Fundamentals of Queueing Theory Gross and Harris [1985]	An established source on queueing models in operations research, this text covers the standard queueing results. One chapter is devoted to queueing networks and another discusses bounds and approximations.
Queueing Systems Kleinrock [1975, 1976]	This two-volume text has been widely used by students of queueing and computer systems. Volume 1 covers the basic theory from standard results to the advanced theory. Volume 2 presents computer applications.
Elements of Queueing Theory with Applications Saaty [1961]	This early text on queueing is now available in a paperback edition. It summarizes the literature through 1960 and devotes a chapter to applications.
Stochastic Modeling and the Theory of Queues Wolff [1989]	A comprehensive treatment of the subject, this text concentrates on the unifying principles behind queueing results. The second half of the book covers the basic theory, priority queues, the GI/G/1 queue, and bounds and approximations for complex queueing systems.

and Odoni [1981] introduce standard queueing models in an accessible way and devote a chapter to the topic of spatially distributed queues where the customers or servers are distributed over a region. These queues, and the associated hypercube model, arise in the deployment of urban emergency services (police, ambulance, or fire engines). At a more advanced level, Heyman and Sobel [1982] devote the last three chapters of their text to queueing systems, and Asmussen [1987] covers a broad range of queueing topics of a more mathematical nature. Whittle [1986] focuses on stochastic processes underlying queueing networks.

Some queueing texts concentrate on special classes of queues. For example, Chaudhry and Templeton [1983] cover bulk queues, a class of queues in which the arrivals or services occur in groups. In their advanced text, Disney and Kiessler [1987] focus on traffic processes within queueing networks. Newell's [1982] text includes queueing models of transportation processes, while Bertsekas and Gallagher [1987] review queueing in the context of delay models for data networks.

Excellent short overviews of queueing theory have appeared in the literature. In a forthcoming book, Cooper expertly reviews the recent work in queueing theory. Kobayashi [1983] offers a concise look at queueing techniques with computer science applications in mind. Bhat [1978] gives a concise presentation of the literature on queueing theory while his earlier paper [Bhat 1969] reviews the first 60 years of research in this area and contains interesting historical material. Taha [1981] offers an applications-oriented perspective on queueing. Other reviews of selected subfields of queueing are the works of Kiessler and Disney [1988] and Teghem [1986]. In a highly interesting and enjoyable collection edited by Gani [1986], some eminent queueing theorists and probabilists give personal accounts of their craft and their contributions to the field. The list of contributors, which reads like a who's who in queueing, includes Bailey, Cohen, Disney, Keilson, Kendall, Neuts, Prabhu, Syski, Takacs, and Whittle.

Queueing Networks

In recent years, many researchers have turned to *queueing network models* to study the performance of manufacturing systems. Briefly stated, in a queueing network, customers receive service at different service centers consecutively. Each service center constitutes a queueing system by itself and may contain multiple machines or servers. The arrivals at this service center are customers that have just entered the queueing network from outside (exogenous arrivals), or those that completed their service at other centers in the network. The movement of customers between the centers is usually assumed to occur according to a Markov chain. This means that when the customer's service is completed at center i, the customer next moves to center j with probability p(i,j). A matrix P = [p(i,j)] specifies these transition probabilities and serves as an input to the model. A network with exogenous arrivals is called *open*, while in a *closed* queueing network there are no exogenous customers and no departures. In this case, a fixed number of customers simply move between the stations without leaving the system. *Jackson networks* constitute a more tractable class of queueing networks. In this system, exogenous customers arrive at each service center according to a Poisson process. Each center has identical machines (servers) and all service times are exponentially distributed.

In a manufacturing environment, the centers may be different machine centers in a job shop and the customer may represent a work order that follows its prescribed routing through these stations until all its operations are completed. This is essentially the environment of East-man Kodak's manufacturing cell. In fact, Karmarkar et al. [1985] used formulas based on queueing network models to study the effect of lot-sizing policies (see the further readings). As Srikar and Vinod [1989] point out, queueing networks for job shops allow a wide range of pa-rameter choices to be studied analytically whereas a simulation study of the same scope is tedious and time consuming.

Trivedi [1982] provides an introductory treatment of queueing net-works. Many recent standard texts devote one or more chapters to this topic [Gross and Harris 1985, Heyman and Sobel 1982, Wolff 1989]. Gelenbe and Pujolle [1987] have written an accessible primer on queue-ing networks, aiming at the reader with little background in queueing theory. Disney and Konig [1985] provide an excellent survey of this area with over 300 references. Buzacott and Shanthikumar [1980] review the use of queueing networks to model flexible manufacturing systems. Bu-zacott and Shanthikumar [1985] develop open queueing network models for dynamic job shops and illustrate their accuracy with examples. Bi-tran and Tirupati [1988] develop approximations for open queueing networks with multiple product classes. Finally, in a review organized around research groups, Buzacott and Yao [1986] examine analytical queueing models of flexible manufacturing systems and assess the strengths and weaknesses of modeling efforts in this area.

6.4 WAITING LINES IN BANKS AND TELEPHONE SERVICES

As in many other manufacturing systems that experience congestion, the waiting lines in Kodak's manufacturing cell represent units awaiting production. A more familiar scenario in everyday life is when individ-uals have to wait in line in such places as banks and grocery stores. Given the aversion of most customers to long delays, reducing waiting times and the length of queues becomes important in these situations. To impart the flavor of queueing models of waiting lines in greater detail, this section focuses on two areas of application. The first area is banking, while the second centers on telephone services.

Queues in Banking

Many banks rely on standard guides to plan the teller staffing require-ments to provide an acceptable level of service to their customers. The level of service criterion may be stated as "no more than five percent of the customers should have to wait more than x minutes." Using standard queueing results, analysts can find the number of service channels (servers) required to meet this service level objective. Deutsch and Mabert [1980] describe an implementation of this approach at 104 branches of the Bankers Trust Company of New York. While the study cost only $110,000, it saved the bank over a million dollars in annual wages.

In an intriguing account, Kolesar [1984] describes another application of queueing models to banking services—this one involving automatic teller machines (ATMs). The bank that commissioned the study was committed to using ATMs and needed to know which locations would benefit most from the installation of additional ATMs. Kolesar's account of this study focuses on the modeling issues in queueing. A comparison of the simplifying assumptions of the queueing model with the waiting process in the real environment, reveals that even this relatively simple system presents the modeler with interesting challenges.

Waiting for automatic teller machines is a familiar experience. ATMs are heavily used after hours when banks are closed. Customers use their cards to gain access to a vestibule that houses the ATMs. When all the ATMs are busy, the customers wait for a free ATM by forming a line within the vestibule. The M/M/c/K queueing model appears to describe this system well; the ATMs act as c parallel servers and the capacity K of the system is the maximum number of customers in the vestibule (see Exhibit 6–4 for the queueing notation). Typically, each facility has two ATMs and can hold about 10 to 12 people.

How good are the assumptions of the M/M/c/K model? Consider the arrival process first. The model assumes arrivals at a uniform rate according to a Poisson process (exponential inter-arrival times with a fixed mean). However, experience clearly shows that the rate of arrivals varies by time of day and day of the week. One of the busiest periods is Fridays at 5:00 P.M., of course! Also, customers tend to arrive in groups rather than singly. Not all arrivals require service: some individuals simply accompany others. While these "partners in queue" do not use the ATMs, they still occupy the waiting area in the vestibule. A further complication is that certain individuals need more than one transaction. These complications alone suggest that the arrival process is what probabilists term nonstationary compound Poisson.

A very important phenomenon that affects the arrival process is *balking*. Some customers may walk up to the facility, observe a long line within the vestibule, and simply decide against entering. Others may enter the vestibule and start to join the line but leave before their turn comes up. If they leave after waiting for some time, their behavior is called *reneging*. A subtler form of balking occurs when the customer learns not to use the facility during some predictably busy hours. While it is clearly very hard to collect good data on the extent of this behavior, a reasonable definition of level of service should take such "lost customers" into account.

As for service times, data collection revealed that the actual service times did not fit the exponential distribution the M/M/c/K model assumes. Moreover, the model assumes that the servers are available continuously although ATMs have some down-time in practice. To test for the effect of service times, Kolesar simulated the behavior of the queue with two servers and a capacity of 12, using the empirically observed service-time distribution. He compared the simulated behavior of this M/G/2/12 model with the analytical results of the M/M/2/12 queue which assumes exponential service times. This comparison revealed the predictions of the latter model to be sufficiently accurate for planning purposes. Following a number of these checks against reality, the M/M/c/K queueing model was used to generate results on waiting times and the percentage of customers that cannot enter the system since they find it filled to capacity upon arrival.

Prior to this study, the bank had used an M/M/c model with infinite system capacity and tended to focus on waiting times as a key measure of service. The results of the queueing model turned management's attention to the percentage of customers lost due to insufficient capacity. Indeed, the results showed that the customers' waiting times did not become too large. The main effect of congestion is that customers are blocked from entering the system since the capacity of the system is saturated. Under heavy traffic, therefore, the percentage of lost customers is a more appropriate measure of service than the waiting time of the customers who are "lucky enough" to get in.

A final point on modeling deserves mention. Kolesar did not use a model that incorporated balking explicitly, for example, by relating the probability of turning away to the queue length the customer sees upon arrival. Although such models have been analyzed, they require parameters that are very hard to estimate (Kolesar sardonically calls them "metaphysical"). Thus, although the effect of balking is real, the model incorporates this effect indirectly through the system capacity K.

Queueing in Emergency Telephone Services

Telephone answering services have long proved to be a rich area for applying queueing models. Larson's [1972] study of New York City's 911 emergency service is an interesting example. He began the study about a month after the inception of the 911 service on July 1, 1968. The New York City Police Department (NYPD) was receiving over 15,000 calls daily at a central communications room in lower Manhattan and had to deal with many unsatisfied users who complained about the long delays. During certain congested periods, such as 8:00 P.M. to midnight on Saturday evenings, 40 percent of the calls were delayed 30 seconds or more. A close look at the data revealed that while the hourly volume of calls showed wide fluctuations (by a factor of eight or more), the number of 911 operators remained relatively constant (it varied by a factor of two). The analysts quickly decided to change the scheduling of operators to respond to the predictable fluctuations during the course of the day.

To find the number of operators required, Larson first tried to define the level of service requirements with a statement of the following form: the fraction of calls delayed T or more seconds should not exceed P. For example, if P equals 0.05 and T is 15 seconds, then at most five percent of the calls experience delays of 15 seconds or more. Once the values of P and T are fixed, a simple M/M/c queueing model provides an expression for the staffing requirements. The required number of operators, denoted by c, is therefore obtained from a relation of the form c = f(T, P). The main output of the study was a collection of seven charts, one for each day of the week, that listed the number of 911 operators recommended for each hour of the day. As the study only reassigned the available manpower, no additional operators were required. The NYPD implemented the new scheduling system in a month. In his entertaining summary of the project, Larson [1988] notes that before the study, 17 percent of all 911 callers experienced delays of 15 seconds or more. The new approach greatly improved NYPD's service: in no hour of the week did the percentage of calls with delays of 15 seconds (or more) exceed five percent.

McKeown [1979] describes another application that used queueing to evaluate the number of lines in a telephone reporting system. The New York State child abuse and maltreatment telephone reporting system was designed to accept reports on or inquiries about child abuse 24 hours a day, seven days a week. Callers dial a single toll-free number and speak to an operator if one is available. If the reporting system does not have an adequate number of lines or operators, the caller receives a busy signal (if all lines are busy) or gets through but is forced to wait on the line until an operator becomes available. Given the nature of the calls, long waits can discourage the caller from reporting an incident altogether. It is therefore desirable to limit the maximum time a caller must wait before reaching an operator.

Two measures of service were used for the New York State Child Abuse Center: (1) the probability of receiving a busy signal, and (2) the probability of having to wait ten seconds or more. McKeown analyzed data on calls to the center and found that the assumptions of Poisson arrivals and exponentially-distributed lengths of calls are justified. He could therefore use standard queueing formulas to compute the number of lines needed to ensure various levels of the first measure of service. These formulas also provided the value of the second measure for different numbers of operators. At the time of the study in May 1974, the Child Abuse Center had enough lines to keep the probability of a busy signal under 0.001 and the probability of waiting more than

10 seconds under 0.03. Over the next three years, the Child Abuse Register experienced a sizeable increase in the volume of calls and added both lines and operators to reduce the probability of a busy signal to essentially zero.

The IRS Taxpayer Information System

Our next example of a queueing application in telephone services involves the Internal Revenue Service's (IRS's) toll-free telephone assistance system. Harris, Hoffman, and Saunders [1987] began their study of this system in 1979 and developed both queueing and simulation models to analyze its performance. Starting in 1974, taxpayers nationwide were able to call the IRS and receive tax information over the telephone. Taxpayers can use the service to request forms, to ask questions about the tax law, to clarify correspondence with the IRS, or to discuss their accounts. Although the calls may actually be long-distance, they never cost the taxpayer more than a local call. This is why the service is designated as "toll-free." In fiscal year 1986, 32 IRS answering stations handled 37.8 million calls from taxpayers. A key characteristic of the IRS system is that it operates under very heavy traffic. About 80 percent of the callers get a busy signal in the filing (peak) season. In the low season this figure decreases to about 40 percent. However, even this lower percentage is much higher than what a commercial operation would find acceptable. Because they fear losing customers to competitors, commercial operations ensure a much higher level of service. The IRS, on the other hand, faces no competition in offering a free service. As Harris, Hoffman, and Saunders point out, this key difference makes the usual queueing models used by commercial operations inapplicable.

Exhibit 6–6 summarizes the process of answering a taxpayer's call. Congestion affects the customers at two points in this process. First, when the customer dials the IRS toll-free number, the call must be assigned to a trunk line. If all trunk lines are full, the caller receives a busy signal. Calls receiving the busy signal are termed *overflow calls*. The next congestion point occurs when the call gets through to the automatic call distributor (ACD) which distributes the calls to the answering agents. If all the agents are busy, the caller hears a recorded message and has to wait until an agent becomes available. In both cases, congestion can result in lost demand. The taxpayer may not try again after receiving a busy signal. *Reneges* occur when the customer reaches the ACD but hangs up after waiting for a free agent for some time. On the other hand, a caller who just failed to get through can place another call to re-initiate the process; such calls are *redials*.

The IRS can reduce congestion and improve service by increasing the number of trunk lines and answering agents. Ultimately, the goal of a queueing model is to relate the requirements for trunk lines (of vari-

EXHIBIT 6–6. The taxpayer calling the IRS for assistance may get a busy signal, receive a message to wait on the line, or get through to an agent directly. Some callers who are asked to wait may renege and hang up before reaching an agent. All callers who fail to reach an agent may try again by redialing.

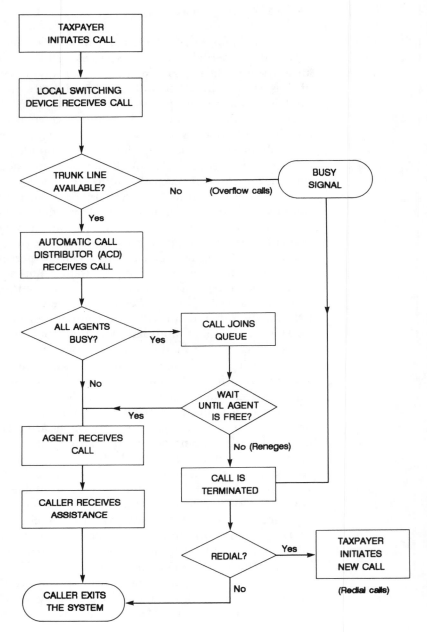

ous types) and agents to the level of service. For this system, however, Harris, Hoffman, and Saunders explain why the traditional M/G/c/c and M/M/c queueing models, which lead to the Erlang-B loss and Erlang-C formulas, are inappropriate for computing these requirements (even though the IRS had used the former model). The gist of their argument is that these models are suitable only for systems where few callers get busy signals and the waiting times are short. The high level of overflow calls and the large number of reneges and redials renders the assumptions of the standard models untenable.

To understand the behavior of the system more completely, Harris, Hoffman, and Saunders developed a detailed simulation model of the operation and validated it with data collected from the IRS site in Baltimore. This model led to important insights into the sensitivity of the system performance to various modeling assumptions. For example, data from actual operations revealed that the service times follow a Weibull distribution rather than the more convenient exponential distribution. Moreover, some calls generate *after-call work* as the agent has to complete certain tasks related to the call after the taxpayer hangs up. A model that combines the after-call work with talk time (using a single service time distribution) ignores the fact that a line becomes available when the talk time terminates (when the taxpayer hangs up), and not when the agent finishes the after-call work.

Even though these refinements are perfectly valid, tests revealed that simulation results are insensitive to the way the service time is modeled: the use of a single exponential service time distribution did not alter the results significantly. Similarly, the simulation runs showed that the results are insensitive to the queue discipline at the ACD (the order in which calls are assigned to agents), so that a FIFO discipline was a safe assumption. On the other hand, the simulation model demonstrated that the system performance was very sensitive to the assumptions about reneging and redialing.

Based on the insights provided by the simulation model, Harris and his coworkers developed a queueing model that captures the key features of the IRS system but suppresses the complications to which the performance of the system is relatively insensitive. This is an interesting case of the fruitful interplay between simulation and queueing models. In this application, the simulation model suggested and justified the simplifying assumptions that made the queueing model mathematically tractable.

The queueing model that Harris and his coworkers developed for the IRS system retains some features of the M/M/c/K queue. Calls arrive according to a Poisson process, and c servers (the agents) handle these calls with exponential service times. The system capacity is K. However, the model includes reneging and redialing as important additional features. The model assumes that individuals renege at a constant rate while waiting in line for agents. Also, each taxpayer who received a busy signal or reneged is assumed to redial with a fixed probability after a random time governed by an exponential distribution. Given values for its seven parameters, the model can calculate such measures of effectiveness as the expected delay for the customers connected, the average utilization of the servers, and the expected system losses.

Harris and his colleagues presented this model to the IRS as an analytical tool to support decisions on staffing and configuring equipment. They also recommended that the IRS collect data to study the redialing phenomenon more thoroughly. The IRS incorporated the estimation procedures for demand and redial probabilities.

Choosing Telemarketing Equipment at L. L. Bean

The telephone service center at L. L. Bean serves as our final example of queueing in telephone systems. L. L. Bean uses about 350 full-time and part-time employees to operate the 24-hour telephone service center for its catalog, mail-order sales. Andrews and Parsons [1989] describe a recent study in which they helped L. L. Bean evaluate automated telephone-operator scheduling systems marketed by different vendors. The role of the scheduling system is to forecast demand and staff the telemarketing operation for 24 hours each day over a seven-day week. Apart from selecting a vendor, the management of L. L. Bean had to establish goals for service levels that optimally balance the cost of losing customers with the cost of providing a high level of service.

Customer behavior at L. L. Bean's telephone service center can be summarized as follows:

1. Call volumes and average service times vary from hour to hour.
2. Not all calls generate orders. Approximately 30 percent of the calls have to do with customer service.
3. A small percentage of customers (about two percent) who have to wait abandon their calls before reaching an operator. However, about 90 percent of those who abandon will call back later.

Since only a small percentage of calls are lost, Andrews and Parsons used a simple M/M/c queueing model for the system (c is the number of telephone agents) and did not attempt to explicitly model abandoned calls. Just as we described for the 911 service study earlier in this section [Larson 1972], the M/M/c model allows one to compute the number of telephone agents based on a service-level target. L. L. Bean's objective was to ensure that no more than 15 percent of calls wait more than 20 seconds before reaching an operator. One can also base the required number of telephone agents on an economic cost/benefit analysis that weighs the cost of adding agents to increase the customer service level against the cost of lost revenues from abandoned calls. Andrews and Parsons used regression analysis to confirm and quantify the relation between the abandonment rate and the percentage of customers that have to wait more than 20 seconds.

The queueing model is at the heart of the company's staffing evaluation model (SEM). SEM computes the staffing requirements hourly based on economic or service level considerations and compares it to the staffing levels proposed by the vendors' systems. Tests with SEM evaluated both the forecasting and the scheduling components of each vendor's system. While the final selection of a vendor took other considerations into account, the evaluation performed by SEM was a valuable aid in L. L. Bean's selection process. The economic approach to setting staffing levels, which balances the costs of understaffing and overstaffing, replaced the vendor's staffing rules in the system selected for implementation. The company estimates that it saves over $100,000 per year in staffing costs alone by using an automated scheduling system.

6.5 OTHER APPLICATIONS OF QUEUEING MODELS

Since the early 1950s, queueing theory has assumed an important place in the MS/OR tool kit. In 1955, the Operations Research Society of America awarded the first Lanchester prize to Leslie Edie for his work on toll collection over the bridges and through the tunnels of New York City. Edie [1954, 1960] analyzed data collected from toll booths at the George Washington Bridge and the Holland Tunnel. A primary goal of the study was to assess the level of service provided to customers and how it varied with the volume of traffic handled by the toll lanes. Edie's detailed description of data collection and modeling issues still makes for good reading. For example, the study revealed that the service time (excluding the wait in line) decreases at high traffic volumes (both the toll collectors and the customers speed up). Since the analysis revealed that right-hand toll booths increase congestion, one result of the study was to reconstruct the toll plaza with left-hand booths only.

In an article that set off an animated debate, Byrd [1978] asked if queueing theory is applicable to problems encountered in practice. In his testy response, Kolesar [1979] pointed out the value of queueing theory in yielding greater insight into the behavior of stochastic systems and cited a number of real-world applications. Despite occasional laments about the theoretical nature of queueing research, applications of queueing in the real world have continued to appear in the 1980s. While we cannot describe the full range of queueing applications here, the following examples should indicate the diversity of the application areas.

Chelst, Tilles, and Pipis [1981] use queueing to model the unloading of coal at Detroit Edison Company's Monroe Power Plant. In this plant, which uses approximately 6.5 million tons of coal annually, four to eight trains transport coal from the mines and unload it at the plant site. Queues build up at the coal unloader which is subject to break-downs, particularly in the cold winter months. In the queueing model, the unloader is the server: it has a fixed number of "customers" corres-ponding to the trains that cycle between the mines and the plant. Chelst, Tilles, and Pipis devised a simple queueing model to evaluate the effects of different unloading procedures on the size and delays of the unloading queue.

Vogel [1979] used queueing theory to model machine maintenance at Becton Dickinson Division, a high-volume manufacturer of hypoder-mic needles and syringes. In this application, arrivals correspond to machine breakdowns and service times represent machine repair times. The role of the server is played by an attendant (operator) who is responsible for several machines. Using simple queueing formulas, Vo-gel determined that the optimal number of machines to assign to each operator is five. This assignment strikes the optimal balance between labor costs of operators and the cost of idle time for the machines. The firm ran an experiment to test this assignment in practice. Based on the positive results of this experiment, the machine operator force in the entire plant was reduced by 115.

Graves et al. [1983] use a queueing model to predict the effect of increasing capacity in general hospital psychiatric units on the flow of patients through public mental hospitals. The general hospital is the preferred facility and is being used increasingly as an alternative to public mental hospitals. Graves et al. construct a model of the flow of patients for the two facilities that treats the general hospital as an M/G/c/c queue. This means that patients are not admitted when the system is full and will have to go elsewhere. The public mental hospital does not turn patients away and is therefore modeled as a GI/G/infinity queue.

In another health services application, Weiss and McClain [1987] model the transfer of patients from an acute care hospital to some other health care facility. Since not enough alternate care facilities are availa-ble, these "backup patients" wait for this transfer in the hospital, even though they no longer need acute care. This waiting time, which is called administrative days, can average between 28 and 62 days. Such long stays cost the patient money and the hospital valuable resources. Weiss and McClain develop a queueing model with state-dependent serv-ice rates for this process and validate it with data from seven hospitals in New York State. The model can help hospitals to predict the impact of backup patients on census predictions for the whole hospital.

Public housing authorities also face a placement problem in provid-ing affordable housing to low income households. Generally, eligible households join waiting lists for different classes of housing units. The decision rules that authorities use to assign households to housing units are called tenant assignment policies. Kaplan [1986] reviews the tenant assignment policies of 10 major US cities and evaluates these policies with the help of a queueing model. He uses the model to derive analytical results on the mean and variance of the applicant waiting times.

Queueing theory is often applied to the deployment of urban emergency units, such as ambulances and fire engines. Kolesar and Swersey [1986] review the applications of queueing and simulation models in this area. Brandeau and Larson [1986] describe an application of the hypercube queueing model [Larson and Odoni 1981, Chapter 5] to ambulance deployment in Boston, where 55,000 telephone calls request emergency medical services each year. In addition to an overview of the hypercube model and its recent enhancements, Brandeau and Larson discuss the data collection effort in great detail. In over two years of use by Boston planners, the model has resulted in estimated annual savings of $150,000.

Green and Kolesar [1984, 1989] use a queueing model to analyze police patrol operations in New York City. The city has 73 police commands called precincts which dispatch police patrol cars independently. Each precinct receives an average of 35,000 police emergency calls per year. Approximately 1,200 police cars, each with two officers, are fielded each day to serve on three nonoverlapping tours of duty. Patrol cars respond to 911 calls, react to incidents they encounter, or perform preventive patrol. The multiple car dispatch (MCD) queueing model Kolesar and Green developed focuses on a single tour of a precinct and assumes that a fixed number of cars are on duty. Emergency calls arrive according to a Poisson process and fall into different priority classes. Each call may require one or more patrol cars: the required number of cars is a random variable whose probability distribution depends on the priority class of that call.

In a meticulous validation study, Green and Kolesar [1989] used detailed data on calls and police car dispatches of three precincts over a 10-day period to test their model. They concluded that the MCD model "is a valid tool for its intended purpose: allocation of police cars across precincts and tours."

In an earlier study, Green and Kolesar [1984] used the MCD model to study the feasibility of decreasing the number of police officers in a patrol car from two to one. They were asked to find how many one-officer cars the city needed to achieve the same average dispatch delay as with the existing two-officer system. Using the MCD queueing model, they determined the increase in the required number of patrol cars and the associated decrease in the number of officers resulting from the change to one-officer patrols. These results indicated that the one-officer patrol program was feasible in New York City and could provide adequate response times with significantly fewer police officers. Green and Kolesar completed the analysis in only four weeks and presented their results to the city officials on July 7, 1981. They recommended that the city undertake a carefully monitored experimental program before implementing the one-officer program in full. In October 1982, the city commissioned an extensive study to develop a one-officer program.

In a related study, Chelst [1988] studied a proposed merger of the fire and police departments in Grosse Pointe Park, Michigan. Under this plan, all emergency personnel would be trained as both policemen and firefighters. Chelst linked a queueing model with a travel time simulation model to predict response time for emergency services. A careful analysis of the operating costs revealed that the merger could save as much as $100,000, provide better response times, and increase patrol coverage.

The studies described in the last section show the importance of customer behavior in waiting lines. Recently, Larson [1987] suggested that researchers should focus more attention on this topic and the broader issue of social justice in queues. The latter topic has to do with inequities that arise in queues. Imagine that you join a queue and a person who arrives after you receives service before you do. In Larson's terminology, you have been victimized by a *slip*, and the second customer derives some satisfaction from having *skipped* over you. Such slips and skips can form two measures of social injustice in queues. Larson's article is a highly readable account of such effects, complete with many queueing horrors!

Our short list of applications leaves out many areas, including the two main areas of computer systems and transportation applications. Krell and Arminio [1982] provide a simple example of delay analysis in a computer network. This highly active area of research is covered in the text by Bertsekas and Gallagher [1987]. Transportation applications occur regularly within the queueing literature. In his text on queueing theory, Newell [1982] describes such applications in transportation as the synchronization of traffic signals, queueing at freeway ramps, and models for rush hour traffic. The bibliography of this text cites some of the better-known queueing models in transportation. Finally, Gilliam [1979] uses queueing analysis in a study conducted by Lockheed Aircraft Service Company to design an international airport in the Middle East. He used standard queueing formulas to determine the congestion at security devices for screening passengers at different levels of passenger traffic through the airport.

6.6 SIMULATION AS A MODELING TOOL

Given a representation of a real-world system and the rules that govern its evolution, a computer can imitate or simulate the behavior of the system as it unfolds over time. Simulation is the generic name for this

MASSACHUSETTS BAY TRANSPORTATION AUTHORITY

12 RIDE TICKET

BETWEEN **BOSTON** AND ALL STATIONS WITHIN **ZONE 7**

084330

Subject To Tariff Regulations

EXPIRES (180) DAYS FROM DATE STAMPED ON BACK.
THIS TICKET IS NON-TRANSFERABLE.

12 RIDE

SERIES 3

class of computer models. Within management science, simulation usually (but not invariably) refers to models of dynamic stochastic systems. The behavior of a stochastic system exhibits randomness. For example, waiting times in queues cannot be predicted with certainty and must be described by a probability distribution. In a simulation run, the computer generates and tracks a sample path of the stochastic system.

The origins of simulation go back to the inception of the Monte Carlo method. Typically, a Monte Carlo simulation models a static stochastic system and samples its behavior repeatedly to obtain information about the expected value of some performance measure or the probability of some event of interest. The idea behind Monte Carlo techniques first occurred to the mathematician Stanislaw Ulam at Los Alamos in connection with the behavior of neutrons in nuclear fission. In his autobiography, Ulam [1976] describes how the idea took form during a long discussion with John von Neumann, while they were driving from Los Alamos to Lamy. In the mid 1950s, the RAND Logistics Laboratory sponsored by the US Air Force simulated large logistics systems to evaluate different operating policies. Over the ensuing years, simulation found acceptance as a standard technique of management science for understanding complex systems. Christy and Watson [1983] report that 89 percent of the firms responding to their survey of industry practice used simulation. Of these firms, 59 percent used simulation in the area of production, 53 percent in corporate planning, 46 percent in engineering, and 41 percent in finance.

Certain advantages of simulation modeling make it a popular technique in practice:

1. Simulation models can incorporate detailed rules governing the behavior of a complex system to allow a degree of realism that most analytical models cannot achieve. A realistic representation of a repair facility was the primary goal of the simulation model Ravindran et al. [1989] developed for the Air Force.

2. Second, because analytical techniques can only rarely provide an exact description of stochastic systems, simulation is often the only technique that can shed some light on the effect of randomness. For instance, since queueing models generally describe stochastic systems under equilibrium conditions, one must often rely upon simulation to obtain information about the transient behavior of systems. Even when analytical solutions or approximations are available, simulation models can validate the analytical results by testing them in a more realistic setting that is closer to the real environment. Taking the study described in Section 6.1 as an example, Karmarkar et al. [1985] used queueing approximations to derive lot sizes for the manufacturing cell. They had to validate these approximations in the more realistic environment captured by the simulation model. Ignall, Kolesar, and Walker [1978] give other interesting examples of the interaction between simulation and analytical models.

3. A simulation model allows the user to evaluate the effect of a policy on the behavior of a system by previewing the system response in a controlled

setting before that policy is implemented. One of the main uses of simulation is to evaluate alternative policies.

4. Simulation models can generate many replications of the system's behavior to allow the user to obtain statistical estimates of the values of interest and to test the sensitivity of the system to its input characteristics.

Despite these strengths, simulation must be used with care. As Law and Kelton [1982] point out, large simulation models are often expensive and time consuming to develop and run. Given the large volume of numbers a simulation model generates, users tend to accept the results of the model uncritically. In reality, however, every simulation model is a statistical experiment that produces estimates of certain system characteristics. Large sample sizes may be needed to obtain statistically defensible estimates. Moreover, the wealth of parameters included in a simulation model often makes it very difficult to obtain reliable sensitivity information. For a large model that is too costly to run repeatedly, the limited sample of replications can exacerbate the problems with statistical significance and sensitivity issues. A user with little statistical training may not realize the sampling error in the estimates produced by a simulation model and may underestimate the sample size required to overcome this. Harris and Marchal [1989] discuss such a case when simulation with a personal computer was used to find the distribution of the net present value of an investment. Annino and Russell [1981] present an entertaining list (complete with cartoons) of implementation pitfalls in simulation analysis.

Simulation Texts

Statistical analysis, stochastic processes, and computer science form the methodological bases of simulation. A number of texts on simulation cover its methodology very competently. In their widely used text on simulation, Law and Kelton [1982] cover the construction of simulation models and their implementation in FORTRAN. Although they include much advanced material on the statistical methodology underlying simulation, their text retains a pedagogical and practical flavor that makes it suitable for students and practitioners. The text includes strong sections on selecting input probability distributions for a simulation model and the analysis of its output. Ross [1990] provides a clear and compact introduction to the probabilistic and statistical building blocks of simulation, and includes some advanced material on simulating certain stochastic processes. The informative but unconventional text by Bratley, Fox, and Schrage [1983] is both a guide to simulation and a compendium of wisdom and advice on the subject. The authors frequently warn against misuses of simulation and suspect methodologies. This text discusses random variate generation in some detail and includes a large collection of generation routines in ANSI FORTRAN. It also devotes adequate space to simulation programming and its languages.

Several texts introduce the basic principles of simulation in an accessible way. Banks and Carson [1984] strike a good balance between simulation programming and the statistical methodology of simulation. In addition to introducing the fundamental techniques of simulation, Hoover and Perry [1989] emphasize simulation languages. The last third of their text is organized as primers for the well-known simulation languages GPSS, SIMAN, and SIMSCRIPT. Solomon's [1983] text has a practical orientation and contains a detailed example that runs through several chapters to illustrate different simulation techniques. This text devotes three chapters to GPSS and provides a listing of a statistical support package in FORTRAN. Carroll [1987] covers simulation programming on a personal computer.

On a more advanced level, Ripley's [1987] terse account of simulation emphasizes random variate generation and statistical issues. The text by Morgan [1984] is more suited to students of mathematics and statistics. Lewis and Orav [1989] cover simulation methodology for problems in both systems simulation and mathematical statistics—areas that use simulation somewhat differently. The authors cover random variate generation in some detail and pay special attention to statistical methods for analyzing simulation output data. They plan a second volume that will concentrate on more advanced topics. Rubinstein [1981] provides a more mathematical treatment of simulation that concentrates on random variate generation, variance reduction, and closes with a chapter on Monte Carlo optimization. Rubinstein [1986] gives theoretical treatments of selected topics in variance reduction, stochastic optimization models, and Monte Carlo optimization methods. A good indication of the advanced research on variance reduction methods in simulation is provided by the November 1989 issue of *Management Science* devoted to this topic.

Commercially available simulation languages facilitate the development of simulation models considerably. Arthur et al. [1986] review and compare some of the more widely used simulation languages. The advances in computer technology continue to transform the underlying structure and the visual interfaces of simulation development tools. Balci and Nance [1989] examine the impact of computing technology and artificial intelligence on the development of simulation models.

6.7 A SAMPLER OF SIMULATION APPLICATIONS

Simulation is now an integral component of the MS/OR tool kit. In an early bibliography of simulation applications, Malcolm [1960] cites over 160 references dealing with the industrial and military uses of simulation analysis. Solomon [1983] includes a number of reprints in her simulation text to illustrate simulation models in such areas as fire fighting, assessing defense procurement policies, risk analysis, analyzing market demand, and manufacturing. The bibliography of this text cites simulation applications from the literature in 12 areas of application. Most of these applications were published between 1974 and 1981. Today, a compendium of simulation applications would likely require an entire book.

In a large class of applications, MS/OR researchers use simulation to evaluate the relative performance of different decision rules in specific systems. The operations of the system can be simulated for each rule to collect statistics on key performance measures that serve as a basis for comparing different rules. For example, detailed job shop simulation experiments have been developed to test scheduling and dispatching rules in dynamic job shops [Baker 1974, Chapter 8]. In one example of such simulation experiments, Bertrand [1983] investigates the performance of a class of rules for assigning due-dates to jobs in a job shop. In another example, Dumond and Mabert [1988] use simulation to evaluate the assignment of due dates in conjunction with activity scheduling procedures for projects with limited resources. Each run of the simulation model tracks approximately 250 projects that span a total of 2,000 days. After a due date is assigned to a project, it is scheduled by a procedure that takes the limited availability of resources into account. The model collects statistics on the difference between the promised due date and the actual completion time of each project. In another simulation experiment, Lee and Adam [1986] investigate the impact of introducing forecast errors into material requirements planning systems. The additional readings include other simulation experiments in manufacturing.

In another class of applications, simulation is used to address specific issues and decisions for a client, a company, or an agency. Exhibit 6–7 collects a sample of simulation studies in this category and groups them by the area of application. This exhibit draws primarily on studies reported in *Interfaces*. Many more applications can be found in publications devoted to simulation modeling including the *Proceedings of the Winter Simulation Conference* and the journal *Simulation*. Certain studies cited in the exhibit use deterministic simulations. This means that the evolution of the system is not subject to uncertainty so that movements or operations follow deterministic rules. One example is the movements of trains over railroad tracks in the study by Welch and Gussow [1986]. Similarly, Bayus et al. [1985] use deterministic rules to simulate the movement of customers between slot machines on the casino floor.

Some studies cited in Exhibit 6–7 are described in other chapters of this book: the models developed by Chao et al. [1989] and Fincke and Vaessen [1988] also appear in Chapter 2; while Chapter 8 discusses

EXHIBIT 6–7. These studies reflect the diversity of applications areas for simulation modeling. In each study, the model was designed to address specific issues of interest to the client organization or the firm conducting the study. The applications are drawn primarily from the journal *Interfaces*.

Author and Company	Issues Addressed	Benefits
Facilities and Equipment Planning		
Swart and Dunno [1981] Burger King	• design the drive-through window to minimize customer wait time	• speedier window service contributed $15 million in annual sales capacity
	• find ways to design kitchens in new restaurants	• model showed that introducing the new special sandwich was not cost effective
	• project the number of workers required	• new labor standards increased profits over $32 million annually
The Process Industries		
Bar-Lev and Pollatschek [1981] Fertilizers and Chemicals Ltd. Haifa, Israel	• decide on the allocation of wagons to the delivery of raw materials (phosphate) to the plants	• the model's results indicated that an additional half shift in unloading saves $60,000 per year; this was implemented by the company
	• compare the benefits of investing in accelerated unloading versus adding new storage facilities (silos)	• company decided to build an additional silo to store phosphate
Golovin [1979, 1985] Exxon	• rapidly assess the impact of new California and federal gasoline blend regulations on refinery production and component inventories; evaluate the changes in operations designed to meet the regulations	• refinery was able to reduce its planned capital expenditure by at least one storage tank; this gave an estimated savings of $1.4 million
	• determine the combination of sulfur removal equipment, octane-improving	• model has grown into a generic multistage production simulation tool that has been used

(continued)

EXHIBIT 6–7. (*Continued*)

Author and Company	Issues Addressed	Benefits
	equipment, and new storage tanks that should be built to meet lead and sulfur phase-out regulations at lowest cost	in over 30 studies that range from facilities investment to resource allocation for refineries, chemical plants, coal mines, and synthetic fuel plants

Manufacturing

Bookbinder and Kotwa [1987] General Motors of Canada	• find the number of automatic guided vehicles (AGVs) needed to transport cars through various phases of assembly • quantify the relation between the number of AGVs and achievable output	• recommended the number of AGVs required in the body-framing system
Fortuin and Korsten [1988] The Philips Group	• evaluate three alternative production systems for manufacturing printed circuit boards • achieve shorter manufacturing lead times by reducing congestion delays	• showed two production systems to be feasible • model indicated that the average lead time can be reduced by a factor of six or seven

Inventory Management

Chao et al. [1989] Electric Power Research Institute	• simulate the changes in the level of inventory of fuel to find the annual costs of inventory • capture variations in supply, demand, and disruptions	• the simulation is one part of a fuel inventory model that has been transferred to over 74 utilities and realized savings of over $125 million
Fincke and Vaessen [1981] Ciba-Geigy	• evaluate the impact of safety stock policies on service levels in the parent and group companies • investigate direct shipments to group companies	• model showed that decentralizing safety stock increases overall distribution costs • quantified the relation between total distribution costs and the parent company service level

EXHIBIT 6–7. (*Continued*)

Author and Company	Issues Addressed	Benefits
Transportation		
Bammi [1990] Northern Border Pipeline	• analyze whether pipe can be delivered within the planned nine months	• model showed that target delivery dates can be met with 20 percent fewer railcars
	• model foreign shipments of pipe, domestic production, and movements of pipe on trains	• savings on leasing costs of railcars amounted to $4.5 million
Dawson et al. [1981] St. Lawrence Seaway Authority	• determine when the capacity of the Welland Canal should be increased to reduce congestion of vessels	• delay construction of a new $2 billion canal for two years
	• model the movement of vessels through the canal in detail to compare different options for increasing capacity	• widen existing canal at a cost of $6 million leads to revenue increases of $3 million per year
		• important spinoffs from simulation analysis included revising the basis for toll charges, improving traffic control, and ranking the components of a $175 million canal improvement program
Welch and Gussow [1986] Canadian National Railway (CN)	• simulate the movements of trains and dispatchers' decisions to find the effects of different factors on rail line capacity	• CN was able to defer expenditures of C$350 million beyond 1990
		• model showed the benefits of computer-aided dispatching and control signals
	• measure train delays for different scenarios	• model suggested appropriate places for converting single-line tracks to double tracks

(*continued*)

EXHIBIT 6–7. (*Continued*)

Author and Company	Issues Addressed	Benefits
Manpower Planning		
Macon and Turban [1981] Florida Power and Light Company (FPL)	• predict the customer waiting time and queue length for energy audits with changes in the level of demand and the number of auditors made available	• helped FPL plan the level at which to offer the audit program and find the required number of auditors
Randhawa, Mechling, and Joerger [1989] Oregon Motor Vehicles Division (DMV)	• evaluate the policy of using receptionists to reduce customer waiting time in DMV stations	• recommendations increased staff utilization and reduced customer waiting times
	• determine when a receptionist is warranted and what functions to assign to this individual	• service level improvement equalled what a nine percent increase in staff can produce
Health Care		
Kwak, Kuzdrall, and Schmitz [1976] Deaconess Hospital St. Louis, Missouri	• evaluate utilization levels of operating and recovery rooms under five policies for scheduling patients for surgery	• model showed that the hospital can improve upon the current policy of randomly scheduling patients for surgery
		• identified four scheduling rules with better performance: each improved the utilization rates of the operating and recovery rooms and reduced the average length of the workday in the recovery room by as much as 21 percent
Lambo [1983] Rural Health Centre Ikire, Nigeria	• evaluate the extent to which different operational and management policies improve the center's operating efficiency and effectiveness	• implemented several policy changes: altered the sequence of tasks at the center, aggregated tasks and divided them among personnel categories
	• obtain more realistic estimates of the impact of manpower decisions made by the linked optimization model	• average time spent by a patient in the center reduced by 45 minutes

EXHIBIT 6–7. (*Continued*)

Author and Company	Issues Addressed	Benefits
Ruth, Wyszewianski, and Herline [1985] Transplantation Society of Michigan	• examine factors affecting demand and supply of kidney transplants in the state • determine how much a given increase in donations reduces the length of the waiting list	• model showed that the waiting list will grow rapidly under current conditions • results indicated that as the donations increase the marginal effect of a donation on reducing waiting lines diminishes
Recreation and Entertainment Bayus et al. [1985] Sands Hotel and Casino Atlantic City	• simulate the movement of customers between groups of slot machines to guide the layout of the casino floor	• the casino used the model to determine the attributes of machines purchased and to design the expansion of the current layout
Farina, Kochenberger, and Obremski [1989] Bolder Boulder, Inc.	• change the physical configuration of the finish line and the release of blocks of runners to remove congestion at the finish line	• eliminate all congestion effects near the finish line in the 1985 race • model was used to fine-tune operations in the 1986 and 1987 races
Smith, Webster, and Heck [1976] US Forest Service	• analyze the effects of different management policies on the quality of the experience of recreational users of a low-density, back-country wilderness area • measure the number of encounters with other parties as an indicator of the degree of solitude	• model examined the impact of the total use level and the effect of smoothing the arrival pattern of users to the Spanish Peaks Wilderness Area in Montana and the Desolation Wilderness Area in California • model used to determine the effects of campsite additions and usage patterns on the West Canada Lakes Wilderness Area in New York

(*continued*)

EXHIBIT 6–7. (*Continued*)

Author and Company	Issues Addressed	Benefits
Government Services		
Monarchi, Hendrick, and Plane [1977] Denver, Colorado	• use the New York City—Rand Institute simulator of fire department operations to test the fire-fighting configurations recommended by a static model • explore effects of station locations, equipment configurations, alarm rates, and dispatch policies upon the performance of the fire department	• reduction of five fire suppression companies by closing obsolete stations and building new ones • maintained about the same level of fire suppression service at lower cost • potential net cost reduction of $2.3 million over seven years
Riccio and Litke [1986] New York City	• investigate how illegally parked cars prevent mechanical sweepers from cleaning the curb • demonstrate that the Department of Sanitation's plan for ticketing cars will reduce the number of illegally parked cars and lead to cleaner streets	• even with a small reduction in the number of illegally parked cars the sweeper's ability to make a street clean would improve significantly • Traffic Department redeployed 30 percent of their mobile enforcement agents to ticket illegally parked cars blocking mechanical sweepers
Military		
Cooper [1980] Ingalls Shipbuilding	• capture all phases of shipbuilding programs (from bidding through manpower scheduling) to assess causes and risks of cost overruns and delays • quantify the impact of delays caused by the Navy (contractor) on program costs to resolve a $500 million claim against the Navy	• model was the sole basis for the majority of the claim, which was settled out of court by the Navy for $447 million • model extended to aid strategic decision making in shipyard operations • the model evaluates bidding policies, marketing, contract management, program

EXHIBIT 6–7. (*Continued*)

Author and Company	Issues Addressed	Benefits
		work management, and resource management; it also forecasts costs
Other		
Russell and Hickle [1986] First National Bank and Trust Company of Tulsa, Oklahoma	• assess the impact of future interest rates on the yield of a portfolio of certificates of deposit (CDs) with different maturities	• model allows the bank to anticipate the cost of its CD portfolio given various interest rate scenarios
Taylor and Evans [1982] General Dynamics Corporation Data Systems Division	• evaluate the increase in data processing throughput if faster tape drives replace existing drives	• model determined that the throughput increases by 23 percent if existing drives are replaced with drives that are 60 percent faster
		• the gain in throughput was enough to make additional space unnecessary; this saved over $1.6 million in projected costs

the larger study for which Riccio and Litke [1986] developed their simulation model. We conclude this section with a more detailed descriptions of two studies cited in Exhibit 6–7.

A major success story concerns the use of simulation modeling at Burger King Corporation. Swart and Donno [1981] describe how Burger King developed a simulation model of restaurant operations in 1979 to improve the productivity of its franchises. The firm collected data from over 40 restaurants in 10 regions of the country. To convince corporate management that the model represents real restaurants, researchers assembled a typical restaurant in a warehouse, staffed it with actual crew members from nearby restaurants, and subjected it to various customer arrival patterns. A comparison of the videotaped results with computer-generated predictions validated the simulation model.

The simulation model became a standard tool for evaluating changes and improving ongoing operations. For example, Burger King used it to determine the optimal distance between the order station and the pick-up window in the drive-through store. The model also evaluated the sales benefit of placing a second drive-through window in series with the first. In another study, the model helped Burger King analyze the impact of introducing new products (specialty sandwiches, for example) on sales by estimating the customer delay caused by this move. According to Swart and Dunno, the overall benefits of the simulation model proved to be remarkable: new labor standards based on the simulation results saved Burger King over 1.5 percent in labor costs, an annual savings of over \$32 million systemwide. The use of the simulation model to design the 300 new units opened each year was estimated to increase profit by over \$3.37 million annually.

The second simulation study we discuss involves an application in health care. Ruth, Wyszewianski, and Herline [1985] developed a simulation model to study the supply and demand of kidney transplants in the State of Michigan. The Transplantation Society of Michigan (TSM) wished to identify the best strategy for increasing the number of kidney donations in the state and wanted to determine the impact of increased donations on reducing the length of the waiting list. The purpose of the simulation model was to analyze the effect of different levels of kidney donation on the waiting list.

The simulation model tracks the supply and demand for kidneys on a daily basis over a period of five years. It keeps a waiting list of potential recipients, a list of kidneys donated on each day, and incorporates a matching process that searches the waiting list for the best candidate to receive each donated kidney. The waiting list is updated daily to reflect the changes in the status of the people awaiting transplants. While the overall structure of the model is simple, the authors decided against using a queueing model since the matching and updating processes are complex and are subject to change over time. In fact, representing the matching process within the model constituted an important modeling issue. The model showed that the waiting lists will continue to grow and that to decrease the length of the waiting list, ever larger increases in the donation list are needed. The authors explain this as follows: "as more kidneys become available, it becomes less likely that there is a compatible recipient left on the list at the particular time a kidney is donated." This means that the kidney is not used or that it must be sent out of state. By revealing the prospect of diminishing returns, the results of the simulation model have important policy implications for agencies like TSM.

6.8 FURTHER READINGS

Related Readings

Karmarkar et al. Paper

- Karmarkar [1987a] develops the M/M/l model with lot sizing and derives the relations in Exhibit 6–2. He also presents the results of a simulated queueing system with batch arrivals and deterministic (batch) service times to show the behavior of the average waiting-time function under more complicated conditions. He then proceeds to generalize the model to handle multiple items.

- Karmarkar, Kekre, and Kekre [1985] analyze batching decisions for a job shop with multiple machines that process multiple items. The shop is modeled as a queueing network where each node represents a machine center modeled as an M/G/c queueing system. The decision variables are the batch sizes for the different items. As described in Section 6.1, the lot size affects both the arrival rate and the waiting time of each item at each machine center. Using queueing formulas to express the waiting times as a function of the batch sizes, the authors formulate an optimization problem that chooses the optimal batch sizes to minimize inventory costs.

- Karmarkar, Kekre, and Kekre [1987] analyze the capacity of a manufacturing cell using an open Jackson queueing network model. The underlying model generalizes the one described in Section 6.1 as it considers the option of increasing the cell's processing capability by using more machines or overtime. The authors present a detailed case study of a cell with eight major machine centers that produces 27 parts, each requiring from three to 12 operations. The performance measure is a weighted sum of manufacturing lead times for the parts. The study shows that increasing capacity can improve both lead times and WIP inventories by 40 percent.

- Bacon and Choudhuri [1987] used the commercial software OPT to compare three lot-sizing tools: economic order quantity, OPT, and Q-LOTS. They ran the experiments for a repetitive batch manufacturing cell with 15 machines and a product mix of 15 parent items. The results showed that the lot sizes determined by OPT and Q-LOTS both outperform the lot sizes based on the economic order quantity by reducing lead times and improving due-date performance.

Ravindran et al. Paper

- Foote et al. [1988] concentrate on the design of the conveyor system at Tinker Air Force Base. Their network model of the materials handling system concentrates on the flows between MRCs to determine the capacity needed for the conveyor system. A shortest path algorithm finds the best paths for the movement of parts.

Background Readings

Karmarkar et al. Paper

- From its beginnings in the metal parts industry, group technology has evolved into an effective approach to standardization across product lines and processes. In their brief but lucid article, Hyer and Wemmerlov [1984] introduce the concept of group technology and describe its role in improving productivity. Snead [1989] covers group technology in much greater detail and examines the different forms this approach takes within manufacturing processes. Chapter 10 of this book is devoted to manufacturing cells and its bibliography contains about 100 references on group technology.

- Zipkin [1986] develops a model for the design and control of a production facility that makes many products in large, discrete batches. The underlying idea is to represent the inventory of each product by a standard model from inventory theory and to then link this model with a queueing model of the production facility. In this way, the sojourn time in the production facility becomes the usual manufacturing lead time for the inventory submodels. This allows the overall model to take the effect of congestion on manufacturing lead times into account. In pursuing this effect, Zipkin's work is related in spirit to the research of Karmarkar et al. [1985].

- Srikar and Vinod [1989] developed a closed queueing network model to evaluate the performance of American Airlines maintenance facility in Tulsa, Oklahoma. This facility, which operates as a large job shop, maintains the landing gears of the company's aircraft fleet. Each gear scheduled for maintenance is disassembled into several component parts and each part visits several work stations in the facility before it is reassembled into gears that are reinstalled on the aircraft. There are 75 part types and 30 work stations. The model is a closed queueing network with multiple job classes. Given a configuration for the job shop, the queueing model can measure the global performance of the shop through such measures as production rates and flow times by part type. Srikar and Vinod imbed this model within a heuristic that searches for superior shop configurations. The model allowed them to plan capacity in anticipation of increased production in the long term.

    Chen et al. [1988] also used a queueing network model to evaluate the performance of a manufacturing system. They developed the model for a facility that fabricates semiconductor wafers. They used several years of data to compare the actual values of key performance measures with the values predicted by the model. They found that the model's predictions were within 10 percent of the observed values.

- Karmarkar [1987b] considers the effect of batch sizes on the delays incurred in deterministic sequencing problems by studying such measures as makespan and flow times. Dobson, Karmarkar, and Rummel [1987] formulate the deterministic problem of batching jobs to minimize flow time as an optimization problem.

Ravindran et al. Paper

- Simulation has long served as a tool for understanding and evaluating the performance of complex manufacturing systems. Carrie's [1988] introduction to simulation of manufacturing systems is aimed at practitioners and requires minimal technical background. Hurrion [1986] has collected a group of articles devoted to simulation in manufacturing, covering such applications as flexible manufacturing systems, production lines, transfer lines, and production control. The presentation is directed towards managers rather than researchers and includes case studies of simulation modeling. Haddock [1988] describes a simulation generator for producing simulation models of flexible manufacturing systems. This generator serves as a preprocessor to the simulation language SIMAN. It accepts data on the manufacturing machine centers and operations and converts these into a simulation model that reports various performance measures to the user.

- Ritzman, King, and Krajewski [1984] have developed a large-scale simulation system called MASS to evaluate the impact of Japanese and American manufacturing techniques on manufacturing performance. The model captures the manufacturing environment through a set of factors including the nature of customer orders, vendor influence, facility design, product structure, process characteristics, inventory policies, and lot sizes. The simulation model has two parts. The first forecasts the orders and develops a master production schedule while the second routes orders through the work stations. By running the model with different settings of the factors, the user can assess which factors are most critical to success. Krajewski et al. [1987] describe the model in greater detail and present their experiments for comparing Japanese (kanban), material requirements planning (MRP), and reorder point systems. Huang, Rees, and Taylor [1983] also performed a simulation study of the Japanese kanban system under operating conditions typical of the American manufacturing environment.

- Cadley, Heintz, and Allocco [1989] developed a simulation model to help design a new electronic assembly shop for AT&T's factory in Montgomery, Illinois. This facility builds a variety of data communications products made out of subassemblies called circuit packs (assemblies of a printed wiring board and electrical components). The new design for the facility consolidated several lines into a single flexible line and adopted a just-in-time approach to production. The authors used the simulation model to analyze such issues as product flow, lot-size determination, buffer sizes, and scheduling and loading rules.

REFERENCES

Andrews, Bruce H. and Parsons, Henry L. 1989, "L. L. Bean chooses a telephone agent scheduling system," *Interfaces*, Vol. 19, No. 6, pp. 1–9.

Annino, Joseph S. and Russell, Edward C. 1981, "The seven most frequent causes of simulation analysis failure—and how to avoid them," *Interfaces*, Vol. 11, No. 3, pp. 59–63.

Arthur, Jeffrey L.; Frendewey, James O.; Ghandforoush, Parviz; and Rees, Loren P. 1986, "Microcomputer simulation systems," *Computers & Operations Research*, Vol. 13, Nos. 2 and 3, pp. 167–183.

Asmussen, Soren 1987, *Applied Probability and Queues*, John Wiley & Sons, New York.

Bacon, Robert E. and Choudhuri, Adi N. 1987, "A manager's dilemma: Lot sizing and/or finite scheduling," University of Rochester, Center for Manufacturing and Operations Research, Working Paper CMOM 87-08, Rochester, New York.

Baker, Kenneth R. 1974, *Introduction to Sequencing and Scheduling*, John Wiley & Sons, New York.

Balci, Osman and Nance, Richard E. 1989, "Simulation model development: The multidimensionality of the computing technology pull," in *Impacts of Recent Computer Advances on Operations Research*, ed. R. Sharda, B. Golden, E. Wasil, O. Balci, and W. Stewart, North-Holland, New York, pp. 385–395.

Bammi, Deepak 1990, "Northern Border Pipeline logistics simulation," *Interfaces*, Vol. 20, No. 3, pp. 1–13.

Banks, Jerry and Carson, John S., II 1984, *Discrete-Event System Simulation*, Prentice-Hall, Englewood Cliffs, New Jersey.

Bar-Lev, D. and Pollatschek, M. A. 1981, "Simulation as an aid in decision making at Israel's Fertilizers and Chemicals," *Interfaces*, Vol. 11, No. 2, pp. 17–21.

Bayus, Barry L.; Banker, Robert L.; Gupta, Shiv K.; and Stone, Bradley H. 1985, "Evaluating slot machine placement on the casino floor," *Interfaces*, Vol. 15, No. 2, pp. 22–32.

Bertrand, J. W. M. 1983, "The effect of workload dependent due-dates on job shop performance," *Management Science*, Vol. 29, No. 7, pp. 799–816.

Bertsekas, Dimitri P. and Gallagher, Robert G. 1987, *Data Networks*, Prentice-Hall, Englewood Cliffs, New Jersey.

Bhat, U. Narayan 1969, "Sixty years of queueing theory," *Management Science*, Vol. 15(B), No. 6, pp. 280–294.

Bhat, U. Narayan 1978, "Theory of queues," in *Handbook of Operations Research*, ed. J. J. Moder and S. E. Elmaghraby, Van Nostrand Reinhold, New York, pp. 352–397.

Bitran, Gabriel R. and Tirupati, Devanath 1988, "Multiproduct queueing networks with deterministic routing: Decomposition approach and the notion of independence," *Management Science*, Vol. 34, No. 1, pp. 75–100.

Bookbinder, James H. and Kotwa, Terrence R. 1987, "Modeling an AGV automobile body-framing system," *Interfaces*, Vol. 17, No. 6, pp. 41–50.

Brandeau, Margaret L. and Larson, Richard C. 1986, "Extending and applying the hypercube queueing model to deploy ambulances in Boston," in *Delivery of Urban Systems*, TIMS *Studies in the Management Sciences*, Vol. 22, ed. A. J. Swersey and E. J. Ignall, North-Holland, New York, pp. 121–153.

Bratley, Paul; Fox, Bennett L.; and Schrage, Linus E. 1983, *A Guide to Simulation*, Springer-Verlag, New York.

Buzacott, John A. and Shanthikumar, J. G. 1980, "Models for understanding flexible manufacturing systems," *AIIE Transactions*, Vol. 12, No. 4, pp. 339–350.

Buzacott, John A. and Shanthikumar, J. G. 1985, "Queueing models of dynamic job shops," *Management Science*, Vol. 31, No. 7, pp. 870–887.

Buzacott, John A. and Yao, David D. 1986, "Flexible manufacturing systems: A review of analytical models," *Management Science*, Vol. 32, No. 7, pp. 890–905.

Byrd, Jack, Jr. 1978, "The value of queueing theory," *Interfaces*, Vol. 8, No. 3, pp. 22–26.

Cadley, John A.; Heintz, Helen E.; and Allocco, Lisa Vogrich 1989, "Insights from simulating JIT manufacturing," *Interfaces*, Vol. 19, No. 2, pp. 88–97.

Carrie, Allan 1988, *Simulation of Manufacturing Systems*, John Wiley & Sons, New York.

Carroll, J. M. 1987, *Simulation Using Personal Computers*, Prentice-Hall, Englewood Cliffs, New Jersey.

Chao, Hung-Po; Chapel, Stephen W.; Clark, Charles E., Jr.; Morris, Peter A.; Sandling, M. James; and Grimes, Richard C. 1989, "EPRI reduces fuel inventory costs in the electric utility industry," *Interfaces*, Vol. 19, No. 1, pp. 48–67.

Chase, Richard B. and Aquilano, Nicholas J. 1989, *Production and Operations Management*, fifth edition, Richard D. Irwin, Homewood, Illinois.

Chaudhry, M. L. and Templeton, J. G. C. 1983, *A First Course in Bulk Queues*, John Wiley & Sons, New York.

Chelst, Kenneth 1988, "A public safety merger in Grosse Pointe Park, Michigan—A short and sweet study," *Interfaces*, Vol. 18, No. 4, pp. 1–11.

Chelst, Kenneth; Tilles, Andrea Z.; and Pipis, J. S. 1981, "A coal unloader: A finite queueing system with breakdowns," *Interfaces*, Vol. 11, No. 5, pp. 12–25.

Chen, Hung; Harrison, J. Michael; Mandelbaum, Avi; Van Ackere, Ann; and Wein, Lawrence M. 1988, "Empirical evaluation of a queueing network model for semiconductor wafer fabrication," *Operations Research*, Vol. 36, No. 2, pp. 202–215.

Christy, David P. and Watson, Hugh J. 1983, "The application of simulation: A survey of industry practice," *Interfaces*, Vol. 13, No. 5, pp. 47–52.

Cooper, Kenneth G. 1980, "Naval ship production: A claim settled and a framework built," *Interfaces*, Vol. 10, No. 6, pp. 20–36.

Cooper, Robert B. forthcoming, "Queueing theory," in *Handbook of Operations Research and Management Science, Volume 2: Stochastic Models*, ed. D. P. Heyman and M. J. Sobel, North-Holland, New York.

Cooper, Robert B. 1981, *Introduction to Queueing Theory*, second edition, North Holland, New York.

Cox, D. R. and Smith, Walter L. 1961, *Queues*, Methuen, London, England.

Dawson, Wayne A.; Lakshminarayan, S. Mohan; Landry, Andre A.; and McLeod, J. Bruce 1981, "Keeping ahead of a $2 billion canal," *Interfaces*, Vol. 11, No. 6, pp. 70–83.

Deutsch, Howard and Mabert, Vincent A. 1980, "Queueing theory and teller staffing," *Interfaces*, Vol. 10, No. 5, pp. 63–67.

Disney, Ralph L. and Kiessler, Peter C. 1987, *Traffic Processes in Queueing Networks: A Markov Renewal Approach*, Johns Hopkins University Press, Baltimore, Maryland.

Disney, Ralph L. and Konig, Dieter 1985, "Queueing networks: A survey of their random processes," *SIAM Review*, Vol. 27, No. 3, pp. 335–403.

Dobson, Gregory; Karmarkar, Uday S.; and Rummel, Jeffrey L. 1987, *Management Science*, Vol. 33, No. 6, pp. 784–799.

Dumond, John and Mabert, Vincent A. 1988, "Evaluating project scheduling and due-date assignment procedures: An experimental analysis," *Management Science*, Vol. 34, No. 1, pp. 101–118.

Edie, Leslie C. 1954, "Traffic delays at toll booths," *Operations Research*, Vol. 2, No. 2, pp. 107–138.

Edie, Leslie C. 1960, "Review of the Port of New York Authority study," *Operations Research*, Vol. 8, No. 2, pp. 263–277.

Erlang, A. K. 1909, "The theory of probabilities and telephone conversations," *Nyt tidsskrift for matematik*, Vol. B20, pp. 33–39.

Farina, Ron; Kochenberger, Gary A.; and Obremski, Tom 1989, "The computer runs the Bolder Boulder: A simulation of a major running race," *Interfaces*, Vol. 19, No. 2, pp. 48–55.

Fincke, Ulrich and Vaessen, Willem 1988, "Reducing distribution costs in a two-level inventory system at Ciba-Geigy," *Interfaces*, Vol. 18, No. 6, pp. 92–104.

Foote, Bobbie L.; Ravindran, A.; Badiru, Adedeji B.; Leemis, Lawrence L.; and Williams, Larry 1988, "Simulation and network analysis pay off in conveyor system design," *Industrial Engineer*, Vol. 20, No. 6, pp. 48–53.

Fortuin, Leonard and Korsten, Antonius T. M. 1988, "Quantitative methods in the field: Two case studies," *European Journal of Operational Research*, Vol. 37, No. 2, pp. 187–193.

Gani, Joseph M., ed. 1986, *The Craft of Probabilistic Modeling: A Collection of Personal Accounts*, Springer-Verlag, New York.

Gelenbe, E. and Pujolle, G. 1987, *Introduction to Queueing Networks*, John Wiley & Sons, New York.

Gilliam, Ronald R. 1979, "An application of queueing theory to airport passenger security screening," *Interfaces*, Vol. 9, No. 4, pp. 117–123.

Golovin, Lewis 1979, "Product blending: A simulation study in double-time," *Interfaces*, Vol. 9, No. 5, pp. 64–76.

Golovin, Lewis 1985, "Product blending: A simulation study in double time: An update," *Interfaces*, Vol. 15, No. 4, pp. 39–40.

Grant, Floyd H., III 1980, "Reducing voter waiting time," *Interfaces*, Vol. 10, No. 5, pp. 19–25.

Graves, Stephen C.; Leff, H. Stephen; Natkins, Judith; and Senger, Michael 1983, "A simple stochastic model for facility planning in a mental health care system," *Interfaces*, Vol. 13, No. 5, pp. 101–110.

Green, Linda and Kolesar, Peter 1984, "The feasibility of one-officer patrol cars in New York City," *Management Science*, Vol. 30, No. 8, pp. 964–981.

Green, Linda and Kolesar, Peter 1989, "Testing the validity of a queueing model of police patrol," *Management Science*, Vol. 35, No. 2, pp. 127–148.

Gross, Donald and Harris, Carl M. 1985, *Fundamentals of Queueing Theory*, second edition, John Wiley & Sons, New York.

Haddock, Jorge 1988, "A simulation generator for flexible manufacturing systems in design and control," *AIIE Transactions*, Vol. 20, No. 1, pp. 22–31.

Harris, Carl M.; Hoffman, Karla A.; and Saunders, Patsy B. 1987, "Modeling the IRS taxpayer information system," *Operations Research*, Vol. 35, No. 4, pp. 504–523.

Harris, Carl M. and Marchal, William G. 1989, "Distribution estimation by computer simulation," *Interfaces*, Vol. 19, No. 3, pp. 33–42.

Heyman, Daniel P. and Sobel, Matthew J. 1982, *Stochastic Models in Operations Research, Vol. 1: Stochastic Processes and Operating Characteristics*, McGraw-Hill, New York.

Hillier, Frederick S. and Lieberman, Gerald J. 1986, *Introduction to Operations Research*, fourth edition, Holden-Day, Oakland, California.

Hoover, Stewart V. and Perry, Ronald F. 1989, *Simulation: A Problem-Solving Approach*, Addison-Wesley, Reading, Massachusetts.

Huang, Philip Y.; Rees, Loren P.; and Taylor, Bernard W., III 1983, "A simulation analysis of the Japanese just-in-time technique (with kanbans) for a multiline, multistage production system," *Decision Sciences*, Vol. 14, No. 3, pp. 326–344.

Hurrion, R. D. 1986, *Simulation*, Springer-Verlag, New York.

Hyer, Nancy L. and Wemmerlov, Urban 1984, "Group technology and productivity," *Harvard Business Review*, Vol. 62, No. 4, pp. 140–149.

Ignall, Edward J.; Kolesar, Peter J., and Walker, Warren E. 1978, "Using simulation to develop and validate analytic models: Some case studies," *Operations Research*, Vol. 26, No. 2, pp. 237–252.

Kaplan, Edward H. 1986, "Tenant assignment models," *Operations Research*, Vol. 34, No. 6, pp. 832–843.

Karmarkar, Uday S. 1987a, "Lot sizes, lead times, and in-process inventories," *Management Science*, Vol. 33, No. 2, pp. 409–418.

Karmarkar, Uday S. 1987b, "Lot-sizing and sequencing delays," *Management Science*, Vol. 33, No. 3, pp. 419–423.

Karmarkar, Uday S. 1989, private communication.

Karmarkar, Uday S.; Kekre, Sham; and Kekre, Sunder 1985, "Lot-sizing in multi-item multi-machine job shops," *AIIE Transactions*, Vol. 17, No. 3, pp. 290–298.

Karmarkar, Uday S.; Kekre, Sham; and Kekre, Sunder 1987, "Capacity analysis of a manufacturing cell," *Journal of Manufacturing Systems*, Vol. 6, No. 3, pp. 165–175.

Karmarkar, Uday S.; Kekre, Sham; Kekre, Sunder; and Freeman, Susan 1985, "Lot-sizing and lead-time performance in a manufacturing cell," *Interfaces*, Vol. 15, No. 2, pp. 1–9.

Kiessler, Peter C. and Disney, Ralph L. 1988, "Further remarks on queueing network theory," *European Journal of Operational Research*, Vol. 36, No. 3, pp. 285–296.

Kleinrock, Leonard 1975, *Queueing Systems, Volume 1: Theory*, John Wiley & Sons, New York.

Kleinrock, Leonard 1976, *Queueing Systems, Volume 2: Computer Applications*, John Wiley & Sons, New York.

Kobayashi, Hishashi 1983, "Queueing models," in *Probability Theory and Computer Science*, ed. G. Louchard and G. Latouche, Academic Press, New York, pp. 53–121.

Kolesar, Peter 1979, "A quick and dirty response to the quick and dirty crowd, particularly to Jack Byrd's 'The value of queueing theory'," *Interfaces*, Vol. 9, No. 2, Part 1, pp. 77–82.

Kolesar, Peter J. 1984, "Stalking the endangered CAT: A queueing analysis of congestion at automatic teller machines," *Interfaces*, Vol. 14, No. 6, pp. 16–26.

Kolesar, Peter J. and Swersey, Arthur J. 1986, "The deployment of urban emergency units: A survey," in *Delivery of Urban Systems, TIMS Studies in the Management Sciences, Vol. 22*, ed. A. J. Swersey and E. J. Ignall, North-Holland, New York, pp. 87–119.

Krajewski, Lee J.; King, Barry E.; Ritzman, Larry P.; and Wong, Danny S. 1987, "Kanban, MRP, and shaping the manufacturing environment," *Management Science*, Vol. 33, No. 1, pp. 39–57.

Krell, Bruce E. and Arminio, Maria 1982, "Queueing theory applied to data processing networks," *Interfaces*, Vol. 12, No. 4, pp. 21–33.

Kwak, N. K. K.; Kuzdrall, P. J.; and Schmitz, Homer H. 1976, "The GPSS simulation of scheduling policies for surgical patients," *Interfaces*, Vol. 22, No. 9, pp. 982–989.

Lambo, Eyitayo 1983, "An optimization-simulation model of a rural health center in Nigeria," *Interfaces*, Vol. 13, No. 3, pp. 29–35.

Larson, Richard C. 1972, "Improving the effectiveness of the New York City's 911," in *Analysis of Public Systems*, ed. A. W. Drake, R. L. Keeney, and P. M. Morse, MIT Press, Cambridge, Massachusetts, pp. 151–180.

Larson, Richard C. 1987, "Perspectives on queues: Social justice and the psychology of queueing," *Operations Research*, Vol. 35, No. 6, pp. 895–905.

Larson, Richard C. 1988, "Operations research and the service industries," in *Managing Innovation*, ed. B. R. Guile and J. B. Quinn, National Academy Press, Washington, D.C., pp. 115–143.

Larson, Richard C. and Odoni, Amedeo R. 1981, *Urban Operations Research*, Prentice-Hall, Englewood Cliffs, New Jersey.

Law, Averill M. and Kelton, W. David 1982, *Simulation Modeling and Analysis*, McGraw-Hill, New York.

Lee, T. S. and Adam, Everett E., Jr. 1986, "Forecasting error evaluation in material requirements planning (MRP) production-inventory systems," *Management Science*, Vol. 32, No. 9, pp. 1186–1205.

Lewis, P. A. W. and Orav, E. J. 1989, *Simulation Methodology for Statisticians, Operations Analysts, and Engineers*, Volume 1, Wadsworth and Brooks, Pacific Grove, California.

Macon, Max R. and Turban, Efraim 1981, "Energy audit program simulation," *Interfaces*, Vol. 11, No. 1, pp. 13–19.

Malcolm, D. G. 1960, "Bibliography on the use of simulation in management analysis," *Operations Research*, Vol. 8, No. 2, pp. 169–177.

McKeown, Patrick G. 1979, "An application of queueing analysis to the New York State child abuse and maltreatment register telephone reporting system," *Interfaces*, Vol. 9, No. 3, pp. 20–25.

Monarchi, David E.; Hendrick, Thomas E., and Plane, Donald R. 1977, "Simulation for fire department deployment policy analysis," *Decision Sciences*, Vol. 8, No. 1, pp. 211–227.

Morgan, Bryan J. T. 1984, *Elements of Simulation*, Chapman and Hall, London, England.

Newell, Gordon F. 1982, *Applications of Queueing Theory*, second edition, Chapman and Hall, London, England.

Randhawa, Sabah U; Mechling, Ann M.; and Joerger, Robert A. 1989, "A simulation-based resource-planning system for the Oregon Motor Vehicles Division," *Interfaces*, Vol. 19, No. 6, pp. 40–51.

Ravindran, A. 1989, private communication.

Ravindran, A.; Foote, B. L.; Badiru, A. B.; Leemis, L. M.; and Williams, Larry 1989, "An application of simulation and network analysis to capacity planning and material handling systems at Tinker Air Force Base," *Interfaces*, Vol. 19, No. 1, pp. 102–115.

Riccio, Lucius J. and Litke, Ann 1986, "Making a clean sweep: Simulating the effects of illegally parked cars on New York City's mechanical street-cleaning efforts," *Operations Research*, Vol. 34, No. 5, pp. 661–666.

Ripley, Brian D. 1987, *Stochastic Simulation*, John Wiley & Sons, New York.

Ritzman, Larry P.; King, Barry E.; and Krajewski, Lee J. 1984, "Manufacturing performance—Pulling the right levers," *Harvard Business Review*, Vol. 62, No. 2, pp. 143–152.

Ross, Sheldon M. 1989, *Introduction to Probability Models*, fourth edition, Academic Press, New York.

Ross, Sheldon M. 1990, *A Course in Simulation*, Macmillan, New York.

Rubinstein, Reuven Y. 1981, *Simulation and the Monte Carlo Method*, John Wiley & Sons, New York.

Rubinstein, Reuven Y. 1986, *Monte Carlo Optimization, Simulation, and Sensitivity of Queueing Networks*, John Wiley & Sons, New York.

Russell, Robert A. and Hickle, Regina 1986, "Simulation of a CD portfolio," *Interfaces*, Vol. 16, No. 3, pp. 49–54.

Ruth, R. Jean; Wyszewianski, Leon; and Herline, Gary 1985, "Kidney transplantation: A simulation model for examining demand and supply," *Management Science*, Vol. 31, No. 5, pp. 515–526.

Saaty, Thomas L. 1961, *Elements of Queueing Theory with Applications*, Dover Publications, New York.

Saaty, Thomas L. 1966, "Seven more years of queueing theory: A lament and a bibliography," *Naval Research Logistics Quarterly*, Vol. 13, no. 4, pp. 447–476.

Smith, V. Kerry; Webster, David B.; and Heck, Norman A. 1976, "The management of wilderness areas: A simulation model," *Decision Sciences*, Vol. 7, No. 3, pp. 524–537.

Snead, Charles S. 1989, *Group Technology: Foundation for Competitive Manufacturing*, Van Nostrand Reinhold, New York.

Solomon, Susan L. 1983, *Simulation of Waiting-Line Systems*, Prentice-Hall, Englewood Cliffs, New Jersey.

Srikar, B. N. and Vinod, B. 1989, "Performance analysis and capacity planning of a landing gear shop," *Interfaces*, Vol. 19, No. 4, pp. 52–60.

Swart, William and Donno, Luca 1981, "Simulation modeling improves operations, planning, and productivity of fast food restaurants," *Interfaces*, Vol. 11, No. 6, pp. 35–47.

Taha, Hamdy A. 1981, "Queueing theory in practice," *Interfaces*, Vol. 11, No. 1, pp. 43–49.

Taylor, Randolph J. and Evans, Walter F. 1982, "Showing that the low-cost route to more data processing capacity will work," *Interfaces*, Vol. 12, No. 4, pp. 1–10.

Teghem, J., Jr. 1986, "Control of the service process in a queueing system," *European Journal of Operational Research*, Vol. 23, No. 2, pp. 141–158.

Trivedi, Kishor S. 1982, *Probability and Statistics with Reliability, Queueing, and Computer Science Applications*, Prentice-Hall, Englewood Cliffs, New Jersey.

Ulam, Stanislaw M. 1976, *Adventures of a Mathematician*, Charles Scribner's Sons, New York.

Vogel, Myles A. 1979, "Queueing theory applied to machine manning," *Interfaces*, Vol. 9, No. 4, pp. 1–7.

Weiss, Elliott and McClain, John O. 1987, "Administrative days in acute care facilities: A queueing-analytic approach," *Operations Research*, Vol. 35, No. 1, pp. 35–44.

Welch, Norma and Gussow, James 1986, "Expansion of Canadian National Railway's line capacity," *Interfaces*, Vol. 16, No. 1, pp. 51–64.

Whittle, Peter C. 1986, *Systems in Stochastic Equilibrium*, John Wiley & Sons, New York.

Wolff, Ronald W. 1989, *Stochastic Modeling and the Theory of Queues*, Prentice-Hall, Englewood Cliffs, New Jersey.

Zipkin, Paul H. 1986, "Models for design and control of stochastic, multi-item batch production systems," *Operations Research*, Vol. 34, No. 1, pp. 91–104.

Lot-Sizing and Lead-time Performance in a Manufacturing Cell

Uday S. Karmarkar

Sham Kekre

Sunder Kekre

Susan Freeman

Complex, multi-item job shops invariably have high levels of work-in-process and long manufacturing lead times because of the queueing delays at work centers. These problems are well recorded (for example, Burbidge [1975]). Estimates suggest that typically only 10 to 15 percent of shop time for a job is spent in actual processing. However, the causes underlying this phenomenon have not been well understood until recently. In particular, Karmarkar [1983a, 1983b] shows that for closed job shops lot-sizing policy is a major determinant of the extent of queueing delays. Yet, most such job shops fail to take this important consequence into account in establishing lot sizes.

We describe two independent attempts to analyze these phenomena: a simulation model developed by Eastman Kodak's Apparatus Division that examined the behavior of a particular manufacturing cell as the lot-size policy for the cell was changed; and an analytical model [Karmarkar 1983; Karmarkar et al. 1983, 1984]. These two approaches afforded on one hand an interesting opportunity to use the analytical model to confirm the empirically observed results from the simulation and to reveal the underlying mechanisms involved. On the other, the simulation provided the means to validate the general model (Q-LOTS) with a specific instance.

SIMULATION OF A MANUFACTURING CELL

The manufacturing cell in question was organized to improve the production of a group of similar parts that had proved to be troublesome because of long production lead times, high in-process inventories, and difficulties in coordinating assemblies. The 13 parts were grouped on the basis of similar process characteristics, and a production cell, separated from the functionally organized shop, was created to produce them. The cell contains 10 major processing work centers with three other minor preparation and finishing operations. Because three of the major centers have more than one machine, there are, altogether, 15 machines in the cell. The work centers include a manual lathe, an NC lathe, and routine operations (drill, punch), as well as certain proprietary metal forming processes which are quite complex. Part flow through the cell is not uniform and varies across parts with some recirculation or multiple visits for certain parts.

The simulation model was motivated by a need to predict and understand the operating characteristics of the cell. One major task was to devise appropriate lot-sizing policies for the cell; for example, to investigate whether the number of setups should be reduced on bottleneck machines. As it turned out, the reverse was, in a sense, the better policy.

The simulation was written in GPSS, which suited the discrete-event nature of the problem. Once the capacities at work centers are fixed, the simulation is driven by the annual demand for each part and the lot sizes chosen. Lots are released at uniform intervals to the cell, and data are collected about queueing times, total lead time, the number of setups made, and work-in-process inventory. While a detailed scientific validation of the simulation against the cell has not been done for various pragmatic reasons, over a year of experience with the cell and the simulation through a variety of parametric changes has convinced its users that the simulation is an accurate representation of cell behavior for the purposes at hand.

RESULTS FROM THE SIMULATION

The simulation was used to study capacity and design problems as well as lot sizing. Initially the characteristics of the

cell were studied under the lot-sizing policies obtained from conventional EOQ models used by an existing production control system. Then the lot sizes were perturbed to examine the consequences. As a first arbitrary attempt, all lot sizes were cut in half. Surprisingly, this did not result in the catastrophic consequences that EOQ models would have foretold. Instead, lead time and work-in-process (WIP) both showed reductions while productivity did not drop. Further across-the-board cuts worked well up to a point, but then lead time and WIP deteriorated abruptly as queues started to appear at various points in the system.

Without recounting all the details, the set of possible lot sizes (a 13-dimensional vector) was searched, guided chiefly by intuition and trial and error. A significant difficulty in this process was caused by the way in which queues would shift to different machines as lot-size patterns were altered. Roughly speaking, the search rules were

(1) Start with fairly large lot sizes,
(2) Reduce all lot sizes until a queue appears,
(3) Increase lot sizes on those parts which have a high setup time on the machine with a queue,
(4) Keep reducing lot sizes on other parts until a queue appears elsewhere, and so on.

Experimentation over several weeks led to substantial improvements, reducing lead times and work-in-process by a factor of over 50 percent compared to the initial results.

THE ANALYTICAL APPROACH

The extant literature on lot-sizing methods by and large does not address the issues of manufacturing lead times and work-in-process. Yet many practitioners and firms have intuitively understood that increasing lot sizes increases production times. Indeed, this is easily demonstrated in the context of a deterministic model [Karmarkar 1983a, 1983b]. Interestingly, this phenomenon is referred to by Magee [1956] in a description of a product cycling problem and by Sugimori et al. [1977] in their discussion of the Toyota Kanban system. It is also mentioned by Sasser et al. [1982] in the Granger Transmission case study. What seems to be less well understood is the countervailing phenomenon that small lot sizes exacerbate the queueing and sequencing delays that occur in complex shops by increasing the load on work centers. While this phenomenon is caused by the higher number of setups, the usual device of using setup costs is an ineffectual and incorrect representation of actual behavior. This is because setup costs are based on a view of capacity as a binding constraint, whereas in job shops, queues effectively discourage high-loading (utilization) levels long before nominal capacity is reached. In essence, the cost of excessively small lot sizes is due to the long lead times and high levels of work-in-process caused by queues.

There have been many studies which model manufacturing facilities as queueing systems [Buzacott 1974, 1980; Koenigsberg and Mamer 1982; Shanthikumar and Buzacott 1981; Solberg 1977; Stecke and Solberg 1981; and Suri 1983]. However, most have not included the effect of lot-sizing policies. One exception is the paper by Zipkin [1983]. Although oriented towards somewhat different concerns, Zipkin has independently developed an approach that is mathematically similar to ours. A paper by Seidmann and Schweitzer [1983] also considers the effect of

batch sizes for the special case of flexible manufacturing systems.

The impact of batch size on lead times can be intuitively understood as follows. Consider a machine or resource at which batches queue up, waiting to be processed. For simplicity, the batches are taken to be alike. Each batch requires a setup plus some processing time which, unlike the setup, depends on batch size. If the rate of arrival of work is held constant and batch size is increased, the time that a batch spends on the machine increases linearly; hence the total work that arrives at the queue while a batch is being processed is greater even though the *number* of batches in queue may not change very much. Thus an arriving batch sees more work waiting ahead of it and also requires more time for its own processing. Since the effect of the fixed setups is diminishing, average queueing time and total time in system eventually increase linearly as batch sizes are increased.

Now consider the impact of reducing batch size. Work arrives at the machine at the same rate but because it does so in smaller batches, the amount of time spent on setups increases. Thus, although the real or productive utilization of the machine remains unchanged, the total work load (intensity) increases. At some point this leads to the buildup of large queues which cause queue times to rise sharply even though processing time per batch continues to drop. Clearly, there is a lower limit on batch sizes at the point where the total processing time plus setup time exceeds the time available on the machine.

In the case where the machine is modeled heuristically as an M/M/1 queue processing identical items, it can be shown (appendix) that the average time T spent in the system by a batch is given by

$$T = \frac{(\tau + Q/P)}{1 - (D/P) - (D\tau/Q)} \quad (1)$$

where D = Total work to be done (units/time)

P = Processing rate at the machine (unit/time)

Q = Batch size

τ = Setup time per batch.

The batch size Q cannot be smaller than $D\tau/(1-D/P)$. For large Q, approximately $T = Q/(P-D)$ where $1/(P-D)$ is the average number of batches in the system. Figure 1 shows a graph of (T) average waiting times versus Q.

This queueing model was extended to the multi-item case [Karmarkar 1983a; Karmarkar et al. 1983] by modeling the facility as an M/G/1 queue where an exact expression is available for the average time in queue. Next, the case of manufacturing systems with many work centers with several machines at each center was modeled as an open network of M/G/c queues [Karmarkar et al. 1984]. The treatment of this case is necessarily heuristic since no exact analysis exists. At each stage

the queueing model was imbedded in an optimization model that determined the best lot sizes for a given objective function. The most general case, which requires the solution of a nonlinear program, has subsequently been coded as a computer program called Q-LOTS. For convenience, we use this term for our analytical approach.

COMPARISON AND VALIDATION

In comparing the two approaches, it is important to remember that

(1) The assumptions underlying the analytical model are quite different from those underlying the simulation mechanism. In particular, the former assumes randomness in arrivals, while the simulation uses a uniform rate of release of work to the cell.

(2) The real cell is a different matter again—the stochastic queueing model may be a better representation of actual behavior since the arrival of batches to the cell is *not* uniform.

The first comparison was qualitative. The behavior observed empirically was explained by the queueing mechanism. In turn, by scaling the lot sizes in the simulation by a constant factor, the characteristics exhibited in Figure 1 were corroborated. Next, Q-LOTS was used to try to determine the best lot sizes for the cell independent of the results from the simulation. Since the objective in the simulation study had been the minimization of average lead times, this was also used as the objective for Q-LOTS. More precisely, the objective function used was the demand weighted lead time for all the parts processed by the cell. Since the work-in-process for a system is given by production rate × lead time, this was also equiva-

Figure 1. Average waiting times (T) as a function of lot size (Q).

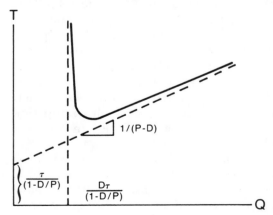

Table 1. Comparison of average lead time (days) and lot sizes (units) by part number as given by Q-LOTS and the best search results. The foot of the table gives the demand weighted average lead times.

Part Number	Q-LOTS Lot Size	Part Lead Time (days)	Best Search Lot Sizes	Lead Times (days)
1	168	9.35	270	13.41
2	112	11.01	168	15.31
3	84	8.50	50	9.63
4	158	4.71	94	4.57
5	179	3.98	90	3.70
6	371	8.35	213	8.86
7	152	3.02	187	2.74
8	128	3.64	170	4.46
9	109	13.73	168	19.52
10	102	11.33	168	15.68
11	109	13.11	168	18.59
12	111	1.90	156	2.46
13	203	8.39	144	8.16
Demand Weighted Lead Time	——	7.26	——	9.08

lent to minimizing the average number of items in process.

When the lot sizes produced by Q-LOTS are compared with the best lot sizes obtained by trial-and-error search on the simulation, the differences are substantial (Table 1). For example, Q-LOTS picks a lot size for part 5 that is twice the search value; the Q-LOTS choices for items 9,

Table 2. Cross-validation results: weighted average lead times (days) predicted by Q-LOTS and the simulation for both sets of lot sizes.

	Lot Sizes From Q-LOTS	Lot Sizes From Simulation
Evaluation on Q-LOTS	8.57	10.66
Evaluation on Simulation	7.26	9.08

10, and 11 are much smaller. Overall, Q-LOTS does better by almost 20 percent than the best search, largely because of its better performance on item 1 (a high volume item) and items 8-12.

In addition to running the Q-LOTS output on the simulation, we also tried to evaluate the search-lot sizes using the analytical model (Table 2). While the predictions of Q-LOTS and the simulation do not match exactly, they are very close with Q-LOTS showing a 20 percent advantage in both evaluations.

The results suggest that Q-LOTS found a slightly better solution than the search. However, it was possible that a better solution could exist (in the sense of performing better on the simulation). To thoroughly search the neighborhood of the Q-LOTS solution on the simulation would have been too time consuming; we tried a simpler alternative. We scaled the lot-size vector Q^* produced by Q-LOTS by a factor α ranging from 0.6 to 2.0 and entered the scaled lot sizes into the simulation and into Q-LOTS. The weighted average lead times for the cell for each of these vectors are given in Table 3. They represent the behavior of the simulation and the analytical model on a ray passing through Q^*. The table also shows predicted work-in-process on a cost basis

Table 3. Comparison of average lead time (days) and WIP($) predicted by Q-LOTS and simulation as the lot-size vector is scaled by a factor α.

Scale Factor a	Average Lead Time (days)		WIP ($)	
	Q-LOTS	Simulation	Q-LOTS	Simulation
0.60	49.56	17.05	391,210	168,140
0.80	9.32	7.90	75,290	65,810
1.00	8.57	7.26	68,840	60,400
1.25	9.06	8.24	72,750	68,860
1.50	9.91	9.16	79,680	76,320
1.75	10.89	10.30	87,650	85,440
2.00	11.95	11.47	96,170	95,910

Figure 2. Comparison of average lead time (days) predicted by Q-LOTS and simulation as optimal lot sizes are scaled.

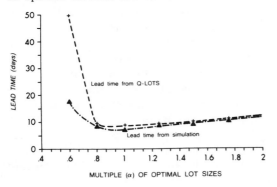

which is slightly different from the unit basis mentioned earlier because of differences in costs across parts. The two measures for the two approaches are graphed in Figures 2 and 3.

The following observations were made from the parametric analysis:

— Q-LOTS corresponds fairly well with the simulation results at large lot sizes and more poorly at smaller lot sizes. However, the simulation becomes unstable in the congestion region. For example, a subsequent simulation run at α

Figure 3. Comparison of WIP($) predicted by Q-LOTS and simulation as optimal lot sizes are scaled.

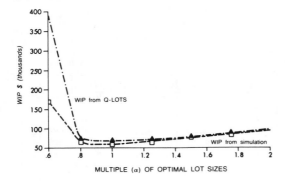

= 0.9 produced an average lead time of 10.29 days and a WIP level of $84,210. Thus the behavior predicted by Q-LOTS at low α is not necessarily an overestimate.

— Q-LOTS appears to find the minimum quite well and generally indicates the qualitative behavior of the objective correctly.

APPLICATION OF THE METHODS

These methods can be applied in closed job shops which are multipart, multimachine manufacturing systems with repetitive batch production either to inventory or for assembly. The methods have potential uses at several levels.

At the scheduling level, the models can be used to devise optimal lot-size policies and to predict the performance of a facility for a given policy. Operationally, these policies can be used to fix lot sizes for batches when fixed batch sizes are desirable. Some limited tests at the detailed scheduling level suggest that even an order-launch approach with these lot sizes is quite successful. An equally important use of the models is to predict the lead times required to produce an order; this can be done using the expected queueing time for a batch given its route through the shop. Knowing these lead times permits the correct release of batches to the shop.

The implementation of such an approach would simply employ the lot sizes and lead times as inputs to a standard MRP system. The lot sizes should not be fixed; rather a range of say 0.8 to 1.5 times the lot size could be used as min-max limits. The advantage of this approach is that it is a top-down approach that requires very little administrative change or modification to existing systems. In addition, a shop-floor control system is not essential. It should be remembered that the models look at average characteristics of the shop and that these will change with the overall production mix. Thus, in principle, a detailed shop-floor system will improve performance; however, we conjecture that this improvement is not great especially relative to the cost of detailed control. Again limited experiments suggest that it is no greater than 10 percent. A theoretical estimate is given by Kekre [1984].

The models can also be used in capacity and design decisions since they are essentially evaluation tools which predict performance. The parameters that might be considered are

— The number and size of machines at work centers,
— Overtime and shift policies,
— Routing of items (if alternatives are available),
— The choice of parts to be made in the cell or facility, and
— The operations or work centers that should be included in the cell.

In fact, the simulation has been used for many of these purposes for this cell. The analytical model has not, but in another paper [Karmarkar et al. 1984] we describe an application of Q-LOTS to capacity analysis in a different manufacturing system.

SUMMARY

We have described a joint project between groups in industry and academia motivated by a common interest in the solution of certain manufacturing problems, although possibly with a differing sense of urgency. Our study provides strong support for the importance of lot-sizing techniques in shop performance and focuses attention on performance issues (lead time, WIP) that have been inadequately treated in the technical literature. Both parties have benefited; the analytical developments provide an understanding of the reasons for the observed phenomena as well as a fast numerical technique for analyzing such systems; the simulation provides validating evidence for the correctness of a complex model.

ACKNOWLEDGMENTS

We appreciate the encouragement provided by John Barnes, Manager of Planning at the US Apparatus Division of Eastman Kodak Company and the support of Ed Sylvestre, Supervisor of the Analytical Services Division of Eastman Kodak, who created the initial opportunity for this collaboration. Support for development of Q-LOTS was provided by the Karres Group and by Case Hunter Inc.

APPENDIX

Using the notation in the text, an expression for the average waiting time in the system is developed assuming that M/M/1 model applied for this model,

λ = arrival rate = D/Q,
$\bar{x}$ = $\frac{1}{\mu}$ = average processing time = $\tau + (Q/P)$,
u = (D/P),
ρ = $\lambda \bar{x}$ = $(D/Q)(\tau + Q/P)$ = $(D\tau/Q) + (D/P)$,
T = the mean time in system.

The results for the M/M/1 model give

$$T = \frac{1}{\mu(1 - \rho)} = \frac{\tau + (Q/P)}{1 - (D\tau/Q) - (D/P)} \quad .$$

The stability condition $\rho < 1$ implies $(D\tau/Q) + (D/P) < 1$ which on rearrangement gives $Q > D\tau/(1 - (D/P))$, a lower bound on the lot size. A lower bound for T is given by

$$T \geqslant \frac{\tau}{(1 - u)} + \frac{Q}{P(1 - u)}$$

which is linear in Q, and is approached asymptotically as Q becomes large.

REFERENCES

Burbidge, J. L. 1975, *The Introduction of Group Technology*, John Wiley and Sons, New York.

Buzacott, J. A. 1974, "On the optimal control of input to a job shop," Working paper #74004, Department of Industrial Engineering, University of Toronto, Toronto, Ontario.

Buzacott, J. A. and Shanthikumar, J. G. 1980, "Models for understanding flexible manufacturing systems," *AIIE Transactions*, Vol. 12, No. 4, pp. 339-350.

Karmarkar, U. S. 1983a, "Lot sizes, manufacturing lead times and utilization," Graduate School of Management, Working Paper No. QM8312, University of Rochester, Rochester, New York.

Karmarkar, U. S. 1983b, "Lot sizing and sequencing delays," Graduate School of Management, Working Paper No. QM8314, University of Rochester, Rochester, New York.

Karmarkar, U. S.; Kekre, S.; and Kekre, S. 1983, "Multi-item lot sizing and manufacturing lead-times," Graduate School of Management, Working Paper No. QM8325, University of Rochester, Rochester, New York.

Karmarkar, U. S.; Kekre, S.; and Kekre, S. 1984, "Lot sizing in multi-item, multi-machine job shops," Graduate School of Management, Working Paper No. QM8402, University of Rochester, Rochester, New York.

Kekre, Sunder 1984, "The effect of the number of items on manufacturing lead time," Graduate School of Management, Working Paper No. QM8418, University of Rochester, Rochester, New York.

Koenigsberg, E. and Mamer, J. 1982, "The analysis of production systems," *International Journal of Production Research*, Vol. 20, No. 1, pp. 1-16.

Magee, J. F. 1956, "Guides to inventory policy, part II. Problems of uncertainty," *Harvard Business Review*, Vol. 34, No. 2 (March-April), pp. 103-116.

Sasser, W. E.; Clark, K.; Garvin, D.; Graham, M.; Jaikumar, R.; and Maister, D. 1982, *Cases in Operations Management*, Richard D. Irwin, Homewood, Illinois.

Seidmann, A. and Schweitzer, P. J. 1983, "Part selection policy for a flexible manufacturing cell feeding several production lines," Graduate School of Management, Working Paper No. QM8217 (October 1982, revised October 1983), University of Rochester, Rochester, New York.

Shanthikumar, J. G. and Buzacott, J. A. 1981, "Open queueing network models of dynamic job shops," *International Journal of Production Research*. Vol. 19, No. 3, pp. 255-266.

Solberg, J. J. 1977, "A mathematical model of computerized manufacturing systems," in *Proceedings of the Fourth International Conference on Production Research*, Tokyo, Japan.

Stecke, K. E. and Solberg, J. J. 1981, "Loading and control policies for a flexible manufacturing system," *International Journal of Production Research*, Vol. 19, No. 5, pp. 481-490.

Sugimori, Y.; Kusunoki, K.; Cho, F.; and Uchikawa, S. 1977, "Toyota production system and kanban system: Materialization of just-in-time and respect-for-human system," *International Journal of Production Research*, Vol. 15, No. 6, pp. 553-564.

Suri, R. 1983, "Robustness of queueing network formulae," *Journal of the Association for Computing Machinery*, Vol. 30, No. 3, pp. 564-594.

Zipkin, P. H. 1983, "Models for design and control of stochastic, multi-item batch production systems," Columbia Business School, Research Working Paper No. 496A, Columbia University, New York.

A letter from John C. Barnes, Manager, Planning, US Apparatus Division, Eastman Kodak Company, states: "We are now planning to establish lot sizes using the analytical model instead of the traditional EOQ approach. The confidence gained has allowed us to commit the manufacturing operation to accomplish a very substantial reduction in planned lead time and, therefore, inventory level. We anticipate . . . that our ability to fulfill schedule requirements will improve markedly as a result."

An Application of Simulation and Network Analysis to Capacity Planning and Material Handling Systems at Tinker Air Force Base

A. Ravindran

B. L. Foote

A. B. Badiru

L. M. Leemis

Larry Williams

Tinker Air Force Base (TAFB), located in Oklahoma City, Oklahoma, is one of the five overhaul bases in the Air Force Logistics Command. It overhauls and repairs six types of jet engines and various aircraft and engine accessories, and it manages selected Air Force assets worldwide. This engine overhaul facility is responsible for logistical support for a series of Air Force engines. Engines are returned from service activities for periodic overhaul or to complete a modification or upgrade. The engine is disassembled, and each part is inspected for wear and possible repair. Individual parts are repaired or modified to a like-new condition or are condemned and replaced with a new part. The majority of the parts are overhauled and returned to service for a fraction of the cost of a new part. A major overhaul may cost less than five percent of the cost of a new engine in terms of labor, material, and replaced parts. Between November 11 and 14, 1984, a fire devastated Building 3001, which contained the Propulsion (Engine)

Division in the Directorate of Maintenance. The division consists of over 2,800 employees and produces over 10 millon component parts and over four million earned hours to support Department of Defense overhaul requirements each year. In February 1985, the Air Force published a statement of work requesting assistance from industry to model and develop a simulation of the engine overhaul process to assist in the redesign and layout of approximately 900,000 square feet of production floor space. Three commercial firms attended an onsite prebid conference to learn the scope of the project, the nature of the data the Air Force could provide, and the time frame in which a finished product had to be delivered. The model was expected to predict the number and type of machines, the personnel, the queueing space required, the material-handling distribution, and the volume between and within organizations. The facility engineers needed various management reports to help them to lay out the plant. The project was to be completed within 120 days. Of the three firms, one elected not to respond, the second bid $225,000 with the first report in nine months, and the third quoted $165,000 to study the problem with an expected project cost of over $300,000. Each was a highly reputable organization with considerable expertise and success in the field. Since TAFB had budgeted only $80,000 and time was running out, TAFB contacted the University of Oklahoma. It had not been considered earlier because of conflicts with class schedules. As the month of May approached, the university became a potential vendor. A contract was let on May 1, 1985, and the first product was delivered by June 15, 1985.

PROJECT SCOPE

The scope of the project was to take advantage of the disaster and forge a state-of-the-art facility for overhauling engines with the most efficient and cost-effective organizational structure and physical layout. The relocation team was charged with developing and implementing a total change in the philosophy of engine overhaul that would maximize flexibility while minimizing facility and plant equipment costs. Of equal importance was the task of developing a means to predict and forecast varying resource requirements as work load mixes changed.

The eight-member relocation team comprised midlevel managers from engineering and production with detailed knowledge of the inner working of the facility plus four faculty members and four graduate students from the University of Oklahoma School of Industrial Engineering. The Corps of Engineers was to construct the building based on specifications

provided by the internal engineering department. Mechanical and industrial engineers designed shop layouts. The university provided the skill and knowledge to develop a capacity-planning and material-handling simulation model using data provided by TAFB. The university team simulated repair activities to a level of detail never attempted or realized before. Its responsibility was to analyze the data available from TAFB and determine what, if any, additional specific data elements were required, to assist in developing techniques to obtain that data from existing systems, to check the data for outliers, and to develop and implement interface programs to obtain data for the simulation model.

The baseline data base consisted of 117 fields with over 2,500 records used to describe the requirements of the organization by individual type of part being repaired. The university used this raw data to create forecasts and net equipment requirements for each individual modular repair center (MRC) based on variable mixes of work loads and resources. The data base provided the following information:

— A work control document (WCD), a unique identifier for each engine part;

— The annual requirement of each end item (engine or subassembly) of which the part to be repaired is a component (the WCD attached to each part carries this information);

— The sequential routes of the part and resource requirements coded by the industrial process code with labor and machine/process time required at each resource;

— The size and weight of the part so that storage and queue space can be estimated, and

— The number of units per assembly (UPA) required of each part to make up the end item.

Prior to the fire, the division was organized along functional operational lines with each department responsible for a specific process, such as machining, welding, cleaning, or inspection. This organization structure was developed in 1974 when engine overhaul functions were consolidated into one organization. At that time, such functional shop layouts maximized equipment utilization and skill concentrations since a typical long-flow part would require 30 to 50 production operations and change organizations only seven to 10 times. Today, the same part requires over 120 production operations and changes organizations as many as 30 to 50 times. This increase has been caused by incremental introduction of technology and by improved repair procedures that offset wear of critical engine parts and reduce replacement costs. The additional repairs increased routing that overburdened the mechanized conveyor system. Since 1974, the only major change was an experiment three years prior to the fire to consolidate one part-type family, combustion cans, into a partially self-contained work center.

The reconstruction period after the fire gave TAFB a unique opportunity to design a modern production system to replace the one destroyed. TAFB manufacturing system analysts changed the repair process from a process specialization type of operation to a family (group) type of operation. Staff from the University of Oklahoma helped to solve the problems associated with long flow times, lack of clear responsibility for quality problems, and excessive material handling. The plan for reconstruction was based on the concept of a modular repair center (MRC), a concept similar to the group technology cell (GTC) concept except that it is more interrelated with other centers than a GTC.

We created and defined the modular repair center concept as a single organization to inspect and repair a collection of parts with similar geometries and industrial processes so as to provide the most economical assignment of equipment and personnel to facilitate single point organizational responsibility and control. An example of such a center is the blade MRC, which repairs all turbine blades from all engine types. With the exception of initial chemical cleaning, disassembly, plating, paint, and high temperature heat treatment, all industrial equipment and processes were available for assignment to an MRC.

Since TAFB lost an entire overhead conveyor system in the fire, implementing the MRC concept required a new conveyor design in terms of routing, size, and location of up and down elevators. The new system needed a conveyor to move parts to their respective MRCs from the disassembly area and to special areas such as heat treatment, painting, or plating and back to engine reassembly. When an engine arrives for repair, its turbine blades are removed and routed via the overhead conveyor to the blade MRC, out to heat treatment, painting, and plating, back to the blade MRC, and finally returned to be assembled back into an engine. A stacker (mechanized inventory storage system) in each MRC handles excess in-process queues that are too large for the finite buffer storage at each machine. One of the functions of the simulation model was to compute the capacity of the buffers and stacker.

DATA ANALYSIS

Standard sources at TAFB provided the information for analysis. The first source, the work control documents (WCD), gives the operation sequences for all the parts. It tells which MRC a part goes to and the sequence of machines the part will visit within the MRC. There are 2,600 different WCDs, with as few as 11 assigned to combustion cans and as many as 700 assigned to the general shop.

The second data source, the engine repair plan, showed how many engines of each type were expected to be repaired each year. We used the fiscal '85 requirements and a projected annual work load of 2,000 engine equivalents to determine how many units of each family type would enter the system.

The third source of data, the TAFB

standard material handling (MH) coding of each part, was based on the size and weight of each part. Parts move on pallets at TAFB. We used the MH coding to estimate the number of parts per pallet (Table 1). TAFB engineers had decided on the shop configuration and location of the MRCs but had not determined their physical dimensions prior to our analysis. The configuration was based on groupings of jet engine parts with similar geometries, metal types, and repair processes (for example, major cases, rotating components). The MRCs are N-nozzle, S-seal, B-bearing housing, GX-gear box, TR-turbine compressor rotor, K-combustion can, BR-blade, AB-after burner, C-case, CR-compressor rotor, ZH-general handwork, ZM-general machining, ZW-general welding. In addition, general purpose shops handle painting, plating, heat treatment, blasting and cleaning. Since several hundred units of each WCD are processed, the facility handles over one-half million units annually. Each WCD is assigned to one of the MRCs and goes through several processes, comprising 25 to 91 operations each. Each MRC handles from 11 to 700 WCDs and has between 19 and 83 processes assigned to it.

TABLE 1. MH (material handling codes). The top chart gives the code for the six different weight categories while the lower matrix expresses the code for 15 different categories of length and width of the base of the part which rests on the pallet. Each number represents a combination of length (L) and width (W), measured in inches. D9, for instance, means a part that weighs 10-25 pounds and has a base whose length is between 12 and 24 inches and whose width is between 24 and 48 inches.

MATERIAL HANDLING CHARACTERISTICS

To conserve space and energy, parts are stored on pallets; in some cases, two different WCDs are stored on the same pallet. Parts that are large in two dimensions but small in a third are stacked. The number of WCDs on a pallet is a random variable depending on how many parts arrive when. To convert a flow of WCDs to a flow of pallets, we used a simple formula to estimate the total number of pallets that would flow between operations given the

Alphameric Code	Weight of Item (lbs.)
A	0-1
B	1-5
C	5-10
D	10-25
E	25-50
F	> 50

W / L	0-6	6-12	12-24	24-48	>48
0-6	1	2	4	7	11
6-12	2	3	5	8	12
12-24	4	5	6	9	13
24-48	7	8	9	10	14
>48	11	12	13	14	15

TABLE 2. Parts/pallet for MH codes. The matrix expresses the number of parts that can be placed on a pallet given the MH code from Table 1. Two parts per pallet can be carried if the part is coded D9. The small values represent fixed loads based on weight and size while the larger values are averages of actual usage, since a pallet can carry many small parts.

Weight Code / Size Code	A	B	C	D-E	F
1	50	30	20	10	5
2	8	8	8	4	4
3	8	8	8	4	4
4	8	6	5	3	2
5	8	6	5	3	2
6	8	6	5	3	2
7	8	6	5	3	2
8	4	4	4	2	2
9	4	4	4	2	2
10	4	4	4	2	2
11	4	4	4	2	2
12	2	2	2	1	1
13	2	2	2	1	1
14	2	2	2	1	1
15	2	2	2	1	1

number of each part type that would move between those two operations.

To obtain the pallet factor estimate OPF (see appendix), we used the TAFB material handling codes (Tables 1 and 2). If $OPF = 0.2$ and 50 units of all types flow from area i to area j per half hour, then $(.2)(50) = 10$ pallets will move on the average per half hour. Other technical details can be found in Foote et al. [1988].

GENERAL MODEL FOR CONVEYOR DESIGN

To establish a basis for building a minimum-size conveyor system to handle the work load, we constructed a network model of the material-handling system. A minimum conveyor system is one that has the least length with the most flexibility and that meets all production volume requirements without logjams. In the network representation, 56 nodes represent (1) different MRCs and their possible associated loading/unloading points, (2) the assembly areas, (3) the possible transfer points in the conveyor, and (4) general purpose shops. Arcs or links in the network represent the possible different sections of the conveyor linking nodes. The arrows on the arcs show the direction items flow (one way or two way). Using the conveyor system drawings, we calculated the distances between all pairs of nodes to find the linear feet of conveyor. The numbers associated with arcs represent these distances. We used Floyd's Algorithm [Floyd 1962], which is analyzed in Dreyfus [1969], to calculate the shortest distance between all pairs of nodes. The algorithm also determines the shortest path, namely, the optimal sequence of arcs (conveyor sections) to travel in order to minimize the total travel time from any department to any other department. Ravindran et al. [1988] cover the details of the conveyor design, including how the random variation in pallet flow on the conveyor was handled and how conveyor bottlenecks were eliminated. Figure 1 shows the old and new layouts and the associated conveyor systems.

COMPUTER GENERATED DATA

From the processing sequence on the work control document and the numbers of engines that need to be maintained, we calculated the flow from each MRC to other MRCs. We wrote a computer program to scan the processing sequence and

FIGURE 1. Conveyor system pre- and post-fire. The top layout shows Building 3001 as it was functionally laid out before the fire. The bottom figure shows the new layout based on a cellular manufacturing organization and conveyor routes optimized by Floyd's Algorithm.

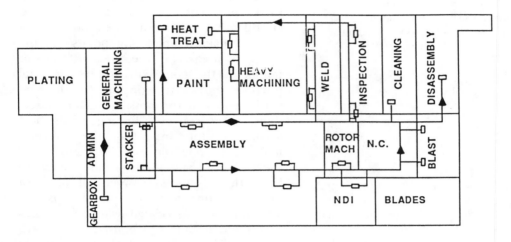

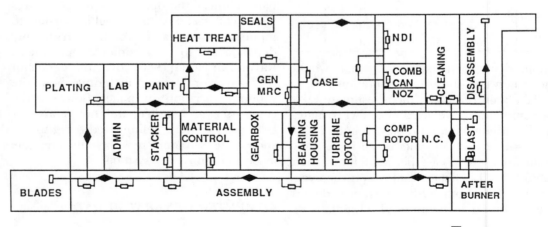

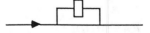

determine when a move out of the MRC would be made. For example, when the process code for heat treatment appeared, the item would move from its MRC to heat treatment and then back to the MRC. The number of items of each type moving was the number of engines times the number of parts of this type per engine. We then summed the movements between each pair of locations over all part types, and converted the movement in terms of parts to pallets moved per half hour.

THE SIMULATION MODEL

We wrote the simulation model, called the Tinker Integrated Planning Simulation (TIPS), using the discrete event orientation in SLAM [Pritsker 1986]; it contains approximately 1,750 lines of FORTRAN code. TIPS is designed to simulate a single MRC at a time. The entities in the model are the WCDs flowing through one particular MRC. Features of the TIPS model include three shifts, transfer to other MRC operations (that is, painting, plating, and heat treatment), and stackers to model WCD storage when machine queue lengths are exceeded. The simulation model is capable of storing 70,000 entities (concurrent WCDs) in an MRC. Despite this, three of the MRCs were so large that they had to be broken into smaller family groups.

Figure 2 illustrates the system concept of the MRC and how material flows inside and to external shops. This allows the stacker to be sized by the simulation; the maximum load will determine the size of the stacker installed.

Tinker Air Force Base supplied the data used to determine the rate of flow of WCDs through each MRC. The data for each MRC came in two sets, the 1985 fis-

cal year data and the data for 2,000 engine equivalents (when the facility would run at full capacity). Both data sets contained a list of the WCDs for the MRC, the operations sequence for each WCD, the corresponding machine process time for each WCD, the corresponding standard labor time for each WCD, the UPA (units per assembly) number for each WCD the data included, and a vector containing the relative frequencies of each WCD. In addition, the projected size of each MRC (for example, number of machines of each type) and information needed to calculate a From-To matrix (for inter- and intra-MRC transfers) was included. We transformed all the data to a format that allowed SLAM to execute the discrete event model.

Two features of the TIPS simulation model make it unique. First, the model was so large that it used the SLAM language at its maximum configuration to run a single MRC. We had to consult with Pritsker and Associates to determine how to extend SLAM's storage limits in the source code. Second, the model integrated both physical (machines) and skill (labor) resources in a single model that supported a bottle-neck analysis, space analysis, and overhead-conveyor-routing analysis. We designed the model for managers and held two training sessions at Tinker AFB to allow managers to use TIPS for decision making.

A final feature of the system is its generality. Originally, 13 MRCs were to be modeled. This expanded to 17. We had three months to develop the model and had to meet the due date. We developed the program using a special format that allowed the model to be restructured for any MRC. Thus, the type of machines, their number, and their operations in an MRC were standard input. The process

FIGURE 2. Sample five-machine MRC configuration. The part shown here has a 1-4-3-painting-5 machine sequence. The inprocess queue area at the machine is limited. When this is full, the overflow goes to the infinite capacity stacker. The simulation computed the maximum stacker storage requirement needed. A route out after machine number three to painting and return after an eight-hour material handling delay is shown. The cross hatching on the machines in the diagram indicates the shifts when they are available. For example, there are six machines of type number one available during the day shift, and only four available during the second shift. If a WCD is on a machine when the shift change occurs, it is assumed that the machine completes processing the WCD prior to the changeover.

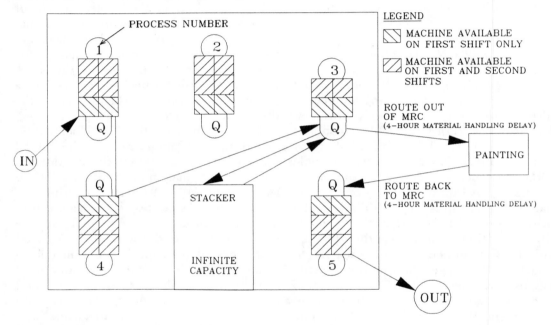

plan for each WCD was an input data set. With this structure, any MRC could be simulated. Some features of the model required special considerations as we constructed the model of the proposed shop configuration:

— Downtime: Machine breakdown affects the flow time and throughput for an MRC. We assumed that after each machine processes a part, a breakdown occurs with probability that depends on the machine. This assumption is based on the

fact that uncompleted work can be finished on other machines and breakdowns are rare. This simplified the code, which helped meet the deadline. The time to repair a machine is exponentially distributed. We based the distributions and parameters used in the simulation on estimates by TAFB personnel.

— Interarrival and service time distribution: Since no data were available on the interarrival distribution of engine inputs, we used a deterministic interarrival time based on the annual volume of that particular WCD. This was reasonable in that repairs of engines are scheduled uniformly over the year. The service time was a truncated normal random variable with the range set at $\mu \pm .05\mu$.

— Labor utilization: The modeling of a WCD being processed on a machine had to incorporate the fact that both a machine and an operator are required to service the part. In addition, sick leave, training leave, and vacations for machine operators are modeled.

CALCULATING THE NUMBER OF MACHINES NEEDED

A prime use of the simulation was to determine the number of machines of a particular type needed in each MRC. The stated objective was to have 95 percent availability for each machine type; that is, 95 percent of the time a machine will be available at a machine center when a component arrives. To determine the smallest number of machines needed to provide 95 percent availability, we first ran the simulation assuming ample machine capacity so that there was no queueing at the machine center. We then used the utilization statistics for the case of ample capacity to determine the minimum number of machines necessary for 95 percent availability.

We had to design the simulation for three shift operations because in emergencies all three shifts are used, and even on one-shift operations, some equipment, such as painting, plating, and equipment designed at TAFB, runs three shifts because it is not economical to duplicate the equipment. Thus, even though most of the equipment is manned for only one shift, the simulation must be run for three shifts per day. When considering a machine center that would operate for only one (or two) shift(s) per day, we had to rescale the utilization statistics from a three-shift day to reflect the shorter work day before calculating the number of machines needed for 95 percent availability.

PROBLEMS WITH LARGE MRCs

Some MRCs were too large to be handled by the simulation model both in terms of unacceptably long run times and memory requirements. As a result, the large MRCs had to be broken up into smaller family groups. For example, we broke the combustion can shop (MRC K) down into six families. (We could do this because the six families in the K shop shared only such entering processes as inspection, and it was easy to split inputs into six groups.) TIPS can handle approximately 70,000 entities (or WCDs) at one time. The run times varied depending on the size of the MRC. For example, the simulation for the estimated repair work load of 2,000 engines for the gear box MRC took approximately one hour to run on an IBM 3081. The run times on a VAX 11/780 were generally eight times longer than the IBM run times. In one specific case, MRC CC2 (one of the smallest families in MRC K), the simulation took 1.5 minutes to run on IBM and 7.8 minutes on VAX. The CC2 shop contains a maximum of five WCDs and can handle up to 73 different processes. It has an annual work load of about 821 parts. By comparison, the gear box MRC handles about 329 WCD types and up to 72 different processes. Its annual repair volume is over 100,000 parts. We used a warm-up period of 13 weeks (one quarter) for each simulation run, and collected statistics on MRCs starting with the 14th week. Simulation outputs were printed in 13-week time intervals to match regular production runs at TAFB. In the early testing, we compared the outputs from different warmup periods (13 and 26 weeks) using a t-test to determine if we needed an extra warmup quarter. The differences in mean values were insignificant.

VERIFICATION

To determine whether the simulation model was working as intended, we took the following verification steps:

(1) We developed the model incrementally. This made it easier to debug the programs.
(2) We analyzed the outputs of each modular component of the overall model for reasonableness (does the output seem to represent real-world expectations?), consistency (does the output remain about the same for similar inputs?), reasonable run time (does the program run longer than expected for the given MRC?), and output (a 10 percent increase in load should show more than a 10 percent increase in waiting time).

VALIDATION

To validate the model, we made a diagnostic check of how closely the simulation model matches the actual system, taking the following steps:

(1) We cross-checked the model assumptions. For example, is the assumption of normally distributed processing time correct?
(2) We compared statistically analyzed results to actual historical data using a representative MRC simulation, checking both average output and range of output.

OUTPUT

The output from TIPS consisted of two documents: the standard SLAM summary report and a custom printout generated by a FORTRAN subroutine. The custom output presented the SLAM output in a format and at a level of detail suitable for prompt managerial decision making. The statistics in the output included

(1) Machine availability by shift for each process,
(2) Maximum queue length in front of each process,
(3) Average processing time,
(4) Average waiting time for each process,
(5) Number of units for each WCD type entering and leaving the system,
(6) Part flow (in units) entering and leaving the stacker for each process,
(7) Time spent in the stacker waiting for a specific process,
(8) Utilization level for each process per shift, and
(9) Total time in the system for each WCD, including waiting time, handling time, and processing time. Labor time is assumed to overlap with processing time.

We wrote supplementary FORTRAN programs to generate certain input data for the TIPS program. For example, we used a bottleneck program to set the initial number of machines available for each process.

The TIPS program is, in effect, the nucleus of an integrated system of management decision aids (Figure 3).

DESIGN CONSTRAINTS

Because the fire was so destructive and because slowing maintenance operations for a long time would seriously affect the

FIGURE 3. The central role of TIPS in shop management. The simulation model is used at Tinker Air Force Base to perform the functions listed, such as capacity planning, production planning, and analysis of part flow, and to provide data for process design, management control, process capability analysis, and process monitoring to determine if production goals are met, and to meet the needs of engineering in designing new overhaul procedures.

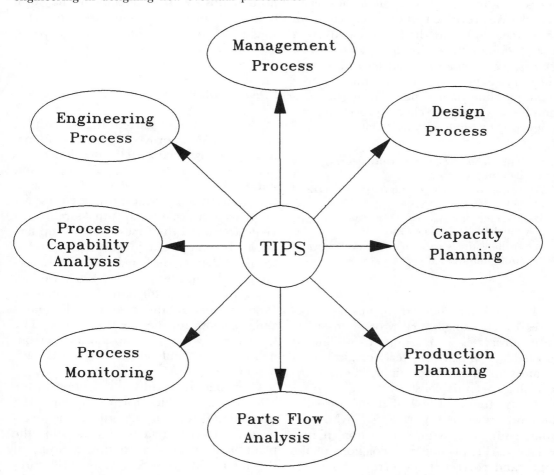

national defense, TAFB set a time limit of three months for designing the analytic computer models. We developed quick approximations of such items as pallet flow so that we could test model validity quickly. The closeness of predicted need to actual need showed that these approximations were acceptable based on the criterion specified by TAFB (plus or minus five percent). The predicted requirements have ranged from 100 to 115 percent of actual need.

INPUT DATA VERIFICATION

The data for the simulation were delivered on magnetic tape and consisted of at least a quarter of a million individual elements. These data were visually scanned on a random basis and anomalies were noted. We reviewed these anomalies in joint meetings. We then developed rules for scanning the entire data set for data errors. These rules formed part of a rudimentary expert system to improve the quality of the data. The following are examples of rules to check processing sequences and time standard data:

(1) The heat treatment can never follow painting,
(2) Labor or machine standard time could never be zero,
(3) Machine time is always greater than or equal to labor time, and
(4) Drilling times can vary between one and four minutes (these ranges were MRC specific).

The program checked for missing processes by checking every process to see if other processes were required to follow or precede it based on technological constraints and then determining if the process plan met this constraint.

Errors found by use of the above rules and others were reported to TAFB personnel for analysis and correction, if necessary. TAFB printed out violations of the rules and corrected the errors. Some errors were transpositions and easily corrected, others necessitated quick time studies or verification of process sequence. Some data rejected by the tests were actually correct. This phase took two months, but it overlapped the design of the simulation and material-handling models. The simulation had to be developed in some detail to calculate the space needed for sequential queues as parts moved from machine to machine and to capture the material-handling sequence and routes as we played what-if games with resources and work-load assignments. We also needed this detail to document and solve bottleneck problems within the flow of a single part or for a combination of parts.

CONCLUSIONS

The Air Force started the project in January 1985, approved the organizational concept in February 1985, developed the industrial process code concept and started data collection for the data base in late January, and created rough-cut capacity plans and organizations in March-April 1985. It wanted the first detailed shop layout to be completed in July 1985, and it required data to meet material and scheduling lead times by June 15, 1985. We had to complete all simulations by September 1985 to finalize the resource allocations and to allow for design lead times. The simulations were used to allocate personnel, machines, and floor space to the various organizations.

Our analysis to aid the transition to the MRC layout included formatting the TIPS simulation program, designing the overhead conveyor system, laying out the plant, and making a routing analysis of the inter-MRC transfers. The TIPS program proved valuable in aiding the transition to the new layout by estimating performance measures (for example, flow-time and queue statistics) that helped determine the number of machines of each type to place in an MRC. In one particular instance, the nozzle MRC, the Production and Engineering Department called for 24 work stations of a particular type. The TIPS analysis indicated that between 11 and 13 work stations were needed. Based on the TIPS results, only 12 work stations were installed and this has proved to be sufficient. At Tinker Air Force Base, simulation proved to be a valuable tool in assessing the effectiveness of the new plans and in determining the right parameters for each new MRC.

The fire at TAFB was a disaster that turned out to be a great opportunity. It would have been very hard to justify dislocating the entire facility for over a year and expending the sum of money required to redesign the facility. In the long run, the benefits of the new system may pay back the cost of the fire with interest.

The University of Oklahoma design team responded to the emergency with accomplishments we are very proud of. We developed and verified a general simulation model in three months, when national consulting firms estimated four times that long. The new system has met design expectations, which is rare. Part flow times have been reduced by 35 to 50 percent depending on size. Labor savings have been $1.8 millon in 1987, $2.1 million in 1988, and continue to rise. $4.3 million was saved in equipment purchases.

Space requirements were reduced by 30,000 square feet. The percent defective has dropped three percent in 1987 and five percent further in 1988. The conveyor system has had no jam-ups due to overloading. Finally, other Air Logistics Centers have adopted the TIPS concept to plan redesign of their facilities and the report [Ravindran et al. 1986] has been distributed for review by over 60 organizations at their request. We have proved that modern management science techniques can be applied quickly and with great impact.

ACKNOWLEDGMENT

We express our appreciation to Margarita Beneke, K. Janikiraman, Wan-Seon Shin, Doug Stewart, and Murali Subramaniam for their assistance in developing and running the TIPS model, to Sandee Boyer for patiently typing several drafts of this paper, and to Hussein Saber for his help with Figure 1. In addition, Stephen Graves, Mary Haight, and two referees have improved the readability of this paper.

APPENDIX

The overall pallet factor is computed by:

$$OPF = \frac{\left\{ \sum_{i=1}^{M} W_i \, P_i \right\}}{\left\{ \sum_{i=1}^{M} W_i \right\}}$$

where

P_i = estimate of pallets/parts given its MH code. For example, if P_1 has code 1A, $P_1 = 1/50 = 0.02$ (see Table 2), $i = 1, 2, \ldots, M$,

W_i = $(N_i)(UPA_i)$, $i = 1, 2, \ldots, M$,

N_i = number of WCDs of type i per year, $i = 1, 2, \ldots, M$,

UPA_i = number of units per WCD_i, $i = 1, 2, \ldots, M$,

OPF = overall pallet factor, and

M = number of WCDs.

REFERENCES

Dreyfus, S. E. 1969, "An appraisal of some shortest-path algorithms," *Operations Research*, Vol. 17, No. 3, pp. 395-412.

Floyd, R. W. 1962, "Algorithm 97: Shortest path," *Communications of the ACM*, Vol. 5, No. 6, p. 345.

Foote, B. L.; Ravindran, A.; Badiru, A. B.,; Leemis, L. M.; and Williams, L. 1988, "Simulation and network analysis in conveyor system design," *Industrial Engineering*, Vol. 20, No. 6, pp. 48-53.

Pritsker, A. Alan B. 1986, *Introduction to Simulation and SLAM II*, third edition, Halsted Press, John Wiley and Sons, New York.

Ravindran, A.; Foote, B. L.; Badiru, A. B.; Leemis, L.; and Williams, L. 1988, "Mechanized material handling system design and routing," *Computers and Industrial Engineering*, Vol. 14, No. 3, pp. 251-270.

Ravindran, A.; Foote, B. L.; Badiru, A. B.,; Leemis, L.; and Williams, L. 1986, "Job shop configuration optimization at Tinker Air Force Base," final technical report, The University of Oklahoma.

7

DECISION-MAKING TECHNIQUES

Faced with government or business problems, a decision maker often must choose among alternative options on the basis of a wide variety of objective and subjective criteria. For example, in choosing the best location for a new manufacturing plant, the decision maker can compare the candidate sites with respect to quantitative and qualitative factors (such as annual operating costs, quality of life, and community receptivity). Even after gathering the required data, the decision maker still needs to integrate the various factors to produce an overall evaluation of each proposed location. The task of a decision model is to formalize and facilitate this process.

Consider first the case of *decision making under certainty* where there is complete information for evaluating each alternative with respect to each of the factors or criteria. A simple scoring decision model is based on scoring the alternatives. We score each city on how well it performs on each factor and then simply select the city with the largest total score. We could also use prespecified weights to take a weighted average of the scores associated with the different decision factors and rank the cities according to total weighted scores. A relatively new procedure, the *analytic hierarchy process* (AHP), could also be used. The idea behind the AHP is to structure the decision factors as a hierarchy spanning several levels. At the top level is the overall goal of the problem (such as selecting the best plant location). The goal is then decomposed into several important factors that affect that decision; some of the factors (such as cost) could be broken down even further (for example, the annual operating costs could be broken down into labor, transportation, and energy costs). The AHP requires the decision maker to judge the relative importance of each decision factor and the relative importance of each alternative with respect to each factor. The output of the process is a weight or priority for each alternative that indicates the decision maker's overall preference. This set of weights forms the basis for ranking the alternatives and selecting the best one. A key strength of the AHP is that it breaks the problem of comparing alternatives down into smaller manageable pieces. The method then combines these limited evaluations into an overall assessment that integrates all of the factors. The first paper in this chapter applies the AHP to an interesting multicriteria decision problem that involves ranking well-known sports records.

Many real-world decision problems contain an element of uncertainty. The decision maker may not have full knowledge of certain problem characteristics or be able to control certain events. For example, suppose we must select the best location for a plant manufacturing a new product, where the entire country is divided into four regions and each region could experience three possible levels of demand for the product (high, medium, and low). We don't know the demands with certainty, but suppose that we can specify the likelihood of occurrence for each demand level through a probability distribution. As the resulting economic impact to the plant can be measured using these probabilities on uncertain future events, we would be making a *decision under uncertainty or risk*. The second paper in this chapter uses a *decision tree* to graphically model problems in which there is a sequence of decisions each of which leads to uncertain future events.

The final paper in this chapter presents an exciting new way of improving managerial decision making—a *decision simulator*. Imagine that we are seated at a desk-top computer terminal. Our decision problem is graphically displayed on the screen, and with the touch of a few keys we can easily generate a solution to the problem. Imbedded in the computer software is a management science model that produces its own solution to the problem. At any time, we can view the decisions and consequences produced by both our solution and the software's solution. We can compare our solution to the MS model's solution and see how they differ. The final paper describes the use of such a simulator in the forest products industry.

7.1 RANKING SPORTS RECORDS

For years, on television and radio, over a friendly drink at the local bar, or in written diatribes on the sports pages, sports aficionados have enthusiastically debated the "greatness" of their favorite athlete's accomplishments. Old timers single out the 511 baseball victories amassed by pitcher Cy Young from 1890 to 1911 as the greatest sports record of all time. Other baseball experts might cry "Foul Ball!" in response—after all, baseball in the late 1800s bore little resemblance to the game played in the "modern era." (Most baseball historians agree that this era starts in 1920. In that year, the "lively" baseball was first used and Babe Ruth hit an astonishing 54 home runs. From the beginning of major league baseball in 1876 through 1919, no player hit more than 29 home runs in a single season!) These experts might propose Hank Aaron's 755 career home runs or Joe DiMaggio's 56 game hitting streak in 1941 as the best marks. Knowledgeable followers of baseball might point out that Joltin' Joe wasn't even the best hitter of 1941. Ted Williams had the best batting average that year—a 0.406 mark that no major leaguer has topped in over 48 years. Although Williams' mark is considered a great feat, seven players since the year 1900 have higher season batting averages (Rogers Hornsby leads the list with a 0.424 average in 1924).

Great sports records are not limited solely to baseball. Followers of professional basketball believe that the single game record of 100 points set by Wilt Chamberlain in 1962 and his record-setting season average of 50.4 points that year will never be surpassed (he played in 80 games and scored an amazing 4,029 points in the 1961-62 season). However, many experts would argue that Chamberlain established his records during a period in which few opposing teams could field an agile player large enough to adequately play defense against him. Chamberlain's athletic ability, his size (he is over seven feet tall and weighs about 275 pounds), and lack of opposition made him the dominant player of the early 1960s. Basketball experts also point out that the current balance of size, speed, and agility found in most team's lineups, coupled with an exhausting season that runs from October to June, might make it difficult for a player (even a superstar like Michael Jordan) to challenge these marks.

Football fans offer Walter Payton's career total of 16,726 yards rushing (amassed from 1975 to 1987) and Eric Dickerson's 16-game single season rushing mark of 2,105 yards in 1984 as the greatest records of all time. Even though O. J. Simpson, in gaining 2,003 yards in the 14-game 1973 season, compiled a better per game rushing average (143.1 yards to Dickerson's 131.6 yards), Dickerson holds the record!

Hockey enthusiasts think that Wayne Gretzky's 215 points scored in the 1985-86 season is a great mark and, since the Great Gretzky is still active, they believe that he or Mario Lemieux, another prolific scorer, might challenge this mark.

Track and field observers point to the individual world record established by Bob Beamon in the long jump. In the 1968 Summer Olympics at Mexico City, Beamon jumped 29′ 2 1/2″. To give some idea of the greatness of this achievement, it wasn't until the 1980 Olympics that the first 28-foot jump took place. However, detractors are critical: the rarified atmosphere of Mexico City along with a tail wind that perhaps was slightly above the legal limit may have unfairly contributed to Beamon's performance. Current long jump followers are watching the progress of Carl Lewis and Robert Emmiyan. Lewis jumped 28' 10 1/4" in 1983, but his performance in the 1988 Olympics was disappointing despite his capture of the gold medal with a jump of 28' 7 1/2". On May 22, 1987 in the city of Tsakhadzor, the Soviet jumper Emmiyan jumped 29' 1"—the second best mark of all time. Admittedly, since the jump was judged only by Soviets and reported only by the Soviet press, some experts are skeptical of this mark.

The large number of outstanding records and the diverse set of qualitative and quantitative issues that affect their merits make determining the greatest active sports records an unusual multicriteria decision problem.

In tackling this decision problem, Golden and Wasil [1987] identify three key tasks: (1) specifying decision factors that separate good records from great records, (2) identifying great records that fall into one of three categories: season, career, and day or single game records, and (3) comparing the great records in each category in order to identify the greatest sports records.

To model this problem, Golden and Wasil apply the analytic hierarchy process. The AHP is a flexible decision-making tool that allows an analyst to combine qualitative and quantitative information to rank alternatives. Exhibit 7–1 lists the four basic steps of the AHP. In the first step, the decision maker structures the problem as a *decision hierarchy* of criteria, subcriteria, and alternatives. Exhibit 7–2 shows the hierarchy for comparing single-season records. The goal of the analysis is to select the best active season record. This goal, which appears at the top level of the hierarchy, is then decomposed into three important criteria for judging the best record. These criteria on the second level are duration of record, incremental improvement, and other record characteristics.

EXHIBIT 7–1. An application of the analytic hierarchy process requires four steps. In Steps 1 and 2, the decision maker represents the relationships amongst the decision factors and makes pairwise comparisons. The algorithm performs Steps 3 and 4 to establish the overall ranking of the alternatives.

Analytic Hierarchy Process (AHP)

Step 1.	Decompose the problem into a hierarchy of interrelated decision criteria.
Step 2.	Use collected data to generate pairwise comparison matrices at each level of the hierarchy.
Step 3.	Apply the eigenvalue method to estimate the relative weights of the decision criteria at each level of the hierarchy.
Step 4.	Synthesize the relative weights of all decision criteria to arrive at overall weights for the alternatives.

EXHIBIT 7–2. The decision hierarchy for determining the best single-season record has four levels. The goal is broken down into three key criteria and each criterion is further decomposed into important subcriteria. At the bottom level are the eight single-season sports records that are to be ranked. All eight records contribute to each of the six subcriteria. This is illustrated by the lines emanating from the node labeled % better than previous record. Though not shown in this figure, similar lines should also be drawn from the other subcriteria. The weight of each criterion and subcriterion is shown adjacent to the nodes of the hierarchy. At the bottom level, there are six different weights associated with each record, although only the weight on the % better than previous record subcriterion is shown.

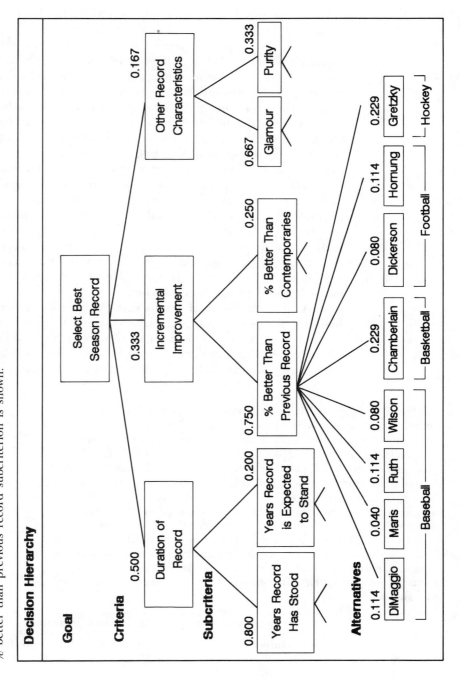

At the third level, each of the second-level criteria is further decomposed into subcriteria. For example, duration of record is broken down into the years the record has stood and the years the record is expected to stand. While quantitative data are available for the first of these, the second (the years the record is expected to stand) clearly calls for subjective assessments. Similarly, the subcriteria under incremental improvement rely on hard data while those under other record characteristics require subjective judgments. At the bottom level of the hierarchy are the decision alternatives, that is, the active single-season records.

Once the decision hierarchy is constructed, the decision maker must assess the importance or weight of each element at each level of the hierarchy. For example, at the second level, the decision maker must evaluate the importance of each criterion, record duration, incremental improvement, and other record characteristics, in selecting the best season record. Instead of directly assigning a weight to each of the three factors, the decision maker must generate entries in a *pairwise comparison matrix*. In the pairwise comparison matrix for the second level shown in Exhibit 7–3, the entries reflect Golden and Wasil's subjective preferences for one factor over another.

At the third level of the hierarchy, three 2 x 2 pairwise comparison matrices are generated, and at the bottom level, the eight records are compared with respect to each of the six subcriteria. This requires another six 8 x 8 matrices. Thus, for the single-season hierarchy, the second step of the AHP results in 10 pairwise comparison matrices.

EXHIBIT 7–3. In developing the entries for the pairwise comparison matrix at the second level of the hierarchy, Golden and Wasil judged duration of record as slightly more important than other record characteristics in its impact on the best season record. Using the widely-accepted 1 to 9 pairwise comparison scale (Exhibit 7–4), they assigned the entry in row 1 and column 3 of this matrix a value of 3 for weakly more important. This indicates that record duration is roughly three times as important as other record characteristics in determining the greatest single-season record. The entry of 1/3 in row 3 and column 1 is the reciprocal of this value of 3 and reiterates the lesser importance of other record characteristics as compared to record duration. Assigning entries in this way produces a *positive reciprocal matrix:* symmetric entries with respect to the diagonal are reciprocals of one another.

Pairwise Comparison Matrix and Weights			
	Duration	Improvement	Other	Weight
Duration	1	3/2	3	0.500
Improvement	2/3	1	2	0.333
Other	1/3	1/2	1	0.167

Using the pairwise comparison matrices as input, Step 3 of the AHP applies the eigenvalue method and produces relative weights of the elements at each level of the hierarchy. For example, the comparison matrix in Exhibit 7–3 implies weights of 0.500, 0.333, and 0.167 for the three criteria. To get some idea of how these weights are derived, suppose that a decision maker has exact knowledge of the relative weights of K elements at some level of the hierarchy. Then the pairwise comparison matrix would be given by

$$A = \begin{array}{c} \\ 1 \\ 2 \\ \cdot \\ \cdot \\ \cdot \\ K \end{array} \begin{array}{cccc} 1 & 2 & \ldots & K \\ \left[\begin{array}{cccc} w_1/w_1 & w_1/w_2 & \ldots & w_1/w_K \\ w_2/w_1 & w_2/w_2 & \ldots & w_2/w_K \\ \cdot & \cdot & & \cdot \\ \cdot & \cdot & & \cdot \\ \cdot & \cdot & & \cdot \\ w_K/w_1 & w_K/w_2 & \ldots & w_K/w_K \end{array}\right] \end{array}.$$

This matrix is reciprocal with respect to the diagonal and has only one linearly independent column (that is, the matrix has rank 1). Moreover, if $w = (w_1, w_2, \ldots, w_K)^T$ is the vector of known weights, then A satisfies:

$$Aw = Kw. \tag{1}$$

The vector w is the principal right eigenvector of the matrix A corresponding to the eigenvalue K.

If the vector of weights is not known, then it can be estimated from the pairwise comparison matrix $\hat{A}$ generated by the decision maker by solving the eigenvalue relation

EXHIBIT 7–4. By assigning a number from 1 to 9 to an entry in a pairwise comparison matrix, the decision maker establishes the importance of one decision factor or alternative over another.

Comparison Scale	
Importance	*Definition*
1	Equal importance
3	Weak importance of one over another
5	Essential or strong importance
7	Very strong or demonstrated importance
9	Absolute importance
2,4,6,8	Intermediate values

If element i has one of the preceding values assigned to it when compared to element j, then j has the reciprocal value when compared to i.

$$\hat{A}\hat{w} \;=\; \lambda_{\max}\hat{w} \tag{2}$$

for ŵ. The matrix Â contains the pairwise judgments of the decision maker, and it is used to approximate A whose entries are unknown. In (2), $\lambda_{\max}$ is the largest eigenvalue of Â, and the corresponding eigenvector ŵ provides the estimated vector of weights. Saaty [1980] has shown that $\lambda_{\max}$ is always greater than or equal to K and that if its value is sufficiently close to K, then the estimated set of weights ŵ solve (1) approximately. This approach to estimating the vector of relative weights from a pairwise comparison matrix is known as the *eigenvalue method*.

Applying the eigenvalue method to the 3 x 3 second-level pairwise comparison matrix produces the set of weights displayed in Exhibit 7–3. Weights at the third level are placed next to the nodes of the hierarchy in Exhibit 7–2. Notice that the weights sum to one. At the bottom level, there are six different weights associated with each record. These weights are produced by applying the eigenvalue method to each of the six 8 x 8 pairwise comparison matrices corresponding to the subcriteria. The weight for each record on the subcriterion percent better than previous record is shown adjacent to each node at the bottom of Exhibit 7–2. The records by Chamberlain and Gretzky receive the largest weights (0.229) on this subcriterion.

The last step of the AHP uses the principle of hierarchic composition to aggregate weights across the various levels of the hierarchy into a composite weight for each alternative. Exhibit 7–5 illustrates this process for Babe Ruth's single-season slugging average record. The weights produced by the six pairwise comparison matrices at the bottom level of the hierarchy are identified in Exhibit 7–5 as "Ruth's Weights." Golden and Wasil selected Ruth's mark as the greatest single-season record. It received the largest overall weight of 0.171 among the eight records in their AHP-based evaluation. The entire process is then repeated to produce separate rankings of career records and day or single game records.

7.2 ANALYSIS OF POSTAL AUTOMATION ALTERNATIVES

In late 1984, the US Postal Service (USPS) had completed the first phase of its postal automation plan. The equipment installed in this phase could optically scan an envelope to identify a nine-digit code (known as ZIP + 4) on the last line of an address and translate it into a bar code. Once this bar code was printed on each envelope, a bar code sorter could then automatically sort the mail to the level of a city block or a building (Exhibit 7–6).

EXHIBIT 7–5. To develop the overall weight for the single-season record set by Babe Ruth (a 0.847 slugging average in 1920), we use the principle of hierarchic composition: we sum the product of a criterion's weight times its subcriterion's weight times the weight of Ruth's record with respect to that subcriterion. For example, the duration of record criterion has a weight of 0.500, one of its subcriteria, years record has stood, has a weight of 0.800, and Ruth's record has a weight of 0.254 on this subcriterion. Thus, the contribution to the overall weight for Ruth's record on this particular branch of the hierarchy is 0.500 × 0.800 × 0.254 = 0.1016. Summing over all branches in the hierarchy produces the composite weight for Ruth's record.

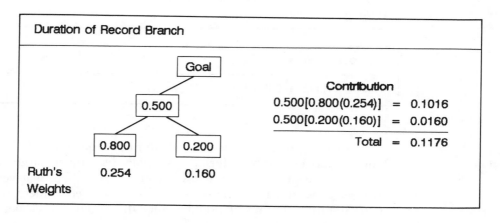

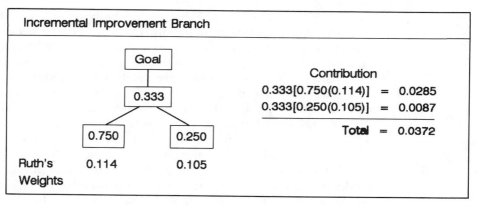

(continued)

EXHIBIT 7–5. (*Continued*)

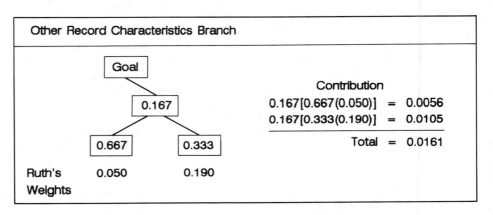

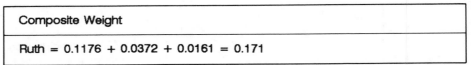

At that time, the postal service did not require the ZIP+4 code but encouraged its use by offering a sizeable discount to large-volume first class mail bearing the nine-digit code. The USPS believed that the ZIP+4 code and the installation of automated equipment would lower costs significantly since it would reduce the number of clerks involved in processing the mail.

In March 1984, with Phase I essentially completed, the USPS began planning its future automation. It had to choose between two technology alternatives: additional single-line optical character readers (SLOCRs) of the type used in Phase I and new multi-line machines (MLOCRs). These two options are illustrated in Exhibit 7–6.

The USPS faced a great deal of uncertainty in developing a strategy for Phase II: it had greatly overestimated the voluntary use of ZIP+4 and found that very few large-volume mailers had adopted it. The savings in labor to be derived from different levels of usage of ZIP+4 were also highly uncertain. In addition, the analysis had to be completed very quickly because the final report was due in a month. To model this complex problem, the USPS turned to an outside contractor. In the article that follows, Ulvila [1987] describes the decision analysis procedure he used for this purpose.

Ulvila needed a modeling tool that could convey the sequential nature of the decision process and account for the major uncertainties likely to affect USPS savings. Moreover, he wanted to display the proce-

EXHIBIT 7–6. In Phase I of its postal automation plan, the US Postal Service installed single-line optical character readers and bar code sorters. In deciding upon its future automation strategy in Phase II, it needed to choose between additional single-line readers and new multi-line readers. The new machines could read four lines of an address, look up the nine-digit code, and affix the code to an envelope. With the new technology, mail could be sorted to the nine-digit level even if the mailer had not used the ZIP+4 code.

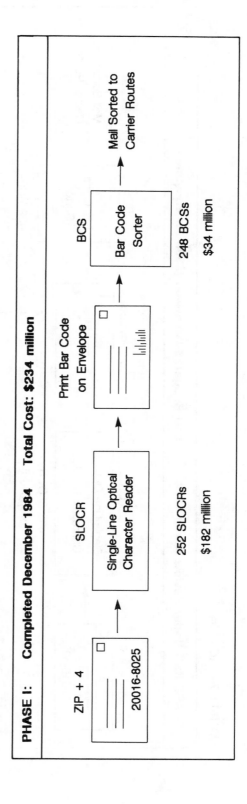

(continued)

EXHIBIT 7–6. (*Continued*)

PHASE II: Under Review March 1984   Total Budget: $450 million ($363 for equipment)

dure on a single sheet of paper so that the client would be able to grasp the full impact of the analysis easily. He decided to analyze the Phase II automation problem using a *decision tree*. The general form of a tree is shown in Exbibit 7–7.

The decision tree for the USPS problem contains six automation options and three major uncertain events: the level of ZIP+4 usage, the savings potential of the various types of new equipment, and the

EXHIBIT 7–7. The square node labeled 1 is a decision node—three courses of action are possible and the decision maker must select the best one. Two of the alternatives (A_1 and A_2) lead to chance nodes. The decision maker does not know which event will unfold, but can attach probabilities to their realization. Thus, the uncertain outcomes of a chance node are described by a probability distribution. Each of the seven paths through the tree results in a payoff. The decision maker calculates the expected payoff of each path and selects the alternative with the largest value as the best course of action. For example, the expected payoff of A_1 is $p_{21}V_1 + p_{22}V_2 + p_{23}V_3$.

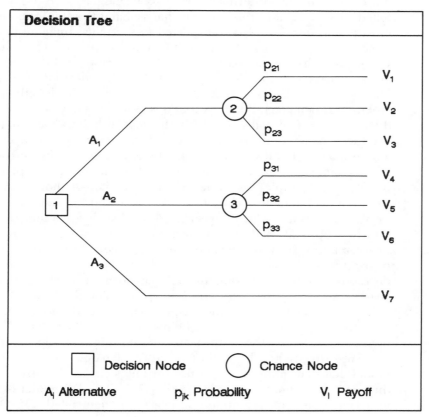

Decision Tree

A_i Alternative p_{jk} Probability V_i Payoff

Decision Node   Chance Node

savings that could be associated with different levels of usage. All the probability distributions used were discrete. Three branches emanated from each of the 47 chance nodes, and there were a total of 100 paths through the tree. Ulvila used the internal rate of return (IRR) and the net present value of cash flows (NPV) to evaluate the six options over the 1985-to-1998 time horizon. Analyzing the expected values of the options revealed that the preferred alternative was to proceed with the Phase II procurement of SLOCRs and simultaneously to continue research into converting SLOCRs into MLOCRs with the intention of performing this upgrade as soon as possible. A detailed sensitivity analysis showed that uncertainty in the cost of purchasing MLOCRs was not important but that other factors, such as the uncertainty in ZIP + 4 usage, contributed significantly to variations in NPV.

7.3 A DECISION SIMULATOR FOR TIMBER PROCESSING

A crew working for a large forest products company is busy cutting down trees in the western US. A 75-foot Douglas fir tree has just been felled, delimbed, and topped—all that remains is a 65-foot stem, which must be cut into logs and transported to the mills. Imagine that you are the worker responsible for deciding how to cut the stem into logs of various lengths. (In the vernacular of the forest products industry, you are known as a "woods bucker.") In making this decision, you must take into account a stem's geometric profile (that is, its length, curvature, taper, and diameter), quality variations (such as knots and rot), and the different types of mills to which the logs will be allocated (each mill produces a different end product such as paper, plywood, or lumber). There may be hundreds of combinations of log lengths and allocations for a single stem, each resulting in a different set of end products and profits. For example, the upper box in Exhibit 7–8 shows a cutting and allocation combination chosen by a woods bucker and the resulting profit. However, the profit associated with such a combination may be far from optimal. Bad cutting decisions can greatly affect the company profit realized from timber and must be avoided. In addition to making near-optimal decisions, you, as woods bucker, must also make these decisions rapidly. The company fells an average of 15 million trees a year or about 100 trees a minute in geographically dispersed areas. As many as six stems per minute require cutting and allocating.

In the paper that follows, Lembersky and Chi [1986] describe the novel way in which they improved stem cutting and allocation decisions for Weyerhaeuser. They constructed a dynamic programming (DP) model that determines the best use for any stem. A simplified version of their DP algorithm is shown in Exhibit 7–9. The DP model is imbedded in a video game-like computer software package called VISION (**V**ideo

EXHIBIT 7–8. The upper box shows a cutting combination chosen by a woods bucker. The woods bucker decides to cut the stem into four pieces: three logs are sent to chip-n-saw mills and a single log is allocated to a fiber mill. This combination can be compared to the optimal solution shown in the lower box. The optimal cutting and allocation decision is produced by the dynamic programming model imbedded in VISION. This exhibit is based on Lembersky and Chi [1984]; however, the mill allocations and log values in the lower box have been added for illustration purposes.

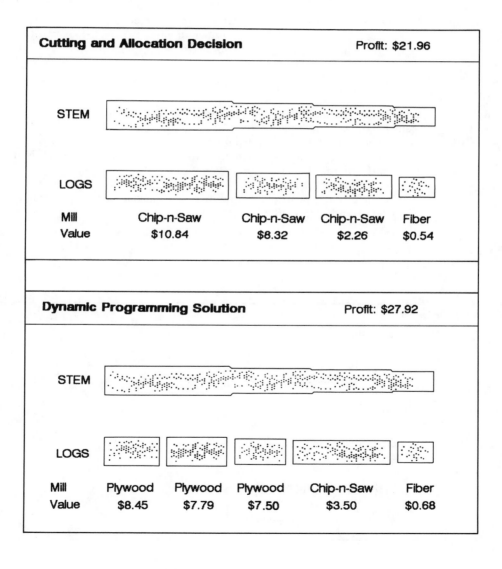

EXHIBIT 7–9. In this simplified formulation of the stem cutting and allocation problem, a dynamic program determines the best way to cut a stem and allocate it to a mill so that its contribution to profit is maximized. In the recursive relationship, $v_m(l_j, d_i)$ and c_j are the value and cost of cutting a log of length l_j from the larger end of the stem and allocating it to mill m. After this log is cut, the remaining stem has length $(i-j)K$.

Dynamic Programming Algorithm

Stem Assumptions

- uniform quality
- no curvature or crook
- constant taper

Parameters

L = length of stem
d = small end diameter
D = large end diameter
M = number of mills to which logs can be allocated

Definitions

$t = (D - d)/L$	taper rate
$l_j = jK$	log lengths are multiples of a constant K
$L = IK$	stem length is a multiple of K
$d_i = d + tiK$	larger end diameter of the partial stem
$v_m(l_j, d_i)$	value of cutting off a log of length l_j from the larger end d_i of this partial stem and sending it to mill m
$c_j = c$	cost of cutting off a log
$f(i)$	maximum possible profit contribution of the partial stem with smaller end diameter d and length iK

Recursion

$$f(i) = \text{maximum } \{v_m(l_j, d_i) - c_j + f(i - j)\}$$
$$1 \leq j \leq \min \{i, N\}$$
$$1 \leq m \leq M$$
where $c_j = 0$ if $j = i$

Illustration of Parameters

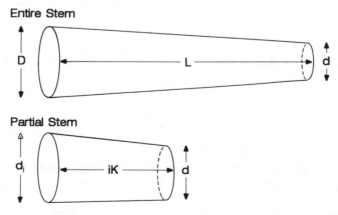

Entire Stem

Partial Stem

Interactive Stem Inspection and OptimizatioN) that allows users to interactively simulate stem cutting and allocation decisions. With VISION, a user (such as a woods bucker, a company manager, or a mill worker) can display a stem on the screen, rotate and inspect it from several perspectives to examine its curvature and other characteristics, cut the stem and allocate the logs, and view the cost implications of the decision. Each user can then compare the profit that results from his cutting and allocation decision with the maximum profit produced by the DP model's solution. This type of comparison is illustrated in Exhibit 7–8. After comparing both solutions and observing the different cuts and allocations, the user can recut the same stem and examine the effects of alternate decisions. As a result of using VISION, the user generally develops improved decision-making skills to take back to the forest floor.

Lembersky and Chi have coined the term *decision simulator* for systems with VISION-like characteristics. Such systems should be easy to use and highly interactive. They should generate believable problem representations and be able to produce immediate feedback from an underlying management science model whose structure is shielded from the user. Lembersky and Chi believe that their approach has produced better decision makers for Weyerhaeuser and enabled the company to increase its profits by over $100 million.

7.4 FURTHER READINGS

Related Readings

Golden and Wasil Paper

- McCallum [1990] tries his hand at ranking sports records in a highly readable article that appears in the popular magazine *Sports Illustrated*. Building on Golden and Wasil's comparison framework, he divides records into three categories and relies on his own subjective judgments and preferences to rate records. However, he does not use a decision-making tool like the AHP in his analysis. Nevertheless, in two of the three categories, McCallum's choice for best record agrees with Golden and Wasil's selection—Wilt Chamberlain's 100-point game as the best single-event record and Babe Ruth's slugging average of 0.847 in 1920 as the best single-season record. McCallum parts company with Golden and Wasil on the choice of best career record. He ranks Jack Nicklaus's victories in 20 major golf championships as the best record in that category.

Ulvila Paper

- For an insightful and informal view of what really happened behind the scenes at the US Postal Service, read the short follow-up note by Ulvila [1988]. In response to brief questions, Ulvila touches on such issues as the amount of taxpayer money that was saved as a result of the analysis.

Lembersky and Chi Paper

- In an earlier paper, Lembersky and Chi [1984] provide additional details about the development of VISION and its application to timber-processing problems, devoting several pages to a typical user session. They then turn to a general discussion of decision simulators (DS), pointing out key issues in designing this class of tools and reviewing several applications that rely upon DS-like systems that incorporate management science models or algorithms.

- Hay and Dahl [1984] describe the materials-flow-planning process for the vertically integrated operations of the Weyerhaeuser Company in an area of the southern United States where the company owns over two million acres of timberlands. Ten facility complexes operate in this area with locations stretching from Oklahoma to Alabama. Each complex includes one or more mills that converts timber into such end products as plywood and paper. Hay and Dahl develop a linear program known as RAS (Region Allocation System) to allow modelers to examine the interaction of such factors as raw material sources, alternative ways of cutting stems, different production facilities, and the demand for end products. A RAS model for a small product line might contain 200 variables and 100 constraints. In developing RAS, Hay and Dahl relied on a DP model similar to the one used by Lembersky and Chi to determine ways of cutting a stem into logs. The many ways of cutting each class of tree stems into logs are then defined as decision variables in the LP. Hay and Dahl also discuss another LP, known as ARBITER, that models the movement of raw material between different complexes over several time periods.

Background Readings

Golden and Wasil Paper

- Since the mid 1970s a considerable body of literature on the theory and practice of the AHP has emerged. By the end of 1988, over 150 applications articles and about 75 theoretical papers had appeared in scholarly and professional journals, in special issues of journals dedicated solely to the AHP, and in textbooks devoted to explaining the methodology and its application. In Exhibit 7–10, we list several sources covering the theory and practice of the AHP.

- One of the first publications about a major application of the AHP concerned the design of a transport network for the Sudan. In the early 1970s, the four main modes of transportation in the Sudan—rail, road, river, and air—formed a transport network that exhibited little connectivity. As a result, the economy of the Sudan suffered and its potential growth was threatened, especially that of the agricultural sector. While the Sudan has vast fertile areas for growing food and its potential exports could feed several hundred million people, agricultural activity on this scale requires an extensive transportation network that the country lacked in the 1970s. The government of the Sudan and the Kuwait Fund for Arab Economic Development commissioned a study to develop an overall transport system for the area by 1985. The full report on the study comprised 1,700 pages, and the AHP played a central role in setting priorities for 103 different projects (such as building a road to connect

EXHIBIT 7–10. A partial list of books and articles that cover the theory and practice of the AHP.

Publication Type	Focus	Reference	Comments
Book	A,T	Saaty [1980]	A comprehensive source and a good introduction to the AHP. Three chapters develop the underlying mathematical theory and two chapters focus on applications in the areas of resource allocation, prediction, planning, and conflict resolution.
	A	Saaty [1982]	This book presents many practical examples in areas such as higher education, public policy, and health care that illustrate the use of the AHP while suppressing much of the complex mathematics. Basic and FORTRAN listings of computer programs for the AHP are included.
	A	Saaty and Vargas [1982]	The goal of this book is to expose readers to applications of the AHP in the areas of planning, resource allocation, and prediction. Fourteen chapters are devoted to such topics as examining the racial conflict in South Africa, predicting the price of oil in 1985 and 1990, selecting an investment portfolio, and analyzing behavior in a match between chess champions.
	A, T	Golden, Wasil, and Harker [1989]	This book presents a unified treatment of the basics of the AHP and its application to important, real-world decision problems. Twelve papers illustrate AHP success stories in areas such as project selection, electric utility planning, medical decision making, and strategic planning.
Article	S	Harker [1989]	A well-written, easy-to-read tutorial that presents an overview of the philosophy and methodology that underly the AHP. Examples are used to illustrate the basic procedure and recent extensions are also described. The mathematical foundations of the method, the supermatrix technique, and alternative modes of questioning in the AHP are also presented.
	S	Golden, Wasil, and Levy [1989]	A complete and comprehensive bibliography of AHP applications. Over 150 published papers are categorized into 29 application areas that range from accounting to

A Application   S Survey   T Theory

(continued)

EXHIBIT 7–10. (*Continued*)

Publication Type	Focus	Reference	Comments
			transportation. Papers that combine AHP with traditional management science techniques like linear programming are also classified.
	S	Zahedi [1986]	A practitioner's guide to the AHP that explains the four-step process in detail and presents a survey of applications in areas such as economics and planning, manpower selection and performance, and portfolio selection. Several extensions to the basic method are also discussed. Nearly 100 references are included.
	T	Harker and Vargas [1987]	This article tries to address many of the concerns that have been raised about the foundations and assumptions underlying the theory of the AHP in (1) its lack of an axiomatic foundation, (2) the ambiguity of questions that a decision maker must answer, (3) the 1 to 9 scale of measure, and (4) rank reversals. Examples and proofs are used to illustrate and correct many of the criticisms about the AHP.

A Application   S Survey   T Theory

major cities) that the Sudan could undertake. This project is described in Saaty [1977a, 1977b],

- Reports on a number of interesting AHP applications have appeared in *Interfaces*, including an analysis of the Falkland Islands conflict [Saaty 1983] and an account on planning national energy policy by the Finnish Parliament [Hämäläinen 1988]. In the first paper, a group of 25 executives attending a seminar on decision making evaluated three options that Great Britain could pursue to resolve the crisis. Two hierarchies were used to model the decision problem. In a three-level benefits hierarchy, options were compared as to their ability to achieve eight different benefits, including saving islander's lives and maintaining Britain's national prestige. The options were then compared in a cost hierarchy on six factors, including political costs and the potential for naval defeat. The ratio of benefit weight to cost weight for each alternative was used to select Britain's best option. In the second paper, Hämäläiner describes a four-level hierarchy used to evaluate new sources of power for Finland, including a nuclear power plant. Several members of Finland's Parliament, along with energy and environmental experts, participated in the analysis. The results of the study received widespread attention in the Finnish media because a microcomputer-based decision aid was used to support planning activities at the national level.

- The proliferation of AHP applications has been greatly facilitated by the availability of a microcomputer package called Expert Choice [1986]. This package operates on the IBM PC, and the commercial version can handle hierarchies with as many as six levels including the goal and up to seven factors or alternatives below each node. A student version is also available.

- Several books are devoted to analyzing sporting events using management science and statistical techniques. Machol and Ladany's book [1976] contains 15 articles that range from an analysis of the optimal time to pull a hockey goalie to a method for handicapping professional football. A companion volume by Ladany and Machol [1977] provides an annotated bibliography of over 45 sports-related papers. Townend [1984] presents an interesting review of how mathematics can be used to explain the mechanics of a sport.

- Some of the most interesting and provocative statistical analyses of baseball have been generated by the Society for American Baseball Research (SABR). Members of the society are known as *saber-metricians:* a neologism combining the acronym SABR with the word for measuring. Bill James is perhaps the best known sabermetrician. His baseball abstract [James 1988] is a well-written, mathematical look at baseball that introduces new statistical measures. Thorn and Palmer [1985] give an insightful and detailed evaluation of baseball and its "new" statistics.

Ulvila Paper

- Decision trees have been used by analysts to model a wide variety of real-world problems, including the evaluation of air-quality-control equipment [Madden, Hyrnick, and Hodde 1983], determining how much to bid for the salvage rights to a ship [Bell 1984], labor contract bargaining [Winter 1985], selecting a home mortgage [Luna and Reid 1986; Heian and Gale 1988], choosing between two wildcat oil ventures [Hosseini 1986], and managing patients with possible appendicitis [Clarke 1987].

- Keeney, Lathrop, and Sicherman [1986] present an interesting, real-world application of decision analysis that uses decision trees and multiattribute utility functions to help Baltimore Gas and Electric Company (BG & E) select a strategy for adding electric generating capacity at one of its sites. Several new technologies for generating electricity were attractive but not yet available. In deciding which technology to adopt, BG & E had to balance uncertain benefits against uncertain costs that would be incurred by waiting for the new technologies. Keeney, Lathrop, and Sicherman describe the detailed decision process that they used to help BG & E analyze the alternative strategies.

- Several microcomputer packages are available for modeling problems using decision trees. McNamee and Celona's book [1987] is a comprehensive guide to analyzing decision problems with the popular SUPERTREE software. The textbook by Samson [1988] includes the student version of the ARBORIST decision tree package.

- The principles of decision analysis are covered in several well-known sources. Keeney [1982] presents a coherent overview of the field designed for the non-decision analyst. He describes the environment and methodolgy of decision analysis, discusses applications, and briefly chronicles the history of the field. Keeney includes a detailed bibliography of over 130 references. Ulvila and Brown [1982] present three real-world case studies on how managers use decision analysis. The case studies focus on the use of decision tree analysis, probabilistic forecasting, and multiattribute utility analysis by large corporations and government departments. The textbook by Samson [1988] is a very good introduction to decision analysis and the book by Keeney and Raiffa [1976] is a comprehensive treatment of utility theory and its application to important decision problems.

Lembersky and Chi Paper

- Faaland and Briggs [1984] examine the problem of determining where to cut a tree into shorter logs in order to maximize the value of the lumber that is then cut from the logs. After reviewing the literature, they develop a dynamic programming technique that combines two optimization activities—cutting the tree into logs and sawing the logs into lumber—in a single model. Computational results are also reported.
- Harrison and de Kluyver [1984] edited a special issue of *Interfaces* that focuses on how management science models have been used in forestry and the forest products industry. Eleven papers cover a wide range of models including the use of decision analysis to plan and manage fires, the development of an integrated decision support and manufacturing control system to maximize the return of a forest products mill, and the use of linear programming by the US Forest Service. Bare et al. [1984] present a comprehensive review of management science applications in forest land management and the forest products industry.
- The decision simulator developed by Lembersky and Chi can be thought of as a "visualization" of a mathematical model. Decision-making aids like Gantt and PERT charts can also be classified as visual models. Bell [1985] gives a history of visual interactive (VI) modeling and assesses its impact on the field of management science, while Kirkpatrick and Bell [1989] present results from a survey of MS/OR practitioners who use commercial software to build VI models. Jones [1988] also discusses the visual representation of MS/OR models and develops a new three-dimensional Gantt chart for machine scheduling.

REFERENCES

Bare, B. Bruce; Briggs, David G.; Roise, Joseph P; and Schreuder, Gerard F. 1984, "A survey of systems analysis models in forestry and the forest products industries," *European Journal of Operational Research*, Vol. 18, No. 1, pp. 1–18.

Bell, David E. 1984, "Bidding for the S.S. Kuniang," *Interfaces*, Vol. 14, No. 2, pp. 17–23.

Bell, Peter C. 1985, "Visual interactive modeling as an operations research technique," *Interfaces*, Vol. 15, No. 4, pp. 26–33.

Clarke, John R. 1987, "The application of decision analysis to clinical medicine," *Interfaces*, Vol. 17, No. 2, pp. 27–34.

Expert Choice 1986, Decision Support Software, McLean, Virginia.

Faaland, Bruce and Briggs, David 1984, "Log bucking and lumber manufacturing using dynamic programming," *Management Science*, Vol. 30, No. 2, pp. 245–257.

Golden, Bruce L. and Wasil, Edward A. 1987, "Ranking outstanding sports records," *Interfaces*, Vol. 17, No. 5, pp. 32–42.

Golden, Bruce L.; Wasil, Edward A.; and Harker, Patrick T., eds. 1989, *The Analytic Hierarchy Process: Applications and Studies*, Springer-Verlag, Berlin, West Germany.

Golden, Bruce L.; Wasil, Edward A.; and Levy, Doug E. 1989, "Applications of the analytic hierarchy process: A categorized, annotated bibliography," in *The Analytic Hierarchy Proc-*

ess: Applications and Studies, ed. Bruce Golden, Edward Wasil, and Patrick Harker, Springer-Verlag, Berlin, West Germany, pp. 37–58.

Hämäläinen, Raimo P. 1988, "Computer assisted energy policy analysis in the Parliament of Finland," *Interfaces,* Vol. 18, No. 4, pp. 12–23.

Harker, Patrick T. 1989, "The art and science of decision making: The analytic hierarchy process," in *The Analytic Hierarchy Process: Applications and Studies,* ed. Bruce Golden, Edward Wasil, and Patrick Harker, Springer-Verlag, Berlin, West Germany, pp. 3–36.

Harker, Patrick T. and Vargas, Luis G. 1987, "The theory of ratio scale estimation: Saaty's analytic hierarchy process," *Management Science,* Vol. 33, No. 11, pp. 1383–1403.

Harrison, Terry P. and de Kluyver, Cornelis A. 1984, "MS/OR and the forest products industry: New directions," *Interfaces,* Vol. 14, No. 5, pp. 1–7.

Hay, Douglas A. and Dahl, Paul N. 1984, "Strategic and midterm planning of forest-to-product flows," *Interfaces,* Vol. 14, No. 5, pp. 33–43.

Heian, Betty C. and Gale, James R. 1988, "Mortgage selection using a decision-tree approach: An extension," *Interfaces,* Vol. 18, No. 4, pp. 72–83.

Hosseini, Jinoos 1986, "Decision analysis and its application in the choice between two wildcat oil ventures," *Interfaces,* Vol. 16, No. 2, pp. 75–85.

James, Bill 1988, *The Bill James Baseball Abstract: 1988,* Ballantine Books, New York.

Jones, Christopher V. 1988, "The three-dimensional Gantt chart," *Operations Research,* Vol. 36, No. 6, pp. 891–903.

Keeney, Ralph L. 1982, "Decision analysis: An overview," *Operations Research,* Vol. 30, No. 5, pp. 803–838.

Keeney, Ralph L.; Lathrop, John F.; and Sicherman, Alan 1986, "An analysis of Baltimore Gas and Electric Company's technology choice," *Operations Research,* Vol. 34, No. 1, pp. 18–39.

Keeney, Ralph L. and Raiffa, Howard 1976, *Decisions with Multiple Objectives: Preferences and Value Tradeoffs,* John Wiley & Sons, New York.

Kirkpatrick, Paul and Bell, Peter C. 1989, "Visual interactive modeling in industry: Results from a survey of visual interactive model builders," *Interfaces,* Vol. 19, No, 5, pp. 71–79.

Ladany, Shaul P. and Machol, Robert E., eds. 1977, *Optimal Strategies in Sports,* North-Holland Publishing Company, New York.

Lembersky, Mark R. and Chi, Uli H. 1984, "Decision simulators speed implementation and improve operations," *Interfaces,* Vol. 14, No. 4, pp. 1–15.

Lembersky, Mark R. and Chi, Uli H. 1986, "Weyerhaeuser decision simulator improves timber profits," *Interfaces,* Vol. 16, No. 1, pp. 6–15.

Luna, Robert E. and Reid, Richard A. 1986, "Mortgage selection using a decision tree approach," *Interfaces,* Vol. 16, No. 3, pp, 73–81.

Machol, Robert E. and Ladany, Shaul P., eds. 1976, *Management Science in Sports,* North-Holland Publishing Company, New York.

Madden, Thomas J.; Hyrnick, Michael S.; and Hodde, James A. 1983, "Decision analysis used to evaluate air quality control equipment for Ohio Edison Company," *Interfaces,* Vol, 13, No, 1, pp. 66–75.

McCallum, Jack 1990, "The record company," *Sports Illustrated,* Vol. 72, No. 1, pp. 58–71.

McNamee, Peter and Celona, John 1987, *Decision Analysis for the Professional with Supertree,* The Scientific Press, Redwood City, California.

Saaty, Thomas L. 1977a, "The Sudan transport study," *Interfaces,* Vol. 8, No. 1, pp, 37–57.

Saaty, Thomas L. 1977b, "Scenarios and priorities in transport planning: Application to the Sudan," *Transportation Research,* Vol. 11, No. 5, pp. 343–350.

Saaty, Thomas L. 1980, *The Analytic Hierarchy Process,* McGraw-Hill, New York.

Saaty, Thomas L. 1982, *Decision Making for Leaders,* Lifetime Learning Publications, Belmont, California.

Saaty, Thomas L. 1983, "Conflict resolution and the Falkland Islands invasions," *Interfaces,* Vol. 13, No. 6, pp. 68–83.

Saaty, Thomas L. and Vargas, Luis G. 1982, *The Logic of Priorities,* Kluwer-Nijhoff Publishing, Hingham, Massachusetts.

Samson, Danny 1988, *Managerial Decision Analysis,* Richard D. Irwin, Homewood, Illinois.

Thorn, John and Palmer, Pete 1985, *The Hidden Game of Baseball,* Doubleday & Company, Garden City, New York.

Townend, M. Stewart 1984, *Mathematics in Sport,* Ellis Horwood Limited, Chichester, England.

Ulvila, Jacob W. 1987, "Postal automation (ZIP+4) technology: A decision analysis," *Interfaces,* Vol. 17, No. 2, pp. 1–12.

Ulvila, Jacob W. 1988, "20/30 hindsight: The automatic zipper," *Interfaces,* Vol. 18, No. 1, pp. 74–77.

Ulvila, Jacob W. and Brown, Rex 1982, "Decision analysis comes of age," *Harvard Business Review,* Vol. 60, No. 5, pp. 130–141.

Winter, Frederick W. 1985, "An application of computerized decision tree models in management-union bargaining," *Interfaces,* Vol. 15, No. 2, pp. 74–80.

Zahedi, Fatemeh 1986, "The analytic hierarchy process—A survey of the method and its applications," *Interfaces,* Vol. 16, No. 4, pp. 96–108.

Ranking Outstanding Sports Records

Bruce L. Golden
Edward A. Wasil

For years, in a variety of informal settings, sports observers have argued the merits of their favorite records or performances. Followers of baseball might debate whether, in 1941, Ted Williams' batting average of .406 was more impressive than Joe DiMaggio hitting safely in 56 consecutive games. Football followers, interested in such glamorous single-season marks as rushing and passing records, might question whether Eric Dickerson's 2,105 rushing yards in a 16-game season was as impressive as O. J. Simpson's 2,003 yards in a 14-game season. The two authors of this paper have had friendly arguments about the merits of many records, including Wilt Chamberlain's record of 100 points scored in a single basketball game. Could a current professional player such as Michael Jordan break Wilt's record? In fact, our sometimes heated discussions led us to pose several questions about the nature of records in sports:

— What makes a "great" sports record?

— What factors separate "good" records from "great" records?

— What are the "great" sports records?

Answering these questions is not a trivial task. However, if we could compile a list of great sports records, it would then be natural to compare these great records in order to identify those records that are indeed the "greatest." Because of the many difficulties raised by this sort of comparison (such as the cross-era nature of the data, the consideration of multiple sports, and even the subjective preferences of the authors), a comparison methodology based on the flexible and widely-applicable notion of analytic hierarchies seemed well-suited to our needs. Our goal, then, is to identify the greatest sports records.

We believe that this effort should be of interest at two levels. First, it is an attempt to carefully consider the primary factors that separate "good" records from "great" records. We would expect this level to be of special interest to knowledgeable observers of sports. Judging by the popularity of recent books on the subject, such as the ones by Townend [1984], Ladany and Machol [1977], and Machol and Ladany [1976], it seems that many operations researchers may be so classified. Second, our analysis is an easy-to-understand, yet nontrivial application of analytic hierarchies. The data are numerous and often difficult to obtain. Each hierarchy is full, and many pairwise comparisons need to be made. The conclusions must be interpreted carefully because of a host of complicating issues. This level should appeal to teachers and users of management science and operations research techniques.

DATA COLLECTION AND RELATED ISSUES

In order to ensure a meaningful comparison, we decided to examine three categories of sports records—season records, career or multiple-year records, and daily or single-game records.

We define a season record as a mark established during a regular "season" of competition not including post-season performances (such as a Super Bowl or World Series). Career marks refer to a lifetime of accomplishment or a record that was set over several years of competition. Daily or single game records refer to records that were set as a result of a one-time performance by an athlete.

To select the great records in each of the three categories, we decided to focus on those records that are measurable achievements and for which historical data could be easily obtained. For example, it is not difficult to measure the magnitude of Bob Beamon's long jump record of 29'2½"—he totally bypassed the 28-foot mark and broke the previous record of 27'4¾" by nearly two feet. In contrast,

consider John McEnroe's crushing defeat of Jimmy Connors in the final match of the 1984 Wimbledon tennis tournament. McEnroe's performance is considered to be one of the finest ever in the men's final. However, his performance cannot be easily compared to performances in finals of previous years.

Based upon our two criteria, we have identified eight season records, 10 career records, and four daily records drawn from baseball, basketball, football, hockey, and track and field as great sports records. These records are listed in Table 1. Certainly this set of records does not exhaust all of the outstanding records but it does contain many of the most widely-noted accomplishments in a variety of sports. With the exception of track and field, the records have been established by professional athletes in team sports. We should point out that Joe DiMaggio's hitting streak, although it consumed only about one-third of a season, is included in the single-season category. Also, Johnny Unitas' record of 47 consecutive games in which he threw touchdown passes is included in the category of career records even though the streak lasted about one-fourth as long as his professional career.

The collection of appropriate data on which to compare the great sports records was quite extensive. For each season record, data was gathered regarding the best marks of all time, the prior best marks, and the marks of contemporaries in the year in which the record was established. An example of such a data set is provided in Table 2.

For each career record, we gathered data regarding the best marks of all time. For each daily record, we gathered data on the best marks of all time and the best prior marks. (Space limitations prevent listing the data for all 22 records. A com-

TABLE 1. Great sports records.

		Sport	Athlete	Year	Record
Season Records					
	Hitting Streak	B	Joe DiMaggio	1941	56
	Home Runs	B	Roger Maris	1961	61
	Slugging Average	B	Babe Ruth	1920	.847
	Runs Batted In	B	Hack Wilson	1930	190
	Scoring Average	BA	Wilt Chamberlain	1961-62	50.4
	Yards Gained Rushing	F	Eric Dickerson	1984	2,105
	Points Scored	F	Paul Hornung	1960	176
	Points Scored	H	Wayne Gretzky	1985-86	215
Career Records					
	Home Runs	B	Henry Aaron	1954-76	755
	Stolen Bases	B	Lou Brock	1961-79	938
	Hits	B	Pete Rose	1963-86	4,256
	Slugging Average	B	Babe Ruth	1914-35	.690
	Strikeouts	B	Nolan Ryan	1966-86	4,277
	Points Scored	BA	Kareem Abdul-Jabbar	1970-86	36,474
	Points Scored	F	George Blanda	1949-75	2,002*
	Yards Gained Rushing	F	Walter Payton	1975-86	16,193
	Consecutive Games,				
	Touchdown Passes	F	Johnny Unitas	1956-60	47
	Points Scored	H	Gordie Howe	1947-80	2,358**
Day/Game Records					
	Points Scored	BA	Wilt Chamberlain	1962	100
	Yards Gained Rushing	F	Walter Payton	1977	275
	Yards Gained Passing	F	Norm Van Brocklin	1951	554
	Long Jump	TF	Bob Beamon	1968	29'2½"

B	Baseball	H	Hockey	*includes point totals from the AFL
BA	Basketball	TF	Track and Field	**includes point totals from the WHA
F	Football		

B   Baseball   H   Hockey   *includes point totals from the AFL
BA   Basketball   TF   Track and Field   **includes point totals from the WHA
F   Football

plete listing with sources is available from the authors upon request.)

Using the data sets, we encountered some difficulties in comparing records. In examining the season records, we notice that some of the records were established over different length seasons. Perhaps the most famous example of a record that was later broken due to a lengthened season is Babe Ruth's 60 home runs. This mark, set in a 154 game season, was broken by Roger Maris in the first year that the baseball season was lengthened to 162 games.

Of course, some records established during a shorter season have not been broken despite a lengthened season. Examples include Hack Wilson's 190 runs batted in (set in a 154 game season) and Paul Hornung's 176 points scored (set in a 12 game season). We hasten to point out that, in Hornung's case, points were scored as a result of touchdowns, points-after-touchdowns, and field goals. Few players today are as versatile as was Paul Hornung. In fact, with the high degree of specialization in football today, there are

TABLE 2. The data set for runs batted in.

Best Marks of All Time		
1. Hack Wilson	1930	190
2. Lou Gehrig	1931	184
3. Hank Greenberg	1937	183
4. Lou Gehrig	1927	175
5. Jimmie Foxx	1938	175
Best Marks Prior to 1930		
1. Lou Gehrig	1927	175
2. Babe Ruth	1921	171
3. Babe Ruth	1927	164
4. Hack Wilson	1929	159
5. Al Simmons	1929	157
1930 Contemporaries		
1. Lou Gehrig		174
2. Chuck Klein		170
3. Al Simmons		165
4. Jimmie Foxx		156
5. Babe Ruth		153

no place kickers scoring touchdowns and no running backs kicking field goals on a regular basis.

A different playing environment can have a major impact on a record achievement. A longer season, a rule change, and equipment improvements can have dramatic effects on the performance of athletes. As examples, consider the introduction of the "lively" baseball and the "bump-and-run" rule in football. These changes probably led to more home runs and more forward passing. In the latter case, increased passing means less running, so that a running record established before the rule change might tend to last longer, other things being equal, since the rule change in some sense encourages a team to pass the football.

Given the fairly large number of records in different sports that we are comparing and the long time span of the various records, it is quite difficult to evaluate all of the changes in the playing environment and their effect on record

achievements. The methodology that we used to compare the records is an attempt to take the effect of such changes into account.

COMPARISON METHODOLOGY

Given the complexity and subjectivity of the decision problem, we decided that the analytic hierarchy process (AHP) might be an appropriate tool to aid us in ranking outstanding sports records.

AHP is a decision-making technique that has been used in a wide variety of settings to rank alternatives. More specifically, AHP is an eigenvalue-based procedure for determining the overall importance of each member of a set of alternatives. The method involves breaking down an intricate problem into a group of disjoint levels comprising a hierarchical structure and then establishing the priorities among the elements of the hierarchy. An example of a hierarchy is shown in Figure 1. The essential characteristic of AHP is that the measurement methodology to assess the priorities is based on the concept of pairwise comparison [Saaty 1980, 1982; and Zahedi 1986].

THE DECISION HIERARCHY

We examined three separate but closely related decision problems. Figures 1, 2, and 3 show the relevant hierarchies and the associated results. For the purpose of explanation, we will focus on single-season sports records. Figure 1 builds upon the analysis provided by Hirdt [1984].

At the highest level of the hierarchy, we seek to select the best active single-season sports record. (An active sports record is one that has not been broken.) At the sec-

FIGURE 1. Single season hierarchy and results.

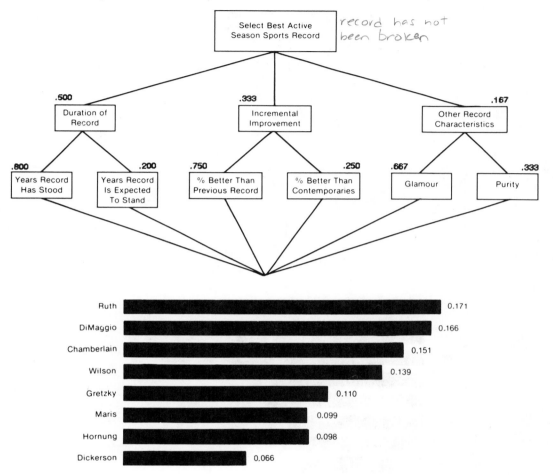

ond level are the key factors or criteria that affect the decision, from our point of view: duration of record, incremental improvement, and other characteristics.

The third level of the hierarchy consists of subcriteria. The subcriteria under duration include the years the record has stood and the years it is expected to stand. The first of these is rather obvious—if a record is old and has not been broken, it is more likely to be a great record. Data are available for comparing records based on this subcriterion. If a record is recent, however, but is expected to last for a long time, it may also be a great record. This subcriterion clearly calls for subjective judgments.

Under the heading incremental improvement, there are two subcriteria— percent better than previous record and percent better than contemporaries. A record that betters both the previous record and contemporary marks by large percentages is likely to be a great record. If a

FIGURE 2. Career hierarchy and results.

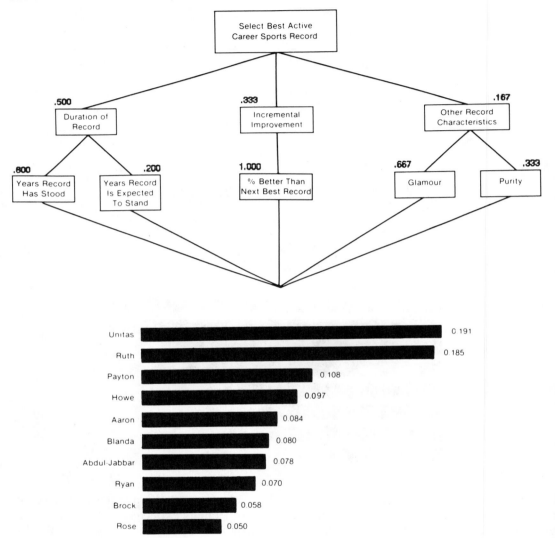

record does well with respect to only the first of these subcriteria, it may be the result of a trend in the sport rather than an outstanding performance. Data are available for comparing records based on these subcriteria.

Under other record characteristics, we have glamour and purity. Great records tend to be well known, often discussed, and glamorous, and some records are more glamorous than others. For example, the home-run leader receives more attention than the stolen-base leader and, in basketball, the scoring leader generally re-

FIGURE 3. Single-day hierarchy and results.

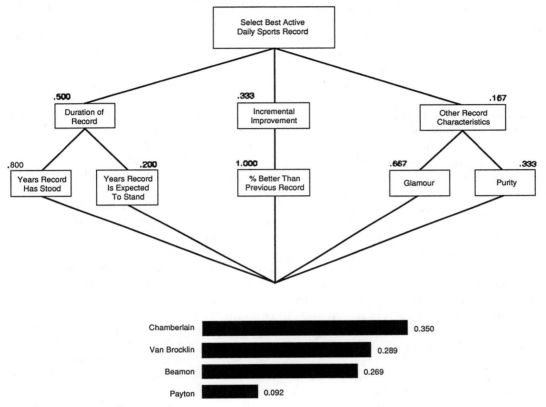

ceives more acclaim than the assist leader. By purity, we refer to the degree to which the record reflects the achievement of a single person. In team sports, record purity is extremely important. Other things being equal, a pure record, such as the number of home runs, is more impressive than an assisted record, such as the number of runs batted in. After all, a home run is the result of a batter's skill, whereas an RBI is often the result of team hitting ability. Each of these two subcriteria requires subjective judgments.

The fourth level or bottom of the hierarchy consists of the various sports records.

DISCUSSION OF RESULTS

With the hierarchies constructed, we generated the appropriate pairwise comparison matrices.

At the second level of each hierarchy, we compared the three key factors—duration of record, incremental improvement, and other record characteristics—as to their impact on the overall selection of the best sports record. This called for a pairwise comparison of the factors. We assigned a numerical value (from 1 to 9) that specified the importance of one factor vis-à-vis another with respect to the overall goal. Admittedly, such assignments are highly subjective. In comparing duration of record against incremental improvement, we felt that duration was slightly more important. In fact, duration is the best single indicator of a record's greatness, in our opinion. Incremental improvement is the second best single indicator. Other record characteristics place third in importance. Our judgments are reflected in the AHP comparison matrix displayed in Table 3.

These pairwise comparisons give rise to the weights shown adjacent to the nodes at the second level of the hierarchy in Figure 1. Duration of record is the most important criteria at this level (receiving a weight of .500), followed by incremental improvement (.333) and other record characteristics (.167).

Each criterion at the second level is further broken down into two subcriteria. Under duration of record, we decided that the years a record has stood is roughly four times as important as the years the record is expected to stand. After all, the first number of years is already known whereas the second number of years is conjectured. The resulting weights are .800 and .200.

Under incremental improvement, we

TABLE 3. A pairwise comparison matrix for the second level of the single-season hierarchy.

	Duration	Improvement	Other
Duration	1	3/2	3
Improvement	2/3	1	2
Other	1/3	1/2	1

found percent better than the previous record to be about three times as significant as percent better than contemporaries because a large percent in the first case almost certainly implies a great record, whereas a large percent in the second case does not. The resulting weights are .750 and .250.

Finally, we gave a slight edge to glamour over purity. For us, it is simply more interesting to debate the merits of well-known records regardless of their degree of purity. The resulting weights are .667 and .333.

At the bottom level of the hierarchy, we formed pairwise comparison matrices that compare the sports records with respect to each subcriterion. In the hierarchy that represents the single-season sports records, six matrices were constructed. That is, we formed six matrices by pairwise comparing the eight season records as to the years the record has stood, the years the record is expected to stand, percent better than the previous record, percent better than contemporaries, glamour, and purity. Three of these matrices (years the record has stood, percent better than the previous record, and percent better than contemporaries) are constructed on the basis of historical data. For example, Hack Wilson's record of 190 runs batted in has stood for 57 years, and Roger Maris's record of 61 home runs has stood for 26 years. When comparing Wilson's record to Maris's record, we computed the pairwise comparison matrix entry by looking at the ratio of Wilson's years to Maris's years and therefore assigned a value of $57/26 \approx 2$. In forming the matrix corresponding to percent better than the previous record, we did not think it appropriate to compare a record holder against himself. Therefore, we eliminated all other marks by the record holder and compared the record against the next best performance by another athlete.

For career and daily records, incremental improvement is decomposed into only one subcriterion—percent better than the next best record in the case of career records and percent better than the previous record in the case of daily records. Measuring the improvement over an athlete's contemporaries, as we did in the case of season records, is not applicable in these categories since the notion of contemporary is somewhat ambiguous. Since four of the athletes are still active (Rose, Ryan, Abdul-Jabbar, and Payton), we decided to adjust the career record by forecasting their career record at retirement. Thus, the number of hits for Pete Rose remains the same (he will probably manage and not play in 1987) and we increased Nolan Ryan's strikeouts by 200, Kareem Abdul-Jabbar's point total by 2,200, and Walter Payton's yards by about 1,800. To simplify data collection, we measured the incremental improvement in this category by calculating the percent improvement over the next best record (as opposed to the previous record).

The remaining three matrices—years record is expected to stand, glamour, and purity—were, for the most part, generated on the basis of our subjective judgments. However, some historical data was used to provide guidance in assessing matrix entries. For example, knowledge about the emergence of a superstar (as in the case of Wayne Gretzky in hockey) or a change in the playing environment can be used to judge the number of years a record is expected to stand.

Based on the comparison matrices at the bottom level of the hierarchy, the weights of each record with respect to the third-level subcriteria were computed. We used the microcomputer software package

Expert Choice to compute these weights.

Finally, the relative weights at all levels of each hierarchy were synthesized to arrive at a set of overall weights for each record. These weights are presented in bar-chart form in Figures 1, 2, and 3. The greatest records in each category are as follows:

— *Season Record:*
   Babe Ruth, .847 slugging average
   Joe DiMaggio, 56 game hitting streak
— *Career Record:*
   Johnny Unitas, 47 consecutive games, touchdown passes
   Babe Ruth, .690 slugging average
— *Daily Record:*
   Wilt Chamberlain, 100 points scored.

We provided two records for each of the first two categories, because the results were close and the weight dropped sharply after the first two alternatives. The resulting weights are such that minor perturbations in the comparison matrices have no impact on our selection of the five truly great sports records.

For the most part, the resulting rankings of sports records in each of the three categories are quite reasonable given the criteria specified in each hierarchy. However, there are two exceptions. We were somewhat surprised that in the daily category Bob Beamon's record was ranked only third best. His low placement in the rankings can be attributed in part to a poor performance with respect to two criteria. Beamon does not score well when compared with Chamberlain and Van Brocklin on the criteria of record longevity and incremental improvement.

Chamberlain's record (set in 1962) and Van Brocklin's record (set in 1951) have each lasted a long time (remember that Beamon's jump took place in 1968). Although Beamon's jump improved the previous record by 6.6 percent and has been cited as the single greatest percentage improvement in a modern day track and field event, Chamberlain and Van Brocklin improved the previous records by 40.8 percent and 18.4 percent respectively. In this case, record longevity and especially incremental improvement appear to be less than perfect indicators of a record's greatness. Beamon's low ranking is also in part attributable to the nature of his sport. That is, the long jump is an individual sport, subject to more or less recognizable boundaries on performance (there are widely agreed upon limits to human performance in running and jumping), whereas Chamberlain's and Van Brocklin's records are the result of team effort. Daily sports records is the only category to mix team sports with individual sports. This appears to make comparing records in this category more difficult to interpret. It may well be that additional factors are needed in order to more fairly compare Beamon's record with the other single-day records.

We also believe that the fourth-ranked career record, Gordie Howe's record of 2,358 points scored, might be ranked higher than it deserves. Although this is an impressive record, it appears to be quite vulnerable because of the superstar nature of one current NHL player—Wayne Gretzky. In only seven seasons, the Great Gretzky already has amassed 1,337 points, a mark good enough for eighth place on the all-time record list. At his average of 191 points a year, Gretzky will only need a bit more than 5¼ seasons to break Howe's record! To be fair, by the time he retires, Gretzky's career point total may be the most impressive career mark around.

CONCLUSION

We hope our results are somewhat provocative, and we invite readers to bring their favorite sports records to our attention, especially if they do not appear on any of our lists.

ACKNOWLEDGMENTS

We thank Joe Horrigan of the Professional Football Hall of Fame, Dennis Buden of the National Hockey League, and Frank Polnaszek of the Hartford Whalers for their invaluable assistance in tracking down several sports records. We also thank Larry Bodin and Larry Levy for their helpful and insightful comments.

REFERENCES

Hirdt, P. 1984, "Gretzkyology: Going by the numbers," *Sport Magazine*, May, pp. 36-37.

Ladany, S. and Machol, R. 1977, *Optimal Strategies in Sports*, North Holland Publishing Company, Amsterdam, The Netherlands.

Machol, R. and Ladany, S. 1976, *Management Science in Sports*, North Holland Publishing Company, Amsterdam, The Netherlands.

Saaty, T. 1980, *The Analytic Hierarchy Process*, McGraw-Hill, New York.

Saaty, T. 1982, *Decision Making for Leaders*, Lifetime Learning Publications, Belmont, California.

Townend, M. 1984, *Mathematics in Sport*, Halsted Press, London.

Zahedi, F. 1986, "The analytic hierarchy process—A survey of the method and its applications," *Interfaces*, Vol. 16, No. 4, pp. 96-108.

Postal Automation (ZIP + 4) Technology: A Decision Analysis

Jacob W. Ulvila

In March 1984, the Office of Technology Assessment (OTA) was asked to review the United States Postal Service's (USPS) strategy of postal automation, in particular, whether the USPS's automation strategy was technically and economically sound, and whether the USPS should continue to procure equipment as planned.

Since October 1, 1983, the USPS had encouraged business mailers to use the nine-digit ZIP code (ZIP+4), such use being voluntary. At about the same time, the Postal Rate Commission approved a discount rate for large-volume first-class mail that used ZIP+4. By March 1984, use of ZIP+4 was still a voluntary program for business mailers.

Concurrently with the movement to a nine-digit ZIP code, the USPS was engaged in a program of postal automation. This program included the acquisition of optical character readers (OCRs) and bar code sorters (BCSs). In June 1981, the USPS awarded contracts totaling $182 million for 252 OCRs to be delivered begin-

ning in the fall of 1982. In December 1981 and August 1982, the USPS awarded contracts totaling about $34 million for 248 BCSs to be delivered beginning in the fall of 1982. Including ancillary equipment and installation expense, this equipment was expected to cost a total of $234 million and was expected to be operational by the end of 1984. It represented phase 1 of the postal automation plan. OTA's review was conducted just prior to phase 2.

The primary rationale for both ZIP+4 and postal automation was economic. Cost savings were expected from reductions in the labor required to sort mail (labor costs account for about 85 percent of total postal costs). Some savings could be expected from automation with the five-digit ZIP code by reducing the number of mail clerks involved in intermediate processing. However, the big gains would come from automation with ZIP+4. ZIP+4 allows sorting to the level of city block, building, or post office box, whereas the five-digit ZIP code allows sorting only to the level of

397

a post office zone or geographical area within a large post office zone. An OCR can read the ZIP + 4 code, translate it into a bar code, and print the bar code on the envelope. BCSs can then sort the letter automatically to the level of carrier routes, eliminating all intermediate sorting. (Additional background information is contained in two reports by the US General Accounting Office, GAO/GGD-83-84 and GAO/GGD-83-24.)

DECISION SETTING

The decision analyzed in March 1984 was whether and how the USPS should proceed with phase 2 of the postal automation strategy. At that time, the USPS had just received bids on an additional 403 OCRs and was planning to solicit bids on an additional 452 BCSs. The USPS had allocated $450 million for phase 2, which included $363 million for capital equipment.

OTA was asked to investigate the advisability of the strategy on both technical and economic grounds. The USPS's strategy was judged to be technically feasible. However, a technology other than the USPS's choice was identified as being worth considering as an alternative [Gingras 1984]. The OCRs that the USPS had purchased in phase 1 and proposed to purchase in phase 2 were single-line OCRs. Single-line OCRs read the last line of an address, which usually consists of the city, state, and ZIP code (either five- or nine-digit). An alternative technology, multi-line OCR was capable of reading up to four lines of an address. OTA concluded that "the preponderance of evidence indicates that multi-line OCR performance is essentially equivalent to single-line for reading nine-digit ZlP mail,

and that multi-line performance is substantially better for reading five-digit ZIP mail to the nine-digit level" [OTA 1984]. That is, a multi-line OCR could read an address, automatically find the appropriate nine-digit ZIP code in a directory, and affix the nine-digit code to an envelope. The mail could be sorted to the nine-digit level even if the mailer did not use the nine-digit ZlP code.

OTA further identified three firms that had proven multi-line OCRs. OTA also indicated that an earlier USPS analysis had underestimated the ultimate performance of multi-line OCRs by "five to 15 percent" and that the combination of a multi-line OCR with a national ZIP + 4 directory (which the USPS had developed) would allow reading, coding, and sorting of at least some five-digit ZIP mail to the nine-digit level.

Economically, the outlook was more complicated. The economic justification for postal automation was the expected savings in labor due to reduced sorting. To achieve the greatest saving, at least with single-line OCRs, required high-volume first-class mailers to use ZIP + 4. However, despite discounts of 0.5 cent to 0.9 cent per piece, very few large business mailers had decided to use ZIP + 4. This, and other evidence, led OTA to conclude that USPS's forecasts of ZIP + 4 usage rates were optimistic and should be subjected to further analysis. In addition, the amount of savings that could be expected at any given rate of usage was regarded as uncertain.

To address this complex and uncertain situation, on February 15, 1984, Decision Science Consortium, Inc. was contracted to perform a decision analysis of postal automation alternatives. The basic modeling approach involved five steps. First, decision options were identified. Second, a probabilistic cash-flow model was developed for each option. Third, results of the model were analyzed. Fourth, the model was briefed at a public workshop held on March 5, 1984. Fifth, the model was refined based on information exchanged during and after the workshop, and the analyses and evaluations were presented to Congress by OTA in June 1984. Details of the model are described below.

THE DECISION ANALYSIS MODEL—ITS STRUCTURE, OPTIONS, AND VALUATION MEASURES

The decision analysis model of postal automation (ZIP+4) technology is shown in Figure 1. Six options were identified:

— *Option A: Single-Line OCR* was the proposed USPS strategy to proceed to pro-

cure 403 additional single-line OCRs as planned. Under option A, there would be no further USPS expenditure on multi-line OCR research, development, or testing.

— *Option B: Multi-Line with ZIP+4* was a decision to cancel the planned phase 2 single-line OCR procurement, initiate testing of multi-line OCRs, and as soon as possible, procure multi-line OCRs rather than phase 2 single-line OCRs, meanwhile retaining the ZIP+4 code. The single-line OCRs already purchased would be converted to multi-line capability.

— *Option C: Multi-Line without ZIP+4* was the same as option B except that the ZIP+4 code would be terminated. The five-digit ZIP code would be retained.

— *Option D: Convert* was a decision to proceed with the phase 2 single-line OCR procurement but simultaneously initiate testing (and any necessary related R & D) on single-line to multi-line conversion and then convert all single-line OCRs as

FIGURE 1. The schematic decision tree of postal automation option shows the six options (A-F), three uncertainties, and two outcome valuation measures (IRR and NPV).

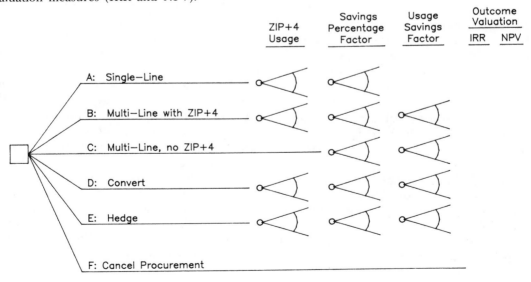

soon as possible, regardless of the level of ZIP+4 use.

— *Option E: Hedge* was similar to option D except that the single- to multi-line conversion would take place only if ZIP+4 use were low at a specified future time (year-end 1987).

— *Option F: Cancel Phase 2 and ZIP+4* was to cancel the phase 2 single-line OCR procurement, terminate ZIP+4, and use the single-line OCRs already purchased to process five-digit ZIP mail.

The evaluation of options was based on the internal rate of return and the net present value of cash flows. This model was thus limited to economic effects, the main reason for postal automation. A discount rate or required rate of return of 15 percent was used, in keeping with USPS policy. A time horizon of 1985 through 1998 was used, which is also the same as that used by the USPS.

UNCERTAINTIES

Three major uncertainties affecting the savings from postal automation were modeled: ZIP+4 usage, savings percentage, and usage savings. Voluntary usage of ZIP+4 was a key uncertainty. The USPS predicted a 90 percent usage level by 1989. However, the USPS had a history of overestimating mailers' usage of new programs. For example, usage of the Postal Service's electronic mail system, E-COM, was only one-third of the original estimate for fiscal year 1983. OTA considered that this degree of overestimation was unlikely, but the USPS's estimate was still considered high. The model treated the USPS predictions as the 95th percentile of the usage distribution. The median usage pattern was that of the five-digit ZIP code when it was initially introduced (it was es-

FIGURE 2. The USPS's estimate of ZIP+4 usage was considered optimistic (high), a median estimate was the rate of five-digit ZIP usage at its introduction, and the low estimate was similar to the pattern for E-COM.

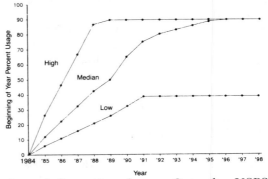

timated from Attachment 2 to the USPS letter to OTA of February 9, 1984 [Jellison 1984]). The usage pattern of E-COM, that is, one third of the USPS estimate in five years, was judged to be the fifth percentile of the distribution. These usage patterns are shown in Figure 2.

The Postal Service also had a history of overestimating the savings potential of new equipment. These savings are modeled by adjusting the USPS's estimated clerk and carrier savings by a multiplicative adjustment factor. The fifth percentile of the distribution on this factor was assessed to be at 80 percent of the USPS's savings. The median was assessed at 90 percent of their estimate, and the 95th percentile at 100 percent of their estimate.

The level of clerk and carrier savings would also vary as a function of usage. This variation was fairly well established for single-line OCRs, but it was uncertain for multi-line OCRs. This was modeled as another multiplicative factor, the percentage of single-line OCR's 90 percent usage savings. For single-line OCRs, this factor equaled .875 times usage plus .2125. The

FIGURE 3. The usage savings factor for multi-line OCRs was the third uncertainty modeled. Variations were due to uncertainties in performance and in the characteristics of mail flow. H = high multi F = .26U + .83. M = median multi F = .36U + .73. L = low multi F = .67 if U < .33, else F = .622U + .465.

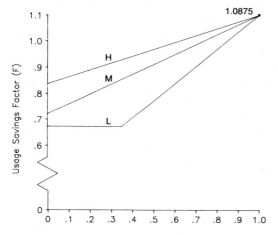

distribution of factors for multi-line OCRs is shown in Figure 3. The fifth percentile was set at the USPS's assessment, which was based on pessimistic assumptions about both the characteristics of the mail flow and the performance of the multi-line OCR, as determined by OTA's technical assessment. The median assessment is based on slightly better performance than the USPS's estimate and the pessimistic assumptions about mail flow are dropped. The 95th percentile, which is shown as the high curve, is a technical judgment of possible performance based on limited test information.

Two other uncertainties were raised: the number of multi-line OCRs that would be needed and the unit price of a multi-line OCR. Estimates of the number of multi-line OCRs needed varied from 655 to 755 and depended on their operating speed and the volume of mail. Estimates of the price per unit varied from the USPS's estimate of $970,000 to a manufacturer's estimate of $769,000. This compares with a unit cost of $750,000 for a single-line OCR. An early explicit analysis showed that the evaluations were insensitive to these uncertainties, so they were not modeled explicitly in the final analysis.

The uncertainties affected the savings from the options differently. Savings from the single-line OCR were affected by ZIP+4 usage and the savings percentage factor. Savings from all options that involved multi-line OCRs and retained ZIP+4 (options B, D, and E) were affected by all three uncertainties. Multi-line without ZIP+4 (option C) was affected by the savings percentage factor and the usage savings factor. ZIP+4 usage did not affect this option because ZIP+4 would be dropped. None of the uncertainties affected the option of canceling the procurement.

All of the uncertainties addressed were continuous variables. However, they were modeled as discrete distributions using the method of Pearson and Tukey [Keefer and Bodily 1983, Pearson and Tukey 1965]. This method represents a continuous distribution as a three-valued discrete distribution, assigning a probability of .185 to the 95th percentile, a probability of .63 to the median, and a probability of .185 to the fifth percentile. Keefer and Bodily [1983] found that this is an excellent approximation to a wide range of distributions. It also has the advantage of requiring only three readily accessible fractiles. This approximation produced a decision tree with nine paths following options A and C and 27 paths following options B, D, and E.

CASH-FLOW ANALYSES

For each path in the decision tree, a detailed cash-flow analysis was developed to determine the internal rate of return and the net present value. Table 1 shows a sample cash-flow analysis for option D (convert) under the condition of high ZIP + 4 usage, a high savings rate, and a high usage savings factor. Investment in single-line equipment and its associated site preparation and program contingency costs would occur in 1985 through 1987. At the same time, research costs would be incurred to develop single-line to multi-line conversion equipment. Conversion equipment would be procured and installed in 1988 through 1990. Maintenance, spare parts, and address information costs would occur throughout the entire horizon of the analysis, 1985-1998. Revenue would be lost due to a rate reduction for mailers who used ZIP + 4. This reduction was 0.5 cent per item of presorted first class mail and 0.9 cent per item of nonpresorted first class mail. The General Accounting Office (GAO) estimated an annual cost of $140 million at 90 percent usage (GAO/GGD-83-24). Savings come from clerk and carrier savings as shown. The net cash flow in a year is calculated as savings minus investment, maintenance, and rate reduction. Also shown is the incremental cash flow, which is net cash flow minus the cash flow associated with option F (cancel the procurement).

Cash-flow analyses for other ZIP + 4 usage rates, savings rates, and usage savings factors were calculated in a similar manner considering the same elements of savings and cost. Analyses for other options were similar but reflected the different timing and cost of equipment and the different savings from that equipment.

Each stream of cash flows was evaluated by its internal rate of return (called return on investment, ROI, by the USPS) and its net present value. The hurdle rate used was the USPS's rate of 15 percent. As shown on Table 1, under conditions of high ZIP + 4 usage and high savings, option D (convert) had an internal rate of return of 111 percent and a net present value of $2.7 billion. Compared with option F (cancel), it had an internal rate of return of 85 percent and a net present value of $2.4 billion. Under this, the most favorable condition, the purchase of single-line OCRs and their subsequent conversion to multi-line capability is a very attractive investment.

The cash-flow analyses were performed using a commercially available spreadsheet computer program, operating on an IBM Personal Computer.

ANALYSIS RESULTS

Cash-flow analyses were conducted for all conditional paths in the decision tree. Figure 4 shows the analysis for option D (convert). Incremental IRRs ranged from about 25 percent to about 85 percent. Correspondingly, incremental NPVs ranged from $0.46 billion to $2.44 billion. Clearly, this was an attractive option. (Because of the well-known problems with internal rate of return, net present value was the primary criterion for evaluation. The following discussions are focused on the NPV evaluations. Conclusions based on IRR are essentially the same.)

From these trees, the expected incremental NPVs were calculated as follows:

Option A $1.3 billion,
Option B $1.2 billion,
Option C $0.9 billion,
Option D $1.5 billion, and
Option E $1.4 billion.

TABLE 1. Cash-flow analysis for option D (convert) at high usage, high savings rate, and high usage savings factor (in thousands of dollars). Under these conditions, net present value is about $2.7 billion and internal rate of return is about 111 percent. Compared with option F (cancel), net present value is $2.4 billion and internal rate of return is 85 percent.

Date	1985	1986	1987	1988	1989	1990	1991	—	1998
Single-line equipment	(140,325)	(140,325)	(113,200)	0	0	0	0	—	0
Site preparation and contingency	(20,077)	(20,077)	(16,147)	0	0	0	0	—	0
Research	(5,000)	(5,000)	(5,000)	0	0	0	0	—	0
Conversion equipment	0	0	0	(43,667)	(43,667)	(43,667)	0	—	0
Maintenance and spares	(27,706)	(34,172)	(36,640)	(42,950)	(57,685)	(98,690)	(86,221)	—	(142,301)
Address information	(32,400)	(30,900)	(15,700)	(16,700)	(18,000)	(19,336)	(20,770)	—	(34,280)
Total investment and maintenance	(225,508)	(230,474)	(186,687)	(103,317)	(119,352)	(161,693)	(106,991)	—	(176,581)
Rate reduction	(58,333)	(88,667)	(117,444)	(136,111)	(140,000)	(140,000)	(140,000)	—	(140,000)
Clerk and carrier savings	161,128	268,953	465,747	711,526	827,240	888,621	1,015,649	—	1,676,253
Net cash flow	(122,713)	(50,188)	161,616	472,098	567,888	586,929	768,657	—	1,359,671
Incremental cash flow	(177,182)	(85,072)	128,190	436,381	536,762	553,493	732,741	—	1,300,394
NPV 2,674,972				Incremental NPV	2,442,773				
IRR 111.3%				Incremental IRR	84.6%				

FIGURE 4. The decision tree analysis of option D (convert) shows all three-point approximations of uncertain factors and the outcome valuations for all paths.

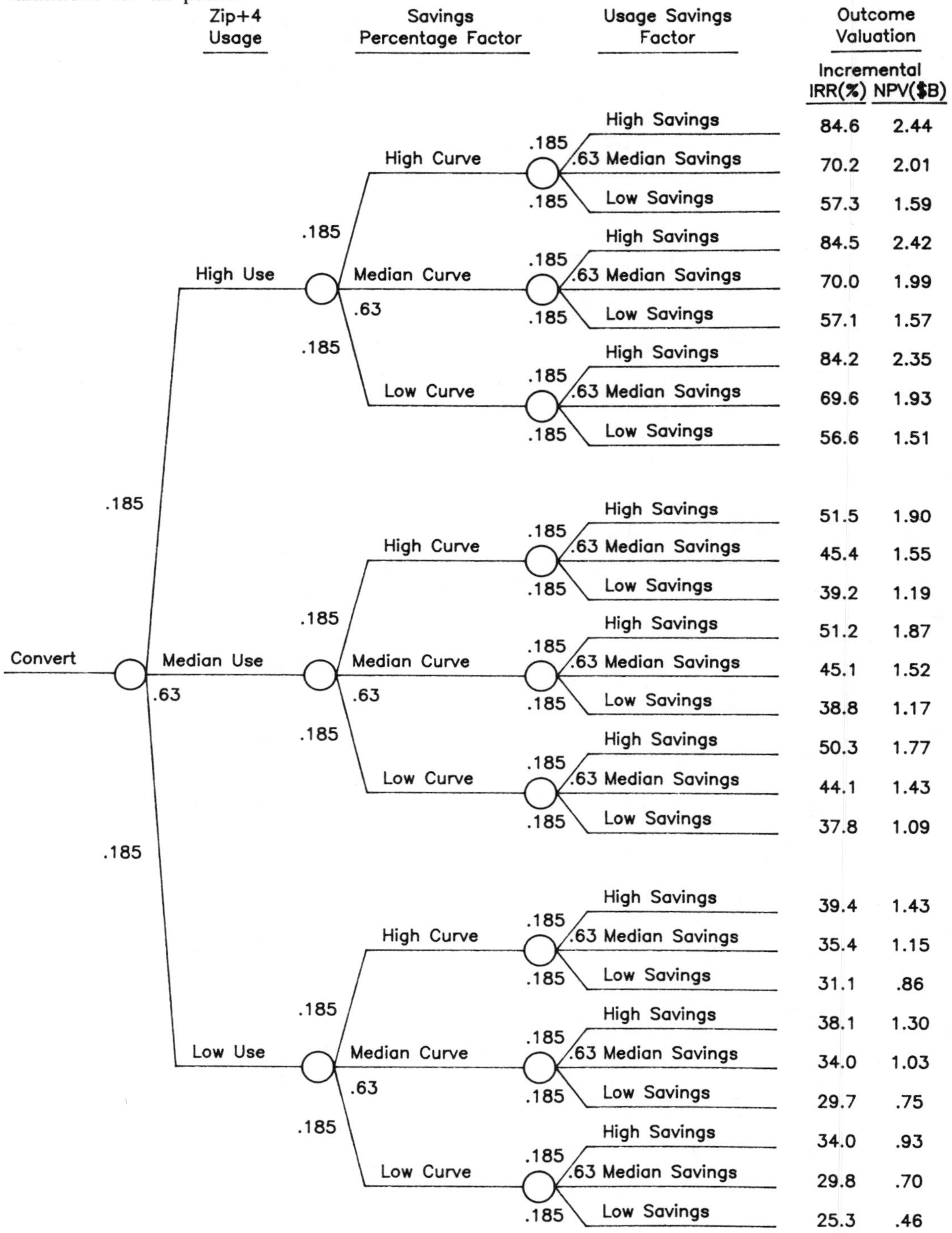

Thus, on an expected value basis, option D (convert) was preferred, followed by options E, A, B, and C. All options were better than canceling (option F).

Next, it was important to consider the uncertainty in the evaluations. Since it was impractical to attempt to assess a utility function for the US government, which would be required for a closed-form analysis, the analysis addressed features of the probability distributions of NPV for each alternative. First, we checked for dominance and found that the NPV from option D (convert) was greater than the NPV from option E (hedge) under all conditions. Thus, option D dominated option E. There were no other cases of strict dominance.

Next, cumulative probability distributions of NPV were developed for each option and compared. These distributions are shown in Figure 5. This comparison shows that option D (convert) dominates

FIGURE 5. The smoothed cumulative probability distributions on incremental net present value show that option D (convert) stochastically dominates option A (single-line OCR), option B (multi-line OCR with ZIP + 4), and option C (multi-line OCR without ZIP + 4).

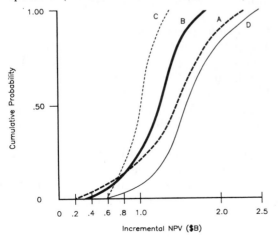

all other options stochastically. That is, for any value of NPV, the probability that option D will exceed that value is greater than the probability that any other option will exceed that value. Thus, option D was preferred regardless of one's attitude toward risk.

Sensitivity analyses were performed which showed, among other things, stochastic dominance by option D conditional on ZIP + 4 usage, conditional on savings percentage factor, and conditional on usage savings factor. A sensitivity analysis on the cost of multi-line OCRs showed this factor to be unimportant.

These analyses were facilitated by Decision Science Consortium, Inc.'s decision tree computer program that operates on an IBM Personal Computer.

CONCLUSION 1: ANY PHASE 2 WAS BETTER THAN CANCELING

Even under the most pessimistic conditions modeled, every phase 2 option considered (A-E) returned greater than 15 percent on cash flows incremental over those anticipated if phase 2 were canceled (option F).

CONCLUSION 2: CONVERT WAS PREFERRED

Purchasing phase 2 single-line OCRs and continuing research on multi-line OCR technology with the intention of upgrading all single-line machines beginning in 1988 was the preferred option on the basis of this financial analysis. Not only did this option have a higher expected value, but it stochastically dominated the other options. That is, for any given net present value (NPV), the probability that option D (convert) exceeded that value was greater than the probability that any other option would exceed that value. Under this condition, the convert option was preferred regardless of one's attitude toward risk taking [Keeney and Raiffa 1976, pp. 134-135]. Convert's financial advantages over the other options was even stronger than stochastic dominance. It also exhibited conditional stochastic dominance.

This conclusion of dominance was a strong one. However, it did depend on the assumptions that went into the model and could change if unanticipated events (outside of those modeled) were to have a selectively adverse effect on the convert option. One possibility, which had been raised by the USPS but discounted in developing this analysis, was that the act of planning for a conversion would cause mailers to dramatically reduce or slow their use of ZIP+4. This seemed highly unlikely for the reason that mailers would make their decisions based on how it affected them (especially by considering the rate incentive) and not based on what the USPS did internally. (Service was almost certain to be identical under single- and multi-line.) The analysis also largely dismissed the argument that the rate incentive would be reduced (and that mailers would act as though it would be reduced) with multi-line OCRs.

The basic reason that convert was preferred so strongly was that the greater savings that would be achieved by the multi-line OCR at any level of usage, even though delayed, outweighed the additional equipment cost of $131 million ($200,000 to convert each of 655 OCRs) and research cost of $15 million.

CONCLUSION 3: UNCERTAINTY IN THE COST OF MULTI-LINE OCRS CONTRIBUTED VERY LITTLE TO THE UNCERTAINTY IN ITS NPV

Varying the cost of a multi-line OCR from a low of $750,000 each (the same as the cost of each single-line OCR — capital and expense) to a high of $970,000 changed the NPV by less than $50 million. This was an immaterial variation. (The analysis used an estimated cost of $850,000.)

CONCLUSION 4: UNCERTAINTY IN USAGE CONTRIBUTED MOST TO VARIATIONS IN NPV

Uncertainty in percentage savings was a close second, and uncertainty in the savings curve was a distant third. Varying the usage of ZIP+4 contributed the most to the variation in NPV of all options except multi-line without ZIP+4 (which had an NPV that was invariant to usage). Varying the savings percentage from 80 percent to 100 percent of USPS estimates contributed somewhat less to the variability in NPV. Variations in the savings curves of multi-line contributed little to their overall variations in NPV except if usage was low (in which case its contribution to variation was a little less than that of savings percentage). For multi-line without ZIP+4, variations due to percentage savings and those due to savings curve contributed about the same to overall variability in NPV.

CONCLUSION 5: PREFERENCES AMONG SINGLE-LINE, MULTI-LINE WITH ZIP+4, AND MULTI-LINE WITHOUT ZIP+4 WERE NOT AS CLEAR-CUT

No stochastic dominance existed among these options. Furthermore, these options exhibited the classical conflict between risk and expected return. Single-line had the highest overall financial risk and highest expected return. Multi-line without ZIP+4 had the lowest risk and lowest expected return. Multi-line with ZIP+4 was in between. Choice among these would depend on a decision maker's attitude toward risk. A risk-neutral or risk-seeking decision maker would prefer single-line; a highly risk-averse decision maker would prefer multi-line without ZIP+4; a decision maker with another degree of risk aversion could prefer any of the three. (This is a comparison among these options only. Convert was preferred to all of these with any risk attitude.)

USE OF THE ANALYSIS

This analysis and the concurrent technical analysis [Gingras 1984] were used as a basis for OTA's report to Congress in June 1984 [US Congress, Office of Technology Assessment 1984]. It provided detailed, quantitative assessments of the economic implications of the strategy options that reflected uncertainties.

The analysis also helped OTA to think creatively about the problem and to generate options. For example, option C (multi-line OCR without ZIP+4) was generated after an early analysis indicated that the labor savings from a multi-line OCR would be large even without any ZIP+4 usage and option E (hedge) was generated after an early analysis indicated that the savings from a multi-line OCR were greatest under the most pessimistic forecasts of ZIP+4 usage.

Some contractual and technical questions were raised about the convert option after the analysis was completed. To address these concerns, OTA generated two additional options with procurements split between single- and multi-line OCRs. Under one option, a 50-50 split procurement, the government would reissue a request for proposal for one-half the number of single-line OCRs and simultaneously initiate testing of the multi-line OCR and single- to multi-line conversion. The other half of the OCRs would be multi-line, and they would be procured as soon as possible. The other option was for a 90-10 split with 90 percent of the single-line OCRs procured immediately.

Results of the completed analysis were used to estimate the evaluations of the new options. This showed that the 90-10 split procurement was about as good as convert. It was between convert and hedge.

Another aspect of this analysis is that it used multiple or plural analyses to arrive at an overall evaluation. These analyses were of two types, technical and economic. Both the USPS and OTA conducted analyses of the technical performance of single- and multi-line OCRs, bar code sorters, and other technologies. Both the USPS and GAO conducted economic analyses of postal operations and the impacts of automation. These analyses used different perspectives and assumptions and produced different results. The decision analysis used these analyses and other information to develop probability distributions on key factors of disagreement and benefited from the different perspectives represented. Decision analyses in general would benefit from deliberate actions to produce plural analyses of decision problems.

ACKNOWLEDGMENT

This paper was supported by the Congress of the United States, Office of Technology Assessment under contract number 433-4660.0 and by the National Science Foundation under award number SES-8420732.

REFERENCES

Gingras, W. P. 1984, *Review of Postal Automation (ZIP + 4) Technology*, Friendship Engineering Company, Friendship, Maryland.

Keefer, D. L. and Bodily, S. E. 1983, "Three-point approximations for continuous random variables," *Management Science*, Vol. 29, No. 5, pp. 595-609.

Keeney, R. L. and Raiffa, H. 1976, *Decisions with Multiple Objectives: Preferences and Value Tradeoffs*, John Wiley and Sons, New York.

Jellison, James V. (Senior Assistant Postmaster General) 1984, letter to Fred B. Wood (Project Director, OTA), February 9.

Pearson, E. S. and Tukey, J. W. 1965, "Approximate means and standard deviations based on distances between percentage points of frequency curves," *Biometrika*, Vol. 52, No. 3–4, pp. 533-546.

US Congress, Office of Technology Assessment (OTA) 1984, *Review of Postal Automation Strategy: A Technical and Decision Analysis* (Technical Memorandum), Office of Technology Assessment, June.

US General Accounting Office 1983, *Conversion to Automated Mail Processing Should Continue: Nine-Digit ZIP Code Should be Adopted if Conditions Are Met* (Report No. GAO/GGD-83–24). General Accounting Office, January 6.

US General Accounting Office 1983, *Conversion to Automated Mail Processing and Nine-Digit ZIP Code— A Status Report* (Report No. GAO/GGD-83-84), General Accounting Office, September 28.

Fred B. Wood, Project Director, Congress of the United States, Office of Technology Assessment, Washington, DC 20510-8024, writes, "The report prepared for OTA by Dr. Ulvila was used by OTA in the preparation of an OTA technical memorandum and testimony to Congress on the subject matter of postal automation. The decision analysis conducted by Dr. Ulvila was the first such analysis on this topic, and made a significant contribution to OTA's own understanding of automation options available to the United States Postal Service. Key elements of Dr. Ulvila's analysis were incorporated into OTA written and oral presentations to Congress and the Postal Service."

Weyerhaeuser Decision Simulator Improves Timber Profits

Mark R. Lembersky
Uli H. Chi

This paper expands on our recent *Interfaces* article [Lembersky and Chi 1984], which we will refer to as LC. It focused on a general approach, decision simulators, for implementing MS/OR algorithms and models. To illustrate the approach, LC also summarized the "VISION" decision simulator at Weyerhaeuser. The current paper describes the background, development, implementation, and benefits of VISION applications in more detail. Elements of LC are repeated here when necessary for completeness.

Weyerhaeuser is one of the largest forest products companies in the world. In 1984, company revenues were over $5 billion, predominantly through domestic and foreign sales of logs and timber, lumber, plywood, and paper products.

Forest products is primarily a commodity industry, which means there is little control over the prices realized from the sale of products. Facing such an environment, efficient utilization of Weyerhaeuser's raw materials base, its trees, is imperative; that, along with costs, is the principal profit factor under company control.

Also, the forest products industry is highly competitive, marked by relatively low profit margins. For example, in 1984 profits as a percentage of sales averaged about 2.5 percent for large, integrated firms. Consequently, even a small percentage increase in raw materials returns produces a disproportionately larger percentage increase in profits.

Weyerhaeuser operations handle a raw materials flow of just under one billion cubic feet each year—that's a volume of wood covering a football field and going four miles high! This large annual flow, divided about equally between the company's western and southern operations, means a very large absolute dollar impact from raw material decisions. Unlike other forest products firms, this flow comes mostly from trees Weyerhaeuser owns; so any increase in value results directly in additional company profits.

For all of these reasons, raw materials utilization decisions are very important to Weyerhaeuser's profitability.

In the mid-70s, a few senior company executives had a sense that better use could be made of the high-valued raw materials from western Douglas fir operations. At that time, no such opportunities were thought to be available in the pine forests of the South.

Achieving improved use of raw materials meant seeking the best use of each individual tree. How a tree is crosscut into logs and what is done with the resulting logs largely determines the return that tree yields. For example, when and in what combinations should the 8½-foot logs be cut that are needed to make 4 × 8 plywood panels instead of cutting the metric length logs required by the export market? When should lumber length logs be cut, and so on? To increase raw material values, individual trees needed to be crosscut and the resulting logs allocated in a way that produced the maximum possible net profit.

This is made more challenging by the field environment where the individual decisions are made. In the western woods, the tree is felled, delimbed, and possibly topped. What remains is the tree stem. The "woods bucker," the worker responsible for making decisions on tree use, must then decide how to cut the trees into logs. He must bear in mind that length, curvature, diameter, and knots are all factors in the value of any particular log. He is not dealing with a raw materials base of interchangeable items: each log is different, each decision on its use is irreversible. Dealing with tree stems is not like dealing with lengths of pipe.

In the South, crosscutting decisions are often carried out at large, fast-moving processing centers that handle the whole stem. The individual trees are smaller, but more crooked. The decisions are just as complex, and each operator is asked to complete several stems a minute, a much faster rate than in the West.

Depending on the decisions the worker makes, the stem can vary in value by 50 percent or more. Because making better decisions on tree cutting and log allocation entails no additional costs, any extra raw material value that can be consistently obtained by improved decisions goes directly into company profits. With Weyerhaeuser's large raw materials flow, the profit increase can be millions of dollars a year.

However, at first glance, making broadly effective improvements in our cutting and allocation decisions seemed difficult. Each year, Weyerhaeuser cuts and allocates approximately 15 million trees, one hundred trees a minute. No two trees are alike and each can be made into a variety of products. The decisions on cutting and allocation are made by hundreds of people in dispersed and often remote geographic areas. The initial proposal to use management science techniques to help improve stem-by-stem decision making was met with skepticism. With so many variables to account for, senior managers asked, how can we go beyond relying on the experience of our men in the field?

The response was what we call VISION. It consists of two elements: first, a dynamic programming optimization procedure that determines the best economic use for any tree; and second, a video-game-like computer system that allows woods and mill personnel, as well as company managers and top executives, to easily grasp what the best use is of any particular tree stem. Together, the result is better decisions in practice.

Funds were initially authorized for VISION in 1976. Weyerhaeuser did not publicize the VISION effort in order to retain its competitive advantage. This secrecy continued until we received a patent on the system in 1982.

DEVELOPING VISION

After the limbs and possibly the top are removed (Figure 1), the tree stem is then crosscut into logs. Each log is allocated to a market, such as export to Japan or sale domestically, or to a company manufacturing facility, such as a lumber mill, a plywood mill, or to one of several types of paper product mills.

The value of a stem is the sum of the revenues produced from each of the invidual logs it is made into, minus the costs associated with cutting the stem and processing the logs.

The revenue Weyerhaeuser derives from any particular log depends on many factors: the log length, curvature, diameter, and taper, its knot and quality characteristics, as well as the market or mill to which it is sent. Log values can vary dra-

matically with these parameters. Figure 2 shows actual data of revenue versus just two parameters, log curvature and length, and also illustrates how the relationship can change significantly with a change in log diameter of only two inches.

Consequently, different decisions on crosscutting and allocating a stem can produce very different log revenues and, therefore, very different stem values (Figure 3).

Finding the optimal cut and allocation decisions for a particular stem can be formulated as a dynamic program. A highly simplified version was included in the appendix of LC. However, a number of analytic and practical difficulties need to be overcome in order to create and exploit a useful formulation. Three of the most significant are

— The algorithm must account for the complex geometry of stems;
— The logs that can be cut from a stem are not simple multiple lengths of each other, for example, eight-foot lumber is not produced from logs half the length of logs yielding 16-foot lumber; metric

FIGURE 1. A tree stem is crosscut into logs and the logs are allocated to a market—such as export to Japan—or to a manufacturing facility— such as for production of lumber, plywood, or paper products.

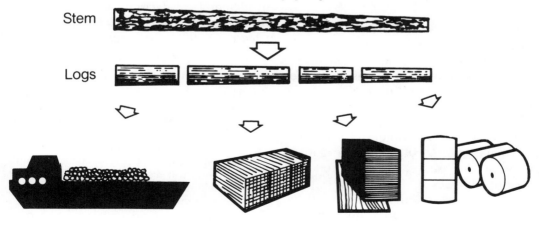

FIGURE 2. Log revenue varies dramatically as a function of log curvature, length, and diameter.

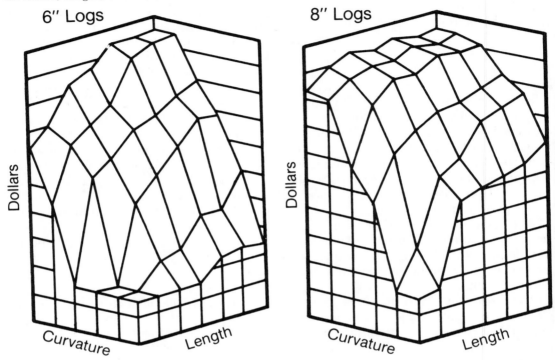

lengths for export must be considered, and so forth; and

— One must have extensive data bases both of stems and of log values as a function of all the important log parameters and possible allocations.

Developing these information bases upon which to rest our dynamic programming algorithm required gathering information on thousands of stems and logs from each of our operating regions. Weyerhaeuser painstakingly collected stem geometry in two-foot increments and entered the physical attributes of each into a stem data base. Next, we had to gather all necessary log values. This required mill tests in many cases.

With this data assembled and with a proprietary dynamic programming al-

gorithm the company developed to handle the complexities mentioned above, we could compute the optimal crosscut and allocation decisions for a stem. However, having this capability and having it actually change field decisions were two different things. Effective implementation was at least equally a challenge.

We faced several obstacles:

— First, we had to convince top management to provide us with the time and the budget to develop an effective implementation vehicle.

— Second, because no two trees are identical, the optimal dynamic programming solutions will also be different. It is not possible to compute a "right answer" that can be implemented for every stem.

— Third, and most important, we had to

FIGURE 3. Different crosscut and allocation decisions for the same stem produce very different log revenues—and therefore very different stem values.

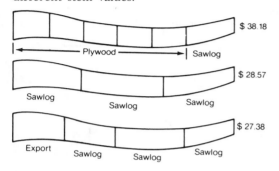

develop a means for transforming better decisions into field worker actions. It was not economically practical nor physically feasible to put computers loaded with the dynamic program in the field with each worker. Nor were these workers going to change their traditional way of cutting and allocating a stem just because some technical folks from corporate headquarters suggested there might be a better way.

Implementation required understanding and acceptance by these decision makers. This implied a great deal of management and worker involvement. Whatever our approach, it had to be easily understood and credible to experienced woodsmen.

VISION was our attempt to meet these challenges. Its name, decoded, suggests its purpose: *Video Interactive Stem Inspection and OptimizatioN*. VISION was our original "decision simulator" used as an implementation vehicle for an optimization algorithm. VISION was designed to provide its user with the opportunity to cut and allocate stems, receive immediate feedback on the economic consequences of those decisions, and see for comparison the dynamic programming decisions and their economic consequences. An illustrated description of the sequence of events in a VISION session is in LC.

VISION allows its user to make decisions, see what revenues they yield, and compare them with the optimal decisions. As a result, the user develops a better understanding of how to optimize the returns available from each tree. It's typical for the first-time user to distrust the optimal solutions and try to beat them. This creates a tremendous challenge. With time, users gradually discover that the dynamic programming cuts and allocations are better decisions than their early ones, and their decisions consistently improve. This improvement occurs at their own pace, with no one looking over their shoulders. When they return to the field, they take their improved decision-making abilities back with them.

We tried to design the system to be easy to learn and use. We didn't want to ask loggers to learn about computers. We wanted them to cut logs. Over 200 persons have interacted with VISION, most of them woods or mill workers. Almost everyone became comfortable with the system in the first five minutes. One logger from Dierks, Arkansas, told us that if we put VISION in his favorite tavern, our employees would pay to play it!

VISION APPLICATIONS AND BENEFITS

VISION has been used in Weyerhaeuser since 1977. The VISION system showed that senior management intuition was correct: raw materials values could be increased in western operations. Contrary to original perceptions, VISION also showed that there were opportunities for increasing raw material values in the South.

Seeing resources in this new way led to many changes in operations. Management used the system to formulate alternative stem-processing strategies and to evaluate their economics. Field workers also built decision skills by spending time with VISION. The most interesting uses involved both strategy changes and individual decisions. An important example of this type of use related to West Coast Douglas fir operations.

The woods buckers in the West make their stem-by-stem decisions using their judgment aided by general strategies called "woods-bucking instructions" printed on a pocket-sized card. Early use of VISION showed that these instructions were producing suboptimal revenues. Weyerhaeuser used VISION both to improve the woods-bucking instructions and to enable buckers to improve their decision-making skills.

Alternative instructions were developed by first computing and displaying the profit-maximizing decisions for sample stems, then studying these decisions for patterns which reappeared for classes of stems, and finally, generalizing these patterns into new woods instructions (Figure 4). This generalization process was aided by a respected field veteran who applied his considerable operational experience and judgment. First, we had to establish the credibility of the dynamic programming algorithm in his mind. He put VISION through its paces and became convinced of the value of the dynamic programming solutions. He then used VISION to compare alternate cutting patterns and construct alternative bucking instructions. Once a number of promising candidate instructions were developed, each was applied to all the sample stems and the resulting aggregate profits compared. The best performing set of instruc-

FIGURE 4. Optimal stem decisions are studied for reappearing patterns that are generalized into new woods bucking instructions; these are compared again with optimal stem decisions. This iterative process employs a respected field veteran.

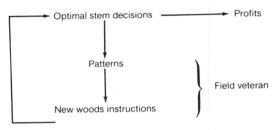

tions was selected. It differed fundamentally from what was then common practice by emphasizing that selected high-value export log lengths be cut rather than instructing that logs be cut where stem quality changed (Figure 5).

We then had to gain the understanding and acceptance of the woods foremen. The foremen used VISION to see the results of cutting and allocating a sample of stems from their region using their old instructions. Then, they were given the new instructions and asked to recut the same set of stems. They were also encouraged to experiment with any other cutting patterns of their own invention. The experienced field expert sponsored and participated in these foremen activities. With their value demonstrated, the foremen readily embraced the new instructions and saw the implications of the dynamic programming algorithm. As a result, their operating regions implemented the new instructions quickly.

These new instructions were put into practice starting in 1977. A careful field audit of cutting practices was completed two years later during 1979. Woods bucker decisions and the values of logs

FIGURE 5. Old instructions emphasize cutting at changes in stem quality (grade breaks); new instructions emphasize cutting high-valued export and domestic log lengths.

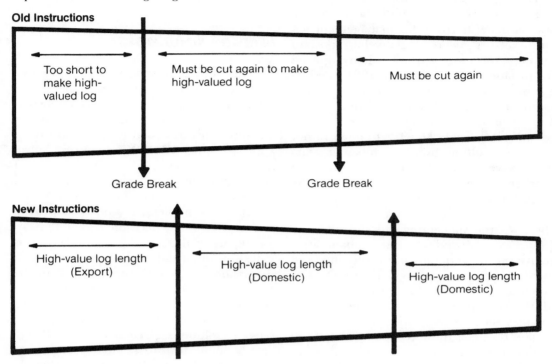

produced were tracked both before and after introduction of the new instructions. The measured difference in value as a result of the new way logs were being cut and allocated was $7 million of additional annual profits, expressed in 1979 dollars.

During the same period, a group of other applications was directed at improving southern raw material values. Region raw material managers, operational superintendents, and operators took part in VISION sessions. By themselves, these activities improved stem-crosscutting and log-allocation decisions. This initial involvement with VISION also spawned many location-specific applications in the South, analogous to the woods-bucking changes in the West. For example, the

manager responsible for raw materials in the Oklahoma-Arkansas region spent many sessions with VISION evaluating the consequences of alternative operating strategies and developing new strategies on the spot. He subsequently implemented new strategies for stem cutting and allocating across his operations. He also became a strong advocate of capital investments in his region that allowed increased control over stem cutting practices. At one location he installed a fully automated system to help achieve optimal cutting and allocation.

In 1979 a careful quantification was also made of the impact across the South. The analysis was requested by the sponsoring group vice-president and reviewed by the chief operating officer. It showed just under $6 million of annual profit increase (again, in 1979 dollars).

Raw material values and therefore the annual benefits from this management science effort were relatively constant through the end of 1980, when adjusted for inflation. However, since 1981, the forest products industry has experienced a significant decline in end-product prices and general raw material values. So, to compute aggregate benefits to date, rather than just multiply by the number of years that have elapsed, the western and southern benefits for each year after 1980 are adjusted for both the decline in raw material values and inflation. For consistency, we put all aggregated dollars on a 1985 basis. We did not put a quantitative figure on the generally improved ability of our workers to adjust to changes, which is nonetheless a benefit of working with VISION. We only included the benefits from changes seen in field operations.

The result of these computations: a $59 million incremental profit contribution to date from the western woods bucking application and a profit increase for our southern operations of at least $42 million so far. Thus, total operational benefits to date are at least $100 million.

And, this is perhaps not VISION's most important effect. As important is that VISION influenced management philosophy from the top on down.

Because a lot of time has passed since our first VISION efforts, we've had the opportunity to observe the staying power of its effects on the company. As timber values have fallen, industry profits have fallen even faster. Fortunately, the nature of the benefits from this management science effort do not decline proportionally to profits. In fact, the ratio of annual benefits to Weyerhaeuser operating profits has steadily increased since 1980 (Figure

6). By 1984, this contribution ratio had grown to over three times its pre-1981 level.

DECISION SIMULATORS

While developing VISION, it occured to us that there were some general features which could be profitably applied to a lot of our management science work. The literature revealed no prior use of an approach with VISION's features. Subsequently, we coined the term *decision simulator* to describe our approach. The term *decision simulator* is intended to suggest that VISION-like implementation tools provide experiences for a decision maker that are analogous to those a flight simulator provides for an airline pilot. A more complete discussion of decision simulators is in LC. Here we wish only to emphasize that decision simulators represent a generic approach to helping implement management science solutions. Systems like VISION can be built for many different applications. Indeed, we've built several other decision simulators ourselves since our first one in 1976. Others have been reported recently in MS/OR journals: We believe that management science practitioners have

FIGURE 6. The ratio of annual benefits from VISION to Weyerhaeuser operating profits has increasd with time.

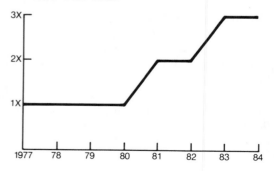

a wide-spread opportunity to exploit the decision simulator implementation approach. Because the ratio of computer cost to performance continues to improve, creating a decision simulator is becoming easier.

IMPACT SUMMARY

We conclude with comments from Donald E. Rush, Group Vice-President for Timberlands, on the impact on Weyerhaeuser of this implementation of management science:

I'm convinced that improved bucking instructions in our western operations led to approximately $60 million more profit, as described in this paper. VISION has changed the West Coast mentality of doing business. We're doing a better job of matching our logs to the marketplace than ever before.

VISION also showed us there was more variation in southern raw material values than we'd believed—and that, consequently, there was an opportunity to upgrade the average value of our southern trees: Implementation in the South led to enhanced profits of over $40 million.

I reviewed these figures carefully and, in fact, reported them to our chief operating officer. They are, if anything, on the conservative side.

I've seen the effect VISION has had on the thinking of even some of our most traditional woods workers. And I've seen the effect this effort has had on the thinking of our top managers— even beyond what I've just described for the South and West.

Top managers were involved in the funding, testing, and implementation of VISION. Our chief executive officer,

George Weyerhaeuser, used it. So did our chief operating officer, myself, and many others. We all realized from our interaction that there was more we could do with our timber resources— and we took action. For example, I've seen us commit many millions of scarce capital dollars to completely automate log processing facilities so that VISION-like procedures can be used on-line to process tree stems. Also, we've funded and developed other systems based on the same principles for such different areas as facility design and truck-routing.

VISION changed our corporate behavior in ways that have made us more money, and these changes have persisted. The contributions to our bottom line have not only held up over the years, but have actually increased in importance over time and under adverse industry economic conditions. This is an advantage unique and exclusive to Weyerhaeuser, an advantage enjoyed currently by none of our competitors.

ACKNOWLEDGMENT

Many persons played significant roles in the efforts described here. Bob Davis supplied his years of field experience and brought his credibility with foremen and workers. Bill Grunow and Lynne Stroh aided implementation of new woods bucking instructions. Doug Hay produced the original dynamic programming algorithm.

REFERENCE

Lembersky, Mark R. and Chi, Uli H. 1984, "Decision simulators speed implementation and improve operations," *Interfaces*, Vol. 14, No. 4 (July-August), pp. 1-15.

8

DECISION SUPPORT
FOR GOVERNMENT SERVICES

Federal, state, and city governments provide a wide range of services important to keeping the public safe and healthy and the living environment clean and accessible. For example, city governments provide a variety of services: police patrol the streets, firemen extinguish blazes, sanitation workers dispose of trash, health care professionals tend to the sick, and highway engineers maintain the roadways. In providing these services, managers at all levels of government encounter many difficult decision problems. Where should a new landfill be located? How should police patrols be deployed to maximize coverage of the city? What size fleet of trucks is needed to remove trash? Over the years, government planners and analysts have relied heavily on management science techniques to model and solve these problems. More recently, their reliance on mathematical models has increased. The fiscal crises of the '70s and '80s forced city and state governments, as well as the federal government, to cut their budgets drastically. Often, this meant a severe cutback in public services. Decision makers now employ MS/OR models to find efficient and inexpensive ways of delivering the same level of services as in the past.

The first paper in this chapter illustrates a relatively new public-sector application area: infrastructure maintenance. Over the last 10 years, management science models have been successfully applied to manage the maintenance of bridges, tunnels, gas pipelines, and roadways. This paper describes the development of a pavement management system that uses a Markov decision model to help the state of Arizona decide which highway segments to maintain each year and how best to repair and preserve them.

In the late 1970s, the Big Apple's luster was severely tarnished: its streets were very dirty and its trash was piling up. The agency in charge, New York City's Department of Sanitation, was labeled an embarrassment and clearly needed to clean up its act. The second paper describes how New York City used four management science models— manpower forecasting, production functions for street cleaning, truck sizing, and assignment of loads to dump sites—to turn New York City around and make it a cleaner place.

8.1 *MAINTAINING ARIZONA'S HIGHWAY SYSTEM*

The Highway Division of Arizona's Department of Transportation (ADOT) is charged with the formidable task of preserving and maintaining 2,200 miles of interstate roadway and 5,200 miles of noninterstate roadway in Arizona. Each year the division's management must allocate a multi-million dollar highway preservation budget by deciding which stretches of highway to repair and what repair actions to use.

In the late 1970s, ADOT's management was worried about several issues related to the highway-preservation decision process. First, the state's seven highway districts were making important maintenance decisions almost autonomously. Each district controlled its share of the funds and decided how to spend the money independently of the other districts. This led to a patchwork of highways in which road conditions varied greatly from one district to another. Since this process resulted in very subjective budget recommendations, the state legislature was reluctant to increase the yearly funding of the preservation program. Second, there was a widening gap between estimated income and expenses. Asphalt, the primary road surfacing material, had tripled in cost between 1975 and 1980, while the revenue from a state tax on gasoline was decreasing due to fuel-efficient vehicles and conservation-minded drivers. Third, money from the Federal Highway Administration, which comprised a major part of ADOT's budget could be used only to preserve interstate highways and roads that met stringent federal standards. However, few roads in Arizona met these standards. In the past, ADOT had not allocated state funds to upgrade roads to federal standards so that they would qualify for federal money. Instead, ADOT chose to regularly resurface only qualified interstate highways.

Faced with the prospect of a widening gap between available funds and preservation requirements and the possibility of widely variable road conditions, ADOT sought a better way of distributing maintenance money. It contracted with an engineering consulting firm to design, build, test, and implement a tool for decision making that could systematically advise ADOT of the best way to maintain roads and stay within its budget. In the first paper, Golabi, Kulkarni, and Way [1982] describe their development of the Pavement Management System (PMS), a state-of-the-art decision support system. PMS collects and stores data on pavement performance and then uses it to build a mathematical model to aid decision making on maintenance. PMS was first implemented in fiscal year 1980–81. ADOT had budgeted $46 million for highway preservation that year—enough for it to keep the same proportion of roads in acceptable condition as it had during the previous six years. The maintenance policies recommended by PMS achieved that goal for $32 million, releasing $14 million of "savings" for allocation to other highway projects.

In order to determine the best long-term and short-term highway maintenance policies, Golabi, Kulkarni, and Way formulated two interrelated Markov decision models. These models form the algorithmic core of PMS known as the Network Optimization System (NOS). The Markov decision process tries to capture the dynamic and probabilistic aspects of pavement maintenance by relating road conditions to maintenance decisions. Exhibit 8–1 lists the four main components of the Markov decision process: variables, states, maintenance actions, and transition probabilities. The condition of the pavement in a one-mile stretch of highway is assessed by measuring four *variables* u, Δu, r, and z that quantify cracking and roughness characteristics of the pavement. These measurements jointly define the *state* of the pavement. For each state, several mainte-

EXHIBIT 8–1. The Markov decision process specifies the effect of maintenance actions on the state of the highway pavement. A state measures four quantities. For example, pavement in state 1 shows five percent cracking; its cracking has changed 2.5 percent during the previous year; roughness is measured as 120 inches of bumps per mile; the index to the first crack is 18 years. Only 120 of the $3 \times 3 \times 3 \times 5 = 135$ possible combinations of the values of the state variables are considered likely. Seventeen different maintenance actions can be undertaken. For example, the second action requires resurfacing a one-mile highway segment with a one-inch overlay of asphalt. Each state has an average of about six maintenance actions that are considered feasible. The transition probabilities to future states depend on the action while in the current state. When the highway is in state 1, two different maintenance actions can be undertaken. When the specified action is a five inch overlay, there is a 0.999 chance that the highway will be in state 1 and a 0.001 chance that it will be in state 9 at the next observed time period.

Variables	Number of Possible Values
u = present amount of cracking	3
Δu = change in the amount of cracking during the previous year	3
r = present roughness	3
z = index to the first crack	5

EXHIBIT 8–1. (Continued)

States

State	u	Δu	r	z
1	5%	2.5%	120 inches/mile	18 years
2				
.	.	.	.	.
.	.	.	.	.
.	.	.	.	.
120				

Maintenance Actions

Action	Description
1	Routine maintenance
2	One inch overlay
.	.
.	.
.	.
17	

Transition Probabilities

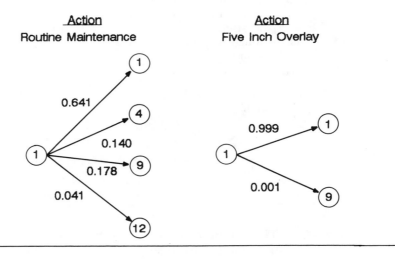

nance *actions* can be undertaken to preserve the road. *Transition probabilities* specify how the future pavement conditions evolve out of the current conditions according to the maintenance actions adopted. Linear programming models are then constructed to find the best long-term and short-term highway maintenance policies. The long-term LP model is given in Exhibit 8–2. The optimal solution to this model tells engineers which maintenance actions to perform for a stretch of highway in a certain state.

EXHIBIT 8–2. The linear programming formulation of the constrained Markov decision process specifies the optimal policy for achieving long-term standards for road conditions. The objective function minimizes the long-term expected average cost of maintaining the highways. Solving the linear program (1), (2), and (5) gives a pure solution by associating a single action a with each state i. However, there are additional requirements. Engineers specify what are acceptable and unacceptable states for the highways. Since the decision variables can also be interpreted as the proportion of roads that are in state i and for which action a is taken, constraint (3) requires ADOT to keep at least a certain proportion of pavement in acceptable states. Constraint (4) limits the proportion of roads in unacceptable states that can be repaired. Due to the presence of constraints (3) and (4), the solution to the entire linear program (1)–(5) can produce a randomized optimal policy.

Input Parameters	*Decision Variables*
c_{ia} = maintenance cost of a mile segment when the road is in state i and maintenance action a is selected	w_{ia} = probability that a one-mile road segment is in state i and action a is selected
$p_{ij}(a)$ = probability of moving from state i to state j when action a is selected	
e_i, l_i = long-range performance standards	

Long-Term Linear Programming Model

minimize $\sum_i \sum_a c_{ia} w_{ia}$
subject to

$$\sum_i \sum_a w_{ia} = 1 \tag{1}$$

$$\sum_a w_{ja} - \sum_i \sum_a p_{ij}(a) w_{ia} = 0 \text{ for all } j \tag{2}$$

$$\sum_a w_{ia} \geq e_i \text{ if i is acceptable} \tag{3}$$

$$\sum_a w_{ia} \leq l_i \text{ if i is unacceptable} \tag{4}$$

$$w_{ia} \geq 0 \text{ for all i and a} \tag{5}$$

The solution produced by the long-term LP required some interpretation. First, the LP sometimes specifies more than one maintenance action for each state. For example, the optimal maintenance policy could recommend taking action a_1 with probability p_1 and action a_2 with probability p_2 when the pavement is in state i. Such randomized policies occur infrequently and the solution never recommends more than two actions for a state. However, when randomized choices do arise, decision makers interpret them in a straightforward way: p_1 represents the proportion of roads in state i that will receive action a_1 while p_2 is the proportion of roads in state i that will receive action a_2.

Second, since the LP model considers only one-mile segments of highway, an optimal solution might specify actions such as a_2-a_1-a_2 for a three-mile stretch of highway. In practice, it might be less expensive to take action a_2 on the entire stretch even though action a_1 may be cheaper when compared to a_2. Such modifications to the optimal solution are permitted as long as the overall project cost does not increase and no inferior actions are taken.

Golabi [1988] informed us that PMS has received industry-wide recognition and acceptance and, to date, is the only pavement maintenance optimization system that has been implemented. In addition to Arizona, the system is used in Alaska, Colorado, Kansas, and Finland. It is also used in Saudi Arabia as part of a comprehensive highway maintenance management system that includes managing structures such as bridges and tunnels and nonpavement elements.

8.2 REFUSE COLLECTION AND STREET CLEANING IN THE UNITED STATES' LARGEST CITY

By any standard of measurement, New York City was filthy in the late 1970s. During that time, the Department of Sanitation was hard pressed to keep more than half of the city's streets acceptably clean. It also had difficulty collecting and disposing of the city's household and commercial refuse efficiently. In all fairness, the size and scope of the problems faced by the department were mind-boggling. Each day an estimated 4 to 5 million pieces of litter weighing more than 100 tons are deposited on the city's 6,000 miles of streets. On a daily basis, the department collects about 12,000 tons of household refuse, and private carters collect another 10,000 tons. The department must then dispose of all 22,000 tons. It also enforces the sanitary code and removes snow. In 1986, the department accomplished these tasks with a work force of about 12,000 employees and a budget of $500 million. About 2,200 workers were dedicated to cleaning the streets.

In 1978, a new sanitation commissioner tackled the difficult task of trying to improve the department's performance. Over a three-year period, many sophisticated scientific methods were employed to analyze streetcleaning and refuse collection problems including the management science models Riccio [1984] describes in the paper that follows. Four MS models—for forecasting manpower needs, for determining production functions for street cleaning, for sizing trucks, and for assigning loads to dump sites—improved the performance of the department. Each model played an important role in transforming what Riccio calls a "municipal embarrassment" into one of the outstanding sanitation agencies in the US. We will briefly describe the models that were used for manpower planning and street cleaning.

For several years starting in 1978, the department collected monthly data on the number of workers needed and the number that were actually available for cleaning the streets, collecting garbage, and performing garage support activities. Workloads were seasonal in nature with manpower needs peaking in the summer months. Such factors as rates of monthly worker attrition and daily absence affected the availability of workers. The manpower forecasting model (Exhibit 8–3) identifies the key factors that determine the need for workers and their availability. An optimization-based search routine produces a solution that predicts the monthly shortages and surpluses of workers. During shortage periods, employees work on their days off and at twice their normal pay. When more workers are available than the department needs, the surplus workers are assigned to extra street-cleaning duties. The model determines the best hiring policy so that total salary and overtime costs are minimized.

The department also developed a way to assess the cleanliness of New York City's streets quantitatively: Project Scorecard. Each month the department samples a mix of 6,000 residential, commercial, and industrial blocks taken from the city's 59 districts. Each block is rated on a scale of 1.0 for spotless to 3.0 for filthy. A rating of 1.5 or less indicates that the block is acceptably clean. The Scorecard rating for each district is the percentage of district streets that are acceptably clean. The city-wide rating is computed by taking a weighted average of the ratings for the 59 districts. Each application of the Scorecard method provides the department with an accurate picture of how well it is doing in the war on litter.

EXHIBIT 8–3. The forecasting model seeks to predict manpower shortages and surpluses for each month. The model determines how many workers to hire in each month so as to minimize the costs for yearly salaries and overtime.

Input Parameters	*Decision Variables*
K = average monthly salary of a worker	H_i = number of workers hired in month i
L_i = number of workers lost due to attrition in month i	P_i = number of workers on payroll in beginning of month i
	Forecasted Quantities
N_i = number of working days in month i	S_i = average daily surplus or deficit of workers in month i
R = overtime cost when working on the assigned day off	

Relationships

$P_i = P_{i-1} + H_{i-1} - L_{i-1} \qquad i = 1, 2, \ldots, 12$

$Q_i = |S_i|$ if $S_i < 0 \qquad i = 1, 2, \ldots, 12$
$\qquad 0$ if $S_i \geq 0$

Manpower Forecasting Model

$$\text{minimize } \sum_i K \cdot P_i + R \cdot N_i \cdot Q_i$$

EXHIBIT 8–4. The street cleaner allocation model helps New York City's Department of Sanitation find the best way of allocating additional street cleaners to each of the city's districts. The optimal solution maximizes the weighted average of the individual ratings for the 59 districts.

Input Parameters	*Decision Variables*
M = total mileage of NYC's streets	X_i = number of additional cleaners assigned to district i
M_i = mileage of streets in district i	
S_i = Scorecard rating for district i	
a_i = Scorecard rating in district i without additional cleaners	
b_i = increase in Scorecard rating for district i for each additional cleaner	

Relationships

$S_i = a_i + b_i \cdot X_i$

$S_i \leq 100$

Allocation Model

$$\text{maximize } S_c = \sum_i^{\cdot} (M_i/M)\, S_i$$

In 1981, the department needed to determine the best way of allocating 450 new street cleaners to the city's 59 districts. In particular, it wanted to know how street cleaners and enforcement agents affected a street's cleanliness. Regression models indicated that there was a significant relationship between the number of days devoted to cleaning and enforcement and a street's cleanliness. The coefficients in these models provided each district with a way to measure the increase in the Scorecard rating when the department assigned an additional cleaner to it. The street cleaner allocation model (Exhibit 8–4) uses these marginal utilities to determine the optimal allocation of the new street cleaners. It turns out that the optimal solution given by this model is somewhat counterintuitive. Clean areas are allocated more new cleaners than the dirty areas since their marginal utilities are quite high. The department implemented a compromise strategy that allocated some cleaners to all districts with the dirtiest ones getting the most new cleaners.

8.3 FURTHER READINGS

Related Readings

Golabi, Kulkarni, and Way Paper

- Golabi [1983] presents many of the theoretical details behind the Markov decision-modeling approach to the problem of maintaining pavement. After discussing the problem's background, the condition variables, and the transition probabilities, he develops two LP formulations of the maintenance problem. The first LP model (briefly discussed in the reading that follows) gives the maintenance policy that maximizes expected benefits. The optimal solution to this model recommends the most expensive maintenance action for each state. Golabi shows how a budget constraint can be incorporated into this model by using the dual problem. The remaining discussion focuses on the linear programs for long-term and short-term cost minimization. Golabi offers several reasons why he prefers the cost minimization model to the maximization approach. He concludes the paper with a brief mention of several successful implementations.

Riccio Paper

- Riccio [1985] discusses the wide variety of programs that the Department of Sanitation used to help clean up New York City in the early 1980s. He focuses on four major areas: (1) measuring street cleanliness, (2) sources of litter, (3) reducing the litter rate, and (4) increasing the cleanup rate. In the first area, he describes the Project Scorecard rating system, while in the second area, he discusses a procedure used to count and categorize the street and sidewalk litter found on 100 blockfaces in New York City. The results of this survey indicated that litter was generated one piece at a time by individuals rather than from litter spilling out of improperly bundled refuse waiting for curbside collection. Nearly 60 percent of street litter consists of food and food-related items, such as napkins, candy wrappers, cups, cup tops, metal and glass containers, straws, and straw wrappers. The pervasiveness of these items points to individuals as the sources of most street litter. Riccio then discusses the various antilittering programs designed to make New York City a cleaner place and the Department of Sanitation's efforts to increase the cleanup rate. The department's strategy includes increasing the number of street cleaners, constructing mathematical models of manpower use, simulating the effects of parked cars on street cleaning, and motivating workers to do a better job.

- Riccio, Miller, and Litke [1986] update the earlier *Interfaces* articles by first reviewing the many street cleaning problems the Department of Sanitation faced in 1980. These problems included a very high percentage of dirty streets, low worker morale, and limited resources to fight the litter war. The authors then briefly describe three different management science models that have helped to improve New York City's cleanliness from 1980 to 1985: (1) regression models relating manpower to cleanliness levels, (2) parametric models relating manpower utilization to factors such as the litter rate and size of the area being cleaned, and (3) Monte Carlo simulations of how illegally parked cars affect street cleaning. The authors point out that these models significantly changed the way New York City addressed the street cleaning problem. Their use led to much cleaner streets and to an annual savings of $12 million in salaries and fringe benefit costs.

- Each day in New York City more than 350 mechanical sweepers are dispatched to clean streets. Since nearly all litter is found very near the curb, it is essential that the mechanical sweepers get close to the curb. In theory, alternate-side-of-the-street parking regulations should keep one side of the street free of parked cars so that the sweepers can get to the curb. In practice, illegally parked cars usually prevent sweepers from getting to the curb at some places along their routes. Along a 10-mile route, as many as 800 cars may block a sweeper. Better coordination between the street-sweeping efforts of the Department of Sanitation and the ticket-writing efforts of the Traffic Department can help solve this problem. The Department of Sanitation proposed that the Traffic Department assign a mobile traffic enforcement officer to ticket illegally parked cars blocking the routes of sweepers in certain districts. The Traffic Department agreed to cooperate provided the Department of Sanitation could demonstrate that this plan would reduce the number of illegally parked cars and that the reduction would lead to cleaner streets. Riccio and Litke [1986] describe their efforts to demonstrate these effects. They developed a Monte Carlo simulation model of street cleaning that consists of four parts: (1) a model that randomly places pieces or piles of litter at the curb, (2) a model that specifies the number and location of illegally parked cars, (3) rules that govern sweeper behavior, and (4) a Scorecard rating model for measuring the cleanliness of a block. The authors vary the number of illegally parked cars on a block from 3 to 17 cars and specify 10 different car spacings. Each street is given a number that signifies its initial dirtiness. A total of 140,000 runs of the simulation model were made. The results of the simulation showed that even with a small reduction in the number of illegally parked cars the sweeper's ability to make a street acceptably clean would improve significantly. The simulation results along with those from a pilot study of the ticketing plan convinced the Traffic Department to redeploy 30 percent of their mobile agents to ticket illegally parked cars blocking mechanical sweepers.

- Riccio, Miller, and Bose [1988] provide some additional insight into how street cleaners, litter enforcement agents, and litter rates affect the cleanliness of New York City's streets. They constructed a set of equations using 12 variables (known as a parametric model) that established relationships between street-cleaning resources, such as enforcement agents and street cleaners, and street cleanliness as measured by the Scorecard rating. The equations contain many constants and factors whose values can be varied in order to measure their effect on the overall rating. The authors used a mainframe computer to test several million combinations of reasonable values. Based on this experiment, they concluded that street cleaners are more effective than litter enforcement agents in keeping New York City's streets clean.

Background Readings

Golabi, Kulkarni, and Way Paper

- White [1985, 1988] presents a survey of real applications of Markov decision processes between 1959 and 1986. The two-part survey lists only papers that describe analyses using real data and results that have been implemented or have influenced the decision-making process. White clusters papers by problem area and provides a short summary of the problem under study, a verbal description of the objective function, notes on implementation of the model, and some general comments for each cluster. Altogether, he surveys 41 clusters containing nearly 60 papers in a wide variety of areas including fisheries management, forestry, reservoir-energy operations, and farming. White points out that only a dozen or so papers describe work in which the final results were actually implemented.

- INTELSAT is a company that provides satellite communication to a large number of member countries (108 countries in 1985). Using demand forecasts, it must develop plans that specify the quantity and timing of satellite purchases while taking into account a wide variety of complex factors, such as the lag time for delivery of a new satellite (from 36 to 48 months), satellite cost (between $30 and $100 million), the remaining lifetime of orbiting satellites, and many other uncertainties. Scherer and White [1985] describe the development of a planning and decision support system (PDSS) designed to help INTELSAT formulate its operational plans. At the heart of PDSS is a spacecraft-purchase-and-launch model that is based on a multiobjective Markov decision process. This model assumes at most 100 spacecraft of up to 10 types with a planning horizon of 10 years. Each spacecraft has a state space of 72 states that span the stages from manufacturing through launching. For example, in state 30, the spacecraft is available for launch, while in state 72, it has suffered a launch failure. Since the very large state space with over 72^{100} elements rendered the problem computationally intractable, Scherer and White simulated the Markov decision process using a Monte Carlo simulation model. This model enabled them to examine three heuristic purchase policies and allowed INTELSAT's management to perform valuable what-if experiments.

- Suppose you've just acquired the assets and liabilities of a securities brokerage firm and you've paid more than net book value. An interesting question that has implications for tax purposes is: What part of the purchase price premium is attributable to the value of the human assets, that is, the pool of account executives? Flamholtz, Geis, and Perle [1984] attempted to answer this question by constructing a finite stationary Markov decision model of the year-to-year movement in sales commissions of account executives. During the year, each account executive is in one of four states: (1) high sales commission, (2) medium, (3) low, or (4) job terminated. They generated one-step transition probabilities by tracking the movements of all account executives over a six year period. Using this model, the authors were able to calculate the total depreciable value of the asset pool, which is the discounted sum of future earnings of the account executives.

- Several excellent books cover the theory of Markov decision processes and its relationship to dynamic programming (DP). Historically, Bellman's book [1957] is the first comprehensive source for much of the early mathematical theory of multi-stage decision processes. Howard's book [1960] is a seminal work filled with interesting examples of Markov processes, such as taxicab operation, baseball batting strategy, and automobile replacement. In this book, Howard describes the powerful policy-iteration method for finding the optimal solution to a sequential decision process. Hillier and Lieberman [1986] present easy-to-follow material on Markov decision processes and applications that is aimed at advanced undergraduate or master's level students. They cover the expected average cost LP formulation and Howard's policy-iteration algorithm and numerically illustrate both methods. Ross [1970] devotes four chapters to the theory of sequential decision making that includes the linear program formulation using the expected average cost criterion. Ross [1983] also discusses the LP model and the policy-improvement method. Denardo [1982] gives a detailed account of recent developments in dynamic programming theory, models, and applications.

Riccio Paper

- Like New York City, most cities use mechanical sweepers to clean streets. Dispatchers may construct the daily sweeper routes manually or drivers may design their own routes. However, when the problem is of the size and complexity faced by New York City, it is difficult for even very experienced dispatchers and drivers to design near-optimal routes manually. Bodin and Kursh [1978] tackled this problem by developing a computer-assisted procedure for routing and scheduling mechanical street sweepers. They performed two pilot studies that applied the procedure to a district in New York City that used eight sweepers to clean 88 miles of streets each day and to 300 miles of central streets and heavily traveled streets in Washington, D.C. The procedure saved one vehicle in New York City and the authors estimate that a city-wide implementation could save $1,000,000 annually. Based on experiences arising from this work, Bodin and Kursh offer advice to practitioners seeking successful implementations of management science models: obtain the cooperation and confidence of key line personnel from the beginning of the modeling process.

- Operations research and management science models have been used in a wide variety of public service applications, including managing the response to disasters using a microcomputer-based decision support system (Belardo, Karwan, and Wallace [1984]); improving flood-forecast response systems using a Markov decision model and a Bayesian learning model (Krzysztofowicz and Davis [1984]); improving educational quality through constrained facet analysis and linear programming (Bessent et al. [1984]); relying on mathematical programming, simulation, and stochastic processes to solve problems in higher education administration (White [1987]); diagnosing housing shortages in Turkey using regression models and input/output analysis (Kavrakoglu et al. [1987]); developing a management information system to plan and monitor the movement of such essential commodities as rice and wheat in India (Ramani and Bhatnagar [1988]); and deploying police officers in San Francisco using an optimization-based decision support system (Taylor and Huxley [1989]).

REFERENCES

Belardo, Salvatore; Karwan, Kirk R.; and Wallace, William A. 1984, "Managing the response to disasters using microcomputers," *Interfaces,* Vol. 14, No. 2, pp. 29–39.

Bellman, Richard 1957, *Dynamic Programming,* Princeton University Press, Princeton, New Jersey.

Bessent, A.; Bessent, W.; Elam, J.; and Long, D. 1984, "Educational productivity council employs management science methods to improve educational quality," *Interfaces,* Vol. 14, No. 6, pp. 1–8.

Bodin, Lawrence D. and Kursh, Samuel J. 1978, "A computer-assisted system for the routing and scheduling of street sweepers," *Operations Research,* Vol. 26, No. 4, pp. 525–537.

Denardo, Eric V. 1982, *Dynamic Programming: Models and Applications,* Prentice-Hall, Englewood Cliffs, New Jersey.

Flamholtz, Eric G.; Geis, George T.; and Perle, Richard J. 1984, "A Markovian model for the valuation of human assets acquired by an organizational purchase," *Interfaces,* Vol. 14, No. 6, pp. 11–15.

Golabi, Kamal 1983, "A Markov decision modeling approach to a multiobjective maintenance problem," in *Essays and Surveys on Multiple Criteria Decision Making,* ed. Pierre Hansen, Lecture Notes in Economics and Mathematical Systems, No. 209, Springer-Verlag, Berlin, West Germany, pp. 115–125.

Golabi, Kamal 1988, private communication.

Golabi, Kamal; Kulkarni, Ram B.; and Way, George B. 1982, "A statewide pavement management system," *Interfaces,* Vol. 12, No. 6, pp. 5–21.

Hillier, Frederick S. and Lieberman, Gerald J. 1986, *Introduction to Operations Research,* McGraw-Hill, New York.

Howard, Ronald A. 1960, *Dynamic Programming and Markov Processes,* The M.I.T. Press, Cambridge, Massachusetts.

Kavrakoglu, Ibrahim; Kaylan, Ali Riza; Özekici, Süleyman; Oüzmucur, Süleyman; and Tamer, Güniz 1987, "A systems approach for the Turkish housing problem," *Interfaces,* Vol. 17, No. 5, pp. 1–10.

Krzysztofowicz, Roman and Davis, Donald R. 1984, "Toward improving flood forecast-response systems," *Interfaces,* Vol. 14, No. 3, pp. 1–14.

Ramani, K. V. and Bhatnagar, S. C. 1988, "A management information system to plan and monitor the distribution of essential commodities in India," *Interfaces,* Vol, 18, No. 2, pp. 56–63.

Riccio, Lucius J. 1984, "Management science in New York's Department of Sanitation," *Interfaces,* Vol. 14, No, 2, pp. 1–13.

Riccio, Lucius J. 1985, "To the 'litter' of the law: Cleaning New York City," *The Journal of Resource Management and Technology,* Vol. 14, No. 2, pp. 95–100.

Riccio, Lucius J. and Litke, Ann 1986, "Making a clean sweep: Simulating the effects of illegally parked cars on New York City's mechanical street-cleaning efforts," *Operations Research,* Vol. 34, No. 5, pp. 661–666.

Riccio, Lucius J.; Miller, Joseph; and Bose, Gautam 1988, "Polishing the big apple: Models of how manpower utilization affects street cleanliness in New York City," *Waste Management & Research,* Vol. 6, pp. 163–174.

Riccio, Lucius J.; Miller, Joseph; and Litke, Ann 1986, "Polishing the big apple: How management science has helped make New York streets cleaner," *Interfaces,* Vol. 16, No. 1, pp. 83–88.

Ross, Sheldon M. 1970, *Applied Probability Models with Optimization Applications,* Holden-Day, San Francisco, California.

Ross, Sheldon M. 1983, *Introduction to Stochastic Dynamic Programming,* Academic Press, New York.

Scherer, William T. and White, Chelsea C. 1985, "A planning and decision-aiding procedure for purchasing and launching spacecraft," *Interfaces,* Vol. 16, No, 3, pp. 31–40.

Taylor, Philip E. and Huxley, Stephen J. 1989, "A break from tradition for the San Francisco police: Patrol officer scheduling using an optimization-based decision support system," *Interfaces,* Vol. 19, No. 1, pp. 4–24.

White, Douglas J. 1985, "Real applications of Markov decision processes," *Interfaces,* Vol. 15, No. 6, pp. 73–83.

White, Douglas J. 1988, "Further real applications of Markov decision processes," *Interfaces,* Vol. 18, No. 5, pp. 55–61.

White, Gregory P. 1987, "A survey of recent management science applications in higher education administration," *Interfaces,* Vol. 17, No. 2, pp. 97–108.

A Statewide Pavement Management System

Kamal Golabi
Ram B. Kulkarni
George B. Way

This article reports the development of a statewide system for maintaining roads in Arizona. The system recommends the best maintenance action for each mile of the 7,400-mile network of highways, and specifies the minimum funds required to carry out the maintenance program. The Markov decision model, on which the system is based, considers both short-term and long-term management objectives, as well as such factors as physical road conditions, traffic densities, environmental characteristics, and types of roads.

Maintaining Arizona's roads is a complex problem. The state covers a large area and its roads vary from heavily traveled interstate highways to sparsely traveled secondary roads, while its climate ranges from the hot deserts of the south to the snowy highlands of the north. Even keeping track of the condition of the roads is difficult let alone knowing the proper maintenance action to take. Experience shows that many factors must be considered in deciding how to maintain a particular mile of the road including its altitude, average temperature, moisture conditions, structural properties, and traffic density. The central question is how poor should each road segment be before it is repaired and which of the many possible repair actions should be taken.

The implementation of the pavement management system to solve this problem resulted in a savings of $14 million in its first year, fiscal year 1980-81, and forecast savings are $101 million over the next five years. Highway management now has close control over costs and maintenance actions, and the system is the focal point of the entire pavement management process in the State of Arizona. A similar system is being developed for the State of Kansas.

THE ARIZONA DEPARTMENT OF TRANSPORTATION

The Arizona Department of Transportation (ADOT) has the responsibility for a road network comprising 2,200 miles of interstate and 5,200 miles of noninterstate highways. The department designs, constructs, preserves, and maintains the extensive road network. It also oversees air, railroad, and public transportation.

This highway network has grown from a few gravel roads to 7,400 miles of paved highways in about 60 years. The state highway system cost over $2 billion and would now cost over $6 billion to replace. ADOT's Highway Division maintains this road network, and also designs and constructs new roads. It is the largest of ADOT's six divisions, employs 2,400 of the 3,700 ADOT employees, and controls 83% of ADOT's $221 million annual budget.

THE NEED FOR A PAVEMENT MANAGEMENT SYSTEM

Until the mid 1970s, ADOT and its predecessor, the Arizona Highway Department, focused on constructing new roads. As the interstate system in Arizona neared completion, emphasis shifted from new construction to preserving existing roads. Several factors contributed to this shift: the network of highways was nearing completion and no extensive new construction was planned; at the same time, the existing highways were aging and required an increasing amount of maintenance to preserve the roads in satisfactory condition. In addition, the Federal Highway Admistration, the source of a major portion of ADOT's budget, has stringent guidelines requiring that a substantial proportion of its subsidies be used on preservation in order to avoid the enormous costs of reconstructing roads in bad condition.

In the mid 1970s, maintenance costs increased dramatically with the rising cost of petroleum-based road surfacing materials.

Because about 40% of highway construction budgets is spent on materials and most of the resurfacing is done with asphalt, the cost of asphalt is very important. Asphalt cost went from $88 per ton in 1975 to $270 per ton in 1980. In 1975, the Arizona Department of Transportation allocated $25 million to pavement preservation (for resurfacing as opposed to spot crack-filling). By 1978-79, the preservation budget had increased to $52 million (Figure 1).

ADOT's management was concerned about the inflationary direction of the budget, particularly in light of the sources of their funds. The maintenance money came from the Federal Government and the Arizona Government. The Federal money could be spent only on interstate highways and roads meeting stringent standards. The Arizona money came from gasoline taxes computed on a unit-per-gallon basis, and these taxes had neither increased significantly with time, nor did the Arizona legislature show any inclination to raise them. Several modern trends were dropping the revenue even further. Although vehicle miles traveled had increased, rates of fuel consumption had decreased because of conservation and increases in automobile efficiency. The

Figure 1. History of preservation fund allocation.

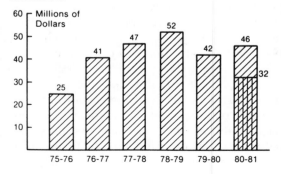

1978 Biennial Statewide Transportation Needs Report to the Arizona Legislature concluded, "It is at best questionable whether current service levels can be maintained, much less improved, even in the event that fuel taxes can be increased."

Intensifying the widening gap between estimated expenses and estimated income in the future was the Federal Highway Administration requirement that its money be spent only on roads meeting its guidelines. Therefore, state funds had to be used to upgrade candidate roads and their shoulders to Federal standards before Federal money could be spent on them for preservation. Few Arizona roads meet all the Federal standards (the average age of an Arizona road is twenty years), and upgrading the roads would consume the state's preservation funds on non-preservation activities. The natural result of this dilemma was that interstate highways which do meet Federal standards got resurfaced regularly (their average age is only ten years) at the expense of the non-interstate roads.

Late in 1977, it became obvious to ADOT's management that they needed a systematic procedure for distributing their maintenance money. Two other issues concerned ADOT's management:

— Decisions about preservation needs and maintenance were made by district engineers. There are seven districts in Arizona which competed for funds. They planned and performed maintenance in an almost autonomous manner. How to spend the district's share of the money was decided on the basis of past experience and the district engineer's expectations for his roads without regard to other districts. Therefore, road conditions could vary widely. In addition, aware of how subjective the resulting budgets were, the state government was reluctant to appropriate additional funds.

— The long-term and short-term effects on road conditions of funding shortages had to be predicted and a systematic procedure designed to cope with predicted budget cuts. It was important to be able to evaluate alternate preservation policies quickly and reliably.

Without a systematic procedure for addressing these partly political questions, the gap between preservation requirements and available State and Federal preservation funds would widen, and the conditions of different roads would vary even more drastically.

OBJECTIVES OF THE STUDY

In early 1978, ADOT contracted with Woodward-Clyde Consultants, an engineering consulting firm based in San Francisco to develop a decision-making tool, termed the Pavement Management System (PMS), for Arizona. A team of management scientists, highway engineers and computer specialists was formed to study the problem. Concurrently, a team was formed at ADOT to help in defining the problem and to provide the necessary data.

The main objective of the study was to develop a decision-making tool to help ADOT maintain its roads in the most desirable condition within its budget. It was important that preservation policies be consistent statewide and that ADOT's considerable investment in roads be protected.

Every year, ADOT is required by the State Legislature to prepare a five-year plan that includes a list of pavements needing corrective action in the first year, as well as tentative plans for the next four years. The PMS had to contribute to this planning process and thus an important objective of the system would be to serve as a basis for devising defensible one-year and five-year budgets and predicting the effect of budget cuts on road conditions. The system had to be relatively easy to use by engineers and flexible enough to allow sensitivity analysis of recommended policies.

COMMUNICATION WITH ADOT'S MANAGEMENT

We recognized that a comprehensive pavement management system requires decision making and coordination of effort at different levels of the organization, as well as the support of upper management. Management support was especially important because the system would require objectives and policy inputs from management and would recommend policies that would have to be approved by management before being carried out. A Pavement Management Steering Committee was formed to obtain the support and input of ADOT's management.

The Steering Committee was composed of upper level managers of ADOT. In addition to the Director of ADOT, the committee included the managers of the Highway Division and the various departments within ADOT: Development, Operations, Transportation Planning, Maintenance, Information Systems, and Materials. The committee also included the representatives from the Federal Highway Administration.

As the project progressed, periodic meetings with the Steering Committee were organized. In an early meeting, various approaches to developing the system were described, and the required inputs and expected outputs were outlined. Throughout the project, we were careful to keep the channels of communication open, to elicit comments, to address the concerns expressed by the committee and sometimes to educate the committee on what operations research could do and what it could not do. We were fortunate to have the full support of ADOT's management throughout the project.

ALTERNATE APPROACHES TO FORMULATION

One could either develop a model that would give the best possible road conditions within the budget limitations by maximizing a benefit function; or develop a model that would give least-cost maintenance policies while achieving and maintaining minimum standards on road conditions.

Roads, no matter what corrective action is taken, deteriorate with time. But deterioration cannot be predicted exactly and hence road conditions are probabilistic in nature. If a rehabilitated road is inspected after, say a year, there is some chance that it will exhibit deficiencies. Of course, the probability of deterioration is strongly dependent on the last corrective action taken. As an example, suppose two cracked pavements are resurfaced by laying one inch of asphalt on one and three inches on the other. While both would be in a desirable condition right after resurfacing, the probability that the first road would develop cracks in one year is larger than that for the second. It was essential that the probabilistic aspect of pavement deterioration should be addressed by the study.

We considered both the benefit maximization and the least-cost approaches and developed mathematical models based on both. Both models were based on formulating the problem as a constrained Markov decision process, and both used linear programming to find the optimal solution. The models, their input requirements, and output characteristics were presented to ADOT's management. ADOT preferred the cost minimization approach and this model was implemented. Their preference was based on several factors: the least-cost model would give them directly the budget required to keep the roads at certain standards; the results were easy to understand and relate to experience; and they could be used directly to show the effect of budget cuts on future road conditions. The goal and objective function of the maximization model, on the other hand, was a subjective benefit function involving trade-offs between road conditions and road categories. While it also gave expected road conditions as a function of the budget, one could not directly set standards and see the effect on budget requirements.

Another reason for using the minimization approach was that it allowed the problem to be decomposed into smaller problems, each addressing all the roads in a particular category (differentiated by traffic density and climate). The linear programs were therefore easier to handle, and the road categories could be expanded later or modified without a need for significant revisions or concerns about computational complexities. The third reason was that the least-cost minimization approach would allow developing a short-term model that would be tied with the long-term model; this could not be achieved easily with the maximization approach.

THE MODEL

The heart of the Arizona Pavement Management System is an optimization model, termed the Network Optimization System (NOS). It recommends preservation policies that achieve long-term and short-term standards for road conditions at lowest possible cost. NOS consists of two interrelated models, a short-term model and a long-term model, and is based on formulating the problem as a constrained Markov decision process that captures the dynamic and probabilistic aspects of the pavement management problem. Linear programming is used to find the optimal solution. Details of the model formulation and some references to the underlying theory are contained in the appendix.

The main components of the Markov decision process are road conditions and types, called (condition) states, and maintenance actions that can be taken. A state is defined as a combination of the specific levels of the variables relevant to evaluating pavement performance. For example, if pavement roughness and the amount of cracking were the only relevant variables, one state might be defined as the combination: (roughness = 50 inches/mile and cracking = 5%). A preservation action might be say: resurface with three inches of asphalt.

In the model transition probabilities link current road conditions and maintenance actions to future road conditions. A transition probability, $p_{ij}(a)$ specifies the likelihood that one mile of the pavement will move from state i to state j in one year, if the preservation action a is applied to the pavement at the present time. A preservation policy for the entire network is the assignment of an action to each state in each time period (year). The probability that a pavement segment is in a given state or condition can also be interpreted as the expected proportion of all pavements that are in that state or condition. This allows the calculation of the proportion of the statewide network expected to be in the given condition in any year for a given maintenance policy.

The performance of the network is evaluated in terms of these proportions. Acceptable and unacceptable states are defined and the objective of the NOS is to find the least-cost policy that would maintain at least a certain proportion of pavements in desirable states, and not more than a certain proportion in undesirable states.

The steady-state optimal policy is independent of the initial conditions of the network. In other words, if the optimal policy is followed, after some length of time that cannot be predicted beforehand, the steady-state condition will be achieved, and henceforth, the proportion of roads in each condition state and the expected budget requirements will remain constant.

However, for planning purposes, ADOT wanted to have control over the time it would take for the roads to reach the steady-state. Moreover, given the uncertainties in the budget they wanted to have the option of imposing different performance standards for the short-term than for the long-term. Furthermore, given the probabilistic nature of road deterioration and budget limitations, ADOT might not be able to follow steady-state policies in a particular year if a large proportion of roads needed immediate repair. Therefore, they needed a short-term model that would accept as inputs short-term performance standards and present road conditions and which, after a specified number of years, T (for example, five years), would achieve the long-term standards. The short-term policies are therefore restricted to those that after T years would upgrade the network to long-term standards while maintaining short-term standards during the first T years.

CONDITION STATES

The variables used to define the condition states were: present roughness (3 levels), present amount of cracking (3 levels), change in amount of cracking during previous year (3 levels), and index to the first crack (5 levels). A total of 135 combinations of these variables are possible. However, 15 of these combinations were considered highly unlikely, which left 120 states.

"Roughness" represents the traveling public's perception of pavements in terms of comfort and the wear and tear on the vehicle caused by rough roads. It is measured by a "Mays Meter" which records the deviations between the axle and the body of the car and adds up the number of inches of bumps per mile. "Cracking" is the highway engineers' rating of the pavement's structural adequacy and its need for corrective maintenance. The road surface is compared to pictures showing different percentages of cracking. "Index to the first crack" is a number that is linked to the last nonroutine maintenance action taken on the road. It is used to account for differences between the probabilities of deterioration of roads with no visible cracks, but with different last nonroutine actions. To understand the significance of the index, consider two road segments A and B. The last nonroutine action on A has been resurfacing with 1″ asphalt and the last action on B, resurfacing with 3″ asphalt. No cracks are visible on either of the two roads, and routine maintenance is planned for the current year. The two roads will have significantly different probabilities of developing cracks during the next year. Since the indices are different, the model assigns these roads to two different states with different probabilities of deterioration. However, once a road shows some cracks the amount of future cracking depends only on the current cracking and on the rate of change in cracking—it is not important anymore to know the last nonroutine action taken, or the time the action was taken. It is worthwhile to note that roads with the same age may behave differently because of other factors (for instance, subsurface moisture and deflection). The net effect of all these factors, including aging, is captured by the two condition variables, cracking and the rate of change in cracking.

To summarize, a state is defined by a vector $(u, \Delta u, r, z)$ where u denotes the present amount of cracking, Δu the change in cracking during the previous year, r the roughness, and z the index to the first crack. The index z changes only if a nonroutine maintenance action is taken.

The statewide network was divided into nine road categories which were defined as combinations of average daily traffic and a regional environmental factor that depends on several climatic conditions; elevation and rainfall were the primary variables used to define the regional factor on a scale of 0 to 5. Since traffic density and the regional factor are independent of the preservation action, each pavement remains in one road category. This, in effect, made nine networks, each of which was characterized by a set of 120 states.

MAINTENANCE ACTIONS

A total of 17 alternate maintenance actions ranging from routine maintenance to substantial corrective measures were selected for asphalt concrete pavements. From this master list, for each state, a set of feasible actions was specified in the model. The average number of feasible actions for each state was about six.

TRANSITION PROBABILITIES

The existing models for predicting road deterioration depend, for the most part, on empirical equations relating long-term deterioration to the pavement's structural properties. While these models are suitable for cases where adequate data do not exist, they were not appropriate for Arizona. Over the years, Arizona had accumulated extensive data on its road conditions, and the corrective actions taken on those roads. To obtain better predictions, we decided to develop regression equations that concentrated on short-term deterioration and used Arizona's data base.

We first considered a set of independent variables that are traditionally used for predicting deterioration: deflection, spreadability, subgrade support, etc. However, the correlations obtained with these variables were rather poor. We then argued that the influence of the engineering and environmental factors was captured by the observed pavement conditions.

Figure 2. The transition probabilities for pavement in condition state 1 under two different actions: routine maintenance or a five-inch overlay.

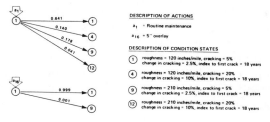

Hence, the present values of the condition variables and the rate of change in these variables should show a strong correlation with future pavement condition, an assumption that was confirmed by the analysis of data (correlation coefficients for regression equations ranged from 0.81 to 0.95). This approach was consistent with the requirements of the optimization model as it requires only *what* (condition) state the pavement would be in, and not *why* it would deteriorate to that state.

With this approach, the independent variables considered were present pavement condition (roughness or cracking), change in pavement condition during the previous year, maintenance actions, traffic densities, and the regional environmental factor. The dependent variables were changes in roughness and cracking in one year.

The (normal) continuous probability distributions of the dependent variables were discretized to give the probability of going from one level of roughness and cracking to another level in one year. It is reasonable to assume that roughness and cracking are probabilistically independent. Thus, if we denote the roughness associated with state i by r_i, the cracking by u_i and the change in cracking in the previous year by Δu_i, we can write:

$p_{ij}(a) = P$ (moving from r_i to r_j in one year under action a) $\cdot P$ (moving from u_i and Δu_i to u_j and Δu_j in one year under action a).

As mentioned earlier, the "index to the first crack" for state j is the same as that of state i if a is a routine maintenance, and is the index associated with a if a is nonroutine maintenance.

The data for the regression equations were derived from a randomly selected group of 270 road segments within the Arizona network. For each road segment, two or three years of data were available, leading to about 700 data points for each regression equation. To verify the accuracy of the predictions, an independent data set of 53 road segments not included in the initial development was selected at random from the ADOT files. Verification was obtained by comparing predictions of roughness and cracking with actual measurements and observations for five years. The correlation coefficient between observed and predicted values was greater than 0.9 for the first year, and between 0.7 to 0.8 for the fifth year (the model needs only one year predictions).

For every feasible action, a pavement in a given condition state can only go to three or four states. Thus, for feasible actions, only 3 percent of the elements in the transition probability matrix were nonzero. Since for each state, six of the seventeen actions are feasible, the number of nonzero $p_{ij}(a)$ is about 2600 (for each road category) or slightly more than 1 percent.

SPECIFYING PERFORMANCE STANDARDS

To set performance standards, we defined acceptable and unacceptable states and ADOT's management specified the minimum proportion of roads required to be in acceptable states and the maximum proportion of roads permitted to be in unacceptable states. The performance standards may vary as a function of average daily traffic (Table 1).

Table 1. Performance standards for the Network Optimization System. Acceptable pavement condition is defined as roughness of less than 165 inches/mile and cracking less than 10%. Unacceptable pavement condition would mean roughness of more than 256 inches per mile or cracking of more than 30%.

Average Daily Traffic	Minimum Proportion of Roads with Acceptable Roughness	Maximum Proportion of Roads with Unacceptable Roughness	Minimum Proportion of Roads with Acceptable Cracking	Maximum Proportion of Roads with Unacceptable Cracking
0 – 2,000	0.50	0.25	0.60	0.25
2,001 – 10,000	0.60	0.15	0.70	0.20
> 10,000	0.80	0.05	0.80	0.10

INPUT AND OUTPUT FEATURES OF THE MODEL

The NOS requires two types of inputs: management inputs and engineering inputs (Figure 3). After the initial implementation of the system, new convenience features were added to the system by ADOT's staff to help organize input data and interpret NOS recommended policies. Using CRTs, input data can be immediately changed and its effect on policies and budget requirements analyzed. We created a separate input data file for each road category so that changes can be made in one category without affecting other categories. Recently, the road categories were expanded from nine to thirteen without much programming effort: the interstate highways were separated from noninterstate highways with each requiring different performance standards. This separation has resulted in additional savings.

The output report summarizes the NOS actions and costs year by year for

Figure 3. Inputs and outputs of NOS.

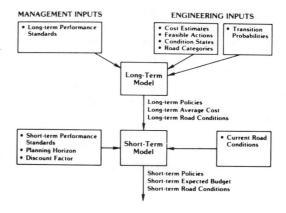

each mile of highway in the ADOT network. The present condition of each mile and the last nonroutine action taken are used to determine its condition state, which is then matched to the NOS output file to determine the appropriate action for the current year. For subsequent years, the NOS predicts the most likely condition state for each mile, the corresponding action, and estimated expected cost.

IMPLEMENTATION

The system was tested with real and hypothetical data, and implemented in May, 1980. After several modifications to facilitate the decision-making procedure and a reorganization of the pavement management process at ADOT, the implementation is now complete.

In the summer of 1980, the Pavement Management Group comprising eleven people was formed at ADOT. The group is responsible for collecting data on road conditions, providing engineering inputs, eliciting management inputs to the system, reviewing inputs with district engineers, running NOS, and recommending rehabilitation policies to the Priority Planning Committee. This committee and its technical subcommittee then organize the recommended policies and schedules into programmed construction projects that are sent to the Transportation Board for review. The Priority Planning Committee is composed of ADOT's upper management; the Transportation Board represents the public and its members are appointed by the Governor. After a public hearing and approval by the Governor, the recommended projects are implemented.

DIFFICULTIES WITH IMPLEMENTATION

To implement the model two difficulties had to be overcome. The first concern was that, because of the performance constraints, the model would not necessarily recommend "pure" strategies, that is, take action a for state i. The policies could be "randomized"—it could recommend that when in state i, take action a_1 with the probability of p_1 and take a_2 with the

probability of p_2. In implementation, this posed no difficulty; cases where this happened were very rare and the model never recommended more than two actions for each state. Because the probabilities p_1 and p_2 could also be interpreted as the proportion of roads in state i for which actions a_1 and a_2 were to be taken, the highway engineers felt comfortable with following the recommendations.

The second concern was more serious. Because the units considered were one-mile road segments, it was possible that the model would recommend, say for a three-mile stretch, that action a_1 be taken on the first and third miles, and action a_2 for the second mile.

Our concern was with the practicality of such a policy, that is, with the economies of scale that were not addressed by the model. ADOT's procedure for grouping individual road segments into construction projects (engineering judgement is used for the groupings) helped overcome this problem. While not many cases with this difficulty appeared, for those that did, if a district considered it more economical to carry out a more expensive action for a particular mile (because, in the previous example, it may be cheaper overall to take action a_1 on all three miles, instead of a_1 - a_2 - a_1, although a_2 by itself may be cheaper than a_1), it was allowed to do so. However, the overall cost of the construction project could not exceed the amount allocated by the PMS to that project and no actions inferior to those recommended by PMS could be taken.

TANGIBLE, DIRECT BENEFITS

The Pavement Management System has changed the pavement management decision process in Arizona from a subjective nonquantitative method to a modern system that integrates managerial policy decisions and engineering inputs through an optimization system. As William Ordway, the Director of Transportation of the State of Arizona, notes, "Unlike industry, state government does not make a profit, but rather is charged by the public with providing the best possible service per tax dollar. This optimization process gives ADOT the confidence that, indeed, it is getting the most benefit for limited funds." The system achieves these public goals and more; the financial impact of the system has been significant.

— During the first year of implementation (fiscal year 1980-81), the Pavement Management System saved $14 million of preservation funds. Because pavement condition data were available since 1974, it was possible to calculate the proportions of roads in acceptable and unacceptable conditions for past years. Those proportions have remained fairly stable over the years. The amount budgeted by ADOT for 1980-81 to keep the network at the same standards was $46 million. Using the PMS and following its recommended policies, ADOT was able to achieve the same standards with $32 million. The long-range standards used in the model (Table 1) were also the historical standards. The $14 million were subsequently spent on other highway related projects. Since the NOS ties present actions and conditions to long-range performance standards, and large fluctuations in total annual expected costs are not allowed, the cost reduction in 1980-81 was not at the expense of either poor future road conditions or very costly measures in subsequent years. This is confirmed by the 1981-1982 preservation budget which is only $28 million to keep the roads above acceptable standards.

There were two reasons for the cost reduction: First, traditionally, the roads have been allowed to deteriorate to a rather poor condition before any preservation action was taken. The roads then required substantial and costly *corrective* measures. The actions recommended by the Pavement Management System are mostly *preventive* measures; that is, it recommends less substantial measures before the road deteriorates to a really poor condition. Analysis shows that less substantial but slightly more frequent measures not only keep the roads in good condition most of the time, but are overall less costly; they prevent the road from reaching really bad conditions that require much costlier corrective measures.

Second, in the past, corrective actions taken were too conservative; it was common to resurface a road with five inches of asphalt concrete. The assumption was that the thicker the asphalt layer, the longer it would take for the road to deteriorate below acceptable standards. While this assumption is correct, the time it takes for a road to deteriorate is not proportional to the asphalt layer. For example, the prediction model shows that there is no significant difference between the rate of deterioration of a road resurfaced with three inches of asphalt concrete and a road resurfaced with five inches. The policies recommended by PMS therefore are less conservative; for example, a recommendation of three inches of overlay is rather rare and is reserved for the worst conditions. It is important to note that the results of the prediction model are not sufficient for determining the optimal maintenance policy. While the prediction model enhances highway engineers' understanding of the general effectiveness of actions, the final recommendation depends on considering the costs versus benefits of *all* actions in the context of short-term and long-term standards, and current road conditions. Given the size of the problem, this would only be possible through the use of a formal optimization model.

— A major source of funds for highway maintenance is the Federal Highway Administration. These funds, called the 4R Funds (for restoration, rehabilitation, resurfacing, and reconstruction), are based on factors such as miles of interstate, the amount of land owned by the Federal Government in the state, and the population. The estimated amount of 4R funds available to Arizona for preservation of the interstate highway during the next five years is $167.5 million. Using the PMS, ADOT estimates that only $91.7 million is needed to maintain the interstate roads in acceptable conditions during the next five years. The surplus of $75.8 million will be allocated to other construction projects over the next five years (Table 2). In addition to the 4R Funds, the Federal Government provides Arizona with funds for maintaining and constructing primary and secondary roads (called the Primary-Secondary Construction Funds, PSCF), of which a minimum of 20% has to be spent on preservation. Traditionally, ADOT has al-

located 50% of these funds for this purpose. Using the PMS, ADOT finds that only 20% of the PSCF is needed for preservation over the next five years. The difference of $25.6 million that would have been spent on preservation of secondary and primary roads will now be allocated to construction projects (Table 2).

The PMS has provided a defensible procedure for preparing one-year and five-year budgets for preservation of pavements. This has helped ADOT's management to justify the revenue requests before oversight legislative committees.

— The use of operations research in pavement management and the success of the Arizona system is influencing the direction of pavement management nationwide. The State of Kansas is in the process of implementing a larger version of the system (20 road categories and 216 condition states), and the Colorado Department of Transportation has accepted a proposal to develop a similar system. Preliminary tests of the Kansas system indicate the model would work for problems at least twice as large as the Arizona problem. Given the amount of interest generated by the system, Kansas and Colorado will probably not be the last states to adopt similar systems.

Table 2. The Pavement Management System's plan for preservation funds needed to preserve present road and cracking conditions for the next five years (1982-83—1986-87), the funds available, and the resulting surplus.

| | (IN MILLION DOLLARS) | | | | | | |
| | Interstate | | | Non-Interstate | | | |
Fiscal Year	Preservation Funds Needed	4R Funds Available	Surplus 4R Funds	Primary-Secondary Funds Needed	PSCF Funds Available	Surplus PSCF	Total Surplus
1982-83	$ 13.2	17.0	3.8	23.1	23.1	0	3.8
1983-84	18.5	28.3	9.8	30.3	36.7	6.4	16.2
1984-85	19.0	37.1	18.1	36.6	43.0	6.4	24.5
1985-86	20.0	37.1	17.1	38.3	44.7	6.4	23.5
1986-87	21.0	48.0	27.0	40.9	47.3	6.4	33.4
TOTAL	$ 91.7	167.5	75.8	169.2	194.8	25.6	101.4

INDIRECT BENEFITS

— The PMS is the focal point in reorganizing the pavement management process in the State of Arizona. As a result, decision making has been centralized and a formal mechanism has been established to integrate management policy decisions, budgetary policies, and engineering decisions. The ADOT management, the district engineers and various divisions within ADOT cooperate in setting objectives and performance standards, and decision making has been transformed into a collective collaborative effort.

— A significant product of the PMS is a coordinated, comprehensive data management system. Although a significant amount of data on pavement performance was collected and stored on the computer prior to developing the PMS, the data were scattered over a number of files maintained by different groups. There was no clear purpose for some of the data being collected. The PMS required consolidating all the data in one centralized system for storage and retrieval. The resulting data management system has proved extremely useful to ADOT personnel at all levels. For example, the district engineers are able to access the latest data on condition of pavements, schedules, and preservation actions on interactive remote terminals in their offices.

— An integral part of the PMS is a set of prediction performance models that provide reasonably reliable predictions of pavement performance under alternative maintenance actions. The prediction model, which is based on an analysis of field data collected over a period of seven years, has enhanced highway and design engineers' understanding of pavement deterioration and the effectiveness of various actions.

ACKNOWLEDGEMENTS

We would like to thank the many individuals who contributed to this study and helped in its implementation, in particular, Fred Finn, Larry Nazareth and Ezio Alviti of Woodward-Clyde Consultants, and Gene Morris and John Eisenberg of ADOT. We would also like to thank Keshavan Nair, Executive Vice-President of Woodward-Clyde Consultants, and William Ordway, Director of ADOT, for their support of this work, and Professor Sheldon Ross for several valuable comments.

APPENDIX: FORMULATION

The Network Optimization System consists of two interrelated models, a short-term model and a long-term model, and is based on formulating the problem as a Markov decision process. The basic theory of Markovian decision processes as a type of dynamic programming model can be found in the books of Denardo [1982], Derman [1970], and Ross [1970]. As described in the body of the paper, for any road category, the long-term model seeks a maintenance policy that minimizes the expected long-term average cost. The requirements are that, for any state i, the proportion of roads remain above a certain level if i is an acceptable state, and below a certain level if i is an unacceptable state. The short-term model seeks a maintenance policy over a planning horizon T that minimizes total expected discounted costs in the first T years subject to short-term standards and to the requirement that the long-term standards would be achieved within the first T years.

As discussed earlier, for any road category, the state of a one-mile road segment at year n, X_n, is defined by the vector $(u, \Delta u, r, z)$, where u denotes the present amount of cracking, Δu the change in the amount of cracking during the previous year, r the present roughness, and z the index to the first crack. Each of the variables can assume between 3 to 5 levels, leading to 120 feasible states. With this definition of the state space, we can restrict ourselves to policies which prescribe actions depending only on the current state of the road. It can be easily seen that the underlying finite Markov chain is irreducible and aperiodic, and hence ergodic.

THE LONG-TERM MODEL

For any policy π (that can be randomized), let w_{ia} denote the limiting probability that the road will be in state i and action a will be chosen when policy π is followed,

$$w_{ia} = \lim_{n \to \infty} P[X_n = i,\, a_n = a].$$

The w_{ia} determine the policy and can be computed from knowledge of the transition probabilities $p_{ij}(a)$ already discussed in the paper. The vector $w = (w_{ia})$ must satisfy

(i) $w_{ia} \geq 0$ for all i and a

(ii) $\sum_i \sum_a w_{ia} = 1$

(iii) $\sum_a w_{ja} = \sum_i \sum_a w_{ia}p_{ij}(a)$ for all j.

Thus, for any policy π, there is a vector $w = (w_{ia})$ which satisfies (i), (ii) and (iii) with the interpretation that w_{ia} is equal to the steady state probability of being in state i and choosing action a when π is employed. The reverse is also true: if a vector $w = (w_{ia})$ satisfies (i), (ii) and (iii), there exists a policy π, such that if π is used then the steady-state probability of being in state i and choosing action a

equals w_{ia}. The w_{ia} can also be interpreted as the proportion of time that the road is in condition i and action a is taken, or alternatively, the proportion of roads that are in state i and for which action a is taken.

The long-term model seeks to minimize the expected average cost while maintaining long-term standards. Since (w_{ia}) is independent of time,

$$q_i = \sum_a w_{ia}$$

is the long-term proportion of roads in state i under a given policy. We seek a policy that would minimize the expected average cost subject to performance constraints on q_i.

Let $c(i, a)$ denote the maintenance cost of a mile-segment when the road is in state i and maintenance action a is chosen. It follows that the expected average cost under policy π equals

$$\sum_i \sum_a w_{ia}c(i,a).$$

Hence, the problem of finding the policy that minimizes the long-term expected costs is

$$\text{minimize} \sum_i \sum_a w_{ia}c(i,a) \qquad (1)$$

subject to

$$w_{ia} \geq 0 \text{ for all } i \text{ and } a \qquad (2)$$

$$\sum_i \sum_a w_{ia} = 1 \qquad (3)$$

$$\sum_a w_{ja} = \sum_i \sum_a w_{ia}p_{ij}(a) \text{ for all } j. \quad (4)$$

Had there been no other constraints to be met, this linear program would give a "Pure" solution—the optimal w_{ia} is positive only if action a is taken for i and it is zero for all but one value of a. However, we have other requirements: we need the proportion of roads in state i to be above a number ϵ_i if i is an acceptable state, and below a number γ_i if i is an unacceptable state (the parameters ϵ_i and γ_i are the long-range performance standards). Hence, we also need

$$\sum_a w_{ia} \geq \epsilon_i \quad \text{if } i \text{ is acceptable} \quad (5)$$

$$\sum_a w_{ia} \leq \gamma_i \quad \text{if } i \text{ is unacceptable.} \quad (6)$$

The long-term problem is therefore, to minimize (1) subject to (2)—(6).

THE SHORT-TERM MODEL

As stated earlier, we want to find a short-term solution such that after a given period T, the steady-state is achieved. We want to minimize total expected discounted costs in the first T periods subject to short-term performance standards. The objective function is

$$\text{minimize} \sum_{k=1}^{T} \sum_i \sum_a \alpha^k w_{ia}^k c(i,a) \quad (7)$$

where α is a discount factor, w_{ia}^k is the proportion of roads in state i in period k for which action a is taken, and T denotes the transition period or the short-term planning horizon.

The short-term constraints are as follows:

Let q_i^n denote the proportion of roads (of the category under consideration) that is in state i in the beginning of period n. In the beginning of the first period, the proportion of the roads in any state i, q_i^1 is known.

Therefore, the proportion of roads in state i for which actions are taken should equal this quantity. In addition, the proportion of roads that are in any state j in the beginning of the kth period must equal the proportion of roads at the end of the $(k-1)$th period. Of course, the decision variables w_{ia}^k must be nonnegative and add to one in each period. Therefore, the constraints are:

$$w_{ia}^k \geq 0 \quad \text{for all } i, a, k = 1, 2, \ldots, T, \quad (8)$$

$$\sum_i \sum_a w_{ia}^k = 1 \quad \text{for all } k = 1, 2, \ldots, T, \quad (9)$$

$$\sum_a w_{ia}^1 = q_i^1 \quad \text{for all } i, \quad (10)$$

$$\sum_a w_{ja}^k = \sum_i \sum_a w_{ia}^{k-1} p_{ij}(a) \quad \text{for all } j$$

and $\quad k = 1, 2, \ldots, T. \quad (11)$

In addition, we require that after T periods, the steady-state solution be attained. The model first solves the steady-state model and therefore it has already obtained the optimal steady-state decision variables (i.e., w_{ia}^*). For computational reasons, we included some tolerance limits so that the steady-state is attained within the specified tolerance, ϕ.

Furthermore, we require that the cost at the end of the Tth year not be significantly different from the steady-state minimum average cost. If the steady-state average cost is denoted by C and the tolerance by ϕ and ψ we have:

$$\sum_a w_{ja}^T \geq \sum_a w_{ja}^* (1 - \phi) \text{ for all } j \quad (12)$$

$$\sum_a w_{ja}^T \leq \sum_a w_{ja}^* (1 + \phi) \text{ for all } j \quad (13)$$

$$\sum_i \sum_a w_{ja}^T c(i,a) \leq C(1 + \psi). \quad (14)$$

Additionally, we require performance standards for the years 1, 2,. . ., T. Let ϵ'_i and γ'_i be the short-term acceptable and unacceptable standards. Then we have

$$\sum_a w_{ia}^k \geq \epsilon'_i \text{ if } i \text{ is acceptable, } k = 2,$$
$$\ldots, T - 1, \quad (15)$$

$$\sum_a w_{ia}^k \leq \gamma'_i \text{ if } i \text{ is unacceptable, } k = 2,$$
$$\ldots, T - 1. \quad (16)$$

Note that since the current proportions in different states are determined by the current condition of the network, and

since we require that at the end of the Tth year the steady-state conditions be achieved, constraints (15) and (16) cannot be specified for $k = 1$ or for $k = T$.

To summarize, the model first solves the steady-state problem, i.e., minimizes (1) subject to (2)—(6). The optimal solution of this LP, the steady-state solution, then acts as a constraint for the short-term model. In the short-term model, we seek to minimize (7) subject to constraints (8)—(16).

REFERENCES

Denardo, Eric J. 1982, *Dynamic Programming*, Prentice-Hall, Englewood Cliffs, New Jersey.

Derman, C. 1970, *Finite State Markovian Decision Processes*, Academic Press, New York.

Ross, S. 1970, *Applied Probability Models with Optimization Applications*, Holden-Day, San Francisco, California.

Management Science in New York's Department of Sanitation

Lucius J. Riccio

In his first year in office (1978), Mayor Koch appointed Norman Steisel Commissioner of New York City's Department of Sanitation. At that time, it could have been said that New York City's Department of Sanitation was a municipal embarrassment. All indicators of performance were way down from their pre-fiscal crisis (1975) values and the media regularly hounded the city administration to make substantial changes in the department's performance.

In three years, Commissioner Steisel was able to turn the department around. The department's record of productivity improvements and management control is generally recognized as the finest in city government and has gained national attention in trade journals as being one of the outstanding sanitation agencies in the country.

There were many components that led to the compilation of this outstanding productivity and management record, not the least of which was the Commissioner's desire for a top-notch planning and evalua-

tion capability. Not long into the job he recruited from without and promoted from within top people trained or trainable in sophisticated management techniques. In the past three years the department has used virtually every scientific management technique from mathematical analyses and computer simulation to advanced human resources management, for example, labor management committees and gainsharing.

NEW YORK'S DEPARTMENT OF SANITATION

Currently, the department has approximately 11,000 employees of which about 6,800 are sanitation workers. It has an operating budget of over $400 million. Its primary responsibilities include: (1) the collection of all household refuse, of which it collects about 12,000 tons a day, (2) the disposal of all refuse collected in the city which includes another 10,000 tons collected by private carters, altogether amounting to approximately 22,000 tons a day, (3) cleaning the streets, (4) snow removal, and (5) enforcement of the sanitary code.

The two major measures of performance for household garbage collection are (1) the PAR Index (Productivity Analysis Report) which measures tons collected per man hour of effort devoted to collection (Figure 1), and (2) loads left out, which is a measure of how well we meet our stated schedules for collection pickup. The first measure indicates how much garbage we pick up, the second indicates how much we leave behind. Another measure of collection performance is the percentage of night trucks. The public is very much against having garbage collected at night for a number of reasons, not the least of which is the noise.

The primary indicator of street cleanliness comes from a program developed by the Fund for the City of New York [Thomas 1980], and now maintained by the Mayor's Office of Operations. That program is called Project Scorecard. Each month over 6,000 block-faces are rated for

Figure 2. Percent of streets acceptably clean, marginal, and filthy by fiscal year. (Source: Mayor's Management Report, January 31, 1982)

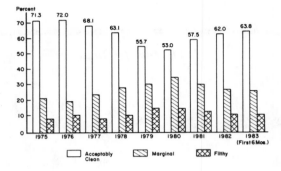

cleanliness according to a well-established scientific procedure and reports are compiled indicating the level of street cleanliness achieved in each subdivision of the city (Figure 2).

The department has maintained good data records for years and, coupled with the sound performance measures, it has been possible to perform a variety of analyses, and various models have been built to assist in either planning or monitoring the department's performance.

MANPOWER CONTROL

One of the first things that was needed was a manpower forecasting model that would facilitate planning the use of manpower and serve as a blueprint for auditing actual usage. Commissioner Steisel proposed the design of such a model and charged Deputy Commissioner Christopher Beemer, Deputy Commissioner Frank Sisto, and Teddy Barra with the task of organizing the data the department had collected over the last several years to make the model a useful prediction tool. Chief Michael Carpinello was

FIGURE 1. Household collection trends according to the productivity analysis report. (Source: Mayor's Management Report, January 31, 1982)

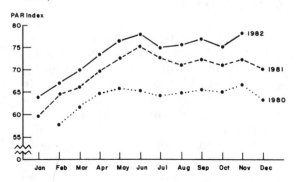

principally responsible for collecting and analyzing the data. The seasonal nature of the department's workload has long been recognized. Because of good data compilation, the department knew how the workload for garbage collection, street cleaning, and garage support changed from month to month. It also knew how the manpower availability changed from month to month. All of the factors that affected manpower need on one hand, or manpower availability on the other, were compiled (Table 1). Historic data were used to determine the seasonal fluctuation in each of these factors. The model that interrelates all of these factors is presented in the Appendix.

The model is used to predict manpower shortages and surpluses. During a period of manpower shortages, overtime would be used to make up for the difference between manpower availability and manpower need. The overtime is quite expensive: when a man works on his predetermined day off, he gets paid at double time. It pays the department to avoid

Figure 3. Output of manpower—forecasting model.

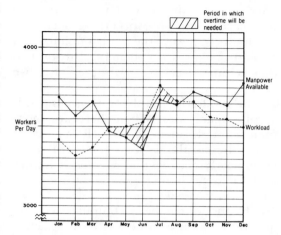

excessive overtime in order to minimize its total costs.

In a graph of the projected manpower availability and workload for a typical year, it can be seen that our workload peaks in the summer and bottoms out in the winter (Figure 3). Because of the nat-

TABLE 1. Factors influencing manpower need and availability.

MANPOWER NEED (workload)	MANPOWER AVAILABILITY

MANPOWER NEED (workload)

Collection
— Tons of Garbage
— Work Rate
— Disposal Site Availability
— Truck Capacity
Cleaning
— Alternate Side and Restricted Parking Regulations (mechanical broom cleaning)
— Litter Baskets
— All Other Street-Motorized Litter Patrol Cleaning
— Special Event and Parade Cleanup
Support
— Garage Manning
— Clerical Support

MANPOWER AVAILABILITY

— Payroll Assigned
— Absence Factor (divided into payroll assigned will yield the number who will show up for work on a given day)
— Medical Duty Assignments (workers injured who cannot be "productive")
— Permanent and Daily Detachments (workers reassigned to do other types of work)
— Attrition Rate
— Hiring Policy

ure of our workload, attrition and the factors that influence absences, it is impossible to hire so that we always have the exact number of workers we need. Because of the way the cost minimization function behaves it is beneficial to hire so that at times we have more men than we need.

The model is useful for projecting this surplus manpower. When there are more than enough men to do all mandated work, the surplus is used for extra street cleaning. Projecting that surplus is important for determining equipment and field supervisory needs.

The model has been computerized and an optimization routine has been attached to yield the optimal hiring strategy to minimize total salary and overtime costs, that is, how many workers should be hired and in what months (see Appendix).

The average daily surplus or deficit of workers in a month is calculated using the manpower forecasting model. The optimization is done by an optimal search routine using several starting points to insure that the global minimum is found.

Each month, actual manpower usage for collection and cleaning and support work is reconciled against our plan. The fit has been excellent. When discrepancies occur, managerial action is taken. For example, excessive overtime was being recorded in the fall of 1981, and we found that losses from attrition had increased, thereby reducing our available manpower below the projected value. The optimal hiring routine was utilized and it was determined that an additional 118 sanitation workers should be hired at that time to minimize our annual costs of production. That is just one example of the many uses of this model.

A key element in determining manpower availability is the absence factor, of which a large component is vacation. The number of vacations that can be taken at any given time of the year is preset through percentages. In the summer months, the prime vacation period, 11 percent of the payroll assigned sanitation workers may take vacations. As it turns out, that is also our peak manpower need period. The manpower forecasting model was used to determine what the percentages should be to eliminate planned overtime in the summer months. This analysis, called "vacation smoothing," shifted some summer vacations into the winter months which is a time of surplus for the department. To satisfy the workers' concerns about reducing vacations in the summer, the department has considered offering an alternate way for the workers to pick their vacation periods. The manpower forecasting model enabled us to determine what the new percentages should be so that we could take full advantage of this surplus in the winter and reduce the overtime in the summer.

PRODUCTION FUNCTIONS FOR STREET CLEANING

Few issues are more directly related to New York City's public image than the cleanliness of its streets. It can be argued that New Yorkers are no more litter-producing than people in other cities, simply that there are more of them. Whether or not that is true, there certainly is enough litter to clean up and it is the responsibility of the Department of Sanitation to do just that. Fortunately we have a quantitative measure of the level of street cleanliness, Project Scorecard, which gives us an accurate, unbiased measure of just how littered our streets are. It is one of the very few scientifically-based and well-constructed measures of performace in the public sector.

Project Scorecard determines the percentage of streets acceptably clean in the following way (Figure 4). A representative sample of block-faces was selected which reflected the residential, commercial, and industrial mix of streets in New York. The sample consists of approximately 6,000 blocks. Each month, each block in the sample is rated by comparing the amount of litter present to a standard that ranges from 1.0 for spotless to 3.0 for continuous piles of litter along and over the curb. A block is considered acceptably clean if its rating is less than 1.5. After all the blocks are rated the percentage with ratings less than 1.5 is calculated. All blocks are rated at least twice. The blocks whose dirtiness varies greatly are rated three or four times to insure accuracy.

In 1975, New York City suffered a severe budgetary crisis when the city almost went bankrupt [Morris 1980]. When the fiscal crisis hit, the function of the department most severely hit with layoffs was street cleaning. As a result, cleanliness levels dropped substantially and, in the few years following the crisis, little attention was paid to getting the streets back in shape.

Figure 4. Project Scorecard rates block-faces on a standard ranging from 1.0 for spotless to 3.0 for filthy. Shown here are blocks rated 1.5 (no concentration of litter, no piles of litter, and large gaps between pieces of litter), 2.0 (litter concentrated, small gaps between pieces of litter), and 3.0 (litter highly concentrated, no gaps in the piles of litter, litter in a straight line along and over curb). A block is considered acceptably clean if its rating is less than 1.5.

When Commissioner Steisel took office in 1978, the critical problems surrounding garbage collection were the department's number one priority. Once substantial productivity gains were made in that area, more attention was focused on street cleaning. In addition, in 1981 the Mayor, the City Council, and the Board of Estimate approved the hiring of 450 additional street cleaners, the first such hiring of street cleaners in six years.

Management science modeling played a role in the allocation of those cleaners. As late as 1981, the department had little understanding of how the use of street cleaners and enforcement agents affected street cleanliness levels. The literature provided some general models but most research had been focused on mechanical broom effectiveness rather than the effects of changes in manning levels [Fleming 1978; Public Technology, Inc. 1982; American Public Works Association Research Foundation 1977; Novotny and Chesters 1981]. Under my direction, Joe Miller built models that indicated the probable payoff in street cleanliness that would be achieved by each incremental increase in manpower in each of the 59 sanitation districts. Data were collected on gross allocations of cleaner manpower for each district and the volume of summonses written for violations of the sanitary code which could affect litter rates. Regression models were then constructed predicting street cleanliness from man-days devoted to cleaning and violations written. Percent acceptably clean was used as the measure of effectiveness because it is the most universally accepted and understood cleanliness measure. The models developed yielded good fits with r^2s ranging as high as .9. The coefficient in the regression for man-days indicated how many workers would be needed to increase the percentage of

streets acceptably clean in that district by one point.

The citywide Scorecard rating is a weighted average of the 59 district ratings. The individual district ratings are weighted according to the proportion of the city's street miles that are in the district.

A very valuable piece of information came out of this model building. Our field supervisors have always been skeptical of the accuracy of Scorecard rating, and it is natural for any agency or organization to resist measures which evaluate performance. However, our model demonstrated that some of their concerns were well founded. Several field supervisors complained that during months in which they devoted a lot of effort to street cleaning, the Scorecard rating did not go up. However, in the subsequent month when street cleaning efforts returned to their typical level, the Scorecard rating would go up. This caused great confusion in the minds of our field leaders.

Our model showed very clearly that a one-month lag in the Scorecard rating was typical when there was a change in the level of cleaning effort. This could be explained by two factors. First, any measurement has a lag to it. The month's Scorecard ratings are an average of ratings from the beginning of the month all the way through to the end of the month. Not all streets are rated every day. Because the Scorecard rating is an average, poor ratings from the beginning of the month will be averaged in with good ratings taken at the end of the month. Secondly, much of our cleaning is mandated by alternate side parking regulations. Extra cleaning is done on secondary or tertiary streets. Streets are classified as secondary or tertiary if they have a low litter rate. It might take two or three weeks for enough litter to build up on those streets for them to become unacceptably dirty.

If, for example, at the beginning of a month they were filthy and if we did extra cleaning in that month, we would get to them but most likely not right away. So at least at the beginning of the month, perhaps the first two weeks, Scorecard raters would rate these streets as not acceptably clean. By the end of the month they would be clean. That month's rating would be an average of the good and the poor ratings and would not reflect the extra cleaning effort. In the second month, many of the ratings on those streets would still be good, because it would take them three or four weeks to get dirty again. So during the second month Scorecard ratings would be higher than the first month when a lot of extra cleaning was done even though extra cleaning was cut back during the second month. This explains the lag effect in the measurement system and is hardly a startling scientific realization, but it has increased our field supervisors' confidence in Scorecard. It has also enabled top management to evaluate more reasonably and more accurately field efforts on street cleaning.

The district specific marginal utilities for cleaners calculated from regression analysis are used to find the optimal allocation of cleaners. The optimal allocation was, of course, a technical solution to what is to a great extent a political decision. Many of the districts that rated very high on the marginal utility ranking were districts that were already quite clean. Making them cleaner would, of course, be a good thing; however there were other districts that were quite filthy and, although their marginal utility of workers would not be quite as high, the "good government" allocation dictated that more workers be channeled into the filthy areas than would

have been allocated according to the optimal model. However, the value of the model was clear. Without this capability we would not be able to predict the payoff of adding workers to various districts.

In the final allocation, most of the 450 street cleaners went to the dirtiest districts but each district got some. Thus the allocation was a compromise between the optimal and the "good government" approach, and as such, had to be considered a complete success. We predicted that the citywide Scorecard rating would rise approximately six points based on our citywide model which indicated that approximately 75 payroll-assigned workers would raise the citywide percent of acceptably clean streets by one percentage point. The results for fiscal year 1982, since September when the additional 450 men went on the streets, have an average of 4.8 percent increase in Scorecard percentage points over the previous year, not a substantial shortfall considering that the allocation was not the optimal one.

Other more theoretical models have been built in an effort to explain why different districts have different marginal utilities with regard to cleaning manpower. A model relating the rate at which litter builds up on the streets and the "passage time" between our cleaning efforts is shown in Figure 5. What we call a "saw tooth curve" model shows that, assuming a street starts out perfectly clean, litter begins to build up at a rate of L. At time t our cleaning crew comes by and makes the street clean again. The cycle repeats. As the litter builds up, at some point (marked by a), the street is no longer rated acceptably clean. At some point, f, the street becomes filthy. The t_a is the length of time that the street is in the acceptably clean range. Then t_a/t is the probability that the street will be rated acceptably clean.

Figure 5. A model of a street's level of cleanliness over time. L = litter rate, a = amount of litter on street above which the street is no longer considered acceptably clean, f = amount of litter on street which causes it to be considered filthy, t_a = time it takes for enough litter to build up on a street with litter rate L so that any more litter would make it not acceptably clean, t_f = time after which street is considered filthy, t = time between cleanings (passage time).

Figure 6. The relationship between cleanliness and filthiness and the time between cleanings.

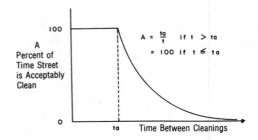

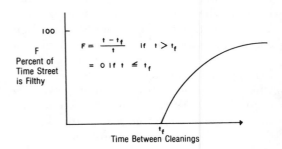

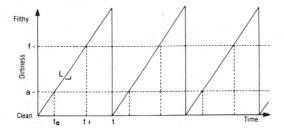

There are several things that the department can do to increase its percentage of acceptably clean streets. First, it can increase manpower to reduce the passage time (Figure 6). Second, the department can make sure that when a street is cleaned, it is spotless after the workers leave. Third, efforts can be made to reduce the litter rate. The primary way for the department to reduce the litter rate is by enforcing the Sanitary Code to prevent such violations as improperly packaged garbage. Improperly packaged garbage, especially by commercial establishments, is a primary source of litter in the streets. Increased efforts at enforcement might have more effect on street cleanliness than reducing the passage time. We are currently investigating the trade-off in investing in those two activities.

Obviously matching the passage time to the litter rate is a key factor. Putting addi-

tional workers into low-litter-rate areas which already have short passage times will have little effect on street cleanliness. Also, putting workers in districts with high litter rates and very long passage times will have little effect at first, but a greater effect once enough workers are added to get the passage time down to the "sensitive" area on the cleanliness versus passage time curve.

INCREASED PRODUCTIVITY THROUGH LARGER TRUCKS

One of the major victims of the fiscal crisis was the city's capital budget. Purchasing new equipment was postponed for several years until the city's budget situation could be straightened out. In 1979, the department began to modernize its collection truck fleet, which was in a sorry state after having no "reinforcements" in many years. At that time, it was recognized that the state-of-the-art in truck capacity had changed substantially since the early 70s. When the department considered purchasing new trucks, it faced the question of what size collection vehicle should be purchased. The typical department truck was a 20-cubic yard, seven-ton capacity vehicle. However, the latest technology made possible a 25-cubic yard, 12.5-ton capacity truck. Although the 25-cubic yard trucks were more expensive, they could, perhaps, yield substantial productivity savings and reduce operating costs.

Under the direction of Chief Joseph Timpone, a model was built to predict whether the larger capacity vehicles would pay off. If the annual manpower savings were greater than the extra capital cost, they were considered a good investment.

The model consisted of work rate (tons per hour collected) and the number of loads produced in a day. For example, let's say that because of the nature of the garbage in a particular district, workers can collect 1½ tons in an hour. Using a seven-ton truck, the workers can collect a full load in about four hours and 40 minutes. Then, they would have to drive the truck to the dump, return to the route and finish out the day. That could mean either doing more collection and dumping a partial load or doing more collection and leaving the truck in the garage with the load to be dumped off-shift by a night worker.

The trip to the dump can take as long as an hour. A 12.5-ton truck would not pack out in 4 hours and 40 minutes, and would save the dump time, thus increasing the time the crew could be on the route collecting garbage. As a matter of fact, at the rate of 1½ tons per hour, in the six hours the workers are actually on the route during a shift they would be able to load out only nine tons. Such a district could use the larger capacity truck.

This model was tested on a number of districts and it was decided that larger capacity trucks should be purchased for use in 11 of the city's 59 districts. Three hundred 12.5 ton trucks were purchased and the savings in operating costs predicted by the model have proved quite accurate. We predicted an eight to ten percent increase in productivity, and although not every district has achieved the percent projected, the average productivity savings for all 11 districts has been nine percent.

ASSIGNMENT OF LOADS TO DUMP SITES

The city has 11 marine transfer stations (locations where garbage is dumped into barges to be tugged to landfills), three landfills, and three incinerators that are dumpsites for the 15,000 tons of garbage the department collects each day and the 10,000 tons private and other carters collect. The department produces between 1,500 and 2,000 loads of garbage every day. Assigning those loads to disposal facilities is a critically important productivity issue. Travel time to and from and queueing time at the dumpsite greatly affect operating costs.

The current allocation of loads to disposal facilities when all facilities are operating has been found to be fundamentally sound. However, difficulties arise (1) when a disposal facility, or set of facilities are shut down for repairs or dredging, or (2) when an incinerator requires more material to burn to avoid losing its continuity of service.

The department has developed a model under the direction of Susan Mentser, and based on prior work done by the staff of Chief Timpone, that assigns loads to dump sites and takes into account queueing effects and disposal capacity. The model has been used for a number of management decisions. For example, if a disposal site has to be shut down for a short time to allow slips to be dredged or a building to be repaired, to which other dump site should trucks be diverted? And, if new types of waste disposal facilities are to be built, such as truck transfer stations or small scale incinerators, where should they be built to minimize overall operating costs? In using the model to determine the number of plants to be built, it was found that productivity costs dominated capital costs in the equation for minimizing overall system costs.

Lastly, the city faces a waste disposal crisis in the next decade: it will run out of landfill space before 1995. New York City will be buried under garbage if it doesn't find a place for its own refuse. Waste-to-energy plants are being designed to meet this crisis. Where should they be built? This model will be helpful in testing the "productivity impact" of different plant locations.

CONCLUSION

These are just some of the issues for which management science modeling and analyses have played an important role in making New York City's Department of Sanitation an efficient, well-run organization. Analyses of this type have now become standard operating procedure in the department and these models have been institutionalized into the department's decision making and policy analysis structure.

REFERENCES

American Public Works Association Research Foundation 1977, *Research on Equipment Technology Utilized by Local Government: Street Cleaning*, National Science Foundation, Washington, D. C.

Fleming, Rodney R. P. E. 1978, Editor, *Street Cleaning Practice*, American Public Works Association, 1313 East 60th Street, Chicago, Illinois 60637.

Morris, Charles 1980, *The Cost of Good Intentions: New York City and the Liberal Experiment, 1960-1975*, W. W. Norton Company, New York.

Novotny, Vladimir, and Chesters, C. 1981, *Handbook of Nonpoint Pollution*, Van Nostrand Reinhold Company, New York.

Public Technology, Inc. 1982, *Performance Evaluation of Street Cleaning Equipment*, Public Technology, Inc., 1301 Pennsylvania Ave. N. W., Washington, D. C. 20004, March 3.

Thomas, John S. 1980, "Scorecard: measuring street cleanliness," in *Helping City Government Improve Productivity: An Evaluation of the Productivity Projects of the Fund for the City of New York*, Frederick O'R. Hayes Associates, 419 Park Avenue South, New York.

APPENDIX: MANPOWER FORECASTING MODEL

$$S_i = A_i - W_i$$

where:

S_i = surplus or deficit of workers on average day in month i,

A_i = average number of workers available to perform mandated jobs on a typical day in month i,

W_i = average number of jobs mandated to be done on a typical day in month i,

$$A_i = [(P_i + H_i - L_i/2 - D_i) / F_i] - M_i;$$

where:

P_i = beginning of month payroll assigned,

H_i = number of workers hired during month i (assumption is workers are hired on the first of the month),

L_i = number of workers lost to attrition during month i (assumption is workers leave at the middle of month, thus $L_i/2$),

D_i = average daily number of workers detached out of bureau to do other work not included in model,

F_i = absence factor. Ratio of workers on payroll, less detached, to workers available for work,

M_i = average daily number of workers on medical duty assignment. These are workers present but due to temporary disability, not able to perform mandated work,

W_i = $G_i + C_i + B_i$;

where:

G_i = average daily number of workers needed to collect garbage,

C_i = average daily number of workers needed to perform mandated cleaning jobs in month i,

B_i = average daily number of workers needed to perform mandated garage support jobs in month i.

The formulation is as follows:

Minimize

$$\sum_{i=1}^{12} P_i \cdot K + Q_i \cdot N_i \cdot R \tag{1}$$

such that $P_i = P_{i-1} + H_{i-1} - L_{i-1}$
$Q_i = S_i$ if $S_i < 0$
$= 0$ if $S_i \geq 0$;

where:

P_i = beginning of month payroll in month i,

K = average monthly salary of a worker,

S_i = average daily surplus or deficit of workers in month i,

Q_i = variable to equal size of deficit when it exists and to equal zero when a surplus exists,

N_i = number of working days in month i,

R = cost of overtime when a worker has to work on the assigned day off,

H_i = number of workers hired in month i,

L_i = number of workers lost to attrition in month i.

The citywide Scorecard rating is a weighted average of the 59 district ratings. It is found as follows:

$$S_c = \sum_{i=1}^{59} \frac{M_i}{M} S_i \tag{2}$$

where:

S_c = citywide Scorecard rating,
M_i = street mileage of district i,
M = total street mileage in city

$$= \sum_{i=1}^{59} M_i \tag{3}$$

S_i = Scorecard rating for district i.

Using the district-specific marginal utilities for cleaners calculated from the regression analyses, the optimal allocation of cleaners is found by the following:

Maximize

$$S_c = \sum_{i=1}^{59} \frac{M_i}{M} S_i \qquad (4)$$

such that $S_i = a_i + b_i X_i$
$\qquad S_i \leq 100$
$\qquad X_i =$ additional street cleaners assigned to district i,

where:

$\qquad a_i =$ Scorecard rating in district i without any additional cleaners.

$\qquad b_i =$ increase in district i's Scorecard rating for each additional cleaner.

TRUCK SIZING MODEL

Determine reduction in number of truck shifts (a crew working an eight-hour shift) with larger truck.

Truck shifts saved per day $= S_c - S_n$

such that $\quad S_n = G/T_n$
$\qquad T_n = T_c + A$ if $T_c + A \leq 12.5$
$\qquad\quad = 12.5$ if $T_c + A > 12.5$
$\qquad A = D \cdot R$
$\qquad T_c = G/S_c,$

where:

$\qquad S_c =$ current total daily truck shifts,

$\qquad S_n =$ total daily truck shifts with larger capacity trucks,

$\qquad G =$ total daily tons of garbage,

$\qquad T_n =$ tons per truck shift collected using larger trucks,

$\qquad T_c =$ current tons per truck shift,

$\qquad A =$ additional tons collected by saving a dump cycle,

$\qquad D =$ time of round trip dump cycle,

$\qquad R =$ crew work rate (tons loaded per hour of work time).

Annual Cost Savings $= (S_c - S_n) \cdot 302 \cdot 3 \cdot I$, where:

$\qquad 302 =$ number of working days in the year,

$\qquad 3 =$ crew size,

$\qquad I =$ daily wages of a sanitation worker.

Determine capital cost of purchasing larger, more costly trucks.

Annual cost $= (C_{25} - C_{20}) (CRF_i^7)$, where:

$\qquad C_{25} =$ purchase price of 25-cubic yard truck (12.5 tons),

$\qquad C_{20} =$ purchase price of 20-cubic yard truck (7.0 tons),

$\qquad CRF =$ capital recover factor for current interest (i) and seven-year life-cycle of trucks.

ACKNOWLEDGEMENTS

The author would like to thank the following people who contributed direction, inspiration, good thinking, or hard work to the models discussed in this paper: Deputy Commissioner Vincent Whitfield, Deputy Commissioner Chris Beemer, Deputy Commissioner Frank Sisto, Chiefs John Doherty, Mike Carpinello, Joe Timpone, Gus Dennis, Bob Hennelly, Ed Sheridan, and Blaze Tramazzo; Mitch Zaretsky, Rick Wolf, Dick Pearlmutter, Fran Heatherington, Barbara Rothenberg, Bob Tsien, Teddy Barra, Larry Milbauer, Rochelle Albee, Valerie Butenas, Joe Miller, Susan Mentser, Karen Bosshart, Ann Litke, all of the Department of Sanitation, and Vincent Fargione of the New York Telephone Company.

Reviews by Sheldon Mann of the Mayor's Office of Operations and the referee for *Interfaces* were extremely helpful in putting this paper in readable form.

In addition, many thanks must go to Deputy Mayor Nathan Leventhal who constantly insists that every effort be made to improve the way government does business.

Most importantly, it must be noted that none of this work could have been done without the support and encouragement of the mayor, Edward Koch, who has created an environment that makes the performance of highly professional work not only a possibility but also an obligation of those who serve the public.

A letter from former Mayor Edward I. Koch of the City of New York states: "I am quite proud of the remarkable record of accomplishment of New York City's Department of Sanitation. The agreement with the union to reduce manning on garbage trucks from three workers to two, the use of larger capacity trucks, using work measurement techniques to extend routes, and the creation and effective deployment of a new street cleaning force are some of the major operational accomplishments Commissioner Norman Steisel has instituted in that agency. Refuse collection productivity is up more than 17 percent over the last two years, and street cleanliness has improved substantially.

Having a strong analytic background himself, Commissioner Steisel knew of the need to have a top technical support staff to help him move his department forward. He created the Office of Operations Planning, Evaluation, and Control (OPEC) to provide him with the operations analysis and planning capability he needed, and hired Dr. Lucius Riccio, who has had extensive government operations planning and research experience, to head that unit.

OPEC's contributions are used to support major decisions affecting millions of dollars of expenditures and the deployment of thousands of workers. As exemplified by the analysis in this article, OPEC has given me and the Department of Sanitation the analytic support necessary to develop strategies and resolve overall service delivery issues."

9

COMPANY-WIDE INTEGRATION OF MANAGEMENT SCIENCE MODELS

This chapter focuses on the company-wide integration of MS/OR models carried out at Citgo Petroleum Corporation, the largest independent refiner and marketer of petroleum products in the US. Citgo's undertaking ranks among the largest implementations of MS/OR models in any company. While the petroleum industry has been a pioneer in using MS/OR models, few applications rival Citgo's experience in showing the pervasive impact of MS/OR models on the flow of information for managerial decision making.

Citgo's effort centered on distributing products from the refinery to over 350 terminals across the country that store the products for wholesale or retail sales. In designing its integrated system, Citgo deployed an impressive array of MS/OR models that included mathematical programming, statistics, forecasting, expert systems, and artificial intelligence. The application of these techniques has resulted in profit improvements of approximately $70 million and has also changed the way Citgo conducts its business. Citgo's integrated system for products planning coordinates pricing, purchasing, distribution, and inventory planning decisions. The main optimization procedure within this system is a large network flow algorithm.

Citgo's project took over two years to implement and cost $20 to $30 million. The late Darwin Klingman, a prominent management science academic and consultant, directed the implementation effort. In the paper included in this chapter, Klingman, Phillips, Steiger, and Young [1987] describe Citgo's project and take a close look at the implementation issues that surrounded it. In a companion paper, Klingman, Phillips, Steiger, Wirth, and Young [1986] focus on the organizational issues of company-wide system integration in a firm such as Citgo. In another paper, Klingman, Phillips, Steiger, Wirth, Padman, and Krishnan [1987] describe some of the technical features of the network optimization model that they implemented at Citgo. In view of the scope and magnitude of this project, we supplement our discussion of the paper presented in this volume with material from the other two companion papers.

9.1 MS/OR MODELS IN CITGO PETROLEUM CORPORATION

In 1985, Citgo's sales exceeded $4 billion and the company sold over 5 billion gallons of product. Approximately 85 percent of Citgo's sales comprise light petroleum products that include four grades of motor fuel (regular, unleaded, and so forth), No. 2 fuel oil, turbine fuel, and several blended motor fuels. As a wholly-owned subsidiary of the Southland Corporation, Citgo supplies the gasoline at most 7-Eleven stores. Citgo's large distribution network, which extends over the eastern two-thirds of the United States, is supplied by its refinery at Lake Charles, Louisiana, spot market purchases, and trades with other refiners (Exhibit 9–1). This network includes five distribution centers and 36 owned or leased terminals for storing petroleum products, and another 350 exchange terminals where Citgo can sell its product through agreements with other petroleum marketers.

In 1983, Southland initiated a major effort to improve its planning and operations by using MS/OR models and implementing a new design for its information systems. Although this project took two years (1984-1985) to implement and cost $20-$30 million, its benefits in 1985 alone were approximately $70 million. The project ranks among the largest implementations of MS/OR models to date and Darwin Klingman, its director, reported directly to Southland's chairman of the board. There must be compelling reasons for a company to undertake an implementation effort of this magnitude. Klingman, Phillips, Steiger, and Young [1987] mention four key factors that necessitated fundamental changes in Citgo's mode of operation:

1. Since 1982, the trend in the petroleum industry has been to decouple the upstream operations of crude oil production from the downstream operations of refining and marketing petroleum products. This restructuring requires companies to make a profit on their downstream operations. Southland's acquisition of Citgo meant that Citgo had to change from an integrated oil company with its own crude production to a profit-making downstream industry. In this market-driven mode, Citgo needed to focus on distribution channels, marketing strategies, the geographical distribution of demand, and pricing decisions.

2. The sources of crude and refined products have proliferated in the last decade. Both can be obtained by purchasing on spot and futures markets

EXHIBIT 9-1. Citgo's distribution network uses pipelines and waterways to carry products from its distribution centers to the terminals that sell them to retail and wholesale customers.

(where prices are notoriously volatile), or by trading with other companies. In this environment, effective decision making requires dramatic increases in the information available to managers.

3. As marketing power shifts from the refiner to the wholesale distributor, sales volume becomes much more sensitive to pricing decisions. Informed pricing, however, depends on the company's ability to track vast amounts of quantitative and qualitative data over time.

4. From 1972 to 1985, the cost of working capital (to finance crude and product inventories plus trade and credit card receivables) increased 30-fold as a result of a ninefold increase in crude prices and a tripling of interest rates. Since downstream profit margins decreased in the same period, tight control over inventory became a necessity.

To respond to these changes, Citgo required vast amounts of information. It also needed well-designed decision support systems to translate data into better decision making. The information had to be current and reliable; small changes can make the difference between large profits or losses. As Klingman and his coworkers point out, the earnings are sensitive to small changes in the mode of operation. Setting the price per gallon a quarter of a cent above the least expensive competitor may result in a loss of 25 percent in sales; an improvement of one in a thousand in the yields of refined products can result in an annual improvement of $3 million in earnings; the diversion of a quarter of a percent of the volume of an input stream into a higher value output stream can earn Citgo $1 million.

The volume of information Citgo tracks is awe-inspiring. Consider, for example, wholesale price and volume forecasts that support marketing and distribution decisions. Citgo develops weekly forecasts, by terminal and by product, for 11 weeks. Considering that Citgo owns or leases about 40 terminals and uses another 350 as exchange terminals, this calls for an extensive set of forecasts. Forecasting retail sales goes beyond this information to capture the weekly retail sales volume of 7-Eleven stores by terminal and by store group. Once forecasts are made, management reviews them and sanctions their corporate use. One key factor leading to Citgo's success was its decision to organize vast amounts of information on forecasts and other data into a single corporate-wide database management system called PASS (Product Acquisition and Supply System).

The authors emphasize the importance of a company-wide data base. The fact that all managers access the same data bank is a key factor in coordinating decisions made by different departments. This represents a fundamental change from Citgo's historical practice of collecting and storing separate operational data banks in various departments.

Integrated Systems and the Associated Benefits

Citgo's comprehensive implementation effort involved a number of different models and systems (Exhibit 9–2). While each model is useful in itself, integrating these models provides Citgo with an added advantage. First, the models draw upon one underlying data bank, thereby ensuring the consistency of the information on which managers base their decisions. Second, the output of one model provides information that other models use. The PASS data base, which captures Citgo's data in an integrated system, serves as a convenient conduit of information from one model to another.

The primary planning tools at Citgo are the refinery LP system and the supply, distribution, and marketing model, known as SDM. Together, the two systems plan the product flow from the acquisition of crude oil through product sales. The refinery LP system is a key tool for operating Citgo's refinery at Lake Charles. In 1984, the annual cost of operating the refinery, excluding crude and feedstock costs, exceeded $700 million. To reduce this cost substantially, the refinery LP model had to be revamped and enhanced.

The SDM model is a large integrated distribution model for short-term operational planning. It uses input data from the PASS data base to optimize the flow of products, plan exchange and trade agreements effectively, and set the amounts of inventory to be stored at the terminals or carried in-transit. SDM requires extensive data. For example, SDM relies upon forecasts of spot market prices (as does the refinery LP system). It also needs forecasts for prices and volumes of wholesale and retail sales. SDM's network optimizer incorporates the price-volume relationship to capture the elasticity of wholesale demand as the price varies. SDM also interacts with TRACS—the strategic marketing deci-

EXHIBIT 9–2. The implementation effort at Citgo involved multiple models and systems. A brief description of the function, technology, and benefits of each model indicates the scope of the project. The figures for benefits are for 1985. The PASS system, which serves as the underlying data base, is not listed but interacts with most systems.

SYSTEM	ROLE OR FUNCTION	TECHNOLOGY	BENEFITS
REFINERY LP	• selecting and acquiring crude and feedstock • planning refinery run levels • setting production levels	• MPSX LP system of IBM • Matrix and report generator software from Haverly Systems	• $50 million in benefits for manufacturing • increased flexibility in gearing production runs to market demand

EXHIBIT 9–2. *(Continued)*

SYSTEM	ROLE OR FUNCTION	TECHNOLOGY	BENEFITS
SDM-SUPPLY, DISTRIBUTION, AND MARKETING MODEL	• selecting markets and setting prices • planning trades and purchases • setting inventory levels and shipping patterns	• Network flow optimization code to solve network problems with 3,000 nodes and 15,000 arcs. • Rule-based systems for exchange agreements and report generation	• $116 million reduction in gasoline and distillate inventories • coordination of distribution and marketing across products and departments
TRACS MARKET PLANNING SYSTEM	• comparing selling options • evaluating existing markets for profitability	• Database management system with rule-based capabilities	• $2.5 million improvement in marketing net profits • evaluation of several new marketing options
FORECASTING MODELS	• developing wholesale price and volume forecasts	• Regression analysis • Econometric modeling	• company uses an official set of forecasts throughout
CRUDE SCHEDULING	• scheduling delivery of crude from storage tanks to refinery	• PC-based optimization procedure	• $20 million reduction of crude inventories
PROCESS CONTROL	• controlling temperature and flow in refinery units • taking corrective action when needed	• Automatic process control • Nonlinear control model	• improvement in product yields and values • lower operating costs
TERMINAL SYSTEMS	• processing transactions and billing at the point of sale • collecting exchange lifting information at terminals	• CATS automated terminal system • OMRON data transmission units	• $9 million reduction in working capital through improved collection of receivables • provides current information to PASS data base

sion support system—to evaluate the profitability of existing and potential markets.

Citgo complemented its large-scale MS/OR optimization models with numerous smaller models, systems, and studies. In increasing its use of automatic process control of refinery operations from under 50 to over 90 percent, Citgo was taking advantage of a tool of long-standing in the process industries. Similarly, Citgo's use of terminal systems for billing and for capturing data at the point of sale enhanced its abilities to obtain timely information. Both of these systems feed up-to-date information into PASS and therefore help complete the company's integrated data bank.

Citgo's integrated system allowed it to reduce its working capital in a variety of ways:

1. A float optimization system led to a reduction of $8.5 million in working capital by controlling the payables associated with crude and product purchases;

2. By managing crude inventories that feed into the refinery, the crude scheduling system reduced working capital by $20 million;

3. The TRACS and SDM systems reduced terminal inventories and imbalances in exchange agreements to reduce product inventories by $116 million. For example, the systems traded off spot purchases against the costs of transportation and in-transit inventory to reduce inventories;

4. By allowing quick data capture and faster billing, the CATS and OMRON systems reduced the delays in collecting receivables. This reduced working capital by $9 million.

Overall, Citgo reduced its working capital by $145 to $155 million between 1983 and 1985. Consequently, it saved approximately $17.4 to $18.6 million annually in interest charges for financing its working capital. This reduction is the combined result of several systems (Exhibit 9–2). Although Klingman and his coworkers played an important role in designing, developing, enhancing, and evaluating all of these models, the centerpiece of their implementation efforts at Citgo was the SDM model.

The Supply, Distribution, and Marketing Environment

Citgo uses a network of pipelines, tankers, and barges to distribute its products from the refinery through five distribution centers to over 350 terminals across the country. Citgo can acquire petroleum products from different sources: it can draw upon its refinery in Lake Charles, purchase products from five major spot markets, or make exchanges and trades with other refiners. A realistic model of Citgo's distribution must incorporate the following elements:

Multiple time periods. Because Citgo's distribution area is so large, products take anywhere from one to five weeks to travel from their supply points to their destinations. For example, refined product from the Lake Charles refinery reaches the Meridian and Birmingham terminals within seven days but takes eight to 14 days to arrive at Charlotte (Exhibit 9–1). Since purchasing refined products or refining crude takes another four to six weeks, the decision to supply product to a distant terminal is made eleven weeks prior to the actual delivery. The distribution model must explicitly model such time lags by using multiple time periods.

Product flows, inventories, and costs. Given the multiperiod nature of the distribution problem, the model must track product flows over time and set inventory levels at each of its terminals, which store product in bulk. It must capture the costs for intransit inventories, for carrying inventory at the terminals, for transportation tariffs, for terminal handling, and for marketing overhead (credit card charges, for example).

Spot market purchases. Citgo must trade off the option of transporting products from its own facilities against the option of purchasing on the spot market. For example, instead of shipping products from Lake Charles to New York, Citgo can supply northeast demand by purchasing from the New York Harbor spot market. The refined products not shipped to the northeast can be used to satisfy Gulf Coast demand. Once its costs for transportation and interest are taken into account, choosing the cheaper option can save Citgo 0.5 to 2.0 cents per gallon. To enhance the profitability of the firm, the distribution marketing model must address these trade-offs in full.

Wholesale price-volume functions. Wholesale demand at each terminal depends on the price offered in its market. Rather than treating wholesale volumes as fixed, the model must incorporate the elasticity of demand.

Exchange agreements. Citgo has ongoing contractual agreements to exchange products with partners in the petroleum industry. For example, Citgo can deliver products from its New York terminal to an exchange partner who will deliver equivalent products to Citgo's exchange terminal in California. This will save Citgo the expense of shipping its own refined products to California. The exchange partner will also benefit since it can satisfy the demand of New York customers without shipping its own refined products from California. Such an agreement is based on Citgo's wholesale and retail demand at the California terminal and the partner's demand in New York. However, exchange imbalances can occur when one partner draws more than the forecasted volume of product. Together with terminal inventories, these imbalances represent the largest component of Citgo's working capital. The model must therefore optimize its use of exchange agreements.

Purchase, sale, trade (PST) agreements. PST agreements are one-time arrangements similar to exchanges but more flexible; they can be one-sided (a purchase or a sale) or trade unlike products (unleaded for premium, say).

The SDM Network Model

Klingman and his coworkers determined early on that a large-scale network flow model captures all of these elements and offers two main advantages. First, since such a model follows the flow of products over the distribution network, managers can easily visualize and understand its structure. Second, although the large number of Citgo facilities and the multiperiod nature of the problem leads to a large network formulation with approximately 3,000 nodes and 15,000 arcs, the fast network flow algorithm solves this problem in approximately 30 seconds of IBM 4381 CPU time. Therefore, repeated optimization runs of the model presented no problems.

The SDM model has a planning horizon of 11 weeks that is divided into six one-week periods and a final five-week period. Since in many cases the product transit times across the distribution network exceed a single week, the model must keep track of product flows across time periods. As refined products move out of Lake Charles towards remote terminals, they pass through various time zones defined by successively larger transit times from Lake Charles (Exhibit 9–3). The standard method for dealing with product flows over *both* space and time is to construct a *space-time network,* a structure we have already encountered in the truckload carrier study of Chapter 3.

A space-time network replicates the physical distribution network by the number of time periods and connects them with arcs that represent movement of products over time. SDM uses two classes of such arcs: *in-transit inventory arcs* represent products that are moving in the pipeline (or on the waterway), while *terminal inventory arcs* capture products that are not moving but are carried as inventory from one time period to the next at the same terminal (Exhibit 9–4). The length chosen for the time periods has an important effect on the structure of the space-time network. For example, if all transit times are small relative to the length of the time period, then products can complete their journeys within a single time period, thereby making in-transit arcs across periods unnecessary. This occurs in the last period of the SDM model since the five-week length of this period allows all product shipments originating in this period to reach their destinations within this same period.

EXHIBIT 9-3. The movement of refined product occurs over space and time. Product bought or refined at Lake Charles in week 1 can reach terminals within time zone 1 within seven days (Meridian or Birmingham, for example). Product not dropped off at those terminals crosses over to time zone 2, where it can satisfy terminal demands during week 2. Atlanta, Spartanburg, and Charlotte all lie within time zone 2, since it takes the product 8-14 days to reach these locations from Lake Charles. As there is not enough time for product to reach these locations in week 1, zone 2 demand in week 1 must be met from initial or in-transit inventory (arrows within boxes). The pipeline that leaves Lake Charles in week 1 to arrive at Atlanta in week 2 represents product in transit. The vertical "pipeline" connecting identical locations represents the movement of inventory from one period to the next at the same location [Source: Klingman, Phillips, Steiger, Wirth, and Young 1986].

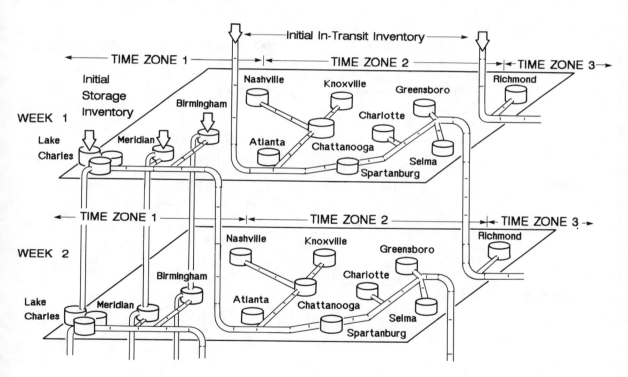

The space-time network structure allows SDM to capture Citgo's operations in great detail. First, the constraints of the model are simple flow balance equations at each node that are easy to visualize. For example, in each period, a Citgo terminal may receive products from the pipeline or waterways, from exchange agreements, trades, or purchases. It uses the products to satisfy wholesale or retail demand, make an exchange delivery, or make a PST delivery. The inventory at the termi-

EXHIBIT 9–4. The Citgo space-time network with two one-week periods and one three-week period shows both time zones and time periods. Nodes for Lake Charles and Meridian, Birmingham, Atlanta, Spartanburg, Charlotte, and Richmond terminals are replicated in each time period. Lake Charles serves as both the refinery and a distribution center (DC). The smallest nodes represent pipeline junctions (C stands for the Colonial pipeline). Paths of physical distribution appear as arcs that join pipeline junctions. For example, the arc that originates at the node above Birmingham in week 1 and terminates at the node above Atlanta in week 2 carries in-transit flow. Inventory arcs join the same terminal nodes across two successive time periods. Supplies and demands appear as triangles. For example, the triangle leading into the Lake Charles node represents refinery supply, while the triangle leading away captures total demand (the sum of retail, wholesale, and exchange demand). Supply triangles leading into the terminals model initial terminal inventory, while those attached to junction nodes capture in-transit inventory. There are no time zones in the last time period since the three-week length of this period is long enough for the product to reach the site with the maximum transit time [Source: Klingman, Phillips, Steiger, Wirth, and Young 1986].

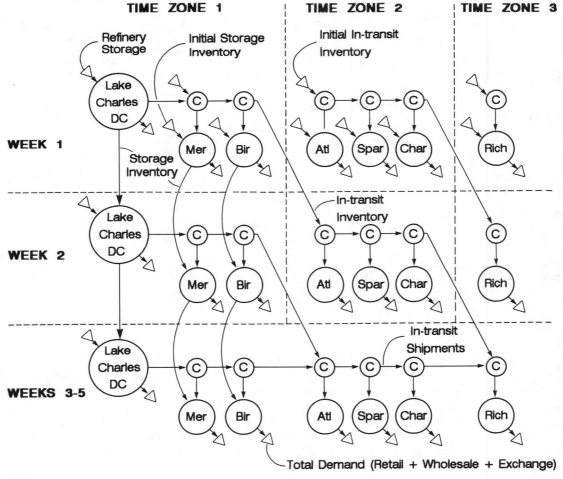

470

nal changes by the difference between the flow of product into the terminal and out of the terminal. A distribution center has some additional options such as spot market sales and purchases. All of the distribution and marketing costs are attached to arcs of the SDM network. For example, the terminal inventory arcs capture the inventory carrying charges while flows to terminals incur transportation costs, as well as marketing, handling, and overhead expenses. The user can control the levels of various activities by placing upper and lower limits on the arc flows. For example, a lower limit on an inventory arc may represent safety stock requirements at a terminal. The objective of the SDM network model is to maximize total revenues less expenses. The revenues are generated by wholesale sales, spot sales, exchange receipts, and PST deliveries. The expenses include refining, spot purchases, exchange deliveries, and PST receipts, plus the costs of transportation, terminal handling, and the time value of money.

SDM sets up a complete network model for each of four different petroleum products—regular, unleaded, super unleaded, and fuel oil. According to Klingman, Phillips, Steiger, Wirth, Padman, and Krishnan [1987], for an unleaded gasoline problem with approximately 3,300 nodes and 15,700 arcs, a typical run takes about 10 minutes. This time includes about three minutes of CPU time on an IBM 4381 mod 2 to load the data into tables, perform data consistency checks, and optimize the problem. The optimization step by itself takes only about 0.5 CPU minutes. The remaining time goes into generating reports, which takes about seven minutes.

Once the model is solved, its results must be communicated to four user groups: (1) product managers who coordinate the operational decisions for a specific product or group of products across the organization; (2) the pricing manager who sets ranges for terminal prices for each product; (3) product traders who are responsible for spot market sales and purchases or trades with other refiners; and (4) the budget manager who generates the monthly and quarterly budgets. As each of these groups needs to consult a different set of outputs from the model, Klingman's team designed reports tailored to the needs of each user group (Exhibit 9–5). The report generation procedure was fully automated to take under 10 minutes. The timely dissemination of these reports was a major factor in coordinating Citgo's operations across functions.

Direct and Indirect Benefits of SDM

The major benefit realized from the SDM model was the reduction of Citgo's product inventory with no loss in customer service. Adjusting for the different levels of sales, Klingman, Phillips, Steiger, Wirth, and Young [1986] estimated that in 1985 Citgo's inventories for automotive gasoline and distillate (distillates comprise No. 2 fuel oil and diesel fuel)

EXHIBIT 9–5. The SDM model requires extensive input information and produces a collection of different output reports. A brief summary of seven major reports shows the information they provide and the users of each report. Each user group finds certain reports of primary interest. The reports present information in units and formats that are familiar to the managers. For example, trades are given in thousands of barrels while the wholesale report uses thousands of gallons [Sources: Klingman, Phillips, Steiger, Wirth, and Young 1986; Klingman, Phillips, Steiger, Wirth, Padman, and Krishnan 1987].

INPUT DATA FILES

Terminal Master Data
Beginning Terminal Inventory
Beginning In-Transit Inventory
Wholesale Demand Forecasts
Retail Demand Forecasts
7-Eleven Demand Forecasts
Exchange Partner Demand Forecasts
Purchase/Sale/Trade Data
Spot, Wholesale, Retail Price Forecasts
Exchange Contract Data
Beginning Exchange Contract Imbalance
Parameter Data
Transportation Route Data
Transportation Link Data
Scheduled Shipments

OUTPUT REPORTS

Report	Information	Units	Users
Infeasibility	Highlights supply and timing problems (for example, forecasted demands higher than potential supply).	MBbl	Product managers, traders
In-transit, Terminal, Exchange, Inventory	Highlights product flows through pipelines and barges, through Citgo terminals and through exchange terminals and exchange paybacks. Allows analysis of critical supply paths along with inventory storage constraints.	MBbl	Product managers
Spot Recommendation	Summarizes model recommended spot purchases and sales; forms the initial strategy for product purchases, geographic trades, and spot purchases and sales.	MBbl	Traders, product managers
Purchases, Sales, Trades	Reports the current status (scheduled shipping date, unscheduled volumes) of all current, completed purchases, sales and trades.	MBbl	Traders, product schedulers, product managers
Wholesale	Summarizes shadow (incremental supply) costs and optimal positions on the price volume curve for each Citgo and exchange terminal.	MGal	Pricing manager

EXHIBIT 9–5. (*Continued*)

OUTPUT REPORTS

Report	Information	Units	Users
Volume Summary	Summarizes volume for each combination of market activity, product, and week.	MBbl	Product managers
Financial Summary	Summarizes sales revenues for each line of business; costs of spot purchases and sales; costs of exchanges; and costs of transportation and handling. Also includes interest expense associated with both terminal and in-transit inventories.	($000)	Budget manager

were reduced by 9.3 and 0.8 million barrels, respectively; as compared to the inventories Citgo would have carried if the 1983 policies had remained in effect. This represents a reduction of $116.5 million in the value of product inventory and translates into an annual savings of $14 million in the interest expenses for carrying inventory.

Beyond direct benefits, the authors point out a number of indirect benefits resulting from improved information flow and coordination. For example, the corporate-wide data base (PASS) that feeds information to SDM provides up-to-date information to all managers. Similarly, the policy of using a single set of official forecasts throughout the organization greatly improves coordination. The increased interdepartmental communication that began in the early phases of SDM's development continued after its implementation as managers came to rely on SDM's outputs. This increased communication has generated new ideas and insights and removed previously held misconceptions—another benefit to Citgo.

9.2 A BRIEF LOOK AT IMPLEMENTATION ISSUES

In Chapter 1, we mentioned the importance of implementation strategy in MS/OR studies. Citgo's project illustrates certain key implementation issues that are common to many integrated MS/OR applications. Without aiming to be comprehensive, the following list collects some of these issues.

Top management commitment. Klingman and his coauthors consider top management support the most important factor in the success of their implementation effort. This opinion is echoed in most of the studies collected in this volume. In addition to the chairman of the board of Southland and the CEO and president of Citgo, the development of the SDM model involved more than 40 managers from all levels of the organization. Such wide commitment at so many levels, while very difficult to obtain, is absolutely necessary for effective system integration.

Data collection. Citgo's SDM model is highly data-intensive. To a large extent, its success and utility relies upon good input data. To ensure the success of data collection, Klingman's team held meetings with Citgo management to assess data requirements. PASS, the comprehensive database management system that interacts with all MS/OR models at Citgo, was an outgrowth of these meetings. Klingman and his coworkers consider PASS a key factor in the successful implementation of their SDM model. Data collected in any firm requires verification. At Citgo, the collected data was checked for inconsistencies and errors. The authors describe the inch-thick log of error messages produced by their code for checking data inconsistencies. Once identified, these errors were corrected and removed over a period of several months.

Assessing information needs. Klingman and his coworkers emphasized the assessment of Citgo's information needs. For example, in revamping the LP refinery model, they investigated the accuracy and integrity of information on costs, yields, and physical measurements. Similarly, they investigated the various types of information the SDM model provides to distinct user groups and designed reports tailored to their needs. Successful model development clearly relies on a careful investigation of information needs. The developers of SDM describe the general principle behind this approach as follows:

> The advantages of beginning with an information assessment are (1) it provides access to top management through both interviews and presentations of study results; (2) major benefits are more likely when information technologies . . . are entwined because the potentials of each suddenly multiply and fresh ideas arise; (3) since most data processing managers don't think like business strategists, and most executives don't really understand what technology can do, management scientists can and should play an important role in such studies [Klingman, Phillips, Steiger, Wirth, and Young 1986, p. 17].

Impact on information flow. Just as assessing information needs must precede model development, after implementation, it is essential to track and evaluate how the model affects the information flows within the company. Citgo, for example, began using a single set of company-wide forecasts and instituted new procedures to generate the budget directly from the SDM model (rather than relying on informal communication between budget analysts and managers). To take full advantage of the information a new model provides, users need training and education.

Citgo's training for its employees focused on using the reports of the SDM model and interpreting its results.

Organizational changes. To the extent that a successful implementation introduces new processes of decision making, it is likely to result in organizational change. At Citgo, the wide scope and integrated nature of the SDM system brought about important changes. To achieve better coordination, Citgo combined the product supply and distribution departments and created a new position of senior vice-president of operations, to whom the combined department reports. More generally, because the SDM model spans multiple functions within the firm, it requires cross-functional coordinated decision making. To convey this to the managers, Klingman and his coworkers held modeling and training meetings of 25 or more managers from different sections of the company. The increased communication between managers from different departments was an important indirect benefit of the model.

The role of MS/OR methodology. Much has been said about the relation between MS/OR practice and its tools. In Citgo's case, this chapter, one factor crucial to success was the fit between the tool used and the application. This fit is far more important than technical sophistication or sheer algorithmic power. At Citgo, the network model served as a conceptual device for following the flow of products over space and time. This facilitated its use as an all-encompassing integrative decision-making system.

9.3 FURTHER READINGS

Related Readings

Klingman, Phillips, Steiger, and Young Paper

- In addition to his reputation as a leading academic, Darwin Klingman was at the forefront of MS/OR practice throughout his professional career. His work at Citgo exemplifies the highest standards of such practice, a success that he replicated in many other projects cited in this chapter. His untimely death in October 1989 was a tragic loss to the MS/OR community. In a moving tribute to his friend and colleague, Fred Glover [1990] cites some of Klingman's lasting contributions to MS/OR.
- Klingman, Phillips, Steiger, Wirth, and Young [1986] describe the implementation process for the SDM model in detail. They present the underlying network model for SDM (our Section 9.1) and go on to describe its implementation. In addition to summarizing the direct and indirect benefits of the model, they address the key challenges of the two-year imple-

mentation effort and point out the main managerial and organizational factors that helped make this implementation a success.

- Klingman, Phillips, Steiger, Wirth, Padman, and Krishnan [1987] focus on the technical details of the SDM network model. The formulation given in the appendix to the paper in this chapter is drawn from their paper. They develop the time/space network underlying SDM and show how to incorporate exchanges and purchase, sale, and trade agreements into this model. One key construct in their model involves the use of nodes called *centroids*. By aggregating flows in an appropriate manner, centroids reduce the number of nodes and arcs required to represent movements of products across time periods. Together with another construct used in modeling exchanges, the use of centroids reduces the number of nodes in the network by approximately 50 percent. The authors also report the size and running times of each of the four network flow problems for regular, unleaded, super unleaded, and fuel oil products. In another paper, Klingman, Padman, and Phillips [1988] review the role of intelligent decision support systems in the context of the Citgo application.

- Mehring and Gutterman [1990] describe the integrated supply and distribution planning model developed for Amoco (U.K.) Limited that covers both primary and secondary distribution activities. Primary distribution focuses on the movement of products from the refinery or other supply sources to the terminals, while secondary distribution covers the movements from the terminals to the customer locations (gas stations, for example). The problem is similar to Citgo's distribution problem, although Mehring and Gutterman used a linear programming model as the basic tool. The LP model incorporates the choice of supply sources for the company's terminals, product exchange agreements, and the shipment of goods to customers. The authors mention that Amoco (U.K.) did not adopt the model for routine planning due to limited resources available for implementation.

- Harrison and Martin [1989] describe a PC-based system to assist United Refining Company (which operates a refinery in Warren, Pennsylvania) in planning its exchange agreements with other refiners. The system uses a network flow code and can solve a typical problem with 450 nodes and over 1,900 arcs in only 10 seconds on an IBM AT microcomputer. The savings from the system are estimated at $150,000 to $200,000 annually, as compared to the manual system used previously.

Background Readings

- The petroleum industry was one of the first industries to adopt mathematical programming models to plan its activities. In 1951, Charnes, Cooper, and Mellon [1952] started their pioneering application of linear programming to a refinery blending problem. As the Texaco gasoline blending system described in Chapter 5 illustrates, work on this class of problems has continued ever since. For example, Uhlmann [1988] implemented a linear-programming based refinery model on a microcomputer. A typical linear program in this application has 2,168 variables and 717 constraints (plus another 333 upper-bounding constraints); its solution time is 414 minutes on an IBM PC/AT. Chapter 5 cites a number of related applications. Bodington and Baker [1990] review the history of the petroleum industry's extensive use of mathematical programming.

- Zierer, Mitchell, and White [1976] applied linear programming to Shell's distribution of products from three refineries to over 100 terminals through transshipment facilities. Their LP formulation of a typical problem had 575 constraints and 1,050 variables. However, their product distribution model was not intended for short-term planning and did not use multiple time periods.

- Optimization has also been applied to the upstream operations of oil and gas production. In their review of the literature in this area, Durrer and Slater [1977] survey optimization models for drilling, oil field development and production planning, and reservoir modeling. Jackson and Brown [1980] describe a linear programming model to evaluate bids for crude oil sales at the Elk Hills reservoir in California owned by the federal government and Chevron. Recent work on the optimal exploitation of oil and gas reservoirs combines mathematical programming with reservoir simulation models [Lasdon et al. 1986]. Dougherty et al. [1987] provide an example of this hybrid approach used by SANTOS, Inc. in the exploitation of the natural gas reservoirs of the Cooper Basin in Australia. They estimate that the model saves three to six million Australian dollars per year.

- In Chapter 3, we briefly mentioned the computer-assisted dispatching system (CAD) that Mobil uses for its tankers. In describing this application, Brown et al. [1987] address many important implementation issues that have to do with the integration of the MS/OR model into a larger interactive planning system. As with Citgo's system, CAD had substantial data requirements and affected the flow of information relating to the distribution system.

  In an earlier work, Brown and Graves [1981] describe their work on dispatching tank trucks in real-time for Chevron USA. In 1980, Chevron's fleet of 300 vehicles delivered 2,600 loads per day to customers out of 80 bulk terminals. Unlike the multi-terminal approach of CAD, Chevron dispatchers considered a single terminal in each dispatch. The network-based procedure solved a typical dispatch of 28 trucks and 103 orders in less than a second of CPU time (on an IBM 3033) and enabled each dispatcher at Chevron to handle up to 400 loads per day, as compared to an industry average of 8 to 150 loads per day at the time. The system was able to reduce transportation costs by about three percent.

- Large-scale network models have proved to be powerful tools in logistics planning. Glover et al. [1979] describe the development of a network model that integrated the production, distribution, and inventory operations of Agrico Chemical Company, a large chemical fertilizer company that mines, produces, and distributes eight principal chemical products to the US and abroad. At the time of the study, Agrico had annual sales of over half a billion dollars, four production plants, 78 distribution centers, and about 2,000 clients. Agrico used the network model in two modes. In long-range planning, the model addressed such decisions as the location and size of distribution centers, the transportation equipment and inventory investment required, and the use of supply, purchase, or exchange opportunities. For short-term planning, the model treated the configuration of plants and distribution centers as fixed and minimized the sum of the following costs: variable production costs, costs of moving the product from plants to customers through the distribution centers, and inventory holding costs. The system used a powerful network flow code that solved a typical network problem with 6,000 nodes and 35,000 arcs in less than a minute. The system saved Agrico approximately $18 million dollars during the first three years of its operation.

- Klingman, Mote, and Phillips [1988] describe an optimization-based logistics planning system for W. R. Grace Company, one of the largest suppliers of phosphate-based chemicals and fertilizers in the nation. This company has three large plants in Bartow, Florida, over 20 regional plants across the country, and 12 regional warehouses. The products flow from the plants in Bartow to regional plants first and proceed to regional warehouses thereafter. The model minimizes the sum of production, shipping, and inventory costs over a planning horizon of 12 months. The authors converted a standard linear programming formulation of this problem into a pure network flow problem with complicating (non-network) side constraints. The network component of this model had 3,408 nodes and 21,564 arcs and there were 288 side constraints. Using a specialized algorithm based on Lagrangian relaxation, Klingman, Mote, and Phillips were able to solve this problem in less than 12 minutes of CPU time on a DEC 20/60 computer. As in the Citgo application, the advantage of the network model went beyond considerations of fast solution times: it communicated the essence of the planning model to managers at W. R. Grace in a visual and easily understandable format.

- Certain complex logistics planning problems combine production and distribution systems. Ever since the well-known work of Geoffrion and Graves [1974] for Hunt Wesson Foods, large scale mathematical programming algorithms have been used to design distribution systems with a facilities location component. Van Roy [1989] describes an example of this class of models for a petrochemical company. The company produces liquified propane and butane at two refineries and ships them in bulk to plants for bottling. The distribution of gas bottles from the plants to the customers occurs either directly or through depots. Some bottles go through transshipment points where large trucks are unloaded onto smaller ones. The problem is to find the location of the bottling plants and the depots, along with the necessary fleet requirements, in order to minimize the total distribution costs. There are 10 potential bottling plant locations, 40 potential depot locations, 40 transshipment points, and 200 customer regions. Planning the fleet sizes needed to carry the bulk or bottled products is a key component of the optimizing system, especially because the company has the option of using overtime or contract carriers. Van Roy uses mathematical programming to solve this problem and reports estimated cost savings of 10 to 25 percent.

- Brown, Graves, and Honczarenko [1987] developed an optimization-based decision support for NABISCO to support its complex production and distribution planning with 100-200 product groups, 10 to 20 bakeries, 200 to 300 facilities (ovens and packing lines, for example), and 120 to 170 customer zones. They developed algorithms that can solve a problem with 40,000 variables (including several hundred binary variables) and 200,000 constraints in less than a minute of computation time on an IBM 3033 computer.

- Powers, Karrenbauer, and Doolittle [1983] argue that complex logistics planning systems should have interface facilities and capabilities designed to enable managers to use the models painlessly. As an example, they describe the interface that they developed for use in the Glidden Coatings and Resin Division of SCM Corporation. Glidden had seven plants, 36 distribution centers, 250 branch locations, and over 5,000 independent dealers. The production-distribution model was used to develop a 10-year plan for the design of Glidden's logistics system.

- In recent years, some large logistics planning systems have been implemented on microcomputers. Carlisle et al. [1987] describe a logistics system they developed for Marshalls, Incorporated, the Massachusetts-based retail chain. Marshalls used the system to optimize the flow of freight from over 350 vendors, through its processing centers, to about 300 retail stores. The system used network flow and network design algorithms and ran on an IBM PC/AT. Blumenfeld et al. [1987] describe a microcomputer-based logistics planning system to study shipping alternatives for GM's component parts. The three plants of GM's Delco Electronics Division make 300 different types of vehicle components (radios, speakers, control devices, and so on) that have to be delivered to GM's 30 assembly plants in North America. In selecting the best shipment sizes and shipping alternatives (direct or through the warehouse, say), the model has to trade off transportation costs against inventory costs: large shipments, for example, reduce transportation costs but increase inventory costs. The authors report that the system lowered logistics costs by 26 percent, thereby saving about $2.9 million per year.

- Advances in the formulation and solution of network models have made it possible to solve large and complex logistics planning problems in practice. As Glover, Klingman, and Phillips [1990] state in their readable tutorial on this class of models, "the cost of solving network problems with 2,400 equations and 500,000 arcs has been reduced from thousands of dollars in the late '60s to less than $100 in the late '80s." These authors go on to describe a host of practical applications of network models. In their earlier reviews, Glover and Klingman [1977, 1982] cite many applications of network modeling in the area of logistics. Magee, Capacino, and Rosenfield [1985] provide a general introduction to logistics systems.

    Starting with the classic work of Ford and Fulkerson [1962] on network flows, a number of comprehensive texts on network optimization cover the techniques that underlie network planning models [Gondran and Minoux 1984, Jensen and Barnes 1980, Kennington and Helgason 1980, Tarjan 1983]. Ahuja, Magnanti, and Orlin [1989] have written a comprehensive survey of network flow algorithms that focuses on recent developments in this field and includes a long list of references. Finally, Simeone et al. [1988] have compiled a useful collection of powerful network optimization codes in FORTRAN.

REFERENCES

Ahuja, Ravindra K.; Magnanti, Thomas L.; and Orlin, James B. 1989, "Network flows," in *Optimization, Handbooks in Operations Research and Management Science, Volume 1,* ed. G. L. Nemhauser, A. H. G. Rinnooy Kan, and M. J. Todd, North-Holland, New York, pp. 211–369.

Blumenfeld, Dennis E.; Burns, Lawrence D.; Daganzo, Carlos F.; Frick, Michael C.; and Hall, Randolph W. 1987, "Reducing logistics costs at General Motors," *Interfaces,* Vol. 17, No. 1, pp. 26–47.

Bodington, Charles E. and Baker, Thomas E. 1990, "A history of mathematical programming in the petroleum industry," *Interfaces,* Vol. 20, No. 4, pp. 117–132.

Brown, Gerald G.; Ellis, Carol J.; Graves, Glenn W.; and Ronen, David 1987, "Real-time, wide area dispatch of Mobil tank trucks," *Interfaces,* Vol. 17, No. 1, pp. 107–120.

Brown, Gerald G. and Graves, Glenn W. 1981, "Real-time dispatch of petroleum tank trucks," *Management Science,* Vol. 27, No. 1, pp. 19–32.

Brown, Gerald G.; Ellis, Carol J.; Graves, Glenn W.; and Ronen, David 1987, "Real-time, wide area dispatch of Mobil tank trucks," *Interfaces*, Vol. 17, No. 1, pp. 107–120.

Brown, Gerald G.; Graves, Glenn W.; and Honczarenko, Maria D. 1987, "Design and distribution of a multicommodity production/distribution system using primal goal decomposition," *Management Science*, Vol. 33, No. 11, pp. 1469–1480.

Carlisle, David P.; Nickerson, Kenneth S.; Probst, Stephen B.; Rudolph, Denise; Sheffi, Yosef; and Powell, Warren B. 1987, "A turnkey, microcomputer-based logistics planning system," *Interfaces*, Vol. 17, No. 4, pp. 16–26.

Charnes, Abraham; Cooper, W. W.; and Mellon, B. 1952, "Blending aviation gasolines: A study in programming interdependent activities in an integrated oil company," *Econometrica*, Vol. 20, No. 2, pp. 135–159.

Dougherty, Elmer L.; Dare, Dennis; Hutchison, Peter; and Lombardino, Enrico 1987, "Optimizing SANTOS's gas production and processing operations in central Australia using the decomposition method," *Interfaces*, Vol. 17, No. 1, pp. 65–93.

Durrer, E. J. and Slater, G. E. 1977, "Optimization of petroleum and natural gas production: A survey," *Management Science*, Vol. 24, No. 3, pp. 35–43.

Ford, Lester R., Jr. and Fulkerson, Delbert R. 1962, *Flows in Networks*, Princeton University Press, Princeton, New Jersey.

Geoffrion, Arthur M. and Graves, Glenn W. 1974, "Multicommodity distribution system design by Benders decomposition," *Management Science*, Vol. 20, No. 5, pp. 822–844.

Glover, Fred 1990, "In memory of Darwin Klingman: A tribute to an esteemed colleague and friend," *Interfaces*, Vol. 20, No. 4, pp. 3–4.

Glover, Fred; Jones, Gene; Karney, David; Klingman, Darwin; and Mote, John 1979, "An integrated production, distribution, and inventory planning system," *Interfaces*, Vol. 9, No. 5, pp. 21–35.

Glover, Fred and Klingman, Darwin 1977, "Network application in industry and government," *AIIE Transactions*, Vol. 9, No. 4, pp. 363–376.

Glover, Fred and Klingman, Darwin 1981, "Mathematical optimization: A successful tool for logistics problems," in *Operational Research '81*, ed. J. P. Brans, North-Holland, Amsterdam, The Netherlands, pp. 453–462.

Glover, Fred and Klingman, Darwin 1982, "Recent developments in computer implementation technology for network flow algorithms," *INFOR*, Vol. 20, No. 4, pp. 433–452.

Glover, Fred; Klingman, Darwin; and Phillips, Nancy 1990, "Netform modeling and applications," *Interfaces*, Vol. 20, No. 4, pp. 7–27.

Gondran, M. and Minoux, Michel 1984, *Graphs and Algorithms*, John Wiley & Sons, New York.

Harrison, Terry P. and Martin, Jack L. 1989, "Optimizing exchange agreements in the refining industry," in *Impacts of Recent Computer Advances on Operations Research*, ed. R. Sharda et al., North-Holland, New York, pp. 217–225.

Jackson, Bruce L. and Brown, John M. 1980, "Using LP for crude oil sales at Elk Hills: A case study," *Interfaces*, Vol. 10, No. 3, pp. 65–70.

Jensen, Paul A. and Barnes, J. Wesley 1980, *Network Flow Programming*, John Wiley & Sons, New York.

Kennington, Jeff L. and Helgason, Richard V. 1980, *Algorithms for Network Programming*, John Wiley & Sons, New York.

Klingman, Darwin; Mote, John; and Phillips, Nancy V. 1988, "A logistics planning system at W. R. Grace," *Operations Research*, Vol. 36, No. 6, pp. 811–822.

Klingman, Darwin; Padman, Rema; and Phillips, Nancy 1988, "Intelligent decision support systems: A unique application in the petroleum industry," *Annals of Operations Research*, Vol. 12, pp. 277–283.

Klingman, Darwin; Phillips, Nancy; Steiger, David; Wirth, Ross; Padman, Rema; and Krishnan, Ramayya 1987, "An optimization based integrated short-term refined petroleum product planning system," *Management Science*, Vol. 33, No. 7, pp. 813–830.

Klingman, Darwin; Phillips, Nancy; Steiger, David; Wirth, Ross; and Young, Warren 1986,

"The challenges and success factors in implementing an integrated products planning system for Citgo," *Interfaces*, Vol. 16, No. 3, pp. 1–19.

Klingman, Darwin; Phillips, Nancy; Steiger, David; and Young, Warren 1987, "The successful deployment of management science throughout Citgo Petroleum Corporation," *Interfaces*, Vol. 17, No. 1, pp. 4–25.

Lasdon, Leon; Coffman, Paul E., Jr.; MacDonald, Robert; McFarland, James W.; and Sephrnoori, Kamy 1986, "Optimal hydrocarbon reservoir production policies," *Operations Research*, Vol. 34, No. 1, pp. 40–54.

Magee, John F.; Copacino, William C.; and Rosenfield, Donald B. 1985, *Modern Logistics Management: Integrating Marketing, Manufacturing, and Physical Distribution*, John Wiley & Sons, New York.

Mehring, Joyce S. and Gutterman, Milton M. 1990, "Supply and distribution planning support for Amoco (U.K.) Limited," *Interfaces*, Vol. 20, No. 4, pp. 95–104.

Powers, Richard F.; Karrenbauer, Jeffrey J.; and Doolittle, George R. 1983, "The myth of the simple model," *Interfaces*, Vol. 13, No. 6, pp. 84–91.

Tarjan, Robert E. 1983, *Data Structures and Network Algorithms*, Society for Industrial and Applied Mathematics, Philadelphia, Pennsylvania.

Uhlmann, Alexandra 1988, "Linear programming on a microcomputer: An application to refinery modeling," *European Journal of Operational Research*, Vol. 35, No. 3, pp. 321–327.

Van Roy, Tony J. 1989, "Multi-level production and distribution planning with transportation fleet optimization," *Management Science*, Vol. 35, No. 12, pp. 1443–1453.

Zierer, T.K.; Mitchell, W.A.; and White, T.R. 1976, "Practical applications of linear programming to Shell's distribution problems," *Interfaces*, Vol. 6, No. 4, pp. 13–26.

The Successful Deployment of Management Science throughout Citgo Petroleum Corporation

Darwin Klingman
Nancy Phillips
David Steiger
Warren Young

In 1983, Southland Corporation, the 7-Eleven convenience store giant and retailer of two billion gallons per year of gasoline through those stores, took a step to integrate vertically by acquiring Citgo Petroleum Corporation, the oil refining and marketing assets of Occidental Petroleum Corporation. Citgo Petroleum Corporation, with 1985 sales in excess of $4 billion, is one of the nation's largest industrial companies, ranking in the top 150 of the Forbes 500 (based on sales).

Southland was determined, at the time of the acquisition, to establish management priorities and procedures that would make Citgo as successful in the downstream petroleum business (refining and marketing) as Southland is in the convenience store industry, while at the same time supplying 7-Eleven stores with quality motor fuels. To achieve these goals, Southland realized that the culture of Citgo had to change. It had to be transformed from an integrated oil company which produced its own crude oil (while part of Occidental) to an independent refiner and marketer of petroleum products. It was essential that the company turn its financial losses around and begin making money in its downstream operation. This meant that Citgo had to fundamentally alter the basis for its decision making, in the process becoming more responsive to the market and less driven by the refining of crude oil.

Toward this end, Southland management made two strategic decisions. First, it established Citgo as a wholly-owned subsidiary with a full debt load. This organizational and financial structure was intended to insure that Citgo make a profit independent of Southland's vast gasoline retailing business and to provide the most basic motivation (economic survival) for improvements in Citgo's operation. Second, in 1983, Southland created a task force composed of Southland personnel, Citgo personnel, and external consultants. The charge given to the task force was to holistically explore ways to improve Citgo's profitability. Darwin D. Klingman, a management science consultant, was appointed director of the task force and reported directly to John P. Thompson, Chairman of the Board of Southland.

We developed various strategies to help Citgo management achieve the goals set by Southland. These involved combining profit center focus, mathematical programming, organizational theory, artificial intelligence, expert systems, decision support systems, and forecasting techniques with the latest information systems technologies. This comprehensive and perhaps unprecedented combination of management science disciplines has resulted in a market-driven, action-oriented management, utilizing sophisticated decision support tools to enhance its economically rational decision-making capabilities.

The results have been impressive. Citgo, which lost money for several years prior to the acquisition and had a pretax loss of over $50 million in 1984, has achieved a pretax profit of over $70 million in 1985. The key to this success has been management science tools, coupled with a new organizational structure endorsing the creative applications of these tools, as well as fortuitous environmental factors. This dramatic turnaround illustrates that a company, effectively managed and focused, can gain a strategic edge by combining management science and information technologies. It also demonstrates that the integration of these technologies multiplies the potentials of each component.

INDUSTRY ASSESSMENT—AN INDUSTRY IN THE MIDST OF AN INFORMATION EXPLOSION

In August 1983, the task force began by evaluating the downstream petroleum industry (refining and marketing) and quickly realized that this was an industry in the midst of an information explosion. This explosion is a function of four major environmental changes that have occurred during the past 15 years, changes that have increased both the number of key decision-making variables and their interaction. It afforded an excellent opportunity for applying management science technologies creatively.

One major environmental change was the increased emphasis in most companies on making a profit from downstream operations. The 1982 deregulation legislation, the industry-wide restructuring that took place between 1983 and 1985, and the decoupling of the upstream (crude oil production) and downstream operations have led to a true downstream profit objective. This is a dramatic change from the historical surrogate of maximizing product volume to monetize crude oil. Previously, companies that owned crude oil refined as much as possible to try to make money on their oil wells, even if this activity led to downstream losses. To realize the downstream profit objective requires much more data and better management science tools in order to address such issues as which markets to serve, how to serve them, what products to sell, which distribution channels to utilize, what prices to charge, and where to buy product.

Another major environmental change is the number of new sources of crude oil and refined product. In the past, the primary sources of crude and product were the company's wells and refineries, with the secondary sources being exchanges of crude or product with a few other industry players. Currently, however, 30 percent of all crude oil refined in the US is imported, and significant amounts are bought on the spot market (the bulk petroleum products market delivering within

48 hours). In addition, crude can be purchased on the futures market (NYMEX) or in short-term netback deals in which the purchase price is dependent on spot market prices on some given date. Refined product can be bought on one of five spot markets as well as through the NYMEX or through purchases and trades with other industry players. The spot and futures markets are highly volatile with prices sometimes changing hourly; therefore, petroleum companies must keep track of many potential sources of crude and product, each of which is more volatile and requires better decision support systems than at any other time in history.

Another critical industry change involves the recent narrowing of the price-volume relationship associated with wholesale (rack) terminal sales. Because the commodity nature of the product is increasing and marketing power is shifting from the refiner to the wholesale distributor (except for major oil companies), the price-volume relationship has become more elastic; that is, setting a price one-quarter cent per gallon above the least expensive supplier might now result in a loss in sales of 25 percent of "normal unbranded volume." By contrast, in the past such an action might not have been significant at all. Furthermore, price-volume relationships change in three ways: (1) historically, as customers react to their perceptions of each company's pricing philosophy; (2) seasonally, as different products proceed through their seasonal demand cycles; and (3) cyclically, as different suppliers take the pricing lead at different points in the above cycles. Massive amounts of quantitative and qualitative information must be accurately gathered, analyzed, and acted upon in order to control terminal inventories and to coordinate refinery production and product purchases, and thereby generate day-to-day profits.

The final important industry change has been the 20- to 40-fold increase in the cost of financing working capital since 1972. This increase resulted from a combination of a nine- to 10-fold increase in crude oil prices along with a two- to fourfold increase in interest rates. It has significantly altered the cost of supplying product to the customer and, as a consequence, can mean the difference between making a profit and showing a loss in today's high-volume, low-profit-margin downstream industry. Companies have reduced inventories and tightened credit terms in order to reduce working capital. This again has increased their decision-making needs.

The industry-wide information explosion continues to overload the decision-making capabilities of many downstream participants and, as such, provides a potentially critical competitive edge to those able to harness it. This, together with Southland's profit-making orientation, led the task force to adopt two highly interrelated goals. The first goal was to provide Citgo decision makers with the best possible management science tools to gather and analyze the information required for economically rational decision making. The second goal was to identify and implement the organizational changes necessary for utilizing management science effectively.

PROFIT IMPROVEMENT ANALYSIS

Starting from the foundation of clearly defined goals, we interviewed Citgo's management to identify areas where harnessing the information explosion could provide significant benefits to Citgo. The resulting financial analysis showed a total potential profit improvement of $55 to $60 million per year in seven major areas: (1) product and crude inventory reductions, (2) accounts receivable and payable, (3) crude oil and feedstock acquisition, (4) variable cost coverage (acquisition, distribution, and marketing costs) on products sold, (5) refinery cost reductions, (6) refinery profit optimization, and (7) personnel reductions.

Next, we identified tools that could be used to realize as much of that potential profit improvement as possible. We will describe the management science tools and organizational changes implemented in three parts: crude oil acquisition and refining, strategic and operational market planning, and working capital control.

MANUFACTURING FOR PROFIT

Like many integrated oil companies, Cities Services Corporation and Occidental Petroleum Corporation (both previous owners of Citgo) operated the Citgo Lake Charles refinery using a strategy of minimizing incremental costs as opposed to manufacturing for profit optimization. The difference between these strategies is illustrated in the 17-month period ending in March 1985, when at times, the price of crude plus the average cost in the industry for processing crude was higher per barrel than the street value of the petroleum products produced. During this "valley of ignorance," refiners operating on the first criterion had significantly higher refinery run levels than those operating on the second criterion.

Based on our earlier assessment of the oil industry, we believed that fierce competition would prevail for at least the remainder of this decade, and the valley of ignorance could easily be repeated. To meet the competition, we wanted to establish procedures, tools, and an organizational culture based on economically rational decision making. This would involve manufacturing for profit. The task force also wanted to produce higher-valued products at a lower cost in an environmentally and operationally safe manner.

The actions taken to improve decision-making capabilities and reduce costs derive from viewing refining as an information-processing activity and establishing (1) data highways for both data acquisition and information dissemination, (2) data repositories for convenient access to all data, and (3) a marriage of the data and data gathering systems with management science techniques to provide management with accurate, timely, and useful information for decision making and planning.

ECONOMICALLY RATIONAL DECISION MAKING

Table 1 identifies the major operating costs (approximate) associated with the Lake Charles refinery for 1984. The best tool for helping management control the three largest operating costs is a refinery LP system. Such a system, if properly developed and used, allows management to gain insights into the refinery operations

Table 1. The major costs of operating the Lake Charles refinery for 1984.

CRUDE & FEEDSTOCK ACQUISITION	$3.3 BILLION
PROCESSING COSTS	$483 MILLION
ENERGY COSTS	$155 MILLION
AVERAGE VALUE OF CRUDE INVENTORY	$140 MILLION
LABOR	$ 64 MILLION
AVERAGE VALUE OF PARTS INVENTORY	$ 12 MILLION

from a holistic perspective that are valuable in optimizing profits. The quality of the decision information provided by such an LP system depends not only on the quality of the model and its use, but also on the quality of the input data. Since the refinery LP input data should be consistent with the data used in other models and for other decision-making activities, the quality of the LP system and its associated data is important to all aspects of the business. Consequently, we began with an audit to determine the quality of Citgo's refinery LP system and its associated data.

The audit disclosed many weaknesses in both the data and the refinery LP system. Much of the data on costs, unit yields, and crude assays were inaccurate and out of date, with the energy cost data for operating the refinery being the worst. Furthermore, much of this data was not maintained independently of the LP system. To correct this, a physical measurements data base was created, using a modern data base management system. This allowed easy accessing and updating of data and replaced data hard-coded into thousands of lines of FORTRAN code or maintained in multiple, partially updated, sequential computer files. This change was critical in establishing consistency between planning and operations and in reaping the potential benefits afforded by the refinery LP system.

Next, we replaced the matrix generator and optimization software in the refinery LP system with Haverly's software for matrix generation and report writing [Haverly Systems, Inc. 1983], and IBM's MPSX linear programming system for optimization [Mathematical Programming System 1982]. These changes reduced run times by a factor of four and made it possible to substantially expand the direct user community because the resulting system was so user friendly.

Once the software was installed and Citgo's original LP model converted, the LP model itself was carefully evaluated to determine where it could be improved. This led to the following enhancements:

— Coker and hydrocracker units were added to the model to reflect fundamental equipment changes in the refinery;
— Capacity limits were added to the model for certain feeder lines;
— The modeling of streams returning from the lube plant was enhanced;
— New spot price forecasts were added and used to value product yields; and
— Multiple time periods were added in order to incorporate inventory costs into the model.

The importance of having a good model cannot be underestimated. For example, a good model will improve product yields, and a one-tenth of one percent increase in overall product yields can result in a \$3 million per year improvement in earnings.

Next, validation and calibration of the new model was initiated. First, the actual inputs and outputs of the refinery were collected for one month. Using the actual crude and feedstock inputs to fix the refinery LP model inputs, the model outputs were then checked against the actual refinery outputs. This was a time-consuming and complex task and one that had to be repeated. Many insights were gleaned from these efforts. For instance, the results indicated that separate and distinct refinery LP models were justified (for example; a three-catcracker model) to reflect which process units were operating. This insight and other insights about details of refinery operations and their portrayal in the LP proved extremely valuable both in determining economically efficient run levels for the refinery and in using the model for crude selection.

Ultimately, the refinery LP system and its associated unit models were recalibrated and completed. The refinery LP system is now used routinely to provide critical decision information in the following areas: crude selection and acquisition economics, refinery run levels, product component production levels, feedstock selection and acquisition economics, unit turnaround options, and hydrocracker conversion.

LOW-COST REFINER

As shown in Table 1, the annual cost of operating the refinery, excluding crude

and feedstock costs, exceeds $700 million. For Citgo to survive, it was essential that these costs be reduced. During our profit improvement analysis study, we identified several areas as targets for cost improvement. These are summarized in Table 2 along with potential benefits and applicable technologies.

ENERGY COST REDUCTION

The annual energy budget for the refinery exceeds $155 million. Except for crude and processing costs, this is the single largest operating budget item. The majority of the energy budget is spent on natural gas, steam, and electricity. The task force conducted an energy audit that disclosed major steam losses and a lack of adequate metering for performing an en-

Table 2. The task force identified several areas as targets for cost improvement, along with their potential benefits and applicable technologies. The benefits and technologies depend on this timeliness and availability of information.

		AREAS OF POTENTIAL IMPROVEMENT				
		HISTORICAL ANALYSIS	ENERGY OPTIMIZATION	UNIT OPTIMIZATION	MAINTENANCE FORECASTING AND SCHEDULING	EFFECTIVE PERSONNEL USAGE
BENEFITS	IMPROVED STREAM FACTOR	X		X	X	
	EXTENDED RUN LENGTH				X	
	IMPROVED OPERATING EFFICIENCY	X	X	X	X	
	OPTIMIZE CONVERSION LEVELS			X		
	RAISE SELECTIVITY			X		
	OPTIMIZE UTILITY MIX		X	X		
	MORE TIMELY PROCESS MODIFICATIONS		X			
	IMPROVED UNDERSTANDING OF VARIABLE RELATIONSHIPS	X	X			
	INCREASED PRODUCTIVITY				X	X
TECHNOLOGIES	GRAPHING	X	X	X	X	X
	STATISTICS	X	X	X	X	X
	REPORTING	X	X	X	X	X
	SIMULATION	X		X		X
	STANDARD ENGINEERING APPLICATIONS		X	X		
	SPECIALIZED ENGINEERING APPLICATIONS		X	X		
	MAINTENANCE PACKAGE	X			X	
	MATHEMATICAL PROGRAMMING	X	X	X	X	X
	DATA BASE MANAGEMENT	X	X	X	X	X
	PROCESS CONTROL	X	X	X	X	X

TIMELINESS AND AVAILABILITY OF INFORMATION

ergy balance on natural gas or electricity. Lack of adequate metering also made it difficult to develop accurate cost data for the refinery LP model, as well as to perform other analyses.

Process control equipment and nonlinear optimization models were installed to measure and optimize energy utilization. The key benefits of this activity have been to provide improved data for planning, to reduce energy consumption, and to balance the energy load by reducing some units' operating levels when other units require high natural gas or steam inputs momentarily, thus reducing energy costs.

UNIT EFFICIENCY

A review of unit operations showed that many existing process control closed loops were being used less than 50 percent of the time. The absence or low use of process control again made it difficult to obtain good data on unit yields and costs. Consequently, process control equipment was installed on all key units. In addition, procedures to evaluate operator performance and train operators were institutionalized to foster continuous use of process control equipment. The resulting dollar savings were printed on the operators' screens as they followed the recommendations for process control.

This technology has proven to be very valuable in controlling the operation of refinery units. Process control automates the 24-hour attention to temperature and flow that is required for efficient and quality refining by creating an accurate historical record of the operations of each refinery unit. The process control readings are maintained and constitute an important data base. This data base is used to analyze operator efficiency, unit productivity,

and failures. It also provides data for scheduling in-process inventories, nonlinear process control cut-point models, and the refinery LP model. Consequently, it has made possible procedures which provide better coordination between planning, scheduling, and cut-point settings. The data base was also instrumental in establishing a $4 million insurance claim when a coker unit was severely damaged.

Refinery unit process control has not only reduced operating costs but has also increased product revenue. This is particularly true in those process units that split input product into several intermediate or final product streams. For example, changing 0.0025 of the volume of an input product stream to a higher valued output product stream in the cokers and hydrocracker increased the overall value by $0.01—0.025 per barrel of input. On a yearly basis, this is worth approximately $1 million on the three process units. Today, process control utilization on all key units exceeds 90 percent.

MAINTENANCE MANAGEMENT

Proper maintenance is essential to insure an environmentally safe and cost-effective operation. Proper maintenance management includes parts inventory control, material procurement, work order generation, job planning and personnel scheduling, cost monitoring and control, equipment history, and preventative maintenance.

To provide these functions, an integrated maintenance information system is being developed in phases at the refinery. The system tracks the $12 million parts inventory and provides part order information. The inventory control function involves issuing and replenishing parts, and it allows for monitoring and controlling these activities. The system also facilitates work order generation, approval, and tracking. The scheduling component of the system uses management science to develop work plans for personnel and instructions for delivering materials when a job is ready to be executed. Cost monitoring and control are substantially enhanced by the availability of timely information. The equipment history and repair parts lists provide valuable information for planning tests of equipment reliability and predicting maintenance work. The benefits of this program include faster processing of work orders, better use of maintenance personnel, lower inventories of parts, and most important, less equipment downtime.

EMPLOYEE EFFICIENCY

At the beginning of 1984, the refinery employed over 1,600 workers; today it is better managed and maintained and it operates more efficiently with 1,200 employees. As a result of many changes, including the automation activities previously discussed, labor costs have been reduced by approximately $15 million per year, and the refinery now has one of the lowest ratios in the industry of personnel per barrel of crude processed.

CRUDE SCHEDULING

Inventories of crude oil represent a major cost to the refinery (Table 1). In addition to the interest costs on inventory, the risk of devaluation is considerable in today's volatile market. For these reasons, the task force recommended that information systems be established that would al-low the refinery to operate effectively with lower inventories. To accomplish this, Citgo's crude oil pipeline was automated, a new tank-gauging system was installed, and a PC optimization-based scheduling system was acquired to schedule delivery and distribution of crude oil from the storage tank farm into the refinery. The first two systems provide accurate and timely data for the optimization-based scheduling system. The resulting information has helped management reduce its crude inventories by approximately $20 million. At the same time, management has been able to reduce processing costs through better sequencing of its various crude inventories.

MANUFACTURING BENEFITS

Today, because of the technological improvements made, the Lake Charles refinery is highly versatile and efficient. It can yield as much as 65 percent gasoline from crude oil (compared to a 50 percent industry average), is capable of producing a large percentage of unleaded gasoline, and can run sour (having a high sulfur content) or heavy (dense) crude. Since the refinery has a number of independent units, it can operate efficiently at several different run levels. Consequently, the refinery is highly flexible, and production runs can be tailored to meet the market environment. This flexibility allows management to use management science tools effectively in responding to market conditions.

Citgo management, with the help of this technology, has made a significant impact on the overall profitability of Citgo. This is vividly illustrated by the following. In 1983, Citgo voluntarily participated in an independent refinery evaluation with

75 other companies. Citgo's rankings on six key measures of refinery performance varied from 38th to 58th, placing it in the middle of the third quartile.

In a 1985 refinery evaluation by the same independent agency, Citgo's rankings rose to the upper half of the second quartile of the refineries that are still operating. Citgo management estimates that the overall benefits of the manufacturing changes coupled with effective management usage were approximately $50 million in 1985. These benefits resulted from improvements in refinery yield, reductions in the cost of labor, and the other programs to reduce costs.

MARKETING FOR PROFIT

We improved Citgo's competitive edge by applying new tools and recommending organizational changes in strategic market planning. We developed a system called TRACS (Tracking, Reporting, and Aggregation of Citgo Segmented Sales) to evaluate the profitability of existing markets. TRACS is a sophisticated data base management system coupled with rule-based artificial intelligence which provides an economic comparison between potential selling options and distribution channels. For example, it can provide comparisons between selling on the spot market and selling at the wholesale rack, or between pipeline distribution and barge distribution. Two important characteristics of TRACS are its ability to evaluate sales at all Citgo owned terminals and all exchange terminals and its inclusion of all variable costs of supplying sales, such as transportation, handling, and marketing overhead costs. It also includes the timing considerations between purchases and sales and the costs associated with financing working capital. Its reporting capabilities include both graphical and tabular output generated on any or all of seven segmentation variables such as geographic location, class of business, and customer.

While not completed until the latter part of 1985, TRACS proved to be very valuable in evaluating (1) a proposed turbine fuel expansion program, (2) customer profitability to determine the risks and possible rewards of additional credit extensions and (3) alternative pricing scenarios for potential crude oil netback deals. Management has been pleasantly surprised at its power and versatility in providing insight into difficult questions. In fact, the insights gleaned from its use have significantly altered Citgo's strategic direction in turbine marketing. During 1986, Citgo used TRACS extensively to evaluate current and potential market segments as part of its strategic marketing-planning effort.

OPERATIONAL PLANNING AND CONTROL

We also applied new tools and concepts for information gathering and analysis in market planning (Figure 1). The planning cycle consists of planning and controlling short-term manufacturing (previously discussed), pricing, supply and distribution, and evaluating profits (that is, performance). The results of the profit evaluation are a valuable aid to decision makers during subsequent planning cycles.

Before these management science tools were implemented, each department at Citgo collected, organized, and stored its own operational data. Because the corporation lacked forecasts of price and volume and departments had limited knowledge of other departments' deci-

Figure 1. The operational planning cycle revolves around the corporate-wide data base, PASS, and uses the management science technologies shown to aid in planning and control.

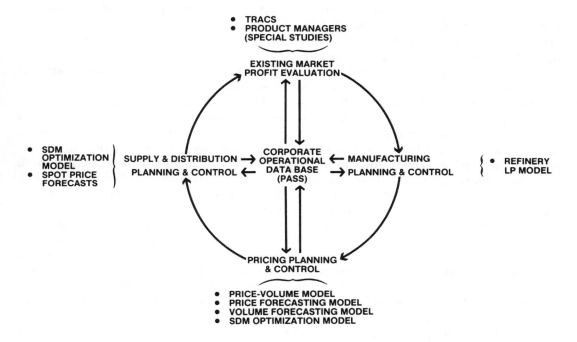

sions, different departments often made operational decisions that were nonoptimal or even conflicting. The first step in breaking down these departmental information walls was the development of the corporate-wide, on-line production acquisition and supply system (PASS), a management data base implemented using ADABAS [Software AG 1984], a state-of-the-art database management system with dictionary, query, and fourth generation language features. Shown in the center of Figure 1, PASS contains up-to-date operational information on such items as sales, inventory, trades and exchanges for all refined products for the past (historical data), present (scheduled activity), and future (forecasts). Much of this data is uploaded from newly installed personal

computers where it is entered by operations personnel using LOTUS 1-2-3. PASS makes all of this information available to all functions and managers. This major change in information flow contributes heavily toward Citgo's improved interdepartmental coordination.

Price and volume forecasting was centralized and improved to feed the PASS database. Historically, Citgo forecasted only total volume and those prices necessary for monthly and quarterly budgets. Consequently, each department developed short-term forecasts for its own needs. Now, using management science techniques, including econometric modeling and regression analysis, Citgo's pricing manager has developed models to provide wholesale price forecasts (based on spot market forecasts, historical time lags, competitive factors, and so forth) and wholesale volume forecasts (based on historical price-volume relationships, assumptions on relative positions within the pricing pack, and so forth). These forecasts are developed by terminal for each of approximately 40 Citgo owned and leased terminals and 350 exchange partner terminals, by product, by line of business, and by week for an 11-week planning horizon. The forecasts are reviewed and approved by both pricing and marketing management before entry into the PASS data base. Once approved, however, they become the official corporate forecasts for use by all departments. Historical data kept in PASS allows easy post-auditing of these forecasts.

Other forecast data collected in the PASS data base include forecasts of retail-sales volumes and of spot market prices. Forecasts of retail-sales volume for the 7-Eleven stores are generated by terminal for each week using a forecasting system developed by each store group. A joint gasoline committee with representatives from both Citgo and each store's group has been established to develop a consistent operating plan. The product traders make spot market price forecasts for the Gulf Coast, New York Harbor, Group III, Chicago, and West Coast spot markets by product and by week. These are reviewed and approved first by a newly organized product committee, next by the vice-president of marketing, and finally by the CEO.

PASS, fed by the information gathering and forecasting systems, provides the on-line, timely, and consistent information needed to improve operational coordination and control. Using a single forecast and other common data keeps all parts of the organization focused and traveling down one path. The amount of information provided by PASS is too massive to be fully analyzed manually by one decision maker or a group of decision makers. Therefore, we developed the SDM system, an optimization-based supply, distribution, and marketing model, so that this data could be used to make economically rational decisions.

The SDM system integrates the key economic and physical characteristics of Citgo's supply, distribution, and marketing for a short-term (11-week) planning horizon. This time horizon incorporates both manufacturing and distribution time lags. The system is used by top management to make many operational decisions, such as where to sell products, what price to charge, where to buy or trade product, how much to buy or trade, how much product to hold in inventory, and how much product to ship by each mode of transportation. All information is provided by location, by line of business, and by week. Thus, the critical timing considerations associated with all of these decisions are incorporated into the model.

The SDM system contains a separate minimum cost flow network model [Glover and Klingman 1977; Wagner 1969] for each product (corresponding to the product managers who work with all supply, distribution, and marketing personnel associated with each product). Each model is generated using input data from the PASS data base, and the optimal solution is aggregated into output reports tailored for use by the individual operational managers. The objective function for the profit-maximization model is calculated as total sales revenue less expenses such as transportation costs, terminal handling costs, and time value of money associated with in-transit and terminal inventory. The constraints of the model include product flow balance (flow in = flow out) for each distribution center (DC) terminal, and so forth, forecasted price/demand functions, inventory capacities, limitations on exchange agreements, spot volume, and purchase/sale/trade (PST) agreements, and so forth. Management also has the option of including preliminary shipment schedules in the model as finalized decisions. Finally, the SDM system employs rule-based artificial intelligence systems to arrive at exchange agreement payback rules for model constraints, and it utilizes an expert system approach to screen output reports to provide management with exception reports which contain notable items (satisfying specified conditions) from all reports.

Due to the complex combination of multiple product sources, distribution timing, trading alternatives, and price sensitive demands, a number of unique modeling techniques were required to control the size of the model and to preserve its network and linear structure. The network framework was important for two main reasons. First, the pictorial aspect of network models proved extremely valuable in working with a broad spectrum of personnel to develop, validate, and implement this integrated model. Second, the rapid solution speed of network models allows management to respond quickly to the dynamics of a commodity market industry by using the SDM system extensively in "what-if" sessions. For example, using a medium-sized computer, an IBM 4381 mod 2, each product model consisting of approximately 3,000 equations and 15,000 variables can be solved using an efficient network optimization code [Glover and Klingman 1982] in approximately 30 seconds. (To run the entire SDM system, model generation requires about two minutes and report processing about seven minutes.) Klingman et al. [1985; 1986] describe a derivation of the entire model in network format and the organizational challenges and key success factors associated with implementing the SDM system. A mathematical statement of the model appears in the appendix.

The SDM system incorporates critical financial and operational variables, thereby supporting a comprehensive working-capital program. The petroleum industry has been a major consumer of management science almost since its inception [Aronofsky and Lee 1957; Aronofsky and Williams 1962; Charnes 1954; Charnes and Cooper 1961; Dantzig 1963; Durrer and Slater 1977; Garvin et al. 1957; Jackson 1980; Manne 1958; Symonds 1955; and Zierer, Mitchell, and White 1976]. Yet, as noted by Liberatore and Miller [1985], very few integrated models for this or any other industry have been developed and implemented. SDM appears to be the only model currently used in the petroleum industry that integrates the supply, distribution, pricing, financing, and sales functions of the short-term downstream petroleum products operations. The SDM system crosses multiple areas of the Citgo organization (supply, distribution, and marketing), integrating the details and trade-offs associated with each area into one model. The model also includes several "new" concepts, such as variable costs of accounts receivable and credit card sales, and the time value of money associated with product inventory and exchange imbalances, which the operational managers have only recently begun to include in their decision-making processes.

The refinery LP system and the SDM system, which are linked together by the spot price forecasts, serve as the primary corporate operational-planning tools. They provide information about material balances and make or buy planning that is economically rational based on forecasts and operational data; in addition, they provide a holistic view of the corporation from crude acquisition through product sales. These systems and their associated data bases, operating in concert, provide management with accurate and timely data and powerful planning support.

Several organizational changes were made to facilitate the cross-functional coordination and implementation of the operational tools recommended by the task force. Four new positions were created and filled: a senior vice-president of refining, supply and coordination to coordinate operational decisions, relying heavily on the SDM system and the refinery LP system recommendations to reach decisions that affect both manufacturing and marketing; an internal management consultant to provide industry specific concepts and integrate them into task force recommendations and models, and to provide liaison between operational managers and the external consultants; and two product managers to integrate and coordinate the SDM system recommendations for their products (one for home heating oil and diesel fuel and another for automotive gasolines). A short-term operating committee (STOC) was formed to develop, coordinate, and communicate changes in operations consistent with the financial objectives established by management.

In addition, Citgo combined the product supply department with the product scheduling department to improve communication and coordination of information flow, as well as to centralize responsibility for overall inventory control. Finally, Citgo structured this new supply and product scheduling department to report to the senior vice-president of refin-

ing, supply and coordination to further aid its efforts to coordinate marketing and manufacturing.

The TRACS system, discussed previously as a tool used in strategic market planning, is also used in the evaluation of operational decisions in order to improve the effectiveness of the operational planning cycle. Here TRACS is used to calculate the marginal profitability of each Citgo sale or group of sales, thereby providing valuable information to the operational managers on the profitability of their decisions.

TRACS is proving to be an important tool for ascertaining difficult-to-obtain information concerning individual and corporate performance. As a result, the performance evaluation process for 1986 has been broadened and made more formal. Citgo management has established specific quantitative goals for both the corporation and individual managers.

The benefits of these integrated information-gathering systems, data base management systems, forecasting models, optimization-based decision support systems, artificial-intelligence-based evaluation systems, and organizational changes have been numerous. They include improved communication and coordination between supply, distribution, marketing, and refining groups; improved data; reduced inventories with smaller variance in inventory levels; elimination of unnecessary product terminals; improved management of exchange agreement and purchase/sale/trade agreements; added insight into pricing strategies; better forecasts; and economically rational decision making.

Citgo management estimates that in the early stages of use, these changes have improved Citgo's net profit by at least $2.5 million in 1985. But more importantly, as the corporation proceeds up the learning curve of using these sophisticated decision aids, the benefits are expected to increase significantly. In addition, based on historical inventory-to-sales ratios, gasoline and distillate inventories have been reduced $116 million, resulting in a $14 million annual reduction in interest expense.

WORKING CAPITAL CONTROL

The task force analyzed Citgo's cash-flow cycle to determine the most effective tools to gather and analyze information on working capital. Figure 2 illustrates the integration of management science tools (LP refinery model, SDM optimization model, forecast models, and so forth) and how these have been coupled with information technologies to multiply the improvement of each.

The profit improvement analysis indicated a significant potential for savings associated with the selection and purchase of products and crude oils. In order to improve the selection of crude oils, Citgo's refinery LP model was substantially modified, as discussed earlier, to enhance the economic evaluation of all possible crudes based on their individual product yields and spot prices. Product purchases, on the other hand, were addressed by the SDM model. Both of these management science models provided detailed and integrated information on optimal quantities and qualities of refined products and crude oils to be purchased.

The control of product and crude oil payables was improved by the acquisition of a payable float optimization system. This system is now incorporated into the corporate payables system and utilizes the standard components of payment-term maximization and disbursement bank selection. It has reduced working capital by an estimated $8.5 million, yielding an annual decrease in interest expense of approximately $1.0 million.

Crude oil inventories, which make up one of the three largest components of Citgo's working capital, require special attention and coordination, especially in view of the current instability of crude

Figure 2. Citgo's working capital cycle illustrates the primary components of working capital and summarizes the tools, data-gathering systems, and studies devised to enhance Citgo's ability to actively manage and control its working capital.

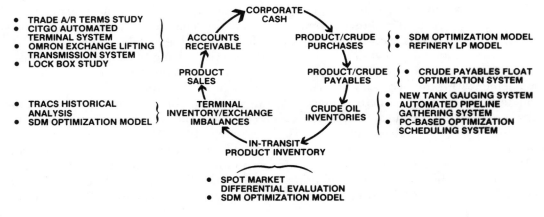

prices. As discussed earlier, we had a new tank gauging system installed at the refinery tank farm, automated the crude oil pipeline gathering system, and implemented a PC-based optimization scheduling system for managing crude inventories. The results of this automation have been impressive; crude inventories have been reduced by $20 million and last minute scheduling changes have been reduced.

To reduce the holding costs of in-transit product inventory, we initially compared the historical spot market prices; for example, we computed the time-adjusted differences between spot market prices at the Gulf Coast and at New York Harbor. This study showed that the average differentials in some spot markets were less than transportation costs plus interest expense. For example, by supplying northeast demand with New York Harbor spot purchases and selling excess refinery production at the Gulf Coast, Citgo could save 0.5—2.0 cents a gallon on average throughout the year. The SDM system fully addresses these optional spot market sources, basing its recommendation on forecasted demand, forecasted spot market prices, transit times, interest costs, and the availability of product on the specific spot markets.

The terminal inventories and exchange imbalances represent the largest component of Citgo's working capital. We implemented two unique systems, TRACS and the SDM optimization models, to provide management with the necessary control information. These systems helped management reduce product inventories (including exchange imbalances) by $116 million.

As a result of several new system and task-force recommendations, the accounts receivable component of working capital, which includes both trade receivables (resulting from the standard terms in the industry of one percent, 10 days, net 11 days) and credit card receivables, has also been significantly reduced. First, an accounts receivable study showed that the average delay between a customer's lifting (purchase) date and payment date was excessive. To correct this, we recommended and management approved the installation of the Citgo automated terminal system (CATS). This is a transaction-processing system at the point of sale which bills the customer at that time and provides accurate and up-to-date inventory levels for each Citgo terminal. We also recommended that OMRON CAT200 units be installed at exchange terminals to rapidly transmit lifting information for billing and thus reduce average collection times. CATS and the inexpensive OMRON units have proven to be highly cost-effective in gathering information for the PASS data base. The task force also recommended that Southland treasury do a lock-box optimization study which was completed and implemented.

These changes affecting receivables have resulted in an actual reduction of $9 million in working capital, or an annual addition to profits of $1.1 million (in reduced interest expense).

In summary, although it is difficult due to the vast changes in areas such as sales volumes and lines of business to calculate the precise changes in working capital, management's best estimate of the reduction in working capital is $145-155 million ($8.5 million for payables, $9 million for receivables, $20 million for crude inventories and $116 million for product inventories) between 1983 and 1985. This yields an annual decrease in interest expense of approximately $17.4 to 18.6 million. In addition, these changes substantially reduce Citgo's vulnerability to falling prices for crude oil and refined product.

SUMMARY

Citgo's implementation of management science tools fed by accurate up-to-the-minute data vividly illustrates how comprehensive and integrated applications of such tools can help companies gain a competitive edge. The integration of these technologies compounds the potential of each, multiplying the gains. The dramatic turnaround of Citgo demonstrates clearly that the petroleum companies that will do best in the 1980s and 1990s are those that come to terms with change and embrace new ways of doing business.

Rarely does a project, spanning only two calendar years, successfully employ and implement, in such a variety of ways and so extensively, the body of knowledge that makes up management science.

The success of the project and its short implementation time is attributable to several factors. Foremost was the support of top management, including Ron Hall, president and CEO of Citgo, John Thompson, chairman of the board of Southland Corporation, and Jere W. Thompson, CEO of Southland Corporation. They created the task force and were receptive to an in-depth study of management information needs and how management science technologies could be effectively employed at Citgo.

A second factor of almost equal importance was the enthusiastic and dedicated support of operational managers during the development and implementation of the resulting systems. Clearly, one person could not run all of the projects discussed. During the organizational restructuring of Citgo, new employees were hired, and ex-

isting employees who supported and were capable of implementing management science tools were promoted. Responsibility for developing and implementing the different systems conceived by the task force was distributed among these employees. The task force director coordinated the teams, which worked simultaneously. This coordination led to another unique aspect of this project, the in-depth integration of the systems.

Specifically, data gathering systems were constructed based on the most recent data-base-management concepts; highly sophisticated optimization-based decision support systems and forecasting models were developed to process the data into management information about the future; and artificial-intelligence-based systems were developed to process the data into management information about the past.

The results of this comprehensive combination of management science disciplines have been impressive. Management has been able to reduce working capital requirements by approximately $150 million. The resulting benefits include an annual decrease in interest expense of approximately $18 million and a substantial reduction in Citgo's vulnerability to falling crude oil and product prices. Citgo management also estimates that the effective usage of these tools improved marketing profits by $2.5 million and refining profits by $50 million in 1985. Thus, the total dollar benefits were approximately $70 million in 1985.

The total cost of the systems implemented, $20-$30 million, was the greatest obstacle to this project. However, because of the information explosion in the petroleum industry, top management realized that numerous information systems were essential to gather, store, and analyze data.

The incremental cost of adding management science technologies to these computers and systems was small, in fact very small in light of the enormous benefits they provided.

ACKNOWLEDGMENTS

As with any project of this size, more people were involved in the support, modeling, data collection, and implementation than can be mentioned. However, we would like to extend special thanks to the following: Ross Wirth for his exceptional efforts in the organizational implementation of the SDM system; Jack Kelsey for developing and supporting the forecasting system and sponsoring the SDM in the pricing department; John Stuart for his accounting systems analysis and for coding TRACS; Jim Galloway for his accounts receivable expertise and assistance; Rudy Gardner for providing exchange expertise and input data; Kurt Spielburg and Jane Reno for quick delivery and installation of the IBM 4381 mod 2; Sharon Kaiser and David Hynes for technical assistance; Ron Hall, Miltford Johnson, Sam Susser, John Dewell, Jim Keynes, and Bill Beckert for their management support and assistance; and John P. Thompson, Jere Thompson, and Clark Matthews II for providing us with the opportunity and financial support to undertake this project.

This research was supported in part by the Center for Business Decision Analysis, the Hugh Roy Cullen Centennial Chair in Business Administration, and the Office of Naval Research under contract N00014-78-C-0222. Reproduction in whole or in part is permitted for any purpose of the US Government.

APPENDIX: AN ALGEBRAIC STATEMENT OF THE CITGO SDM MODEL

The following index sets are defined:

I = mode (pipe or water),

J = distribution center (DC),

K = centroid (the point in a distribution route that is a specified number of time periods away from the nearest preceeding DC),

L = Citgo owned and leased (TA) terminals,

M = exchange contract,

N = exchange terminals,

P = purchase/sale/trade (PST) agreements,

T = [1,2,3,...,7] = time periods, and

V = set of segments in linearization of the price/volume function.

Subsets of the index sets are defined as follows:

$I(j)$ = all modes associated with DC, $j \epsilon J$,

$I(j,k)$ = all modes associated with DC, $j \epsilon J$ and centroid $k \epsilon K$,

$K(i,j)$ = all centroids associated with mode $i \epsilon I$ and DC, $j \epsilon J$,

$K(l)$ = all centroids associated with terminal $l \epsilon L$,

$K(m)$ = all centroids associated with exchange contract $m \epsilon M$,

$K(p)$ = all centroids associated with PST agreement $p \epsilon P$,

$L(k)$ = all Citgo and TA terminals associated with centroid $k \epsilon K$,

$M(k)$ = all exchange contracts associated with centroid $k \epsilon K$,

$M(n)$ = all exchange contracts associated with exchange terminal $n \epsilon N$,

$N(m)$ = all exchange terminals associated with exchange contract $m \epsilon M$, and

$P(k)$ = all PST agreements associated with centroid $k \epsilon K$.

The variables are defined as follows:

R_t = refinery supply, for all $t \epsilon T$,

MI_{ijt} = DC mode in-flow, for all $j \epsilon J$, $i \epsilon I(j)$, $t \epsilon T$,

MO_{ijt} = DC mode out-flow, for all $j \epsilon J$, $i \epsilon I(j)$, $t \epsilon T$,

SP_{kt} = spot purchases, for all $k \epsilon K$, $t \epsilon T$,

SP_{ijt} = spot purchases, for all $j \epsilon J$, $i \epsilon I(j)$, $t \epsilon T$,

SS_{kt} = spot sales, for all $k \epsilon K$, $t \epsilon T$,

SS_{ijt} = spot sales, for all $j \epsilon J$, $i \epsilon I(j)$, $t \epsilon T$,

CI_{ijkt} = centroid in-flow, for all $k \epsilon K$, $j \epsilon J$, $i \epsilon I(j,k)$, $t \epsilon T$,

CO_{ikt} = centroid out-flow, for all $k \epsilon K$, $j \epsilon J$, $i \epsilon I(j,k)$, $t \epsilon T$,

CO_{lkt} = centroid out-flow, for all $k \epsilon K$, $l \epsilon L$, $t \epsilon T$,

W_{svt} = wholesale volume, for all $v \epsilon V$, $s \epsilon L \cup J \cup N$, $t \epsilon T$,

S_{rt} = storage inventory, for all $r \epsilon J \cup L$, $t \epsilon T$, where S_{r0} equals beginning inventory,

T_{kt} = in-transit inventory, for all $k \epsilon K$, $t \epsilon T$, where T_{k0} equals beginning inventory,

XD_{mt} = exchange imbalance down-flow, for all $m \epsilon M$, $t \epsilon T$, where $XD_{m0} = 0$,

XU_{mt} = exchange imbalance up-flow, for all $m \epsilon M$, $t \epsilon T$, where $XU_{m0} = 0$,

BO_{kmt} = bulk shipments out of centroids, for all $m \epsilon M$, $k \epsilon K(m)$, $t \epsilon T$,

BI_{kmt} = bulk shipments into centroids, for all $m \epsilon M$, $k \epsilon K(m)$, $t \epsilon T$,

PR_{kpt} = PST receipts, for all $p \epsilon P$, $k \epsilon K(p)$, and

PD_{kpt} = PST deliveries, for all $p \epsilon P$, $k \epsilon K(p)$, $t \epsilon T$.

Finally, define the parameters, which will be subscripted over the appropriate indices as follows:

c = costs,

lb = lower bounds,

ub = upper bounds,

d = demands where these values are denoted by non-negative numbers, and

s = supplies where these values are denoted by non-negative numbers.

Minimize:

$$
\Sigma_{t \epsilon T} \; [c_t R_t \; + \; \Sigma_{j \epsilon J} \; \Sigma_{i \epsilon I(j)} \; (c_{ijt} \; SP_{ijt} \; - \; c_{ijt} \; SS_{ijt}) \\
+ \; \Sigma_{k \epsilon K} \; (c_{kt} \; SP_{kt} \; - \; c_{kt} \; SS_{kt}) \\
+ \; \Sigma_{j \epsilon J} \; \Sigma_{k \epsilon K} \; \Sigma_{i \epsilon I(j,k)} \; c_{ijkt} \; CO_{ijkt} \\
+ \; \Sigma_{k \epsilon K} \; \Sigma_{l \epsilon L(k)} \; c_{lkt} \; CO_{lkt} \\
+ \; \Sigma_{l \epsilon L} \; (c_{lt} \; S_{lt} \; - \; \Sigma_{v \epsilon V} \; c_{lvt} \; W_{lvt}) \\
+ \; \Sigma_{j \epsilon J} \; (c_{jt} \; S_{jt} \; - \; \Sigma_{v \epsilon V} \; c_{jvt} \; W_{jvt}) \\
- \; \Sigma_{n \epsilon N} \; \Sigma_{v \epsilon V} \; c_{nvt} \; W_{nvt} \\
+ \; \Sigma_{m \epsilon M} \; (c_{mt} \; XD_{mt} \; - \; c_{mt} \; XU_{mt}) \\
+ \; \Sigma_{m \epsilon M} \; \Sigma_{k \epsilon K(m)} \; (c_{kmt} \; BO_{kmt} \; - \; c_{kmt} \; BI_{kmt}) \\
+ \; \Sigma_{p \epsilon P} \; \Sigma_{k \epsilon K(p)} \; (c_{kpt} \; PR_{kpt} \; - \; c_{kpt} \; PD_{kpt})].
$$

Subject to
Lake Charles DC:

$$
R_t \; + \; \Sigma_{i \epsilon I(j)} \; (MI_{ijt} \; - \; MO_{ijt}) \\
- \; \Sigma_{v \epsilon V} \; W_{jvt} \; + \; S_{j,t-1} \; - \; S_{jt} \; = \; d_{jt} \\
\text{for } j = \text{Lake Charles, } t \epsilon T.
$$

DC:

$$
\Sigma_{i \epsilon I(j)} \; (MI_{ijt} \; - \; MO_{ijt}) \\
- \; \Sigma_{v \epsilon V} \; W_{jvt} \; + \; S_{j,t-1} \; - \; S_{jt} \; = \; d_{jt} \\
\text{for all } j \epsilon J, \; j \neq \text{Lake Charles, } t \epsilon T.
$$

Inbound Mode Node:

$$\Sigma_{k \in K(i,j)} \ CO_{ijkt} + SP_{ijt} - MI_{ijt} = 0$$
for all $j \in J$, $i \in I(j)$, $t \in T$.

Outbound Mode Node:

$$MO_{ijt} - SS_{ijt} - \Sigma_{k \in K(i,j)} \ CI_{ijkt} = 0$$
for all $j \in J$, $i \in I(j)$, $t \in T$.

Centroid:

$$\Sigma_{j \in J} \ \Sigma_{i \in I(jik)} \ (CI_{ijkt} - CO_{ijkt})$$
$$- \ \Sigma_{l \in L(k)} \ CO_{lkt} + \Sigma_{p \in P(k)} \ (PR_{kpt} - PD_{kpt})$$
$$+ \ SP_{kt} - SS_{kt} + T_{k,t-1} - T_{kt}$$
$$+ \ \Sigma_{m \in M(k)} \ (BI_{kmt} - BO_{kmt}) = 0$$
for all $k \in K$, $t \in T$.

Citgo/TA Terminals:

$$\Sigma_{k \in K(l)} \ CO_{lkt} - \Sigma_{v \in V} \ W_{lvt}$$
$$- \ S_{lt} + S_{l,t-1} = d_{lt}$$
for all $l \in L$, $t \in T$.

Exchange Contracts:

$$\Sigma_{k \in K(m)} \ (BO_{kmt} - BI_{kmt}) + XU_{mt}$$
$$- \ XU_{m,t-1} - XD_{mt} + XD_{m,t-1}$$
$$- \ \Sigma_{n \in N(m)} \ \Sigma_{v \in V} \ W_{nvt} = d_{mt} - s_{mt}$$
for all $m \in M$, $t \in T$.

PST Receipt:

$$\Sigma_{k \in K(p)} \ PR_{kpt} = s_{pt}$$
for all $p \in P$, $t \in T$.

PST Delivery:

$$\Sigma_{k \in K(p)} \ PD_{kpt} = d_{pt}$$
for all $p \in P$, $t \in T$.

Bounds:

$$lb_t \le R_t \le ub_t,$$
for all $t \in T$,
$$MI_{ijt} \ge 0,$$
for all $j \in J$, $i \in I(j)$, $t \in T$,
$$lb_{ijt} \le MO_{ijt} \le ub_{ijt},$$
for all $j \in J$, $i \in I(j)$, $t \in T$,

$$lb_{kt} \le SP_{kt} \le ub_{kt},$$
for all $k \in K$, $t \in T$,
$$lb_{ijt} \le SP_{ijt} \le ub_{ijt},$$
for all $j \in J$, $i \in I(j)$, $t \in T$,
$$lb_{kt} \le SS_{kt} \le ub_{kt},$$
for all $k \in K$, $t \in T$,
$$lb_{ijt} \le SS_{ijt} \le ub_{ijt},$$
for all $j \in J$, $i \in I(j)$, $t \in T$,
$$lb_{ijkt} \le CI_{ijkt} \le ub_{ijkt},$$
for all $k \in K$, $j \in J$, $i \in I(j,k)$, $t \in T$,
$$lb_{ijkt} \le CO_{ijkt} \le ub_{ijkt},$$
for all $k \in K$, $j \in J$, $i \in I(j,k)$, $t \in T$,
$$lb_{lkt} \le CO_{lkt} \le ub_{lkt},$$
for all $k \in K$, $l \in L$, $t \in T$,
$$lb_{svt} \le W_{svt} \le ub_{svt},$$
for all $v \in V$, $s \in L \cup J \cup N$, $t \in T$,
$$lb_{rt} \le S_{rt} \le ub_{rt},$$
for all $r \in J \cup L$, $t \in T$,
$$T_{kt} \ge 0,$$
for all $k \in K$, $t \in T$,
$$lb_{mt} \le XD_{mt} \le ub_{mt},$$
for all $m \in M$, $t \in T$,
$$lb_{mt} \le XU_{mt} \le ub_{mt},$$
for all $m \in M$, $t \in T$,
$$lb_{kmt} \le BO_{kmt} \le ub_{kmt},$$
for all $m \in M$, $k \in K(m)$, $t \in T$,
$$lb_{kmt} \le BI_{kmt} \le ub_{kmt},$$
for all $m \in M$, $k \in K(m)$, $t \in T$,
$$lb_{kpt} \le PR_{kpt} \le ub_{kpt},$$
for all $p \in P$, $k \in K(p)$, $t \in T$, and
$$lb_{kpt} \le PD_{kpt} \le ub_{kpt},$$
for all $p \in P$, $k \in K(p)$, $t \in T$.

REFERENCES

Aronofsky, T. S. and Lee, A. S. 1957, "A linear programming model for scheduling crude oil production," *Transactions AIME*, Vol. 69, No. 4, pp. 389–403.

Aronofsky, T. S. and Williams, A. C. 1962, "The use of LP and mathematical models in underground oil production," *Management Science*, Vol. 8, No. 4, pp. 394–407.

Charnes, A. 1954, "A model for programming and sensitivity analysis in an integrated oil company," *Econometrica*, Vol. 22, No. 2, pp. 193–217.

Charnes, A. and Cooper, W. W. 1961, *Management Models and Industrial Applications of Linear Programming*, two vols., John Wiley and Sons, Inc., New York.

Dantzig, G. 1963, *Linear Programming and Extensions*, Princeton University Press, Princeton, New Jersey.

Durrer, E. J. and Slater, G. E. 1977, "Optimization of petroleum and natural gas production—A survey," *Management Science*, Vol. 24, No. 1, pp. 35–43.

Garvin, W.; Crandall, H.; John, J.; and Spellman, R. 1957, "Applications of linear programming in the oil industry," *Management Science*, Vol. 3, No. 4, pp. 407–430.

Glover, F. and Klingman, D. 1977, "Network application in industry and government," *AIIE Transactions*, Vol. 9, No. 4, pp. 363–376.

Glover, F. and Klingman, D. 1982, "Recent developments in computer implementation technology for network flow algorithms," *INFOR*, Vol. 20, No. 4, pp. 433–452.

Haverly Systems, Inc. 1983, *Matrix Generation System*, 78 Broadway, P.O. Box 919, Denville, New Jersey 07834.

Jackson, B. L. 1980, "Using LP for crude oil sales at Elk Hills: A case study," *Interfaces*, Vol. 10, No. 3, pp. 65–70.

Klingman, D.; Phillips, N.; Steiger, D.; Wirth, R.; Padman, R.; and Krishnan, R. 1985, "An optimization based integrated short-term refined petroleum product planning system," CBDA 123, Center for Business Decision Analysis, The University of Texas, CBA 5.202, Austin, TX 78712. (To appear in *Management Science*.)

Klingman, D.; Phillips, N.; Steiger, D.; Wirth, R.; and Young, W. 1986, "The challenges and success factors in implementing an integrated products planning system for Citgo," *Interfaces*, Vol. 16, No. 3, May-June, pp. 1–19.

Liberatore, M. J. and Miller, T. 1985 "A hierarchical production planning system," *Interfaces*, Vol. 15, No. 4, pp. 1–11.

Manne, A. S. 1958, "A linear programming model of the US petroleum refining industry," *Econometrica*, Vol. 26, No. 1, pp. 67–106.

Mathematical Programming System Extended/370 1982, International Business Machines Corporation, Data Processing Division, 1133 Westchester Avenue, White Plains, New York 10604.

Software AG 1984, ADABAS, North American Incorporated, 11800 Sunrise Valley Drive, Reston, Virginia 22091.

Symonds, G. H. 1955, *Linear Programming: The Solution of Refinery Problems*, Esso Standard Oil Company, Public Relations Department, New York.

Wagner, H. 1969, *Principles of Operations Research with Applications to Managerial Decision*, Prentice-Hall, Englewood Cliffs, New Jersey.

Zierer, T. K.; Mitchell, W. A.; and White, T. R. 1976, "Practical applications of linear programming to Shell's distribution problems," *Interfaces*, Vol. 6, No. 4, pp. 13–26.

John P. Thompson, Chairman of the Board, and Jere W. Thompson, Chief Executive Officer of The Southland Corporation attest that "When Southland acquired Citgo Petroleum Corporation on August 31, 1983, our management had already ascertained Citgo's enormous potential as a future contributor to the operational and financial success of Southland. However, we also knew that Citgo would have to undergo significant restructuring to realize its potential in a fast-changing industry environment that traditionally had not favored refining and marketing operations . . .

"We have been very gratified at the success that this approach, with its heavy dependence on management science and cooperative effort, has achieved at Citgo. The numerous systems that were developed for Citgo . . . have become an integral part of the Citgo operation, saving many millions of dollars that otherwise would have been lost profits. In 1985, the combination of a dynamic new management team, these innovative management science systems, and a significant improvement in refining industry market conditions during much of the year contributed to Citgo's turnaround in profitability from a 1984 operating loss that exceeded $50 million.

"Finally, the study conducted by the task force has not only contributed to this profitable condition, it has provided us with a more thorough understanding of

Citgo's operations, thereby enabling us to improve Citgo's organization and operations and enhance its profitability in the years to come. We look forward to future management science developments which might provide even greater advantages to Southland in what is becoming an increasingly competitive business climate."

CONCLUSIONS

We hope that the applications of MS/OR presented in this book have succeeded in imparting the flavor, richness, and challenges of applying the expertise represented by our field. No set of readings can fully communicate all the aspects and ingredients of MS/OR practice. To the reader, papers in this book may seem like the "slicer-dicer" demonstrations one sees on television or at county fairs: The demonstrator turns an apple into, say, a swan with only a few strokes of the special tool. Replicating this feat at home, however, requires much more than the instructions given in the user's manual. Similarly, successful MS/OR applications combine technical expertise with a rare bend of art, common sense, educated judgment, and communications skills.

A great many of the applications collected in this book reflect "big MS/OR." These studies are major undertakings, require the joint efforts of many experts, and generally extend over a long stretch of time. Needless to say, "little MS/OR" is also alive and well. Many smaller studies of more limited scope continue to provide valuable guidance. Understandably, academic MS/OR publications highlight the first successful implementation of a technique and tend to ignore its repeat applications over time. From the practitioner's viewpoint, however, all repeat applications present new challenges and generate novel insights into how organizations change.

A thread of common characteristics runs through the successful implementations presented in this book. We will conclude this book by reflecting on these characteristics. The following principles, which are drawn from the readings, have been noted often by other observers of MS/OR practice.

1. *Be opportunistic.* Select problems that management considers important and define projects that are very likely to succeed. Projects are most likely to succeed in areas where management discerns a strong need for improvement. A number of the papers report that managers recognized the need for change because of severe market and competitive pressures. Such pressures go a long way in "selling" the need for an MS/OR study.

2. *Find a champion within top management.* The readings repeatedly emphasized the role of top management support in providing the momentum for change. Organizationally, few advantages rival the benefit of having an advocate for the study at the top.

3. *Start simple and keep it simple.* An MS/OR study that appears arcane has little chance of winning support. It is better to start with simpler concerns that are readily understandable and familiar to all. One successful consulting firm starts all projects as exercises in data retrieval and reporting. After capturing the company's data and instituting clear and timely procedures for reporting it, managers begin to ask questions that go beyond information retrieval and require modeling and analysis.

4. *Keep the user foremost in mind.* The successful applications described in this volume depend on the analysts paying close attention to the users' needs and preferences. Users must help design the types and formats of reports they would like to see. Involving the end user in system design is a tested implementation principle that pays back in faster system acceptance and easier communication of results.

5. *Score early victories.* As MS/OR projects can last a long time, early victories are essential to the professional health (and employment) of MS/OR practitioners. One way of achieving an early victory is to start with a short but highly informative project that clearly shows the benefits of the modeling effort. Another common way is to divide a big project into phases, each of which provides useful information to management, sometimes long in advance of completing the project in full. Ideally, some of the earlier phases will result in modules that are quite valuable in themselves (a forecasting system, for example).

6. *Use the preliminary study to gain support and reduce risk.* In some applications reported in this book, a preliminary model was constructed to convince management of the potential benefits of a full-scale project. The scope of this preliminary model may range from a simple cost-benefit analysis to a complex model that is neither short nor simple, as in a simulation study. Its main role is to assess the potential benefits of the larger project and to avoid the risks of embarking upon a much larger study needlessly.

7. *Communicate your results throughout the process.* Communicating the structure and results of the model to other members of the firm is a major ongoing enterprise in most successful studies. Using multi-function teams and involving a broad spectrum of management facilitates communications and leads to system acceptance.

8. *Allow the model to evolve.* Analysts should not be afraid of changing the model, even after it is documented and implemented. Models are not icons but evolving representations of reality. Few reasonable managers require that a telecommunications system or a database system remain fixed and rigid over time. There is no reason to hobble MS/OR models with such requirements either.

Practitioners of MS/OR can easily find other points to add to this informal list. Good reports of applications should present a more realistic picture of MS/OR implementation, and raise questions about the factors that affect its success. If the papers collected in this book have accomplished this for the reader, then our purpose in preparing this book has been well served.